"Heinze's deep roots in the Lutheran and Anglican traditions plus his lifelong investigation of the multifaceted aspects of the Reformation have resulted in a magnificent history of that period that is concise, lucid, and beautifully written. The most recent scholarship is cited plus appropriate citations from primary sources which contribute to a most balanced and judicious narrative. The endnotes must be read, for they contain fascinating observations of the author. The bibliography is comprehensive and the key to the newest scholarship.

"Scholars will find Heinze's insights provocative, and anyone interested in church history will find this volume to be the best introduction to one of the critical turning points in Western history."

Robert V. Schnucker, former managing editor and book review editor, *16th Century Journal*; professor of religion, University of Northern Iowa

"Containing fifteen highly competent chapters assessing the extent and validity of the contemporary fashion for '*revisionism*,' Dr. Heinze's new book provides the student world with an up-to-date text. Readers will welcome the way he evaluates the paradoxical nature of the sixteenth-century *reformations* as not only radical crises but also a series of essentially conservative events altogether loyal to the timeless truths underlying a great Christian tradition.

"*Reform and Conflict* merits high praise for surveying the byways as well as the highways criss-crossing a tortuous terrain. Truly, as a guide to three-dimensional history in the most complex of periods, it will prove invaluable."

Peter Newman Brooks, fellow emeritus in ecclesiastical history, Robinson College

"For anyone looking for a comprehensive, well-written, and up-to-date history of the Reformation, *Reform and Conflict* should be their first choice. Professor Heinze explains complex topics lucidly and accurately. Historiographical issues are covered fairly. All of the important subjects of the Reformation are given substantial coverage while the human dimension of the era and the various people involved with these events is rightly emphasized. *Reform and Conflict* will be a welcome addition to the bookshelves of scholars and the general reading public while at the same time it will serve as a fine textbook for use in the college classroom. The excitement of the age of the Reformation along with its triumphs and tragedies come alive in this book."

Ronald H. Fritze, dean of arts and sciences, Athens State University

"*Reform and Conflict* is a well-written and insightful work by a ripe scholar of Reformation history. It is well-balanced in its approach to the period—just traditional enough to serve as a sound source to learn the rudiments of the Reformation movement and just cutting-edge enough to make the reader aware of the new social history and current gender studies. University students seeking a reliable guide to this era will find it both useful and delightful, and any member of the lay reading public who wishes to know more about Luther, Calvin, and their ilk will discover an enjoyable read. I commend it to one and all."

Robert D. Linder, university distinguished professor of history,
Kansas State University

REFORM AND CONFLICT

From the Medieval World to the Wars of
Religion, A.D. 1350–1648

RUDOLPH W. HEINZE

The Monarch History of the Church, Vol. 4

John D. Woodbridge and David F. Wright,
Consulting Editors

Tim Dowley, Series Editor

MONARCH
BOOKS
Oxford, UK

Originally published in the United States of America by Baker Books in 2005.
Reproduced from the original setting by agreement.

First published in the UK in 2006 by Monarch Books
(a publishing imprint of Lion Hudson plc),
Mayfield House, 256 Banbury Road, Oxford OX2 7DH.
Tel: +44 (0)1865 302750 Fax: +44 (0)1865 302757
Email: monarch@lionhudson.com
www.lionhudson.com

ISBN-13: 978-1-85424-690-5 (UK)
ISBN-10: 1-85424-690-9 (UK)

Distributed by
Marston Book Services Ltd, PO Box 269,
Abingdon, Oxon OX14 4YN.

Unless otherwise stated, Scripture quotations are taken from the Holy Bible,
New International Version, © 1973, 1978, 1984 by the International Bible
Society. Used by permission of Hodder & Stoughton Ltd. All rights reserved.

Scripture marked RSV is taken from the Revised Standard Version of
the Bible, copyright 1952 [2nd edition, 1971] by the Division of Christian
Education of the National Council of the Churches of Christ in the United
States of America. Used by permission. All rights reserved.

The text paper used in this book has been made from wood independently
certified as having come from sustainable forests.

British Library Cataloguing Data
A catalogue record for this book is available from the British Library.

Printed and bound in Malta by Gutenberg Press

CONTENTS

MAPS AND ILLUSTRATIONS

PREFACE

The "textbook mentality" that an assertion is true because it is written down, is utterly alien to any historical outlook.

David Bebbington[1]

Although the past does not change, the way in which historians view and explain it is in a constant state of flux. New research, new methods, and new questions regularly shed new light on the past. As a result, historians can never rest secure that their previous study of a period, no matter how detailed and thorough, can be relied on without qualification to instruct a new generation of students. Those who were privileged to be taught Reformation history by the great scholars of the past generation will always appreciate what was learned from outstanding historians such as Roland Bainton, Harold Grimm, A. G. Dickens, and G. R. Elton. However, just as these scholars revised past interpretations, so, in turn, their students have suggested new ways of understanding the Reformation.

One of the unfortunate aspects of revisionism in historical studies is that too often the new generation of historians is overly critical of what their forefathers taught. As a result, they abandon previously hard-won insights and present a radically new view of the period. This book is an effort to take seriously the interpretations resulting from new research as well as what the great scholars of the past believed about the Reformation. It also includes insights that I have gained from four decades of teaching Reformation history to students on two continents. Although the effort to synthesize interpretations that present radically contrasting explanations may not please all who read this volume, I hope it will be of help in better understanding a complex movement.

The title of this work conveys both the greatness and the tragedy of the Reformation. It was a paradoxical period in the history of the Christian church since the church emerged from the century and a half labeled "the Reformation era" both stronger and weaker. The Reformation brought moral and doctrinal reform to all the branches of the Western Christian church, but reform was achieved at the cost of conflict and bitter divisions between Christians that also weakened the church. Today both Protestants and Catholics can look back to the Reformation as a period that has greatly influenced what they believe and practice. They can also rightly revere the great church leaders of that era who provide an inspiring example of commitment and courage. However, those leaders had their share of human weaknesses, and they often reacted to fellow Christians with whom they disagreed in a very un-Christian manner. They also contributed to the conflicts that divided Christendom and resulted in the terrible blood-letting that characterized the final century of the Reformation era. Reform and conflict combined to produce a church that was very different in 1650 from what it had been in 1500. We have gained much from the reform aspects of the Reformation, and hopefully what we learn from the conflicts can help us to avoid making similar mistakes in the future.

I'm grateful to Baker Books for their sponsorship of this series and in particular to the members of the staff who worked on this volume including my project editor Paul Brinkerhoff, acquisitions editor Chad Allen, copyeditor Lois Stück, and Kathleen Strattan, who produced the index. I also appreciate the work of the staff at Monarch Books in London, and especially Tony Collins, for their contributions. I am pleased to dedicate these efforts to my wife, Mildred, and to my children, Phillip, Lisa, and Michael. Through the many years I spent in research and writing, they put up with a husband and father who was often absent and who was so absorbed in Reformation studies even when he was at home that they seldom had his full attention. I am especially grateful to my wife and daughter because they patiently read this manuscript when it was at its roughest stage and tirelessly corrected my spelling, punctuation, and grammar. In addition they encouraged me by regularly telling me that they enjoyed what they were reading despite all the errors. I also wish to thank my classes at Concordia University, Oak Hill College, and Wheaton College, who taught me as much as I taught them and whose reactions to my teaching were of great value in helping formulate my approach to the Reformation.

I particularly want to mention the members of my final class at Wheaton—Philip, Matthew, Joel, Christopher, Reginald, Martha, and Heather—who were first exposed to the material in this book in lecture form. I am grateful to another former student, Ron Fritze, whose scholarly reviews, which he shared with me even before they were published, helped me to appreciate better the contributions of postrevisionists in the debates about the English Reformation. I wish to thank Wendy Bell, the librarian at Oak Hill College, as well as the staff of the Wheaton College library, and especially John Fawcett, who assisted me in finding the resources to write this work. I owe a great debt of gratitude to those who taught me Reformation history or who encouraged me and guided my research. Among the many who might be mentioned, Nelack Tjernagel, Robert Kingdon, Frank Larkin, Harold Grimm, A. G. Dickens, and G. R. Elton stand out as the men who had the greatest influence on me. Finally, my friend and former colleague Wayne Lucht, who served for many years as the editor of *Lutheran Education*, and Tim Dowley, the editor of the series, lent me the benefit of their expertise in reading the manuscript and making suggestions for alterations.

Rudolph W. Heinze
Wheaton, Illinois
April 2005

WRITING THE HISTORY OF THE REFORMATION

Can we doubt that there has ever been any age which has seen so many admirable things in so short a time? So many changes in kingdoms, religions and estates? One capable of explaining everything with care, and in terms of circumstances and motives, as that noble Paduan author [Livy] did for Roman history, could create a work and monument quite as excellent as those of antiquity.

Johann Sleidan[1]

Early Histories of the Reformation

Johann Sleidan (1506–1556) wrote the above words in July 1537 to describe the age in which he was living; less than a decade later he took up the challenge of writing the first history of the Reformation era. Sleidan recognized both the difficulty and the importance of writing an accurate history. He had witnessed the Reformation from both sides of the religious divide, having served as secretary to a French Catholic cardinal, as councillor to the Protestant city of Strasbourg, and as an observer at the Council of Trent. He began his *Commentaries on Religion and the State in the Reign of Charles V* in the midst of the first German religious war, and it was published in 1555, the year of the peace treaty that first gave legal recognition to the schism in the church created by the Reformation. Although Protestant in his sympathies, Sleidan tried to be fair in relating the story of the Reformation. He stated that "nothing adorns the writing of history more than truth and candour" and

11

maintained he had "taken the utmost care that neither of these may here be found wanting."[2] Nevertheless, Catholics regarded his work as heretical and unscholarly, while Protestants criticized it for its moderation toward Catholics and for revealing Protestant weaknesses that they would have preferred to have remained hidden. Yet the book became a best seller, possibly because the subject matter was so compelling and the author recognized the great drama of the age in which he was living.

Even before he began his research, Sleidan was perceptive in his view of his age. An era of drastic changes in church and state, it included reform and schism in the church, civil conflicts, and wars between kingdoms. Although historians today are no longer so confident that the Reformation era witnessed the end of the Middle Ages and the beginning of the modern era, major changes certainly occurred in Europe over a relatively short period of time. Writing the history of the Reformation is not an easy task because the conflicts and divisions that occurred in the church have made it especially difficult for those who are committed to the Christian faith to write about the period without being influenced by their own religious beliefs. Although Sleidan tried to write an impartial history,[3] those who followed him made no pretense to objectivity.[4]

Shortly after the first of the religious wars ended, a group of Lutherans, led by the conservative Lutheran leader Matthias Flacius Illyricus, produced a thirteen-volume work based on manuscript sources collected from libraries and archives throughout Europe. The work, entitled the *Magdeburg Centuries* and published between 1559 and 1574, demonstrates that thorough research does not necessarily lead to impartial history. The *Magdeburg Centuries* was a Protestant polemic that divided the history of the church into three periods: ancient, medieval, and modern. Although the narrative did not go beyond the thirteenth century, the theme of the work was that the purity of the church in the ancient period was lost in the medieval period and restored in the Reformation. It presented the papacy in the worst possible light and included malicious gossip, such as the legend of a female Pope Joan, as historical fact.[5]

Not surprisingly the *Magdeburg Centuries* was answered by an equally biased Catholic work. Between 1588 and 1607 Caesar Baronius, an Italian cardinal, published in twelve volumes his *Ecclesiastical Annals*, which surveyed from a Roman Catholic perspective the history of the church to 1193.[6] Although his study was based on impressive historical research, including archaeological evidence, religious polemic rather than a search for historical truth was again the dominant motivation for the work.

In the four centuries since the publication of Sleidan's work, the trends established in those early histories have continued. Historians operating from the perspective of their personal religious convictions continued to write partisan histories; they were often based on thorough and careful research, but their conclusions were influenced more by religious bias than the evidence. Both Roman Catholic and Protestant scholars praised or denounced the Reformation on the basis of their own religious convictions. Protestants defended the Reformation by arguing that the medieval church had become so corrupt that the Reformation was almost inevitable, and they tended to describe the Reformers in such positive light that many biographies were little more than hagiographies. Roman Catholic scholars, who viewed the Reformation as a disaster that divided the church and opened the door to the secularization of society, presented a positive picture of the medieval church to show that the Protestant Reformation was unnecessary. They had a negative opinion of the Reformers and described their achievements in a pejorative way, while maintaining that the Catholic Reformation brought true reform to the church.

Scholars representing different Protestant traditions also frequently disagreed with one another. Lutheran scholars were often unfair in their assessment of Calvin and Zwingli, while portraying Luther as a man almost without fault—at least after he had separated himself from the Roman Catholic Church. Scholars from the Reformed tradition were often highly critical of Luther, while Calvin and Zwingli were their heroes. Both Protestants and Catholics used the label "Anabaptist" as a term of contempt to describe the left wing of the Reformation, while Mennonite scholars presented Anabaptists as the true heroes and heroines of the Reformation.

Recent Developments in Reformation Research

While partisan histories abounded in the centuries following the Reformation, some historians continued the tradition of Sleidan and sought to write objective history, attempting to understand the past for its own sake rather than to defend an ideological position. The growth of ecumenical understanding among Christians has led to a significant decrease in partisan histories, as historians of all religious persuasions have shown greater understanding and appreciation of other points of view. Since the 1960s, interest in the Reformation has increased greatly as new research and new methodologies have resulted in radical revisions of previously held beliefs. Historians no longer write about a single Reformation because they recognize that the era experienced multiple reform movements that differed too significantly from each other to be included under one label.[7] They also recognize the positive achievements of the late medieval church, and some even question the necessity for the Reformation, not just its appeal and impact. New approaches to Reformation scholarship and new areas of research have greatly expanded our understanding of the period and corrected some misunderstandings. However, there remain many unanswered questions, and historians continue to debate conflicting interpretations and to investigate new topics, neglected by previous generations, such as the role of women in the Reformation and how the Reformation affected ordinary men and women.

One of the major new trends in Reformation studies is the writing of social history by scholars particularly concerned about how reform movements affected people's lives. These studies have drawn on new resources. Earlier studies concentrated on the political and theological aspects of the Reformation and used traditional sources such as the writings of the Reformers, correspondence of princes and councillors, decisions of imperial diets, and city chronicles. Scholars seeking to understand how the Reformation affected the people are turning to publications that were designed to influence public opinion, such as broadsides and pamphlets. Autobiographies and personal letters are also utilized to supply insights into the private lives of the men and women of sixteenth-century Europe. Local city and church archives, council minutes, wills, records of church courts, consistories, and ecclesiastical visitations are studied to answer questions about the impact of the Reformation that an older generation of historians either ignored or answered on the basis of assumptions rather than hard evidence.

The result of all this new research is to make us still more aware of the human drama of the Reformation—much of it heroic, but also often tragic. The bitter rivalries that developed between people pursuing similar goals, the broken friendships, the vitriolic attacks between fellow Reformers, as well as the courageous martyrs who were the victims of prejudice and hatred are all part of the human drama of the Reformation. Reformation history is exciting for many reasons— there were heroes and heroines on both sides of the religious divide, but there were also many whom the modern world would consider villains. Even the most impressive characters had their full share of weaknesses.

Terminology

Recent studies have also questioned some of the standard termi-
nology used in earlier works. We have already noted that contemporary historians prefer to use the title *Reformations*, since the singular,
Reformation, suggests a unified movement. If this book had been written
in the mid-twentieth century, it might well have been titled "Renaissance
and Reformation." Today, however, the term *Renaissance* is also suspect
because it carries the connotation of a great revival of culture at the end
of what was once mistakenly called the "Dark Ages." Even the phrase
"origins of the Reformation" has been called into question because it
suggests that the Reformation was bound to occur, and it can lead to
studying the late Middle Ages largely to uncover factors that made the
Reformation inevitable. Historians point out that the Reformation was a
complex series of events, and to speak of "origins" is to suggest a greater
unity in those events than actually existed.[8]

Some scholars are even uneasy about the use of the term *Protestant*
to identify the movements that split from the medieval church. The
term first originated at the Second Diet of Speyer in 1529 when by a
majority vote the German Estates rescinded an earlier decision of the
first Diet of Speyer in 1526. That diet had left it to each political entity
within the Holy Roman Empire to decide how it would implement the
Edict of Worms of 1521, which banned Lutheran teaching. Utilizing the
freedom granted by the 1526 diet, a number of princes and imperial
cities had introduced or promoted Lutheranism. When the Second Diet
of Speyer took away this freedom, six princes and fourteen imperial cities objected, using a legal process called *protestatio*. They maintained
that the religious agreement of the previous diet should remain in force
until a national assembly could be called to make a final decision. As a
result they were called by some the "protesting estates" or "protesting
ones." "Protesting ones" was changed to "Protestant" toward the end of
the sixteenth century when it was translated into English and French.
The term was also eventually used in Germany, originally to refer to
Lutherans, since it was Lutheran princes who protested at the Diet of
Speyer, but it was later applied to all Reformation traditions. By the
end of the eighteenth century the term *Protestantism* had become the
regular designation for those who broke away from the medieval church.
Since it was not used in this fuller sense during the Reformation itself,
some historians are reluctant to use it. They prefer the term *evangelicals*, "followers of the gospel," which was how the Reformers and their
followers often described themselves. Another term sometimes used in

place of Protestant is *Reformation churches*. However, since the term *Protestant* has had such wide usage, the meaning of the word is quite clear today, and it seems legitimate to continue using it to describe those who seceded from the Church of Rome during the Reformation.

Reform and Conflict 1350–1650: An Overview

As we take up again the history of the period almost 450 years after Sleidan finished his work, it is evident that some of his observations still hold true. The changes that occurred were so radical that a medieval Rip van Winkle who went to sleep in 1350 and woke up in 1650 would certainly not recognize the world as the same one in which he was born. As Sleidan noted, many of those changes were admirable. All branches of the church in Western Europe experienced significant administrative, moral, and doctrinal reform that brought major changes to the church. However, reform was accompanied by conflict between those who were committed to the beliefs and practices of the medieval church and those who believed massive doctrinal and moral reform was necessary. There was also conflict between those committed to different approaches to reform and to different theologies.

The Reformation resulted in a lasting schism in a church that, at least in Western Europe, had retained its essential unity for more than one thousand years. The legal existence of more than one Christian church was difficult to accept after a millennium of religious unity, and it was only reluctantly acknowledged when it became evident that neither dialogue nor suppression could restore the church's unity. Religious divisions together with political, social, and economic factors led to military conflict that plagued Europe between 1550 and 1648. At a local level, parishes, villages, guilds, and families also experienced conflict as bitter hatreds replaced harmonious and even loving relationships. Those terrible conflicts helped in the long term to undermine the cause of reform and, at least in some respects, the Reformation lessened rather than increased the impact of the church upon society. This study takes its title from these two characteristics of the Reformation era: reform and conflict. We also look at the period that preceded the Reformation, not as a prelude to the Reformation but as a period in its own right, during which the church also experienced reform and conflict.

The initial section is devoted to an overview of the pre-Reformation period. The first chapter describes the setting in which the events took place, surveying late medieval society and the role of the church in that society. The second chapter applies the overall theme of the study to the late medieval church: the reform movements of the late Middle Ages are examined in an effort to determine what they achieved and why they failed to meet the concerns of many in that society who continued to be extremely critical of the church. Although it is evident that the late medieval church was meeting the religious needs of society more effectively than previous generations of Protestant historians were willing to concede, enough people were alienated from the church to support the Protestant Reformation. The cause of that alienation will be examined in the second part of the chapter, which deals with conflicts in the church.

In the third chapter we examine the events that led to the outbreak of the sixteenth-century Reformation. Since Martin Luther was the primary protagonist in those events, this chapter will be devoted to examining his life, the development of his theology, and the events that resulted in his leading the way to a lasting schism in the church. The next stage of the Reformation era saw the establishment of a number of different reform movements and a great expansion of the Reformation churches. Lutheranism spread throughout much of Germany and Scandinavia, while new urban movements came into existence in Switzerland and Germany. Radical reform movements sprang up throughout Europe, led by people who rejected the approach and theology of those called the "Magisterial Reformers" because they worked with the magistrates or rulers. In Geneva, John Calvin led a reform movement that would be imitated throughout much of Europe. Although King Henry VIII initiated a Reformation in England for reasons that had little to do with church reform, the English church also experienced a Protestant Reformation that reached fruition in the reign of Henry's daughter Elizabeth. The Protestant Reformation was also firmly established in Scotland at this time. Each of these reform movements is covered in separate chapters. In addition, the impact of the reform movements on a major section of European society is described in the chapter entitled "Women and the Reformation."

When efforts to heal the breach between the Church of Rome and the growing Protestant movement failed, the papacy called its own reforming council, which defined the theology of the medieval church in opposition to Protestantism and introduced significant moral and spiritual reform within the Roman Catholic Church. Catholic reform reached well beyond the borders of Europe in an aggressive missionary enterprise that brought Christianity not only to the Portuguese, Spanish, and French colonies in the New World but well beyond the boundaries of European empires to the farthest reaches of the Asian continent. Protestants, although much less energetic in their missionary enterprises, also attempted to bring the gospel to Native Americans in the English colonies. Missionary enterprise and developments in non-Western branches of the church are discussed in a separate chapter.

The sad result of the competing reform movements was theological and military conflict. The first of two chapters on these conflicts deals with the theological struggles. Although normally fought with words rather than guns, these were often almost as vicious as the military conflicts in the vitriolic language used and the hatred generated. In addition to conflicts between Protestants and Catholics, Protestants fought each other: Lutherans, Zwinglians, and Calvinists engaged in vicious debates, and there were also deep divisions within Lutheranism and Calvinism. All parties were critical of the Anabaptists and were generally involved in persecuting them. In their turn, Anabaptists were also divided among themselves and sometimes resorted to violence in pursuing their objectives.

Military conflict is the subject of the penultimate chapter. During the last century of the Reformation era, Germany, France, the Low Countries, and England were torn apart by bloody religious wars. When neither party was able to annihilate the other, they eventually had to agree to compromise settlements, dividing the area between the competing confessions. Only the English Civil War, fought between Protestants rather than between Protestants and Catholics, had a different result. A logical concluding year for the Reformation era on the European continent is the Peace of Westphalia of 1648, which ended the Thirty Years' War. In England it is necessary to add another decade since the English Civil War was followed by the restoration of the Stuart dynasty in 1660.

Having told the story of the Reformation era in terms of reform and conflict, the final chapter examines the lasting impact of the Reformation, summarizing its effect upon the arts, science, economics, political thought, and education and then investigating how it affected the religious beliefs of the average person and to what degree the sought-after reform was actually achieved. It concludes by looking back across three centuries of church history and asking how significant were the "changes in kingdoms, religions and estates" that Sleidan noted in his description of his own age. He obviously thought they had huge significance, and until recently so did most historians. However, today historians are asking hard questions about the impact of the Reformation. What was the overall impact of the Reformation? How much did it change Europe and the world? To what degree was it the beginning of the *modern world*?

1

CHURCH AND SOCIETY IN THE LATE MIDDLE AGES

▼

Everywhere is woe, terror everywhere. . . . I am not mourning some slight distress but that dreadful year 1348, which not merely robbed us of our friends, but robbed the whole world of its peoples. . . . Will posterity credit that there was a time when . . . almost the whole earth was depopulated? . . . Can it be that God has no care for the mortal lot?

Francisco Petrarch[1]

Now, indeed, may every thoughtful spirit thank God that it has been permitted him to be born in this new age, so full of hope and promise, which already rejoices in a greater army of nobly-gifted souls than the world has seen in the thousand years that have preceded it.

Matteo Palmieri[2]

Late medieval people lived in a world of striking contrasts. It was an era of death and disaster when many felt they were living in the end times, but it was also an era of creativity, expansion, and hope for a brighter future. The above statements, both of which were written by medieval humanists, exemplify the paradox. At the beginning of this period, Francisco Petrarch (1304–1374) lamented the terror of the Black Death, which took such an enormous toll of human life and brought so much suffering. At the end of the period, Matteo Palmieri (1406–1475) was one of many humanist scholars who felt they were living in a wonderful age of cultural "rebirth," which historians have called the Renaissance. Both the disasters and the achievements of the age were to have a profound effect on the church, and to understand the history of the Christian church in the late Middle Ages, one must first look at the environment in which it ministered. The *way* in which the church ministered to that society is discussed in the second half of this chapter.

The Calamities of the Late Middle Ages

The fourteenth century has been labeled "calamitous,"[3] and there could hardly be a more fitting adjective to describe a period when the people of Europe were afflicted by a series of terrible natural and man-made disasters. Climatologists have identified a gradual shift to a colder and wetter climate that reached its most severe point in the mid-fourteenth century, and climate changes resulted in a number of serious problems. Although the average temperature fell only slightly, it was enough to cause major floods, a shorter growing season, and crop failures. A particularly serious crop failure occurred in 1315, when the summer rainfall became such a deluge that chroniclers compared it with the Old Testament flood. Crops failed throughout Europe, resulting in famines so severe that there were grim reports of people eating their own children and the bodies of hanged criminals. Floods, heavy snowfalls, and colder temperatures persisted throughout the century, and as if that was not enough, swarms of locusts and earthquakes added to the misery of the people of Europe. It is not surprising that many thought the final judgment and return of Christ were imminent.

Natural disasters contributed to economic problems. The previous two centuries had witnessed significant economic expansion, as new land was brought under cultivation while urbanization and commerce flourished. By the fourteenth century, however, all the land that could productively be brought under cultivation had been used, and the amount of land under cultivation actually declined as some marginal land had to be abandoned because it could not bear continued usage. Climate change further undermined the land's productivity. The expanding economy of the previous period, which had brought much prosperity to Europe, was replaced by a depression that added to the hardship of the masses and resulted in significant social tensions. In the cities, guilds were closed to new members, while in the countryside nobles sought to impose heavier burdens on the peasantry. Unemployment and underemployment resulted in a declining standard of living for the masses of Europe, and the economic oppression of the power elite finally became unbearable, resulting in a series of urban and peasant revolts. At the beginning of the century, discontented workers rose against their oppressors in Flanders and Northern Italy. In 1378 Florence experienced a major revolt of poor laborers, who even seized control of the city for a period. Rural discontent led to peasant revolts in France in 1358 and England in 1381. Although some lower-class revolts had temporary success, the ruling classes were able to suppress them and impose even heavier burdens upon the poor.

The problems of the late Middle Ages were complicated by the man-made tragedy of war. Late medieval warfare was particularly destructive to the civilian population because armies lived off the land, looting, raping, and sometimes massacring the local population. A retreating army often practiced a scorched-earth policy, destroying crops and fields in order to demoralize a hostile population and deny the advancing army food supplies. Soldiers were normally recruited from the lower classes and were paid very little—sometimes nothing—so they had to rely on the spoils of war for subsistence. When a war was over, armies were disbanded as soon as possible, resulting in roving bands of ex-soldiers plaguing the countryside. Such banditry only added to the misery of the population and the turmoil of the era. France and Italy were particularly troubled by such banditry because of the almost constant wars that afflicted those areas.

In 1337 England and France, two of the most prosperous and advanced countries in Western Europe, began a war that lasted for over a hundred years. Although this conflict was temporarily halted by a number of truces, lasting peace was not finally restored until 1453, and it left one of the richest areas of Europe devastated, with a particularly disastrous effect on the peasantry. A French diarist, describing the plight of the peasants, decried the atrocities committed by the English forces and their Burgundian allies in what had been one of the most prosperous areas of France. They were, he stated, "pillaging everywhere, so . . . it was impossible to till the soil or sow anywhere . . . most of the peasants abandoned work in the fields and were in despair." Complaints were greeted with mockery "and their men behaved worse even than before," so that the peasants complained that "Saracens would treat us better than the Christians do."[4] After the Hundred Years' War ended, England went on to experience civil war, the so-called "Wars of the Roses," which did not end until 1485 and provided new military opportunities for the English soldiers who had fought in the Hundred Years' War.

Italian cities likewise engaged in almost continuous wars. Cities fought each other, and factions within cities fought civil wars. When one faction was defeated, its leaders were expelled and their property confiscated. From exile, they plotted their return and, when and if they were strong enough, attacked and deposed their opponents, further disrupting the life of the city. The folly of war was evident to sensitive people such as Petrarch. Commenting on a war between Florence and Pisa in 1372, he told the story of "a fool" who questioned the rationality of war: "Would that our warmakers might ponder his words! So might a war never be begun, or it might be ended before we should sink under war's ravages and calamities, after which indeed peace will come. That peace will be good, though it be all too late; it would be much the best, if it could come in time. But men's ears are shut against wise counsels. The ultimate triumph of war, they say, is total madness."[5]

North of the Alps, Germany was also afflicted by "total madness." What is today Germany was part of the Holy Roman Empire, ruled by an elected emperor who was constantly struggling against centrifugal forces in his empire. Civil wars raged between rival claimants to the throne, and in the course of those wars, the emperor's authority was diminished even further as local authorities gained increasing power at his expense. Although the Golden Bull of 1378[6] regularized the method of electing the emperor, the empire continued to be divided, without a strong central authority.

The troubles of the emperor were complicated by a new threat from the East that increased as the period progressed. During the previous two centuries, Western armies had launched a series of military expeditions against the Muslim rulers of the Near East. Although these Crusades had some initial success, resulting in the establishment of Western crusader states in Palestine, Lebanon, and Syria, the Muslims gradually regained the territory they had lost, and by 1291 the last of the crusader states was eliminated with the fall of Acre. Muslim success against Western armies led one disillusioned crusader to lament that "God who used to keep watch over us is now asleep, but Mahomet works with all his might."[7] From a Western perspective, God slept for two centuries as Muslim advances continued at the expense of the eastern Holy Roman Empire, which had survived for almost a millennium after the fall of the western empire.

The new enemies of the Holy Roman Empire were the Ottoman Turks, who emerged from a small emirate in the late thirteenth century to become the primary power in the Balkans in the next two centuries. Their gradual conquest of the Balkan Peninsula took place under a series of able military leaders and involved a number of humiliating defeats for the Christian rulers of the area. One of the worst defeats occurred at the Battle of Kossovo in 1389, where the Turks defeated a combined force of Serbs and troops from other Balkan states and killed most of the Serbian nobility. When the West became alarmed and counterattacked with a new Crusade, they were annihilated at Nicopolis in 1396. The humiliation was accentuated by the fact that important figures, including a marshal of France, the heir to the Duke of Burgundy, and two cousins of the French king, were taken captive and huge ransoms had to be paid to secure their release. Although the Mongol leader, Tamerlane, who defeated the Turks at Angora in 1402, temporarily halted the Turkish advance, it resumed again under the aggressive leadership of Sultan Mohammed II in the second half of the fifteenth century.

Constantinople, the capital of a once mighty empire, which was now only a shadow of its former glory, finally fell to the Turks in 1453. Although this had long been expected, the West was shocked and the pope called for another Crusade. Nothing came of this, however, and the Turkish advance into the Balkans continued as Montenegro, Albania, Serbia, and Bosnia were incorporated into the Turkish Empire. In 1480 the Turks even occupied the Italian city of Otranto, but the king of Naples quickly recaptured it. Mohammed II died the following year, and the West had a temporary respite from Turkish attacks as the Turks fought their own internal battles[8] and set about the conquest of Syria and Egypt. In 1520 Suleiman the Magnificent resumed the advance. Six years later, the king of Bohemia and Hungary was killed at the Battle of Mohacs and the Turks were at the gates of Vienna. Throughout the Reformation era, the Turkish menace, described as "the scourge of God," was part of the rhetoric of Reformers and political leaders. As we shall see, it would have a major impact on the Reformation.

The Black Death

At the same time as the people of Europe were suffering the calamities of weather, war, revolts, and depression, they also faced a still more serious problem that killed more of the European population than the sum of all the other disasters. It came without warning and without the people of that society really knowing what was happening. The Black Death first reached Europe in 1347. It probably began in China and spread across Russia to the Crimea, where the Tartars were besieging the Genoese trading post in the city of Caffa. The infection began in the Tartar camp, and the Tartars spread the plague to the besieged garrison by catapulting the bodies of the dead into the city. When the Genoese fled, they took with them the plague, and by the time their ship reached Messina in Sicily, most of the crew were dead or dying. Thus the plague made its entry into Europe, where it spread quickly and easily, as people had no natural immunity. In the three years between 1348 and 1351, the plague swept across the whole of Europe, taking a terrible toll on its population. Although it abated temporarily, new outbreaks occurred in 1362 and 1375, and during the next century the plague returned at least once every decade.

The plague was spread by fleas that lived on black rats. When fleas bit a human, a pustule formed at the point of the bite. By the third day, the lymph nodes began to swell and hemorrhaging occurred under the skin. The infected person suffered excruciating pain, neurological disorders, wild anxiety, and terror, from which death was a blessed relief. In addition to the bubonic form, which affected the lymph nodes, a pneumonic strain also developed that was even more contagious. Contemporaries called it "the pestilence," but five centuries later a German historian gave it the name the Black Death,[9] not because people turned black (although the victims did have black spots or blotches due to bleeding under the skin), but because it was so frightening as a result of its virulence. It spread easily from person to person, so that if a person came into contact even with the clothes of sick people, he or she was likely to be infected. Priests and doctors who came to minister to the sick often died, and many people became so fearful that they avoided the sick, whose suffering was thereby increased. In many instances it was the most caring clergy who died, because it was they who ministered to the sick and dying. One fortunate survivor was a fourteenth-century Mother Teresa, named Catherine of Siena. When the plague struck her hometown of Siena, Italy, in 1374, she and her followers ignored the danger to themselves and continued to minister to the plague victims.

We do not know how many people died, because detailed death statistics were nonexistent in the fourteenth century. However, evidence from surviving documents such as manorial rolls, ordination lists, and city records makes it possible to estimate the likely death rate. On the basis of such evidence, it is believed that one third of the population of Europe may have died in the three years 1347–1350, although recent historians have argued that the death toll was even higher. Death rates were worse in the cities and towns, where people lived in very crowded conditions and sanitation was especially poor. Sometimes there were not enough people left alive in a town to bury the dead. At the height of the plague, average life expectancy, which had been thirty-four in 1300, fell to seventeen. Although some historians are not convinced that society suffered major psychological damage, it is difficult to believe that the Black Death did not have a significant impact on the overall outlook of the society. No modern war has caused anywhere near the proportion of deaths that resulted from the plague, and we know how profoundly the death rates of the two twentieth-century world wars affected Western society. The psychological effect must have been all the worse in a society in which people had no idea why they were suffering or how to combat the plague. People waited helplessly for the onset of the disease or, if they fled hoping to escape it, they often only spread it to new areas.

A deeply religious society struggled to explain why God was allowing his people to suffer so terribly. Petrarch was not alone in asking the question, "Can it be that God has no care for the mortal lot?" It seemed that God had turned against his people and nobody knew why. Some thought God was punishing Christian society for its sins, and there were those who felt they could take upon themselves the punishment for that society. In 1349 the town of Tournai witnessed the spectacle of about two hundred people beating themselves and each other with rods and whips to atone for the sins of society. Called Flagellants, they first appeared in 1260, when Europe was suffering an earlier series of disasters. A new wave of flagellant groups appeared in 1349, in response to the Black Death, and spread throughout much of present-day Belgium, Holland, Germany, Switzerland, and parts of eastern France. They were banned by Pope Clement VI in 1349 and officially condemned by the Council of Constance in the following century.

Flagellants were one of the strange responses to the plague, but they hurt only themselves. Other people blamed the Jews for the suffering of society, and large numbers of Jews were massacred by angry mobs in 1348–1349. Such massacres were often linked with the appearance of Flagellants. In Mainz, where the largest Jewish community in Germany lived, a massacre started in the midst of a Flagellant meeting, and the entire Jewish community was killed. Often the authorities did little to help the Jews, and those who did were often attacked themselves.

Fortunately these aberrant responses were not universal. In fact, many people were drawn closer to the church. At a time when death was so prevalent, it is not surprising that people thought more seriously about the afterlife and the way they could assure themselves of it. There was a higher involvement in church life in the late Middle Ages, and as we shall see, practices associated with life after death became especially popular.

The Renaissance

At the same time that Europe was suffering these terrible calamities, it also experienced great cultural vitality. The period has often been called the Renaissance, a French word meaning "rebirth." At one time historians believed the culture and learning of the classical period were "reborn" at the end of what was often called the "Dark Ages." They regarded the Middle Ages as a dark, unenlightened period when culture stagnated and the learning of classical antiquity was lost. The idea of a Renaissance was also tied to the Reformation because it was believed that once learning was reborn and people began to think for themselves, they rebelled against the shackles of a church that had held them in subjugation and told them what to think. The nineteenth-century Swiss historian Jakob Burkhardt viewed the Renaissance as the period that gave birth to the modern world, and he stressed that during this period the modern ideas of individuality and the pursuit of fame emerged.[10] Although this interpretation was based on a faulty understanding of the Middle Ages and a failure to appreciate its cultural achievements, clearly there was a great outburst of cultural creativity and increased interest in classical studies in the fourteenth and fifteenth centuries that helped transform learning in Western Europe and had a major impact on the Reformation.

As we have already noted, those living during the late Middle Ages, such as Matteo Palmieri, sometimes thought of themselves as living in an age of enlightenment and rebirth or recovery of the classical heritage. Contemporary writers such as Petrarch (1304–1374), Boccaccio (1313–1375), and Vasari (1511–1574) used similar metaphors of rebirth and renewal to describe the age in which they were living. The recovery of the classical heritage and its application to their own age was a central concern, and there was great optimism about what could be achieved. In 1338 Petrarch expressed great confidence in the future, commenting: "There is perhaps a better age in store; this slumber of forgetfulness will not last forever. After the darkness has been dispelled, our grandsons will be able to walk back into the pure radiance of the past."[11] His hopes were to be realized in the following century as more and more classical manuscripts became available and scholars began to learn Greek again. In the half century before the fall of Constantinople, scholars brought some 250 ancient manuscripts to Italy to save them from a feared Turkish invasion. The availability of these manuscripts sparked great interest in language and textual criticism.

Architects and sculptors were also interested in learning from the classical past, which often led them to the ruins of ancient Rome. Filippo Brunelleschi (1377–1446) spent time in Rome studying ancient architecture and later applied his discoveries to designing the magnificent dome of the cathedral in Florence and the Foundlings' Hospital, that city's first true Renaissance building. Donatello (1386–1466), who traveled to Rome with him, applied what he learned about classical sculpture to his incomparable bronze statue of David. Using as a model a Roman equestrian statue of Marcus Aurelius, he also produced the *Gattemelata*, the first life-size, bronze equestrian statue since the classical period. Other Florentine artists also broke from medieval tradition: Masaccio built on the work of the earlier Florentine artist Giotto, painting figures in a lifelike setting and depicting real human emotions, in contrast to the flat, nonrealistic style of the Middle Ages.

Florence was both the most important early center of Renaissance culture and one of the largest and most prosperous cities in Europe. After 1434 it was ruled by the Medici family, who had amassed wealth in banking and were especially generous patrons of the arts. Under their patronage the arts flourished, culminating in the great triumvirate of Renaissance art: Raphael (1483–1520), Michelangelo (1475–1564), and Leonardo da Vinci (1452–1519). From about the 1470s Rome began to challenge Florence as cultural leader when the Renaissance papacy became great patrons of the arts, finally supplanting Florence in the sixteenth century. The enormous scale of the papal projects lured some of the greatest artists to Rome. In 1506 Pope Julius II invited Michelangelo to Rome to build a grandiose tomb for the pope, but before the artist could complete the project, Julius suddenly gave him a new assignment, for which posterity will be forever grateful. Michelangelo spent the next three years on his back on a high scaffold painting the ceiling of the Sistine Chapel. He stayed in Rome for much of the rest of his life, making significant contributions to various building projects, including the Farnese Palace and classical buildings on the Capitoline Hill. Near the end of his life, Michelangelo became the chief architect for the completion of St. Peter's basilica. In 1508 Raphael was invited to Rome by Julius to direct the decoration of the staterooms in the Vatican. He painted his celebrated Madonnas in Rome and died there in 1520. Although da Vinci painted the *The Last Supper* and *Mona Lisa* in Milan and Florence respectively, he also worked on the Belvedere Palace in the Vatican for Pope Leo X, the son of Lorenzo de' Medici. Ironically, Leo's planned completion of the building of St. Peter's was partially financed by the indulgence sale that Luther protested against in the *Ninety-five Theses*.

Renaissance Humanism

The Renaissance also had a major impact on the Reformation through the work of a group of intellectuals who have been labeled "human-ists"—scholars dedicated to restoring classical antiquity. The humanists were specialists in literature and the humanities, particularly concerned with the liberal arts and studies of the humanities. Drawing their inspi-ration from the classical past, they sought not only to collect as many manuscripts as possible but also to acquire an accurate picture of the classical age by striving to achieve an accurate text. With this aim, they compared manuscripts to emend faulty readings and identify inter-polations and forgeries, pioneering the methods of textual criticism. They were also concerned to restore the Latin language to its classical excellence and bitterly criticized what they considered the inadequate, bastardized Latin of the Middle Ages.

A good example of the concerns, methods, and criticism integral to Italian humanism is found in the career of Lorenzo Valla (1407–1457), a Latin translator and philologist, one of whose concerns was to teach his age to write Latin the way Cicero wrote it. In 1441 he published a work entitled *Elegances of the Latin Language*, in which he attempted to purge Latin of its medieval blemishes. He also made a critical study of the Vulgate, the Latin translation of the Bible, which was the official Bible of the medieval church, and suggested that the church's system of penance and indulgences rested on a mistranslation: he maintained that the Greek word *metanoia*, which the Vulgate translated *paenitentia* (penance), was more properly translated "repentance." Erasmus's inter-est in biblical studies was stimulated by Valla's work and his acceptance of Valla's translation of *metanoia* was to influence sixteenth-century Reformers.

Valla's best-known work was entitled *On the Falsely Believed and Lying Donation of Constantine*, which he wrote while under the protection of Alfonso, king of Aragon, Sicily, and Naples. It was fortunate he had a powerful protector, because it constituted a vicious attack on the papacy. Using the methods of textual criticism, Valla argued convincingly that a supposed fourth-century document called the Donation of Constantine was a forgery. The document, which the papacy maintained was written by Emperor Constantine after Pope Sylvester had supposedly cured Constantine of leprosy, awarded the papacy far-reaching powers, stating that the papacy was to have superiority over the patriarchs of Alexandria, Antioch, Jerusalem, and Constantinople as well as the oversight of Rome and the western lands of the empire. Valla argued that the language of the document probably belonged to the eighth rather than the fourth century, and it was highly unlikely that Constantine would have made such a grant or that Pope Sylvester, whose main concerns were spiritual, would have accepted it. Valla used his scholarship to launch a direct attack on the papacy, suggesting that the papacy may well have been responsible for the forgery and that later popes defended what they knew to be false. He also argued that the papacy's usurpation of temporal power had led to the corruption of the church, and he urged the people of Rome and rulers of Europe to deprive the pope of his temporal powers. It is not surprising that Valla was summoned before the Inquisition and accused of heresy; however, since Valla was protected by King Alfonso, the case was withdrawn. More surprising is the fact that Valla ended his career in the service of the papacy. When King Alfonso moved toward reconciliation with Rome, Valla decided it might be wise to make his own peace with the papacy, and he wrote Pope Eugenius IV a letter of apology, requesting pardon. Although Eugenius ignored his request, his successor, Pope Nicholas V, forgave Valla and made him papal secretary. Valla's exposé of the Donation of Constantine was suppressed for years but was printed in 1517, and the Reformers drew heavily on its arguments in their attacks on the papacy.

Another concern of some Renaissance intellectuals was to attempt to harmonize conflicting religious beliefs. Few were more committed to this than a fourteenth-century German man named Nicholas of Cusa. Educated at Heidelberg, Padua, and Cologne, Nicholas received a doctorate in canon law in 1423. He was a churchman, philosopher, theologian, and scientist, and in an age of great hostility between Islam and Christianity, he worked hard for their reconciliation. Before the fall of Constantinople, he had been trying to unite the Eastern and Western churches; when the city fell, he wrote a treatise in which he sought a path to lasting peace with Islam. He recommended calling a conference of wise men representing different countries and religions to meet in Jerusalem in an attempt to create "one orthodox faith." He also studied the *Qur'ân*, and although he stated that by denying the resurrection and the deity of Christ the *Qur'ân* was in opposition to fundamental Christian belief, he also wrote that, by accepting the prophets and Christ as a prophet, the principles of the *Qur'ân* derived from Christian teaching.

The same effort to find a universal faith was one of the objectives of the Florentine Academy and its two leading figures, Marsilio Ficino (1433–1499) and Pico della Mirandola (1463–1494), who sought to discover a global spiritual harmony and a unity of all philosophies. Ficino believed truth could be found in all religious sources and greatly admired Plato.[12] In view of the humanist concern to achieve spiritual harmony, it is not surprising that in the sixteenth century humanists would also play a leading role in trying to heal the schism resulting from the Reformation.

Economic Growth, New Technology, and Expansion

While the Italian Renaissance was reaching a high point of cultural achievement, the economy of Europe was slowly recovering.[13] New technologies and industries helped stimulate economic expansion, which resulted in growing urbanization. Most towns and cities had been hard hit by the population decline resulting from the plague, but around the middle of the fifteenth century the population of Europe began to increase gradually, and an increasing population meant greater demand for goods, which in turn helped stimulate economic growth. However, not all areas benefited. Some regions, such as northern Italy and Burgundy, had a flourishing economy, often based on the textile industry and growing urbanization, while other areas continued to suffer economic deprivation and depression. The largest cities in Europe were in northern Italy: Venice may have had as many as 100,000 inhabitants; Milan was equally large, while other Italian cities, such as Florence and Rome, had populations of over 40,000. In contrast, large northern cities such as Bruges and Ghent probably had no more than 30,000 inhabitants, and in Germany only a few cities were larger than 20,000. In England, only London was as large. Economic growth was supported by and encouraged developments in banking, which led to the growth of a money economy. Technological innovations also helped to stimulate the economy.

Major technological breakthroughs in mining led to a significant increase in the amount of silver and copper available to support the growing economy. The invention of ventilation systems and suction pumps to remove water from the mines, which made it possible to mine at greater depths, occurred at the same time as major improvements in smelting techniques. The boom in copper mining coincided with the opening of new markets, which partially resulted from technological progress in shipbuilding. In the fifteenth century the Portuguese developed the caravel, whose maneuverability and ability to withstand heavy seas provided the type of ship needed to continue the exploration of the coast of Africa launched by Prince Henry the Navigator in 1418. In 1488 Bartholomew Diaz rounded the Cape of Good Hope, and a decade later Vasco da Gama reached India. The Portuguese found that copper and bronze artifacts were in great demand in India and West Africa, so the increased supply resulting from new mining technology proved very helpful to them in their new commercial empire. While Diaz was returning to Lisbon in triumph from his voyage to the Cape of Good Hope, a relatively unknown Genoese sea captain named Christopher Columbus was also in the city, trying to convince the king of Portugal to support an even more audacious undertaking. Four years later, supported by the rulers of neighboring Spain, Columbus took three ships (two of them caravels) across the Atlantic Ocean and opened up two continents to European colonization and economic exploitation.

The new mining technology also had an interesting impact on the Reformation. Mining added significantly to the wealth of one of the richest families in Europe, the Fuggers of Augsburg. They had accumulated enough money in the textile industry to become bankers and, in return for loans to the Hapsburgs, they obtained mining concessions. They then added to their fortune by mining silver in the Tyrol and copper in Hungary. As we shall see, the Fuggers played a role in the events that led to the outbreak of the Reformation. Among the rulers who benefited from the mining boom was Frederick the Wise of Saxony, because many of the silver mines were in the part of Saxony ruled by him. Frederick used some of that wealth to found a new university at Wittenberg and to pay the salary of a young teacher named Martin Luther. Luther's father, Hans, who was the son of a peasant, became prosperous as the result of investing in copper mining, making it possible for him to afford an excellent education for his gifted son. The wealth produced by new industries brought about the founding of universities north of the Alps, thereby increasing educational opportunities. Before the middle of the fourteenth century universities were located almost exclusively in Italy, France, and England. By the end of the fifteenth century, however, there were twenty-three universities outside that area, and the total number of universities in Europe had more than doubled. Many of these new universities were in Germany, where they would play an important role in the Reformation.

Even more significant for the Reformation was the new printing technology. Although block printing had existed for some time, around the middle of the fifteenth century a German goldsmith, Johannes Gutenberg, made the critical breakthroughs that gave birth to a large-scale printing industry. His most important discovery was the invention of movable type, which was combined with the development of an ink that would adhere to the metal type. The alteration of existing winepresses into screw-and-lever printing presses made possible the printing of pages of type. One of the early products of Gutenberg's new invention was the Gutenberg Bible, printed about 1455. It was only the first of many religious works made available at an affordable price by the new technology. Within a half century of the appearance of Gutenberg's Bible, printing presses had been set up all over Europe. By 1501 over 110 locations throughout Europe had at least one press—and some places had many more. Venice, for example, had approximately 150 presses. Printing not only made it possible to mass produce books and pamphlets at a fraction of their previous cost but also ensured uniformity of texts and helped avoid the copying mistakes that were all too prevalent in hand-copied manuscripts. One sixteenth-century observer praised the inventor of printing as having performed a divine service to learning. He noted that one man, using a printing press, could in a single day match the productivity of many scribes over an entire year. Printing made it possible for Luther's *Ninety-five Theses* to spread throughout Germany in two weeks and throughout Europe in a month.

The Role and Theology of the Church

The society of the late Middle Ages differed dramatically from modern European society because of the all-encompassing role of the Christian church. By 1500 Christianity had been the official and only tolerated religion in Western society for over a thousand years. Although Jews and Muslims lived within the borders of what was called Christendom or the *Corpus Christianum* (Christian body), they were considered outsiders. Christendom consisted of those who professed the true faith as defined by the church. Although there were political subdivisions within Christendom, and struggles took place within the body, the unity of the church and common allegiance to the church gave medieval society a fundamental unity. Since Christendom involved a thorough intertwining of secular and spiritual, one of the problems faced throughout the

Middle Ages was whether the spiritual or the secular leader should be head of that single Christian society. The secular leader was, in theory, the emperor, who headed a polyglot collection of political and spiritual jurisdictions that historians have called the Holy Roman Empire. The spiritual head of Western Christendom was the pope, and throughout the Middle Ages there were struggles between the emperor and the papacy over the limits of their jurisdictions. There were many areas of overlapping authority. For example, bishops were powerful secular rulers who controlled a great deal of land and wealth, but they were also princes of the church with major spiritual responsibilities and authority. An ongoing question was who should have the right to select bishops. Both the emperors and the papacy claimed that right at various periods, and both needed to control the bishops because their exercise of authority depended on having bishops who were sympathetic to their goals and objectives.

By the opening of the sixteenth century, despite the fact that the papacy had lost its struggle with secular authorities, the church continued to wield enormous power and influence. The church was the largest landowner in some parts of Europe, and large numbers of people were members of the clergy—in some areas as much as 10 percent of the population. The papacy itself was a major political force, controlling large areas of land in central Italy and elsewhere, and the church possessed enormous wealth. In addition the church touched the lives of the people of Christendom in almost every area, providing not only for their spiritual needs but also for their social life.

Life was in many ways governed by the ecclesiastical calendar: Saints' days provided holidays, and the major church festivals filled the drab lives of late medieval people with color, pageantry, and drama. The church's sacraments marked every important event in a person's life from birth to death, beginning with baptism and ending with extreme unction. Although life on this earth came to an end with Christian burial, the church's services did not end with death because the most important function of the church was to provide for life after death. In the late Middle Ages, when so many died prematurely, people always lived in the presence of death. Consequently, the church's teaching on how a person could gain eternal life and on the sacraments, which were the means the church provided to help in that quest, were very important to the average person. Although a central question for medieval people was, "What must I do to be saved?" most of them probably understood only the most basic theology.

Much medieval theology had been defined in the first five centuries of the Christian era and was expressed in a series of creeds, beginning with the Apostles' Creed, which best expressed what most people understood about the faith, as it was the one they were expected to know and on which they were examined at confession. The Nicene Creed, which taught the doctrine of the Trinity, was certainly not as well-known or understood, although it was recited at mass. The Athanasian Creed, which defined the relationship between the two natures of Christ, was recited on special days.

Beyond those creedal definitions, there was much diversity in the theology of the Western church. Historians are becoming increasingly aware that the traditional picture of a monolithic church, whose doctrinal position was clearly defined and which allowed very little freedom of thought, belongs in the realm of mythology. Doctrinal pluralism, uncertainty, and even individualism were all characteristic of the late medieval church. One modern commentator maintains that "nobody could be quite sure exactly what was the official teaching of the Church on certain matters."[14] Even in the areas in which doctrinal definitions were clear, they had not been worked out with the precision that would come with the Reformation. Two vitally significant doctrinal topics, on which there was at least basic agreement but where there remained questions, concerned justification and the sacraments. Because both subjects were to become the source of much division during the Reformation, we need to look at what the medieval church taught about them.

As has already been noted, some of the most important questions in medieval theology were those that dealt with life after death. The promise of eternal life was especially important to medieval people because they were constantly confronted with the reality of death. In late medieval society, a man might expect half his children to die before they reached adulthood, and he might lose two or three spouses during his lifetime. The doctrine of justification dealt with the question of how sinful human beings can be made right with God and thereby have life after death, and it was the subject of considerable debate among theologians in the late Middle Ages. Although there was agreement that justification did not take place in a moment but was a lifelong process made possible by the atoning death of Jesus Christ, how far the process was the responsibility of the individual sinner was under debate. The diagram that follows illustrates that part of the church's teaching on which there was basic agreement.

Medieval Doctrine of Justification

God

Sacraments   **Heaven**

Saints

Average
Person

Purgatory

Death

Those Who
Reject Grace

Birth

Hell

According to the church's teaching, the process of justification began shortly after birth, when babies born to Christian families were baptized. It was believed that the sacrament of baptism provided forgiveness for original sin and created faith. Before baptism, a person was unable even to respond to God's call, but after baptism he or she could respond and cooperate with God. Justification was understood as meaning "to make righteous"; God provided the means by which people were made righteous, but the individual also contributed. The sacraments were the vehicles God used to infuse grace to sinners, beginning with baptism.

Throughout life, sacraments aided in the process of justification. When an individual sinned, as all people did frequently, the sacrament of penance offered the opportunity for forgiveness and restoration. It consisted of two parts: the confession of sins and "satisfaction." One was expected to be contrite, that is, to be sorry for one's sins and confess them to a priest, who offered absolution, which removed the guilt or the eternal punishment for sin. Yet there remained a temporal punishment that was dealt with by satisfaction, which the priest prescribed and which might consist of alms-giving, prayers, going on pilgrimage, or some other meritorious work.

When sinners came to the end of their earthly lives, they were offered the sacrament of extreme unction. After death they went to one of three possible places. Those who had rejected God's grace, or had never received it, would go to hell, where they would suffer eternal torment—often vividly portrayed in painting, sculpture, and popular literature. Those who lived exceptionally saintly lives, and for whom the process of justification had been completed by the time of their death, would go directly to heaven. The majority of people, however, had not done sufficient satisfaction or penance to expiate the temporal punishment of sin, so they would go to purgatory, where the works of satisfaction would be completed. Once that had happened, they would go to heaven; so although the suffering of purgatory was excruciating, it was temporary—in contrast with the unending suffering in hell.

The church's teaching on justification clearly gave God the central role, since infused grace made salvation possible. The belief that salvation depended on free choice and rejected the need for infused grace was labeled Pelagianism, which had been condemned as heresy in the early Middle Ages.[15] In the late Middle Ages there was no question that human beings needed God's grace to be saved, but their role in the process was debated. One point of view, expressed in the works of theologians such as William of Ockham (1280–1349) and Gabriel Biel (1420–1485), placed a strong emphasis on the human contribution to salvation and is often labeled semi-Pelagianism. While rejecting a full Pelagian position, these theologians tried to preserve human responsibility by arguing that, although God could save human beings entirely by grace, he had chosen to set up a system in which human merit would be rewarded. Even though it was not sufficient to earn salvation, God chose to recognize meritorious human effort, which thereby became a necessary contributing factor to salvation. Biel explained his position in a rational and convincing manner: "No doubt he [God] could have simultaneously made us his friends and accepted our work as meritorious without this gift of grace. But how could we have remained in friendship with God without the assistance of grace? Thus God has established the rule [covenant] that whoever turns to him and does what he can will receive forgiveness of sins from God. God infuses assisting grace into such a man, who is thus taken back into friendship."[16]

A second position on justification is associated with the name of Pelagius's fourth-century opponent, Augustine of Hippo. Augustine taught that human beings were saved solely by the grace of God, and a group of late medieval theologians, called Augustinians, held firmly to his position. They considered their opponents to be Pelagians because they placed too much emphasis on what human beings contributed to their salvation and not enough on the grace of God. Among those who held this position were an Augustinian monk, Gregory of Rimini, and his contemporary, Thomas Bradwardine, an Oxford professor of divinity who was later appointed archbishop of Canterbury.[17] In 1344 Bradwardine wrote a treatise against the semi-Pelagian view, which he entitled *The Case of God against the Pelagians*. He included a statement

on justification that sounds very similar to the teaching of the Protestant
Reformers two centuries later: "All those who are children of Christ are
justified and are just, not because of themselves but because of Christ.
. . . Grace is given to you, it is not a payment. For this reason it is called
grace, because it is freely given. With preceding merits you cannot buy
what you have already received as a gift. Therefore the sinner has received
first grace in order that his sins might be forgiven."[18]

Bradwardine and the other Augustinians held a bleaker view of human
potential than their opponents. They believed that without God's direct
help humans were totally lost in their sin and could not even respond to
God. Sinners in no way deserved God's grace and mercy, so it was clearly
an unmerited gift. However, despite their affinity to the teaching of the
Protestant Reformers, the Augustinians were not Protestants "born out
of due time," because they were committed to the pattern of salvation
illustrated above. Justification was a process and, for most people, part
of that process was time spent in purgatory. The doctrine of purgatory,
which would be rejected by all the Protestant Reformers, was a critical
part of the theology of the late medieval church and played a central
role in popular religious practice.

The belief that there is an intermediate state after death before one
enters heaven became a part of the church's official teaching during the
Middle Ages. Although it is found in some early fathers, such as Clement
of Alexandria, Ambrose, and Origen, and was clearly taught by Pope
Gregory the Great in the seventh century, it was not until the thirteenth
century that Thomas Aquinas provided a detailed exposition of this
belief, which was officially defined as church doctrine at the Councils
of Lyons in 1274 and Florence in 1437.

A series of practices was developed in the course of the Middle Ages
to help reduce the length of time spent in purgatory. One method was
to arrange for masses to be said for a person's soul after death. Wealthy
people had the opportunity to invest in the health of their souls by setting aside an endowment that would provide for a chantry chapel and
support a priest who would say masses for their souls. The chapel might
simply be an altar in a space partitioned off in a church or cathedral,
or it might be a separate building attached to the church. People who
could not afford such an endowment individually could join an association called a confraternity, a group of laypeople who paid subscrip-
tions to support a priest to say masses on behalf of deceased members.
Confraternities were often based around a guild and served a social as
well as a religious function. Although this provision for masses to be
said or sung for souls in purgatory occurred already in the early Middle

Ages, the practice became particularly widespread and popular in the late Middle Ages.

People could also take advantage of other practices the church taught that helped souls in purgatory. One popular method was going on pilgrimage and viewing relics—physical objects associated with Christ, the saints, or some spectacular miracle. Some of the wealthier rulers in Europe amassed huge collections of relics; for example, Martin Luther's prince, Frederick the Wise of Saxony, spent five days in Jerusalem in 1493 collecting relics. He then invested a vast amount of money rebuilding the castle church in Wittenberg to house his collection of more than ten thousand relics, which included the body of one of the children massacred by Herod, milk from the breast of the Virgin Mary, and straw from the stable where Christ was born. Albrecht of Brandenburg had a collection of relics that it was believed would liberate those who viewed them from over 39 million years in purgatory. Although today there is no question that most of the items revered as relics were bogus, few medieval people were skeptical of the claims made, and opposition to the cult of relics was rare.

A further way in which time in purgatory could be shortened was through indulgences, initially granted to people who had done an exceptional work of piety, such as going on a Crusade. In the late Middle Ages, however, the church began selling indulgences, and the papacy argued they were based on the surplus merit that Christ, the Virgin Mary, and the saints had accumulated through their especially holy lives. In 1342 Pope Clement VI issued the papal bull *Unigenitus*, which stated that this surplus merit could be dispensed by the pope through indulgences that would partially or fully remit temporal punishment for the sins of the person who purchased the indulgence. In 1476 Pope Sixtus IV issued a further papal bull, *Salvator noster*, which stated that indulgences could be applied to the souls of the departed in purgatory.

In the course of the Middle Ages, a series of doctrinal definitions dealt with the sacraments. Initially theologians disagreed about the number of sacraments. In the eleventh century, Peter Damian stated there were twelve sacraments, while in the following century Hugh of St. Victor wrote a major work on sacraments in which he listed as many as thirty. In the same century, Peter Lombard, who wrote the standard textbook of medieval theology, fixed the number at seven, a number accepted by Thomas Aquinas in the following century and formally affirmed at the Council of Florence. Five sacraments—baptism, confirmation, penance, the Eucharist, and extreme unction—applied to all Christians; the final two—matrimony and orders—did not. Normally a person could only participate in one or the other of the final two, since ordination was the sacrament of entry into the priesthood, and priests were not allowed to marry.

The most important sacrament for medieval worship was the Eucharist, doctrines about which had been the source of a good deal of theological debate until in 1215 the Fourth Lateran Council closed part of the debate by defining the doctrine of transubstantiation. The council decreed that: "His [Christ's] body and blood are truly contained in the sacrament of the altar under the forms of bread and wine, the bread and wine having been changed in substance by God's power into his body and blood. . . . Nobody can effect this sacrament except a priest who has been properly ordained according to the church's keys which Jesus Christ himself gave to the apostles and their successors."[19]

The doctrine of transubstantiation led to the practice of giving only bread to communicants in order to avoid the danger of spilling the wine, which—according to that doctrine—was the very blood of Christ. This practice was justified by the doctrine of concomitance, which stated that the body and blood are in both elements, so the laity received both even when they were only given the bread. The Eucharist became the center of the medieval worship service and the act of consecration the high point of the mass because this was when the ordinary elements of bread and wine were changed in substance into the glorious body and blood of Jesus Christ, the Lord of the universe. This occurred behind a screen, and the congregation, standing in the nave of the church where the laity normally worshiped, knew it had happened only by the ringing of a bell and the elevation of the host (the consecrated bread).

The doctrine of transubstantiation led to many practices that Protestants later called "idolatry." The host was reserved in a special place in the altar with a light burning before it. Priests and laypeople bowed to the altar, acknowledging the presence of the body of Christ. The consecrated host was venerated and carried in Corpus Christi processions. Although people were required to go to confession and communion at least once a year, they normally came to mass only to be in the presence of Christ and witness this great miracle. The average person viewed the consecrated host as having miraculous powers, and people sometimes surreptitiously took it home to use in ways that would have horrified the church, such as feeding it to a sick cow in the hope that the animal would be healed. In such ways the official theology of the church could be misunderstood by the average person or adapted to fit his or her perceived needs.

Popular Religious Belief and Practice

Religious beliefs and practices in the late Middle Ages were not limited to what the church taught and provided. Popular religious practices and beliefs sometimes differed greatly from official religion, and in some instances they posed a challenge to the church. While the church's ministrations were designed to provide for the life beyond, popular religion was often more concerned with the present life. Rites that were quite different from the church's rituals developed to protect crops and animals, to protect against disease, to help in childbirth, and to deal with infertility and impotence. For such purposes, the rituals of the church were sometimes adapted or parodied. Superstition, magic, occult practice, and astrology were all acceptable elements of the belief systems of medieval people, who were also easily attracted to charismatic figures who claimed to be prophets with a special word from God and who sometimes posed a serious threat to the church and to social order.

One example of the social disruption caused by popular prophets is the events associated with the "Drummer of Niklashausen," a cowherd named Hans Boehm, who claimed he had a vision of the Virgin Mary commanding him to preach. In 1476 he appeared in the village of Niklashausen, Germany, and began preaching. According to one account: "He preached violently against the government and the clergy, also against pointed shoes, slashed sleeves, and long hair. He also claimed that water, pasture, and wood ought to be held in common by all and that tolls and export payments should be abolished. The whole country, he said, was mired in sin and wantonness and, unless our people were ready to do penance and change their wicked ways, God would let all Germany go to destruction."[20]

Boehm's preaching, combined with reports of his vision, had an amazing effect and stimulated a mass pilgrimage. According to the same account, people confessed their sins, cut off the points of their shoes (pointed shoes were then in fashion), trimmed their hair, and threw away their adornments. The drummer became such a figure of adoration that people tore off tufts from his cap, believing they had power to cure illness. The drummer also attacked the clergy, and his pilgrims chanted a song:

O God in heaven, on you we call, *kyrie eleison*.
Help us seize our priests and kill them all, *kyrie eleison*.[21]

Eventually, when the drummer told his followers to bring weapons to church, the authorities intervened, and the bishop of Würzburg sent armed retainers to arrest him. Although the drummer was arrested and thrown into prison, the mob attacked the prison crying out that the Virgin Mary would protect them from harm by the authorities. Nevertheless, the soldiers fired on the crowd, killing and wounding many. The drummer and three others were burned at the stake and their ashes thrown into the river, but people dug up the soil from the spot where the drummer had been executed, took it home, and treasured it as a sacred relic.

This account exemplifies the mass frenzy and threat to social order that could arise from popular religion. Understandably the church was constantly trying to control unofficial religion, and in that effort it often incorporated elements of popular belief and practice into official religion. For example, liturgical practices that had originated outside official channels were incorporated into the regular liturgy. Dramatic and symbolic reenactments of biblical stories, such as Palm Sunday processions with Christ on an ass, clergy and people creeping barefoot on their knees to kiss the cross on Good Friday, and the opening of the tomb on Easter Day, became part of the liturgical cycle, celebrating key feast days in the church calendar such as Palm Sunday, Good Friday, Easter, Ascension, and Pentecost.

The cults of saints and of the Virgin Mary were an especially important part of late medieval popular piety, and intense devotion to the Virgin Mary was so fundamental that it was accepted, although not necessarily endorsed, by the church. Mary was viewed as a mediator between sinful human beings and her glorified Son, often viewed as a judge rather than a Savior. Popular works such as Herolt's *Miracles of the Blessed Virgin* described remarkable miracles performed by Mary, including raising people from the dead. A related form of popular piety was a general devotion to the saints, who also served as intermediaries and who were believed to provide help in this life for everything from toothaches to safety in travel.

Connected with this devotion to Mary was the popular practice of pilgrimage. Pilgrims from all over Europe undertook long and often dangerous journeys to sites associated with saints, such as St. Albans in England, or Santiago de Compostela in Spain, which was reputed to be the burial place of the apostle James. Rome, which was associated with both Peter and Paul and was the residence of the papacy, was also a place where a great number of relics could be viewed and was understandably one of the most popular pilgrimage sites.

The church played an important role in the lives of late medieval people, and its ministrations were very popular. In an age of calamities,

contrasts, and conflicts, the church served an especially important function. Even though most people probably could not follow the intricacies of
Christian theology, they understood enough to find comfort and meaning
for their lives. Although they also sought religious experiences outside
the official channels of the church that were sometimes in conflict with
the church's teaching, unless they were directly opposed to Christian
belief, the church itself often sanctioned such popular religious beliefs
and practices. This example of tolerance suggests that the church was
serving the religious needs of society effectively; however, many articulate voices in society disagreed, arguing that the church was failing in
almost every area and was in desperate need of reform.

Many reform movements in the late Middle Ages sought to deal with
the problems in the church, and the church was also torn apart by internal conflicts throughout much of the period. This has led to a major
debate among historians about the health of the late medieval church
and the degree to which its failures help explain the Reformation. The
conflicts that plagued the late medieval church and efforts at reform in
the pre-Reformation period will be examined in the next chapter.

2

REFORM AND CONFLICT IN THE LATE MEDIEVAL CHURCH

▼

Observe how many behave, who live strictly under the monastic discipline. They seldom go out, they live retired, they eat the poorest food; they work hard, they talk little, they keep long watches; they rise early, they spend much time in prayer, they study much, and always guard themselves with discipline.

Thomas à Kempis[1]

Almost as happy as the theologians are those men who are commonly called "religious" and "monks"—though both names are quite incorrect, since a good part of them are very far removed from religion. . . . Everyone despises this breed of men so thoroughly that even a chance meeting with one of them is considered unlucky, still they maintain a splendid opinion of themselves.

Desiderius Erasmus[2]

The Historical Debate

The above descriptions of monasticism, found in works that were best sellers in the pre-Reformation period, give us some idea of the challenge facing historians as they try to assess the late medieval church. The first quotation is taken from one of the classic devotional works of the late Middle Ages, Thomas à Kempis's *The Imitation of Christ*. Written in the early fifteenth century, it became one of the most popular books of devotion for clergy and laity alike, with seven hundred manuscripts and numerous printed editions in less than a century. *The Imitation of Christ* was one of many devotional works written in the century preceding the Reformation that testify to the health of the late medieval church. In contrast, the second quotation is taken from Erasmus's *In Praise of Folly*, a scathing attack on monks, parish priests, theologians, the hierarchy of the church, and religious practices. Benefiting from the printing press, Erasmus was the first best-selling author in the history of printing, with *In Praise of Folly* appearing in more than six hundred editions. Although Erasmus's book was probably the most widely read of the literature criticizing the church, it was certainly not alone. So many treatises advocating reform were written in the century preceding the Reformation that they have still not been adequately studied. So while many people thought the church was in desperate need of reform, others believed it was healthy, serving the religious needs of society impressively—and they supported it generously in a variety of ways.

The constant and often strident criticism suggests that the church had very serious problems. Many articulate voices were aware of these problems, were extremely critical of the church, and insisted on reform. The protest literature was often critical of the parish clergy, who were accused of being immoral, greedy, unconcerned about the religious welfare of their parishioners, and inadequate for their jobs. The higher clergy, especially the papacy, were accused of disgracing the offices they held. The large amount of fifteenth-century literature criticizing religious abuses provides evidence for those historians who explain the Reformation in terms of the failure of the late medieval church. Those who hold this view often contrast the church of the High Middle Ages (1050–1300) with that of the late Middle Ages (1300–1500) and paint a convincing picture of continuing decline, especially evident in the decline of the papacy. Popes such as Innocent III (1198–1216), who dominated their society and who were impressive in their moral behavior, contrast dramatically with Renaissance popes such as Alexander VI (1492–1503) and Leo X (1513–1521), who were little more than local Italian princes competing with other rulers of Europe and certainly less than impressive in their personal morality.

Yet other evidence suggests that the church was healthy, popular, and in the process of reform. The growing movements of lay piety, the popularity of lay confraternities and mass endowments, the steady stream of devotional literature produced by the new art of printing, and a considerable revival of preaching all testified to a healthy, vibrant church. The popularity of the church is illustrated by the laity's spending large amounts of money building and renewing churches, contributing to endowments for chantry priests, participating in pilgrimages, and supporting the churches in other ways. For example, in Suffolk, England, approximately half the parish churches were substantially remodeled during the fifteenth century. Laypeople also spent large sums of money on relics and endowing masses. Confraternities became so popular that there were ninety-nine such bodies in the city of Hamburg alone in 1517, and this pattern of newly founded confraternities was repeated in many cities. Such evidence has led historians who have studied these expressions of devotion[3] to conclude that the late medieval church was certainly not in a state of decline. It had, in fact, great vitality and was meeting the religious needs of society impressively. They argue that the constant repetition of the same criticism may reflect higher expectations rather than a decline in the church. The heretical movements of the late Middle Ages, once considered forerunners of the Reformation, were, these historians contend, relatively small movements in contrast to the great support the medieval church enjoyed from the majority.[4] Although reforms were necessary, the fact that the need for reform was recognized itself testifies to the health of the church. The wide and enthusiastic support of the church by most of the laity indicates that heretical movements were likely to attract little popular support.

How does one reconcile these two dramatically contrasting views of the late medieval church, both based on surviving evidence? In the first instance, some of the apparently contradictory evidence is not, on closer examination, really contradictory. The late medieval church had great strengths and major weaknesses, and the evidence that reveals its strengths helps explain why the church was so popular with many people. However, even allowing for the hyperbole characteristically found in the works of ardent Reformers, the church clearly had serious problems, some of which resulted from the incessant conflicts that raged throughout the period. The conflict over the leadership led to a schism in the papacy and eventually to conflict about who held the final authority in the church. Such conflict diverted the attention of the hierarchy, causing them to misuse the resources of the church to fight opponents and making the papacy very suspicious of reform movements that threatened their power. There were also conflicts between laity and the clergy, sometimes labeled "anticlericalism," leading to some of the most outspoken criticism of the clergy.

Although a profusion of conflicts plagued the late medieval church, a plethora of reform movements was also a characteristic of that church. Pious bishops who worked hard to reform their dioceses were not uncommon and, in the great tradition of the Middle Ages, monastic orders aided the cause of reform. There were also other movements that did not originate in the established institutions of the church. Significant lay movements such as the Brethren of the Common Life, the group with which Thomas à Kempis was associated, made important contributions to the spiritual life of the laity. Humanists were some of the most outspoken advocates of reform, and they were especially vocal in pointing out the weaknesses of the church. In this chapter we will first examine the conflicts in the late medieval church to discover how they helped undermine its health, but we will also survey the reform movements in an effort to present a balanced picture. The chapter concludes with some suggestions on how conflicting evidence on the condition of the late medieval church might be reconciled and how the unresolved problems provide the background to the Reformation.

The Conflict in Leadership

The conflicts between emperor and papacy over the leadership of medieval society, mentioned in the previous chapter, initially resulted in some important victories for the papacy. However, in these struggles the papacy dissipated its prestige by misusing spiritual weapons such as excommunication in what many perceived as a political struggle. At the end of the thirteenth century, Pope Boniface VIII came into conflict with Philip the Fair of France and issued a papal bull entitled *Unam Sanctam*, which made extreme claims for papal power. Although the bull claimed that "it is altogether necessary to salvation for every human creature to be subject to the Roman pontiff,"[5] it did not persuade Philip to subject himself to Boniface VIII. Instead, he accused the pope of gross immorality and heresy and sent an army into Italy to capture the seventy-year-old pontiff and bring him back to France for trial. Although Boniface escaped, he died shortly afterwards, and a Frenchman, the archbishop of Bordeaux, who took the title Clement V (1305–1314), was elected to replace him. Clement spent his pontificate traveling around France, finally settling in Avignon, a papal territory in southern France, where he died in 1314. The College of Cardinals, now largely French since Clement had added twenty-three French cardinals, elected another French pope, John XXII (1316–1334), who stayed on at Avignon.

For the next seventy-three years, popes resided at Avignon. Petrarch called it the Babylonian Captivity of the Church, suggesting that the popes were the captives of the French king whose territory surrounded the papal enclave at Avignon. The Avignon popes have received a great deal of criticism, not all of it entirely fair. Although Clement's successor, John XXII, had more than his share of faults and was more of a politician than an effective spiritual leader,[6] his successor, Benedict XII (1334–1342), was a committed reformer. He was followed by Clement VI (1342–1352), who was largely responsible for the nefarious reputation of the Avignon popes. Clement was a lavish spender of questionable morality, whose luxurious court resembled that of a secular ruler rather than the spiritual head of Christendom. The abuses of his court were especially evident to intellectuals such as Petrarch, who was so appalled by it that he called it "the sewer of the world." Other great minds of the age, such as Marsiglio of Padua (1275–1342) and William of Ockham (1285–1347), made similar criticisms.

Many respected and saintly people in Europe cried out against the immorality surrounding the papacy at Avignon and demanded the pope return to Rome. Catherine of Siena (1347–1389), who was later canonized in 1461, was particularly horrified by the conduct of the papal court, voicing the opinion of many when she said it was wrong for the bishop of Rome to be absent from Rome, and bombarding the pope with indignant letters demanding his return to the holy city. St. Bridget of Sweden (1303–1373), founder of the Brigittine order and canonized in 1391, joined Catherine in demanding that the pope return to Rome. She was unrestrained in her criticism of papal abuses, stating that the pope was "like to Lucifer in envy, more unjust than Pilate, harsher than Judas, and more abominable than the Jews."[7] Such pressure, and his own belief that the bishop of Rome should reside in Rome, finally brought Gregory XI (1370–1378) back to Rome in 1377, where he died the following year.

The French cardinals then had the problem of electing a new pope in the face of a Roman mob. They did not completely succumb to intimidation because they elected a Neapolitan, who took the title Urban VI (1378–1389). Although Naples was in Italy, it was allied with France, so Urban was in a sense a compromise candidate. Shortly after his election the mob, not knowing who had been elected, broke into the conclave, causing the cardinals to flee in terror. Urban seemed like a good choice at a time when the church was in desperate need of reform.

He was a committed reformer, determined to root out worldliness from the clergy, beginning at the top with the Curia and the cardinals, and to eliminate corrupt practices. However, he was also given to violent rages, paranoia, and an inflated sense of his own authority. Urban was so abusive to the cardinals that they concluded they had made a terrible mistake in electing him.

Gradually the cardinals left Rome and went to Anagni, where they declared that the coercion of the mob made Urban's election invalid. They deposed Urban, went back to Avignon, and elected as his replacement Cardinal Robert of Geneva, who took the title Clement VII (1378–1394). This resulted in a massive problem for the church: which of the two popes elected by the same set of cardinals was the true pope—the man who had been elected first, but supposedly under pressure from the mob, or the man elected second? There seemed to be no way to resolve the problem. Urban deposed the cardinals who had deposed him and selected twenty-nine new cardinals, so there were then two sets of cardinals as well as two popes. The final result was what has been labeled the "Great Schism."

The church had experienced many papal schisms in the course of its history but never one in which the same set of cardinals had elected two popes. Europe was thoroughly divided, since some areas supported the Roman pope, while others supported the pope residing at Avignon. As might be expected, northern and central Italy supported Rome and France supported Avignon. The empire was divided as England, the enemy of France in the Hundred Years' War, supported Rome while Spain supported Avignon. Rulers also switched allegiance. In 1398 France withdrew its recognition of Avignon, but just when the Roman pope seemed to be gaining, Sicily and Genoa fell away from him. Since both popes had their own sets of cardinals, schism did not end with the death of either Clement or Urban because the two sets of cardinals elected respective successors.

During the period of the Great Schism (1378–1415) there were four Roman popes but only two Avignon popes. Urban died in 1389 and was succeeded by Boniface IX (1389–1404), who was immediately excommunicated by the Avignon pope, Clement. Boniface responded in kind by excommunicating Clement. When Clement died in 1394, there was hope that the schism could be ended if the Avignon cardinals did not elect a new pope. However, they elected Pedro de Luna, a man of irreproachable morals, but entirely the wrong candidate if they hoped to heal the schism. He took the title Benedict XIII (1394–1423) and proved to be unshakable in his conviction that he was the legitimate pope. His obstinacy helped to prolong the schism even after the rulers of Europe, as well as the majority of church leaders, were committed to end it. By the time Benedict died in 1423 the schism had ended for all but himself and his four remaining cardinals, but the means used to end the schism created a new conflict over who had the final authority in the church.

The Conflict over Authority

The conflict over leadership between the rival popes led a number of university scholars to question how far the pope had the right to the sole governance of the church, with some beginning to argue that the final authority in the church was a council rather than the papacy. In the first five centuries of the church's history, the great doctrinal controversies had been resolved by councils, and the new theorists called for a return to some sort of conciliar government. Although not rejecting the primacy of the papacy, they maintained that the final authority in the church resides in the whole body, and while they accepted that the pope was superior in authority to any other single person in the church, they claimed he was not superior to the whole church body as represented in a general council.

In 1393 the University of Paris stated that if the competing popes, after being "urged in a brotherly and friendly manner," would neither resign nor accept arbitration, there was "a third way which we propose as an excellent remedy for this sacrilegious schism. We mean that the matter shall be left to a general council." One of Benedict XIII's original supporters, Pierre D'Ally, whom Benedict had appointed to a bishopric, broke with Benedict when he failed to support efforts to heal the schism. He argued that where there were "several contenders for the Papacy so that the whole Church obeyed no single one of them . . . the Church can and should assemble a general council without the authority of the Pope."[8]

That is precisely what happened in 1409, when cardinals from both parties joined together to issue a call for a council to meet at Pisa. Although neither of the rival popes accepted the council and instead called councils of their own in opposition, the Council of Pisa received the support of most of the courts of Europe and was attended by more than five hundred prelates. This council attempted to resolve the schism by deposing both the competing popes and electing a new pope, Alexander V (1409–1410). However, neither of the deposed popes recognized the deposition, and both retained enough support to continue to press their claims. So the conciliar movement, at least in its initial stages, rather than resolving the problem, complicated it, as there were now three rivals all claiming to be the true pope.

When Alexander V died in 1410, John XXIII (1410–1415)[9] was elected in his place, and there was a real possibility of three lines of popes continuing. John was a poor choice. He had been a pirate earlier in his life, and although he later became a doctor of law and was an excellent administrator, his morals were highly questionable. He was also unscrupulous in his political dealings and hardly the man to restore the spiritual prestige of the papacy. Fortunately, he did not remain pope for long. Although he managed to establish himself briefly in Rome, he was forced to flee in 1413 when the king of Naples retook the city. John XXIII then turned to the German Emperor Sigismund for aid, but the emperor required John to call a new council as a condition of receiving imperial assistance. As a result, John reluctantly called the Council of Constance, which began meeting in 1414.

The Council of Constance was one of the most impressive councils in the history of the church. A contemporary listed 12,460 people who attended. Among them were 2 popes, 33 cardinals, 47 archbishops, 145 bishops, 93 suffragan bishops, 132 abbots, 155 priors, 5,000 spiritual lords, 29 dukes, 32 princes, 141 counts, 71 barons, 1,500 knights, and 217 doctors of theology. This impressive gathering, sponsored by the emperor, succeeded in solving papal schism. It met from 1414 to 1418 in the lakeside city of Constance and resolved the conflict in leadership by deposing all three popes and electing a completely new pope, who took the title Martin V (1417–1431). Fortunately, this did not result in four popes because both John XXIII and the Roman pope resigned. Although Benedict failed to recognize his deposition and remained in his castle in Spain anathematizing opponents until his death in 1423,[10] the rest of Christendom accepted the decision of the council.

The papal schism was healed and the council sought to ensure that schism could not happen again by issuing two decrees attempting to give councils a permanent place in the governance of the church. The decree *Sacrosancta* stated that a general council representing the whole church held its authority directly from Christ, and everyone, including the pope, must obey its decrees in matters pertaining to the faith, the abolition of schism, and reform. A second decree, *Frequens*, provided for regular meetings of councils. It ordered that a new council should meet in five years followed by a second council seven years later. Thereafter councils should meet every ten years.

The decisions of the Council of Constance might have resolved the entire conflict over authority if the papacy had been willing to accept the council's solution—but it was not. Even though Martin owed his position to a council and had supported the conciliar movement as a cardinal, once he became pope he consistently fought to restrict the authority of councils and resisted all reforms that would diminish papal authority. Although, in obedience to *Frequens*, he called a council to meet in Pavia in 1423, he dissolved it the following year when it began to show antipapal tendencies. In response to public pressure, he called another council seven years later, which began to meet at Basel in 1431, but Pope Martin V died before it began its real work.

Martin's successor, Eugenius IV (1431–1447), who was strongly opposed to the conciliar movement, quickly came into conflict with the council. From the beginning of his pontificate he sought to undermine it and to restore the full authority of the papacy over the church. Shortly after becoming pope, Eugenius dissolved the council, but when it refused to disperse he had to back down, withdraw his bull of dissolution, and accept humiliating terms. However, when radical members of the council attempted drastically to curtail papal power, Eugenius gained support from the moderates. In 1437 he moved the council to the Italian city of Ferrara, and two years later it was transferred to Florence. Many of the delegates resisted these moves and stayed at Basel, but the pope's success in negotiating an agreement with the Eastern church won him much additional support. The conflict in authority reached a new intensity when the remaining delegates at Basel deposed Eugenius IV and elected an antipope, Felix V, in 1439. By this time Europe was tired of schism, and Eugenius won the day. The antipope resigned in 1449 and the Council of Basel moved to Lausanne, where it voted its own dissolution.

Less than half a century after the seeming triumph of the conciliar movement, Pope Pius II issued the papal bull *Execrabilis* (1460), which in the strongest possible language prohibited appeals to a council in opposition to the pope, calling councils "erroneous and damnable." Although Pope Julius II (1503–1513) called another council on the eve of the Reformation, it was clearly controlled by the papacy. The victory of the papacy over the conciliar movement was definitively stated in the papal bull *Pastor Aeternus*, which was issued in 1516 by Pope Leo X (1513–1521). It declared that the pope "alone has the power, right and full authority, extending beyond that of all councils, to call, adjourn and dissolve the councils." The bull also repeated the radical claims for papal authority made by Boniface VIII at the beginning of the period, stating that "it is necessary for the salvation of souls that all Christian believers be subject to the pope at Rome."[11] The papacy had won the conflict over authority; however, its potential for bringing meaningful reform was undermined in the ensuing struggle that diverted the attention of the church's leadership. Furthermore, although the papacy had regained its authority over the church, the men elected to papal office in the next half century had little commitment to reforming the church, and their moral behavior sometimes suggested that rather than leading a reform movement, they themselves needed to be reformed.

The Renaissance Papacy

The popes who ruled the church in the half century before the Reformation were often good administrators, effective political and military leaders, as well as great patrons of the arts, but they were generally not impressive spiritual leaders. Rather than leading the way to meaningful reform from above, as the popes had done in the High Middle Ages, the Renaissance popes concentrated their efforts on patronizing Renaissance culture, rebuilding the city of Rome, promoting the interests of their relatives, and expanding the holdings of the Papal States. They were often shamelessly nepotistic, appointing incompetent relatives to high positions in the church and using the resources of the church to enrich their families. As a result of concentrating on Italian politics, the Renaissance papacy often seemed little more than one among many Italian powers engaged in local struggles rather than the universal head of Christendom. Some of the men who held papal office during this period were notoriously immoral and disgraced their office by their lifestyle and pursuit of worldly power; others were able and largely moral men who made major contributions to the Renaissance culture. Unfortunately, the best of the Renaissance popes held office at the beginning of the period and the worst in the half century that led up to the Reformation.

Nicholas V (1447–1455) was first of the true Renaissance popes, and one of the best. His contribution to learning and culture was massive. He founded the Vatican library, collecting an impressive number of books in Latin and Greek, and sent emissaries throughout Europe to find more manuscripts. He also inaugurated the physical rebuilding of Rome, whose buildings had suffered serious deterioration during the Avignon papacy and the Great Schism. In 1450 Nicholas presided over a great jubilee, which drew thousands of pilgrims to Rome, and it seemed as though the papacy had recovered its prestige after the disasters of the previous century. Nicholas V also showed some support for church reform by sending legates, including the former conciliar theorist, Nicholas of Cusa, throughout Europe on missions of reform. The final years of his pontificate were darkened by the fall of Constantinople in 1453, and before he died two years later, Pope Nicholas V began to plan a Crusade to liberate that city from the Turks. The next two popes, Calixtus III (1455–1458) and Pius II (1458–1464), were also committed to a Crusade against the Turks, but neither was successful in that effort. Pius had been an accomplished author before he became pope, and his election was acclaimed by the humanists. He was a serious churchman and even composed a letter—which was never sent—to the Turkish sultan, in which he attempted to refute the teachings of the *Qur'ân*, summarized the Christian faith, and urged the sultan to convert to Christianity and be baptized. Although he was guilty of using the papal office to enrich his relatives, Pius II stands with Nicholas V as one of the best of the Renaissance popes.

Sadly, those who followed Pope Pius II did not have the same spiritual commitment. Pope Paul II (1464–1471) was a pompous and vain man, who initially rose to high office in the church because his uncle was Pope Eugenius IV. He missed the opportunity for significant reform and concentrated his efforts on collecting works of art and restoring the monuments of ancient Rome. He loved display and extravagance, and his court resembled that of a secular ruler.

Paul II's successor, Pope Sixtus IV (1471–1484), was an equally lavish spender. He bought the papacy by bribing the cardinals, and his coronation tiara cost 100,000 ducats, which was over one-third of the papal income. Sixtus IV initiated a policy that proved disastrous to the reputation of the papacy, as he became involved in duplicity and the unscrupulous behavior that characterized the wars between the Italian states. He fought a series of wars and shifted alliances as it suited him, with no concern for morality or fidelity. He devoted his energies to enriching his family, making his favorite nephew a cardinal at the age of twenty-six. Another nephew was involved in an infamous conspiracy that led to the murder of Giovanni de' Medici and wounding of Lorenzo de' Medici in 1478. The assassins selected a singularly inappropriate time and place—high mass in the cathedral in Florence—but this did not deter the pope from continuing to support his nephew. When the dead man's relatives took revenge by murdering the killer, Sixtus IV excommunicated the entire city of Florence. During his pontificate he created thirty-four cardinals, six of whom were his nephews. The result of this type of nepotism, which other Renaissance popes also practiced, was the creation of a largely Italian College of Cardinals, drawn from some of the richest Italian families. In 1431 half the cardinals were non-Italians, but by 1492 only one of the twenty-three cardinals was not an Italian. Sixtus IV's greatest claim to fame was that he continued the rebuilding of Rome, completed the establishment of the papal library, and commissioned the Sistine Chapel, which is named after him. Unfortunately, those were not the sort of accomplishments the church most needed at a time when the cries for reform were becoming ever more strident.

Sixtus IV's successors disgraced the papal office even more blatantly. When Innocent VIII (1484–1492) became pope by bribing the now notoriously secular cardinals, he already had sixteen illegitimate children, whom he openly acknowledged, giving them honors and riches at the expense of the church. To raise money, Innocent VIII turned the sale of indulgences into a business and created numerous unnecessary new offices—which he also sold—in the papal Curia, thereby creating a new vested interest that would resist any real financial reform. He abandoned his predecessor's policies of seeking to unite Christendom against the Turks, as he found a useful new source of revenue by agreeing to keep the sultan's fugitive brother in confinement in return for a payment of forty thousand ducats annually and the lance that supposedly pierced Christ's side during the crucifixion.

When Innocent VIII died, the cardinals again succumbed to bribery and elected one of their own number, Roderigo Borgia, who as Pope Alexander VI (1492–1503) was possibly the most notorious pope of all time. The author of a sympathetic history of the papacy comments: "Roderigo was a worldly and ruthless man, and at the time of his election was already the father of eight children, by at least three women. That such a man should have seemed a fit successor to Peter speaks volumes about the degradation of the papacy."[12]

Alexander VI continued to keep a mistress even after he became pope, when he was already in his sixties. People seemed to believe he was capable of the most despicable deeds, including assassination and murder, and although the worst stories about him are probably not true, he was certainly a thoroughly secular ruler and unscrupulous politician who devoted himself to advancing the interests of his children. The most infamous of these was Cesare Borgia, whom Alexander made bishop of several sees when he was still only eighteen. Cesare's reputation was equally notorious, and he was accused of any number of murders, including that of his own brother. It is believed that Niccolo Machiavelli's classic work on Renaissance statecraft, *The Prince*, which portrays the ruler as having no moral restraints in advancing the good of the state, was modeled on Cesare. It is not surprising that a city ruled by the Borgias was a place of lawlessness and corruption, and travelers visiting Rome described it as a city full of criminals, where "money, power, and lust governed everything."[13] The many pilgrims who visited Rome during the jubilee year, 1500, returned home with stories that shocked the pious people of Germany and other northern countries. It is, therefore, not surprising that they had very little sympathy for Rome when one of their own came into conflict with the papacy two decades later.

When Pope Alexander VI died in 1503, the cardinals selected a reformer, Pius III, as the next pope. Unfortunately, he died after being in office less than a month and was succeeded by one of Sixtus IV's nephews, Julius II (1503–1513). By comparison with Innocent VIII and Alexander VI, Julius was a great improvement, being a man of some integrity and a great patron of the arts. Future generations will be forever grateful to him for commissioning Michelangelo to paint the ceiling of the Sistine Chapel and initiating, in 1505, the building of a new St. Peter's to replace the basilica of St. Peter. Pope Julius II was also a clever diplomat and a good military leader, who expanded the territory of the Papal States. Had he been a secular prince, Julius II would have been considered an outstanding ruler, but he was hardly an impressive spiritual leader. Although he called the Fifth Lateran Council in 1512, which met for five years, its reforming successes were negligible, largely because the head of the church was not committed to a policy of reform. Julius is well depicted in Raphael's painting, which shows him in armor astride a horse, as the victorious leader of a successful state rather than a prince of peace.

The impression many had of Julius II is revealed in an anonymous tract first published in 1517. Probably written by Erasmus,[14] it was so widely circulated that a contemporary stated that "everyone here is reading the little book on Pope Julius excluded from heaven—and it is strange how few condemn it."[15] The work contains an imaginary dialogue between St. Peter and Julius as the pope appears at the gates of heaven demanding to be welcomed into heaven with ceremonies befitting his office. In the dialogue, Peter contrasts Julius's lifestyle and values with those of Jesus Christ. While Julius brags of his accomplishments and revels in the wealth, military power, and adulation he received as pope, Peter reminds him what Christ and the apostles taught about true Christian values. When Julius states "this is all new to me," Peter responds with a telling condemnation of the way Julius has carried out his office as pope: "I suppose so; how would you have had leisure to leaf

through the Gospels, to read and reread Paul's epistles and mine, when
you were occupied with so many embassies, alliances, schemes, armies,
triumphs? Even the other arts prefer a mind free of sordid interests; but
the discipline of Christ requires a heart completely cleansed of every
taint of earthly concern."[16] The dialogue ends with Peter refusing to
allow Julius to enter and Julius threatening: "I shall wait a few months
and, when I have built up my forces, knock you out of there, unless you
come out to surrender."[17]

The *Julius Exclusus* reveals the way many in Europe viewed the
Renaissance papacy at the time of the Reformation and helps explain
why Luther's attack on papal abuses, which came in the pontificate of
Leo X (1513–1517), was so popular. The son of Lorenzo the Magnificent,
Pope Leo X was a typical Renaissance prince and devious politician,
whose main concern was to protect the papal possessions in Italy and
his native Florence as well as promote the interests of his family. He was
recklessly extravagant, amassing huge debts and using the resources of the
church to support his ostentatious lifestyle. Although he was an affable
man, with a great passion for the arts, he was not equipped to respond
effectively to what would prove to be one of the greatest challenges in
the history of the church. Leo X failed to understand either the seriousness of the situation or the theological questions that were at the base of
Luther's protest. Moreover, his behavior and that of his predecessors had
undermined the prestige and popularity of the papacy. The Renaissance
papacy left a wonderful artistic heritage for future generations, but to
a great extent it also helped prepare the way for the Reformation. As a
result of papal misdeeds, the sixteenth-century Protestant Reformers had
a receptive audience when they criticized the papacy, and they gained a
following that they might not have had if the Renaissance papacy had
not disgraced the highest office in the church.

Anticlericalism

Another area of conflict in the late Middle Ages was between the laity
and the clergy, which some historians have labeled "anticlericalism."
Criticism of the clergy has been taken to indicate that many of the laity
were anticlerical. There is no doubt that such criticism was widespread,
and much of it deserved. Bishops were often notorious for their ostentatious lifestyles and failure to carry out their spiritual duties. In France
many of the bishops were nonresident royal officials, exclusively from the
upper classes and often the younger sons of the nobility. Some German

bishops were rulers of important areas of the empire, with great secular power, and they lived and behaved much like the other princes in the empire. Three of them, the archbishops of Cologne, Mainz, and Trier, were imperial electors; since there were in all only seven electors, these three were especially powerful and their positions particularly prized. Like the Renaissance popes, many of the bishops were far more devoted to the secular power and wealth their office brought them than to their spiritual duties. Parish priests were also often criticized for their vices, including avarice, ignorance, and unchastity. Some deserved that criticism, but others certainly did not. Visitation records reveal that many parish priests carried out their duties admirably. As is still the case today, however, immoral clergy inevitably attracted more attention than those who faithfully carried out their duties.

Criticism of the clergy was not limited to their moral faults. Overinvolvement in and commitment to secular enterprises, pride, and claims to a privileged status on the part of the clergy as well as the demands of clerical taxation were the subject of numerous complaints from the laity. Clergy were often so involved in protecting their rights and privileges or seeking preferment or material gains that a society that expected a more spiritual clergy was understandably critical of them. Some of that criticism simply expressed disgust and anger, and some revealed a sincere desire for meaningful reform; whether it can all legitimately be viewed as an expression of anticlericalism is debatable. The term *anticlericalism* is ambiguous and can be defined in ways ranging from opposition to the very idea of a clergy set apart to criticism of individual clergymen.

Extreme forms of anticlericalism do not seem to have been common, since the laity clearly were not opposed to the church or to the clergy as a class, and they accepted the need for a sacerdotal priesthood. As mentioned earlier, people continued to give large sums of money to the church and were often very supportive of their local clergy. There is also little evidence that lay rulers were alienated from the church, so criticism is not necessarily a sign that the laity were anticlerical. Rather, it suggests that a society that was deeply concerned about spiritual matters was inevitably critical of clergy who neglected those matters. The laity did not want to do away with the spiritual estate; they simply wanted to reform the church and its clergy. But the demand for reform was real and reflected definite abuses. The steady stream of criticism from every quarter, including some of the best minds of the period, cannot be explained away as being merely the result of higher expectations. Nor does it simply reflect the kind of criticism that might be expected in any age because of the publicity given to a few bad clergy. There was too much criticism from too many quarters to be ignored. It suggests that the church had serious failings and that the need for reform was evident to some of the most articulate members of that society.

Reform from Above

Although the need for reform was evident, it was less clear how it could actually be achieved. The complexity of the church's structure, the vested interests against reform, and the sheer size of the problem made reform easier to desire than to achieve. The most desirable kind of reform, because it was likely to be effective and would avoid the danger of schism, would have been a reform movement initiated by the papacy. This is the way the church had been reformed in the High Middle Ages. As we have seen, however, the Renaissance papacy was not really committed to reform, and the church hierarchy was in a sense trapped by the very system it helped create. Its leaders were unwilling to give up the power and luxury that they enjoyed. Another possible avenue of reform, common in previous ages, was reform led by new or reformed monastic orders. Although a number of reformed monastic orders were established in the late Middle Ages and movements committed to a strict observance of the monastic rule (such as the Observant Augustinians and Franciscans) became popular, their overall impact on the wider church was limited.

Diocesan bishops also sometimes initiated reform in their dioceses. Bishops were expected to exercise oversight of the clergy and to discipline those living immoral lives or neglecting their duties. The Fourth Lateran Council in 1215 had ordered bishops to hold diocesan synods and make visitations at regular intervals. Yet because of the size of many dioceses and the obstacles the bishops faced in their visitations, even those who were diligent and committed found it difficult to carry out their responsibilities effectively. In practice, the state of the clergy in various parts of Europe varied greatly. In some places, especially in country villages, the parish system had broken down. Priests were often poorly educated or not educated at all. Parishes often lacked the resources to support the clergy adequately, and much of the church's wealth had been diverted to secular uses. Thus a prelate sincerely seeking to bring reform to such parishes faced serious obstacles. A bishop who was committed to the cause of reform was also likely to meet significant resistance from the clergy, whose poverty made them resent any reform efforts that might further diminish their income or place more burdens on them. Nevertheless, there are numerous examples of fifteenth-century bishops who took seriously their responsibility to oversee their clergy. They made visitations, issued reforming decrees, exhorted their clergy to be more diligent in carrying out their spiritual responsibilities, and disciplined those clergy who were leading immoral lives. Yet even the efforts of able, conscientious bishops were insufficient to bring about the widespread and thorough reform that was needed. Reform from above, without a reformed papacy, was not likely to succeed in a hierarchical church.

Lay Piety and Mysticism

Another type of reform in the late Middle Ages might be labeled "reform from below," as it originated outside the official channels of the institutional church. It often involved lay associations founded for the purpose of spiritual renewal, whose strength lay in their potential to enhance the spiritual lives of individuals and bring reform to the wider church through Christians who had experienced renewal.

The best known of these lay associations was the Brethren of the Common Life, founded by Gerard Groote (1340–1384), who, after spending two years in the Carthusian Order, left to become a missionary preacher. He gathered around him laymen and clerics who desired to live a common life but not separate themselves from the world. Living like monks, they kept a common household, involving physical and menial work as well as regular prayer, but they did not take vows. Some members were priests and others laity, but they lived together in common. One member, Jan Busch (1399–1480), called their piety the "*Devotio Moderna*," and they were regarded by some as offering an alternative to the monastic system. Members also wrote works of piety, such as *The Imitation of Christ*, mentioned earlier, which strongly emphasized private prayer and moral self-renewal. Some of their beliefs were similar to those taught later by the sixteenth-century Reformers; for example, Wessel Gansfort (ca. 1420–1489), who served as spiritual adviser to the school for the Brethren in Zwolle, was greatly appreciated by Luther. Indeed, when Luther read Gansfort's works, he commented: "My opponents could get the idea that Luther fetched everything from Wessel."[18] However, although Wessel held positions similar to Luther on questions such as justification, he remained loyal to the traditions of the church and did not teach the Reformation doctrine of *sola scriptura*. Despite

some affinities with later Protestant teaching, the Brethren's approach
to reform was not radical, and they did not pose a real threat to the
existing system.[19]

The second form of popular piety was mysticism, and it posed a
greater threat to the church because it emphasized personal religion
over against the corporate religion of the official church. Mystics sought
to unite their will with God's will by contemplation and prayer, and
they emphasized a direct personal relationship with God that could be
achieved outside the official channels of the church, posing a threat
to a church that contended that the church and its sacraments were
the sole means of access to God. The older form of mysticism was
largely confined to monasteries and involved withdrawal from the
world; however, in the late thirteenth century, mysticism came out of
the cloister and began to teach a form of mysticism open to all. One
of the influential leaders of late medieval mysticism was a Dominican
friar, Johannes Eckhart (1260–1337), whose speculative philosophical writings led him to be accused of heresy at the end of his life.[20]
Eckhart regularly preached to large lay audiences, and in his sermons
he maintained that the soul's union with God could be achieved by
those who earnestly desired it and were prepared to abandon all to
achieve it. Eckhart's influence was carried into the next generation
by two other Dominican preachers, Johann Tauler (1300–1361) and
Henry Suso (d. 1366), who spread the mystical teaching throughout
the Rhineland.

A lay movement called the Friends of God, inspired by the preaching of the mystics, emerged in the fourteenth century. It began in
Switzerland and spread down the Rhine Valley to the Netherlands.
Although primarily a middle-class movement, it included people from
all classes, including women, and its members were committed to living lives of piety, love, and holiness. In the High Middle Ages, such a
movement might have become a monastic order, like the Franciscans
or Dominicans, but the Friends of God remained a lay movement.
Its best-known member, Rulman Merswin of Strasbourg, attacked
the corruption of the church, which he contrasted with the spiritual
quest of the Friends of God. Although mysticism as expressed by
the Friends of God might have posed a threat to the institutional
church, it never became a widespread movement and was strongest
in or before the fourteenth century. By the end of that century, the
Friends of God group had virtually disappeared, and although mysticism continued to have an impact, it was not as significant as it
had been earlier.

Christian Humanism

The reform movement that was most articulate in its criticism of the church on the eve of the Reformation was humanism. Although Italian humanists such as Lorenzo Valla challenged the church through their scholarship, the most serious challenges were posed by the Christian humanists of northern Europe, who were inspired by the example of their Italian predecessors. They were equally interested in ancient manuscripts but had a particular interest in the original source-texts of Christian antiquity, such as biblical manuscripts and documents relating to the early church. They were also extremely critical of the dominant medieval theological system known as Scholasticism. Scholasticism developed in the thirteenth century with the recovery of Aristotelian logic, and scholastics such as Thomas Aquinas (1225–1275) used the logic of Aristotle to demonstrate the rationality of the Christian faith and to systematize theology. Although Scholasticism initially attracted some of the best medieval minds, including creative thinkers such as Duns Scotus (1265–1308) and William of Ockham (1284–1347), by the end of the Middle Ages scholastic theologians tended largely to repeat earlier arguments. Humanists satirized the tedious and seemingly irrelevant philosophizing of late medieval scholastics, claiming that they were seeking to answer questions that nobody except them seemed to be asking.[21]

The greatest and most influential of the northern humanists was the man whose criticism of monasticism was cited at the beginning of this chapter, Desiderius Erasmus (ca. 1467–1536). Often called "the Prince of the Humanists," Erasmus was the dominant intellectual figure of his age, admired even by those whom he attacked. Born in the Netherlands, he was the illegitimate son of a priest who was himself a humanist who knew both Latin and Greek. When both his parents died, Erasmus was sent by his guardians to a school in Deventer, where he lived in a hostel run by the Brethren of the Common Life. In 1487 he entered monastic life as an Augustinian canon. He was ordained priest in 1492 and three years later began his studies at the University of Paris. Paris was a center of Scholasticism, and the tedious debates of the scholastic theologians bored Erasmus and alienated him from such study of theology. In 1499 he made his first trip to England, where John Colet, later Dean of St. Paul's, encouraged him to study the New Testament. Erasmus returned to the Continent in 1500 and began an intense study of Greek. After spending three years in Italy, he returned to England in 1509 to teach Greek and lecture in divinity at Cambridge University. In 1516 he published an annotated edition of the Greek New Testament with his own Latin translation,

Desiderius Erasmus (ca. 1467–1536).
Illustration from Beza *Icones*.

followed by a second edition in 1519, which was to have a profound effect on the Reformation and would provide the basis for Luther's German translation.

By the time the Reformation began, Erasmus was the most famous scholar in Europe. The major European universities sought his services, as did the most powerful princes of his day. King Henry VIII of England, King Francis I of France, and the king of Hungary all wrote him personal letters inviting him to their countries. Emperor Charles V made Erasmus a royal councillor and paid him a pension, and even Popes Leo X and Adrian VI showed him great respect and invited him to Rome. Erasmus was a gifted, witty, and urbane scholar who charmed all he met; his persistent attacks on abuses in the church and calls for reform could not be ignored.

This chapter began with an example of Erasmus's attack on monasticism, taken from *In Praise of Folly*, which was written in 1511 when he was at the height of his popularity. Although Erasmus poked fun at the weaknesses and vices of men in all walks of life and satirized the superstitious practices of contemporary popular piety, he was particularly critical of the clergy. He lambasted the papacy for ostentatious living, pursuit of power, and failure to imitate Christ. His criticism of cardinals and bishops for imitating the lifestyle of secular rulers was equally devastating, and even lowly parish priests were not spared Erasmus's sarcastic witticisms. They were accused of pursuing their own material gain with the same fervor as their superiors and of neglecting their spiritual responsibilities. Some of his wittiest comments were reserved for the scholastic theologians, whom he accused of being so "incredibly arrogant and touchy" that he was reluctant to write about them. He feared "they might rise up en masse and march in ranks against me with six hundred conclusions and force me to recant. And, if I should refuse, they would immediately shout heretic."[22]

Even though Erasmus's orthodoxy would become suspect and his books were placed on the Index of Prohibited Books after the Reformation began, he was always loyal to the church. The purpose of his writings was to make the church aware of the need for reform and to encourage the kind of reform that would make the faith more meaningful to the laity. He defended his attack on scholastic theology by insisting that he was not attempting to undermine the church's teaching but rather to enhance it. He attacked all outward forms and practices that were performed with a wrong attitude, and he lashed out at hypocrisy wherever he detected it. He emphasized a biblical faith based on Christ's teaching in the Gospels and stressed inner piety rather than outward observance of ceremonies.

Although it has long been argued that humanism as represented by Erasmus helped prepare the way for the Reformation,[23] some historians have questioned this connection. There is no doubt that humanists provided the tools that the Reformers used—such as Erasmus's edition of the Greek New Testament—but there were fundamental differences of theology and approach to reform between the Protestant Reformers and humanists such as Erasmus. After the Reformation began, Erasmus broke publicly with Luther, and although some humanists joined the Reformation, others opposed it. Humanism seems to have appealed largely to the educated minority rather than the masses, since the humanists stressed reform through education and learning, which tended to appeal to an educated elite and not to the general public—or even to many of the clergy. Consequently humanism was not likely to bring widespread reform to all levels of the church.[24]

Heresy

Another effort to reform the church from below went well beyond humanism, as its proponents attacked the doctrines as well as the morals of the late medieval church. Two major reform movements that were condemned as heresies by the church began during the period of the Babylonian Captivity and the Great Schism. The first was initiated by an Englishman, John Wycliffe, and the second, which owed much to Wycliffe's teaching, was led by the popular Bohemian preacher John Hus.

John Wycliffe was an Oxford philosopher and theologian who began as a fundamentally orthodox theologian, attacking the abuses of the church and supporting the king in his controversy with the papacy. As his attacks on the church continued, however, he became more radical. He began to teach that the Bible was the only true source of authority

John Wycliffe (ca. 1330–1384).
Illustration from Beza *Icones*.

and that all men should read it and study it. A word-for-word English translation of the Bible, apparently the work of Wycliffe's disciples, appeared in 1382, and a decade later a more polished and readable version came out, which remained the only English translation until Tyndale brought out his translation in the 1520s. Although in 1377 Pope Gregory XI issued several bulls condemning aspects of Wycliffe's teaching, John of Gaunt, the king's uncle, protected him. As Wycliffe became more radical, he began to lose this support. He was not censured for advocating the authority of the Bible or for supporting a vernacular translation—the authority of the Bible was readily accepted in the Middle Ages, and vernacular translations were not unusual on the Continent. However, when Wycliffe rejected the doctrine of transubstantiation, it cost him the support of John of Gaunt. In May 1382 the archbishop of Canterbury summoned a council in London that condemned Wycliffe's ideas, and he was forced to leave Oxford.

Wycliffe spent his final years as a parish priest in Lutterworth, Leicestershire. In those years his opposition to the church and to traditional Catholic doctrine became sharper and more fundamental. Certain aspects of his teachings posed a particular threat to the church. For example, he argued that since a sinful person had no right to authority or property, the secular authority could deprive a churchman of his property if he abused it. He also maintained that the true church was an invisible church, made up of all the elect, rather than the visible church on earth with its corrupt hierarchy. In addition, he asserted that popes and cardinals were not necessary for the government of the church and unworthy popes ought to be deposed. He contended that the Bible was the sole source of authority in the church and did not accept any church practice not found in the Bible. Wycliffe died in December 1384 after suffering a stroke during a service. Since he had not been excommunicated, his body was buried in consecrated ground. However, in May 1415 the Council of Constance pronounced him a heretic, and in 1428 Pope Martin V ordered that Wycliffe's bones be exhumed and burned at the stake. Although one doubts if that postmortem punishment bothered Wycliffe, his followers the Lollards suffered persecution that continued into the sixteenth century.

Another group influenced by Wycliffe, and who also suffered persecution, were the followers of John Hus in Bohemia. Hus was born of peasant stock and admitted he originally became a priest for money and prestige, but he became spiritually more zealous as he studied. He was a gifted preacher, and in 1402 he was appointed preacher at Bethlehem Chapel in Prague, which had been founded in 1391 to provide preaching in the vernacular. Shortly before Hus's appointment, the teachings of Wycliffe reached Bohemia through Czech students who studied at Oxford. These teachings became extremely popular, and efforts to ban them only increased their popularity. Hus was clearly influenced by them, although he seems never to have adopted Wycliffe's rejection of the doctrine of transubstantiation, his followers insisted that the laity be given both bread and wine in communion. Hus particularly denounced the abuses of the church, preaching powerful sermons in the vernacular and writing a treatise on the church entitled *De Ecclesia*, in which he questioned whether the pope was the vicar of Christ: "If he who is to be called Peter's vicar follows in the paths of virtue, we believe that he is his true vicar and chief pontiff of the church over which he rules. But, if he walks in the opposite paths, then he is the legate of antichrist at variance with Peter and Jesus Christ. No pope is the manifest and true successor of Peter, the prince of the apostles, if in morals he lives at variance with the principles of Peter and if he is avaricious."[25]

Hus lashed out against the abuses and immorality of the clergy in bitter invective and was uncompromising in his demands for reform. Although he made enemies, he also had great popular support. He was eventually excommunicated by the archbishop of Prague, and

John Hus (ca. 1372–1415). Illustration from Beza *Icones*.

he went into voluntary exile in the villages of southern Bohemia, writing books and preaching in barns, fields, towns, and forests.

When the Council of Constance was convened in the fall of 1414, Hus was invited. He accepted the invitation, even though his friends warned him he was walking into a trap. He received a safe-conduct from Emperor Sigismund, but this was ignored when he arrived in Constance, and he was thrown into prison and never given an opportunity to defend his ideas or reply to specific charges. When he tried to argue his case, he was shouted down. Sigismund justified his violation of the safe-conduct by claiming Hus was a great heretic and deserved no protection. Sigismund even told the court that if Hus recanted, it should not save him because he could not be trusted. Hus refused to recant on the grounds that this would be perjury because he had never taught the errors ascribed to him—one of which was that he was the fourth person in the Godhead. He was condemned to death by burning at the stake and died singing "Jesus, son of the living God, have mercy on me."

Hus's death sparked a national protest movement in Bohemia, where his followers took over the church. In 1420 the Four Articles of Prague were published, demanding freedom of preaching, the eucharistic chalice for the laity, an end to worldly power wielded by churchmen, and punishment of grave sins committed by clerics. The Hussites, as Hus's followers were called, divided into two major groups. The Taborites were the more radical, rejecting any practice or belief not found in the Bible, including veneration of saints, prayers for the dead, transubstantiation, and indulgences. They lived communally, conducted services in the vernacular, and allowed laypeople, including women, to preach. The Utraquists were more moderate and worked to reach a compromise that would allow the chalice to the laity. Emperor Sigismund, who became heir to the Bohemian throne when the old king died, tried to take Bohemia by force, launching a number of Crusades. However, the Hussites, led by the blind military leader Jan Zizka, an innovator in military technology, withstood attack after attack until Zizka's death in 1424. While the Taborite movement was eventually defeated, the Utraquists arrived at a compromise agreement at the Council of Basel in 1431, which granted the eucharistic cup to the laity. Hus remained a national hero, and remnants of the Hussites in Bohemia continued as the Bohemian Brethren, who joined the Reformation in the sixteenth century.

A third late medieval reformer who was declared a heretic was the Italian Dominican monk Savonarola, who attempted to reform the city of Florence during the pontificate of Alexander VI. Initially Savonarola

Girolamo Savonarola (1452–1498). Illustration from Beza *Icones*.

enjoyed much success, condemning the vanity and immorality of the city and calling for the establishment of republican government. A great bonfire was built on which people burned their gambling equipment, cosmetics, false hair, and magic and lewd books. Savonarola also brought about major reforms in Florence and denounced Pope Alexander VI and the corrupt papal court, but finally he made too many enemies. He was excommunicated by Alexander, abandoned by the Florentine government, and arrested. Under torture, he confessed to false prophecy and political conspiracy, and he was executed in May 1498.

These are the most prominent examples of late medieval heresy. The degree to which these movements had widespread support or were forerunners of the Reformation has been much debated. Wycliffe has been called the "Morning Star of the Reformation," and it was once argued that his teaching and his followers, the Lollards, prepared the way for the English Reformation. Today historians tend to question that interpretation as well as the degree to which late medieval heresy had a significant impact. They maintain that the popularity of both Wycliffe and Hus was relatively short-lived and that, even though the movements they inspired survived, they did not affect large numbers of people. However, these movements were certainly signs that discontent with the church was serious enough to cause some people to risk horrible death to bring reform. In addition, Wycliffe and Hus also anticipated some of the teachings of the Reformers, and their followers would eventually identify with the Reformation.

The Late Medieval Church—an Appraisal

The late medieval church exhibits a curious mix of reform and conflict. People living at the time were both supportive of the church and extremely critical of its failings. The stream of criticism that continued unabated throughout the period reflects that many felt the church was failing to live up to the standards they expected. A society that took its religion seriously enough to spend huge sums of money on its churches and religious practices expected the church and its ministers to reflect the teaching of Jesus Christ in the way they lived their lives and carried out their ministries. Immoral and ignorant priests and materialistic bishops, who seemed to have little concern about religious matters, were more offensive to that society than they might have been to a more materialistic society. Whether the church had suffered a decline or the standards of people in the late Middle Ages were higher is a question open to debate. There was certainly much health and vitality in the late medieval church, and it seems that many people were satisfied with the way their religious needs were being met. Yet others were not happy about the way the church was carrying on its ministry, and they were unrelenting in their criticism. Those most involved in the reform movements of the late Middle Ages were often those most critical of the failings of the clergy. The fact that the hierarchy failed to respond adequately to these cries for reform created a situation in which there were substantial numbers of discontented people who provided a potentially responsive audience for the sixteenth-century Reformers. The theology of the late medieval church posed another problem: although many found the teachings and ministrations of the church provided comfort in the face of life's tragedies and assurance of eventual salvation, others who sincerely sought to find an answer to their religious quest were disappointed. Rather than finding peace and a loving God, the church's teaching about justification, purgatory, hell, and a God of judgment filled them with fear and dread. One such person was a gifted, high-strung, German monk named Martin Luther, whose personal religious struggles initiated the sixteenth-century Reformation.

3

MARTIN LUTHER AND THE ORIGIN OF THE LUTHERAN REFORMATION

▼

Venal indulgences were promulgated by Tetzel, a friar of the Dominican order and a most audacious sycophant; at the same time, Luther, who was ardent in the pursuit of holiness . . . published his own propositions on the subject of indulgences. . . . These he affixed to the church contiguous to the castle of Wittenberg, on the day before the festival of All Saints, in the year 1517. . . . Such was the origin of a controversy, in which Luther, not as yet suspecting or imagining the future overthrow of rites and ceremonies, forcibly enjoined moderation, for he did not at that time himself entirely reject the indulgences . . . this flame would gradually spread far and wide.

Philip Melanchthon[1]

Shortly after Martin Luther's death in 1546 his good friend and colleague, Philip Melanchthon, wrote this description of the event that began the Reformation. Although some of what he wrote has been called into question,[2] there is no doubt he was right to say Luther had no intention of beginning a revolution when, in 1517, he wrote the *Ninety-five Theses* questioning the sale of indulgences. What seemed at the time a minor

event led eventually to a lasting schism in the church, which none of
the leading participants desired or anticipated. The man at the center
of this ecclesiastical revolution was a relatively unknown German monk
and university lecturer. Although he had a brilliant theological mind and
a fierce temper, Luther was not the kind of person whose background
suggested he would one day rebel against the church to whose service
he had dedicated his life. What was it that changed him from a loyal
son of the church to its most feared opponent? How did a reasonable
effort to reform an obvious abuse become a movement that challenged
some of the most fundamental beliefs of the medieval church and led
to a lasting schism? Such are some of the questions we will explore in
this chapter.

Luther's Life and Career to 1512

Martin Luther was born in Eisleben, a small town in Saxony, on 10
November 1483. His father, Hans, was the eldest son of a landowning
peasant. Since it was the custom in that part of Germany for the youngest
son to inherit the land, Hans left the family farm to pursue a career. His
career was helped by his marriage to Margaret Lindemann, the daughter
of a successful burgher family in Eisenach. A year after their second
son, Martin, was born, the family moved to the town of Mansfeld, the
center of a flourishing copper-mining industry. Hard work, frugality, and
loans—probably guaranteed by
his wife's family—brought Hans
economic and social advancement. Before he died in 1530, he
became part-owner of six mine
shafts and two copper smelters
as well as a respected member
of Mansfeld society. Success did
not, however, come easily. Hans
remained in debt for most of his
life, and his children learned from
him the importance of frugality
and discipline.

As an adult, Martin Luther had
unpleasant memories of the strict

Martin Luther (1483–1546).
Illustration from Beza *Icones*.

discipline he experienced as a child. Although psychoanalytical historians have used the comments Luther made about his upbringing in their effort to explain Luther's rebellion against the church, his experiences seem to have been quite typical of a child growing up in late fifteenth-century Germany.[3] Luther clearly had a strict upbringing, but there is also evidence of genuine love in his family. Luther's father recognized his son's academic gifts and provided the means for him to receive an excellent education. He began school in Mansfeld at the age of six or seven and stayed there until he was fourteen. In 1497 he was sent to Magdeburg, a major city, to continue his studies. Luther mentioned later that he went to a school run by the Brethren of the Common Life, but since they do not seem to have had a school in Magdeburg, it is more likely that he lived in a hostel run by the Brethren. After a year in Magdeburg, he went to Eisenach, where his mother's relatives lived. He spent three happy years there surrounded by his relatives, forming good and lasting friendships and receiving an excellent education. Two teachers there were particularly helpful to Luther, and one became a lifelong friend. They recognized his gifts and probably recommended that he continue his education at the University of Erfurt. His father, although still in debt at the time, continued to finance his son's education; so Hans presumably recognized that Martin had special gifts that, with the proper education, would make it possible for him to have a better life than his parents.

Erfurt was one of Germany's oldest universities and the third largest, so at the age of seventeen Luther was thrown into an environment quite different from the small towns in which he had received most of his previous education. Not surprisingly, he was not overly successful in his first degree, ranking thirtieth in a class of fifty-seven in his baccalaureate examination. However, he improved considerably in his master's examination, where he ranked second out of seventeen candidates. Luther's father was proud of his son, addressing him as Master Martin. The son of a copper miner had risen well above his family's status, and Hans had even greater ambitions for his son. He hoped that Master Martin would become a lawyer and not only earn a fine living but also be able to provide for his parents in their old age. Yielding to the wishes of his father, Luther began the study of law in May 1505, and his proud father gave him a very expensive gift, a copy of the *Corpus Juris Civilis*—the major legal text for the age—to aid him in his studies. Martin's future direction seemed set until he had an experience that changed the entire course of his life.

Luther had just begun his legal studies when he made a trip home to Mansfeld, possibly because his father summoned him to arrange a

marriage or perhaps because Luther was already beginning to have
some doubts about whether he should pursue a legal career. Before
he began his legal studies, Luther had a number of experiences that
may have made him think deeply about death and the health of his
soul. In 1505 an outbreak of the plague in Erfurt took the lives of two
of his examiners. Earlier Luther himself had a brush with death when
he accidentally cut an artery in his thigh. He later commented that he
had experienced intense spiritual turmoil and had spent some time
reading the Bible.

We do not know what transpired during his visit with his parents, but
as he was returning to Erfurt a sudden thunderstorm broke and he took
refuge under a tree. When lightning struck nearby, possibly knocking
him to the ground, he cried out in fear, "Help me, St. Anna, and I will
become a monk."[4] It is not unusual for people in a terrifying situation
to make promises of this nature, but normally, when the danger is over,
they renege on what they had said impulsively in that moment of terror.
Although Luther admitted that he later regretted his vow, to the amaze-
ment of his friends (who tried to dissuade him) in July 1505 Luther
entered an Observant order of the Augustinian Hermits in Erfurt. Many
years later Luther could still recall how appalled his father was at his
decision: "In your paternal affection you feared for my weakness, since
I was then a youth, just entering my twenty-second year. . . . Your own
plan for my future was to tie me down with an honorable and wealthy
marriage. Your fears for me got on your mind and your anger against
me was for a time implacable."[5]

People hearing this in the twenty-first century may find it difficult
to understand why Luther would abandon the prospect of a promising
career that was likely to bring him economic prosperity and recognition
in order to enter a monastery where he had to give up all his possessions.
However, sixteenth-century people believed profoundly in the reality of
heaven and hell and that life on earth was only a brief pilgrimage but
life after death lasted for eternity. Depending on what one did in this
life, the afterlife would be spent either in everlasting bliss or everlasting suffering. The importance of life on earth was that it determined
where you would spend eternity. Luther's brush with death had made
him vividly aware both of how transient this life is and of how uncertain
he was about his own salvation.

As noted in an earlier chapter, medieval theology taught that justification was a process dependent on the grace of God in Jesus Christ
in which human effort played a major role. Depending on where one
placed the emphasis, this theology could provide comfort or it could

be a fearful dogma. For many it offered a safe way to salvation, made possible by the mercies of God in Jesus Christ. Although the system demanded some human contribution, divine help was also assured, and eventual salvation was promised to those who remained in the process. For others, the system was a source of fear and dread, especially if it was understood in terms of those late medieval theological traditions that placed such a great emphasis on human merit, because they never knew if they had done enough to merit salvation. Although the church never taught that people were saved solely by their good works, at a popular level the emphasis on the human contribution to salvation was so strong that many probably believed that their salvation was largely dependent on their own effort.

The popular religion to which Luther had been exposed as a boy emphasized the terrible suffering the damned endured for eternity in hell. Christ was pictured as a judge whose role was to decide whether people deserved heaven or hell on the basis of their works. Christ was portrayed sitting on a rainbow with a lily extending from his right ear—signifying the redeemed—and a sword—symbolizing the fate of the damned—protruding from his left ear. On his right side angels ushered the redeemed into paradise, while on the left devils dragged the damned from their tombs to cast them into hell. When Luther entered the monastery, he feared the latter might be his own fate, since he was well aware of how far he had failed to achieve the standards that he believed God demanded. He became a monk so he could spend all his time seeking to please God and earning his own salvation. He later said that he had thought, "If I were to enter a monastery . . . and serve God in cowl and tonsure he will reward and welcome me."[6]

Luther later said that his first year in the monastery was peaceful. He was fully occupied in the strenuous routine that began with worship at 2:00 a.m., followed by six more services in the course of the day. His time was spent in worship, prayer, and meditation, and at least for the first year that seemed to calm his troubled spirit. Less than two years after he entered the monastery he was ordained priest and celebrated his first mass. It was a grand occasion. Though his father was still not fully reconciled to his son's disobedience in entering the monastery, he made him a very generous gift of twenty guilders and brought about twenty guests to the service. What should have been a festive occasion became a crisis, however, when in the midst of celebrating the mass, Luther was overcome with the realization that he was totally unworthy to come into the presence of God. As he came to that portion of the mass where the priest says, "We offer unto thee, the living, the true, the eternal God," he became terrified and struggled to continue. He later wrote that he thought:

> I, who am ashes, dust and full of sins, am addressing the living eternal and true God. Therefore it is no wonder that he who prays trembles and shirks back. Thus long ago when I was still a monk and for the first time read those words in the Canon of the Mass: "Thou therefore, most merciful Father" and also "we offer to Thee, the living, the true, and the eternal God," I used to be completely stunned, and I shuddered at these words. For I used to think "With what impudence I am addressing so great a Majesty, when everybody should be terrified when looking at or conversing with some prince or king."[7]

The crisis that Luther experienced at his first mass was indicative of his overall spiritual problem. He was overwhelmingly aware of the holiness and perfection of God and equally aware of his sinfulness. He believed that in order to meet with God one needed to possess holiness from within, and in his honest self-examination he knew he did not possess that holiness. Even his most noble acts were marred by sinful thoughts, and although he made full use of confession,[8] fasting, self-punishment, and prayer, he was never satisfied that he had done enough to atone for his sins. In various sources written later in his life, he described the anguish he felt and his desperate effort to appease a righteous God. Despite his efforts, Luther found himself overwhelmed by his inadequacies. He was only too aware that he could not meet what he considered God's standards of true contrition and full confession. He viewed Christ as a "severe and terrible judge" who was unapproachable; therefore, he could not go to him for comfort and forgiveness. No matter how hard he tried, he remained plagued by the realization that his efforts could never fully appease a righteous God. He described his efforts to please God by his works of piety as a hopeless endeavor to achieve the impossible. "I tortured myself with prayer, fasting, vigils and freezing; the frost alone might have killed me. . . . What else did I seek by doing this but God, who was supposed to note my strict observance of the monastic order and my austere life? I constantly walked in a dream and lived in real idolatry, for I did not believe in Christ: I regarded Him only as a severe and terrible Judge portrayed as seated on a rainbow."[9] Although his fellow monks jested with him and told him that he demanded too much of himself, they could not comfort him, because his understanding of justification did not make allowances for human frailty.

Luther received significant help in his spiritual struggles from the vicar-general of his order, Johann von Staupitz, whose Augustinian understanding of justification emphasized the mercies of God in Jesus Christ. Staupitz came from a noble family and had been a child-hood companion of the Elector Frederick the Wise of Saxony. When Frederick wanted to start a new university at Wittenberg in 1502 he summoned Staupitz, who was appointed to a professorship in biblical studies and became dean of the theological faculty. Although Staupitz was a busy man, he spent time with this gifted new member of the order who was so absorbed in his spiritual struggles, pointing Luther to the suffering Christ. He told Luther that he had a mistaken picture of Christ and should view Christ as a Savior and friend rather than a severe judge. Staupitz also had a sense of humor that must have aided Luther in some of his difficult times. At one point he told Luther to go out and commit a real sin, such as murdering his parents, rather than worrying so much about what Staupitz called his "hobby horses and pet sins."[10] Even after Luther and Staupitz had taken different paths on the road to reform, Luther still acknowledged his debt to his former mentor; in 1523 he wrote to him, "It was through you that the light of the gospel first began to shine out of the darkness into my heart."[11]

While Luther was struggling with these spiritual problems, he contin-ued his studies in theology and began a teaching career. In 1508 Staupitz sent Luther to the Augustinian monastery in the city of Wittenberg to lecture on Aristotle at the newly founded university. His first stay there was very short, as the following year he was transferred to Erfurt where for two years he lectured on theology and continued his own theological studies.

In 1510 Luther was sent on a mission to Rome by his monastic order. He undertook the long and arduous journey with enormous excitement because he expected to receive great spiritual benefits and also aid his deceased relatives.[12] He hoped to benefit his soul by viewing the col-lection of relics that exceeded anything he could find elsewhere. Forty popes and seventy-six thousand martyrs were buried in Rome, and the relics included the rope with which Judas hanged himself, a piece of Moses's burning bush, the chains of St. Paul, and one of the coins that was paid to Judas for betraying Christ. It was claimed that the steps in front of the Lateran were the very ones that had once stood in front of Pilate's palace, and if one crawled up all twenty-eight steps on hands and knees repeating the Lord's Prayer for each step, a soul would be released from purgatory. In a sermon that he preached the year before he died, Luther stated that when he arrived at the top of the stairs, which he had climbed to free his grandfather from purgatory, the thought kept coming to him, "Who knows whether this is true?"[13] It may be questioned whether Luther remembered this episode accurately over three decades later, but there is no doubt that Luther, who had expected so much from Rome, was bitterly disappointed by his experience. He was shocked by the incompetence, ignorance, venality, and immorality of Italian priests, and he was especially distressed about their irreverence toward the Eucharist and that they rushed through the mass so they could say six or seven to his one. He found the holy city a thoroughly secular city, and he left disillusioned.

Shortly after his return, Staupitz asked Luther to take his place as professor of biblical theology at the university, and in April 1511 Martin moved to the small town of Wittenberg, where he would spend the remainder of his life.[14] Staupitz also encouraged Luther to continue his studies and take the degree of doctor of theology, but the young monk was not easily convinced. In a conversation in the courtyard of the monastery in Wittenberg, Luther pleaded his ill health and maintained that the workload would be so great that it would result in his death. Staupitz replied, "The Lord has big plans. He needs good and wise people who can assist Him in heaven as well. When you die, you will there have to be His adviser."[15] Even if Luther was not convinced by this argument, he was submissive to authority and obeyed his superior. The following year he received his doctorate, and in 1513, a year later, Luther began his lectures in biblical theology at the University of Wittenberg. He was also appointed preacher for the Augustinian monastery and the city church. In the midst of his demanding work, he continued to experience spiritual crises that played a role in the gradual change that took place in his theology. "I didn't learn my theology all at once," Luther later commented. "I had to ponder over it ever more deeply, and my spiritual trials were of help to me in this for one does not learn without practice."[16]

Luther's Theological Development

Luther's theological development in his first decade as university lecturer has been a subject of intense study and historical controversy. Some time between 1512 and 1519 he came to a new understanding of justification that led to a radical break with the medieval tradition. Although historians continue to debate the dating of his so-called "Reformation breakthrough," it is clear that it emerged from Luther's study of Scripture as he prepared for his lectures at the university.

Even though the Bible was widely read and studied in the Middle Ages, the study of Scripture had not been an important part of Luther's theological education at Erfurt, which centered on the writings of the late medieval scholastics. In addition, the most commonly used exegetical method tended to obscure the real meaning of the text. The standard method of biblical interpretation was known as the *Quadriga* because it sought a fourfold meaning in the passages of Scripture. One meaning was literal, but three were spiritual and nonliteral: the allegorical meaning expressed the doctrinal teaching of the text, the tropological sought its moral teaching, and the anagogical pointed to the future fulfillment of God's promises. Although this method did have some useful results, what the biblical writer was actually trying to communicate was often lost in the effort to find a fourfold meaning to the text. Theologians tended to use the Bible as a series of proof texts to support theological propositions. Even though writers such as Nicholas of Lyra (1265–1349) had argued that the literal sense must be given priority, the *Quadriga* remained dominant.

The study of Scripture received a great stimulus from the contributions of the humanists at the end of the Middle Ages. While not abandoning the medieval method entirely, they placed greater emphasis on a return to the sources and a more careful scholarly study of the scriptural text in order to determine its real meaning. They also produced linguistic and grammatical aids for biblical study, as well as new editions such as Erasmus's Greek New Testament.

Luther became a prolific reader of the Bible while he was in the monastery. Although he struggled with the meaning of some passages, he came to love the Bible and turned to it rather than the writings of theologians as he sought answers to the problems that troubled him. With the discovery in the late nineteenth and early twentieth centuries of Luther's early lectures on Psalms, Romans, Galatians, and Hebrews, it became possible to trace his theological development. He began lecturing on the Psalms in the summer of 1513 and continued those lectures until October 1515. There were already signs in those lectures that his theology was changing. In his best-selling biography of Luther, the great Reformation scholar Roland Bainton suggested how a new understanding of the words of Psalm 22, "My God, my God, why hast thou forsaken me?" helped to change Luther's view of Christ.

> The reference to Christ was unmistakable. . . . What could be the meaning of this? Christ evidently felt himself to be forsaken, abandoned by God, deserted. . . . Why should Christ have known such desperations? Luther

knew perfectly well why he himself had had them: he was weak in the presence of the Mighty: he was impure in the presence of the Holy . . . but Christ was not weak: Christ was not impure; Christ was not impious. Why then should he have been so overwhelmed with desolation? The only answer must be that Christ took to himself the iniquity of us all. He who was without sin for our sakes became sin and so identified himself with us as to participate in our alienation. . . . What a new picture this is of Christ! . . . The judge on the rainbow has become the derelict on the cross.[17]

In those early lectures on the Psalms and Romans, Luther moved from a view of justification that placed the emphasis on what man does to one that placed the emphasis on what God does. This was the Augustinian position, which Staupitz also held, but it was still medieval because justification was considered a process in which the sinner was gradually made righteous.

The event that led to Luther's new understanding of justification is called "the tower experience," because he once stated that it happened in the tower of the monastery.[18] Although Luther described it as a critical turning point in his theological development, scholars are divided over when it occurred and what actually took place. In the preface to the first volume of his collected Latin works, written in 1545, Luther stated that the experience occurred while he was giving his second lectures on the Psalms, which would place it in 1518. Historians have long questioned Luther's dating, maintaining that his memory may well have been faulty, since his account of the experience was written almost thirty years after the event, and they generally prefer to date it somewhere between 1513 and 1515. Recently it has become more common to accept Luther's dating. Although dating the tower experience may seem a minor point, it is important for explaining the outbreak of the Reformation. "If an early date is chosen, the consequence is that [Luther's new understanding of justification] inevitably led to the dispute with Rome." On the other hand, "if the late date is chosen" then "it was the sharp debate with traditionalist opponents that led him to his new conception of God's righteousness and of justification."[19]

A second problem is determining what Luther actually discovered. Once again scholars have offered a variety of solutions, but there is still no consensus about the content of Luther's new theology or how it differed from medieval theology.[20] In his account, Luther described the experience in graphic detail. He maintained that he was struggling with the meaning of a text in Paul's Epistle to the Romans that used the phrase, "the righteousness of God" (RSV). He claimed he found the verse especially difficult because he had been taught to understand it as "the formal or active righteousness, as they called it, with which God is righteous and punishes the unrighteous sinner." However, after meditating on that verse "day and night," he began to understand that the writer was speaking of "the passive righteousness with which a merciful God justifies us by faith." Luther described the impact of that discovery as opening him to a new understanding of the entire Bible. "Here I felt that I was altogether born again and had entered paradise itself through open gates. There a totally new face of the entire Scripture showed itself to me."[21] He said he found a similar teaching in Augustine, but the latter "did not explain all things concerning imputation clearly."[22]

What did Luther actually discover that had such a profound effect on him? As we have already pointed out, scholars do not agree. But Martin Brecht, who is probably the leading Luther scholar of our age, believes the meaning and significance of Luther's discovery is quite clear: "The essential centre of Luther's discovery consists in the recognition that in Christ, God's son, true man and true God, God freely gives us his righteousness, wisdom and strength. This is the content of the gospel and this faith believes and therefore is justified."[23] Rather than being dependent on our own righteousness, we are covered by Christ's righteousness and "everything which Christ has is ours and is given to us unworthy ones freely out of pure mercy."[24] Luther first expressed his new belief clearly in his sermon on *Two Kinds of Righteousness* in 1519, which provides an essential key to understanding his Reformation breakthrough. In this sermon he stated:

> Through faith in Christ, therefore, Christ's righteousness becomes our righteousness and all that he has becomes ours; rather, he himself becomes ours. Therefore the Apostle calls it "the righteousness of God" in Rom. 1: For in the gospel "the righteousness of God is revealed . . . as it is written 'the righteous shall live by his faith.'" Finally in the same epistle, chapter 3, such a faith is called "the righteousness of God." . . . This is the righteousness given in place of the original righteousness lost in Adam.[25]

Luther's new view of justification meant that justification could no longer be viewed as a process in which the sinner was made righteous. In the medieval view, righteousness was something God worked within human beings, and they cooperated in achieving it. For Luther, the righteousness by which God justified sinners was not worked within them. It was always external and fully depended on the righteousness of Jesus Christ. Furthermore, it was achieved in a single stroke through

faith. Luther "saw himself as a man already saved and not merely plod-
ding along the road to salvation. . . . The Christian life with its required
good works was not the condition of salvation but its consequence."[26]
Although justification was to be understood as *declaring* the sinner to be
righteous rather than *making* him or her righteous, this did not mean
that the believer ceased to be a sinner. The Christian is both justified
and a sinner at the same time. Even though believers are fully righteous
through faith, they also remain fully and completely sinners. There is
an ongoing struggle between the new nature created by Christ and the
old sinful nature that continues throughout the believer's life. The new
nature, however, is no longer under any compulsion to do good works
for the sake of justification. Rather, it struggles against the old and seeks
to do the will of God in response to God's love in Jesus Christ. In the
sermon on *Two Kinds of Righteousness*, Luther described the second
form of righteousness as that which God works within us. It is, Luther
states, "the product of the righteousness of the first type, actually its
fruit and consequence."[27]

Luther's "Reformation breakthrough" made the break with the medieval church almost inevitable. All those aspects of medieval teaching and
practice that were a part of the process of becoming righteous became
unnecessary, including meritorious works, purgatory, the infusion of
grace through the sacraments, a priesthood that mediates between
unrighteous man and a Holy God, indulgences, and the popular religious practices associated with those teachings. Sinners stand before
God throughout their lives clothed in Christ's righteousness, and they
do not need to earn merit because they already have all the merit they
could possibly need, since Christ earned it. They have direct access
to God because they are righteous, and when they die, they will be
taken directly into his presence. While they live, they do not need to
worry about their standing before God because, assured by faith that
they are righteous before God, they can freely serve him without any
concerns about rewards or punishments, in freedom motivated by the
love that God has shown them in Jesus Christ. The church was not a
mediating body between the righteous God and unrighteous human
beings; rather, its role was to teach the Scriptures and administer the
sacraments in order to create and strengthen faith. Purgatory had no
place in the new theology, and the practices associated with it, such as
indulgences, were therefore unnecessary. Although Luther did not come
to realize the full implications of his discovery immediately, it would
eventually lead him to break with much of the theology and practice
of the medieval church.

The Indulgence Controversy and the Beginning of the Reformation

If we accept Luther's dating of the tower experience, it came after the event that began the Reformation, the writing of Luther's *Ninety-five Theses* in October 1517. They were written to protest against some questionable theology and serious abuses in the sale of indulgences. In his university lectures Luther had become increasingly critical of abuses in the church. While he loved the church and refused to have anything to do with the sectarian Hussites, in a similar way to Hus he attacked the extravagant, unspiritual lifestyle of the church hierarchy, the profaning of holy things, the immoral lifestyle of clergy, and aspects of monasticism. While Luther was criticizing immoral prelates, he still maintained that they were to be obeyed. Even his protest about the sale of indulgences was not intended as a rebellious act but to alert the church to the way in which the indulgence sellers were hurting the reputation of the papacy. According to official teaching, indulgences could remit the temporal punishment for sin or commute the act of satisfaction ordered by the church. A careful distinction was made between the eternal punishment for sin, for which Christ had earned forgiveness, and temporal punishment, imposed by the church in the form of satisfaction. In addition, it was clearly taught that those who received indulgences must be contrite and make confession. However, sometimes those technicalities were overlooked in the zeal to sell indulgences.

In 1515 Pope Leo X issued a plenary indulgence with the intent of using the proceeds to complete the building of St. Peter's. The sale became intertwined with German politics when half of the proceeds were designated to help pay the debt which Albrecht of Brandenburg, the twenty-four-year-old brother of Elector Joachim of Brandenburg, had incurred in order to become archbishop of Mainz in 1514. Mainz was not only the largest archdiocese in Christendom, it also had one of the seven votes in the choice of the emperor, and since the ruler of Brandenburg was also an elector, this put two of the seven votes into the hands of one family. Albrecht's election was technically illegal, according to existing church law, since he was below the required canonical age for an archbishop and was already the archbishop of Magdeburg and administrator of the see of Halberstadt. For this reason a papal dispensation was necessary, which Leo was quite willing to grant in return for a substantial sum of money that he planned to use in his building project. Albrecht agreed to pay the pope twenty-nine thousand Rhenish gold gulden, but since he did not have such a large sum of money available, he borrowed it from the Fugger banking house. In a complex three-cornered arrangement, Leo X agreed that Albrecht would receive half the proceeds of a sale of indulgences, which could be used to repay the Fuggers, while Leo would receive the other half to finance the completion of St. Peter's.

The sale was carefully organized, and the product was advertised so as to make it especially appealing to anyone concerned about escaping the pains of purgatory or aiding their relatives who were already in purgatory. The indulgence would, according to the instructions issued by Albrecht, provide plenary "remission of all sins" and the punishments of purgatory would be "totally wiped out." In addition, an indulgence purchased on behalf of those already in purgatory would fully remit their punishment, with "no need for the contributors to be of contrite heart or to make oral confession." This made it seem that money alone could release a soul from the terrible sufferings of purgatory. A popular slogan used by indulgence preachers emphasized the automatic nature of the transaction: "As soon as the coin in the coffer rings, the soul from purgatory springs." The preachers were instructed to present the great advantages to be derived from the indulgence "in the most effective way" and explain "them with all the ability they have."[28]

One of the most effective salesmen was a Dominican monk named John Tetzel, who had sold indulgences for the Fuggers and the papacy since 1504. Supposedly, he once boasted that he had saved more souls by indulgences than St. Peter had by the gospel. He was also well paid for his services, receiving a substantial salary, travel expenses, and a large bonus. Tetzel was a superb salesman and knew how to arouse public interest. He started by entering town in a solemn procession with the papal coat of arms and the bull of indulgence borne aloft on a gold-embroidered velvet cushion. A cross was set up in the marketplace, and Tetzel gave sermons on hell, purgatory, and heaven. He especially appealed to the consciences of his audience when he pointed out how they could aid their deceased parents in purgatory.

> Don't you hear the voice of your wailing dead parents and others who say, "Have mercy upon me, have mercy upon me, because we are in severe punishment and pain. From this you could redeem us with a small alms and yet you do not want to do so." Open your ears as the father says to the son and the mother to the daughter. . . . We created you, fed you, cared for you, and left you our temporal goods. Why are you so cruel and harsh that you do not want to save us, though it only takes so little? You let us lie in flames so that only slowly do we come to the promised glory."[29]

Although Frederick the Wise did not allow the indulgence salesmen into his territory, in the spring of 1517 Tetzel was in a town near
Wittenberg, and Luther's parishioners went to hear him and to buy
indulgences. When they returned to Wittenberg, they expected to receive
absolution without any show of contrition or commitment to amend
their lives. They felt they had purchased their way into heaven.

Luther was concerned for the salvation of his parishioners and furious that the indulgence preachers were misleading people for financial
gain. Although Luther never heard Tetzel, he had listened to reports from
his parishioners in the confessional and was horrified. He had already
preached against indulgences and the way in which the indulgence
preachers were misleading people. He had also written a *Treatise on
Indulgences* in which he spoke out against the abuses, while still accepting their legitimate use. On 31 October 1517 Luther wrote a polite letter
to Archbishop Albrecht of Mainz expressing his concern about the false
understanding the indulgence preachers were conveying to the ordinary
person. He was particularly distressed that "simple folk" believed "that
when they have purchased such letters they have secured their salvation" and "that the moment money jingles in the box souls are delivered
from purgatory." Along with the letter he enclosed *Ninety-five Theses*,
which he had written on indulgences so that the archbishop could "see
that the opinion on indulgences is a very varied one." It is likely that
he posted the document on the church door in Wittenberg after he sent
the copy to Albrecht.[30]

What in the long term became one of the most significant documents
in the history of the church was written by a loyal son of the church
who was seeking to reform an abuse. It was not a call to revolution
or even an appeal to the common people. It was written in Latin and
directed to the academic community, as is evident from the introductory
statement: "Out of love and concern for the truth, and with the object
of eliciting it, the following heads will be the subject of a public discussion at Wittenberg under the presidency of the reverend father, Martin
Luther. . . . He requests that whoever cannot be present personally to
debate the matter orally will do so in absence in writing."[31]

The *Ninety-five Theses* were written in anger, but they were not intended
to attack the use of indulgences or the papacy even though Luther clearly
questioned some of the powers claimed for indulgences. For example,
he denied the power of indulgences to remit sin or to release souls from
purgatory and maintained that they could only excuse the penalties
imposed by the church (theses 5–11). Furthermore, he maintained that
they had no value without repentance and "any Christian whatsoever,

who is truly repentant, enjoys plenary remission from penalty and guilt, and this is given him without letter of indulgence" (thesis 36). Luther also called into question the belief in the "treasury of merit" on which indulgences were based (theses 56–66). He was particularly concerned that the purchase of indulgences should not generate a false sense of security and detract from works of charity (theses 41–43). He even argued that the pope was being slandered by the "unbridled preaching of indulgences," which makes it difficult "for learned men to guard the respect due the pope against false accusations, or at least from the keen criticisms of the laity" (thesis 81). In the theses that followed (theses 83–89) Luther listed some of those "keen criticisms," which included questioning why the pope did not "empty purgatory for the sake of most holy love and supreme need of souls . . . if he can redeem innumerable souls for sordid money with which to build a basilica, the most trivial of reasons" (thesis 82). Luther ended by warning against the false sense of security engendered by indulgences: "Let them thus be more confident of entering heaven through many tribulations rather than through a false assurance of peace" (thesis 95).[32]

There is no evidence that the debate that Luther called for actually took place. The *Theses* were probably posted in manuscript and were circulated among a small group of Luther's friends. Probably without Luther's knowledge printers obtained a copy, they were translated into German, and in a short time printed copies had spread throughout Germany and beyond its borders. Luther was completely surprised by the reaction. He claimed he had not intended to create "so great a tumult," but that is precisely what happened. Not surprisingly, Tetzel attacked Luther, calling him a heretic in the tradition of Hus and Wycliffe, and an even more vicious attack came from a man Luther had considered a friend, Johann Eck, a theologian at the University of Ingolstadt in Bavaria. Revealing a particular talent for invective, Eck called Luther "a heretic, rebellious, presumptuous and impudent as well as sleepy, simple-minded, unlearned and a despiser of the pope."[33]

But Luther also received considerable support and even acclamation. In April 1518 he attended a meeting of his order in Heidelberg, where he engaged in a disputation in which he defended the theology of Augustine but did not even mention indulgences. He was well received and returned in triumph. He next wrote a lengthy exposition of the *Ninety-five Theses*, which was sent as an appeal to the pope. In the dedication, Luther expressed his confidence that the pope would judge the matter fairly, writing: "I put myself at the feet of your Holiness with everything that I am and have. . . . I will regard your voice as the voice of Christ, who speaks through you."[34] Despite the humble and submissive tone of the dedication, Luther was not backing down. Rather he defended what he had written earlier, stating he would accept no authority other than the Scriptures and calling for a reformation of the church.

Although in the spring of 1518 it seemed as though the indulgence controversy was little more than a quarrel among German theologians, after some initial delay, preparations were being made in Rome to deal with this troublesome German monk in summary fashion. In December 1517 Albrecht had forwarded the documents Luther sent him to Rome, confident that the pope would know how to counter "such error;"[35] but Leo X was not qualified to deal with serious theological questions. He seemingly did not understand the seriousness of the situation,[36] and when he reacted, he did so in a way that only worsened the developing crisis.

Probably under pressure from Dominicans, who considered themselves the defenders of orthodoxy and held important positions in the Curia, a pompous sixty-two-year-old Dominican theologian, Sylvester Prierias, was delegated to write a reply to Luther. He did so in three days, largely ignoring the questions Luther had raised in his *Ninety-five Theses*, relying on threats and sweeping claims for the power of the papacy. These included a statement that "whoever does not hold to the teaching of the Roman Church and the pope as an infallible rule of faith, from which even Holy Scripture draws its power and authority, is a heretic."[37] Emperor Maximilian, who was convinced Luther was a dangerous heretic, had already agreed to execute the ecclesiastical condemnation with the imperial ban. On 23 August Leo empowered Cardinal Cajetan, who was papal legate to the meeting of the German princes that was to take place in Augsburg, to arrest Luther so that he might be brought to Rome to be tried before a papal court.

Although Luther did not take Prierias's attack seriously,[38] the summons to Rome was an ominous sign because Luther knew that a fair trial was highly unlikely, and he was well aware of what had happened to Hus. In desperation he appealed to his prince, Frederick the Wise, through George Spalatin, Frederick's secretary and personal chaplain, who would play a key role as intermediary between the professor and his prince.[39] Frederick was an amazing man. Even though he believed in relics and indulgences, held different theological views from Luther most of his life,[40] and would have preferred that Luther react in a more conciliatory manner, he consistently supported Luther and demanded he receive a fair hearing. Even after Cajetan warned Frederick that if he continued to back Luther he would bring dishonor on his house, the elector would not abandon the man Cajetan called that "shabby little friar."[41] Many reasons have been offered for Frederick's tenacious support of Luther, but probably the most convincing is that he was a Christian prince who was not prepared to abandon one of his subjects, especially a prominent professor at his university, without indisputable evidence that he deserved punishment. Frederick was true to his epithet, in that he knew how to play the political game; he was also in a position of power because Emperor Maximilian was nearing the end of his life, and Frederick was one of the seven men who would elect the new emperor. All this played a critical role in saving Luther's life and the Reformation.

In September 1518 Frederick made arrangements for Cardinal Cajetan to give Luther a hearing in Augsburg. Luther went, convinced he would eventually go to the stake. "Now I must die," he thought, "what a disgrace I shall be to my parents."[42] Cajetan was a learned theologian and knew Luther's attack on indulgences was not actually heretical. Initially he tried to disarm Luther with friendliness, and Luther treated him with great respect, but they made no progress on resolving their differences. In their three meetings Cajetan consistently insisted that Luther recant and stop disturbing the peace of the church, while Luther declared that he could not recant until he was proved wrong from the Holy Scriptures. The third interview was particularly stormy and ended with both men shouting at each other. After the meeting, Cajetan wrote to Frederick, urging him to cease protecting Luther either by sending Luther to Rome or exiling him from Saxony.

On 9 November 1518, Pope Leo X issued the bull *Cum Postquam*, clarifying many of the disputed points on indulgences. It stated that indulgences applied only to the temporal penalty for sin and not to the guilt, which must be remitted through the sacrament of penance. It also stated that only the temporal penalties on earth and in purgatory could be diminished through indulgences and not the eternal pains of hell. However, it affirmed the treasury of merit, which Luther had called into question, and stated that the pope could draw on that treasury for the benefit of the dead in purgatory. The bull repeated the arguments that Cajetan had been using against Luther, defended the pope's right to issue indulgences, and condemned the views of all monks and preachers who stated a contrary view.

Luther recognized his dire predicament, especially since it was not clear that Frederick would continue to support him. On 25 November he wrote to Spalatin, "I daily expect condemnation from the city of Rome, therefore I am setting things in order and arranging everything so that if it comes I am prepared and girded to go as Abraham, not knowing where, yet most sure of my way, because God is everywhere."[43] Staupitz even urged Luther to leave Wittenberg and join him in Salzburg. Luther was ready to leave when he received word from Spalatin that Frederick wanted him to stay, writing to Cajetan on 8 December absolutely refusing to deliver Luther to the pope unless he was proved guilty of heresy by an impartial judge or council.

The Imperial Election and the Leipzig Debate

Elector Frederick's importance increased dramatically as the life of the old Emperor Maximilian came to an end. Charles, the Hapsburg king of Spain, the most likely candidate to succeed him, was the one Pope Leo X least favored because he already ruled large areas of Europe;[44] adding the Holy Roman Empire to his possessions would make him so powerful that Leo feared he would dominate the papacy. Consequently, Leo was especially anxious to avoid alienating one of the electors. When he heard that Maximilian was on his deathbed, Leo dispatched Karl von Miltitz, a Saxon nobleman, to gain Frederick's goodwill by presenting him with the highly regarded "Golden Rose of Virtue," which was given to one ruler annually for outstanding service to the church.

Miltitz, who met with Luther in January, acted with great duplicity in an effort to gain credit for resolving the problem. He treated Luther respectfully and sought a solution that would be acceptable to all parties—which really meant not confronting the issues. Luther was cooperative and also sought to find a resolution, promising to refrain from further attacks on his adversaries if they would do likewise. He even wrote a humble letter to the pope stating that he had not wished to harm the church and that he had urged people to remain loyal to the church, while still defending his actions, but the letter was never sent. Meanwhile Miltitz, anxious to convince the pope he had been successful, submitted a distorted account of the meeting that led Leo to believe Luther had submitted. In March he wrote Luther calling him "my beloved son," and no longer the "son of perdition,"[45] even inviting him to Rome where he could repeat his recantation, offering to pay his traveling expenses.

Emperor Maximilian died on 12 January 1519, and despite efforts by Pope Leo X to find an alternative candidate, including even Frederick the Wise, Charles was elected on 28 June 1519. His election created a radically new political situation. Emperor Charles V was now the most powerful European prince since Charlemagne, but the nineteen-year-old emperor had his own problems. His great power worried the other rulers of Europe, especially the king of France, Francis I, whose kingdom was surrounded by Hapsburg power and who became Charles's implacable enemy and was almost continuously at war with him. In the east the Ottoman Turks under Suleiman the Magnificent (1520–1566) threatened the border of the empire, crushing the Hungarians at the Battle of Mohacs in 1526 and laying siege to Vienna in 1529. The political situation was to have a major effect on the Reformation. The papacy was often more concerned about curtailing the emperor's power than about the Reformation, while Charles's attention was constantly diverted by his political problems, so he was unable to deal effectively with the developing schism in his empire. He also needed the support of the Lutheran princes against the Turks, so he could not afford to alienate them.

Shortly after the election of Charles V, the Lutheran Reformation entered a new stage as a result of the Leipzig Debate, which began the day before the election. This debate pitted Luther and his colleague at the University of Wittenberg, Andreas Bodenstein (called Karlstadt after his birthplace), against Luther's old antagonist, Eck. Karlstadt had responded to Eck's attack on Luther's *Ninety-five Theses*, and the two had engaged in written debate. Eck then challenged Karlstadt to a public oral debate. Luther was not initially involved because he had promised Miltitz to keep silent unless he was attacked. However, Eck's response to Karlstadt in December 1518 was clearly directed against Luther's position, so Luther felt justified in replying. Eck was delighted because, as he admitted in letters, he had always intended to engage in debate with Luther, and now he had his opportunity. He was convinced that Luther had strayed beyond the boundaries of orthodoxy in his position on papal authority and hoped to win prestige for himself by openly exposing Luther's heresy in the debate.

The debate was held at the University of Leipzig from 27 June to 16 July 1519, and it began with Karlstadt and Eck discussing questions about freedom of the will and the necessity of grace in order to do good works. Eck was the more able debater, and Karlstadt, hampered by a poor memory, was ridiculed by his opponent because he regularly needed to consult the piles of reference books he had brought with him. Eck clearly got the better of Karlstadt, and it was not until Luther entered the debate, on 4 July, that two more equal adversaries were pitted against each other.

Eck intended to trap Luther into statements that would identify him with the convicted heretic John Hus, who was especially hated in Leipzig because during the Hussite wars in the previous century the Bohemians had raided across the border into Saxony.[46] Eck's effort to establish guilt by association with a condemned heretic was largely successful. When he pointed out that Hus held the same position on papal authority as Luther, the latter responded that "not all the articles of Hus are heretical." The ruler of ducal Saxony, Duke George, was shocked, and it is reported he shouted in a voice that could be heard throughout the hall: "May the plague take him."[47] Eck's trump card was that Hus's views had been condemned as heresy at the Council of Constance, which eventually forced Luther to question the authority of councils and to insist on the sole authority of Scripture. At one point the debate became so heated that Luther switched from Latin to German, maintaining he was being "misunderstood by the people." He then made his most radical statement in German:

> I assert that a council has sometimes erred and may sometimes err. Nor has a council authority to establish new articles of faith. A council cannot make divine right out of that which by nature is not divine right. Councils have contradicted each other. . . . A simple layman armed with Scripture is to be believed above a pope or council without. . . . Neither the Church nor the pope can establish articles of faith. These must come from Scripture. For the sake of Scripture we should reject pope and council.[48]

That was precisely what Eck wanted Luther to say, and he responded, "This is the Bohemian virus, to attach more weight to one's own interpretation of Scripture than to that of popes and councils."[49]

The debate continued with a discussion of purgatory and indulgences, but there was a surprising amount of agreement on both issues. Although Luther had still not rejected a belief in purgatory, he would not accept the passage from 2 Maccabees, which Eck cited as a scriptural defense, arguing that it was from the Apocrypha rather than the canonical Scriptures. Eck made no attempt to defend the abuses of the indulgence preachers, but he once again criticized Luther's questioning of papal power. In his final speech Eck reemphasized a point that was to haunt Luther throughout the early years of the Reformation; he questioned how Luther could set himself up against centuries of church teaching as being the sole person to understand Scripture correctly.

Luther went home with a new problem. He was disappointed with the debate, but more significantly he realized that he held beliefs similar to those of a man he had once hated as a heretic. After reading Hus's treatise on the church in February 1520, he wrote: "I have taught and held all the teachings of John Hus, but thus far did not know it. John

Staupitz has taught it in the same unintentional way. In short we are all Hussites and did not know it. Even Paul and Augustine are in reality Hussites."[50]

By this time, however, Luther had also arrived at a position on justification that was significantly different from Hus's doctrine, and he later differentiated himself from the Bohemian reformer by pointing out that, while Hus attacked abuses, he attacked the doctrines of the medieval church. Although Eck believed that he had won the debate and the Universities of Cologne and Louvain condemned Luther, the Universities of Paris and Erfurt, which had been assigned the role of judges, failed initially to render a verdict. Two years after the debate, Paris finally responded by condemning Luther; however, their report failed even to mention the Leipzig Debate.

Meanwhile Luther had become a German hero. Students now flocked to Wittenberg, and Luther received significant support from the humanist community. Printers loved Luther because he provided them with a product that often sold out as soon as it became available. Between 1517 and 1520 nearly 400,000 copies of Luther's various publications were sold. (The Catholic theologian Johannes Cochlaeus once complained that all the printers were "secret Lutherans.")

Eck and Luther both wrote in defense of their positions, but Eck was not satisfied with simply attacking Luther in print. A few days after the debate ended, he wrote to Frederick the Wise urging him to act against Luther. Frederick did not respond, but Eck had more success with Pope Leo X when he wrote to him in October 1519 suggesting he condemn Luther for holding the Hussite heresy. In the spring of 1520, Eck went to Rome and helped prepare the bull of excommunication against Luther.

By 1520 Luther had grown considerably more radical. He was also incredibly productive. In the half year following the Leipzig Debate, he wrote sixteen treatises and over a hundred sermons, which reveal a new Luther. They were obviously written in haste and, since Luther seldom revised his initial draft, he sometimes overstated his case. Nevertheless, in contrast to the Luther who had hoped to bring reform within the context of medieval Christianity, the new Luther was not at all cautious about how radically he broke with the tradition and practice of the medieval church. In 1520 he wrote three tracts expressing views that could clearly not be reconciled with medieval orthodoxy. In addition, although the papal bull excommunicating Luther was written before any of them was published, Pope Leo X would have had no trouble finding evidence for condemning Luther as a heretic in those tracts. They illustrate how radical Luther had become as he began to understand more and more the implications of his new theology.

The Tracts of the Year 1520

Luther's first tract, the *Open Letter to the Christian Nobility of the German Nation Concerning the Reform of the Christian Estate*, was published in August 1520. In it Luther asked the German nobility to reform the church because, he maintained, the clergy had grown indifferent to the cause of reform. He argued that the papacy and its supporters had built three walls to protect themselves against any effort to reform the church. The first of those walls was the claim that the spiritual power was superior to the temporal power, and because it was a separate estate the temporal power could not interfere in the spiritual realm. The second wall was the contention that only the pope could interpret Scripture, and the third wall was that the pope alone could summon a council.

Luther demolished the first wall with the doctrine of the priesthood of all believers. "It is pure invention," he wrote, "that pope, bishops, priests and monks are to be called the spiritual estate, while princes, lords, artisans, and farmers are called the temporal estate." In a radical revision of accepted medieval beliefs, he asserted that "all Christians are truly of the spiritual estate, and there is among them no difference except that of office."[51] On the basis of the New Testament texts that mention priesthood, he maintained that the whole body of believers in Jesus Christ, clerical and lay alike, is the true priesthood. The clergy are not distinguished by some indelible character given at ordination. No one becomes a priest when a bishop consecrates him, since all baptized Christians are already priests. However, not everybody is called to exercise the office of the ordained ministry, so the congregation may select one of their number to act in the place and stead of the whole congregation. A priest is nothing else than an officeholder, and the medieval division of society into two estates was "a piece of deceit and hypocrisy."[52]

Luther then attacked the second wall by stating the "claim that only the pope may interpret Scripture is an outrageous fancied fable"[53] that was not supported by a single biblical text. Holy Scripture is open to all and can be interpreted by all true believers who seek the guidance of the Holy Spirit. The third wall collapsed with the others because, Luther insisted, there was no scriptural support or historical evidence for the pretense that only the pope has power to call a council.

In the second part of the book Luther castigated the pope and the cardinals by launching an unrestrained attack on the worldliness and immorality that was so prevalent in Rome and which he claimed was so terrible in its "contempt of God that Antichrist himself could not possibly rule more abominably."[54] The third part of the tract contained a long list of matters that Luther felt needed reform, including the abolition of papal power over the state and the creation of a German church with its own court of final appeal. He also called for religious and moral reform for the whole of Christendom.

The *Open Letter to the Christian Nobility* was written in German and directed to a popular audience. Two months later Luther wrote a tract in Latin entitled *The Babylonian Captivity of the Church*, addressed primarily to the clergy. In it he attacked the entire medieval sacramental system. He discussed all seven sacraments but argued that only baptism, communion, and penance were instituted by Christ. (He would later also deny that penance was a sacrament.) The Eucharist received the greatest amount of attention. Luther maintained that Rome had held the church in captivity in a similar fashion to Israel's exile in Babylon, and he identified three captivities in the celebration of the Eucharist. The first was withholding the cup from the laity, the second was the doctrine of transubstantiation, and third was the conception of the mass as a sacrifice. It is not surprising that *The Babylonian Captivity* is considered the most revolutionary of Luther's early tracts, since in it he identified with beliefs held by individuals who had been condemned as heretics and thereby struck at the heart of medieval orthodoxy. By insisting that both bread and wine be given to the laity, he was knowingly accepting the Hussite position. Wycliffe was condemned for rejecting the doctrine of transubstantiation, and in questioning that doctrine Luther was treading on especially dangerous ground because the Fourth Lateran Council in 1215 had made it a required part of the church's theology. Finally, when Luther denied that Christ's sacrifice was repeated in the Eucharist, he was setting himself in opposition to a doctrine that was the basis for much of medieval piety.

The third tract owed its origin to another meeting between Luther and Miltitz, which took place in October 1520. At that meeting Miltitz tried again to resolve the conflict by persuading Luther to write a conciliatory letter to the pope accompanied by a devotional booklet. Luther agreed, and both were published in November 1520. Even though Luther sought in this letter to be conciliatory, he did not back away from any of his previously expressed positions, and he certainly lacked tact. He addressed Pope Leo X as an equal and stated that the Roman Church had become so immoral that "even Antichrist himself, if he should come, could think of nothing to add to its wickedness." He even stated that Leo's advisers and a corrupt Curia had misled him so that he was "a lamb in the midst of wolves." Luther ended by telling Leo that he had included a treatise dedicated to him "as a token of peace and good hope," which contained "the whole of Christian life in brief form."[55]

Although it is hard to believe that the letter could have contributed anything to reconciliation, the treatise, entitled *The Freedom of the Christian*, differed markedly in tone and content from the two earlier tracts. It was conciliatory and devotional rather than polemical, and it contained a beautiful summary of Luther's new doctrine of justification and its implications for Christian living. It began by stating two seemingly contradictory propositions: "A Christian is a perfectly free lord of all, subject to none. A Christian is a perfectly dutiful servant of all, subject to all."[56] A Christian is totally free because he no longer lives under the law but under the gospel. Christ has done everything necessary for his salvation, and "he needs no works to make him righteous and save him, since faith alone abundantly confers all those things." Christ's righteousness had become his, "and all sin is swallowed up by the righteousness of Christ."[57] Although the Christian is free from the need to do good works for justification, this very freedom makes him a willing slave. Because he has experienced the love of God in Jesus Christ, he is compelled out of love and gratitude to God to serve his neighbors unselfishly. Even though he is free from the need to do good works, he makes himself the slave of others. Although, in contrast to the earlier tracts, Luther did not attack the teaching of the medieval church in acrimonious language, *The Freedom of the Christian* was nevertheless also radical in that it was based on Luther's new theology, which denied many of the teachings and practices of the church.

Excommunication and the Diet of Worms

By the end of 1520 Luther had clearly broken with the church, and it is not surprising that he was excommunicated in the same year. However, the bull of excommunication was prepared before any of the pamphlets appeared. In fact, Luther wrote *The Freedom of the Christian* after the bull had been published in Germany. The bull, entitled *Exsurge Domine*, from the opening words "Arise O Lord and judge thy cause," was largely the work of Eck. It claimed that "a wild boar" had invaded the Lord's "vineyard" and the destructive nature of the boar's activities were enumerated in a list of forty-one errors taught by Luther that the bull stated could no longer be tolerated. The majority of the condemned articles were directed against Luther's views on the sacrament of penance, indulgences, and purgatory. Eck's influence is evident in the inclusion of Luther's statement made at Leipzig that "certain articles of John Hus, condemned by the Council of Constance, are most Christian, true and evangelical."[58]

The bull was published in June 1520, and Luther was given sixty days to recant before the excommunication went into effect. Those who distributed the bull often met resistance from angry mobs, who resented a German hero being condemned by Rome. Luther's response to the bull was anything but conciliatory. On 10 December 1520, exactly sixty days after the bull had been delivered to Wittenberg, students and faculty from the university built a bonfire and burned copies of scholastic writings and canon law. In a dramatic act of defiance, Luther, shaking with emotion, stepped out of the crowd and threw the papal bull into the flames, supposedly saying, "because you have confounded the truth (or saints) of God, today the Lord confounds you. Into the fire with you!"[59] On 3 January 1521 Luther's excommunication was formally pronounced in another papal bull that declared him a heretic outside the law and stated that those who gave him protection would also be considered heretics. The break with Rome was now complete, but since the papacy would have difficulty enforcing the bull without the cooperation of the secular authorities, the critical event in Luther's condemnation would occur in April 1521, when Luther appeared before the imperial diet meeting in the town of Worms.

On 6 March 1521, two months after the papal excommunication went into effect, Emperor Charles V cited Luther to appear before the Diet of Worms. The citation was issued over the objections of papal nuncio Girolamo Aleander, who maintained that since the church had already condemned Luther's teachings, the role of the secular authority was simply to execute the papal sentence. Charles was also reluctant to have Luther come before him in a public meeting. He finally agreed to have Luther appear before the Diet of Worms as a concession to Frederick the Wise, who insisted that Luther not be condemned without a hearing, and because the German princes feared a popular uprising if Luther were not given a fair hearing. It was agreed, therefore, that Luther would be summoned under a safe-conduct, but there was to be no disputation. He would simply be given an opportunity to recant. Luther knew he was facing a critical test and went to Worms in great anxiety. Although he was enthusiastically greeted in city after city as he made his two-week journey from Wittenberg to Worms, he knew only too well what had happened to Hus, who also had an imperial safe-conduct. When greeted with an ovation at Erfurt, he commented, "I have had my Palm Sunday, I wonder whether this pomp is merely a temptation or whether it is also the sign of my impending passion."[60]

Luther arrived in Worms on 16 April 1521. The following day at 4:00 p.m. he appeared before the emperor, the electors, the princes, and all the estates of the empire. Luther was so intimidated by this awesome assembly that his statements could barely be understood. He was confronted with a pile of books and asked by the official inquisitor, Johann von der Ecken, the chancellor of the bishop of Trier, if he acknowledged the books as his and if he wished to retract what he had written. Luther responded in a voice barely audible that the books were his and that he had also written others. In response to the second question he requested additional time for deliberation. Although Luther was given another day to consider his answer, he was warned of the destructive effects of persisting in his views. He was told to consider "the general peace and quiet of Christendom" and not "to rely on his own private opinion" or to "overthrow the universal Christian religion, to incite the world, to confuse the lowest with the loftiest, and to seduce so many godly minds and souls."[61] That night he wrote out a few notes, which have survived and betray no agitation, but it is hard to believe he was not troubled by the warnings he had received as he considered the most difficult decision of his life. If he refused to recant, he might well suffer the fate of Hus, but even more frightening was that it would mean insisting he was right in opposition to a millennium of church teaching and risk bringing division and turmoil to the church he loved.

The following day Luther was kept waiting for two hours before he was ushered in to give his response at 6:00 p.m., but this time he appeared confident and well prepared. When he was again asked whether he was prepared to defend all his books or if he wished to retract anything he had written, he tried to avoid a direct answer. He pointed out that his books dealt with many different subjects. Those that dealt with faith and the Christian life were neither sharp nor polemical, and even his opponents would find nothing objectionable in them. Other writings were directed against the papacy and the papists, who by their doctrines were destroying the church. If he recanted them, he would only be adding to papal tyranny. Although he was willing to acknowledge that some of his tracts were "more severe than befits my religion or my profession,"[62] he was not prepared to retract them unless proven wrong by the Holy Scriptures.

Ecken responded to Luther's defense by pointing out that heretics had always taken refuge in the Scriptures and Luther should not be so arrogant as to believe that he was the only person who truly understood the Scriptures. Ecken concluded his remarks by asking for a direct answer from Luther without evasion: Was he or was he not willing to recant? Luther then gave a direct answer, "without horns and without teeth," in a speech that has become famous: "Unless I am convinced by the testimony of the Scriptures, or by evident reason (for I put my faith neither in popes nor councils alone, since it is established that they have erred again and again and contradicted one another), I am bound by the scriptural evidence adduced by me, and my conscience is captive to the Word of God. I cannot, I will not recant anything, for it is neither safe nor right to act against one's conscience. God help me. Amen."[63]

Luther then left the hall, but his hearing was not over. The emperor was prepared to condemn him, but the electors convinced him to establish a commission to examine Luther's writings with the purpose of pointing out his error and gaining a recantation. Luther met for several more days with a group led by the archbishop of Trier, who tried to persuade him to back down. Standing firm must have been particularly difficult in that context, because he was dealing face-to-face with reasonable men who engaged in nonpolemical discussions with him, but Luther held his ground. He would not recant what he had written unless he was proven wrong from the Scriptures. He met with the committee until 25 April, when he asked for permission to leave for Wittenberg the following day.

The course of history may have been changed because a twenty-one-year-old emperor kept his promise of a safe conduct and Luther was later allowed to leave Worms under a new safe conduct. The Emperor Charles V did not take action against Luther until 26 May 1521 when he promulgated the Edict of Worms, accusing Luther of heresy and disobedience to established political authority and placing him under the imperial ban. All subjects of the emperor were forbidden to assist or even communicate with him on pain of being arrested and having their property confiscated. All Luther's books were ordered to be burned, and the papal bulls against him were to be enforced. Luther was now a hunted outlaw, under sentence of death. He would live with that sentence the remainder of his life, but he survived because his prince, Frederick the Wise, continued to protect him. Frederick had arranged for Luther to be abducted by knights in the Thuringian Forest on his way home from Worms and taken to Wartburg Castle, overlooking Eisenach, where he remained in disguise for ten months.

The opening stages of the Reformation were over. Both the church and the state had condemned Luther, but he had not been silenced. The next stage of the Reformation would witness the spread and consolidation of the German Reformation and the appearance of other reform movements. Returning to the questions posed at the beginning of this chapter, it is clear that Luther's change from a reformer to a revolutionary occurred gradually. The response to his initial call for reform played a major role in that change, but probably the critical factor was the change in Luther's theology that likely occurred after 1517. Melanchthon's assessment, in that first Luther biography, was correct. He had not intended to start a revolution "but was desirous of tranquillity," yet "little by little he was dragged into other subjects."[64]

4

THE CONSOLIDATION AND SPREAD OF THE LUTHERAN REFORMATION

▼

> I shall remain here in seclusion till Easter, and write postils, and translate
> the New Testament into German, which so many people are anxious to
> have. . . . Would to God that every town had its interpreter, and that this
> book could be had in every language and dwell in the hearts and hands
> of all.
>
> Martin Luther[1]

Luther wrote those words from Wartburg Castle in December 1521 to
John Lange, his fellow Augustinian monk, who had been his friend in
Erfurt, informing him of his intention to begin a task that would occupy
him for the remainder of his life. One of Luther's greatest legacies to the
Reformation and to the German language was his German translation
of the Bible, begun in Wartburg Castle. It was not the first translation
of the Bible into German; even before the Reformation began, there
were at least eighteen different German translations and, at the time
Luther wrote, Lange was engaged in translating the Gospel of Matthew.
However, Luther's translation was to prove by far the most influential

and would play a major role in the spread and consolidation of the Lutheran Reformation. Although Luther had never wanted to split the church, the events of the previous two years, which included his excommunication by the church and his condemnation by the state, meant his effort to reform the church would lead to schism. Despite Luther's reluctance to have his followers use his name, the result would be a "Lutheran" Reformation.[2]

Luther at Wartburg Castle

After being abducted as he returned from the Diet of Worms, Luther spent ten months at Wartburg Castle. He grew a beard and a head of curly hair and remained in semiconfinement disguised as *"Junker Jorg"* (Sir George), a knight. Although safe from his enemies, Luther's time at Wartburg was one of the very difficult periods of his life as he struggled with doubts, depression, and constant physical problems. The rich food bothered his stomach, and he suffered from constipation as well as insomnia, at one point going five days without sleep. He also found the separation from friends and followers difficult, while the attacks of Satan were for him real and continuous. He wrote, "I can tell you in this idle solitude there are a thousand battles with Satan. It is much easier to fight against the incarnate devil—that is, against men—than against spiritual wickedness in heavenly places. Often I fall and am lifted again by God's right hand."[3]

Luther wrote to his friend Philip Melanchthon complaining that he was so overwhelmed with physical and spiritual problems that "for the last eight days I have written nothing nor prayed nor studied,"[4] and he contemplated leaving to go to Erfurt to get medical help. Despite all the problems and his complaints about his own laziness, the period at Wartburg Castle was one of the most productive of Luther's life. In less than a year he wrote twelve books, which set out some of the major teachings of the Lutheran Reformation, as well as translating the New Testament.

The first of these books, entitled *On Confession: Whether the Pope Has Power to Require It*, attacked one of the major sources of the power of the medieval priesthood and a long-standing practice of the medieval church. The Fourth Lateran Council in 1215 had established the requirement that the laity must confess their sins to a priest at least once a year. Luther concluded that this was not necessary since Christ provided that Christians confess their sins to one another. When attacked by James

Latomus, a member of the Louvain University faculty, Luther responded with a treatise that dealt with the central questions of sin, grace, and the nature of man and which provided one of the most thorough explanations of his doctrine of justification. In July he responded to an attack by Jerome Emser, the chaplain of Duke George of Saxony, with a sarcastic reply in which he stressed again the doctrine of the priesthood of all believers.[5] In October Luther wrote a treatise entitled *On the Abolition of Private Masses* in response to events in Wittenberg, where Karlstadt and others were introducing radical innovations. Arguing that both bread and wine should be given to the laity, Karlstadt declared that those who did not do this were committing a sin. He also declared that vows of celibacy were sinful and should be broken. In September Melanchthon celebrated the sacrament with students, with everyone receiving both elements, and in October the Augustinian cloister suspended private masses. Luther's treatise displayed a balanced approach and a pastoral heart. While supporting the abolition of private masses and the laity receiving both bread and wine in communion, he argued that no one should be coerced into making these changes, and those who continued to celebrate the mass in the old way should not be condemned for it. He also confessed that he had struggled with doubt and had often asked himself, "Are you the only wise man? Can it be that all the others are in error and have erred for so long a time? What if you are mistaken and lead so many people into error who might all be eternally damned?"[6]

The following month Luther wrote another treatise in response to events in Wittenberg. When Augustinian brethren began to leave the monastery in large numbers, Luther felt it necessary to provide a justification for their action so that they could leave with clear consciences. In a very personal work dedicated to his father, Luther dealt with this subject in a balanced way. He had already rejected the idea that Scripture required celibacy, and he now argued that the vow of chastity was contrary to reason and human nature. He particularly attacked the spirit and the intent in which vows were taken. Most monks, he maintained, took their vows because they hoped to win merit, and that was clearly wrong. However, he allowed that if a monk took his vows trusting solely in the merits of Jesus Christ, monasticism was not wrong. He also argued that such vows were not perpetual and binding, since Christian liberty should allow both the taking and the revoking of a vow. However, he cautioned against *insisting* monks and nuns leave the cloister, since they should have full freedom to make that decision for themselves.

While at Wartburg Castle, Luther also prepared a collection of short sermons to aid pastors who could not write their own. But his most important work was the translation of the New Testament into German, which he accomplished in the incredibly short period of eleven weeks. He found it an extremely challenging task, as he strove to produce a translation that spoke to the people of Germany in a language they understood. Again and again he struggled to find just the right word and to employ expressions that were in common use among ordinary people. For example, he rejected the Vulgate translation of the angel's greeting to Mary, pointing out that Germans would misunderstand "Hail Mary, full of grace." "What German would understand that, if translated literally? He knows the meaning of a purse full of gold, or a keg full of beer, but what is he to make of a girl full of grace? I would prefer to say simply, '*Liebe Maria*.' What word is more rich than the word, '*liebe*'?"[7]

Luther also produced prefaces and commentaries to help his readers understand the text. In his prefaces he gave preference to some biblical books over others. For example, he stated that the Gospel of John was superior to the other three Gospels because John dealt with Jesus's preaching, while the others stressed his works. He called John, the Pauline Epistles, and 1 Peter "The true kernel and marrow of all the books," while he called James "an epistle of straw" because "it has nothing of the nature of the gospel about it."[8] When Luther returned to Wittenberg in March 1522, he brought with him the draft of his translation of the New Testament. Melanchthon went through the manuscripts, dealing with problems in the Greek, and in September 1522 it was published. Although Luther did not profit from it—he was distressed that he did not even receive free copies—it was a great success for the publishers. A second printing appeared in December, and it is estimated that some 200,000 copies of the New Testament were sold between 1522 and 1534. It took Luther another twelve years to translate the Old Testament, so the first complete Wittenberg Bible did not appear until September 1534. The German Bible, which communicated so effectively in the common language of the people, would have a major effect on the spread of the Reformation and also on the development of the German language.

The Disturbances at Wittenberg and Luther's Return

The disturbing events in Wittenberg that motivated a number of the treatises mentioned above were the result of Luther's followers introducing more radical reforms than either Luther or Elector Frederick was prepared to accept. Late in 1521 Karlstadt and an Augustinian monk, Gabriel Zwilling, began preaching fiery sermons stirring up the people. Zwilling was so effective in his preaching that some called him a second Luther. Karlstadt celebrated communion on Christmas Day 1521 without priestly vestments and giving both bread and wine to the laity. He also advocated that clergy be compelled to marry. Zwilling even stated that the monasteries should be dissolved and the monks and nuns insulted in public. Mobs stirred by this preaching began to carry out acts of violence, breaking into churches and destroying altars and saints' pictures.

At the same time three men from the nearby town of Zwickau arrived in Wittenberg. Labeled the "Zwickau Prophets," they caused further uproar in Wittenberg. Led by Nicholas Storch, a weaver, who had to leave Zwickau because of his radical teaching, they also included Thomas Drechsel, a blacksmith, and Marcus Thomas, a former Wittenberg student. Claiming direct revelation from the Holy Spirit, they preached radical doctrines, including the rejection of infant baptism and the denial of the need for a professional ministry or even organized religion. They emphasized special revelation through visions and dreams and the imminent return of Christ. Luther's colleagues Melanchthon and Justus Jonas were impressed with their claims, Melanchthon so strongly that he asked the Elector Frederick to recall Luther, who alone, he felt, could respond adequately. On 13 January 1522 Luther advised Melanchthon on how to recognize false prophets: "First of all, since they bear witness to themselves, one need not immediately accept them: according to John's counsel, the spirits are to be tested. If you cannot test them, then you have the advice of Gamaliel that you postpone judgment. Thus far I hear of nothing said or done by them that Satan could not also do or imitate."[9]

Meanwhile the town council introduced some innovations, including Karlstadt's way of celebrating the Eucharist. The elector found himself in a difficult position because an imperial diet had forbidden any kind of religious innovation. Frederick did not want to stand in the way of truth, but he could not allow disorder. Therefore, on 17 February 1522, he ordered all innovation stopped and the old order restored until a general decision could be reached for Germany. Luther, who had at first been pleased with some of the changes, even chiding the elector for moving too slowly, was distressed by the violence and disruption of society. Despite the express order of the elector not to return, Luther traveled back to Wittenberg on 6 March disguised as an Augustinian hermit. He preached eight sermons in the city church, which had a profound effect on the situation. Named after the Sunday when he began preaching them, they were called the *Invocavit* Sermons. In them Luther expressed his concern, not so much about the reforms but about the way in which they were being introduced. First, he admonished those who had initiated the changes for neglecting Christian love, which considers the weakness of others and does not become impatient or cause offense. He also warned against the use of force and the neglect of Christian freedom. In religious matters, he maintained one must only use persuasion and preach the gospel to bring about change. Even the mass should not be abolished by force, because "There are many who would be compelled to consent to it and yet not know where they stand, whether it is right or wrong. . . . We must first win the hearts of the people. But that is done when I teach only the word of God, preach the gospel and say: Dear lord or pastors abandon the mass, it is not right, you are sinning when you do it. . . . but I would not make it an ordinance for them, nor urge a general law."[10] Luther also stated that no changes should be made in rites or ceremonies that do not jeopardize faith. Decisions concerning nonessentials such as marriage of clergy, monasticism, fasting, and the proper use of images and pictures should be left entirely to the individual conscience.

Luther's sermons had an immediate impact. One student commented: "Like Paul, Martin knows how to feed [the people] with milk until they have matured and are ready for solid food." Another student stated, "All week long Luther did nothing other than to put back into place what he had knocked down, and he took us all severely to task."[11] The sermons effectively dealt with the problem. The Zwickau Prophets left town,[12] and Zwilling recognized the error of his ways and was reconciled to Luther, who even recommended him for a parish position. But Karlstadt persisted in his beliefs and became even more extreme in his actions. He had always sought academic honors and held doctoral degrees in theology, civil law, and canon law as well as holding the prestigious position of professor in the university and archdeacon in the church; now he renounced all his honors. Karlstadt dressed in peasant's clothing and asked to be addressed as "brother Andy." He left Wittenberg in the summer of 1523 and became a parish pastor in Orlamunde, where he became quite popular in the parish and gained a great deal of support throughout Germany. He was also on friendly terms with Thomas Müntzer, one of the leaders of the Peasants' Revolt, although he rejected violent revolution. When the Peasants' War broke out in Germany, Karlstadt found himself identified as a rebel, even though he tried to persuade the peasantry to avoid violence. Luther gave him refuge in July 1525 in Wittenberg on condition that he abstain from further public activity. But Karlstadt left Saxony in 1529, spent years wandering around Germany, and eventually ended up in Switzerland where he identified himself with Zwingli's theology. In 1534 he was appointed to the post in Old Testament theology at Basel University. He also worked with Bucer for the reconciliation of the Protestant Reformers. He died of the plague in December 1541 having had a remarkable and influential career. He was prolific in his writings, producing some ninety printed works in his lifetime.

The Peasants' Revolt

The events just described reveal Luther at his best; three years later an event occurred that showed him at his worst. In 1524 and 1525 the peasants of south Germany and Austria rose in rebellion to protest against economic changes that were leading to increasingly heavy burdens being imposed upon them. The revolt broke out in the summer of 1524 in the Black Forest region and spread to Upper Swabia and Württemberg. By the spring of 1525 it had spread throughout Germany. In March peasant leaders gathered at Memmingen and drew up a list of their objectives in the form of Twelve Articles. Most of the articles expressed economic and social grievances, but they were given a religious justification. Luther's doctrines of the priesthood of all believers and of Christian freedom were interpreted in socio-economic terms to mean equality of social status and freedom from feudal dues. Article three, for example, stated that "Christ has redeemed and purchased us without exception by the shedding of his precious blood, the lowly as well as the great. Accordingly, it is consistent with Scripture that we should be free and we wish to be so."[13]

The Twelve Articles impressed Luther, although he had originally ignored the uprising. In April he responded with a tract entitled *Admonition to Peace: A Reply to the Twelve Articles of the Peasants in Swabia*. Calling the peasants "dear brothers and friends," he expressed sympathy for their cause and chided the princes and nobles for their treatment of the peasants, stating that the revolt was the result of their resistance to the gospel and their exploitation of the peasants. Luther warned the peasants, however, that followers of Jesus Christ cannot resort to force in order to correct wrongs: a Christian is forbidden to resist the government with force, even if the government is oppressive. He concluded by stating that both the peasants and the authorities were wrong and should submit to arbitration in order to find a legal solution.

From 21 April to 4 May Luther traveled around Saxony preaching to the peasantry and experiencing the revolt and the destruction it brought firsthand. However, he found his influence was inadequate to stop the violence. At Nordhausen hecklers interrupted his sermons and the violence continued unabated. By the end of April, some forty monasteries as well as a large number of castles and the cities of Erfurt and Salzungen had fallen to the rebels. Frederick the Wise, who was near death,[14] clung to the hope that a peaceful solution could be negotiated with the rebels and seemed unwilling to respond with force. By May Luther could no longer contain himself. In anger, he attacked the peasants in a tract entitled *Against the Murdering and Robbing Hordes of Peasants*, a fierce and uninhibited denunciation of the peasants that accused them of acting "like mad dogs," revealing that their statements in the Twelve Articles claiming they were acting in the name of the gospel "were nothing but lies." Luther pointed out that the peasants had sinned by breaking their obedience to the rulers whom they had sworn to obey, starting a rebellion, and cloaking "this terrible and horrible sin with the gospel." In Luther's mind, people who acted like this deserved no mercy, so he showed none in the words he selected to describe how one should deal with the rebels: "Therefore let everyone who can, smite, slay and stab, secretly or openly, remembering that nothing can be more poisonous, hurtful or devilish than a rebel. It is just as when one must kill a mad dog: if you do not strike him, he will strike you and a whole land with you."[15]

The princes did not need Luther's advice to crush the peasants. They were already reacting when he wrote the pamphlet, and by the time it was published the peasants had been defeated by a combined Protestant and Catholic force at the Battle of Frankenhausen on 15 May. The princes were determined to teach the peasants a lesson, and a bloodbath followed just as Luther's pamphlet reached the public, which made Luther seem even more brutal. The pamphlet was a terrible example of Luther allowing his temper, rather than reason, to dictate his reactions. It was also clearly a setback for the reform movement. Although Luther tried to explain and justify his tract and appealed to the princes for clemency in a number of individual cases, the damage had been done. It is not surprising that the Lutheran movement lost some of its popular support.

The Organization and Spread of Lutheranism

Despite the negative impact of the Peasants' Revolt, the Lutheran Reformation continued to spread. Wittenberg became a center of missionary activity as students studying at the university returned to their homes, carrying with them the beliefs of the Reformation. Printing played a major role in the spread of Lutheranism. Pamphlets, which were published in quarto size and normally included woodcut illustrations, flooded Germany. Art in the form of woodcuts was effectively used to reach the nonreading public. Political cartoons were another visual method used to attack and satirize the opposition and popularize the teachings of the Reformation. By 1525 Lutheranism had been established in such major German cities as Erfurt, Magdeburg, Nuremberg, Strasbourg, and Bremen. Other German principalities, including Hesse, Brandenburg, Brunswick-Lüneburg, Schleswig-Holstein, Mansfeld, and Silesia, had become Lutheran by 1528. As Lutheranism spread throughout Germany, leaders were faced with the challenging task of organizing the church and providing an educated preaching clergy to propagate and maintain the faith. In addition the church needed forms of liturgy that would make Luther's teachings a part of the regular worship service.

One of the pressing needs of the new church was for some type of supervision to bring order out of the chaos and to ensure that the clergy were paid. In 1527 John the Steadfast (1525-1532), who became the ruler of Saxony after the death of his brother Frederick, decided to conduct a visitation of the churches in his territories. Not surprisingly, the visitors found a variety of different conditions in the parishes. Although some clergy had enthusiastically embraced the new faith, others had little or no understanding of what Luther taught. Some could not even repeat the Ten Commandments or the Lord's Prayer, and many were totally ignorant of biblical teaching. In order to provide a simple means for educating both laity and clergy, Luther prepared a *Small Catechism* in 1529 for the laity and a *Large Catechism* for the instruction of clergy and heads of households. In the preface to the *Small Catechism* he described what he called "the deplorable, miserable condition which I discovered lately when I, too, was a visitor." In typical Luther fashion he described the situation in emotive terms:

> The common people, especially in the villages, have no knowledge whatever of Christian doctrine, and, alas! many pastors are altogether incapable and incompetent to teach. . . . Nevertheless, all maintain they are Christians, have been baptized and receive the [common] holy Sacraments. Yet they . . . cannot . . . recite the Lord's Prayer, or the Creed, or the Ten

Commandments: they live like dumb brutes and irrational hogs; and yet, now that the Gospel has come, they have nicely learned to abuse all liberty like experts.[16]

The deplorable state of the church revealed by the visitation resulted in Elector John the Steadfast having Melanchthon draw up an ordinance entitled *Instruction of the Visitors to the Pastors*. It provided for the discipline of recalcitrant clergy and a general order of worship as well as the supervision of the clergy in each of the four districts of Saxony by a superintendent who would report to the elector. Although Luther preferred a church independent of the state and considered the visitation an emergency expedient in which the prince would serve as a temporary bishop, the interim solution would become the permanent pattern for the church in Germany.

After some hesitation, Luther prepared a vernacular liturgy, which was first used in Wittenberg at Christmas 1525. It was a modified version of the old Latin rite that retained much of the medieval service and yet allowed freedom in the use of externals such as vestments and ornaments. Two essential parts of the new service were preaching in the vernacular and congregational hymn singing. In unequivocal terms, Luther expressed his belief in music as a means of communicating the faith and uplifting Christians: "He who despises music, as do all the fanatics, does not please me. For music is a gift and largesse of God, not a gift of men. Music drives away the devil and makes people happy; it induces one to forget all wrath, unchastity, arrogance and other vices. After theology, I accord music the highest place and the greatest honour."[17]

Luther himself wrote many hymns including "A Mighty Fortress," which became a kind of anthem of the Reformation. Before Luther's death a large number of hymns were available in a series of different editions for every occasion, and the Lutheran Church had acquired a reputation for being a "singing church."

The First Lutheran Confessions

As Lutheranism grew, the Lutheran secular rulers created political structures to protect themselves against the power of Emperor Charles V. In 1522 a new pope, Adrian VI, demanded enforcement of the Edict of Worms, but the diet meeting at Nuremberg avoided taking a strong stand. It simply stated that everyone was to "avoid debatable subjects that await the determination of the proposed council of the church."[18] In 1526 a new diet met at Speyer, at a time when Emperor Charles V especially needed the support of the German princes in his struggle with France and the Ottoman Empire. This diet effectively suspended enforcement of the Edict of Worms until a council or national assembly could be held and left it to the individual rulers to "so live, govern and deport ourselves as we severally hope and trust will be answerable before God and the Imperial Majesty."[19] Two days later the Turks won the Battle of Mohacs, in which the Hungarian king, Louis II, was killed. As a result, Charles V became even more dependent on the support of the German princes as the Turks advanced to the eastern border of the empire. However, the toleration gained in 1526 was short-lived. The Second Diet of Speyer in 1529 repealed the 1526 decree, and the Edict of Worms was reimposed. While most principalities complied, six of the territorial princes, joined by fourteen free cities, drew up a strong protest to the emperor. The "protesting estates" provided the basis for the term *Protestant*, which was eventually applied to all who left the Roman Catholic Church.

In 1530 Emperor Charles V made a major effort to achieve reconciliation and a common front against the Turks. He was in a particularly strong position because he had repulsed the Turks at Vienna, defeated the combined forces of the French and the papacy in Italy, and been crowned emperor by Pope Clement VII at Bologna in February. A diet was called at Augsburg, and Elector John the Steadfast asked Luther, Jonas, Bugenhagen, and Melanchthon to draw up a statement of faith, which became known as the Augsburg Confession. Luther traveled with the elector and his party as far as Coburg, the southernmost castle in Saxon territory. Since he was still an outlaw, it was not safe for him to leave Saxony, so he remained at Coburg for five months while his colleagues sought to achieve reconciliation at Augsburg. Although Melanchthon drew up the Augsburg Confession, Luther fully approved it. After reading the first draft, he commented that it "pleases me very much and I know nothing to improve or change in it, nor would this be appropriate, since I cannot step so softly and quietly."[20]

The confession had trodden "softly and quietly" in the sense that it emphasized the common ground between the two camps. It was divided into two parts: the first contained the chief articles of faith, and the second explained the Lutheran position with respect to such issues as giving the cup to the laity, denial of the sacrificial character of the Lord's Supper, opposition to the celibacy of the clergy, and abrogation of monastic vows. Throughout, it stressed that those signing the confession did not intend to depart from the Catholic faith or to create any new doctrines, and it went out of its way to condemn the innovations and heresies of the Anabaptists. It also avoided controversial topics such as purgatory, the veneration of saints, transubstantiation, and the priesthood of all believers, although it clearly taught the Lutheran position on justification. It also included a statement that laid down minimum requirements for the unity of the church: "To the true unity of the Church it is enough to agree concerning the doctrine of the Gospel and the administration of the Sacraments. Nor is it necessary that human traditions, that is, rites or ceremonies, instituted by men, should be everywhere alike."[21]

The Roman Catholic theologians drew up a response to the Augsburg Confession called the Confutation of the Augsburg Confession, defending the Catholic position from Scripture and tradition and refusing to make any concessions on the points in dispute. The emperor had the Confutation read to the assembly and insisted that the Lutheran princes accept it. They refused, and after a number of other efforts to achieve some agreement failed, Melanchthon drew up the Apology for the Augsburg Confession. It was seven times as long as the Augsburg Confession and placed a much greater emphasis on the differences between the Catholic and Lutheran positions. It was also considerably more belligerent in tone. The Apology was clearly not intended to be a reconciling document, and when the emperor refused even to receive it, the Lutheran delegation left. The effort to heal the breach had failed.

In 1531 the Lutheran principalities responded to a growing concern that Emperor Charles V was about to attack them by organizing a defensive league known as the Schmalkaldic League, by which the Lutheran princes and cities promised each other mutual assistance if the emperor attacked. Luther had consistently refused to justify such an alliance on the grounds that the Bible taught obedience to the authorities, but he was finally convinced by the legal arguments that the princes presented to him. They maintained that the German constitution allowed princes to resist the emperor when he violated the law of the land. The league originally included the rulers of Saxony, Hesse, Braunschweig-Lüneburg, Anhalt, and Mansfeld as well as the cities of Magdeburg and Bremen, but it grew to include a number of other important territories, such as Brandenburg and Württemberg, as well as numerous free cities.

In 1532 the Turks attacked Vienna, and Charles was forced to make further concessions to the Lutherans. A truce, called the Peace of Nuremberg, postponed the religious settlement and stipulated that no attacks were to be made against the Lutheran estates before the meeting of a general church council. In 1533 Charles was faced with the additional threat of an alliance against him between France and the papacy. His continuing political problems probably saved the Lutheran Reformation because they constantly diverted his attention and prevented him from using imperial might to suppress Lutheranism at a time when the movement was still relatively weak. Meanwhile, the Schmalkaldic League grew stronger and the Lutherans became increasingly alienated and less willing to compromise. When the pope finally summoned the long-delayed church council in 1537, the Lutheran princes asked Luther to draw up a new statement of faith. The resulting confession, known as the Schmalkald Articles, was a dogmatic declaration of the Lutheran position. Luther, who felt at the time that he was near death, considered it a final statement of his doctrine and his faith. The Schmalkald Articles asserted Lutheran doctrine in such a radical and uncompromising way that one historian calls them "a virtual Lutheran declaration of independence from Rome."[22]

Luther's Later Years

When Luther wrote the Schmalkald Articles, he had less than a decade to live. Although plagued by both illness and controversy during those years, his life was greatly enhanced by his wife and family. In 1525, during the Peasants' War, Luther married a nun named Katherine von Bora, who had fled the Wittenberg nunnery two years earlier with eleven other nuns. All the others had married or left, but Katherine remained and stubbornly refused to marry the man Luther had suggested as a possible husband. She said, however, that she would be willing to marry Luther or his colleague Amsdorf. Luther was probably influenced in his decision when he paid a visit in April to his father, who said he was happy Luther had left the monastery and hoped he would now marry and have heirs. Luther later stated that he had married to please his father, upset the pope, "make the angels laugh and the devils weep," and seal his testimony.[23]

Luther was forty-two years old and Katie was twenty-six when they married on 13 June 1525. Luther honestly admitted at the time: "I feel neither passionate love nor burning for my spouse, but I cherish her."[24] Genuine affection grew in the years ahead as Katie turned out to be the perfect helpmate for Luther. She was strong in the areas where Luther was particularly weak. Luther thought money was for spending or giving away, he never worried about debt, and his income was limited because he refused to accept any payment for his preaching or his publications, which could have earned him a great deal.[25] Katherine had to find a way to bridge the gap between earnings and expenditure. She did so by running a farm, gardening, breeding pigs, brewing beer, and taking in lodgers. In 1532 Elector John the Steadfast gave Luther the Augustinian monastery together with its lands. It was a three-story building with forty rooms on the ground floor alone, so the Luthers had plenty of room for students as well as guests, and the house was regularly filled with people. In fact, life there was at times so chaotic that it is a wonder Luther was able to work. When Prince George of Anhalt considered staying with Luther during a visit to Wittenberg, he was advised that he might prefer a more peaceful place: "The home of Luther is occupied by a motley crowd of boys, students, girls, widows, old women and youngsters. For this reason there is much disturbance in the place, and many regret it for the sake of the good man, the honorable father. . . . As the situation now stands and as circumstances exist in the household of Luther, I would not advise that your Grace stop there."[26]

The Luther household was blessed with six children—three boys and three girls.[27] Luther loved his children dearly and was a good father to them despite his busy life. He also came to love and appreciate Katie, as is evident from his many references to her. When he spoke of Paul's Epistle to the Galatians, the epistle he loved best, he called it "my Katherine von Bora." He once confessed his sin was that he trusted Katie more, and expected more from her, than he did from Christ. Luther's appreciation of marriage deepened during his twenty years with Katie, and one suspects he was describing his own experience when he wrote, "the first love is drunken. When the intoxication wears off, then comes the real married love."[28]

Katie also took care of Luther in the numerous illnesses that plagued him during the last decade of his life. Until 1524 Luther enjoyed reasonably good health, but from 1527 onward his health began to deteriorate quickly. A year earlier he had suffered from a kidney stone, which he reportedly rid himself of by eating a heavy meal of fried herrings and cold peas with mustard. In April 1527 he was stricken by tightness in the chest, dizziness, and fainting spells and had to give up preaching for a time. In July 1527 he experienced periods of weakness that made him think he was about to die, and he was also seized by serious depression. These attacks, which he called *Anfectungen*, continued throughout his life; when they occurred, he was seized by overwhelming feelings of alienation from God and despair. In a letter to Melanchthon he described how he felt: "I spent more than a week in death and in hell. My entire body was in pain, and I still tremble. Completely abandoned by Christ, I labored under the vacillations and storms of desperation and blasphemy against God. But through the prayers of the saints God began to have mercy on me and pulled my soul from the inferno below."[29]

Attacks of dizziness continued, and Luther again had to give up preaching for two months in 1532. He also had a running sore in his leg that bothered him for the remainder of his life. In addition he suffered from kidney stones, gout, constipation, and hemorrhoids. These physical disorders, combined with the pressure of overwork, endless controversy, and constant personal attacks may explain, but not excuse, his bad temper and his vicious attacks on opponents.

Luther never had much patience with those who disagreed with him, but as he grew older he became even more scathing in his attacks on his opponents. Although he was not alone in the use of scurrilous language, since it was commonly used in sixteenth-century controversies,[30] his unreasonable attacks on opponents at the end of his life detract from his reputation. He launched some of his harshest attacks on his Catholic opponents, maintaining that because they were the enemies of the gospel he could no longer pray for them, and his prayers now included curses against the papacy. He also attacked Anabaptists and those Reformers who differed with his eucharistic theology, even questioning their salvation,[31] and we have already noted his acrimonious attacks on the peasants. However, Luther's most disgraceful tract was entitled *Of the Jews and Their Lies*, written in 1543. It differed markedly from an essay he wrote in 1523, entitled "That Jesus Christ Was Born a Jew," in which he urged that the Jews be treated compassionately and permitted to work and trade in Christian society with the hope that they might "hear our Christian teaching, and witness our Christian life," and eventually be converted. He even expressed sympathy when they were converted, commenting, "If some of them should prove stiff-necked, what of it? After all, we ourselves are not all good Christians either."[32] Twenty years later Luther expressed a very different attitude. Disappointed that the Jews had not converted to Christianity in large numbers and in reaction to erroneous rumors that Jews were trying to convert Christians and had even circumcised them, he launched a vicious attack on them. He stated that their synagogues and schools should be burned, their houses should be destroyed, their rabbis should be forbidden to teach, their religious books should be taken from them, and they should be forbidden to carry on commercial activities and be forced to work as day laborers on the land.

It was not only Luther's opponents who found him obstinate and difficult; he was also often a burden to one of his most gifted friends,

Philip Melanchthon (1497–1560).
Illustration from Beza *Icones*.

Philip Melanchthon, who several times wanted to leave Wittenberg. At times Luther recognized and expressed regret for his temperamental weaknesses. At one point he explained to his wife, "Wrath just won't turn me loose. Why, I sometimes rage about a piddling thing not worthy of mention. Whoever crosses my path has to suffer for it—I won't say a kind word to anyone. Isn't that a shameful thing?"[33]

Luther believed that the Christian was both saint and sinner at the same time, and his life and personality tended to confirm his theology. The other side of Luther that remained with him all his life and made him a very attractive personality was his sense of humor, which included his ability to joke about and even laugh at himself. He also knew how to enjoy the good things of life, including his family, good beer, good food, and good companionship. As mentioned earlier, he was a great lover of music, which he considered one of God's greatest gifts, maintaining that it drove away the devil, healed the soul, and raised one's spirits. Despite his pomposity in controversy, in his calmer moments Luther was a humble man who recognized his own weaknesses. He never considered his own works worthy of collecting for publication, and when his friends insisted on printing a collection of his works at the end of his life, he wrote an apologetic introduction pointing out they could find much better writings from such men as Melanchthon: "My books . . . were prompted or rather dictated by the bewildering pressure of events, and consequently resemble the 'primitive and disordered chaos' so that even I can no longer sort them out with ease. For these reasons I desired hitherto that all my books should be buried in perpetual oblivion, to make room for better ones."[34]

Luther died in February 1546 after mediating in a quarrel between the two counts of Mansfeld. His last words, in response to his friend Justus Jonas's question, "Do you want to die standing firm on Christ and the doctrine you have taught?" was a resounding *"Ja!"*[35] Almost twenty years earlier, when Luther thought he was about to die, Justus Jonas recorded a more detailed confession. It reveals the man described in this chapter, who was certain of the faith he taught, impatient of those who taught differently, ready to admit his weakness, and passionately devoted to the service of God as he understood it: "I am fully conscious and certain that I have taught correctly from the word of God, according to the service to which God pressed me against my will: I have taught correctly about faith, love, the cross, and the sacraments. Many accused me of proceeding too severely. Severely, that is true, and often too severely: but it was a question of the salvation of all: even my opponents."[36] Katie outlived Luther by four years, dying with words that would have made Luther happy: "I will cleave to the Lord Christ as a burr to the cloth."[37]

The Spread of Lutheranism outside Germany

By the time Luther died, Lutheranism had already spread well beyond the borders of Germany. Its acceptance outside Germany and the permanence of its impact varied from place to place. Its greatest and most lasting success was in Scandinavia, where it was inextricably intertwined with the political struggles of that region and was imposed from above by the political authorities, as it had been in much of Germany. In the eastern part of Europe, where there was no strong central authority, it sprang from below as the nobles were influenced by Lutheran teaching and demanded concessions from the monarchs on religious matters.

Turning first to Scandinavia, the present five countries of that region—Finland, Sweden, Norway, Denmark, and Iceland—had temporarily achieved a dynastic unity by the Union of Kalmar in 1397, although each area retained its own laws and customs. The Danish king at the beginning of the Reformation was Christian II (1513–1523), who invited his uncle, Frederick the Wise, to send a Lutheran theologian to teach at a Danish university. Karlstadt went there briefly, but after the Edict of Worms, Christian lost interest, probably because he wanted to avoid offending Charles V. King Christian II was deposed in 1523, and his successor, Frederick I, who had been influenced by Lutheranism, encouraged Lutheran preachers to spread the Reformation. He received the support of nobles, who enriched themselves by seizing church property. When Christian II attempted to regain the throne, Frederick joined the Schmalkaldic League, but he died in 1533, after which the country was plunged into a three-year civil war. The victor in that war was Christian III (1536–1559), who was committed to Lutheranism, and at a national assembly held in Copenhagen in 1536 it was introduced as the state religion. In 1537 a Lutheran pastor (rather than, as traditionally, the archbishop of Lund) crowned the new king, signifying the change in religion that had occurred. King Christian III then began to reorganize the Danish church.

Norway, which had supported Christian III's opponent in the civil war, was forced to accept Lutheranism after his triumph, and superintendents were appointed to replace Catholic bishops. Iceland, which had belonged to Norway, became a Danish province, and Reformation was also introduced from above. In both areas, the effort to impose Lutheranism met with stiff resistance. On the other hand, the Reformation in Sweden and Finland (which was united to Sweden) was directly linked with the struggle for independence from Denmark. Christian II had imposed his rule on Sweden in a brutal way, and in 1521 he massacred many of the Swedish nobles. A young nobleman, Gustavus Eriksson, later known as Gustavus Vasa (1523–1560), led the fight against the Danes, and in 1523 he was chosen king by a Swedish diet. The new Swedish king faced major problems because the country was virtually bankrupt after the civil war. The church owned about one-fifth of the land in Sweden, and it is not surprising that this provided a great temptation for a bankrupt state, especially since Pope Leo X had supported the Danes in their effort to suppress the Swedish revolt. Thus national interests set the stage for the adoption of Lutheranism in Sweden even before the victory of Lutheranism in Denmark. The Diet of Vesteras in 1527 provided for the confiscation of Swedish church property and for the teaching of the gospel. In the years that followed, Lutheranism was gradually introduced under the leadership of the king. After Vasa's death, the accession of Sigismund of Poland, who was a Roman Catholic, led to the calling of a National Synod in 1593, which reaffirmed Lutheranism, in order to forestall the reintroduction of Catholicism.

In contrast to the imposition of the Reformation from above in Scandinavia, in eastern Europe merchants and university students from western Europe introduced the Reformation. Poland was already a weak monarchy, and the king lost even more power when nobles began to convert in large numbers to Lutheranism. Lutheran ideas also made progress in the towns and even among some bishops along the Baltic coastline in the early 1520s. Efforts by the Roman Catholic Church to suppress these movements failed, and in the 1540s Calvinism (see chapter 7, "Calvin and Calvinism") began to make inroads. In 1555 a diet suspended the jurisdiction of ecclesiastical courts, thereby giving legal recognition to Protestantism. In 1573 the Compact of Warsaw granted religious liberty to all religious groups. However, the experiment in religious toleration

failed as the militant Catholicism of the Catholic Reformation eventually suppressed Protestantism, and Poland eventually became one of
the most strongly Roman Catholic countries in Europe.

In Bohemia the Hussite movement was initially receptive to
Lutheranism, which also spread into neighboring Moravia. But efforts to
achieve a union between Lutherans and older Bohemian religious groups
failed, and Bohemian Protestantism was to become a victim of suppression from above later in the Reformation era. The spread of Lutheranism
to Hungary, Austria, and Transylvania was aided by the large number
of Germans who lived in those areas. In Transylvania, Germans who
had lived there since the twelfth century readily accepted Lutheranism,
and a bishop was elected to head a church that adopted the Augsburg
Confession as its doctrinal statement; however, Calvinism eventually
displaced Lutheranism. Austria was at the heart of the Hapsburg lands,
but each division of Austria had a great deal of local autonomy, making
it difficult for the Hapsburg ruler, Ferdinand, to suppress Lutheranism.
Although a number of Protestant leaders were executed, important nobles
converted to Lutheranism, and their sons were sent to study at Lutheran
universities such as Wittenberg. Several cities also joined the Lutheran
movement, but by the end of the Reformation era, Austrian Lutheranism
also succumbed to the Catholic Reformation.

The Peace of Augsburg 1555

German Lutheranism also faced the prospect of suppression after
the death of Luther. Emperor Charles V finally lost patience with the
Lutheran princes when all his efforts to reunite the church by negotiation failed, and as a result he decided to use force. In July 1546, only a
few months after Luther's death, the emperor launched the long-delayed
attack. Although initially the Lutheran princes had a larger army and conducted a successful campaign, they were divided in their leadership and
failed to follow up their victories. The emperor received reinforcements
from the Netherlands and Italy, and he also persuaded the Lutheran
ruler, Maurice of Saxony, to switch sides by offering John Frederick's
electoral title as a bribe. In April 1547 Charles's able commander, the
Duke of Alva, won a major victory at the Battle of Mühlberg, where John
Frederick was captured. Fifteen months after Luther's death, Wittenberg
was occupied by the emperor's forces, and John Frederick lost his electoral office as well as most of his territory. John Frederick and Philip

of Hesse were imprisoned, leaving the emperor in complete control of Germany, except for the cities of Magdeburg and Bremen.

Charles V then reimposed Catholicism through the so-called Augsburg Interim, which was to have effect until the meeting of a general council. Although some concessions were made on the questions of clerical marriage and giving the cup to the laity, the other articles of this settlement reaffirmed the Roman position including papal primacy and the seven sacraments. If the Augsburg Interim had been successfully enforced, the Reformation in Germany would have been suppressed, but Charles's victory had come too late to stamp out Lutheranism. In the two and a half decades since the Edict of Worms, the Lutheran movement had gained too much strength and had become too embedded in Germany to be suppressed by a military victory.

Charles found that he could only enforce the interim where his troops were stationed; other Lutheran principalities resisted passively, by not enforcing the interim, or actively, by refusing to accept it. Magdeburg, which had successfully defended itself against Charles's troops, became a center of resistance and was joined by other German cities, including Hamburg, Bremen, Lubeck, and Göttingen. The emperor's old enemies also plagued him. The pope, who was concerned about the emperor becoming too powerful after his victory, withdrew his troops, and the Turks were preparing to attack again in Hungary. Meanwhile the new French king, Henry II, made an alliance with Maurice of Saxony, who was disillusioned with the emperor and no longer willing to betray the Lutheran cause. Maurice led the fight against Charles V, and although it cost him his life, the imperial forces did not prevail, and Charles was forced to give up the effort to subdue the Lutherans. Prematurely aged from his many troubles, his body painfully racked with gout, which he had suffered since he was in his twenties and which was exacerbated by his gluttony, Emperor Charles V finally gave up. He resigned all his offices and retired into a Spanish monastery, where he continued his unhealthy eating habits and died in September 1558.

The Hapsburg Empire was now divided. Charles's son Philip was to rule Spain, Burgundy, and the Italian possessions, while Charles's brother Ferdinand, who held the imperial title, was to rule Germany and the eastern lands. Before he resigned, Charles delegated Ferdinand to negotiate a peace with the Lutherans. Aware that such a peace would require religious concessions he felt he could not make in good conscience, he entrusted these negotiations to his brother, who agreed to the Peace of Augsburg in 1555. By its terms, the Lutheran princes, imperial knights, and free cities were guaranteed security equal to that of the Catholic estates. However, it applied only to those Protestants who adhered to the Augsburg Confession, so Calvinists and other Protestants were excluded. It also proclaimed the principle that each ruler would determine the religion of his domain and all subjects must conform, a principle termed by seventeenth-century jurists *Cuius regio, eius religio* (Latin, literally, "whoever the king, his religion"). An exception to that rule was made in the case of ecclesiastical princes such as bishops or abbots. Anyone dissatisfied with the religion of his area had full liberty to move to another principality. The Peace of Augsburg ended the first phase of the German Reformation with the political authorities clearly in control of the church. Lutheranism had received toleration, but other problems remained to be resolved, and Calvinism, which was excluded from the settlement, had already made major inroads in Germany. In addition, serious divisions had developed among Lutherans. Not surprisingly, the Peace of Augsburg proved to be a temporary settlement.

Luther's Influence

In the century following the Peace of Augsburg, Luther's influence on the movement he started became even stronger than it was when he was alive. He was increasingly portrayed as an unblemished hero and an authority for the Lutheran churches. A recent study has pointed out that Luther's image was used in three different ways. First, he was viewed as a prophet who replaced the authority of popes and councils and as an authority for interpreting Scripture. Second, he served as a teacher whose writings were used by his followers as authoritative guides to confront false teaching and for establishing true doctrine. Third, he was regarded as a prophetic hero whom God used for the liberation of the church and the German people from papal oppression. Luther was also portrayed as a miracle worker and venerated in much the same way as medieval saints had been. Miracles were even attributed to his image. Stories spread about a picture of Luther that supposedly emerged unscathed from fires that burned down the house in which it hung. The miracle of the "incombustible Luther" was attributed to divine intervention.[38] Luther also became the subject of numerous biographies. Although more has been written about Luther than almost any other figure in European history,[39] thorough research does not guarantee objectivity, and it should not surprise us that radically contrasting pictures of the Reformer have been presented by his historians.

Shortly after Luther's death, Melanchthon wrote his biography of Luther, presenting a very positive picture of the author's friend and colleague. At the same time, Luther's enemies constructed a very different picture. In 1549 Johannes Cochlaeus published a biography of Luther that presented his life and work in extremely negative terms. These early, biased writings by contemporaries supplied later historians with the evidence to construct the kind of Luther who best fitted their preconceptions.[40] What followed was a series of biographies that sought either to discredit Luther totally or to praise him uncritically, depending on the confessional allegiance of the author. Only in the last century have polemical works been replaced by more objective studies that sought to uncover the "real" Luther rather than one fitting the author's religious beliefs.

The quincentennial commemoration of Luther's birth in 1983 resulted in an avalanche of publications, but many of them presented a Luther who fit the twentieth century better than the sixteenth. Everybody was anxious to claim Luther for their own and to make him relevant to modern problems. Even the communist government of the German Democratic Republic, which had formerly denounced him as a tool of the princes and an enemy of the people, now portrayed him as a hero. However, in order to achieve their goal of presenting a Luther who was acceptable to the modern world, historians had to ignore those aspects of Luther's beliefs and character that are less palatable to modern attitudes. The problem with this approach was that it created a Luther who would have been out of place in the sixteenth century! In a review of the quincentenary publications, the well-known Tudor historian Geoffrey Elton reminded his readers that although the "real" Luther might not be "attractive to the twentieth century," he may have a great deal to teach our own age. Elton perceptively observed that even though our world "lacks the Christian convictions concerning Satan, his works and the fall which inspired Luther, it has good cause to think sin rampant enough and destructive of peace and good conduct. It will not even care about the meaning of Luther's theology for this or that theme of modern concern, but it might even so get help from Luther. . . . But if it is to gain from Luther it must turn to the real Luther—furious, violent, foul-mouthed, passionately concerned."[41]

This is the Luther we have sought to portray. Despite his personality defects, or maybe partially because of them, he helped to change the course of history and left a rich heritage to future generations.

5

THE URBAN REFORMATION: ZURICH, BASEL, AND STRASBOURG

▼

> The imperial registers drawn up at the Diet of Worms in 1521 list a total of eighty-five cities under the title of "free and Imperial Cities." . . . At that time some sixty-five of these cities could be considered directly subject to the empire. The great majority of them, more than fifty, in some way officially recognized the Reformation during the sixteenth century. Over half of the cities became and remained Protestant.
>
> Bernd Moeller[1]

The above evidence, taken from Bernd Moeller's classic 1962 essay on imperial cities and the Reformation, suggests that the oft-quoted statement that "the Reformation was an urban event"[2] has some substance. This is not to suggest that the cities were the only areas that adopted the Reformers' teaching or that they were even the most significant. In fact, since only 10 percent of the population of Germany lived in cities, if the appeal of the Reformation had been limited to an urban environment, its overall support would have been limited. However, clearly the Reformation had a substantial following in the cities, and most

Reformers were especially active in the urban areas. Some spent their entire ministries in cities (including Zwingli, Bucer, and Oecolampadius, the three we will be discussing in this chapter, as well as John Calvin). The explanations for the success of the urban Reformation are varied; however, the fact that people lived in close proximity to one another and that there was a higher literacy rate in the cities were important factors. The Reformed preachers could readily find an audience in the cities, and many of their converts were able to read the Scriptures and the Reformation literature. Although Lutherans had a good deal of success in the German cities, some historians have argued that the theology of Reformers such as Zwingli and Bucer had an even greater appeal to urban populations. They contend that whereas Luther's theology placed a greater emphasis on the individual, the starting point for the urban Reformers was the community.[3] We will examine some of these questions in this chapter as we trace the course of the urban reformation in three major cities—Zurich, Basel, and Strasbourg.

Zwingli and Zurich

Controversy and divisions among Reformers plagued the Reformation from its onset. One of the earliest conflicts occurred between Luther and the Swiss reformer Ulrich Zwingli. Their theologies reflected their different backgrounds as well as the different environments in which they worked. However, they also had much in common: they were almost the same age, they each spoke a dialect of the German language, and both came from peasant families. Zwingli was born on 1 January 1484 in the town of Wildhaus, in the Toggenburg Valley, which was part of the Swiss confederation. The confederation was a group of virtually autonomous regions, or cantons, joined in a loose union. Although they were able to cooperate in the face of a common enemy, such as their ancient adversary the Hapsburgs, the regions that made up the confederation had very little in common, not even a common language. They ranged geopolitically from the rural cantons of central Switzerland, with their largely agricultural economies, to commercial centers and industrial cities such as St. Gall, with its linen industry, and Basel, a center of the printing industry. Zurich, which had a population of six thousand, was a center of trade and ruled over the surrounding rural areas.

Zwingli's family was reasonably prosperous. His father was an administrative official in his local area, serving as chief magistrate for the district. Like Luther's father, he had the financial means to provide his son

Ulrich Zwingli (1484–1531).
Illustration from Beza *Icones*.

with an excellent education, and he recognized Ulrich's intellectual abilities, sending him first to learn reading and writing from his uncle, a priest at the nearby town of Wessen. At the age of ten young Ulrich was sent to Basel, where he studied Latin. He then went to Bern, where he continued his Latin studies under Heinrich Woeflin, a proponent of humanism. Zwingli almost became a friar because he had an excellent voice and the Dominicans, who were interested in his musical gifts, persuaded him to enter as a novice.

Zwingli's father, however, was not prepared to have his son become a friar, so he removed him from Bern and sent him to the University of Vienna, a center of humanist studies. Thus, in contrast to Luther's monastic experience, Zwingli had a strong humanist emphasis in his training that would influence his theology. Zwingli completed his studies at the University of Basel, receiving his bachelor's degree in 1504 and his master's in 1506.

After completing his formal education, Zwingli received an appointment to a parish in Glarus, where he served as priest for a decade. While at Glarus he was able to study the classics as well as the church fathers and especially Augustine. He also taught himself Greek and read the works of Erasmus, becoming an avid follower of the "Prince of the Humanists," whom he met in Basel in 1516. When Erasmus's Greek New Testament was published in 1516, Zwingli is said to have memorized Paul's epistles in Greek. His admiration for Erasmus continued even after the Zurich Reformation began, although he eventually broke with Erasmus,[4] maintaining that he was simply too weak to carry his followers into the fullness of reform. In 1513 Zwingli served as chaplain to a contingent of Swiss mercenaries fighting for the pope against the French, and in 1516 he witnessed the massive defeat of Swiss soldiers by the French at Marignano, where an estimated ten thousand died. He then became a vocal opponent of the mercenary trade,[5] which made him unpopular in Glarus because this trade was especially lucrative for the leading citizens of the town. As a result, Zwingli left Glarus in April

1516 and transferred to the parish of Einsiedeln, where he became a very popular preacher. Einsiedeln had a shrine of the Black Image of the Virgin that attracted numerous pilgrims, and Zwingli's preaching skills became widely known. When the prestigious position of People's Priest in Zurich's great minster became vacant, he was a leading candidate. Although he had to defend his sexual misconduct with a young woman,[6] the electors were obviously willing to excuse this, because in December 1518 Zwingli was elected to the position.

By the time Zwingli took up his new post, according to his own testimony he had already begun to preach what he called "the Gospel of Christ,"[7] maintaining that he had learned it from Scripture rather than from Luther, who had published his *Ninety-five Theses* more than a year earlier. "Before anyone in this area had even heard of Luther, I began to preach the gospel of Christ in 1516. . . . I started preaching the gospel before I had even heard Luther's name. . . . Luther, whose name I did not know for at least another two years, had definitely not instructed me. I followed holy scripture alone."[8]

On 1 January 1519, his thirty-fifth birthday, Zwingli began a series of sermons in the minster, preaching directly from the Greek text. In contrast to Luther, who preferred to retain the traditional method of preaching from the set Gospel and Epistle lessons of the church calendar, Zwingli began with Matthew and preached sequentially through the New Testament. Following the humanist approach of seeking truth directly from the original sources, Zwingli's central doctrine was *sola scriptura* (by Scripture alone). In a sermon entitled *Of the Clarity and Certainty of the Word of God*, published in 1522, he stated:

> No matter who a man may be, if he teaches in accordance with his own thought and mind his teaching is false. But if he teaches you in accordance with the Word of God, it is not he that teaches you, but God who teaches him. . . . When I was younger, I gave myself overmuch to human teaching. . . . But eventually I came to the point where, led by the Word and Spirit of God, I saw the need to set aside all these things and to learn the doctrine of God direct from his own Word.[9]

Zwingli was a superb preacher with a wonderful voice as well as great rhetorical skill. He attracted large audiences, including people from the surrounding areas who came to hear his sermons on market days. His popularity increased when Zurich suffered an outbreak of the plague in autumn 1519, and he stayed to minister to the sick and dying, eventually catching the infection himself and coming very close to death.

The first challenge to traditional Catholicism came in 1522 over what seems like an insignificant issue. Zwingli had been preaching from the Bible for over two years when the printer Christopher Froschauer, who had become Zwingli's close friend, invited him to a gathering at his house during Lent attended by a group of his workers. They then deliberately broke the Lenten fast by cutting up a sausage and eating it. Although Zwingli did not eat because he was concerned about giving offense, on 23 March he defended the action in a sermon, arguing that breaking a fast was not a sin, and the church could not punish those involved. His sermon, entitled *Freedom of Choice in Eating*, was published, and the bishop of Constance, under whose jurisdiction the city fell, sent a delegation to the city on 7 April to protest about the violation of canon law. When called before the council, Froschauer defended his actions on the basis of biblical teaching and stated that, if church leaders punished them for things that were not contrary to the word of God, the council should come to their defense and "protect our godly rights." He also defended Zwingli, stating that "God has given Zurich a better preacher than can be found in all of Germany."[10]

A second issue arose in the summer of the same year when Zwingli and a number of other ministers petitioned the bishop of Constance to sanction clerical marriage. Once again Zwingli was convinced by his study of Scripture that the prohibition on clerical marriage in the medieval church was based on human rather than divine law. It was not taught in the Bible, and since the gift of chastity had not been given to all men, priests should be allowed to marry. In Switzerland, as elsewhere, the rule of celibacy was widely violated; many priests lived openly with women and raised families with the full knowledge of their bishop, who added to his income by fining priests for children born out of wedlock.[11] However, marriage continued to be strictly forbidden, so unsurprisingly the bishop rejected their appeal. In the years that followed, the bishop's objections were ignored as the rule of celibacy was generally abandoned in Zurich and city officials accepted this situation. Zwingli married Anna Reinhart in 1522, but he kept his marriage secret until April 1524 when a public marriage ceremony was held in church. Meanwhile, Zwingli attacked many other aspects of medieval church practice in his sermons, including intercession to saints, indulgences, pilgrimages, and veneration of the Virgin Mary. He received significant support from the city government when an order was issued that all preaching must be based on the Holy Scriptures.

In November 1522 Zwingli resigned his position as People's Priest and received a new authorization to preach, this time from the council.

(His original authorization had come from the bishop, so this move signified his independence from episcopal authority.) In January 1523 he was offered the opportunity to defend his views at a public debate. In preparation, he put forward *Sixty-seven Theses*, which indicate how far he had moved from the position of the medieval church. They not only attacked forced fasting and clerical celibacy but also rejected belief in purgatory, the sacrificial mass, the need for a priestly mediator, and the special status of the clergy. The debate was heavily weighted in favor of Zwingli, since arguments were confined to Scripture, and he was declared the winner. However, the Zurich authorities still refused to order an immediate end to many traditional religious practices. Popular outbreaks of iconoclasm led to a debate on the question of images and the mass in October 1523. This disputation also ended in victory for Zwingli, but the magistrates were committed to a policy of slow change, which Zwingli accepted. They were prepared to remove images and abolish the mass only when they felt the majority of the community was ready to accept such changes.

Accordingly, eight months later, on 15 June 1524, the council authorized the removal of all images from the churches and the brightly colored painted walls of the cathedral were whitewashed over. In addition, Zwingli objected to the music used in the medieval service because he felt it distracted from, rather than enhanced, the true worship of God. Consequently, organ music, congregational singing (except psalms), and choirs were eliminated from the service. In 1527 the organ in the minster, which had been silent for several years, was removed and chopped up. In December 1524 the Dominican and Augustinian monastic houses were confiscated, and on 14 April 1525 the mass was officially abolished, to be replaced by a simple service in which communion was administered from a table in the nave. The words of Scripture were read, and the congregation received both bread and wine. In contrast to Luther, Zwingli was not prepared to accept that practices not specifically forbidden by Scripture could be retained. The Bible must be the final authority in all matters involving the church, and practices that were not clearly biblical must be eliminated.

As is evident, the Reformation in Zurich proceeded slowly, with the city government playing a major role in bringing about the changes. Zwingli held a corporate view of society and did not distinguish between the realms of the church and the state. In his *Sixty-seven Theses* he contended that "all the rights and protection that the so-called spiritual authority claims belong to secular governments provided they are Christian."[12] The magistrates, he believed, exercised authority on behalf of all the inhabitants of the city, who were the same people who made up the church. Zwingli was, therefore, willing to have the city government exercise control of public morals through a Court of Domestic Relations, which was established in 1525, and a Court of Morals, established the following year. He differed from Luther and Calvin in that he was even willing to have the town council exercise the right of excommunication and exclusion from the Lord's Supper, although initially he had some reservations about this. Between 1525 and 1530 Zwinglian ideas and practices spread rapidly in Switzerland and among southern German cities including Ulm, Strasbourg, Augsburg, Lindau, Memmingen, Frankfurt, and Constance. Some scholars believe that Zwingli's corporate approach had a greater appeal to cities, which would help explain why many of the cities of south Germany found Zwingli's position more appealing than Luther's, which emphasized the individual's relationship with God. In addition, they argue that Luther's doctrine of justification by faith alone ran contrary to urban concerns about public morality.[13]

Conflicts with Anabaptists and Luther

The slow pace of reform and Zwingli's position on church and state were rejected by a group of Radical Reformers led by Conrad Grebel, who wanted more rapid change and eventually adopted the position that, rather than being identical to the whole of the community, the church must be a gathered community of true believers who voluntarily separate themselves from the world. They were to become the first Anabaptists, who will be discussed in the next chapter. Zwingli also came into conflict with Luther, with whom he had differences in a number of areas. We have already noted Zwingli's rejection of images and much of the musical heritage of the Middle Ages, which Luther found not only acceptable but even beneficial to worship. In addition, Luther and Zwingli may have differed in the importance they placed on the doctrine of justification by faith. Luther was most concerned about the individual believer's relationship with God, while Zwingli was more concerned about the moral and spiritual renewal of Zurich.[14] The differences between Luther and Zwingli were most pronounced on the sacraments, and particularly the Eucharist. Although both rejected the medieval doctrine of transubstantiation and the sacrificial mass, Luther continued to believe that "the true body of our Lord Jesus Christ" is distributed in the sacrament "in and under the bread and wine."[15] He based his understanding on a literal interpretation of the words of Jesus recorded in Matthew 26:26,

"This is my body." He also believed that the Eucharist was efficacious for the true believer in that it would result, as the Scriptures promised, in forgiveness of sin and the strengthening of faith.

Zwingli had a very different understanding both of the benefits received from the sacrament and the nature of Christ's presence. His interpretation of Christ's statement, "This is my body," was influenced by a Dutch humanist, Cornelius Hoen, who had come to believe that Christ's words could not be taken literally and that the word *is* must be understood as meaning "signifies." Luther rejected Hoen's explanation as avoiding the clear meaning of the scriptural words, since there was no suggestion in the text that Christ was employing a figure of speech when he used the word *is*. He reacted even more strongly to Karlstadt's contention that Christ was pointing to himself rather than the bread when he said, "This is my body," and tended to associate Zwingli's belief with Karlstadt's radical doctrines, which he so abhorred. Zwingli maintained that Luther was ignoring the meaning of John 6:63, "It is the spirit that gives life, the flesh is of no avail" (RSV) which made it clear that a physical receiving of Christ's body and blood in the Eucharist was unnecessary. In addition, Acts 1:9 states that Christ had ascended into heaven where, as Christians confess in the Apostles' Creed, he is "at the right hand of God." Consequently his physical body could not be present in the Eucharist. Whereas Zwingli tended to emphasize the distinctiveness of Christ's two natures without denying their unity, Luther argued that "our faith maintains that Christ is God and man, and the two natures are one person, so that this person may not be divided in two."[16] Luther believed that the attributes of Christ's divine nature are communicated to his human nature; therefore he is omnipresent and the human body of Christ is ubiquitous, meaning he can be in many places at the same time without the limits imposed by space or time. Luther also maintained that Zwingli misunderstood what it means to be "at the right hand of God." Rather than indicating a specific place, it means to share in God's almighty power. Finally, Luther placed a much greater emphasis on the Eucharist than Zwingli, who made preaching the center of worship and suggested that communion be celebrated only three or four times a year. Luther, while placing a strong emphasis on preaching, believed word and sacrament should be united in Christian worship, and he maintained communion should be celebrated every week.

The differences between Luther and Zwingli were accentuated by the fact that they expressed their views in a series of publications in which they not only stated their differing theologies but in which they also engaged in inordinate name-calling. As usual, Luther excelled his opponent in his use of abusive language, although Zwingli's responses inevitably fueled Luther's anger. In 1525 Zwingli stated his theological position in a work entitled *On True and False Religion*. On the question of whether Christ's body and blood are truly received in the Eucharist, he cited John 6:63 and attacked the position held by Luther as being "opposed by all sense and reason and understanding and by faith itself."[17] Luther responded with a publication whose title, *That These Words of Christ "This Is My Body" Still Stand Firm against the Fanatic*, suggested that it was not intended to be a friendly dialogue. Zwingli answered in a treatise that was meant to be moderate and irenic. It was even entitled, *Friendly Exposition of the Eucharist Affair to—Not against—Martin Luther*. Although the tone was moderate, the overall message was that Luther was wrong and should admit his mistake and humbly submit to Zwingli's view. Luther clearly did not consider it a "friendly exposition," stating that the work was "full of pride, accusations, stubbornness, hate and almost every wickedness, even though couched in the best words."[18] In Luther's response, entitled *That These Words of Christ "This is my Body" etc. Still Stand Firm against the Fanatic*, he accused his opponent of being in league with the devil for persisting in a teaching that was blasphemous and threatening to salvation. Zwingli responded in June 1527 by accusing Luther of being a papist, claiming his "formulations came from a brothel."[19] Luther reached a high point of invective in his reply, which warned that Zwingli's books were "the prince of hell's poison. For the man is completely perverted and has entirely lost Christ."[20] Zwingli struck the final blow in the battle of publications by accusing Luther of dealing with theology like "a sow in a flower garden."[21]

Considering the vicious polemics exchanged between the two men, it is surprising that they agreed to meet in the year following the last exchange. They did so reluctantly and only at the urging of the Lutheran prince, Philip of Hesse, who was concerned that the emperor might attack because he was enjoying a brief respite from his conflicts with the French king, Francis I, and with the pope. To meet this potential threat, evangelicals needed to establish a common front against a common threat. The meeting took place at Philip's castle in Marburg and included many of the leading figures in both camps. Rather than pit the two hot-headed chief opponents against each other, the meetings began with a meeting between Zwingli and the irenic Melanchthon, while Luther met with the equally mild-mannered Oecolampadius. Although Zwingli and Melanchthon reached some agreement, the plenary session, which began the following day, revealed the deep divisions between the two sides on the Eucharist. Luther took his stand on Christ's words, "This is my body," which he felt proved his point that the Bible teaches the real presence of Christ in the sacrament. He supposedly even wrote the Latin words *Hoc est corpus meum* (this is my body) in chalk on the table and covered it with the velvet tablecloth. Zwingli and Oecolampadius were equally sure that John 6:63, "The flesh is of no avail," proved their point that the physical presence of Christ's body and blood was unnecessary.

The meeting had some very tense and explosive moments, and the differences between the two men seemed insurmountable. At one point, when Zwingli accused Luther of not having a single passage of Scripture on which to base his argument, Luther tore off the tablecloth and stated, "'This is my body!' Here is our Scripture passage. You have not yet taken it from us, as you set out to do, we need no other. My dearest lords, since the words of my Lord Jesus Christ stand there *Hoc est corpus meum*, I cannot truthfully pass over them, but must confess and believe that the body of Christ is there."[22]

Although the discussions continued the following day, no agreement was reached on these critical differences. When they realized they would not be able to agree, both Luther and Zwingli revealed a softer side. Luther first thanked Oecolampadius "for giving me your views not with bitterness but friendship" and turned to Zwingli and said, "Mister Zwingli despite your anger I thank you as well. I apologize if I have been harsh to you. I am only human. I really wish the issue could have been resolved to our mutual satisfaction." Zwingli responded, "Doctor Luther I ask you to forgive my anger. I have always wanted your friendship and I still do."[23] It was a good way to end a meeting that had been so acrimonious, and there were more good things to come. At the end of the meeting, the participants signed a statement in which they expressed agreement on fourteen points of doctrine, and on the fifteenth point they stated: "Although we are not at this time agreed, as to whether the true Body and Blood of Christ are bodily present in the bread and wine, nevertheless the one party should show to the other Christian love, so far as conscience can permit, and both should fervently pray God Almighty, that, by His Spirit, He would confirm us in the true understanding."[24]

It was a beautiful statement and might well have provided the bridge for further discussions and eventually unity, but sadly, in the months following Marburg, both sides forgot their commitment to "show to the other Christian love." Less than a month after the colloquy ended, Zwingli wrote to Jerome Vadian, the reformer of St. Gall, stating that "if ever anyone was beaten it was the foolish and obstinate Luther."[25] Writing to his friend Nicholas Gerbel, a Strasbourg humanist, shortly after the meeting ended, Luther clearly explained what he meant by

Christian love. He stated that although "we ought to have charity and peace even with our foes . . . we plainly told them, that unless they grow wiser on this point they may indeed have our charity, but cannot by us be considered as brothers and members of Christ."[26]

Even at the Diet of Augsburg of 1530, the two parties were not able to establish a common front against the threat posed by the emperor. The Lutheran princes would not allow the Strasbourg theologians, led by Martin Bucer, to sign the Augsburg Confession because of their differences on the Eucharist. Strasbourg, therefore, joined with Constance, Memmingen, and Lindau to present a separate confession of faith, written largely by Bucer, called the Tetrapolitan Confession, in which he attempted to minimize the differences with the Lutherans. Zwingli circulated his own, more radical, confession, the *Fidei Ratio*, which was ignored by the emperor. Despite Bucer's efforts to reach agreement with Luther, he remained adamant in resisting any compromise statement.

Meanwhile, Zwingli was faced with problems from the Catholic cantons in Switzerland. A brief conflict, shortly before the Marburg Colloquy met, resulted in a victory for Zurich, sealed in the first Peace of Kappel in June 1529. However, a second war began in 1531, in which Zurich's poorly led, unprepared, and outnumbered army was decisively defeated at the Battle of Kappel. Zwingli, who accompanied Zurich's army clad in armor and wielding a battle-ax, was wounded in the battle. Heinrich Bullinger, Zwingli's successor in Zurich, wrote an account of the battle in which he stated that the enemy found Zwingli's wounded body on the battlefield and killed him, quartered and burned his body, mixed his ashes with dung, and scattered them so his followers could not recover his remains. Bullinger ended his account with words of praise for the fallen Reformer, commenting that "all those who knew him were constant in their praises."[27] Luther was an exception; on hearing of Zwingli's death, he commented that those who take the sword would also perish with it.

Zwingli's Successors

Zwingli's death did not bring an end to the Reformation in Zurich. His successor, Heinrich Bullinger (1504–1575) was not only a very able replacement but also considerably more moderate than his predecessor both in temperament and in theology. After the death of Zwingli, he became the pastor of the great minster in Zurich and the *Antistes*, the Zwinglian equivalent of a medieval bishop. He was a prolific writer and had an influence that ranged well beyond Zurich. Bullinger was particularly respected in England, where his advice was regularly sought in the course of the English Reformation. During the Marian persecution, he welcomed English exiles to Zurich, including a number of men who were to become bishops in the Elizabethan church. He also wrote some twelve thousand letters to political and religious leaders throughout Europe and in the four decades after Zwingli's death made Zurich a center of international Protestantism. During his lifetime Bullinger published 119 separate works, and his *Decades of Sermons*, a collection of sermons on Christian doctrine that he began to publish in 1549, were more widely read in some parts of Europe than even Calvin's *Institutes*. His *Commentaries on the Pauline Epistles* were equally widely read and went through seven editions.

Bullinger was also to have a major impact on Reformed theology, as he was involved in the writing of three Reformed confessions. In 1536 he joined theologians from a number of Swiss Reformed cities, including Basel, to write a confession of faith for the Swiss Protestant churches, known as the First Helvetic Confession. Martin Bucer and Wolfgang Capito, two of the Strasbourg Reformers, adopted the confession and hoped to use it as a means of coming to an agreement with the Lutherans. Although Luther's initial reaction to Bullinger was favorable, when he and the other Swiss Reformers refused to accept the Wittenberg Concord, in which Bucer came to an agreement with Luther on the Eucharist, Luther reacted strongly against Bullinger and turned again to polemics. In 1549 Bullinger came to an agreement with Calvin in the *Consensus Tigurinus*, which became the basis for the Reformed doctrine of the sacraments. Finally, Bullinger drafted the Second Helvetic Confession in 1566, which became one of the most influential and comprehensive Reformed statements of faith in the sixteenth century. It was adopted by the Reformed churches of France, Hungary, Poland, and Scotland.

Although Bullinger generally followed Zwingli in his theological position, he differed in a number of areas. For example, his sacramental theology gave greater significance to the Eucharist than Zwingli had, and on predestination he taught single predestination of the elect to salvation by God's eternal decree, in contrast with Zwingli's belief in double predestination, the belief that God foreordained some to salvation and others to damnation. Bullinger believed that damnation was the result of human sinfulness and the rejection of God's grace rather than God's eternal decree. On the question of state control of the church, he agreed with Zwingli and taught that the Christian community was rightfully under the Christian magistrate. Excommunication should therefore be in the hands of the magistrate and not, as Calvin would insist in Geneva, in the hands of the church.

Bullinger was a caring and generous man, who provided for Zwingli's family after his death. Bullinger had married Anna Adlischwyler in 1529, and their marriage was particularly productive, resulting in six sons and five daughters. He also took in a student, Rudolf Gwalther, at the age of thirteen and raised him like a son. When Bullinger died in 1575, Gwalther (1519–1586) became his successor, preserving the Zurich model of a state church and helping to spread the influence of the first Zurich Reformer by editing three volumes of Zwingli's works and translating some of his German works into Latin. Finally, Gwalther continued his mentor's influence on the English Reformation, where his model of the state church was particularly popular. Zwingli's successors ensured that his influence would continue as they joined with Calvin in establishing the Reformed branch of Protestantism. Zwingli also had a significant influence on the Reformation in the other two cities covered in this chapter, Basel and Strasbourg. The men who led the reform in these cities, Johannes Oecolampadius and Martin Bucer, were with Zwingli at Marburg, and both were influenced by humanism, which would play a major role in bringing the Reformation to the two cities.

Humanism and the Reformation in Basel

Basel was a logical place for the Reformation to blossom because it had been a center of church reform in the late Middle Ages. The controversial Council of Basel, which opposed Pope Eugenius IV and sought to maintain the position on authority decreed by the Council of Constance, met there from 1431 to 1449. Even after Eugenius IV transferred the council to Ferrara, the delegates continued to meet at Basel and appointed an antipope, Felix V, in 1439. Although the council finally submitted to the legitimate pope in 1449 and the schism was healed, there was a long tradition of antipapal activity in Basel and a deep commitment to reform.

Basel was equally a center for humanism. It was home to the humanist scholar Thomas Wyttenbach, who influenced Zwingli while he was studying in Basel and who was committed to church reform and opposed Scholasticism, monastic vows, and indulgences. In 1521 Erasmus moved to Basel and attracted many other men committed to the humanist type of reform. In addition Basel was an important publishing center; the printers Froben and Amerbach were located there, and from their presses flowed a continuous stream of books, including many of Erasmus's works.

Although Erasmus and the humanists were committed to the reform of the church and held many positions in common with the Protestant Reformers, including their emphasis on the Scriptures, there were also clear differences. This dissimilarity is illustrated most graphically in the break that occurred between Luther and Erasmus. Initially, Luther and Erasmus showed great respect for one another, and Erasmus had welcomed Luther's efforts at reform and defended him. However, as the controversies surrounding the Reformation became more heated, Erasmus urged both parties to seek a solution through arbitration. He was first and foremost a scholar who could see good and bad on both sides of an issue and therefore found it difficult to take sides. He also preferred to stay out of controversy. However, in trying to take a middle position, he found himself attacked by both sides. Initially Erasmus was quite comfortable in the liberal atmosphere of Basel, where he was able to continue with his writing as well as editing and translating works of the church fathers. But three years after he moved to Basel, he came into conflict with Luther. Although he would have preferred to avoid it, the break with Luther was, in a sense, forced upon him when he was urged by the Catholic side to write against Luther. He finally did so in August 1524, when he published his *Diatribe on Free Will*.

The *Diatribe* was a carefully written, well thought-out tract in the tradition of scholarship to which Erasmus was committed. He stated his position in a clear and concise manner as he contended that human beings have conditional free will and their good deeds are meritorious in God's sight. The Bible, he maintained, would not command good works unless man was capable of doing them. For Erasmus, the denial of free will was a dangerous doctrine, because it might discourage human beings from seeking to do good works. Although he accepted that the will is in bondage because of the fall, in accord with the teachings of the medieval church he also argued that we have a restricted freedom to do meritorious works. Erasmus wrote his work in one sitting, and he received congratulations for it from Pope Clement VII, Emperor Charles V, and King Henry VIII of England, who himself had written against Luther.

Luther responded in a work that was four times as long, entitled *The Bondage of the Will*. It was one of Luther's most important works, and he later called it, along with his catechism, the best expression of his thought. He argued that the divine will was immutable, that it determined all things, and that we can contribute nothing to our salvation. Grace is an act of full, free forgiveness that God initiates and in which he alone preserves us. Man cannot by his own reason or strength respond to God, and "in all things pertaining to salvation or damnation" he "has no free will, but is a captive, servant and bond slave, either to the will of God, or to the will of Satan."[28] Luther also asserted that Erasmus's effort to find a middle way was unacceptable:

> I will not accept or tolerate that moderate middle way which Erasmus would, with good intention, I think, recommend to me; to allow a certain little to free will, in order to remove the contradictions of scripture and the aforementioned difficulties. The case is not better, nor anything gained by this middle way. Because, unless you attribute all and everything to free will, as the Pelagians do, the contradictions in Scripture still remain, merit and reward, the mercy and justice of God are abolished. . . . Therefore, we must go to extremes, deny free will altogether and ascribe everything to God.[29]

Luther ended his tract on a positive note by stating that he had been aided by Erasmus's work, and even though Erasmus was wrong on this point, he honored and respected him. However, in typical Luther fashion, he added a remark undermining some of the positive things he had said about Erasmus, concluding that, "God has not willed yet nor granted you to be equal to the subject matter of this debate."[30]

The controversy did not end there. Erasmus considered Luther's tract an attack on his person, and in 1526 and 1527 he responded to Luther caustically, completing the break between himself and the Reformation. When the Reformation came to Basel, Erasmus moved to Freiburg, where he lived until 1535, when he returned to Basel to supervise the printing of his edition of Origen; he died there the following year. The last years of his life were filled with a good deal of sadness, as both sides attacked him, and the University of Paris censured some of his writings. During the Catholic Reformation, Erasmus's writings were even placed on the Index of Prohibited Books. In the bitterness and vitriol of the Reformation, this gentle scholar found himself out of place. However, when he died, he was fittingly given a magnificent funeral in a city that had by then adopted the teachings of the Reformers. Despite his rejection of the Reformation, the movement owed a great deal to him. It was said that "Erasmus laid the egg that Luther hatched." His appeal to the Bible as the ultimate authority in religious matters, his Greek New Testament, his attacks on Scholasticism, and his biting satires on the abuses in the church all helped to prepare the way for the Reformation.

Johannes Oecolampadius

The man who brought the Reformation to Basel was also deeply indebted to Erasmus and to humanism. Johannes Oecolampadius was born in Germany in 1482. His original name was Huszgen, but, under the influence of humanism, he changed his name to Oecolampadius, which means "lantern" or "shining light." He studied at a number of universities, including Heidelberg, Tübingen, and Basel. At Heidelberg he met the humanist scholar Jakob Wimpfeling and became a prominent member of the humanist circle. He also came to know Philip Melanchthon and his great uncle, Johannes Reuchlin, who encouraged him to study Greek and Hebrew. Oecolampadius was an excellent linguist, lecturing in Greek at Heidelberg and writing a Greek grammar while also gaining greater proficiency in Hebrew. He also became a close friend of Wolfgang Capito, who was to be his first biographer. Both men came to Basel in 1515 when Capito was appointed professor of theology at the university and preacher at the minster while Oecolampadius worked with Erasmus, helping him finish his notes and the commentary to his edition of the Greek New Testament. In 1518 Oecolampadius completed his doctorate in theology and at the age of thirty-six might have looked forward to a promising career as a humanist scholar had not the Reformation changed the direction of his life and ministry. He was preacher and confessor at Augsburg Cathedral when he first came into contact with Luther's teaching. In 1520 he entered a Brigittine monastery near Augsburg so he could, in quietness and solitude, read the church fathers and Luther and attempt to resolve the conflict he was feeling as he struggled to decide between Luther and his opponents. He ended his study by concluding that Luther was closer to the truth than his opponents. He left the monastery and returned to Basel in 1523, where he lectured on Isaiah at the university.

Oecolampadius came into contact with Ulrich Zwingli in early 1523, and a close friendship developed. By this time he had accepted Luther's doctrine of justification by faith alone and defended it publicly. He also advocated the marriage of priests and used his pulpit to disseminate the teachings of the Reformers. As he became more strongly Protestant, his friendship with Erasmus was threatened, especially after he seemed to support Luther in the debate over free will. Oecolampadius now led his newly adopted city into the Reformation, but it was not an easy path because Basel was deeply divided and there was a great deal of opposition. Basel had become a center for publication of Luther's writings, which the town council had welcomed for the economic benefits they brought to the town—but they also brought with them doctrine that many did not welcome. By 1522 some of the Basel preachers were calling for a Reformation, and the example of Zwingli's Zurich was making an impact. The Lenten fast was broken, and the city was becoming increasingly divided. In 1523 the council issued an order to the clergy that they were to preach only the gospel and avoid attacking others. In 1524, when the council appointed Oecolampadius to be pastor of St. Martin's Church, it included the condition that he should not introduce innovations into the service without the authorization of the council. The bishop and the university, which was still largely Catholic, opposed Reformation teaching, and the council tried to remain neutral. In order to avoid more disunity in the city, a censorship law was introduced in December of 1524.

In the following year, Oecolampadius published his position on the Lord's Supper, which was clearly Zwinglian; this made the council even more cautious, and it abandoned plans for a disputation on the Eucharist. Oecolampadius then began to innovate on his own. After preaching two sermons on the subject to prepare his congregation, he abandoned the mass. Although the council continued to try to steer a middle course, they gradually adopted the position of the Reformers as they began to secularize the monasteries and the endowments of the church. In 1527 they released the clergy from saying the mass and people from attending. However, at the same time as they were releasing the clergy from saying the mass, they welcomed the new bishop of Basel and tried to maintain toleration by proclaiming in February 1528 that citizens should not hate each other because of differing religious views. In the same year Oecolampadius, who was now forty-five years old, married the twenty-six-year-old widow Wibrandis Rosenblatt (whose story will be related in the chapter on women of the Reformation).

In 1528 the triumph of the Reformation in neighboring Bern gave the final impetus to reform in Basel. On 6 January 1529 the Council of Basel ordered a public disputation about the mass to be held in June. However, many in Basel were not prepared to wait that long. In February the town guilds sent an ultimatum to the council, and when it continued to hesitate, an angry crowd began to tear down images in the churches. Erasmus had urged moderation and waiting for meeting of a general council of the whole church to be held, and he was deeply distressed by these violent measures, which he described in a letter in May 1529:

> The smiths and workmen removed the pictures from the churches, and heaped such insults on the images of saints and the crucifix itself, that it

is quite surprising there was no miracle, seeing how many there always used to occur whenever the saints were even slightly offended. Not a statue was left either in the churches, or the vestibules, or the porches or the monasteries. The frescoes were obliterated by means of a coating of lime; whatever would burn was thrown into the fire and the rest pounded into fragments. Nothing was spared for either love or money. Before long the mass was totally abolished so that it was forbidden either to celebrate it in one's own house or to attend it in the neighboring villages.[31]

Erasmus left Basel a month before he wrote this letter, and nearly all the professors at the university emigrated. Catholic leaders on the council were dismissed, and evangelical preachers were installed in the churches. Preachers were ordered to base their messages on the exposition of the Bible, with sermons at 8:00 a.m., 12:00 noon, and 4:00 p.m. on the Lord's Day. The council completed the imposition of Reformation doctrine and practice in all city churches when it published an order of service and church discipline in April 1529. In the same year, Oecolampadius participated in the Marburg Colloquy, where, while clearly disagreeing with Luther's position, he had sought to be a peacemaker. Even after the failure of the colloquy, he continued to work to find agreement with Luther. He failed in that effort and also failed in the effort to limit the council's authority over the church by placing excommunication in the hands of the church. Two years after the victory of the Reformation in Basel, which owed so much to him, Oecolampadius died in the presence of his wife and children. The last month of his life was saddened by the news that his friend Zwingli had been killed at the Battle of Kappel. The Reformation in Basel, to which Oecolampadius had contributed so much, was complete by the time of his death and is an excellent example of how urban Reformation was accomplished in a city that had experienced the reform movements of the late Middle Ages but where the council moved slowly and cautiously in introducing the new teachings because of deep divisions among the citizens.

The Reformation in Strasbourg

Like Basel, Strasbourg had a reforming tradition in the late Middle Ages, which also helped prepare the way for the Reformation. The leading figure in the late medieval reform movement was Geiler von Kaisersberg, who preached in Strasbourg between 1478 and 1510. He was an outstanding preacher, and from his pulpit he sought to bring about spiritual and moral reform in Strasbourg. He was severely critical of clergy and the abuses in the church, and he attacked in strong language those popes who had obtained their office by bribery. He also stressed the importance of Scripture as the basis for doctrine and morals. He sounded almost Protestant when he wrote, "Neither pope nor emperor have the right to pass decrees contrary to divine law, and if they do so, one is not only allowed to disobey but obligated by one's conscience not to observe them."[32] However, while he lauded the Scripture as a source of authority, he still upheld the teaching authority of the church and disapproved of vernacular translations of the Bible and having laypeople read the Bible without guidance. Finally, he would not have agreed with the Reformation principles of the priesthood of all believers or justification by faith alone.

In the end, Geiler despaired of institutional reform, looking rather to the reform of individuals, who would "keep God's commandment and do what is right so that he may obtain salvation." Although he would not have agreed with some of its central doctrines, he did help to prepare Strasbourg for the Reformation. Furthermore, when reform came to Strasbourg, the differences between his preaching and that of the Reformers were not always recognized. For example, when the city council was questioned by Pope Adrian VI about the spread of the "Lutheran heresy," they reminded the pope of "Dr. Geiler's" preaching "a very long time before the Lutheran question arose." They maintained that, although there was very little difference between his preaching and that of the Reformers, he had not only "preached in the cathedral" but had "enjoyed the support of bishop Albrecht."[33]

In view of its medieval tradition of Reformed preaching, it is not surprising that the Reformation came to Strasbourg through preaching. The first of the Reformation preachers was Matthew Zell (1477–1548), People's Priest in the chapel of St. Lorenz in the cathedral, who began his evangelical preaching in 1522. His sermons on Romans drew large crowds, and when he was refused permission to use the pulpit in the nave, which Kaisersberg had used, he preached from a portable one. In the following year, several of the city parishes installed Reformed preachers. Between 1522 and 1524 the city was clearly divided between those who agitated for the installation of Reformed preachers, attacking the privileges of the old church, and members of the ruling oligarchy, who remained committed to the position of the medieval church. Some of those seeking to establish the Reformation in Strasbourg were enthusiastically committed to Zwingli's teaching, but others were more inclined to adopt the Lutheran position, partly for the political advantages of joining the Lutheran alliance. In a similar fashion to Basel, the divided council moved slowly in introducing the Reformation. The mass was finally abolished in 1529, the same year that Basel imposed Protestant services and the Marburg Colloquy failed to achieve unity, which forced Strasbourg to decide between adopting a pro-Swiss foreign policy and joining the Lutheran alliance. The Zwinglian group was initially successful, and this led, as we have already noted, to Strasbourg joining with three other cities to submit a separate confession at the Diet of Augsburg. After the diet, the group, whose priority was achieving a political alliance with the Lutheran princes, succeeded in convincing the council to sign the Augsburg Confession, and Strasbourg joined the Schmalkaldic League in 1531.

Although Matthew Zell began the Reformation in Strasbourg, three other men made major contributions. We have already met two of them, Wolfgang Capito (1478–1541) and Martin Bucer (1491–1551). The third was Caspar Hedio (1494–1552). All three men were greatly influenced by humanism, and both Capito and Hedio had been involved in the Basel Reformation. Capito was a friend of Erasmus and had assisted in the production of the Greek New Testament; he was also a close friend of Oecolampadius. Capito not only wrote the latter's biography, but he married his widow, Wibrandis Rosenblatt, when Oecolampadius died in 1531. Capito came to Strasbourg in 1523 and became provost of St. Thomas's Church, where he delivered a series of theological lectures to the clergy and leading laymen of the city, through which many were converted to Reformation theology. He also continued his humanist scholarship, producing a Hebrew grammar in 1525 and commentaries on Habakkuk, Hosea, and Genesis in Latin. In addition, Capito worked for reconciliation with the Lutherans by signing the Wittenberg Concord in 1536, and he devoted much of the final five years of his life to an unsuccessful effort to persuade theologians of Zurich and Basel to subscribe to the Wittenberg Concord. Caspar Hedio, who was also a Christian humanist, initially served as a minister in Basel. He moved from there to Mainz, and in November 1523 he was nominated to be the main preacher in the Strasbourg Cathedral. While spreading the Reformation through his preaching, he also continued his scholarly pursuits, translating patristic and medieval writers into German.

Martin Bucer

The fourth and most influential Strasbourg reformer was Martin Bucer, whose influence would stretch well beyond the borders of his

adopted city. Unlike the other major Reformers, Bucer grew up in relative poverty. He was the son of a cooper and a midwife, and his parents
sent him to live with his grandfather in Schlettstade, where he attended
Latin school. In 1506, at the age of fifteen, he entered the Dominican
order, which transferred him to the convent in Heidelberg in 1516, where
he earned his master's degree at the university and learned Greek from
Johannes Brenz, who was later to become one of the leading Lutheran
Reformers. Bucer also read the works of Erasmus and was influenced
by him; he was present at the Heidelberg Disputation in 1518, where
he heard Luther, who had a lasting influence on his life and theology. In
1521 Bucer's petition for release from his monastic vows was granted,
and after serving as a chaplain in the court of Franz von Sickingen and,
in May 1532, becoming one of the first Reformers to marry, he settled in
Strasbourg, where Zell persuaded the town magistrates to allow him to
give daily expositions of the New Testament. The people of the parish of
St. Aurelius were so impressed with him that they elected Bucer pastor
of St. Thomas's Church in the spring of 1524. In the years that followed,
he played a major role in establishing and organizing a Protestant church
in Strasbourg through his publications and his personal influence with
the council. In 1534 he published a new church order as well as a catechism, and in 1538 he published a work entitled *Concerning True Pastoral
Care*, which set forth his vision of a truly Reformed church.

Bucer, Capito, and Hedio all held Erasmus in the highest esteem,
and their theology was influenced by humanism. While holding to central beliefs of the Reformation,
Bucer placed an especially strong
emphasis on the transformation that faith in Christ brings
about in a Christian's life. He
also stressed church discipline,
which was designed to aid in
that transformation. In his lectures on Ephesians, delivered
in England near the end of his
life, he listed five marks of the
church. The fifth of those marks
was "righteousness and holiness
of life."[34] Christians who did not
display "holiness of life" were to

Martin Bucer (1491–1551).
Illustration from Beza *Icones*.

be "kept in check by excommunication and every form of discipline, to be administered by faithful shepherds and teachers and elders chosen from all the ordinary members of the Church."[35] Discipline was meant to help the individual Christian progress in piety and to aid in the transformation of society. Bucer identified four church offices: pastors, teachers, elders, and deacons. Discipline was to be in the hands of the lay elders, rather than the magistrates, as was the practice in Zurich. However, the Strasbourg city council was not prepared to allow this, and it would only be in Calvin's Geneva, after a long struggle, that Bucer's ideal would be realized. He also differed from Zwingli on the Eucharist. Although he was on Zwingli's side at Marburg, afterwards his main aim seems to have been to unite Luther and the Swiss. In that effort he was sometimes deliberately ambiguous on the Eucharist, although he made statements that affirmed a belief in the "real presence" of Christ in communion.

In the effort to achieve reconciliation and to initiate dialogue between competing parties in the church, Bucer truly became an international figure. He traveled thousands of miles throughout Europe and played a role in the organization of the church in many south German cities, including Ulm, Frankfurt-am-Main, and Augsburg. He also had an influence on the Reformation in a number of other European countries. Bucer's greatest success in the effort to achieve reconciliation was the agreement that he reached with Luther in 1536, known as the Wittenberg Concord. Luther was always very suspicious of Bucer and sometimes used harsh language to describe his efforts to bring people together. However, with the help of Melanchthon, Bucer finally succeeded in arriving at an agreement with Luther. He began his efforts to achieve an agreement in 1530, while the Diet of Augsburg was still in session, and even traveled to Coburg to meet Luther, but he left the meeting disappointed because no agreement was reached. After the meeting he described Luther as "a man who often loses his way and nevertheless is insufferable about returning to it, who fears the true God and seeks to glorify him from his heart, but who only becomes more agitated when admonished." He wisely concluded, "This is the way God has given him to us, and this is how we must accept him."[36] Bucer continued his efforts in the years that followed, but it was difficult to convince Luther, who was always suspicious of any Zwinglian tendencies, that Bucer did not hold Zwingli's beliefs on the Eucharist.

In December 1534 Melanchthon met with Bucer and found his position on the Eucharist acceptable; however, Luther continued to be suspicious, writing, "The more I reconsider the matter . . . the less favorable

I am toward this hopeless union."[37] Finally, in May 1536 Bucer and Capito, with a number of others, met with Luther and his colleagues in Wittenberg. Although Luther was still suspicious of their motives, in the end they overcame the remaining obstacles, as the group from Strasbourg accepted the real presence of Christ's body and blood in the sacrament. They also insisted that they had never taught that the elements were only symbols and agreed that if Zwinglians taught a symbolic presence, they were in error. A problem concerning whether or not the "ungodly" also receive Christ's body and blood was resolved by substituting the biblical expression "unworthy," and agreeing that they received it to their damnation. Melanchthon was given the task of drawing up the agreement, which was signed on 29 May 1536. Although Bucer and Capito cried tears of joy that they had reached an agreement, it was achieved largely because the group from Strasbourg was willing to accept an essentially Lutheran position. As a result, efforts to get the Swiss to accept the Wittenberg Concord failed, and the divisions between Lutherans and Zwinglians continued.

Bucer was also active in the effort to heal the divisions between Catholics and Protestants. He was unwilling to accept that the breach with Rome was permanent and was convinced that unity would eventually be restored. He led the Protestant side at ecumenical discussions with Catholics in Hagenau, Worms, and Regensburg in the early 1540s before the Council of Trent made permanent the divisions of Christendom. With his Catholic counterpart, John Gropper, Bucer wrote a compromise formula known as the Book of Regensburg, which, it was hoped, might be acceptable to both sides. The book provided a basis for the discussions at the colloquy held in Regensburg in 1541, which will be discussed in more detail in chapter 10. Although the participants were able to agree on the doctrine of justification, the colloquy failed because they could not resolve their differences on the Eucharist. Less than a decade after the failure of the colloquy, Emperor Charles V defeated the Lutheran princes militarily and attempted to bring his own brand of unity with the Augsburg Interim in 1548. Bucer, who was then fifty-eight years old, was forced to leave his beloved Strasbourg and flee to England, where he lived the remaining two years of his life and had a lasting influence on the English Reformation. He also influenced the most important of the second-generation Protestant Reformers, John Calvin, who spent more than three years in Strasbourg and even accompanied Bucer to the Regensburg Colloquy. Although Calvin was at times critical of Bucer's readiness to compromise, he always acknowledged his debt to him.

In conclusion, we return to the question introduced at the beginning of this chapter: Was there a particularly urban theology that had a special appeal to people who lived in cities? Moeller and others believe there was, and they contend that because the urban Reformers made their starting point the community rather than the individual, as Luther did, their theology was more in accord with the communal experiences of city dwellers. Although that interpretation has much to commend it, we cannot ignore the fact that Lutheranism also appealed to many people who lived in cities, and the similarities between the urban Reformers and Luther are much greater than the differences. Consequently, it seems that the effort to draw distinctions between Lutheranism and the Reformed faith in their appeal to people who live in cities may not be enough to explain the urban Reformation. The urban Reformation certainly had its unique features and unique leaders, but it was a part of a wider movement that had a more universal appeal.

6

The Radical Reformation

▼

Michael Sattler shall be delivered to the executioner, who shall lead him
to the place of execution and cut out his tongue, then forge him fast to a
wagon and thereon with red-hot tongs twice tear pieces from his body;
and after he has been brought outside the gate, he shall be plied five times
more in the same manner.

Trial and Martyrdom of Michael Sattler[1]

The above account of Michael Sattler's execution is shocking even in an
age when brutal executions were common. Sattler was certainly not the
type of man who might be considered such a danger to society that he
needed to be executed in a terrible way to deter others from following
in his path. Formerly the prior of a monastery, he was the author of the
Schleitheim Articles, which included an article that stated Christians
should not resort to violence even in the defense of the faith. Sattler was
clearly a man of peace, who took seriously Jesus's command "to learn
from him, for he is meek and lowly of heart,"[2] so why was he treated in
such a brutal fashion? Why were those who were labeled Anabaptists
considered such a serious threat that they needed to be eliminated and
executed in a manner that would strike terror in the hearts of those who
might be inclined to accept their teaching? What were their defining

beliefs, and what justifies grouping the many different movements we will be discussing in this chapter under the label "Radical Reformation"?

These are some of the questions we will be confronting in this chapter, but the answers are not as clear as we might like. In contrast to what was called the Magisterial Reformation, because it was carried out with the cooperation of the established authorities or magistrates, the Radical Reformation splintered into many small sects with contrasting theologies and approaches to reform. The various groups that have traditionally been given the label "Anabaptist" were so different from each other that it is difficult to justify treating them together as a single movement. Even their methods of achieving reform differed radically, ranging from Michael Sattler's pacifism to Thomas Müntzer's readiness for, and even advocacy of, violence to achieve his goals. Historians writing about the Radical Reformation have added to the confusion because they have sometimes been more influenced by their preconceptions than by historical fact in arriving at their interpretations, which have varied so greatly over the centuries that it is difficult to believe they are talking about the same movement.

Interpretations of the Radical Reformation

Both Protestant and Roman Catholic historians have described the Radical Reformation in a very negative way. The Magisterial Reformers considered the Anabaptists a threat to correct doctrine as well as to the proper order of society, and the radical, violent wing of the movement seemed to confirm their fears. Roman Catholics were equally intolerant of the Anabaptists, whom they considered to be a tool of the devil. Not surprisingly, the history written by historians representing those traditions was neither fair nor accurate.[3] The twentieth century witnessed a dramatic change in Radical Reformation studies, which some historians have called "Free Church historiography."[4] Since scholars from mainline denominations had either neglected the study of the Radical Reformation or described the Anabaptists in a very negative way, a group of scholars—of whom Harold S. Bender, the editor of the *Mennonite Quarterly Review*, was the most prominent—sought to correct the misrepresentations. They were, as a rule, fine scholars, and the Mennonite tradition of historical studies certainly deserves our respect. However, since they were reacting against the unfair treatment of their tradition in earlier works, they tended at times to go to the opposite extreme. Although historians in this school acknowledged the abuses that took place in areas such as Münster, where a violent form of communal Anabaptism was established, they attributed these aberrations to persecution. The mainline Anabaptist movement, they maintained, was peaceful and tolerant, and its ongoing tradition was found in people such as Menno Simons and the Mennonites, who followed his teaching. They presented their forefathers as courageous believers who had kept the faith despite terrible persecution and who provided an impressive martyr tradition for their descendants. In the words of James Stayer, "the historiographical outcome was to make the ugly duckling of the Reformation into its most beautiful swan."[5]

The distinguishing mark of Anabaptism, according to the Free Church interpretation, was a view of the church that differed radically from that of Roman Catholics and the Magisterial Reformers, who continued the medieval pattern in which the church encompassed the whole of society. In contrast, Anabaptists sought to restore the New Testament understanding of the church as a gathered community, separate from the wider society.[6] Anabaptists were persecuted because they not only refused to conform to the state churches of their day, but they rejected participation in government, war, oaths, and courts of law. They were a threat to the accepted understanding of church and society, and so they were persecuted. Even the name *Anabaptist* (which means "rebaptizer") was an unfair term because they rejected infant baptism as invalid baptism; and therefore, when they baptized adults, they did not consider this a second baptism. Their enemies used the term to identify them by a particular characteristic and also to make them subject to the death penalty under Roman law.[7]

Although Free Church historiography made an important contribution to a better understanding of Anabaptism, its conclusions have been challenged by a new generation of historians who have sought to arrive at a more balanced view of the movement, uninfluenced by confessional loyalties. One of the major turning points in Anabaptist studies was the publication of George Williams's monumental work in 1962 entitled *The Radical Reformation*.[8] Although he was indebted to the Free Church historiography, Williams's study transcended the denominational histories of the past. In a sense, he tried to achieve the impossible by classifying all the divergent Anabaptist groups and identifying the common characteristics that gave unity to the movement. He believed the Radical Reformation "was as much an entity" as either the Magisterial or the Catholic Reformation, describing it as "a radical break from the existing institutions and theologies in the interrelated drives to restore primitive Christianity and to prepare for the imminent advent of the Kingdom of

Christ."[9] He identified three major divisions of the movement, which he labeled Anabaptists, Spiritualists, and Evangelical Rationalists. Although Williams's work is indispensable for any serious study of the Radical Reformation, some of the leading scholars in Anabaptist studies have also questioned his conclusions.[10]

In recent years a number of new trends can be detected in Anabaptist studies. Some scholars have rejected the effort to separate the Anabaptists from the more violent manifestations of the Radical Reformation or the mainline Protestant movement, arguing that "the Anabaptists were . . . the legitimate children of the early Reformation movement and the Peasants' War."[11] The Lutheran Reformation began with Luther's radical break with tradition; the beliefs expressed in his early Reformation writings, including his advocacy of the priesthood of all believers, involved the rejection of some of the core beliefs of the medieval church upon which medieval society was based. However, Lutheranism was later institutionalized and the original radical spirit lost. The same process occurred in Switzerland. By contrast, Anabaptism maintained the anti-clericalism of the original Reformation as well as the social radicalism that was implied in Luther's early writings, and some were prepared to use violence in the pursuit of their objectives.

While certain scholars have emphasized the radical nature of Anabaptism, others have pointed out that not all the groups normally labeled Anabaptist were radical. Some were, in fact, more conservative and closer to medieval Catholicism than the mainstream Reformers. The so-called Spiritualists, such as Sebastian Franck and Caspar Schwenckfeld, never openly broke with the medieval church, although they rejected many of the religious observances of the church as unnecessary. Other Anabaptists, including Hans Denck and Hans Hut, rejected the Reformation doctrines of *sola scriptura* and justification by faith, teaching a doctrine of justification that had more in common with the beliefs of the medieval church than with the Reformation. The enormous diversity of the movement has led other scholars to despair of identifying any unifying beliefs in the movement, pointing out that there really is no way of distinguishing genuine Anabaptists from what the Free Church historians considered "perversions." Hans Goertz, one of the leading scholars in Anabaptist studies today, maintains that "there is no historical answer to the question of which among the many Anabaptist groups were the genuine Anabaptists."[12]

The Radical Reformation began in two places at approximately the same time. The earliest leader was Thomas Müntzer, who centered his activities in Germany and reacted against Martin Luther. Shortly after

Müntzer began to attack Luther, a group of Radical Reformers in Zurich, led by Conrad Grebel, broke with Zwingli. Although Grebel and his followers are normally identified with the peaceful wing of the movement and Müntzer was clearly a part of the violent wing, they were in contact with one another, and Müntzer had an influence on the Swiss Anabaptists. In September 1524 Grebel and the Swiss Anabaptists wrote a letter to Müntzer that was filled with praise for him. They called him and Karlstadt "the purest proclaimers and preachers of the divine word," and stated that his writing on baptism "pleases us greatly." While praising Müntzer, they denounced both Luther's and Zwingli's halfhearted attempts at Reformation, commenting that Müntzer was "far purer than our people here and those in Wittenberg, who slide each day from one distortion of Scripture into another and from one blindness into a still greater one."[13] Clearly those who originated the Radical Reformation had a great deal in common; however, there were also significant differences. Since Müntzer's rejection of the Lutheran Reformation slightly predated the Swiss Anabaptists' attack on Zwingli, we shall begin by telling his story.

Thomas Müntzer

Like Luther, Thomas Müntzer came from Saxony, was born into an economically respectable home, and was also well-educated. After studying at Leipzig, Frankfurt, and Wittenberg, he was probably ordained in May 1514. His first contact with Luther may have been made in 1518, during his stay of perhaps a few months in Wittenberg, where he attended lectures on St. Jerome. He also must have become acquainted with Karlstadt at this time. One of the great debates in Müntzer studies has been the degree to which he was influenced by Martin Luther; Lutheran scholars have argued that Müntzer began as a disciple of Luther but became radicalized and broke away from Luther's thinking. Recently the tendency, especially among German scholars, has been to ascribe more significance to the influence of late medieval mysticism on Müntzer rather than any decisive influence from Luther.[14] Although initially he was a follower of Luther, this was really only a superficial attachment. The major influences on Müntzer were Johannes Eckhart, John Tauler, and the work entitled *German Theology*. Whereas Luther broke radically from the mystics in his doctrine of justification, Müntzer continued to follow the mystical tradition. For Luther, the final authority was Scripture but, like the mystics, Müntzer emphasized the inner word.

Whatever the basis of Müntzer's thought, initially he and Luther were very friendly. He attended the Leipzig Debate in July 1519, and Luther recommended him for a temporary position in Zwickau, substituting for a humanist preacher. At this time Müntzer seemed to be a committed disciple of Luther. Curiously, the first recorded instance of someone being called a "Lutheran" was in a Catholic polemic against Müntzer in 1519. When he wrote to Luther in July 1520, asking him for advice about a controversy with local Franciscans, he signed the letter "Thomas Müntzer, whom you brought to birth by the gospel," and called Luther a "model and beacon to the friends of God."[15] His attitude toward Luther was to change markedly in the following years. In 1524 he wrote a tract in which he spoke of Luther as "the unspiritual soft-living flesh in Wittenberg, whose robbery and distortion of Scripture has so grievously polluted our wretched Christian Church." In the same tract he also referred to him as "Father Pussyfoot" and "Dr. Liar."[16] Clearly something had gone wrong in the relationship between the two men!

The break between Luther and Müntzer began after the latter was appointed pastor of St. Catherine's Church in Zwickau. Müntzer was an extremely effective preacher and gained the support of many of the poor weavers and laborers. He was also beginning to distance himself from Luther as he started to teach direct inspiration by the Holy Spirit as well as millennial beliefs. One of Müntzer's opponents in Zwickau warned Luther that Müntzer "has confused everything with his crazy mouth and his doctrines."[17] When his supporters used violence in pursuit of their objectives, Luther withdrew his support of Müntzer, although he was not involved. Müntzer then left Zwickau to go to Bohemia, where on 1 November 1521 he published what is known as the *Prague Manifesto*. In it he proclaimed that God was going to do wonderful things and that there would be a great renewing of the world through the Holy Spirit, in which the Czechs would have a central role. He wrote that "the new church will begin here, this people will be a mirror for the whole world," and he summoned them "to help in this defense of God's word." Speaking like an Old Testament prophet, he also warned them, "if you refuse, God will let you be struck down by the Turks in the coming year."[18] The Manifesto failed to convince the Prague authorities, and Müntzer was expelled from the city in December of 1521. He then returned to Germany, and in a letter written to Melanchthon in March 1522 revealed his impatience with the slow pace of the Lutheran Reformation. Although he still spoke highly of Luther, he also commented, "Our most beloved Martin acts ignorantly because he does not want to offend the little ones . . . but the tribulation of Christians is already at the door. . . . Leave your dallying, the time has come. . . . You delicate biblical scholars, do not hang back."[19]

Müntzer's letter was written after Luther's return from Wartburg Castle to confront the troubles in Wittenberg that were the result of Karlstadt's effort to implement the Reformation without delay. During the same period the so-called Zwickau Prophets, led by the weaver Nicholas Storch, brought additional confusion as they claimed direct inspiration of the Holy Spirit. Luther's experience with the Zwickau Prophets as well as with Karlstadt and others associated with troubles at Wittenberg was to have a profound effect on his attitude toward the Radical Reformation, as he always associated Anabaptists with Storch and the Zwickau Prophets. Philip Melanchthon once wrote that all the Anabaptists were brought into the world by a "single stork." Although Müntzer maintained he had nothing in common with the Zwickau Prophets, Luther continued to associate him with violence and the radical doctrines of the Prophets. In the spring of 1523 Müntzer was appointed pastor of St. John's Church in Allstedt, and he remained there until August 1524 in what was the most productive period of his ministry. At Allstedt he wrote the first Reformed liturgy in the German language, which was marked by an emphasis on popular participation even to the degree that the whole congregation said the words of consecration in the Eucharist. He married a former nun, carried on a parish ministry, and tried to make his peace with Luther. In a letter dated 9 July 1523 he addressed Luther as "father" and tried to assure him that he had nothing in common with the Zwickau Prophets. He maintained that he had "no intention of saying anything I cannot verify through a clear text of Scripture," and said he wished to restore their friendship. He concluded, "May the Lord protect you and restore the old love."[20] Luther, however, did not react favorably to Müntzer's effort at reconciliation; rather, he accused him of abusing Scripture and advised the Allstedt leadership to withdraw support.

Müntzer then broke completely with Luther and began to attack him. He considered Luther the leader of a halfhearted reformation based on a biblical intellectualism, which blocked true faith and the sanctified life. He may have been carried away by his success as a preacher, as the people of Allstedt flocked to hear his sermons. Moreover, he concluded that he was called to lead a true reformation, and he felt his chance had come to displace Luther when he was given the opportunity to preach a sermon to Duke John, the brother of the Elector Frederick the Wise, and John's son, John Frederick. The sermon was delivered on 13 July 1524 at the ducal palace in Allstedt. In the sermon Müntzer called for the princes to lead the way and to be prepared to use violence to establish the kingdom of God. He took as his text the second chapter of the book of Daniel, where Daniel explained the handwriting on the wall to King Nebuchadnezzar, proclaiming:

> A new Daniel must arise and interpret for you your vision. . . . If you want to be true governors, you must begin government at the roots, and, as Christ commanded, drive his enemies from the elect. For you are the means to this end. . . . Christ says it sufficiently . . . every tree that bringeth not forth good fruit is rooted out and cast into the fire. . . . For the godless person has no right to live when he is in the way of the pious. The sword is necessary to wipe out the godless. . . . That this might now take place, however, in an orderly and proper fashion, our cherished fathers, the princes, should do it, who with us confess Christ. If however, they do not do it, the sword will be taken from them.[21]

We do not know how the princes reacted to the sermon, but other rulers clearly did not approve of what Müntzer was preaching and doing in Allstedt. Ernest of Mansfeld, whose territory abutted Allstedt, forbade his subjects to attend Müntzer's sermons, and Müntzer responded by threatening him. The authorities became even more concerned about his radicalism when Müntzer created a paramilitary group of about five hundred members, called the League of the Elect, which used violence against a chapel dedicated to the Virgin Mary in the vicinity of Allstedt.

Luther was horrified at Müntzer's activities and beliefs since he abhorred violence or direct action and distrusted the claims of special revelation. In July 1524 he wrote to Elector Frederick the Wise urging him to act against what he called "the rebellious spirit." Although he conceded the radicals' right to preach, he stated that "when they want to do more than fight with the Word, and begin to destroy and use force, then your Graces must intervene . . . and banish them from the country."[22] On 1 August Duke John summoned Müntzer to Weimar and forbade him to publish or preach. Expecting to be expelled, Müntzer fled Allstedt a week later. Before leaving, he attacked Luther in his treatise *An Explicit Exposure of the False Faith of the Unfaithful World*, in which he reiterated his view that true faith came through the experiencing of the Holy Spirit and attacked Luther viciously as one who sought honor for himself and as the "defender of the godless." In Müntzer's view Luther was the tool of established authorities and had acquiesced in the oppression of the common people. Müntzer published another attack on Luther in Nuremberg before becoming pastor of a church in Mühlhausen. In spring 1525 he came into contact with the peasant uprising, which had broken out in the previous summer and fall in southwest Germany, spreading to central Germany in the spring.

In May 1525 Müntzer went to Frankenhausen, where a contingent of about nine thousand peasants had gathered. He became their leader and inspired them with assurances that God was on their side and would make them invincible in battle. So the peasants, armed largely with farming tools, confronted a professional army with cavalry and artillery. We should not be surprised at the result of the battle. When it became clear God was not providing the help Müntzer had promised, the peasants broke ranks and fled. The battle ended with a horrible slaughter of peasants, while the opposing army suffered only a few casualties. Afterwards, three hundred peasants were beheaded, but Müntzer did not even die with dignity. In the midst of the slaughter, he left the field of battle and hid under a bed in a house in town. He was discovered, tortured, and brutally executed after he had signed a confession and recantation.

After the defeat of the revolt Luther wrote a tract in which he maintained that Müntzer had been a tool of the devil. Luther's lack of sympathy for him is in striking contrast to the adulation Müntzer later received from Communist historians, who viewed him as a great hero of the people in contrast to Luther, who, they maintained, betrayed the people's cause and allied himself with the princes. Today historians have a more balanced view of Müntzer. He was clearly a gifted and dedicated man, and his influence on the Radical Reformation was considerably greater than a previous generation of historians recognized. However, he was also a tragic figure, who was misled by his conviction that he was God's prophet sent to inaugurate a new order. His willingness to resort to violence in the pursuit of that objective ended in disaster, both for Müntzer and for those who trusted his leadership.

The Swiss Brethren

Müntzer's break with Luther and the vicious polemics with which they attacked each other had a number of striking parallels in Zurich. A group that included Conrad Grebel (1498–1526), Felix Mantz (1498–1527), and George Blaurock (1492–1529) and who had initially supported Zwingli became disillusioned with the slow pace of reform and Zwingli's unwillingness to establish a church in Zurich that was in accord with what they considered New Testament teaching. Grebel came from a prosperous patrician family and had an excellent education, having studied in Basel,

Vienna, and Paris. In October 1521 he returned to Zurich a convinced humanist. In accord with the humanist commitment to learning biblical languages, he joined a group that studied Greek and Hebrew with Zwingli, and through Zwingli's teaching he was converted from humanism to evangelical Christianity. Grebel was initially a great admirer of Zwingli and even wrote a Latin poem praising him as the restorer of the gospel. He also participated in the public disputations in January and October 1523 that led to the establishment of the Reformation in Zurich. However, in the second disputation he began to have doubts about his mentor's commitment to a thoroughgoing Reformation when Zwingli accepted the view that decisions about the mass should be left in the hands of the council. When the council decided in December 1523 to continue the mass temporarily to avoid a schism in the community, Grebel tried to convince Zwingli that a new council should be elected that would not tolerate practices contrary to biblical teaching. Zwingli's rejection of Grebel's plan led the latter to believe that Zwingli was more interested in pleasing the magistrates than in implementing biblical teaching. In December 1523 he wrote his brother-in-law that "whoever thinks, believes, or says that Zwingli is performing his duties as a shepherd, thinks, believes, and speaks impiously."[23]

Grebel then joined others who were disillusioned with the pace of reform in Zurich to gather in secret meeting houses where they could worship in accord with what they considered New Testament teaching. Among those who joined Grebel were Felix Mantz and George Blaurock. Mantz was the illegitimate son of a priest, who had received an excellent education and had a thorough knowledge of Latin, Greek, and Hebrew. He joined Zwingli in 1519, but in the years that followed he also became disillusioned with the pace and nature of reform in Zurich. He signed the letter to Müntzer mentioned earlier and became one of the protagonists in a debate about baptism that took place in January 1525. Mantz died a martyr's death after playing a leading role in spreading Anabaptist beliefs in the neighboring Swiss territories.

Blaurock, whose real name was George Cajakob,[24] was a Swiss priest who broke with the medieval church when he married in 1523. He came to Zurich and, after first following Zwingli, joined the group led by Grebel who opposed Zwingli. He was a powerful preacher and founded the first Anabaptist congregation in Zollikon near Zurich in 1525. He was also the first to be baptized by the group in January 1525.

Baptism was not originally the central issue in the conflict between the Swiss Anabaptists and Zwingli. In fact, they did not initially reject the medieval view of the church as including the entire community. It

was only after they failed to gain control of the Zurich Reformation that
they began to argue that the true Christian church must be a gathered
community separate from the wider society. The essential sacrament
for the medieval understanding of the relationship between church and
community was infant baptism. Baptism made all who were born to
Christian parents—which included the vast majority of the European
population—members of the church shortly after they were born. The
rejection of infant baptism was, therefore, a critical aspect of the new
Anabaptist view of the church, and in January 1525 Grebel and Mantz
debated with Zwingli on the question of baptism in the Zurich council
chamber. The council decided in favor of Zwingli's position and ordered
Grebel and Mantz to stop holding meetings with their followers. However,
they not only continued their meetings but shortly afterwards took a
decisive step in the break with the official Reformation in Zurich. After
praying for God's guidance, Grebel baptized Blaurock. A contemporary
chronicle, written from an Anabaptist viewpoint, described what happened:

> When the prayer was ended, George of the house of Jacob stood up and
> asked Conrad Grebel, for the sake of God's will, to baptize him with a true
> Christian baptism on his own faith and confession. With that request and
> desire, he knelt down again, and Conrad baptized him, since there was no
> ordained minister there to do it for him. And then the others asked George
> to baptize them in the same way, which he did according to their request.
> And so in the highest fear of God, they gave themselves to the name of the
> Lord, each authenticating the other in the service of the Gospel, to learn
> and to keep the faith. And that was the beginning of the separation from
> the world and its evil works.[25]

The Swiss Anabaptists also began to apply a literal interpretation
of the Bible to relations with the state. Following the Sermon on the
Mount, they refused to swear oaths or to perform civic duties, and in
accord with the practice of the early church described in Acts 2, they
advocated practicing community of goods. Initially they had significant
successes in Zurich and other parts of Switzerland. People stopped
baptizing their children, and large numbers of adults were baptized in
towns throughout German Switzerland, sometimes by immersion in
rivers. The movement spread to Bern, Basel, and St. Gall. In St. Gall,
where Grebel's brother-in-law was a leader of the Reformation, even
the authorities were sympathetic. However, at the very time that the
movement was spreading, the Peasants' War was raging in Germany, and
although Grebel and Mantz spoke out against using violence to defend

the gospel, violence also broke out in Switzerland. In addition, the excesses practiced by more extreme Anabaptists cost them the support of people who had originally been sympathetic to, or at least tolerant of, the movement. For example, in June 1525 groups from Zollikon came to Zurich shouting in the streets and warning the city of the impending judgment unless they repented within forty days. They even identified Zwingli with the beast of Revelation.

The Zurich authorities responded to what they considered a serious threat to the stability of the city by imprisoning or banishing the Anabaptist leaders. In March 1525 Grebel, Mantz, and Blaurock were imprisoned, and other Anabaptists were captured and tortured. The council also decreed that "if any one hereafter shall baptize another, he will be seized by our Lords and according to the decree now set forth, will be drowned without mercy."[26] Although Grebel, Mantz, and Blaurock were successful in escaping from prison, Mantz was recaptured and in December 1526 was bound hand and foot and pushed from a boat into the Limmant River, thereby becoming one of the first of many Anabaptist martyrs. Grebel, weakened by imprisonment, had died of the plague six months earlier, and Blaurock, who was captured with Mantz, was sentenced to be beaten through the streets and then expelled. Blaurock became an itinerant evangelist in central Europe, establishing many congregations in the Tyrol, but in 1529 he was caught and burned for heresy.

Michael Sattler and the Schleitheim Articles

Persecution led to the dispersion of the original Swiss Brethren to other areas, including Germany, where a new leader appeared in the person of Michael Sattler (1490–1527), just about the time that Mantz was executed. Sattler had been prior of the Benedictine monastery near Freiburg, but when peasants seized the monastery during the Peasants' War in 1525, he left and came into contact with the Swiss Brethren. He was rebaptized in 1526 and became an Anabaptist leader. After evangelizing around Zurich, he moved to Strasbourg, where he met Martin Bucer and Wolfgang Capito, who were so impressed by him that after his death they considered him a Christian martyr. In February Sattler met with a group of Swiss and south German Anabaptists in the small town of Schleitheim on the Swiss-German border, and they wrote what is considered the first Anabaptist confession of faith. Sattler wrote most of the confession, which Anabaptists called the "Brotherly

Union," and historians have labeled it the Schleitheim Articles or Schleitheim Confession. It contained seven articles that outlined the major Anabaptist beliefs.

In the first article, which called infant baptism "the first abomination of the pope," it was stated that baptism should be given "to all those who have been taught repentance and who believe truly that their sins are taken away through Christ."[27] The second described the ban, or excommunication, stating that believers who had fallen into sin should be dealt with according to the provisions of Matthew 18.[28] The third article revealed a Zwinglian view of the Eucharist, which was called the "breaking of bread." The fourth maintained that true believers must separate themselves from the ways of the world, and the fifth described the role of the pastors, who were to be elected by the congregation. The sixth and seventh were lengthy articles that dealt with the use of the "sword" and taking of oaths. Both were forbidden to Christians, who were not even to serve as magistrates because "the rule of government is according to the flesh, that of Christians according to the Spirit."[29] Although only the Swiss Anabaptists and the Hutterites fully accepted the Schleitheim Articles, they had such widespread publicity as an expression of Anabaptist belief that both Zwingli and Calvin wrote refutations of them.

While returning from Schleitheim, Sattler and his wife were arrested. A copy of the Schleitheim Articles was found on Sattler, and he was taken to Rottenberg, where he was brought to trial along with his wife and nine others for violation of Catholic doctrine and practice. One of the charges was that he had taught nonresistance toward the Turks. According to the Anabaptist account of the trial he responded that if the use of the sword were right, he would prefer to use it against those who claimed to be Christians and persecuted God-fearing people. Sattler was convicted and sentenced to suffer the terrible death described at the beginning of this chapter. When his wife refused to recant, she was also executed by drowning in the Neckar River.

The public display of brutality, which was a common way of intimidation in the sixteenth century, was clearly intended to frighten others from joining the movement. However, it seems to have had the opposite effect. The account of Sattler's death was read and carried about by other Anabaptists to give them courage to live their lives as Sattler had. The type of cruel execution that Sattler had experienced was repeated over and over again in both Protestant and Catholic areas. Although recent studies suggest that the number of executions was not as great as was once thought, nevertheless at least two thousand Anabaptists were executed in the sixteenth century. Of those executions, 85 percent took place in Catholic areas, where even those who recanted were executed. Protestants tended to rely on imprisonment or exile to suppress Anabaptism, and they used indoctrination to try to get them to recant.[30] Although we rightly condemn the terrible persecution of Anabaptists, historians are grateful for the information supplied by the trial records, which provide an invaluable source for studying not only the Radical Reformation but also women of the Reformation, since many of the Anabaptists martyred were women.

Michael Sattler was one of many Anabaptist leaders who suffered martyrdom. In fact, almost all of the well-educated and able people who led the first generation of the Radical Reformation were either executed or died young. Recent research suggests that the total number of Anabaptists was considerably smaller than once thought; the groups were normally no larger than one hundred people. They were also far from unified as a movement. However, initially they experienced a period of rapid expansion, which especially frightened the authorities. A contemporary chronicle, written by an Anabaptist sympathizer, explained the appeal of the movement:

> The Anabaptists spread so rapidly that their teaching soon covered, as it were, the land. They soon gained a large following, and baptized many thousands, drawing to themselves many sincere souls who had a zeal for God. For they taught nothing but love, faith and the need of bearing the cross. They showed themselves humble, patient under much suffering; they break the bread with one another as an evidence of unity and love. They helped each other faithfully, called each other brothers, etc. They increased so rapidly that the world feared an uprising by them, though I have learned that this fear had no justification whatsoever. They were persecuted with great tyranny, being imprisoned, branded, tortured and executed by fire, water and the sword. In a few years very many were put to death. Some have estimated the number of those who were killed to be far above two thousand. They died as martyrs, patiently, and humbly endured all persecution.[31]

They also had some impressive leaders in the first stage of the movement. Although they were often in contact with one another and influenced each other, they also differed radically from one another. The three diverse individuals discussed below provide an example of the unity and diversity of the first generation of the Radical Reformation.

Other Early Anabaptist Leaders: Hubmaier, Denck, and Hut

Balthasar Hubmaier (1480–1528), Hans Denck (1500–1527), and Hans Hut (1490–1527) were in contact with each other during various stages of their careers and even influenced each other to the degree that Hubmaier probably baptized Denck and Denck baptized Hut. However, there were also major differences between them. Hubmaier was what has been called a "Magisterial Anabaptist" because he was prepared to accept a state-sponsored church and believed that Anabaptists could be magistrates. Hut was a man of action and a charismatic evangelist who carried on the tradition of Thomas Müntzer in his apocalyptic emphasis and rejected totally Hubmaier's view of the relationship between church and state. Denck was a Spiritualist and an outstanding scholar who preferred to avoid dogmatic controversy. Both Hubmaier and Denck were well-educated, while Hut was a book peddler who had a limited education and disdained professional scholars. All three had some involvement in the Peasants' War and were influenced by the teaching of Thomas Müntzer. They died within a year of each other. All suffered persecution; however, only Hubmaier was executed.

Hubmaier held a doctorate in theology and is normally considered the best Anabaptist theologian. He was born in Bavaria and received his first degree from the University of Freiburg in 1503. He received his doctorate from the University of Ingolstadt, where Eck, Luther's opponent at the Leipzig Debate, taught, and after completing his degree Hubmaier gave lectures at the university. He then became the cathedral preacher in Regensburg, during which time he was zealously anti-Semitic and deeply committed to Catholic practice, being partly responsible for the large Jewish community being expelled and their synagogue leveled. A chapel dedicated to the Virgin Mary was built on the same site, and Hubmaier became its chaplain. In 1521 he accepted a call to the Austrian town of Waldshut, where his theology began to change after he read the letters of Paul as well as the writings of Erasmus, Melanchthon, and Luther. By 1523 Hubmaier was a convinced Protestant, and after a disputation in 1524, Waldshut was won for the Reformation. Hubmaier was also in contact with Zwingli and other Swiss Reformers. When Archduke Ferdinand, the brother of Emporer Charles V and the ruler of Austria, threatened Waldshut, Hubmaier went to Schaffhausen, where he wrote one of the earliest pleas for religious toleration.

Hubmaier returned to Waldshut in October 1524, and having read Karlstadt's works and possibly Müntzer's, he began to move in the direction of the Radical Reformation. He was also in contact with the Zurich radicals, and in April 1525 he was baptized in Waldshut along with sixty others. Afterwards he baptized approximately three hundred people and wrote an excellent defense of believer's baptism. Hubmaier and the city of Waldshut then became involved in the Peasants' War, and when the peasants were defeated, Hubmaier fled to Zurich, where he was arrested, tortured, and forced to recant. After he was allowed to leave Zurich, he joined other Anabaptists going to Moravia, where a more tolerant attitude prevailed. He settled in Nicolsburg, where he was successful in converting both the bishop and the temporal ruler, Count Leonhart von Liechtenstein, to Anabaptist beliefs.

Anabaptism literally became a state religion in Nicolsburg as some two thousand Anabaptists settled under the benevolent rule of Liechtenstein. Hubmaier even had his own printer, who published his numerous writings on a variety of subjects. Among these was a tract entitled *On the Sword*, in which he rejected the statement in the Schleitheim Articles that a Christian could not be a magistrate. However, Hubmaier's state-sponsored Anabaptism was short-lived. When his old enemy, Ferdinand, became ruler of Bohemia and Moravia in 1527, he had Hubmaier extradited and brought to trial in Vienna, where he was burned at the stake in March 1528. Three days later his wife was drowned in the Danube.

Hubmaier may well have baptized Hans Denck, who followed a different path and taught a different theology. Denck was the son of well-educated parents in Upper Bavaria. From 1517 to 1519 he studied at the University of Ingolstadt, where he mastered Latin, Greek, and Hebrew and read the mystical as well as the humanist writers of the day. After serving as a language teacher in Regensburg, Denck went to Basel, where he worked as a proofreader and attended Oecolampadius's lectures at the university. Through Oecolampadius's influence, Denck was appointed headmaster of the St. Sebald School in Nuremberg, where he came under the influence of Müntzer and Karlstadt, the former staying with him for a month in 1524. Denck was expelled from Nuremberg in 1525 when the Lutheran clergy became concerned that his theology had strayed far from the major tenets of Lutheranism. He eventually ended up in Augsburg where Hubmaier, who stayed in Augsburg for two months, probably baptized him after he left Zurich en route to Nicolsburg in 1526. In the same year Denck baptized the fiery evangelist Hans Hut, but Denck once again came into conflict with Lutheran ministers and moved on to Strasbourg, where he engaged in a disputation with Bucer, who unfairly labeled him "the Anabaptist pope."

Since Denck was a man who preferred to avoid dogmatic controversy, he left Strasbourg in December 1526 and went to Worms, where he published two important works and assisted Ludwig Hatzer in a translation of the Old Testament prophets, which was published in April 1527. In the next seven years this work went through twenty-one printings and was used by both Zwingli and Luther in their translations of the Old Testament. However, Denck again came into conflict with the authorities, so he left Worms and eventually ended up in Basel. Disheartened by the setbacks suffered by the movement and disillusioned with the divisive and sectarian character of the Radical Reformation, Denck wrote a confession under the influence of his former teacher, Oecolampadius, in which he moderated some of his earlier views, including his beliefs about baptism. Fittingly, this gentle scholar, who sought to avoid controversy and was ill-suited to be the leader of a movement, was not asked to die a martyr's death. In November 1527 at the age of thirty-one, he died of the plague.

At his trial in 1528 Hans Hut was described as "a clever fellow, rather tall, a peasant with light brown cropped hair and a blond moustache," and it was said that he baptized "almost on the run."[32] Although Denck had baptized him, Hut was radically different from Denck in his background, personality, and approach to reform. In contrast to the scholarly Denck, Hut was self-educated, a craftsman rather than an academic, and a man of action who became one of the most successful Anabaptist evangelists. He heard Müntzer preach an apocalyptic sermon at Frankenhausen in the spring of 1525 and became convinced that the Peasants' War was the prelude to Christ's second coming. As a result, he joined the peasants and barely escaped with his life when they were defeated at Frankenhausen. Disappointed and convinced that the peasant uprising had been premature and that they had sought their own glory, Hut went home but was still convinced Christ was returning soon.

Hut came to believe that the Turks were an instrument of God's judgment and that their conquests were a sign that the return of Christ was imminent. In fact, he set the date for the second coming as Pentecost 1528, which meant there was little time left. Hut, therefore, set off on a frantic itinerant ministry in which he rushed from place to place preaching and baptizing. His travels took him to Nicolsburg, where he engaged in a disputation with Hubmaier in May 1527. Hut rejected Hubmaier's defense of an alliance between the magistrates and Anabaptists, while Hubmaier in turn was critical of Hut's apocalyptic preaching, maintaining that he and his followers "gave simple folk the idea of a definite time for the last day . . . and thereby induced them to sell their possessions and property."[33] Count Leonhart von Liechtenstein was so alarmed by Hut's radical ideas that he imprisoned him in the castle, but Hut managed to escape and went to Austria, where he went from town to town, preaching, baptizing, and founding congregations. In August 1527 Hut went to Augsburg to attend a meeting of Anabaptist leaders, but this was to be Hut's last stop on his journeys, because in September he was arrested and brought to trial. However, he died in his cell on 6 December 1528 before the trial was complete. Nevertheless the authorities continued his trial; his dead body was tied to a chair in court, and he was sentenced to be burned at the stake the following day.

Hut, Denck, and Hubmaier not only disagreed with each other, they were also opposed to some of the core beliefs of the Protestant Reformation. In 1527 Hubmaier wrote a treatise on freedom of the will in which he attacked the Protestant doctrine of bondage of the will, which he considered nothing more than an excuse for continuing to live in sin. In a clever parody of Protestant teaching, he caricatured those who denied free will, arguing that it resulted in "evil" people blaming "all of their sin and evil on God." They excused their sins by saying, "It must be God's will that I be an adulterer and run after harlots. Well, God's will be done! After all who can thwart the will of God? If it were not God's will, I would not sin. When God wills it, I will stop sinning."[34] Hut and Denck both rejected the Reformation doctrines of justification by faith alone and *sola scriptura*. In accord with the beliefs of the medieval church, they both viewed justification and sanctification as one process, accepted the authority of Scripture plus tradition, and believed that the final authority rested with the inner word.

The Radical Fringe of the Radical Reformation

Hut's extremism and emphasis on the inner voice led to some very bizarre manifestations of the Radical Reformation after his death. Representative of such was a group from the village of Uttenreuth in Franconia, where Hut had preached. This group, who were labeled the Uttenreuth Dreamers because they took Hut's teaching on dreams and revelations literally, was led by Hans Schmid. About sixty-five people joined his sect, which was characterized by the members having dreams and visions in which God spoke to them directly. One of the strangest characteristics of the sect was their attitude toward marriage: the Spirit revealed to them that their marriages were sinful—because they had not followed God's voice in choosing their spouses—and revealed to them whom they were to marry instead. Sixteen couples were then "wed by the Spirit." Married couples whose marriages were not in accord with the Spirit's wishes were allowed to live together but not have sexual relations. Some Dreamers even referred to themselves as God and were convinced that the end of the world was very near. When Schmid was arrested in April 1531, the authorities were horrified at what they uncovered, and in June he and two other members were executed while the other Dreamers were flogged and expelled from the village.[35]

The Uttenreuth Dreamers were a small, insignificant sect, probably unknown outside the immediate vicinity of the town after which they were named. In contrast, the violent manifestations of the Radical Reformation in northwest Germany and the Netherlands were well known throughout Europe and played a major role in discrediting Anabaptism both in the eyes of contemporaries and future generations of historians. These revolutionary groups owed their inception to the followers of a charismatic leader named Melchior Hoffman, a furrier who became a Lutheran lay preacher in Livonia. Influenced by Karlstadt, he came to reject Luther's sacramental theology and began to preach a radical, apocalyptic message, eventually abandoning his Lutheranism and allying with the Zwinglians. In 1529 Hoffman went to Strasbourg, where he came into contact with Anabaptists and was converted to the movement in 1530. He then began proclaiming that Christ would soon return and that Strasbourg would be the place where he would establish his kingdom. The Strasbourg authorities were not impressed, however, and in April 1530 Hoffman fled Strasbourg because the council had ordered his arrest.

Hoffman then began to preach his apocalyptic message in the Netherlands, where natural disasters, including famine, plague, and floods, combined with economic problems and the appearance of three comets between 1531 and 1533 helped to convince people that the end of the world was at hand. As a result, Hoffman gained a large following who considered him a prophet of God and believed fervently in his prophecies. Unfortunately for Hoffman, he also believed in his prophecy. When one of his followers prophesied that Hoffman would be arrested in Strasbourg and would spend six months suffering in prison before the coming of the new era, Hoffman returned to Strasbourg, where he was arrested on 20 May 1533. He greeted his arrest with jubilation, because he expected it to be a crucial step in the fulfillment of the prophecy. According to a contemporary account, "When Melchior saw that he was going to prison, he thanked God that the hour had come. . . . And with this he went willingly, cheerfully and well comforted to prison."[36] Hoffman's joy at having the first part of the prophecy fulfilled was eventually dissipated when Christ did not return and Hoffman remained in a

Strasbourg prison. After ten years, he died a broken and forgotten man, disillusioned with the revolutionary actions of his followers.

Although Hoffman eschewed violence, his disciples, the so-called Melchiorites, did not. After his imprisonment, his followers divided into two groups. One group, represented by Obbe Philips, rejected the militant application of Hoffman's teaching.[37] The second group, led by Jan Matthijs, believed the use of the sword was justified to destroy the ungodly and usher in the kingdom of God. Matthijs was a baker who, after converting to Anabaptism, took up a self-appointed position of leadership. He declared that he was the prophet Enoch, and he traveled around Holland proclaiming that God would soon establish his thousand-year kingdom on earth and destroy the tyrants. He eventually ended up in the city of Münster,[38] where a Lutheran pastor, Bernhard Rothmann, had prepared the way for what was to follow. Rothmann, who began as a Lutheran, was responsible for leading the city of Münster to adopt the Reformation in 1533. However, when Rothmann rejected infant baptism, both Lutherans and Catholics united against him and tried to evict him from the city. They were unable to do so because he was so popular among the people. In January 1534 Rothmann was baptized by Matthijs, who then took up the leadership of the Münster Anabaptists.

Matthijs was joined in Münster by a twenty-four-year-old convert, John Beukels of Leyden, who had been a journeyman tailor but, after failing in that trade, had become an innkeeper in Leiden. Matthijs declared that Münster, rather than Strasbourg, was where Christ would return, and after the Anabaptists gained control of the city council on 23 February 1534, Matthijs became the effective ruler of Münster. He then tried to turn Münster into the New Jerusalem, and his policies appalled moderate Anabaptists. The library was burned, and all books except the Bible were destroyed. Communal ownership was introduced, the towers of all the town churches were destroyed, and Matthijs insisted that all citizens be rebaptized—those who refused were exiled. Approximately two thousand citizens were expelled,[39] but others who responded to Matthijs's call for Anabaptists to come to the "holy city of Münster" took their place, as approximately 2,500 new immigrants came to the city. Others tried to come too, but the authorities stopped them before they could reach Münster. Horrified by reports of what was happening in Münster, the Catholic bishop joined Protestants to lay siege to the city. On 4 April 1534 Matthijs, convinced that the Lord had made him invincible, led a sally against the armies besieging the city and was killed in the attack.

John Beukels then took over the leadership in Münster and introduced even more radical measures. The city council was dissolved, and leadership

John Beukels of Leyden (ca. 1509–1536).
Illustration from Beza *Icones*.

was placed in the hands of twelve men, who called themselves "The Twelve Elders of Israel." Severe penalties were introduced for even minor offenses: among the sins punishable by death were backbiting, gossiping, and complaining, in addition to blasphemy, adultery, and lewd conduct. The most controversial measure was the introduction of compulsory polygamy in July 1534.[40] Rothmann managed to find a biblical defense for this practice, citing the example of the Old Testament patriarchs and Genesis 1:28 ("be fruitful and multiply," RSV). He also pointed out that since 1 Timothy 3:2 says a bishop must be the husband of one wife, it can be assumed that other male believers were allowed more than one. One might argue that the policy had some justification since 70 percent of the population were women; however, it was not at all popular, and there was a great deal of resistance despite the threat of severe penalties for those who did not comply.[41] Beukels showed how strongly he supported the measure by taking for himself sixteen wives. Rothmann eventually took nine wives, but most of the leaders limited themselves to two or three.

After repulsing an attack by the besieging armies in September 1534, John Beukels had himself anointed and crowned king with great pomp and ceremony, citing the example of King David. However, his kingship was short-lived. With the town suffering from famine after the long siege, the besieging armies finally broke through the wall and, after a fierce battle, slaughtered almost all the inhabitants. Rothmann probably died in the battle, but Beukels and two of his leading associates were captured. Although Beukels made a partial recantation, he was, nevertheless, publicly tortured to death with the other two men on a platform in Münster. The bodies of the three men were placed in iron cages and hung from the tower of St. Lambert's Church as a warning to all who might be tempted to follow in their path. It had taken sixteen months to capture the city, and the rulers of Europe were horrified at what had transpired in the besieged city. In April 1535, two months before the city fell, the German Estates expressed their fear that if the Münster insurrection were not crushed, it would result in "irreversible disadvantage and damage, secession, uprising and insurrection of the common man." In the end, they feared that it would "lead to the ruin and disruption of the Roman Empire and of all authority and honesty."[42] In view of this fear, it is not surprising that Anabaptists suffered even more persecution in the years following the fall of Münster.

The Hutterites and the Mennonites

While the Münster debacle helped to discredit the Radical Reformation, it was short-lived, as were the vast majority of the Anabaptist groups. In contrast, two of the movements that were committed to pacifism survived persecution and have continued to the present day: the Hutterites and the Mennonites. The Hutterites were the earlier of the two, having originated in a group of Anabaptists who rejected Hubmaier's Magisterial Anabaptism. Two hundred of them, influenced by Hans Hut, left Nicolsburg under the leadership of Jacob Wiedmann and settled in Austerlitz, having committed themselves to sharing all their possessions. Others joined the group, and a new settlement was started in Auspitz, but divisions soon developed within the group. At this point Jacob Hutter entered the scene. He was not the founder of the group that later came to be identified by his name, but he played a major role in its survival. He was originally a hatter, and he traveled extensively in the pursuit of his trade. At one point in his travels, he came into contact with the Anabaptists and was converted to their beliefs and baptized. He became the leader of the Anabaptists in the Tyrol when George Blaurock, whose missionary efforts had contributed to the founding of the Anabaptist congregations in the region, was executed. Persecution forced the group to move to Moravia, where Hutter's sense of calling and leadership skills brought peace to the feuding Anabaptists. He was also responsible for transforming their unstructured communalism into a well-organized community with full economic sharing.

The Hutterites prospered for the next two years under Hutter's leadership until the impact of the Münster affair resulted in a new wave of persecution. Ferdinand, the Hapsburg ruler of the area, forced the reluctant nobles to expel the Anabaptists in 1535, but they survived by living in caves and forests. However, Hutter and his wife were hunted down and arrested; he was whipped, immersed in freezing water, and burned at the stake in February 1536. In that same year the persecution abated and the Hutterites again found refuge in Moravia, where they thrived despite sporadic persecution. By the end of the sixteenth century they had established seventy settlements in Moravia and Slovakia with approximately twenty thousand people living in them. The Hutterites suffered greatly during the Thirty Years' War, and many migrated to Transylvania and the Ukraine. In the nineteenth century a small group settled in North America, where they have survived and prospered.

The second Anabaptist group that survived the Reformation era also took the name of a leader who was not actually responsible for founding the movement. Menno Simons (1496–1561) is in some ways comparable to Hutter in that he rescued a movement that was deeply divided. After the defeat of the Münster Anabaptists, the militant Melchiorites continued under the leadership of Jan van Battenburg, the illegitimate son of a nobleman. His followers continued to practice polygamy and organized themselves into terrorist gangs that attacked "the godless" by burning crops and robbing churches, monasteries, and manor houses. Although Battenburg was captured and executed in 1538, his lawless bands continued to plague the Low Countries for several more decades. Fortunately, the violent Melchiorites were far outnumbered by a pacifist group represented by David Joris (1501–1556), whom Battenburg sought to have murdered. Joris, who accepted Hoffmann's apocalyptic beliefs and combined them with a spiritualism that emphasized the baptism of the Spirit and the inner light, allowed his followers to conform outwardly to the established religion while hiding their true beliefs in order to avoid persecution. Although he became the most important Anabaptist leader in the Netherlands after the fall of Münster, his leadership did not last. Tiring of his ambulant existence, Joris settled in Antwerp under the patronage of a wealthy supporter and spent his time writing books. In 1544 Joris moved to Switzerland, where he died in 1556, having abandoned many of the Anabaptist beliefs including adult baptism.

Following Joris's departure, the majority of Melchiorites became followers of a new leader named Menno Simons, who rejected the violence of Münster, the mystical apocalyptic emphasis of Hoffman, and the spiritualism of Joris as well as the compromises Joris was willing to make in order to avoid persecution. Simons was a Catholic priest in Friesland who gradually adopted Protestant beliefs through the reading of Reformation pamphlets and the study of Scripture. When he first came into contact with Münsterites in 1534, he had been studying Scripture for eight years and had formulated his own theology, which was totally opposed to the violence practiced at Münster.[43] Early in 1536 Simons came into contact with Obbe Philips, was baptized, married, and left his parish. In 1540 when Philips renounced Anabaptism, Simons became the leader of the Philips group.

Through his writings and preaching, Simons sought to organize the scattered Melchiorite groups into congregations. From 1542 on, he was a hunted man because the authorities put a price on his head. He preached and baptized at night, moving through the Rhineland, around Cologne, and up the Baltic coast as far as Danzig, always one step ahead of the authorities. By 1545 his followers, who were being called "Mennists," had grown significantly in numbers as the result of his tireless efforts. Simons finally settled in the province of Holstein, where he died a natural death in 1561. Throughout his ministry he emphasized pacifism and nonresistance, and he was also concerned that churches practice discipline in order to maintain the health of the community. He viewed the church as a gathered body of believers who were separate from the wider society, and he was thoroughly committed to a biblically based theology. Although the Mennonites splintered internally after Menno's death, they continued to grow in strength. In 1570 they achieved toleration in the Netherlands, and although they were divided into six different factions, by the end of the sixteenth century there may have been 100,000 Mennonites in the Low Countries, giving them a membership only slightly less than the Reformed church. In 1660 a Mennonite pastor produced a book known as the *Martyr's Mirror*, which recounted their earlier sufferings; it became one of the most important Mennonite books.

The Radical Reformation: An Assessment

The groups and leaders discussed in this chapter are only a sample of the many different movements and individuals associated with the Radical Reformation.[44] They illustrate its incredible diversity and why it is so difficult to identify the unifying characteristics of the entire movement. The authorities and the Magisterial Reformers considered the Anabaptists a radical threat because they applied the principles of the Reformation in an uncompromising way and drew conclusions that threatened the established order in both church and state. For example, they took the Reformation teaching about the priesthood of all believers literally, in contrast to the Magisterial Reformers, who became uneasy as they began to realize it could lead to uneducated laity challenging the clergy. The fact that Anabaptists refused to baptize infants threatened a principle at the heart of medieval society—the identification of the civic and the religious communities. The Magisterial Reformers never abandoned this concept as they, along with their Catholic opponents, found it difficult to envisage any other type of Christian society. The Anabaptist rejection of infant baptism carried with it a conviction that individuals must make their own choice as to whether they want to be a part of the church; so their church necessarily became a gathered community, separate from wider society.

The Anabaptists were Radical Reformers in the sense that they applied literally the Reformation principle of *sola scriptura*. Once the Magisterial Reformers attacked the traditional sources of authority in the church, the doors were open to those who wanted to approach the Scriptures in a literal way. Much of what the Magisterial Reformers taught about doctrines such as baptism and the Trinity depended partly on an interpretation of Scripture based on the tradition and teaching of the church. Having rejected that authority, the Radical Reformers questioned whether doctrines like infant baptism were actually taught in Scripture, and the most radical even questioned the doctrine of the Trinity. They also wanted to introduce reforms immediately and to eliminate anything that they believed violated scriptural teaching, such as the mass, images, and monasticism. In each case, the Magisterial Reformers were worried about the disruption that this would cause to society and to tender consciences, and they were not prepared to move as quickly, looking to established authority to ensure that things were done decently and in order. The issue that most distressed Reformers such as Luther was that radicals like Thomas Müntzer were prepared to appeal to an even higher authority than Scripture—the direct inspiration of the Holy Spirit—which would lead to a totally subjective criterion of truth. The Münster debacle was a frightening example of what could happen when this approach was taken to an extreme. The Anabaptists were mainly sincere and courageous men and women who were willing to suffer terrible torture and death for what they believed; yet some were prepared to use violence to impose their own beliefs. The Radical Reformation had its most lasting impact through movements that rejected violence, such as the Hutterites and the Mennonites, who preserved and institutionalized some of the best traditions of the Radical Reformation.

7

CALVIN AND CALVINISM

▼

> Being of a disposition somewhat unpolished and bashful, which led me
> always to love the shade and retirement, I then began to seek some secluded
> corner where I might be withdrawn from the public view. . . . In short,
> while my one great object was to live in seclusion without being known,
> God led me about through different turnings and changes, that He never
> permitted me to rest in any place, until, in spite of my natural disposition,
> He brought me forth to public notice.
>
> John Calvin[1]

John Calvin wrote the above account in 1557 as he looked back on his
life and career, one of the few times he indulged in public self-analysis.
By his own admission he was a very secretive man who would have preferred to avoid the public eye, but, ironically, he was to become one of
the best known of the Protestant Reformers and probably had a greater
influence on future generations than any of the others. Although Luther
was the originator of the Reformation, it was Calvin who was responsible
for its spread throughout much of Europe, and it was Calvinism that had
the greatest impact in North America. Calvin also produced the most
important work of Protestant systematic theology, the *Institutes of the
Christian Religion*, which even today continues to be well-respected and
extensively studied. Although Calvin wrote clearly and communicated

169

very effectively, he is not an easy person to know because he was so private; in contrast with Luther, he seldom said much about himself.

Calvin is one of those historic characters whom people tend either to love or to hate. Possibly even more than Luther, he has been an object of veneration by his loyal followers and vicious vilification by those who find his theology and his actions abominable. According to the author of a popular Reformation textbook, he was "one of those strong and consistent men of history whom people either liked or disliked, adored or abhorred."[2] Both his detractors and his admirers have misrepresented him. He has, for example, been portrayed as a pompous bigot and an unfeeling dictator,[3] but those who believe Calvin was an uncompromising dogmatist who delighted in polemics will find it difficult to reconcile this view with his approach to the Scriptures. In the introduction to his *Commentary on Romans*, he points out that in interpreting Scripture, "God has never so blessed his servants that they each possessed full and perfect knowledge of every part of their subject." This was so that "we should be kept humble," and since full agreement could not be achieved "in the present life," Calvin maintained that exegetes should avoid attacking each other in a polemical fashion.[4] Those who have read Calvin's commentaries will know that they are particularly useful because Calvin concentrates on making clear the original meaning of the text rather than using the text for extensive dogmatic commentary. Some of Calvin's treatises reveal him as a peacemaker. Maintaining that the devil had stirred up the controversy over the Lord's Supper in order to "impede the advance of the gospel," Calvin criticized both parties at the Marburg Colloquy. "Both sides erred . . . in that they did not listen to each other patiently and were not really committed to finding the truth together."[5]

Calvin's admirers misrepresented him as much as did his detractors. William Bouwsma, one of Calvin's best-known biographers, points out that Calvin's followers have practically made him into an idol who could do no wrong. The statue of Calvin in Geneva is an excellent example of how his admirers have too often portrayed him:

> Here Calvin stands more than twice as large as life, stylized beyond recognition, stony, rigid, immobile, and except for his slightly abstracted disapproval of whatever we might imagine him to be contemplating, impassive. Drained of his humanity, this man, who was singularly eloquent about the universality of human frailty and who was constantly looking within himself for reminders that no human being is ever free from the struggle with his own sin and weakness, has been converted into a strangely ambiguous icon to create an impression and to stimulate a degree of veneration.[6]

This image of Calvin contrasts with Calvin's own statement in a letter to Melanchthon where he wrote, "In the church we must always keep an eye on how far we defer to men. For it is all over with her when one person, no matter who he is, has more authority than everyone else."[7] In order to portray accurately the *real* Calvin, we must get behind the hero worship of those who idolize him as well as the scurrilous attacks of those who despise him. We must engage in "the quest for the historical Calvin" by basing our assessment on the historical evidence rather than on our preconceptions or confessional alliances. When we uncover the *real* Calvin, we will find that the quest was well worth the effort.

Calvin's Early Life and Career

Calvin was born in Noyon in Picardy on 10 July 1509, twenty-six years after Luther, so he was very much a second-generation Reformer. Calvin was only learning to read while Luther was lecturing at the University of Wittenberg, and he was only eight when Luther published his *Ninety-five Theses*. Although Calvin and Luther never met and their personalities were radically different, the two men seem to have admired each other. When Luther read some of Calvin's writings, he was very impressed; in a letter written in October 1539 he stated that he was pleased that Calvin was serving in Strasbourg. In turn, Luther's friends reported that Calvin was high in Luther's favor.[8] Although Calvin was at times critical of Luther's extreme language, he regularly defended him against his detractors. In his treatise responding to the Roman Catholic theologian Albertus Pighius (1490–1542), Calvin summed up his opinion of Luther stating that "we regard him as a remarkable apostle of Christ, through whose work and ministry, most of all the purity of the Gospel has been restored to our time."[9] Calvin considered himself a follower of Luther and

John Calvin (1509–1564).
Illustration from Beza *Icones*.

not the founder of a rival movement, but he clearly did not consider Luther's theology the final word. Rather he viewed his own work as building on that of his predecessor.

Like Luther, Calvin came from an upwardly mobile family. His grandfather had been a cooper or boatman in a village in Picardy, and his father left the family home and moved to Noyon, where he, like Luther's father, was successful in a new vocation. By the time Calvin was born, his father was the bishop's notary, and he had even higher ambitions for his bright young son, John. He first sent John to be educated with the sons of the aristocratic De Montmors family, where he would learn the manners of an aristocrat. When John was eleven, his father obtained a church benefice for him, which provided him with income for further study at the University of Paris, where he would be trained for a career in the church. Calvin had completed the arts course, in which he became proficient in Latin and philosophy, when the direction of his studies was changed. Whereas Luther had moved from the study of law into the study of theology, Calvin took the opposite path. As he was about to begin the serious study of theology, his father had a quarrel with the cathedral chapter of Noyon and advised his son to leave the study of theology and pursue a law degree.

Since Calvin could not study civil law in Paris, which only provided for the study of canon law, he moved to Orleans late in the year 1527. Two years later he moved on to Bourges to continue his legal studies. When his father died in May 1531, he abandoned the study of law to pursue what had by now become his overriding interest, humanist literary studies. Calvin came into contact with humanism in Paris where he developed friendships with the Cop family. The father, Guillaume Cop, who was the king's physician, had a circle of humanist friends and corresponded with Erasmus. Calvin also acquired a number of friends among the evangelical-minded humanists, and after his father's death, he returned to Paris in 1531 to pursue literary studies. His first publication in 1532 was a typical humanist commentary on Seneca's *De Clementia*. Even after his conversion to evangelical Christianity, Calvin remained sympathetic to humanism and always held Erasmus and the great French humanist Lefèvre d'Étaples in high esteem.

Some time between August 1533 and May 1534 Calvin experienced an evangelical conversion, which he described in his *Commentary upon the Book of Psalms* in 1557. This was the same work from which the statement quoted at the beginning of this chapter was taken. He described the event as having occurred after he was "withdrawn from the study of philosophy and was put to the study of law," to which he applied himself "faithfully . . . in obedience to the will of my father." However, according to Calvin, God had a different plan for his life:

> Since I was too obstinately devoted to the superstitions of popery to be easily extricated from so profound an abyss of mire, God by a sudden conversion subdued and brought my mind to a teachable frame, which was more hardened in such matters than might have been expected from one at my early period of life. Having thus received some taste and knowledge of true godliness, I was immediately inflamed with so intense a desire to make progress therein, that although I did not altogether leave off other studies, I yet pursued them with less ardour.[10]

Although there is no mention of going through a period of great spiritual turmoil as Luther did, in his treatise against Pighius, Calvin indicated that he understood Luther's struggle. In response to Pighius's accusation that Luther's tormented conscience suggested he must have been a "very monster from hell," Calvin responded that the godly often experience "fearful tortures of conscience."[11] Although he did not state that he had experienced those "fearful tortures," his empathy with Luther's struggle suggests that he might well have had similar experiences.

On All Saints' Day 1533 the new rector of the University of Paris, Nicholas Cop, who was Guillaume's son, preached a sermon in which he attacked the scholastic theologians of the Sorbonne and presented his ideas on justification. Although he intermingled the statements that seemed to be inspired by Lutheranism with the biblical humanism of Erasmus and with more traditional Catholic piety, and the theology revealed in the address was not radically different from that of the French humanists, he offended the conservative faculty of the Sorbonne. As a result, Cop was not only deposed as rector, but he was called to answer charges before the parliament of Paris. Rather than undergo a trial by what was likely to be a biased court, Cop fled the city; Calvin, who may have had some involvement in the writing of Cop's sermon, also chose to leave Paris.[12] Calvin spent the next year traveling around France under an assumed name.

In October a group of radical French Protestants posted placards in Paris, Orleans, and a number of other cities denouncing the mass.[13] This infuriated the king and led to widespread persecution. When a number of Protestants were burned at the stake, including one of Calvin's associates, Calvin left France and went to Basel, where Nicholas Cop had also taken refuge. From there he arranged for the publication of the first edition of the *Institutes of the Christian Religion*, which he completed writing in August of 1535 and published in Basel in March 1536.

Calvin's Theology

The *Institutes* clearly delineate Calvin's theology and were to become the most important Protestant book of systematic theology. Calvin had two purposes in writing. In the prefatory address to King Francis I of France he stated that his initial purpose was to provide "a kind of rudiments, by which those who feel some interest in religion might be trained to true godliness." It was intended to be a catechism, or primer, to help French Protestants understand and defend their faith and therefore, according to Calvin, it was "written in a simple and elementary form adapted for instruction."[14] The second purpose was to inform Francis I about the true teachings of the faith that was being slandered and unjustly persecuted in France, so that he would understand that French Protestantism was not, as its enemies maintained, cause for "sedition and impunity for all kinds of vice."[15] The 1536 edition was a very short handbook, consisting of six chapters dealing with the law, the creed, the Lord's Prayer, the sacraments, false sacraments, and Christian liberty.[16] Calvin produced a second Latin edition in 1539 that was three times as long as the original edition. In the same year he translated the *Institutes* into French for those who could not read Latin. An expanded Latin edition was published in 1543, followed by a French translation in 1545. A fourth Latin edition appeared in 1550. The final Latin edition was published in 1559, and once again a French translation was produced the following year. The greatly expanded 1559 edition, which became the standard edition, differed radically from the original version. It was no longer a manual for new believers "written in a simple and elementary form"; rather, it had grown into a sophisticated theological textbook that dealt with some of the most complex doctrines of the faith in significant detail.

One excellent example is the doctrine of double predestination, which was to become a central doctrine for later Calvinists. In the 1536 edition it is mentioned on only two occasions and given no great prominence. The section dealing with predestination largely emphasized the way in which that doctrine brings reassurance to the people of God. The doctrine assumed greater importance as the *Institutes* were expanded, and in the 1559 edition, four chapters were devoted to it. Calvin described predestination as "the eternal decree of God, by which he determined with himself whatever he wished to happen with regard to every man. All are not created on equal terms, but some are preordained to eternal life, others to eternal damnation; and, accordingly, as each has been created for one or other of these ends, we say that he has been predestined to life or to death."[17]

The development of this doctrine was partially in reaction to the teachings of Jerome Bolsec, who in 1551 asserted that God's decrees to election and reprobation were based on his foreknowledge of who would and would not have faith. Although Bolsec was banished from Geneva, Calvin defended the doctrine again the following year. Predestination was never the center of Calvin's theological system, as it would become for later Calvinists; rather, it was an ancillary doctrine that Calvin believed was clearly taught in Scripture and which was designed to explain why some accepted the gospel and others rejected it. Calvin did not try to explain why God made the choice, because this involved probing the inscrutable judgments of God, and it was "not fitting that human beings should with impunity pry into things which the Lord has been pleased to conceal within himself."[18] Calvin taught predestination as a pastoral-orientated doctrine that was designed to comfort believers because it assured them that their salvation was not dependent on their own efforts. He was also careful not to define the doctrine beyond what he considered the clear teaching of Scripture. Calvin's followers gave much more prominence to the doctrine of predestination than it had in Calvin's theology, and they defined it in considerably greater detail as they began to debate the chronology of the divine decrees and the extent of Christ's atonement for sin. Theodore Beza, Calvin's successor, taught that the decrees of election and reprobation preceded the fall into sin of the first human beings. This position has been given the complex title "supralapsarianism" (above or before the fall), while those who held the opposing position, which was called infralapsarianism (below or after the fall), believed these decrees came after the fall. The controversy about the extent of Christ's atonement would also divide Calvin's followers, as some argued that Christ died only for the elect and others that he died for all humankind.

Predestination is discussed in book 3 of the *Institutes*. Before Calvin broached that subject, he had already discussed how human beings can know God, the nature of man, the work of Jesus Christ, and the doctrine of redemption. Although Calvin believed that every human being has a natural knowledge of God and that a general knowledge of God can be acquired through observing his creation, he believed this knowledge was inadequate and distorted. A true knowledge of God can only come through biblical revelation. The Bible reveals that humans have fallen from the original pristine state in which they were created and that human beings are incapable of saving themselves. Therefore, God sent a redeemer in the person of Jesus Christ who was both God and perfect man. He lived the perfect life in our place "that he might present our flesh as the price of satisfaction to the just judgment of God, and in the same flesh pay the penalty which we had incurred."[19]

The benefits of Christ's redeeming death are appropriated by faith, which Calvin defined as "a firm and sure knowledge of the divine favor toward us, founded on the truth of a free promise in Christ, and revealed to our minds, and sealed on our hearts by the Holy Spirit."[20] Calvin was in full agreement with Luther that justification was not based on any merit earned by human beings through their righteous deeds; it was solely and utterly dependent on the mercies of God in Jesus Christ. According to Calvin, justification was "the acceptance with which God receives us into his favor as if we were righteous . . . and consists in the forgiveness of sins and the imputation of the righteousness of Christ."[21] In addition to having Christ's righteousness imputed, the believer is regenerated so that his or her attitude and motivation are changed. The result is a sanctified life. In contrast to Roman Catholic theology, Calvin clearly distinguished between *justification* and what later theologians would call *sanctification* but did not separate them since both flowed from the believer's union with Christ: "The believer's union with Christ leads directly to his or her justification. Through Christ, the believer is declared to be righteous in the sight of God. Second, on account of the believer's union with Christ—and not on account of his or her justification—the believer begins the process of becoming like Christ through regeneration. . . . Calvin asserts that both justification and regeneration are the results of the believer's union with Christ through faith."[22]

Like Bucer, Calvin tried to find a middle road between the two extremes of Lutheranism and Zwinglianism in his eucharistic theology. He cautioned that "we must neither, by setting too little value on the signs, dissever them from their meanings to which they are in some degree annexed, nor by immoderately extolling them, seem somewhat to obscure the mysteries themselves."[23] Although Calvin could not accept Luther's belief that Christ's body and blood were enclosed in the bread and wine, he insisted that we partake of Christ in the sacrament in a unique way "by the secret and incomprehensible power of God."[24] He rejected Luther's view of the ubiquity of Christ's body, arguing it could not be in the bread because Christ is in heaven at the right hand of God. Nevertheless, he also rejected the Zwinglian belief that the bread and wine were mere symbols or signs of the body and blood of Christ and insisted that the believer truly communes spiritually with Christ in the Eucharist. Calvin described what he called the Lord's Supper as more than "a vain or empty sign"; he insisted that "truly the thing there signified he [God] exhibits and offers to all who sit down at that spiritual feast, although it is beneficially received by believers only who receive this great benefit with true faith and heartfelt gratitude."[25]

Calvin's First Stay in Geneva (1536–1538)

After publishing the first edition of the *Institutes*, Calvin visited the Duchess of Ferrara in Italy who was a cousin of the king's sister, Marguerite of Angoulême, and, like her cousin, sympathetic to the cause of reform. A number of French evangelicals had gathered at her court as a place of refuge after the Affair of the Placards (discussed in chapter 14). Calvin stayed only a few weeks, and after a brief stop in Basel, he returned to France to put his affairs in order because he planned to leave France permanently. He had decided to move to Strasbourg, where he could study in peace and live a secluded life as a scholar. However, as a result of the war between France and the Holy Roman Empire, the direct route to Strasbourg was blocked by the opposing armies; consequently, Calvin took a detour through Geneva, planning to stay no longer than one night in that city, which was at the time in the process of religious and political transition.

Geneva was a small city of approximately ten thousand inhabitants before the Reformation. It had been ruled by a bishop in the Middle Ages, but in the fifteenth century the dukes of Savoy gained control of the bishopric, and the bishops became virtual puppets of the dukes. Nearly all the bishops, who were members of the Savoyard dynasty, were absentees, and some were not even ordained. Although Geneva was under the control of Savoy, the city retained a measure of self-governance. The male citizens elected four syndics who selected a council made up of about twenty-five members. A second council, called the Council of Two Hundred, was established in 1527. In the first quarter of the sixteenth century a group of revolutionary townsmen, who sought independence and closer links with the Swiss confederacy, resisted Savoy's dominance and gained the support of the cities of Bern and Fribourg. In 1527 the bishop fled the city, and efforts by Savoy to regain control were defeated with the help of Bern in 1536. Bern, which had adopted Protestantism in 1528, encouraged Geneva to do the same and in 1533 sent a group of Protestant preachers including Guillaume Farel (1489–1565), who, although twenty years Calvin's senior, was to become his close friend and co-worker in Geneva. However, according to his testimony, Calvin entered into the

Guillaume Farel (1489–1565).
Illustration from Beza *Icones*.

relationship unwillingly and only in response to some questionable tactics used by Farel.

Calvin came to Geneva three months after the city had accepted the Reformation, in May 1536, and pledged "to live according to the law of the gospel and the word of God and to abolish all papal abuses."[26] However, the implementation of that mandate would be extremely challenging in a city that was only superficially Protestant. When Calvin arrived for what he thought was only going to be an overnight stay, Farel was convinced that this was a providential act of God to provide him with the help he needed. Calvin was not easy to convince. He wrote:

> Farel, who burned with an extraordinary zeal to advance the gospel, immediately strained every nerve to detain me. And after having learned that my heart was set upon devoting myself to private studies, for which I wished to keep myself free from other pursuits, and finding that he gained nothing by entreaties, he proceeded to utter an imprecation that God would curse my retirement, and the tranquillity of the studies which I sought, if I should withdraw and refuse to give assistance, when the necessity was so urgent. By this imprecation I was so stricken with terror, that I desisted from the journey which I had undertaken.[27]

Calvin quickly found he had taken on an immense task. When, in the year of his death, Calvin looked back at those early days in Geneva, he remembered the overwhelming obstacles facing Farel and himself as they began their work of trying to transform Geneva into a truly Reformed city. Calvin remarked, "When I first arrived in this church there was almost nothing. They were preaching and that's all. They were good at seeking out idols and burning them, but there was no Reformation. Everything was in turmoil."[28] Calvin was determined to bring real change to Geneva, so in January 1537 he presented an ecclesiastical ordinance along with a new catechism that would have subjected the citizens of Geneva to a degree of moral control that they were not yet ready to accept. He also sought to place the power of excommunication in the hands of the ministers rather than the state. Not surprisingly, Calvin was not very popular. He recalled that "I have been saluted in derision outside my door in the evening by fifty or sixty arquebus shots." And he added, "You may well imagine how this could astonish a poor, timid scholar such as I am and always have been."[29]

Pressure was also coming from Bern to follow the pattern of reform that had been established in that city. The Reformation in Bern was in turn influenced by Zurich, where the civil government controlled many aspects of church life, including discipline and liturgy. However, Bern also retained many of the aspects of medieval worship, which had been eliminated in Geneva, including the use of baptismal fonts, wafer bread in the Lord's Supper, and the celebration of traditional Christian holy days such as Christmas, Annunciation, and Ascension. When the newly elected Geneva magistrates ordered the restoration of these forms, Calvin resisted. The issue at stake was state control of the church rather than simply the restoration of forms that Calvin found objectionable. Therefore, he refused to obey and even preached against the government's actions. In reaction, the magistrates forbade preaching by Calvin or Farel, who ignored the ban. Calvin also refused to administer communion at Easter because he believed the community had first to be reconciled before they could commune together in the sacrament. This action resulted in expulsion rather than reconciliation, as both Calvin and Farel were dismissed from their posts and left the city in April 1538.

Calvin in Strasbourg (1538–1541)

Calvin's experience in Geneva caused him to doubt whether he had truly discerned God's call. With some degree of relief he now concluded that his original plan to devote his life to scholarship was more in accord with his gifts and God's direction than the ministry into which Farel had lured him. He was planning to settle in Basel, where he could pursue his scholarly interests, when Bucer, who was seeking a pastor for the large, French-speaking congregation that had settled in Strasbourg, resorted to the same tactics Farel had used to bring Calvin to Geneva. Once again Calvin was diverted from his original intention. According to Calvin's account:

I resolved to live in a private station, free from the burden and cares of my public charge, when that most excellent servant of Christ, Martin Bucer, employing a similar kind of remonstrance and protestation as that to which Farel had recourse before, drew me back to a new station. Alarmed by the example of Jonah which he had set before me, I still continued in the work of teaching. And although I always continued . . . studiously avoiding celebrity, yet I was carried, I know not how as it were by force to the imperial assemblies, where willing or unwilling, I was under the necessity of appearing before the eyes of many.[30]

In contrast to his experience in Geneva, the decision to go to Strasbourg was one of the most rewarding of Calvin's career. Although he spent only three years in Strasbourg, they were some of the happiest in his life. He was able to use his gifts as a teacher lecturing on the Bible at the Strasbourg Academy and found the work as minister of the French émigré church rewarding, proving to be a good pastor who did not neglect his pastoral duties despite all the other demands on his time. He also found time for scholarship and was able to complete the expanded edition of the *Institutes* as well as the French translation mentioned earlier. In 1540 Calvin published a commentary on Romans, which was the first of his many volumes of biblical commentaries. He also responded to the Catholic humanist reformer, Jacopo Sadoleto (1477–1547), who sought to win Geneva back to Roman Catholicism, with a brilliant defense of the Reformation that won him international acclaim. In addition, he wrote a *Short Treatise on the Lord's Supper*, published in 1541, and a Psalter that included metrical versions of nineteen psalms in French with melodies.

Sloth was never one of Calvin's faults, and in the midst of his teaching, pastoral duties, and scholarship, he also managed to attend a number of international conferences called to heal the schism in the church. In February 1539 a conference was held in Frankfurt, with further meetings at Hagenau, Worms, and Regensburg. Calvin attended three of the meetings, including the Regensburg Colloquy in April 1541, where Protestants and Roman Catholics came very close to arriving at an agreement.[31] Calvin met Philip Melanchthon at the Frankfurt meeting, and they became lifelong friends. Although they differed on many issues and had different personalities, their common commitment to scholarship and desire to heal the breach in the church drew them together. Shortly after the meeting in Frankfurt, Calvin commented in a letter on the different approaches of the two men and some of Calvin's objections to Lutheran practices: "I have plainly told Philip to his face how much I disliked that over abounding of ceremonies; indeed, that it seemed to me the form which they observe was not far removed from Judaism. When I pressed him with the argument, he was unwilling to dispute with me about the matter, but admitted that there was an overdoing in these either trifling or superfluous rites and ceremonies."[32]

Melanchthon was always attempting to find a way to reconcile the differences between the Reformers and heal the breach in the church. In an effort to express the Lutheran view on the Lord's Supper in a way that would be acceptable to the Reformed cities, he changed article 10 of the Augsburg Confession on the Lord's Supper. The article in the original Augsburg Confession stated "that the Body and Blood of Christ are truly present and are distributed to those that eat in the Supper of the Lord; and they reject those that teach otherwise."[33] The revised version simply read, "Concerning the Lord's Supper, they teach that with bread and wine are truly exhibited the body and blood of Christ to those who eat in the Lord's Supper," and it did not include the condemnation of "those that teach otherwise." Calvin found the statement acceptable and signed the so-called *Variata* of the Augsburg Confession. Luther may also have accepted it, but later orthodox Lutherans rejected it, and the Book of Concord of 1580 would include only the original version.[34]

In addition to all his other activities, Calvin learned important lessons on the implementation of religious reform from Martin Bucer and the other Strasbourg Reformers. The church organization that Calvin would later introduce to Geneva was in many ways a copy of the Strasbourg model. In addition, Calvin observed the outstanding system of education developed by Johann Sturm (1507–1589), which he later copied in Geneva. The Strasbourg period was not only a time of productivity and learning but also a time of great personal happiness for Calvin, who felt he had finally found the place God had intended for him. He became a citizen of Strasbourg in August 1540 and married in the same month. Calvin had begun searching for a wife in the previous year when he became convinced, partly by the example of Martin Bucer's happy marriage, that he too should have a wife. He approached his new venture in the same carefully reasoned way that he approached other problems, and he was so convinced he should marry that he even reserved a date with Farel, whom he hoped would officiate at the wedding. However, he still needed to find the right woman, and in a letter to Farel he described the attributes that he was looking for in a bride: "I am none of those insane lovers who embrace also the vices of those they are in love with, when they are smitten at first sight with a fine figure. This only is the beauty which attracts me: if she is chaste, if not too nice or fastidious, if economical, if patient, if there is hope that she will be interested about my health."[35]

Before he found the person who met his specifications, he rejected a number of possibilities and almost gave up looking.[36] But just when he had given up hope, he found Idelette de Bure, the widow of an Anabaptist, who had two children. She and her husband, who had been convinced by Calvin to change his theology, were members of Calvin's congregation, and when Idelette's husband died of the plague in the spring of 1540, Martin Bucer suggested that Calvin should consider taking the widow for his bride. He took his friend's advice and in August married Idelette. In contrast to Luther, Calvin left very little information about his relationship with his wife for future historians to use in their biographies. However, the few comments he made in letters to friends suggests that she turned out to be just what he needed in a wife; he once described her as "the faithful helper of my ministry" and called her "the best companion of my life."[37] She bore Calvin three children, but all died shortly after birth. After nine years of marriage Calvin also lost his wife, who died at the age of forty. Calvin was devastated. He wrote to his friend Farel, "I do what I can to keep myself from being overwhelmed with grief. . . . May the Lord Jesus . . . support me under this heavy affliction."[38] Although Calvin was only forty when Idelette died, he never married again.

Calvin spent most of his married life in Geneva, because in September 1541 he had very reluctantly left his happy life in Strasbourg to return to Geneva. He was invited to go back because the situation at Geneva had changed in the three years he was at Strasbourg. The inadequacies of the ministers who replaced Calvin and Farel, as well as the dominance of Bern, were particularly distressing to those Genevans who had continued to support Calvin and Farel. When they won a majority on the city council, after an abortive attempt by Bern to gain more control over Geneva, a delegation was sent to Strasbourg in September 1540 to see if Calvin could be persuaded to return. He was not at all grateful for the invitation. In fact, he was horrified at the prospect of leaving his happy life in Strasbourg and returning to the place where he had suffered so much. He stated in a letter to Farel that he would rather "submit to death a hundred times than to that cross on which I had to perish daily a thousand times over." In another letter he tried to explain why he was so opposed to going back to Geneva: "Whenever I call to mind the wretchedness of my life there, how can it not be but that my very soul must shudder at any proposal of my return. . . . Now that by the favour of God I am delivered, who will not excuse me if I am unwilling to plunge again into the gulf and whirlpool which I know to be so dangerous and destructive."[39]

Farel, who was happily settled as a pastor in Neuchatel, continued to urge Calvin to go back to Geneva. Others joined in the chorus urging Calvin to return, including Bullinger, who pointed out that Geneva was of vital importance to the Reformation. Calvin agonized for a year before accepting the invitation, and when he did, it was because he could not escape the conclusion that God was calling him back. He had written to Farel in response to an earlier letter, "Had I the choice at my own disposal, nothing would be less agreeable to me than to follow your advice. But when I remember that I am not my own, I offer up my heart, presented as a sacrifice to the Lord."[40]

Although Farel did not return, Calvin continued to correspond with him in letters that reveal his most private thoughts that he did not confide to others. They provide a unique source of information for historians seeking to uncover the *real* Calvin. Unfortunately, the two friends had a falling out in 1558 when Farel decided to marry the daughter of a widow who, having fled persecution in France, was staying at his house with her son and daughter. Had he decided to marry the widow there would have been no problem, but the daughter was seventeen years old and Farel was sixty-nine. Calvin was horrified and rebuked Farel with sharp and bitter words for putting the Reformation at risk and providing ammunition for its Catholic critics, but Farel, nevertheless, proceeded with the marriage. Seven years later the bride would be a widow, but not before Farel had fathered a son. He named his son after Calvin, whom he continued to respect even after the friendship was disrupted by Farel's marriage. They had one last meeting in Geneva before both Reformers died, and in a final letter to his old friend, written three weeks before Calvin's death, Farel spoke "of our seamless partnership which was so beneficial to the church of God that its fruits await us in heaven."[41]

The Genevan Reformation 1541–1564

Calvin was welcomed back to Geneva in grand style. He was given a black velvet robe trimmed with fur and, more importantly, a house on the Rue de Chanoines near the cathedral, to which Idelette and her two children were brought from Strasbourg in a carriage. The warmth of his welcome did not deflect Calvin from pursuing a program that some in the council would find unpalatable. Within six weeks of his arrival he submitted to the magistrates a new set of Ecclesiastical Ordinances that placed a strong emphasis on church discipline. In a statement to the council he warned:

> If you desire to have me for your pastor, correct the disorder of your lives. If you have with sincerity recalled me from my exile, banish the crimes and debaucheries which prevail among you. . . . I consider the principal enemies of the gospel to be, not the pontiff of Rome, nor heretics, nor seducers, nor tyrants but bad Christians. . . . Of what use is a dead faith without good works? Of what importance is even truth itself, where a wicked life belies it and actions make words blush? Either command me to abandon a second time your town and let me go and soften the bitterness of my afflictions in a new exile, or let the severity of the laws reign in the church. Re-establish there pure discipline.[42]

The Ecclesiastical Ordinances were designed to achieve that "pure discipline" so that Geneva could become what Calvin considered a truly Christian city in its beliefs and conduct. Following the Strasbourg pattern, four church offices (pastors, elders, deacons, and doctors) were instituted, with the elders and pastors responsible for church discipline.[43] The ordinances specified that the elders were "to keep watch over the lives of everyone, to admonish in love those whom they see erring and leading disorderly lives and, whenever necessary, to report them to the body which will be designated to make fraternal corrections."[44] The pastors were to meet weekly as a group, presided over by Calvin, when they would discuss biblical passages and seek to maintain doctrinal purity. Together with the elders, they formed the Consistory, which met every Thursday to deal with church discipline. Calvin believed that the Consistory should possess the power to excommunicate, but the magistrates intended to retain this right and limit the Consistory to making recommendations. The Ecclesiastical Ordinances avoided conflict on this issue by some clever circumlocution, providing that if a person stubbornly persisted in sin after being admonished three times, "he shall be excommunicated and the matter shall be reported to the authorities."[45] When the Consistory's power to excommunicate was definitely confirmed in 1555, Calvin won a decisive victory, which differentiated the Geneva Consistory from similar institutions elsewhere in Europe.

Until recently, our knowledge of what happened at the Consistory meetings was fairly limited. Although the Consistory had a secretary who kept a record of the Thursday meetings, they were written in haste and in a very difficult hand, which only an expert in sixteenth-century French paleography can read. Consequently, scholars have too often used a printed transcript of selections from the registers made in 1853, which include only 5 percent of the total cases, contain errors, and also concentrate on the more spectacular cases while leaving out the ordinary ones that made up most of the business of the Consistory. In 1987 a group of scholars began to produce a scholarly edition of all the Consistory records, which will enable future historians to acquire a fuller and more accurate understanding of the Consistory's work.[46]

The records already published reveal that the Consistory did a great deal of positive work in attempting to reconcile disputes between Christians as well as carrying out its better-known function as a court of discipline. According to the editor of the Consistory records: "The Consistory served as a counselling service by establishing a mechanism to resolve disputes between family members, neighbours, and business partners. They would be summoned before the Consistory and given an opportunity to talk their problems out. Sometimes the problem would be worked out at that session. At other times, the Consistory would organize a later public service of reconciliation."[47]

The Consistory also encouraged learning by urging people to attend religious services, which were available every day of the week at different times, as well as catechism sessions, which met in the parish church after Sunday services. When acting as a court of discipline, the Consistory excommunicated about five people a week for a variety of offenses including sexual immorality, quarreling, blasphemy, and the use of Catholic practices, which were called "superstition." Excommunication was lifted when the person showed signs of repentance. That normally meant that they were seldom barred from more than one of the quarterly communion services. Since the Consistory could not impose criminal sentences, cases that might result in more severe punishment, such as that of Michael Servetus, were heard before secular courts. The Consistory did not show any deference to prestigious citizens or to people who held political power, and Calvin's readiness to punish them for moral lapses led to some serious tensions between church and state.

Although Calvin's effort to reform the morals of Geneva has been heavily criticized and he has been portrayed as an authoritarian dictator, the effort to regulate morals was not unusual in sixteenth-century cities. Before the Reformation Geneva, like other cities, had laws on moral issues such as drunkenness and prostitution, but in the early sixteenth century they were not strictly enforced. Furthermore, Calvin's power was in reality extremely limited since the only position he held in Geneva was that of an ordinary pastor. He had no greater authority than any other minister, and for most of his time in Geneva he was a foreigner who did not even have the right to vote.[48] He was an employee of the city and could be dismissed and even expelled from the city at the whim of the government.

Although the Consistory achieved success in changing the moral behavior of Genevans, Calvin was not always successful in attaining his objectives, especially when his policies came into conflict with long-established Genevan customs. For example, Genevans often frequented the large number of taverns, which the Genevan ministers believed were not good for the moral health of the city; so in April and May of 1546 laws were enacted closing the taverns and replacing them with cafes under the supervision of the city government. Some of the morally objectionable practices that commonly occurred in taverns, such as cursing, dancing, and gambling, were forbidden; in addition, patrons were required to pray before they could be served food or drink, and a French Bible was placed on every table to stimulate edifying conversations. The law was, understandably, very unpopular, and it was withdrawn when it became evident that the consumers were not prepared to accept this infringement on their social activities. Although people living in the twenty-first century will find some of the Consistory's actions objectionable,[49] it is important to remember that the Geneva Consistory was not unique. Many other cities possessed similar institutions, and the punishments they ordered were often far more severe than those given by the Geneva Consistory for the same crime.

Opposition to Calvin in Geneva

It is not surprising that Calvin faced a good deal of opposition in his effort to reform Geneva. Citizens often resented the discipline imposed on them, and since the Consistory did not distinguish between prominent citizens and those without power and influence, Calvin sometimes came into conflict with members of the government, including some who had formerly supported him. Some citizens even named their dogs after Calvin—which was not intended as a compliment—and according to Calvin's own account, "they set dogs at my heels and they caught at my robe and my legs." Others deliberately mispronounced his name, calling him "Cain."[50] They also called him "that Frenchman," which reveals resentment at the fact that their city was being taken over by foreigners. Geneva had become a city of refugees as Protestants fleeing from persecution flocked to Geneva; most came from France, but they also came from Italy, Britain, the Netherlands, and Germany. By 1560 almost half the population of Geneva was made up of refugees, and it was really these foreigners, especially the French, who brought about the triumph of Calvin's program after 1555.

Calvin also encountered opposition from people who objected to his theology. Sebastian Castellio was a humanist scholar whom Calvin met in Strasbourg. When Calvin returned to Geneva, he invited Castellio to join him and become rector of the Latin school. However, the friendship cooled when Castellio challenged some of Calvin's theological positions. When the newcomer sought acceptance as a minister, the council examined him, in the course of which he commented that he did not think the Song of Songs belonged in the Canon because it was obscene. He also expressed disagreement with the statement in the Geneva catechism about Christ's descent into hell. When the council refused him admission to the office of minister, Castellio decided to leave Geneva, and Calvin even offered to write a recommendation for him. After a brief time in Lausanne he returned to Geneva, but he did not win any friends among the Geneva ministers when he denounced them for drunkenness, impurity, and intolerance. This resulted in his expulsion, and Castellio went to Basel, where he eventually became professor of Greek at the university. By then he was totally alienated from Calvin, and he later became one of the most vocal critics of Calvinism.

Another of Calvin's theological opponents was Jerome Bolsec who, as noted earlier, was responsible for Calvin having to define more precisely his doctrine of double predestination. Bolsec had been a Carmelite monk; after being converted to Protestantism, he settled near Geneva. He then began to attend the weekly theological discussion meetings in Geneva, and although he agreed with Calvin's theology on most points, he clearly disagreed with him on predestination. In October 1551 he attacked Calvin's doctrine of double predestination, maintaining it made God the author of sin. As a result Bolsec was imprisoned and put on trial for heresy, found guilty, and exiled from Geneva for life in December 1551. Bolsec never forgave Calvin, and after a brief period in Bern, he went to France and converted back to Roman Catholicism. He expressed his hatred of Calvin by writing a biography in which he was unrestrained in his attacks on Calvin and his character. Just as Cochlaeus had attempted to discredit Luther's morals, Bolsec charged Calvin with greed, financial misconduct, and sexual sins.

Calvin also encountered dangerous political opposition from a faction who exploited popular hostility to Calvin as a French immigrant. Ami Perrin was the leader of a faction in the council that had been responsible for bringing Calvin back to Geneva in 1541. He and his father-in-law, however, opposed the power of the Consistory, partly because they were summoned to appear before it several times. Although they supported the Reformation, they were opposed to Calvin's system of discipline, and for that reason they were later referred to as "libertines."[51] By 1552 they were in control of the city government and prepared to challenge Calvin's effort to keep the right of excommunication in the hands of the church, exercised through the Consistory. At this point the ambiguity of the statement in the Ecclesiastical Ordinances benefited Calvin's opponents. Although Calvin believed it vested the right of excommunication in the Consistory, his opponents, led by Ami Perrin, held that the city council held that right. In March 1553 the syndics demanded that the Consistory give them a list of all excommunicated persons, together with the reasons for their excommunication. When the Consistory refused, matters were at an impasse, and Calvin, feeling that he had failed, was ready to give up the effort to change Geneva. The records note that "M. Calvin has remonstrated and asked that the council will not be displeased if, since he sees that some wish him ill, and many grumble and turn away from the word, he goes into retirement and serves no longer."[52] Although the council turned down his request, Calvin was at the low point of his influence in Geneva when a number of unexpected developments led to a drastic change in his position and saved his program of reform.

In August 1553 Michael Servetus, a Spaniard fleeing the authorities in France, stopped briefly in Geneva on his way to Italy. Servetus was born in Spain to a well-to-do family, and he received an excellent education. He was an independent thinker who, having lived in a country where there were large numbers of Muslims and Jews, came to the conclusion that the major block to their conversion was the doctrine of the Trinity, which he came to believe had no biblical support. After rejecting Roman Catholicism, he moved to Basel, where his unorthodox views got him into trouble with Oecolampadius, so in 1531 he moved to Strasbourg. At the age of twenty he published *On the Errors of the Trinity*, in which he questioned the doctrine of the Trinity. The book was severely criticized, and Servetus promised to publish a recantation. His recantation was published in 1532 under the title, *Dialogues on the Trinity*, but it was clearly not a recantation. Although he expressed his views more moderately and stated that the arguments in his first book were not well thought out, he did not actually recant the theological position presented in that book. As a result he had to leave Strasbourg, spending the next twenty years in France, where he studied medicine and published a book that became a best seller. He may also have made significant contributions to the discovery of the pulmonary circulation of blood. Servetus clearly had a promising future in medicine, but he could not resist again becoming involved in theological controversy. In 1546 he began to correspond with Calvin, beginning with polite doctrinal queries that eventually turned into very hostile exchanges.

When Servetus sent Calvin copies of some papers he was writing on infant baptism, Calvin sent him pages from the *Institutes* dealing with the subjects in question. Servetus returned them with annotations showing where Calvin was wrong along with an account of his own views on the Trinity. Calvin was furious with what he called Servetus's "arrogant boasting," and when Servetus expressed an interest in coming to Geneva, Calvin remarked in a letter to Farel, "Servetus lately wrote to me and coupled with his letter a long volume of his delirious fancies. . . . He takes it upon himself to come hither, if it be agreeable to me. But I am unwilling to pledge my word for his safety, for if he shall come I will never permit him to depart alive."[53]

These were ominous words, but Servetus was not deterred. He wrote another book entitled *Restitution of Christianity*, which he sent to Calvin and in which he questioned doctrines concerning the Trinity, original sin, infant baptism, and justification by faith. He also attacked Calvin. Following this, he was arrested and imprisoned for heresy in France, Calvin's information possibly resulting in the local authorities taking action against him.

Servetus managed to escape by climbing over a garden wall and decided to go to Italy. Unfortunately for him, he took the route through Geneva, and on Sunday he decided to go to church to hear Calvin preach. He was recognized at the service, arrested, and brought to trial. Convicted and facing execution, he drew up his own charges against Calvin, whom he described as an evil sorcerer who deserved execution. He did not help his case by the abusive language he used against Calvin, whom he called a "worthless and shameless twister,"[54] and it is not surprising that he was convicted of heresy. Although Calvin endeavored to have Servetus beheaded rather than burned at the stake, this effort was not successful, and on 27 October 1553 Servetus, accompanied to the stake by Farel, who urged him at every step to recant, was burned to death. The Geneva Council justified this ultimate punishment because of the threat that they maintained Servetus's teaching posed to the eternal salvation of many souls. The charge read in part: "He blasphemes detestably against the Son of God, saying that Jesus Christ is not the Son of God from eternity. He calls infant baptism an invention of the devil and sorcery. His execrable blasphemies are scandalous against the majesty of God, the Son of God and the Holy Spirit. This entails the murder and ruin of many souls."[55]

Although future generations have judged Calvin harshly for his role in the Servetus affair, in his own age most people praised him, and it helped him win the day in Geneva. Even Melanchthon, who was known for his gentleness, congratulated him, stating: "I have read your writing in which you have clearly refuted the horrible blasphemes of Servetus.... I maintain that your magistrates acted with justice in having put to death a blasphemer, after having regularly judged the affair."[56] The one strident voice of criticism came from Sebastian Castellio, whose book *Should Heretics Be Persecuted?* condemned the burning of Servetus. Castellio argued that those who claim to be followers of Jesus Christ should deal with others in love and mercy, as he did. This certainly meant that the burning of heretics could not be justified, and, although Castellio did not accept Servetus's views, he argued for freedom of expression and tolerance of diverse views. Today we have no trouble recognizing that Castellio was right, but in the sixteenth century Calvin's action had much more support than Castellio's plea for tolerance. We need to be careful in judging Calvin by the standards of future generations—he was simply accepting the standards of his age. All the Reformers accepted the death penalty as legitimate punishment for serious crimes, and all but Luther accepted that it should be applied to heretics. A large number of people were burned at the stake throughout the Reformation period, but Servetus was the only person executed in Geneva for his religious opinions during Calvin's lifetime.[57] Furthermore, it was the Geneva Council, and not Calvin, who condemned Servetus to death, although clearly Calvin approved.

Although Servetus's execution earned Calvin the reproach of future generations, in his own time it gained him a good deal of support. It clearly enhanced his reputation as a defender of orthodoxy among Protestants and helped to discredit his opponents, but it did not immediately lead to the triumph of his policy. In fact, in November 1553 the Council of Two Hundred stated unequivocally that the final decision on excommunication and excluding people from the Lord's Supper should rest with the council. Calvin, of course, would not accept this, and the struggle dragged on. But with Calvin's increased prestige, the balance of power was shifting, and in the February 1554 elections, Calvin's supporters won an overwhelming victory. One reason for the growing political strength of Calvin's friends was that French émigrés had been granted the right to vote. Between 1550 and 1650 the population of Geneva increased from 13,100 to 21,400, largely as a result of Protestant refugees fleeing persecution in their own countries. The majority of the refugees were from France, where many had been quite well-to-do. They were also well-educated and of high social standing, so the Geneva authorities, who were struggling with financial problems, saw the advantage of tapping the resources of these prosperous Frenchmen. Consequently, in April 1555 they were given bourgeois status, including the right to vote.

At the same time, the opposition to Calvin became involved in an affair that thoroughly discredited them and led to the exile or execution of their main leaders. On the evening of 16 May 1555, a group of Calvin's opponents, including Perrin, gathered in two taverns for supper. Upset by their political losses and fearful of the growing French émigré influence, they engaged in angry rhetoric. Finally, fortified by good food and too much drink, they took to the streets, setting out to burn down a house they believed was full of armed Frenchmen. It was neither a planned conspiracy nor a major uprising, and they quickly dispersed when ordered to do so by the authorities. However, their actions were seen by Calvin and his supporters as an effort to overthrow the Geneva government and slaughter the French refugees; therefore, the so-called conspirators were arrested, brought to trial, and sentenced to death for treason. Perrin and some of the leaders fled the city, so their sentences could not be carried out, but others paid the supreme price for their folly.

Calvin had now definitively won the day in Geneva. Even before that victory, he had already succeeded in winning the battle over the right of excommunication. Although the council had stated in November 1553 that the right rested finally in their hands, Calvin and the Consistory continued to fight that decision. In January 1555 they got the Geneva councils to agree that they would abide by the Ecclesiastical Ordinances, which, in fact, confirmed the existing practice and meant that the Consistory would have the final word on excommunication.

Another essential part of Calvin's program was also achieved in the last decade of his life—the establishment of the Geneva Academy as a place to provide the education that Calvin believed was essential to his program. Although earlier he had tried hard to get the council to act on this matter, it was unwilling to provide the necessary funding until January 1558. It took another year to establish the academy, but on 5 June 1559 it was opened with Theodore Beza as the first rector. The academy flourished in the years that followed, and within five years there were one thousand students in the preparatory college and three hundred in the academy. Most of the students were foreigners, and, as might be expected, in the first four years 114 of the 160 students came from France. The majority of them were pastors who would go back to France to pastor the Calvinist churches in their homeland.

Calvin only achieved these successes at the very end of his life, and he died five years after the founding of the Geneva Academy. Like Luther,

Calvin suffered from ill health much of his life, and as he grew older the problems became more severe. Although he continued to carry on his ministry despite his frequent illnesses, he became increasingly weak. He no longer attended the Consistory meetings regularly, and on 6 February 1564 he preached his last sermon. On 6 April he wrote to Bullinger describing his physical condition:

> Although the pain in my side is abated, my lungs are so full of phlegm that my breathing is difficult and short. A stone in my bladder has been very troublesome for the last twelve days. An ulcer in the haemorrhoid veins tortures me even when sitting down or lying in bed, so that I could not bear the agitation of riding. Within the last three days the gout has also been very troublesome. You will not be surprised, then, if so many sufferings make me lazy. I can hardly be brought to take any food. The taste of wine is bitter.[58]

On 27 April Calvin met with the members of the Little Council for a final admonition and prayer for divine guidance in their governance of the city. He thanked them for all they had done for him and asked them to excuse him "for having performed so little in public and in private compared with what I ought to have done." He also thanked them for "having borne patiently with my vehemence, which was sometimes carried to excess."[59]

The following day, Calvin called his fellow ministers to his bedside, and in a long, rambling address he described the hardships he had experienced in his ministry and his effort to teach correct doctrine and to interpret the Scriptures accurately. He urged them to remain at peace with one another, avoiding "bickerings or sharp words." He also urged them not to make changes or innovations, not because he wanted "out of ambition that what I have established should remain and that people should retain it without wishing for something better, but because all changes are dangerous and sometime hurtful."[60] In a poignant farewell, each of the ministers shook his hand before leaving. Calvin died on 27 May and was, as he requested, buried in an unmarked grave.

Theodore Beza

Calvin was succeeded by the man who would later write his first biography, Theodore Beza. In the latter years of his life, Calvin and Beza had become close friends, and in his final address to the Genevan ministers Calvin urged them to support Beza, "for the charge is great and so weighty that he might well sink under the load."[61] There was, in fact, little danger of that happening because Beza was more than adequate for the challenges that faced him as Calvin's successor. He was eight years younger than Calvin, but his background was similar. He was born in France, the son of a member of the minor nobility, and like Calvin, he studied law and became enamored of humanist studies. In 1539 he moved to Paris to pursue his humanist interests, but rather than becoming a humanist scholar, he was converted to the Reformed faith and the course of his life changed dramatically. In 1548 he fled to Geneva, but because there were no openings for him there, he accepted a call to teach Greek at the Lausanne Academy and later became its rector.

Beza became the first rector of the Geneva Academy in 1559 and remained in Geneva for the rest of his life. As a close friend of Calvin and spokesman for the Reformed cause at the Colloquy of Poissy in 1551, which sought to bring peace to the church in France, he was Calvin's logical successor (see chapter 14 for a discussion of the colloquy). He became the moderator of the Venerable Company of Pastors and held that post until 1580. Beza played a major role in the definition and expression of Calvinist thought in the second half of the sixteenth century, and many of the beliefs that would later be identified as "Calvinism" stemmed from his teaching. He would also be one of the leaders in the religious colloquies that sought to heal the breach between Lutherans and Calvinists and in the colloquies and synods that took place in France in the period of the religious wars. He continued to be productive even in his declining years, publishing a treatise on the Lord's Supper in 1593 and serving as professor in the academy until 1599. Six years later, he died in Geneva at the age of eighty-four.

Calvinism

Although Calvin did not want a personality cult to develop around him and certainly did not approve of his followers being called by his name, after his death the term *Calvinist* came into common use to describe those who followed his teachings. Calvin's Lutheran opponents, concerned about the inroads Calvin's teachings were making in Germany, first devised the term *Calvinism* as a way to distinguish the Reformed faith from Lutheranism. Although Calvin objected to the use of his name to describe his followers, at the time the term was first used he was close to death, and his protest went unheeded. Thus the term

Calvinism came into common usage to describe the beliefs of those who held to the Reformed faith. In the second half of the sixteenth century that faith spread throughout much of Europe, with France the first area to be heavily affected. In Calvin's lifetime perhaps ten thousand refugees came to Geneva, the vast majority of them from France, and some later returned to aid in the establishment of Calvinism in their homeland. Although Calvin did not initially encourage the organization of Reformed churches in France, after 1555 there was a rapid and massive spread of Calvinism. In 1562 it is estimated there were as many as 1,750 French congregations, with a membership of about two million people—approximately 10 percent of the French population. Calvinism made its greatest impact among artisans in the urban areas and among the nobility; in some areas as many as 40 percent of the nobles became Calvinists. Between 1555 and 1562 Geneva sent to France at least eighty-eight ministers who had come to Geneva as refugees and were trained in pastoral and preaching work. When, after 1552, French Calvinists were faced with suppression by the government, Calvin would not sanction resistance unless it was led by princes of the blood. Although Calvinism was not especially militant during Calvin's lifetime in its political philosophy of resistance to those who persecuted them, after his death French Calvinists became more radical, especially after thousands of them were slaughtered in 1572 in the St. Bartholomew's Day Massacre.

Calvinism also spread to German states and cities, including the Palatinate, Nassau, Brandenburg, Wesel, and Bremen, although it was not accepted as a legal religion until 1648. Lutherans were particularly alarmed when Frederick III, Elector of the Palatinate, adopted the Reformed faith in 1561 because he was one of the seven electors who elected the emperor. He subsequently dismissed all Lutheran ministers and theologians and replaced them with Calvinists, and in 1563 two of his theologians, Kaspar Olevianus (1536–1587) and Zacharias Ursinus (1534–1583), prepared the Heidelberg Catechism, which was to become one of the standard Reformed catechisms. Calvinism also made inroads into the eastern part of Europe, including Hungary and Poland, and was particularly successful in the Netherlands, where Lutheran influence had initially been strong but Calvinism began to spread in the 1550s. In the 1560s the Low Countries were thrown into religious war as the Spanish overlords sought to suppress the Calvinist movement (see chapter 14 for a discussion of the war). Calvinism also spread to the British Isles; when the English Protestant religious settlement was finally established in Elizabeth's reign, its theology could be described as moderate Calvinism. Some of the most committed English Calvinists were those people we

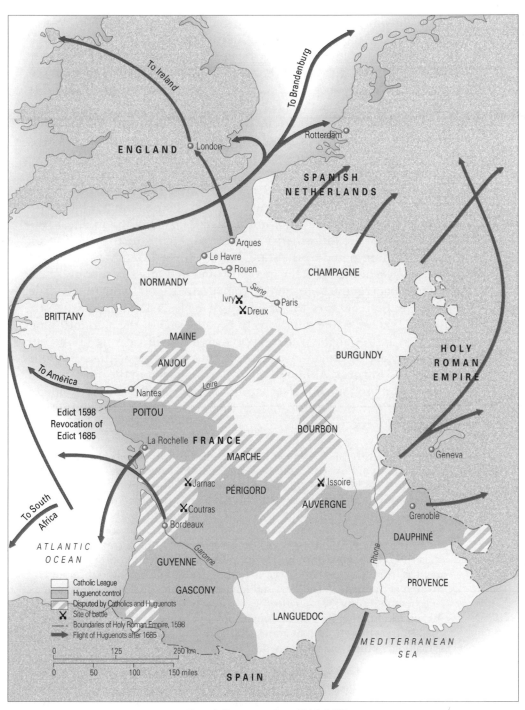

French Protestantism 1560–1683.

call the Puritans, who eventually spread Calvinism to the New World, where it would have a massive influence. Scotland at the same time became strongly Calvinist, under the leadership of John Knox.

After this brief overview of the spread of Calvinism, we return to the quest with which we began this chapter. Calvin was an able and humble man but like Luther had his share of faults, and his actions are not always easy to defend. He fought a long and hard battle to turn Geneva into what his disciple John Knox would call the "most perfect school of Christ that ever was in this earth since the days of the apostles."[62] Although many would question this description of Geneva, many dedicated men and women saw in Geneva an ideal to be copied and tried to introduce what Calvin had achieved in Geneva in their home countries. Calvin's achievements in Geneva were impressive;[63] possibly the greatest was that he alone of the Reformers was successful in protecting the church from being dominated by the state. He also turned Geneva into a great center for spreading the Reformed faith and in doing so probably had a greater impact on the Reformation than even Luther. In the first decade of the twentieth century the professor of ecclesiastical history at Yale, Williston Walker, wrote what was to become one of the standard biographies of John Calvin. Walker appreciated Calvin's strong points but was also aware of Calvin's weaknesses, and he wrote with scrupulous honesty and fairness. Although many have engaged in the quest for the "historical Calvin" since Walker wrote his biography, his description of Calvin remains a perceptive analysis that presents a useful summary of Calvin's major motivation:

> Whether friend, disciple, or foe, none could fail to recognize Calvin's transcendent ability. He might be slandered, the worst of motives might be imputed to him by traducers, but none who knew him could doubt his devotion to his cause. With all his frequent arrogance towards men, Calvin's spirit was humble towards God. To do and to teach his will was undoubtedly his prime intention; and if Calvin too often identified the divine purpose with his own wishes the error does not detract from the sincerity of his consecration. He submitted to his long bodily enfeeblement as from the wise hand of God. In the crises of his life, his conversion, his first settlement in Geneva, and his return to the difficult ministry in that turbulent city, he sacrificed ease, scholarly honours, and personal inclination to what he deemed the imperative voice of God. He put God first. In the strength of that conviction that God had chosen his task, he fought his battles and did his work.[64]

8

ORIGINS OF THE ENGLISH REFORMATION

▼

> Be it enacted by the authority of this present Parliament that the King our sovereign lord, his heirs and successors kings of this realm, shall be taken, accepted and reputed the only supreme head on earth of the Church of England.
>
> English Parliament, Act of Supremacy[1]

The above legislation, enacted by the English Parliament in 1534, illustrates one of the central differences between the English Reformation and the other European sixteenth-century Reformations. The statute, which is entitled the Act of Supremacy, declared that the head of the state was also the head of the church in England. Although, as we have noted, the Reformers accepted state control of the church—with the important exception of Geneva—only in England was it decreed in such an explicit manner by the legislative body of the state. According to the wording of the act, the king had always been the supreme head of the English church, but the papacy had usurped that power; therefore, Parliament was setting things right by ordering that the king and his successors be "taken, accepted and reputed the only supreme head on earth of the Church of England." Although, as we shall see, religious motivations were not entirely absent, the needs of the state were the primary consideration in the legislation that initiated the English Reformation, and each stage of the Reformation was legislated by Parliament. In 1941 Maurice Powicke began what would become one of the standard brief studies of the English Reformation with the following comment:

> The one definite thing which can be said about the Reformation in England is that it was an act of State. The King became the head of the Church, the King in Parliament gave a sanction to the revised organization, formularies, liturgy, and even in some degree to the doctrine of the Church. The King's Council and Ministers took cognizance of ecclesiastical affairs. The King co-operated with the bishops and convocation in the government of the church and he appointed commissions to determine appeals in ecclesiastical cases.[2]

Although Powicke described the initial stages of the English Reformation accurately, historians continue to debate why these events took place as well as their impact on the English people and the English church.

The Debate about the English Reformation

Before the rise of what has been labeled "revisionism," the standard interpretation of the English Reformation was found in A. G. Dickens's classic work, *The English Reformation*, first published in 1964.[3] Dickens maintained that religious motivations played an important role in bringing about the English Reformation and that the late medieval church in England was in dire need of reform. For Dickens, the late medieval movement called Lollardy[4] provided evidence of anticlericalism and widespread dissatisfaction with the church that reflected the attitude of many English people. Although Lollardy was not strong enough or widespread enough to produce the Reformation on its own, Dickens argued that it was a forerunner of the sixteenth-century Reformation. In addition, the impact of the Continental Reformations spawned a nascent Protestant movement centered largely in the universities, and many people were attracted by the Protestant doctrine of justification by faith alone. Although King Henry VIII, who broke with Rome largely over his marital problems, would have been satisfied with a settlement that was Catholic but rejected the papacy, Protestantism had already made significant inroads in England by the time of the king's death. In the reign of his son, Edward VI, a full-scale Protestant Reformation was introduced, but when Edward died, Henry's oldest daughter, Mary, tried to restore Roman Catholicism. She failed because she misunderstood her people, whom she thought would be eager for the return of the old faith. When this did not prove to be the case, she turned to persecution, which not only failed to eradicate Protestantism but also undermined the last hope that Roman Catholicism had in England. It is, therefore, not surprising that her sister, Elizabeth, who understood the English people in a way that Mary never did, was able to introduce an enduring Protestant settlement. Despite opposition from the revitalized Roman Catholicism of the Catholic Reformation and the more zealous Protestants who were not satisfied with the settlement, the Elizabethan Settlement survived.

Dickens's interpretation was first seriously challenged by J. J. Scarisbrick's Ford Lectures in 1982, published two years later under the title *The Reformation of the English People*. Christopher Haigh and Eamon Duffy joined Scarisbrick in questioning Dickens's interpretation, presenting the major revisionist arguments in a number of well-received works.[5] They maintained that the late medieval church was very popular among the general population and in the process of being reformed. Protest movements such as Lollardy were insignificant, and Protestantism had made little progress in England before the king became involved. Consequently, when Henry VIII broke with the pope, he had to impose his Reformation on an unwilling nation, and he almost failed. In his son's reign, Protestantism was only a thin veneer over the basic Catholicism of the English people, and so Mary was welcomed and her effort to restore Catholicism would have succeeded had she lived long enough. Unfortunately for the Catholic cause, Mary reigned for only five years, while her sister, Elizabeth, had almost half a century to impose her religious settlement on the kingdom. Even then Elizabeth did not have complete success. According to Haigh, at the end of her reign she had created "not a united Protestant England, but a deeply divided England."[6]

Revisionism has stimulated a great deal of research into areas that had been somewhat neglected, and it has helped to encourage new approaches to research.[7] These studies reveal that the English Reformation was a good deal more complex than either Dickens or the revisionists imagined. The so-called "postrevisionists" have pointed out the weaknesses in the arguments of both sides in the debate. They maintain that too often revisionists have failed to appreciate the real attraction of Protestant doctrines such as justification by faith, while Dickens, who clearly recognized that appeal, failed to give adequate attention to the continuing strength of Roman Catholicism. While the new generation of scholars accepts the revisionist argument that the Catholic hold on the majority of the population was strong and that most people were satisfied with their religion, they also recognize that anticlericalism did play a significant role in the English Reformation. Furthermore, the English monarchy, which did not have a standing army, a bureaucracy, or a paid police force, was incapable of imposing its will on the kingdom without the cooperation of the power elite who served as its law-enforcement officials and who sat in Parliament. While postrevisionists agree that England did not become a Protestant country until after 1570, they believe there were a significant number of Protestants in England before 1559. They also stress that those who were converted to the Reformed faith had distinct advantages over the majority who remained loyal to medieval Catholicism in the positions they held, their commitment, and their conviction that God was on their side.[8] The account of the English Reformation presented in this chapter and the following one attempts to combine insights found in Dickens, the revisionists, and the postrevisionists to present a balanced picture that takes into consideration the most recent scholarship.

Lollardy and Anticlericalism

The debate over the English Reformation stimulated a renewed interest in the study of Lollardy, which was once considered a forerunner of the Reformation.[9] We have already noted its origins in the teachings of John Wycliffe, and although he died in 1384, his followers continued to promulgate his teachings. In 1394 a group of knights formulated what were called the Twelve Conclusions, which provided a statement of Lollard beliefs that were presented to Parliament. They were stridently anticlerical and condemned many of the practices of the late medieval church, including the subordination of the English church to Rome. They maintained that the church had "been blind and leprous many years by the maintenance of a proud prelacy."[10] Although Lollardy initially had some support at court, its demands were far too radical to be given serious consideration, and in the years that followed, Lollards began to suffer serious persecution.

In 1401 a statute with the descriptive title "The Statute on Burning Heretics" was enacted, and when a Lollard nobleman, Sir John Oldcastle, sought to seize power in 1414, the movement was thoroughly discredited. Despite persecution, however, Lollardy survived as an underground movement, surreptitiously circulating copies of the Bible in English—

which Lollards had translated—and other Lollard works. It is difficult to determine the number of Lollards because they met in secret and normally continued to attend their parish church. They placed a strong emphasis on preaching, and their central concern was that a vernacular Bible should be in the hands of the laity. One of their most remarkable achievements was the production of a sermon cycle, consisting of two sermons for each Sunday as well as sermons for special days in the church year.[11] There is very little evidence of Lollardy during the period 1430–1460, perhaps because the Wars of the Roses diverted the attention of the authorities. However, in the first decades of the sixteenth century a series of prosecutions initiated by bishops uncovered a number of Lollard cells. The renewed persecutions resulted in thirty-five executions and revealed that Lollardy had survived in some of the major population centers of England including London, Bristol, East Anglia, Kent, and East Sussex as well as the Chilterns and Cotswolds.

Despite an abundance of new research,[12] it is still difficult to know how strong Lollardy was in the first quarter of the sixteenth century and to determine its impact on the Reformation. Since our knowledge of the movement is based to a great extent on heresy trials, it may be that there were many Lollards who were not discovered by the authorities and that the court records reveal only the tip of the iceberg. On the other hand, revisionists maintain Lollardy was a tiny minority movement that had little impact on the Reformation.[13] In some areas trial records reveal that Lollardy was especially strong among wealthy and influential people. Furthermore, in areas such as Amersham possibly as many as 10 percent of the population were Lollards.[14] Although Lollardy was not strong enough or widespread enough to pose a substantial danger to the church or to suggest that the majority of the English people were dissatisfied with the church or anticlerical, Lollards in some respects did anticipate the Reformation. Although they did not teach the major Reformation doctrine of justification by faith alone, their emphasis on reading the Bible in the vernacular and preaching, as well as their anticlericalism, all may have helped prepare the ground for the English Reformation.

Revisionists believe that the majority of the English people were happy with their church, and they have provided a substantial amount of evidence to document that conclusion.[15] However, clearly there were substantial numbers of people in late medieval England who were very critical of the church and its clergy, and it is normally a minority who initiate a revolution. Although the Lollards were the most radical critics of the church, others were also so strident in their attacks on both the church and the clergy that it was once assumed that the English were generally anticlerical in the years preceding the Reformation. Although some serious questions have been raised about the degree of English anticlericalism, one has to ignore or explain away a good deal of evidence to argue that it was nonexistent.[16] Criticism of the clergy was common, and some of the most widely read works of the pre-Reformation period, such as William Langland's *Vision of Piers Plowman* and Geoffrey Chaucer's *Canterbury Tales*, presented the clergy in a most unfavorable light. The clergy were often criticized in sermons, and moral Reformers were sometimes especially critical. Reformers such as Thomas Gascoigne, the chancellor of Oxford University in the mid-fifteenth century, William Melton, Chancellor of York in the sixteenth century, as well as the humanist reformer, John Colet, described the failings of the clergy in specific terms. Although revisionists question whether committed Reformers can be trusted to present an accurate picture of the clergy's moral state, the consistent criticism of the clergy in the pre-Reformation period suggests a degree of anticlericalism in elements of the population in England.[17]

Humanism and Early English Protestantism

Among the most persistent critics of the clergy were the English humanists. The first generation learned their skills in Italy, where a number of them studied during the reign of King Henry VII (1485–1509). When Erasmus first came to England in 1499, he was greatly impressed with the men of learning he met there. During that visit he wrote to a friend in Italy:

> I now scarcely miss Italy, but for the sight of it. When I listen to my friend Colet, I seem to hear Plato himself. Who would not marvel at the perfection of the encyclopedic learning in Grocyn? What could be keener or nobler or nicer than Linacre's judgement? What has Nature ever fashioned gentler or sweeter or happier than the character of Thomas More? But why should I catalogue the rest? It is marvellous how thick upon the ground the harvest of ancient literature is here everywhere flowering forth.[18]

The men Erasmus mentioned would become some of the leading figures in English humanism during the reign of King Henry VIII (1509–1547). Although Erasmus never learned to speak English, he returned to England a number of times and had a significant impact on the development of English humanism, and some of the men he mentioned in his letter also influenced him. During his second visit to England in 1505, John Colet (1467–1519) encouraged Erasmus to make his translation of the New Testament. Between 1510 and 1513, while he was working on his translation, Erasmus lectured at Cambridge, where he influenced a new generation of English humanists.

Although some humanists acquired high positions in the English church, they continued to be critical of its failings. Colet became the dean of St. Paul's Cathedral in London and used his position to encourage church reform. Shortly after Henry VIII ascended the throne, Colet preached a sermon in which he castigated the worldliness of the clergy, calling for "the reformation of the Church's estate" and maintaining that "nothing hath so disfigured the face of the Church as hath the fashion of secular and worldly living in clerks and priests."[19] John Fisher (1469–1535), who became bishop of Rochester in 1504, was equally critical in his sermons of the failings of the clergy. Some humanists also rose to high positions in the state. Sir Thomas More (1477–1535) chose to follow a legal career, eventually becoming Henry VIII's chancellor. Erasmus wrote *In Praise of Folly* at More's house and dedicated it to him. In the year before the publication of Luther's *Ninety-five Theses*, More published his best-known work, *Utopia*, which portrayed an ideal commonwealth in a tolerant society.

The years preceding the beginning of the Reformation on the Continent were the halcyon days of English humanism. The men associated with the movement were often close friends who admired Erasmus and his scholarship. They freely pursued their own scholarship, criticizing the church as well as scholastic theology, while debating academic and theological questions in the congenial atmosphere of More's house in Chelsea. When the Reformation began, the comfortable world of humanism was thoroughly disrupted, and the humanists had to make a choice between the new theology and the old. Conservatives such as More and Fisher had no trouble making their choice; they now turned their literary skills against the teaching of the Reformers and wrote fiercely polemical tracts in opposition to Reformation theology, as well as attacking Luther personally. However, when their king broke with Rome, they faced a much more difficult decision. They eventually suffered martyrdom for the church they had once freely criticized.

As we know, Erasmus also broke with Luther, but others who were schooled in that same humanist tradition became the first generation of English Protestants. They were largely centered at the universities, especially at Cambridge where Erasmus had taught, and a group of them met regularly to discuss the new theology at a pub in Cambridge called the White Horse Inn. Although "there were few if any strict Lutherans" in England, "we can nevertheless discern signs of broadly 'evangelical' influence in Cambridge from the mid-1520s onwards."[20] Many of the first generation of English Protestants also died as martyrs, and their stories were included in the account by John Foxe (1517–1587) of the English Reformation, popularly called the *Book of Martyrs*.[21]

Thomas Bilney (1495–1531) was the first Protestant martyr. He had a humanist background and was, according to his own testimony, attracted to Erasmus's Latin translation of the New Testament because he wanted to read good Latin, but in reading the New Testament he came to believe the doctrine of justification by faith alone. According to Foxe, Bilney was "a godly man . . . but of little stature" and a "great preacher." He was responsible for the conversion of a number of other early Protestants, including Hugh Latimer (1485–1555), who called Bilney "meek and charitable, a simple good soul not fit for this world."[22] Although he seems to have been orthodox in most doctrines, including transubstantiation, Bilney was arrested in November 1527 and convicted of heresy. Persuaded by his friends to recant, he was, nevertheless, imprisoned in the Tower for twelve months and only freed after reaffirming his recantation. As a sincere man of conscience, he was deeply troubled by his recantation, and he returned to preaching the doctrines that had led to his heresy conviction. This resulted in his being arrested once again, and as a relapsed heretic he was shown no mercy. In August 1531, after hearing mass and receiving the Eucharist, he was burned at the stake.

Bilney was responsible for the conversion of Robert Barnes (1495–1540), who also had a humanist background, having studied at Louvain at the same time that Erasmus was there. Barnes returned to England with a doctor of divinity degree and became prior of the Austin Friars in Cambridge. He seems to have been the unofficial leader of the group that met at the White Horse Inn, but in December 1525 he ran into trouble for a sermon he preached at St. Edward's Church, Cambridge, on Christmas Eve. Although he maintained he was not a Lutheran, he was brought to trial, convicted, and assigned to do public penance. He was also imprisoned, but when he learned he was to be burned, he tricked the authorities by writing a suicide note, leaving his clothes with the note, and pretended he had drowned himself.[23] While they dragged the river for his body, Barnes fled to the Continent. He eventually came to Wittenberg, where he became a friend of Luther and a convinced Lutheran. After Henry VIII broke with Rome, Barnes returned to England and was used by Thomas Cromwell in his effort to establish an alliance between England and the Lutheran princes. However, in the conservative reaction at the end of Henry VIII's reign, Barnes was accused of heresy and burned at the stake in July 1540.

The most significant of the early English Protestant martyrs was William Tyndale (1495–1536), because he was responsible for a new English translation of the Bible that was to play a critical role in the English Reformation. Tyndale was born in Gloucestershire and took his master's degree at Oxford in 1512. He then spent a brief time in Cambridge, but he does not appear to have been associated with the White Horse Inn group.[24] Tyndale was a very learned man who spoke seven languages and was also extremely independent, not becoming a follower of any one man. Rather, his major concern was to make the Bible available to the people of England in their own language. Tyndale explained that he was committed to translating the Bible into English because: "I had perceived by experience how that it was impossible to establish the lay people in any truth except the scriptures were plainly laid before their eyes in their mother tongue, that they might see the process, order and meaning of the text."[25]

Although manuscript copies of the Lollard translation continued to be circulated surreptitiously, it was an inadequate and inaccurate translation, having been made from the Latin Vulgate translation rather than the original languages. Tyndale was committed to producing a translation based on the original Greek and Hebrew texts of the Bible and one that would be printed so it could be published in large quantities. He initially offered his services to the humanist bishop of London,

Cuthbert Tunstall (1474–1559), who had aided Erasmus in his New Testament translation. In less tense times Tunstall might have been prepared to support Tyndale's project, but during these times, even a scholarly humanist like Tunstall was reluctant to support any project that might seem to encourage Luther's teaching.

Having been turned down in his effort to obtain church support for his translation, Tyndale turned to illegal means.[26] After

William Tyndale (1495–1536).
Illustration from Beza *Icones*.

acquiring financial support from some cloth merchants who were involved in importing Luther's works from the Continent, Tyndale went to Germany in April 1524 to work on his translation. In a little over a year the first copies of the New Testament were being printed in Cologne. The first print-run was almost confiscated by the authorities when one of the printers, who had drunk too much German beer, bragged about the work going on in his shop. Tyndale managed to escape with the printed sheets and took them to Worms, where the printing was completed in the spring of 1526. Within a short time copies were being smuggled into England, where the authorities tried to buy them and destroy them to get them off the market. Tyndale was quite happy to have them sold, even though he knew they were to be destroyed, because as he said, "The whole world will cry out upon the burning of God's word." Furthermore, he could use the money he received "to correct the said New Testament"[27] and print a better second edition.

Tyndale eventually moved to Antwerp, where he began the translation of the Old Testament in the safety of the English community and with support from English merchants. Before he died, he revised his New Testament translation at least twice, and in 1530 he translated the Pentateuch.[28] In May 1535 he was betrayed by a fellow Englishman named Henry Phillips, who was probably in the pay of the new bishop of London, John Stokesley. Phillips, who posed as Tyndale's disciple, tricked him into leaving the house where he was staying and led him out into the streets where two law officers were waiting in ambush. Tyndale was arrested, imprisoned, and condemned as a heretic. In October 1536 he was executed by being "strangled first by the hangman and afterwards with fire consumed." According to Foxe, as he died, he cried out in "a loud voice, 'Lord! Open the King of England's eyes.'"[29]

Although that never happened to the degree that would have satisfied Tyndale, his translation helped to "open the . . . eyes" of his countrymen to the Bible. He is rightfully called the father of the English Bible,[30] and his translation was truly a masterpiece that communicated the biblical message effectively and accurately. According to David Daniell's biography of Tyndale, "The 1526 New Testament . . . is triumphantly the work of a Greek scholar who knew that language well, of a skilled translator who could draw on the Latin of the Vulgate and Erasmus, and German, for help when needed, but above all of a writer of English who was determined to be clear, however hard the work of being clear might be. The word of God must speak directly in a way that can be understood by the reader alone."[31]

Tyndale also included prologues that presented an evangelical understanding of the text so the reader was likely to be influenced in a Protestant direction when reading the English Bible. By the time of his death Tyndale's New Testament was widely disseminated throughout England, and there is evidence that some of those who read it were clearly affected in the way Tyndale had hoped. Dickens illustrated this by citing a letter written by Robert Plumpton, who came from a family that would later be known for its Catholic commitment. In 1536 Plumpton sent his mother a copy of Tyndale's New Testament and wrote to her expressing his excitement about the doctrine found in the prologues that taught Luther's doctrine of justification by faith alone: "Dearly beloved mother in the Lord, I write not this to bring you into any heresy, but to teach you the clear light of God's doctrine. Mother you have much to thank God that it would please him to give you license to live until this time, for the gospel of Christ was never so truly preached as it is now."[32]

The King's Great Matter

While the Reformation theology was making its first converts in English universities and Tyndale was beginning work on his English translation, the official English reaction to the Reformation was what one might expect from a good Catholic country. In response to Pope Leo X's bull ordering that Luther's books be destroyed, a book burning was held at Cambridge. A far more elaborate book burning, attended by a host of English peers and bishops as well as foreign dignitaries, was held at St. Paul's in London on 12 May 1521. Henry VIII's reaction to Luther's theology was also extremely negative. He not only commissioned Fisher and More to write in opposition to Luther, but in 1521 he published his own response to Luther's *Babylonian Captivity* entitled *Assertio Septem Sacramentorum* (Defense of the Seven Sacraments), which earned him the title *fidei defensor* (defender of the faith).[33] Henry VIII had always been jealous of the king of France's title as "most Christian king" and was pleased that he could now call himself *fidei defensor*. However, he would be "defender of the faith" only so long as it did not conflict with what he considered the welfare of the kingdom he believed God had given him to rule. Less than a decade after Henry proudly accepted his new title, a conflict developed that eventually resulted in the legislation cited at the beginning of this chapter. As a result, King Henry VIII added another royal title that was an expression of his rebellion against papal authority, while still not giving up the title that the pope had awarded him. He would from then on be called "king of England and France, *Defender of the Faith*, Lord of Ireland and *in earth Supreme Head under Christ of the Church of England*."

The events that resulted in the legislation that granted Henry VIII his title as "Supreme Head" are related to a dynastic question. The so-called Wars of the Roses pitted the white rose of York against the red rose of Lancaster, as two rival families fought a protracted struggle for the throne of England. In 1485 an obscure Welshman named Henry Tudor was crowned King Henry VII after the Yorkist king, Richard III, was defeated and killed at the Battle of Bosworth Field. Henry Tudor, who had an extremely questionable legal claim to the throne, had become the leader of the Lancastrian party because the more legitimate claimants were killed in the course of the wars. Consequently, in order to secure the Tudor dynasty on the throne of England, Henry VII needed to win support by giving England good government and producing male heirs to continue the line. He was successful in both endeavors. Although Henry VII had two sons, by the time he died, his elder son, Arthur, had also died. Consequently, the hope of the Tudor dynasty and peace in England depended on his surviving son, who in 1509 was crowned King Henry VIII.

In contrast to his father, the seventeen-year-old new king was an impressive figure who looked as people expected a king to look. Henry VIII was tall, well-built, and, according to one contemporary description, "the handsomest potentate I ever set eyes on."[34] He was also an excellent athlete, a fine musician with a good voice, and a composer. He excelled at archery, was an excellent horseman, and competed successfully in tournament jousts. He also had a good intellect, had a grasp of theology, and could communicate in a number of languages. Soon after his father's death, Henry VIII married his brother's widow, Catherine of Aragon, the daughter of Ferdinand and Isabella of Spain. It was an excellent match because it tied the house of Tudor, with its questionable royal claim, to one of Europe's well-established dynasties. Since marriage to one's brother's widow was contrary to canon law, Henry had to acquire a papal dispensation before the marriage could take place. This was easily acquired, because Pope Julius II was happy to oblige one of Christendom's powerful new monarchs.

Henry VIII's reign began marvelously. He seemed to love his new queen, who was six years his senior, and the first years of their marriage were marked by an unending round of parties at which Catherine was always by her husband's side. At the same time Henry engaged in the favorite sport of English kings—war with France—and had a number of military successes.

The main thing that marred the early years of Henry's reign was Catherine's failure to bear a male heir. She had numerous pregnancies, which included a number of males, that ended in miscarriages, still-births, or early mortality. Finally in 1516 Catherine bore a child who survived—a girl whom they named Mary. Unfortunately, Mary did not solve Henry's problem because it was not at all clear that the English would accept a queen to rule the country. The last time a female succession was attempted, the country was torn apart by a terrible civil war,[35] so Henry still needed a male heir to assure a peaceful succession. After Mary's birth, he told the Venetian ambassador that they were still young and "if it was a daughter this time, by the grace of God the sons will follow."[36] However, sons did not follow, and by 1525 Catherine was no longer young and was considered past childbearing.

Henry VIII, who was an amateur theologian, found his answer to why Catherine had not been able to give him a male heir in the Bible. Leviticus 19:21 reads, "If a man take his brother's wife, it is an unclean thing, he hath uncovered his brother's nakedness; *they shall be childless*." Of course Henry was not childless, but he conveniently overlooked that weakness in his argument as he convinced himself that God was punishing him for living in sin with his deceased brother's wife. He also had a ready solution to his problem. In 1527 he commissioned his chancellor, Thomas Wolsey (1473–1530), to secure an annulment of his marriage from Pope Clement VII (1523–1534). Under normal circumstances, the pope would have been only too willing to oblige a monarch who had been so loyal to Rome, but in the same month that Wolsey began the process that should have resulted in an annulment, the troops of Emperor Charles V sacked the city of Rome. The pope, who was now practically a prisoner of the imperial army, could not risk offending the emperor, who as Catherine of Aragon's nephew was not prepared to have his aunt's marriage declared invalid. Clement was in an impossible position, so for two years he delayed, hoping something would occur that would resolve his dilemma.[37]

Initially Henry VIII's desire to end his marriage to Catherine seems to have been motivated by his conviction that his marriage was contrary to God's law and by his concern for a peaceful succession, so that his people would not again have to experience the horrors of civil war. However, in the same year that he began the procedure to annul his marriage, another less noble motivation complicated the situation. The thirty-six-year-old monarch fell in love with a twenty-year-old lady at court named Anne Boleyn (1507–1536). She was not a great beauty,[38] and a marriage to Anne would not bring England any political benefits. Wolsey, who hoped Henry would marry a French princess, was totally opposed, but Henry was unrelenting in his pursuit of Anne. He even wrote her passionate love letters, which have survived and provide historians with the means of studying the development of their relationship.[39] It is clear from the letters that Anne was coy in the way she responded to the king's affections and was not prepared to give in to his desire for a sexual relationship outside of marriage.[40] Consequently, Henry became all the more anxious to end his marriage to Catherine so he could marry Anne, but the pope, out of necessity, continued to use delaying tactics.

The Henrician Reformation

In 1529 King Henry VIII called Parliament in an effort to put more pressure on the pope. This provided a forum for the church's critics to enact legislation reforming abuses such as pluralism and nonresidence that had long been criticized by Reformers. These statutes were the first in a number of acts passed by what has traditionally been called the "Reformation Parliament" because it enacted the legislation that gradually separated the English church from Rome. One of the most significant Reformation statutes was called the Act in Restraint of Appeals, which forbade appeals to courts outside the country for rulings made in English courts. This was justified because "this realm of England is an Empire," and therefore there was no jurisdiction superior to the jurisdiction of its government.[41] The act made it possible for an English court to annul the king's marriage without the danger that its decision might be appealed to Rome. This legislation was needed because in the early months of 1533 it was discovered that Anne was pregnant. It was now necessary to act very quickly so that the expected heir would not be illegitimate. In January 1533 Henry secretly married Anne, and in March Parliament passed the Act in Restraint of Appeals. On 23 May the archbishop of Canterbury's court declared that Henry VIII's marriage to Catherine was not valid, and on 1 June Anne Boleyn was crowned queen of England. All this was done with brilliant timing, because on 7 September the new heir was born. Unfortunately, for Henry there was one matter that the king and his advisers had not been able to control. To Henry and Anne's great disappointment, the baby was a girl, whom they named Elizabeth.[42] A year later Parliament passed the Act of Supremacy, and the first stage of the English Reformation was complete.

Henry VIII's marital problems had led to a Reformation in England that in its first stage involved little more than a change in the government of the church, as the king replaced the pope as the head of the church in England. The changes were accepted with relatively little resistance, but Henry showed no mercy to those who continued in their allegiance to the papacy. The best-known Catholic martyrs were John Fisher and Thomas More, both of whom were executed in 1535. By the time Henry VIII added his new royal title, he had two new advisers committed to a more radical Reformation. In 1533 Thomas Cranmer (1489–1556) was appointed archbishop of Canterbury and Thomas Cromwell (1485–1540) became the most important figure in the royal government. Both men were sympathetic to Protestantism and worked closely together to introduce evangelical doctrine into the first doctrinal statements of the English Reformation, the Ten Articles of 1536 and the Bishops' Book of 1537.[43] An extremely significant step that would aid in the spread of Protestant teaching was an order in the 1538 royal injunctions that a Bible in English be placed in every parish church.

The most disruptive event of the Henrician Reformation was the dissolution of the English monasteries. In 1535 Cromwell instituted a commission to investigate the state of the monastic houses in England. The report, which cited a significant number of moral lapses in the monasteries, provided justification for a parliamentary statute in March 1536 that ordered the lesser monasteries (those with an income of less than two hundred pounds a year) to be dissolved and their property ceded to the king.

THOMAS
CRANMER.

The dissolution of the monasteries helped set off the only major rebellion against the Henrician Reformation. Robert Aske, the leader of the revolt in Yorkshire, called it a "pilgrimage" to emphasize its religious motivations, but economic and social questions were also involved in the revolt. The Pilgrimage of Grace, which affected seven northern counties, lasted through the autumn and winter of 1536–1537. Despite the fact that the rebels raised an

Thomas Cranmer (1489–1556).
Illustration from Beza *Icones*.

army of thirty thousand, they quickly disbanded when the king promised to negotiate. Henry VIII used the excuse of a new revolt that broke out in January 1537 to take his vengeance on the rebel leaders. The Pilgrimage of Grace also helped bring about the final step in the dissolution of the monasteries, as the crown now put pressure on the abbots and priors of the larger monasteries, some of whom had supported the rebels, to surrender their properties to the crown. This was later confirmed by an act of Parliament. The dissolution involved a huge transfer of property from the church to the monarchy, and beginning in 1539, the crown sold or granted these lands to laymen, who now had a vested economic interest in not overturning the Henrician Reformation.

By the time the Pilgrimage of Grace began, both Catherine of Aragon and Anne Boleyn were dead. When Catherine died of natural causes in January 1536, Henry and Anne rejoiced, but Anne's joy was short-lived. In the same month that Catherine died, Anne miscarried, and the fetus was found to be male. The imperial ambassador reported that "the king had certainly shown great disappointment and sorrow."[44] Henry blamed Anne for failing to give him a male heir, and in the months that followed she clearly fell from the royal favor.[45] Henry also became increasingly suspicious of Anne and her relations with other men. In May 1536 five men, including her own brother, Viscount Rochford, were accused of adultery with the queen; Rochford was also accused of incest. They were all executed within the month, and on 19 May 1536 Anne was also executed.[46] The next day Henry was betrothed to Jane Seymour. He married her ten days later, and on 12 October 1537 she gave birth to the long-awaited male heir, who was named Edward. She had served the king and the kingdom well, but it cost her life. Twelve days after Edward's birth, Jane died from puerperal fever. Henry married three more times in the remaining decade of his life,[47] but he did not have any more children. The future of the English Reformation now lay in the hands of Henry's three children: Mary, Elizabeth, and Edward.

The final years of King Henry VIII's reign were characterized by what has often been called a conservative reaction, as Henry became concerned about the religious diversity that was beginning to appear in the kingdom. In November 1538 he issued a royal proclamation that complained of individuals "using some superstitious speeches and rash words of erroneous matters and fanatical opinions both in their preachings and familiar communication." The proclamation forbade the importation of English books or the printing of English books without official approval as well as the printing of Bibles in English with annotations or prologues. A draft proclamation drawn up in April 1539 lamented the disputes between factions "in church, alehouses, taverns and other places and congregations" and threatened parliamentary legislation to resolve the problem.[48] In the same year Parliament passed the Act of Six Articles, which the king revised in his own hand and which threatened those who denied transubstantiation with the death penalty and confiscation of their property, even if they recanted. It also stated that communion in one kind was sufficient for the laity; clerical celibacy, private masses, and auricular confession were to continue; and vows of chastity were to be kept. In July 1540 the conservative faction convinced the king that Thomas Cromwell was a heretic as well as a traitor, so he was removed from power and executed. At the same time others who had worked with him, such as Robert Barnes, were also executed for heresy. However, Thomas Cranmer survived, and when in January 1547 the king breathed his last, Archbishop Cranmer was at his bedside. Although Henry was noted for casting aside his servants when they no longer served his purposes, he never abandoned Cranmer, even protecting him when his conservative enemies sought to destroy him in the last years of the reign. Having survived Henry VIII's reign, Cranmer was in position to play a vital role in Henry's son's reign in preparing a fully Protestant settlement.

The Edwardian Reformation

Since Edward VI was only nine years old when his father died, a regency council made up of sixteen men chosen by the king was set up to rule in his stead. Shortly after Henry VIII's death, his councillors ignored the terms of his will and the boy king's uncle, Edward Seymour, the Duke of Somerset, became the Lord Protector. Somerset then controlled the government, and Cranmer led the church as archbishop of Canterbury. Both men were committed to a Protestant settlement, and the young king was fully supportive. At his coronation, Cranmer called upon Edward VI to imitate the Old Testament boy king, Josiah, who had inaugurated a religious reformation in ancient Israel and wiped out all aspects of pagan worship. Edward, who had been trained by humanist tutors sympathetic to Protestantism and who read his Bible daily, was only too happy to take up that role. However, his archbishop wisely moved cautiously in carrying out a program of reform, because support for a Protestant Reformation was still relatively limited.[49]

The fact that reform was introduced in gradual stages helped to avert the kind of resistance that might otherwise have developed. Rather than forcing unwelcome changes upon people, Archbishop Cranmer sought to change their minds and win their hearts through a program of instruction in evangelical theology, done partly through twelve homilies or sermons written by him. In July 1547 a series of injunctions was issued that ordered that these homilies, which taught the Reformation doctrine of justification by faith alone and stressed the sole authority of Scripture, be read in all parish churches every Sunday. Since the homilies were designed to educate the population in Reformation theology, competition from sermons that might teach otherwise was restricted and eventually entirely forbidden.[50] The injunctions also ordered that instruction in the creeds, the Lord's Prayer, and the Ten Commandments be given and that the Gospel and Epistle lessons be read in English.

More drastic reforms followed when Parliament met at the end of the year. Communion in both kinds was ordered, and the Six Articles as well as the heresy acts were repealed. The chantry endowments were confiscated, in a statute that specifically attacked the doctrine of purgatory. In 1548 ceremonies using candles, ashes, palms, holy bread, and holy water were ended, and it was ordered that images be taken out of the churches. Although these changes struck at the heart of popular religious practices, the most sensitive area of change involved the worship service and especially the Eucharist. A royal proclamation issued in December 1547 reveals the type of eucharistic debates that were occupying the English church. It complained that people were arguing about whether Christ's body and blood were present "really or figuratively, locally or circumscriptly, and having quantity and greatness or but substantially and by substance only, or else but in a figure and manner of speaking." Rather than probing "mysteries as lieth hid in the infinite and bottomless depth of the wisdom and glory of God," which "our human imbecility cannot attain," the proclamation ordered that people were to limit themselves to the clear words of Holy Scripture when discussing the Eucharist.[51]

Liturgical changes were introduced very cautiously and gradually because they were most likely to meet with resistance.[52] In December 1548 a four-day debate on the Eucharist was held in the House of Lords that revealed the deep divisions among the bishops. Although Cranmer no longer believed in Christ's corporal presence in the bread and wine,[53] when he put together the first English prayer book he avoided a clear statement of that doctrine which might unnecessarily offend conservatives.[54] Protestants and Catholics were not even agreed on what to call the sacrament. Roman Catholics called it the mass, but Protestants, as a rule, found that title too suggestive of Catholic doctrine, which they considered idolatrous. The title given to it in the 1549 prayer book reveals deliberate ambiguity about eucharistic theology as it is called "the supper of the Lord and the Holy Communion commonly called the mass."[55] The prayer book did not include a doctrinal statement, and even the catechism, which the book contained, did not discuss the sacraments. No specific statement on the Eucharist appeared until 1550, well after the publication of the first prayer book. In January 1549 Parliament approved the first English prayer book and ordered its use throughout the kingdom. It replaced a confusing mélange of books that had been used in the English church[56] and drew on the best liturgical traditions of the past as well as more modern Catholic and Protestant reform liturgies. While leaving no doubt on the essential doctrines of the Reformation, Archbishop Cranmer showed great moderation in balancing traditional and Reformed rites. Linguistically the prayer book has been hailed as a masterpiece. Peter Newman Brooks calls it "by any standards, a remarkable achievement," pointing out that Cranmer's "liturgy was not merely an English, or national, rite of the Reformation era, but a book of prayer and worship deeply rooted in the Catholic tradition of the Western Church."[57]

Beauty of language and a cautious approach to eucharistic theology were not sufficient to satisfy those who rightly felt the religion that had been so important to them was being undermined by the English prayer book. The people in the western counties, who sometimes did not even speak English, were offended by an exclusively English service. When the prayer book was introduced in Devon and Cornwall, the common people, often led by their priests, broke into open rebellion. The rebellion, sometimes called the Prayer Book Rebellion, lasted from June until August 1549, and although the rebels had economic and other complaints, religious concerns were dominant in the statement of grievances they drew up. Fortunately for the government, the gentry of the area did not support the rebellion, and therefore it was relatively easy to suppress. A considerably more serious rebellion, which was clearly motivated by economic grievances, broke out in the heartland of England in the spring and summer of the same year. It had its greatest success in East Anglia, where it was led by Robert Kett; consequently, it is often called Kett's Rebellion. For three weeks the rebels held the important city of Norwich, and although it also was eventually suppressed, the uprising led to the downfall of the Duke of Somerset, who was arrested and imprisoned in October 1549. Somerset was executed on trumped up charges of treason in January 1552.

John Dudley, Earl of Warwick and later Duke of Northumberland, now took over the leadership, and the Reformation continued in an aggressive manner. By the end of 1549 a royal circular to the bishops ordered destruction of all Latin service books. In the following year evangelicals replaced conservative bishops in six dioceses, and parish churches were stripped of altars, ornaments, and plate. In 1552 the Church of England also received a new liturgy because the 1549 prayer book did not please radical Protestants, who felt it was still "too Catholic." It may well be that Archbishop Cranmer had always intended to produce a second, revised, prayer book,[58] but he was committed to introducing liturgical change gradually.

Cranmer was assisted in the revision of the prayer book by the wise advice of Martin Bucer, who had fled Strasbourg at the time of the Augsburg Interim and was given a professorship at Cambridge.[59] Cranmer and Bucer had much in common, and Bucer had already assisted the archbishop of Cologne, Hermann von Wied, when he sought to introduce a moderate reformation in his diocese. Bucer chose his words carefully when he commented on the 1549 prayer book, stating that he "found nothing . . . which was not taken from the word of God, or at least upon a reasonable interpretation was not opposed to it." However, he stated that he had reservations about "a few small points which if they were not fairly interpreted might seem to be insufficiently consistent with the word of God."[60] Bucer discussed those "few small points" in an extended critique that has been labeled the *Censura*. Most of his suggestions were adopted in the revised prayer book, which eliminated the ambiguities in the 1549 prayer book and the ceremonies that might be interpreted in a Catholic sense. The new prayer book left no doubt about what to call the Eucharist, entitling it "The Lord's Supper or Holy Communion." It also moved away from a Lutheran interpretation of the Eucharist: the words said at the distribution of the elements were changed so that they stressed the memorial understanding of Christ's presence in the elements. The 1549 words, "The body of our Lord Jesus Christ which was given for you preserve your body and soul unto everlasting life," were changed to, "Eat this in remembrance that Christ died for you and feed on him in your hearts by faith with thanksgiving."[61]

Even that was not sufficiently clear for some radical Protestants. John Knox (1513–1572), who had come to England from Geneva in 1549, objected to the rubric that said that people should kneel at communion because he feared that this suggested a real presence of Christ in the elements. Therefore he argued for the insertion of a revised rubric that stated clearly that kneeling did not indicate an intention to adore the elements or the presence of Christ's natural body in the elements. When Cranmer was asked by the Privy Council to make this modification, he objected strongly. He wrote a very sharp letter to the Privy Council, which was somewhat out of character for Cranmer and indicated how strongly he felt about the matter: "I know your lordships' wisdom to be such that I trust ye will not be moved with these glorious and unquiet spirits, which can like nothing but that is after their own fantasy and cease not to make trouble and disquietness when things be most quiet and good order. If such men should be heard, although the book were made every year a new, yet should it not lack faults in their opinion."[62] Despite Cranmer's objections the rubric, called the Black Rubric (not as a value judgment but because of its color in the text), was inserted into the book.

By the end of King Edward VI's reign, those whom Cranmer called the "glorious and unquiet spirits" were agitating for more change. For example, when the Zwinglian Protestant John Hooper (d. 1555) was appointed bishop of Gloucester, he objected to the service specified in the new Ordinal of 1550, which retained the traditional vestments and included the saints in the oath of supremacy.[63] Once again Cranmer was confronted with more radical Protestants, who objected to his moderate pattern of reform. Although Hooper won the day on the question of the saints, which the young king deleted from the oath of supremacy with his own pen, he was coerced to use the vestments by the threat of imprisonment.

Archbishop Cranmer made one more contribution to the Edwardian Reformation before King Edward VI's death. He had hoped that a general council of Reformers would draw up a united doctrinal statement for a Reformed church, but when this failed to happen, he wrote his own statement of faith for the English church. Its Forty-two Articles avoided statements that might needlessly divide Protestants over issues on which the Bible was not entirely clear. The articles were, however, very clear in proclaiming the central Reformation doctrines of justification by faith and the sole authority of Scripture. The Forty-two Articles were promulgated in June 1553. Less than a month later they became irrelevant when King Edward VI died and his successor returned the Church of England to a pre-Reformation theology.

What was the impact of the Edwardian Reformation? Did England become a Protestant country during the five years of Edward VI's reign? In 1977 Geoffrey Elton wisely commented that "the question should really be not whether the Edwardian Reformation made England Protestant (an achievement for which it hardly had time), but whether Englishmen on the whole accepted or resisted the pressures to receive the Protestant faith." Whereas Elton maintained that "acceptance, varying from patient to eager, was the commonest reaction,"[64] revisionist historians have argued that resistance was more common and that Protestantism had made relatively little impact on the kingdom during Edward VI's short reign. Historians can find evidence for both points of view because the surviving documents make it very difficult to determine the religious beliefs of the average English person. As Norman Jones has pointed out, "One of the problems besetting historians of the Reformation is the refusal of the people they study to clarify their religion. Sometimes it seems that they had no idea what they believed in."[65] As might be expected, since it involved dramatic changes in religious belief and practice, there was resistance to the Edwardian Reformation. The second Edwardian prayer book included, for the first time, fines for nonattendance at church, probably out of concern that people would stay away from the new services. People also disrupted services and expressed their boredom openly when listening to the homilies, but the surprising thing is not that there was resistance to such a radical change in religion but that there was so little resistance. There seems to be little doubt that the people of England were divided in their religious beliefs at the end of Edward VI's reign. Although evangelicals clearly remained a minority, they had made an important impact in some of the most important areas in the kingdom, including the southeast and the Bristol area. Edward's successor, his half-sister Mary, would find that restoring Catholicism was not as easy as she might have hoped. She would also have trouble getting people to come to church, and people who were willing to surrender their lives rather than their faith would result in her being called "bloody Mary" by future generations.

The Marian Reaction

King Edward VI died on 6 July 1553 at the age of fifteen; one wonders how the history of England might have changed had Edward lived to adulthood. He was a brilliant young man and at the age of fourteen was already participating in government affairs. However, in May 1553 his health began to deteriorate rapidly, and in order to protect what had been achieved during his reign he cooperated in an effort to change the succession. His two half-sisters, Mary and Elizabeth, were excluded and Lady Jane Grey, the fourteen-year-old granddaughter of Henry VIII's younger sister, was declared his successor. On 21 May 1553 she was married to the son of John Dudley, Duke of Northumberland. The teen-age queen was so unprepared for the role she was being asked to play that she fainted when the council informed Jane that she was queen. She had good reason to be terrified, because the effort to change the succession was doomed to failure from the beginning. Even Protestants were not prepared to support a queen with a questionable legal claim to the throne in place of the legitimate heir. Consequently, Mary had little trouble deposing her rival, and even the Duke of Northumberland, who quickly realized that Jane's cause was hopeless, abandoned his daughter-in-law and proclaimed Mary queen on 20 July. It did not, however, save his life. Although Mary was initially generous in her treatment of those who had supported Jane, Northumberland was executed before Mary's reign was a month old. At his death, Mary scored her first victory in her effort to restore the old faith, as Northumberland recanted and confessed his heresy. Unfortunately for Mary's policy, the ease with which she achieved her first adjuration may have led her to believe that the commitment to their faith of other Protestants was equally shallow.

Mary was thirty-seven years old when she became queen, and to that point her whole life had been a tragedy through no fault of her own. She had seen her mother disgraced, and she was herself declared illegitimate and removed from the succession by act of Parliament. The father whom she loved had ignored her and forced her to pay homage to her sister, whom she considered a bastard. Unhealthy and unwanted as a child, Mary had lived her early adult life in the background, with her religion her only comfort. But now, as queen, she would have the chance to achieve her one great ambition in life and restore the church to its rightful position. She was confident that England was basically loyal to the old faith, and she fully expected to accomplish her task with limited opposition. Although she seems to have inherited the intelligence and governmental skills of the Tudors, her judgment was at times clouded by her deep religious commitment. In the end, she failed to achieve a lasting restoration of the Catholic faith in England, and historians have long debated why she failed in that effort. As might be expected, Protestants had a facile explanation for her failure. Foxe considered it the well-deserved judgment of God: "We shall never find any reign of any prince in this land or any other, which did ever show in it (for the proportion of time) so many great arguments of God's wrath and displeasure, as were to be seen in the reign of this queen Mary, whether we behold the shortness of her time, or the unfortunate event of all her purposes."[66]

Those who did not blame Mary's failure on her religious policies tended to blame it on her character weaknesses and her ineptness as a ruler. Geoffrey Elton reached a high point of invective when he called her "arrogant, assertive, bigoted, stubborn, suspicious and . . . rather stupid."[67] Catholic historians were, of course, more sympathetic. Revisionists are impressed with Mary's achievements in the brief period that she was queen and blame her early death as well as the failure to have an heir for her lack of success in achieving a more permanent restoration of Catholicism.[68]

Mary began her reign by informing her subjects that, although her "conscience is stayed in matters of religion," she did not intend to "compel or constrain other men's consciences" except as God would persuade them "through the opening of his word unto them by godly, virtuous and learned preachers."[69] However, when one of those "godly, virtuous and learned preachers" spoke at Paul's Cross the following day, he had to be rescued from an unruly mob who stormed the pulpit. Clearly not everybody was prepared to welcome the restoration of the old faith. The next time one of those "virtuous and learned preachers" preached in London, two hundred of the queen's guard surrounded the preacher, and the sermon proceeded without incident. Although some resisted Queen Mary's efforts to restore the old religion, most rejoiced and welcomed the return of the images, forms, and ceremonies that had been so important to their spiritual life, and in many places these were restored even before the government began its legislation on religion. John Hooper, who was imprisoned after Mary came to power, wrote to Bullinger from his prison cell in September 1553 expressing his distress at what was happening in England: "The altars are again set up throughout the kingdom; private masses are frequently celebrated in many quarters; the true worship of God, true invocation, the right use of sacraments, are all done away with; divine things are trodden under foot, and human things have pre-eminence."[70]

Initially Mary moved slowly and cautiously. Early in her reign a proclamation forbade unlicensed preaching, but the queen continued to insist that she did not intend to force her religion on anyone. Catholic bishops, some of whom had been imprisoned during Edward's reign, replaced Protestants in a number of dioceses, and some Protestant bishops exchanged their episcopal thrones for a prison cell, among them Archbishop Cranmer, Nicholas Ridley (1502–1555), Hugh Latimer (1485–1555), and John Hooper. They were arrested and imprisoned in the early months of Mary's reign on charges of treason, since the heresy laws had not yet been reinstated. When Parliament met in October

1553, it repealed the Edwardian religious legislation and reversed the annulment of Henry's marriage to Catherine of Aragon, thus absolving Mary of bastardy. Parliament was, however, not passively compliant in bowing to Mary's will. The repeal act was debated for five days, and a substantial number in the House of Commons voted against the legislation.[71] Furthermore, the Act of Supremacy was not repealed, and the heresy laws were not restored. Thus Mary had to live with the title she hated, "Supreme Head of the Church of England," until Parliament finally repealed the act at the end of 1554.[72] In March 1554 the queen issued a set of injunctions that, among other things, deprived all priests who had married during Edward's reign of their benefices.[73] The injunctions also ordered bishops to "diligently travail for the repressing of heresies and notable crimes, especially in the clergy, duly correcting and punishing the same."[74] This did not lead to rampant persecution, possibly because the heresy laws were not revived until the end of the year, and initially Mary was quite happy to allow Protestants to leave England. Approximately eight hundred men, women, and children left England to go into exile on the Continent. Since the Lutheran cities did not welcome them, most went to Zurich, Frankfurt, or Geneva.

Mary's major concern in the first year of her reign was to find a husband and proceed with the all-important task of producing an heir, which was vital for the future of Catholicism in England. Time was of the essence because of Mary's age, but there was little consensus on whom the queen should marry. Mary eventually decided for herself and negotiated a treaty with Emperor Charles V to marry his son, Prince Philip, who was later to become Philip II of Spain. Mary made her decision against the advice of her councillors and with the opposition of Parliament, who presented a petition to the queen in November 1553 urging her not to proceed with the Spanish marriage. Nevertheless, the marriage treaty was signed in January 1554. In the same month, opposition to Mary was expressed in a serious rebellion when about three thousand Kentish men, under the leadership of Thomas Wyatt, rose in revolt against Mary's policies and marched on London.

Although Wyatt was motivated partly by his Protestant sympathies, it seems that many of those who followed him were primarily responding to the fear of Spanish tyranny being imposed on England as an aftereffect of the match between Mary and Philip.[75] Wyatt came very close to ending Mary's reign less than a year after it had begun, but the queen courageously rallied her troops as the rebels stood at the gates of London, and the one serious rebellion Mary faced was defeated. After their defeat, Wyatt and about one hundred of his followers were executed.

Sadly, Lady Jane Grey and her husband, who had not even been involved in the rebellion, were also executed. The queen's half-sister, Elizabeth, whom the rebels had planned to put on the throne, was temporarily imprisoned in the Tower, but fortunately for the future of Protestant England, Mary did not execute her.

Prince Philip and Queen Mary were married in July 1554. Philip was eleven years her junior, and even though he was very attentive to his bride in public and she seems to have fallen in love with him, there is no indication that he returned that affection. He had married in obedience to his father, and as a dutiful son he did what was expected of him. Emperor Charles V, English Catholics, and the queen were delighted when it was announced at the end of November that Mary was pregnant; the future for Catholic England looked bright. Mary also rejoiced when in the same month Cardinal Reginald Pole (1500–1558) arrived in England[76] to absolve the realm formally of sin and restore the kingdom to papal obedience. He later replaced Cranmer as archbishop of Canterbury. The queen ended the year on a high note as Parliament repealed the legislation that had initiated King Henry VIII's Reformation and restored the heresy laws.

Queen Mary had another six months of successful rule, and then things began to go terribly wrong. First the pregnancy went wrong, because the queen had never really been pregnant. The baby was expected in April, and onlookers could respond to the emperor's inquiry "How goeth my daughter's belly forward?" that the Queen was clearly showing physical signs of pregnancy.[77] But by the summer it was quite clear that Mary had not been pregnant.[78] Prince Philip left England at the end of August 1555 to join his father in the Netherlands, and he stayed to govern his Continental possessions when Charles V abdicated. Despite Mary's pleas for him to return, he did not come back to England until March of 1557, and he stayed only long enough to persuade his wife to ally England with Spain in a senseless war against France. Although Queen Mary continued to pray for a miracle, and shed many tears as she prayed,[79] there would be no Catholic succession.

In the same year that Mary discovered she was not really pregnant, she initiated the most disastrous policy of her reign. On 4 February 1555 John Rogers (1500–1555), a Protestant minister who had assisted in the production of an English Bible, was burned at the stake. He was the first of nearly three hundred Protestants executed in the remaining years of Mary's reign. When one compares these figures with the thousands who were executed on the Continent, Mary does not seem to deserve the label "bloody Mary," which Protestants gave her. However, by English standards, the numbers were shocking. During the first twenty years of the Reformation approximately sixty people had been executed for heresy, only two of them in Edward VI's reign. In the century and a half preceding the Reformation, possibly as many as one hundred Lollards had been executed; but in Mary's short reign almost twice as many were executed as in the previous two centuries. Why Mary initiated the policy and what were its long-term effects on English Christianity have been subjects of much speculation. The most likely answer to the first question is that Mary was distressed by the persistence of Protestants in maintaining their faith and worship and what she considered blasphemous attacks on the mass. Despite laws outlawing the use of the Edwardian prayer book, Protestants continued to worship in secret in many different places, including cellars, cemeteries, back rooms of pubs, barges, and the houses of powerful sympathizers. Exiles produced and smuggled into England a flood of scurrilous attacks on Mary, her bishops, and the mass. Mary was concerned that unless the virus of heresy was annihilated, it would affect others and threaten their eternal salvation; she hoped the fires would purify the land.

It is likely that Mary and her bishops hoped that, when faced with the flames, many Protestants would react as the Duke of Northumberland had and abjure their heresy or that they would die like cowards and thereby disgrace their faith. They "wanted converts, not martyrs,"[80] and they tried especially hard to break down the resistance of Protestant leaders. John Hooper was the first Protestant bishop to be executed. He was put to death in his cathedral city, and although his persecutors tried hard to break his resistance and his execution was particularly brutal, he died courageously after forgiving his executioner. According to Foxe, his last words were, "Lord Jesus receive my spirit."[81] Ridley and Latimer, who were executed in Oxford in October 1555, died with equal courage, remaining firm in their faith.

The most important bishop to be executed was the man who had played the central role in the English Reformation, Thomas Cranmer. Mary had good reason to despise Cranmer because as archbishop of Canterbury he had been responsible for so much of what particularly distressed her about the events of the past two decades, from the annulment of her mother's marriage to the prayer books she believed imposed so much false teaching on her beloved people. It would be a particularly serious blow to English Protestantism if Cranmer recanted his faith, so every effort was made to achieve that goal. He was imprisoned for two and a half years and kept isolated from his friends most of that time. He was sixty-six years old, in ill health, and, therefore, quite vulnerable to the clever arguments advanced against his position. As a scholar, Cranmer was committed to openness and discussion, but with no one to support him in his beliefs, he finally broke. In what may have been his last letter, he wrote to his friend Peter Martyr at the end of 1555 expressing his confidence that God would be with him in his weakness. He concluded with the words, "I pray God to grant that I may endure to the end."[82] Initially it seemed as though that prayer was not answered, because shortly after he wrote that letter he signed a recantation. It was the first of six that he was pressured to sign, but in the end he also stood firm, withdrawing his recantations and stating that because the hand that had signed the recantations had betrayed him, it would be the first to burn. Foxe recorded his death: "Fire being now put to him, he stretched out his right hand, and thrust it into the flame, and held it there a good space, before the fire came to any other part of his body: where his hand was seen of every man sensibly burning crying with a loud voice, 'this hand hath offended.' As soon as the fire got up, he was very soon dead, never stirring or crying all the while."[83]

Mary had two more years to reign after Cranmer's death, but her failure to have an heir meant the Catholic reaction would not survive her death. The last year of her reign was particularly bitter. The persecutions, which may initially have provided popular entertainment,[84] became more and more unpopular as most of the victims were ordinary people, including sixty women. More and more people came to support rather than jeer the martyrs, and as a result the burnings were eventually held in secret. Although Cardinal Pole made a valiant effort to bring real reform to the English church and to teach people the Catholic faith, the challenges facing him were overwhelming. Possibly as many as half the population was under twenty years of age and had never known the religion their parents and grandparents had once found so meaningful. The monastic lands were not restored, although Mary did reestablish some religious houses. Although Pole was not prepared to concede the loss of the church lands, there was little chance that the gentry, who had paid good money for them, would be willing to give them up. There was also very little progress in restoring the religious guilds and chantries, which were linked to the doctrine of purgatory. At the same time England suffered a series of natural disasters, which some believed were the judgment of God upon an apostate land. Bad harvests due to inclement weather resulted in a serious famine, while outbreaks of plague took a terrible toll of life. Possibly as many as 20 percent of the English population died in those final years of Queen Mary's reign, and to add to Mary's distress, in January 1558 England lost her last Continental possession when Calais fell to the French.

Queen Mary died on 17 November 1558, just twelve hours before Archbishop Reginald Pole also departed this earth. Only one of King Henry VIII's children remained alive, and after Mary's death, the daughter of Anne Boleyn peacefully ascended the throne as Queen Elizabeth I (1558–1603). Ironically, the English Reformation had begun because Henry VIII felt he needed a male heir to assure a peaceful succession, but the English people readily accepted both his daughters. Elizabeth would, in fact, prove to be an excellent ruler who dealt with a particularly challenging situation in an impressive manner. England had experienced three religious changes in eleven years, and the wars of religion were already beginning to plague Continental countries. Elizabeth was faced with the challenge of arriving at a religious settlement that could unite a divided country and protect England from the same tragic conclusion to the Reformation era that was being experienced on the Continent. How she achieved this will be covered in the next chapter. We will also tell the story of still another Reformation that occurred in England's northern neighbor, Scotland, at about the same time that Elizabeth was attempting to consolidate the English Reformation.

9

The Scottish Reformation and the Elizabethan Settlement

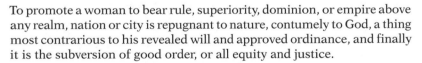

> To promote a woman to bear rule, superiority, dominion, or empire above any realm, nation or city is repugnant to nature, contumely to God, a thing most contrarious to his revealed will and approved ordinance, and finally it is the subversion of good order, or all equity and justice.
>
> John Knox[1]

Those are the words with which John Knox began his infamous tract, *The First Blast of the Trumpet against the Monstrous Regiment of Women*.[2] Although the tract was directed against Mary Tudor and Mary of Guise, the regent in Scotland, it seriously impaired his relationship with Queen Elizabeth I of England. As a result, it may well have played an important role in changing the location of his reforming activities. He seems to have been planning to return to England with the other Marian exiles when Mary Tudor died, but not surprisingly, he found he was no longer welcome there. Knox himself recognized, to use his own words, that "my first blast hath blown from me all my friends in England,"[3] and as a result he returned to Scotland, where he was to play a major role in the Scottish Reformation. In the long run, both Knox and the Scots may have benefited from the change of direction forced upon him as the result of his tract. As we shall see in the second part of this chapter, he probably would not have been able to achieve his goals in England; however, he proved to be perfectly suited for leading the Reformation in his native Scotland.

The Reformation in Scotland

The Reformation in Scotland was almost as complex as the English Reformation, and we should not be surprised that historians of the Scottish Reformation are not agreed on some central questions. Revisionism in the interpretation of the Scottish Reformation predated even English revisionism.[4] Scottish revisionists maintain that the church in Scotland was not as corrupt as the evidence seems to suggest and as a previous generation of scholars believed. They also question the degree to which the Reformation in Scotland was Calvinist and Presbyterian. For example, Gordon Donaldson has argued that its theology was no more Calvinist than the English church's, and Presbyterianism did not really emerge in a doctrinaire fashion until the late 1570s. Others who maintain that a commitment to certain aspects of Presbyterianism was a central plank of the Scottish Reformers' position from the beginning have challenged these views.[5] Finally, in a similar fashion to English Reformation revisionism, historians are questioning the degree of popular support for the Reformation and the speed with which it spread. One thing that is not in doubt, however, is that the political situation in Scotland and the relationship between Scotland, England, and France played a major role in the Scottish Reformation. So we must begin by describing the political situation.

In the Middle Ages, England tried a number of times to conquer Scotland but was unsuccessful. Resistance to the English led by people such as William Wallace (1272–1306) became part of Scottish folklore. Scotland also had a long-standing relationship with France, and England always felt uneasy about the strong French influence on their northern border. King Henry VII tried to resolve the Scottish problem by a marriage alliance between his oldest daughter, Margaret, and King James IV (1473–1513) of Scotland. However, even though their son, King James V (1513–1542), was Henry VIII's nephew, the French influence again became paramount when James V married Mary of Guise, a French Catholic. During the reign of Henry VIII England fought three wars with Scotland, the second ending disastrously for King James V when the English forces decisively defeated his army at the Battle of Solway Moss in 1542. Two weeks later James V died, leaving as his heir a six-day-old baby named Mary Stuart, who would later become known as Mary Queen of Scots (1542–1587). During her minority, a regent, the Earl of Arran, ruled Scotland. Although he tried to keep England happy by initially playing the role of England's ally, Arran eventually also turned to France. In the last years of his reign, Henry VIII fought both Scotland and France. The Scottish war continued into his son's reign, and the Duke of Somerset (Lord Protector for King Edward VI) devoted much effort and expense to an unsuccessful attempt to maintain control of the northern kingdom. Mary Stuart was sent to France when she was still a young girl, where she was brought up as a Catholic; meanwhile her mother, Mary of Guise, became regent in Scotland in 1554. In 1558 Mary Stuart married the heir to the French throne, who became King Francis II (1559–1560) the following year.

Protestantism first penetrated Scotland during the reign of King James V, partly through the import of Luther's books. Although in 1525 the Scottish Parliament passed an act forbidding this trade, it did not stop the growth of Scottish Protestantism. In addition, Tyndale's English Bible translation was widely circulated in Scotland. One of the earliest Scottish Protestants was Patrick Hamilton (1504–1528), a member of an important noble family closely related to the king. He was a humanist who had studied in France and Germany before he became a teacher at the University of St. Andrews in 1523. While at St. Andrews, Hamilton became attracted to Luther's teaching and wrote a book that led to his being accused of heresy by the archbishop of St. Andrews, David Beaton (1494–1546). As a result, Hamilton fled to Germany, where he visited Wittenberg. When he returned to St. Andrews early in 1528, Beaton asked him to appear before him claiming he wished to debate. Instead of being engaged in a debate, Hamilton was accused of heresy, brought to trial in a church court, and convicted within twelve hours. He was then executed by being burned at the stake, but in his courageous death he made many converts. According to one account, although it took six hours before he died, Hamilton "never gave one sign of impatience or anger, nor ever called to heaven for vengeance upon his persecutors."[6]

The next Protestant martyr in Scotland was George Wishart (1513–1546), who was also of noble birth. He had spent a good deal of time on the Continent and in England before returning to Scotland in 1543. During the next few years he traveled around Scotland, entering churches to preach hour-long sermons against Catholic practices and spreading

his Protestant beliefs. He was protected by a group of armed followers, one of whom was John Knox, who accompanied him as a kind of
bodyguard carrying a two-handed sword. It is likely that Wishart played
a role in Knox's conversion to Protestantism, and much of our information about Wishart's ministry comes from the *History of the Reformation*
that Knox wrote between 1559 and 1572.

Wishart eventually also fell victim to Beaton, the militantly anti-
Protestant archbishop who executed five Protestants in 1544 and who
twice tried to have Wishart murdered. In 1546 Beaton succeeded in
having Wishart arrested, condemned as a heretic, and burned at the
stake. Beaton signed his own death warrant when he executed Wishart,
however, because the Scottish nobles who followed Wishart were determined to get their revenge on the archbishop. Two months after Wishart's
death, a group of sixteen Scottish nobles entered Beaton's castle at St.
Andrews and murdered him. When Beaton saw his assassins coming at
him with weapons drawn, he supposedly cried out, "I am a priest. Ye
will not slay me!"—but he was sadly mistaken if he thought that would
deter a group of angry Scottish nobles bent on revenge. One of them
cried out as he raised his sword, "The blood of Wishart cries a vengeance
upon thee and we from God are set to avenge it."[7] After stabbing him
repeatedly, they hung his body over the castle wall for all to see; they
then took over the castle.

John Knox joined the group at the castle after Beaton's death and
became their preacher. They held the castle until July 1547, when a
French fleet captured the castle and took its garrison to France. The more
important prisoners were put in other castles, but those of humble birth
such as Knox were condemned to serve as slaves on French galleys.

The Career and Contribution of John Knox

John Knox might have spent the rest of his life as a galley slave, and
it probably would have been a relatively short life in view of the terrible
conditions to which galley slaves were subjected. However, after an
imprisonment of nineteen months, Knox was released, possibly as the
result of the direct intercession of King Edward VI. Knox then went to
England, where he was initially welcomed by Archbishop Cranmer and
the council. He spent five years in England, at first serving congregations at Newcastle and Berwick near the Scottish border. In 1551 he was
appointed as one of the six chaplains to Edward VI and not only had the
opportunity to preach before the king, but was invited to become the

John Knox (1513–1572).
Illustration from Beza *Icones*.

bishop of Rochester and vicar of an influential London church. To his credit, he turned down both these prestigious appointments. He was unhappy with the first Edwardian prayer book, and even the second prayer book did not fully satisfy him, because he insisted on adding the "black rubric" against Cranmer's strong objections. When Edward VI died, Knox fled to the Continent, going first to Geneva where he met Calvin, then to Zurich to meet Bullinger, eventually settling in Frankfurt-am-Main, where he became involved in a controversy that was to be a preview of the divisions that would occur in the Elizabethan church.

The disputes at Frankfurt were published by a group of English Puritans in 1574 under the title *Brief Discourse of the Troubles Begun at Frankfurt*. One group, which included John Knox as one of its major leaders, felt the 1552 prayer book was still not Protestant enough. They revised it by deleting vestments, the litany, oral responses, the *Te Deum*, and other aspects of the liturgy that they felt detracted from the proper worship of God. The new order of service, which was drawn up in 1555, later became the Book of Common Order, the official worship book of the Church of Scotland.

Another group of exiles, led by Richard Cox, who had helped Archbishop Cranmer write the 1552 prayer book, were adamant that there should be no change from the English usage. In Cox's words, they must "do as they had done in England and . . . have the face of an English church." Knox replied, "The Lord grant it to have the face of Christ's church."[8] With another exile named William Whittingham, Knox appealed to Calvin, who gave a very cautious response, which sounds somewhat like Luther's *Invocavit* Sermons. Calvin agreed that the 1552 prayer book contained some things that needed changing but felt they could be tolerated for a time. He urged Knox and Whittingham to be generous to those who were not yet prepared for more changes. Both sides resorted to questionable political maneuvering, and the opposition eventually persuaded the city authorities to expel Knox, who had in any event already returned to Geneva. There he became pastor of a refugee English congregation that included a number of his supporters from the Frankfurt congregation. The Geneva congregation, which was ruled by elders and two elected pastors, would provide a model for the later development of Presbyterianism. The order of worship introduced in February 1556 was a foretaste of the type of worship that English Puritans later sought in place of the prayer book. The service was entitled "The Interpretation of Scripture," pointing to the centrality of the sermon, singing was limited to psalms, and set prayers were abandoned. The major part of the service was a sermon, followed by questions and discussion. The Eucharist was celebrated once a month with the minister and the congregation sitting together at a table.

Knox was very impressed with Geneva, which he called "the most perfect school of Christ that ever was in earth since the days of the Apostles."[9] He probably would have been happy to stay there; however, the Reformation was spreading in Scotland and preachers were needed, so he accepted the invitation to return in September 1555. He spent nine months there preaching Reformation theology in various parts of the kingdom and urging people to cease attending mass. His success in persuading people alarmed the authorities, so in May 1556 he was summoned to Edinburgh to face charges of heresy. However, the regent, Mary of Guise, intervened and canceled the summons. Although she was a committed Roman Catholic, Mary did not want to do anything that would make the French alliance unpopular. Knox wrote her a letter thanking her and inviting her to become a Protestant or at least to grant toleration to Protestants. Mary treated the letter with contempt, and six weeks after writing the letter, when his congregation in Geneva asked him to return, Knox went back to Geneva with his wife and his mother-in-law.[10]

Having two females in the household did not soften Knox's attitude to women when he felt they were acting in violation of divine law. He was still bitter about his experiences with Mary of Guise and especially distressed by the persecution his fellow believers were suffering in England at the hands of another Mary. In anger, Knox wrote his infamous tract, which was directed primarily against Mary Tudor, queen of England, although it was filled with bitter denunciations of women rulers and offensive remarks on the female sex in general, whom he described as "weak, frail, impatient, feeble and foolish." His shocking conclusion was that, if afflicted by a female sovereign, the faithful had a duty to remove her. He specifically applied this principle to Mary Tudor, stating that

Parliament "ought to remove from honor and authority that monster in nature; so call I a woman clad in the habit of man, yea, a woman against nature reigning above man."[11] Later Knox would argue that Christians should overthrow any idolatrous sovereign, whether male or female, and he condemned as sinful the teaching, commonly held by the other Reformers, that one is obligated by God's Word to obey rulers. Knox did not win many friends by publishing his *First Blast of the Trumpet*—even among his Protestant supporters. Calvin was especially upset that the book was published in Geneva and, after he read it, not only dissociated himself from Knox's position but banned its sale in Geneva. The timing could hardly have been worse. Mary Tudor died a few months after the publication, and Queen Elizabeth I ascended the English throne. Although Knox's tract clearly was not directed against her, Elizabeth never forgave him.

Meanwhile the Reformation was progressing in Scotland, and Protestant congregations were being established in a number of important cities, including Edinburgh. In December 1557 a group of nobles known as the Lords of the Congregation drew up a covenant to establish the Reformed faith in Scotland. In January 1559 Knox again returned to Scotland, and his inflammatory preaching led to popular outbreaks of iconoclasm. With the English supporting them, the Lords of the Congregation took up arms against Mary of Guise and her French allies. Scotland was saved from a protracted civil war when Mary of Guise died, and in July of 1560 the Treaty of Edinburgh provided for the withdrawal of both English and French troops, leaving the Scots free to devise their own religious settlement, which they did when the Scottish Parliament met in August 1560.

The so-called Reformation Parliament abolished the mass as well as papal jurisdiction and adopted a Scottish confession of faith that was broadly Calvinist in theology. In addition, the *First Book of Discipline*, which had been compiled by a committee that included Knox, set up a system of superintendents, in place of bishops, to govern the church. Knox also attempted to set up the Geneva pattern of church organization in Scotland, which would permit the church to control its own theology, select its own ministers, and retain the power of excommunication. A system of local and national church assemblies was set up to ensure that the church would remain independent of the state, but it was never fully put into effect. Knox also provided the Scottish church with its own liturgy. In 1564 the liturgy used at Frankfurt, entitled the Book of Common Order, was adopted as the official book of worship for Scotland. Knox served as minister of the Church of St. Giles, the great parish church of Edinburgh, and began writing his *History of the Reformation*, which recorded the story of the Scottish Reformation from his point of view. He lived twelve more years, during much of which time he was subject to a new woman ruler who was also a committed Roman Catholic.

Mary Queen of Scots

Mary Stuart returned to Scotland in August 1561 after her husband died when she was eighteen years old. She had left Scotland when she was only five years old and had grown up in the luxury of the French court, where she was used to adulation rather than criticism. Consequently, she was hardly prepared to face the problems confronting her in Scotland, which included the indomitable John Knox, who was unremitting in his criticism of her. When she first arrived, the English ambassador, Thomas Randolph, commented that everyone seemed to be impressed by Mary except Knox, who "thundereth out of the pulpit" against her.[12] Randolph may have been overstating the case, because clearly some Protestants were so distressed about her attending mass that they tried to force their way into the royal chapel to disrupt the service the first Sunday after Mary's arrival. She found herself in an especially difficult position, because she was a committed Roman Catholic trying to rule what was now largely a Protestant country. How well she performed that task is a matter of ongoing debate. Depending to some extent on their confessional allegiances, historians have either been highly critical of her or unrestrained in their praise of her courage and her faith.[13]

Mary continued to worship as a Roman Catholic in her own chapel while allowing—and even favoring—the growth of the Reformed Scottish church. But her lenient policy toward Protestantism did not win her any friends among either zealous Catholics or equally committed Protestants. She certainly did not win the heart of John Knox, who preached sermons against her from the pulpit of St. Giles that were so scathing that they became a source of embarrassment even to the Protestant nobility. In his *History of the Reformation* Knox stated that he had six interviews with the queen, in which he did not mince words in denouncing her idolatrous religious practices. He reported that at one point he harangued her so much that she was reduced to "howling" and shed floods of tears. Although this story has often been repeated in histories of the Scottish Reformation, one needs to be somewhat careful about accepting it completely, because we are entirely dependent on Knox's account for the information about his interviews with the queen.

A debate that took place in June 1564 between Knox and the queen's supporters gives us some idea of what Mary was facing. In the debate Knox was accused of calling Queen Mary a slave of Satan and stirring up people against her. Knox responded that Mary was a rebel against God because she insisted on maintaining the mass. When it was pointed out that Mary was sincerely convinced that the mass represented the true faith, Knox responded that the people who sacrificed their children to Moloch in the Old Testament were also convinced that their religion was true, but they were still rebels against God.

Queen Mary's eventual downfall was not brought on by her confrontations with Knox. Rather it was her questionable taste in men that resulted in disaster for this impetuous queen. In July of 1565 she married a handsome eighteen-year-old Scottish nobleman named Henry Stewart, who held the title Lord Darnley. At first glance it seemed like a good choice, since he was a Roman Catholic and had a distant claim to both the English and Scottish thrones. However, he turned out to be a highly unstable, petulant young man and a very inadequate husband for the vivacious queen. He also became insanely jealous of Mary's close relationship with her Italian secretary, David Riccio, whom he suspected was having an adulterous relationship with his wife. Protestant nobles who suspected Riccio of being a papal agent conspired with the jealous husband, and on the evening of 9 March 1566 a band of twenty men led by Darnley broke into the queen's room in Holyrood Palace. They dragged the screaming Riccio from the room where he was having supper with Mary and stabbed him to death.

Although Knox may not have been involved in the plot,[14] he later defended the murder in his *History of the Reformation*, commenting, "That vile knave David was justly punished the 9th of March in the year of God 1565 for abusing of the commonwealth and for his other villainy." He called the murder a "just act" and stated that the murderers were "most worthy of all praise."[15] Mary clearly did not consider the murderers "worthy of praise," and she did not wait long to get her revenge. Less than a year after Riccio's murder, on the night of 9 February 1567, the house where Lord Darnley was staying was blown up by gunpowder, and he was found strangled in the garden. The man suspected of having carried out the murder was James Hepburn, the Earl of Bothwell, who was also Mary's lover. Mary might still have managed to survive the scandal of her husband's murder if she had not married Bothwell three months after Darnley's death. This was too much even for Mary's supporters, and the nobility rose against her. She was captured, and her infant son, James, who was born the previous summer, was crowned king. Although Mary escaped and managed to raise an army, on 12 May 1568 her forces were defeated by an army led by the Earl of Moray, who had been appointed regent for the infant James. Mary then fled to England, where she caused her cousin Elizabeth a series of problems that will be discussed in the second half of this chapter.

Although Knox was by then an old man and physically ill, he continued his ministry even when he had to be carried into the pulpit to preach. He gave his last sermon at St. Giles on 9 November 1572, and five days later he died. Knox left a mixed legacy. He made a major contribution to the Scottish Reformation, which was, in the final analysis, remarkably successful.[16] Those who stand in the tradition that he helped to establish in Scotland venerate him as one of the great heroes of the faith; others judge him on the basis of his vicious attacks on his opponents and his antifemale rhetoric. Even making allowances for the prejudices of the age, one would not want to defend what Knox wrote in the *First Blast of the Trumpet*, and his vitriol is embarrassing even to his most fervent supporters. However, Knox felt he was expressing the judgment of God rather than his own opinion. At the end of his life he wrote: "Many have complained much and loudly, and do still complain of my too great severity, but God knows that my mind was always free from hatred to the persons of those against whom I denounced the heavy judgments of God."[17] In the final analysis, despite his weaknesses or perhaps partially as the result of them, there are few more colorful figures in the Reformation than John Knox. Thomas Randolph, the English ambassador, provides us with an interesting contemporary appraisal of Knox that takes into consideration both his strengths and his weaknesses. He praised Knox's preaching, maintaining that "the voice of one man is able in one hour, to put more life in us than 500 trumpets continually blustering in our ears," but he also commented: "I commend better the success of his doings and preachings than the manner thereof."[18]

Andrew Melville and Scottish Presbyterianism

After Knox's death, others took over the leadership of the Scottish Reformation. During the minority of Mary's infant son, James VI (1567–1625), Protestant regents ruled the kingdom. During that period the Scottish church began to follow the English pattern of church government, and Protestant bishops were introduced in 1572. That policy was abandoned four years later, and in 1578 a Second Book of Discipline proposed a presbyterian type of church government. Although the word *presbytery* was not used in the book, it provided for local assemblies, provincial synods, and a national synod. It excluded bishops and proposed parity of ministers. By 1581 the word *presbyterian* was being used to describe the system. Presbyterianism is normally associated with Andrew Melville (1545–1622), the youngest son of a Scottish noble family and one of the new leaders of the Scottish Reformation. He was well-educated, having studied in Paris and Geneva, where he came under the influence of Theodore Beza. In 1574 Melville returned to Scotland to become principal of Glasgow University and in 1582 moderator of the Scottish church's general assembly. He was so committed to a Presbyterian church polity that he rejected all attempts to win him away from that conviction by offering him a bishopric.

As moderator of the general assembly, Melville helped to bring about the ratification of the Second Book of Discipline, which has been called the "Magna Charta of Presbyterianism." Presbyterianism differed from the episcopal system partly in that it was a more egalitarian type of church government. All ministers were of equal rank, and the government of the church as well as church discipline originated at the congregational level rather than being imposed from above by bishops, who were often selected by the king. At the congregational level, ministers and lay elders formed what was called in Scotland a *session*. Groups of congregations were bound together by a regional governing body, called a *presbytery*, which examined candidates for ministry and ordained them. The local presbyteries sent representatives to regional synods, and at the top of the governing pyramid was a national synod that set policy for the whole church. The adoption of the Second Book of Discipline did not, however, mean the triumph of presbyterianism, since opposition continued, especially from those who believed that episcopacy was the type of church government ordained in Scripture. For example, Patrick Adamson, the archbishop of St. Andrews, claimed that "the office of a bishop . . . hath the ground of the word of God, and in purity hath continued from the days of the apostles to this time," and he contended that claiming "equality of pastors . . . is anabaptistry."[19]

King James VI also opposed the presbyterian polity because it both eliminated his dominant position in the selection of church leaders and involved the separation of church and state. In May 1584 the so-called "Black Acts" reaffirmed state control of the church as well as government by bishops. However, despite the fact that the acts remained law,

James VI (1567–1625).
Illustration from Beza *Icones*.

Presbyterians continued with the unofficial development of their system. James VI became even more opposed to the Presbyterians when Andrew Melville lectured him in a meeting in 1596, reminding him that he was subordinate to the church and calling him "God's silly vassal."[20] Melville was soon to find out that he had considerably overstepped the boundaries of a subject's relationship to his sovereign, for in 1606 James imprisoned Melville for some satirical verses he wrote, and he spent four years in the Tower of London. After his release he went into exile in France, where he died in 1622.

When Queen Elizabeth I died in 1603, King James VI of Scotland also became King James I of England (1603–1625). Shortly after he became king, Puritan ministers confronted him with a petition asking for changes in the English religious settlement, and he agreed to meet with them at what is known as the Hampton Court Conference. When one of the Puritan ministers present made a careless statement that reminded James of Scottish Presbyterianism, he replied that a presbytery "agreeth with a monarch as God and the Devil. Then Tom and Dick shall meet and at their pleasure censure me and my Council and all our proceedings."[21] In the years that followed, King James, and after him his son Charles I (1625–1649), attempted to assert royal control over the Scottish church through the episcopate and suppress presbyterianism. This effort eventually contributed to the outbreak of the English Civil War, which will be discussed in a later chapter.

The Elizabethan Settlement

While Scotland was experiencing its Reformation, the English Reformation was being consolidated under the rule of Queen Elizabeth I

(1558–1603). She possessed great gifts that would be used to good effect in dealing with the challenges that faced her as she ruled a very divided country. She also had her share of weaknesses. "Her vanity was notorious, her tongue sharp and despite her declared intention 'to live and die a virgin,' sexual jealousy soured many personal relations." In addition, she had a tendency to vacillate when facing difficult decisions.[22] Nevertheless, she understood her people and knew how to manipulate their emotions so that she was able to retain their love and loyalty even when they opposed her policies.

When Elizabeth came to power, the Church of England had experienced three religious changes in eleven years. A religious war had just ended in Germany, while France and the Netherlands were about to be thrown into similar and protracted wars. Elizabeth was determined to protect her country from what was happening on the Continent, and she succeeded in doing so. However, in her effort to maintain a religious settlement that might spare England the horror of religious war, she faced strong opposition.

It is difficult to be certain about Elizabeth's personal beliefs because she had to hide them for much of her life, and she became very skilled at telling people what she knew they wanted to hear. For example, she told the imperial ambassador that she planned to return to religion as it had been in her father's reign, since she knew the emperor would be happier with an English church that was still Catholic in doctrine even if it did not accept papal supremacy. In fact, Elizabeth probably would not have been happy with her father's theology because it is likely she was an evangelical in her personal belief, although she was not sympathetic to the more radical Protestants. She was more "Catholic" in the sense that she preferred celibate clergy as well as ceremony and decoration in worship. She also did not believe every parish needed a preaching minister and preferred the homilies to sermons whose content she could not control. Although Elizabeth was eager for a settlement that would unite the kingdom, religious toleration was clearly not something she or her ministers thought desirable. William Cecil, her chief minister, maintained that "the state could never be in safety, where there was toleration of two religions. For there is no enmity so great as that of religion and they that differ in the service of God can never agree in the service of their country."[23]

The settlement was enacted in the face of significant opposition, but in contrast to what was once believed, the opposition came from conservative Catholics rather than radical Protestants.[24] Two parliamentary statutes formed the basis of the settlement. The first was an Act of Supremacy in which Queen Elizabeth I was declared "Supreme Governor" rather than "Supreme Head" of the Church of England—there were those who felt uncomfortable with anybody but Christ being called the head of the church, especially if that person was a woman. This was followed by an Act of Uniformity, which, following the pattern of the Edwardian acts, ordered the use of a single worship service and provided for a graduated scale of penalties if it was not used. The prayer book to be used was the one authorized by Parliament in the "fifth and sixth year of the reign of King Edward the Sixth," which was the 1552 prayer book. However, a number of changes were made, including "the form of the Litany altered and corrected, and two sentences only added in the delivery of the sacrament to the communicants." In addition the so-called "ornaments rubric" provided that "the ornaments of the Church and of the ministers thereof" would be those that were in use "in the second year of the reign of King Edward the Sixth, until other order shall be therein taken by the Queen's Majesty."[25]

The first of those alterations removed the prayer from the litany that asked for deliverance from "the tyranny of the bishop of Rome and all his detestable enormities." Although this change pleased Roman Catholics, radical Protestants considered it a fitting prayer. The second change was of greater significance. The two sentences added to the liturgy were taken from the 1549 prayer book. When the bread was distributed in communion, the minister was to say, "The body of our Lord Jesus Christ which was given for thee, preserve thy body and soul unto everlasting life." When he shared the wine he was to say, "The blood of our Lord Jesus Christ which was shed for thee, preserve thy body and soul unto everlasting life." These two sentences were added to the 1552 words, which were, "Take and eat this in remembrance that Christ died for thee and feed on him in thy heart by faith with thanksgiving," and "Drink this in remembrance that Christ's blood was shed for thee, and be thankful."[26]

The significance of the change was that it enabled those who believed in a real presence of Christ's body and blood in the Eucharist, which included Calvinists and Lutherans, to read their theology into the 1549 words. On the other hand Zwinglians, who viewed the sacrament as a memorial feast in which the bread and wine were mere symbols, could focus on the 1552 words, which emphasize the memorial aspects of the sacrament. The third addition, the "ornaments rubric," was to be a source of ongoing controversy in the years that followed. It was understood as providing for the restoration of the vestments that were in use in the 1549 prayer book, which would have helped Catholics to worship using the prayer book because at least in ministerial dress the service resembled the Catholic service, but more extreme Protestants were not happy with vestments associated with the priests of the medieval church because they associated them with the doctrine of the sacrificial mass. Another ingredient of the settlement was a theological statement called the Thirty-nine Articles, which was adopted in 1563. It was a revision of the earlier Forty-two Articles, dropping certain statements, including the specific denial of the real presence in the Eucharist.

Although the settlement had been established by 1563, most scholars agree that England was still a long way from becoming a Protestant country. Even the justices of the peace, who were expected to enforce the settlement, were not reliable Protestants. In 1564 an inquiry into their religious beliefs revealed that "scantly a third part was found fully assured to be trusted in the matter of religion."[27] The church also lacked an educated preaching ministry who might be able to convert the kingdom to the Protestant faith. For example, the bishop's visitors gave the following report on the Sussex churches in 1559: "Many churches there have no sermons, not one in seven years, and some not one in twelve years, as the parishes have declared to the preachers that of late have come thither to preach. Few churches have their quarter sermons according to the Queen's Majesty's injunctions. . . . The ministers there for the most part are very simple."[28]

When Elizabeth became queen, the zealously Catholic Marian bishops and the most committed priests resigned their posts. All the bishops, except the obscure bishop of Llandaff, refused to take the oath of supremacy, so they were deprived and replaced with Protestants. About four hundred other Marian clergy either resigned their posts or were deprived between 1559 and 1564. In order to fill the vacant episcopal posts, Elizabeth had to rely heavily on the returning Marian exiles, some of whom had adopted a more radical form of Protestantism during their Continental sojourn in cities where Calvinism or Zwinglianism prevailed. She did, however, manage to find a man to serve as archbishop of Canterbury who was not tainted by a stay on the Continent during the Marian period. Matthew Parker (1504–1575), who had been one of Anne Boleyn's chaplains and held the post of dean of Lincoln at the end of Edward's reign, had stayed quietly in England during Mary's reign and managed to survive. He was Elizabeth's choice for the most important position in the English church, both because of his identification with her mother and because he had not been a Marian exile. Parker proved to be an outstanding choice, and he led the fledgling Elizabethan church through the first decade and a half of its existence.

The Puritan Challenge

Parker was faced with many challenges, not the least of which was providing the type of educated ministry that was essential for a Protestant church. He also found that some of his best clergy were often the most obstreperous in arguing for changes in the settlement—a group of committed, well-educated Protestants whom others called Puritans.[29] Their enemies first used the term to deride them, and later generations have had difficulty defining who should be included under the label.[30] They were unpopular not only among Catholics but also among less zealous Protestants. One Elizabethan pamphlet stated, "The hotter sort of Protestants are called Puritans,"[31] and "hot prots" were not to everyone's liking. They were often portrayed unfairly; for example, one contemporary slander described a Puritan as a person "who loves God with all his soul, but hates his neighbour with all his heart."[32] Henry Parker, writing in 1641, left us a more accurate description of a Puritan. He pointed out that although their "dissent in ecclesiastical policy" resulted in them suffering abuse, "those whom we ordinarily call puritans are men of strict life and precise opinions, which cannot be hated for anything but their singularity in zeal and piety."[33] In fact, many Puritans were deeply committed Christians and impressive ministers who worked hard, often in opposition to the queen, to convert England to their sort of Protestantism. Although they did not fully accept the settlement, in the end they played the major role in bringing to England a new kind of committed, zealous Protestantism. They were also very able theologians who were, as a rule, solid Calvinists. Many of them had spent the Marian years in Reformed cities such as Zurich and Geneva, where they had come into contact with the best Reformed practices. We have already noted that in Frankfurt differences between different groups of exiles over the form of worship led to a major controversy. This was the forerunner of the conflicts that broke out in Elizabeth's reign when Puritans, who felt the Elizabethan prayer book was not Protestant enough, sought to introduce revisions throughout her reign.

Another group of committed Elizabethan Protestants have been called "Conformists" because they were happy to accept the Elizabethan Settlement as adequate for the time. Many of them had also been in exile but had returned to take up positions of leadership in the Elizabethan church. Although they too would have preferred a settlement that did not include the elements that Puritans considered too Catholic, the Conformists considered these issues secondary to the larger question of establishing a Protestant church. Whereas most English Protestants were prepared to accept that things not explicitly forbidden in Scripture could be used in the church, Puritans insisted that "anything that cannot be justified by scripture is unlawful in worship."[34] Edmund Grindal (1519–1583), a returning exile who later became archbishop of Canterbury, expressed the attitude of Conformists in a letter he wrote to Bullinger in 1567:

> We who are now bishops, on our first return, and before we entered on our ministry, contended long and earnestly for the removal of those things that have occasioned the present dispute, but as we were unable to prevail, either with the Queen or the Parliament, we judged it best, after a consultation on the subject, not to desert our churches for the sake of a few ceremonies, and those not unlawful in themselves, especially since the pure doctrine of the gospel remain in all its integrity and freedom.[35]

This comment contrasts dramatically with the position of another returning Marian exile named Thomas Sampson. On his return he stated that he could not accept ecclesiastical office in the Elizabethan church until the queen would "concede to the clergy the right of ordering all things according to the word of God."[36] Grindal and other Conformists considered some of the questions about which Puritans felt so strongly *adiaphora*, which literally means "matters of indifference." On these matters, a variety of different practices and beliefs might be permitted in the church because they are neither commanded nor forbidden in the Bible. But Sampson and other Puritans rejected the concept of *adiaphora*: "all things"—including relatively minor manners—needed to be "ordered according to the word of God." Sampson did eventually accept the position of dean of Christ Church, Oxford, but he refused to conform on those matters that violated his conscience, and this helped bring on the first controversy involving Puritans in the Elizabethan church. It is called the Vestiarian Controversy because it involved the question of vestments and clerical dress; however it also concerned other liturgical and ceremonial matters.

When the Elizabethan Settlement was enacted, many believed it was only the first step in eliminating Catholic practices from the church. They believed that the phrase in the ornaments rubric that stated that the ornaments should be in use "until other order shall be therein taken" meant that changes would soon be introduced that would eliminate the vestiges of Catholicism in the settlement. Initially the bishops allowed significant freedom so that clergy who did not conform to the specified clerical dress or who took communion standing rather than kneeling were not disciplined. The queen, however, was not happy when she learned of the laxity in enforcing the settlement. In January 1565 she wrote a public letter to Archbishop Parker in which she complained of "diversity of opinions and especially in the external, decent and lawful rites and ceremonies to be used in the churches" and ordered that "varieties, novelties and diversities" were to be investigated and corrected.[37] Parker, who did not want to enforce the rules about clerical dress strictly, tried to find middle ground. In March 1566 a directive drawn up by Parker and four bishops was published under the title *Advertisements*. Some concessions were made, and clergy were no longer expected to wear vestments at communion but only "a comely surplice with sleeves."[38] However, on other matters in dispute it stipulated that communion was to be received kneeling rather than sitting or standing and fonts were to be used in baptisms.

The *Advertisements* provided what most would have considered a reasonable compromise solution. Even Bullinger, writing from the Continent, urged the Puritans to conform, warning them about hiding "a contentious spirit under the name of conscience."[39] In the same letter he asked them to consider whether they would "not more edify the church of Christ by regarding the use of habits for the sake of order and decency, as a matter of indifference . . . than by leaving the church . . . to be occupied hereafter, if not by evident wolves, at least by ill-qualified and evil ministers."[40] Most accepted this advice, and although a number of London clergy were suspended for refusing to conform, only a handful of them lost their licenses permanently.[41] A few of the deprived London ministers began to minister in private houses and other buildings, where they preached and administered the sacrament. The best known of these was a service held in Plumbers' Hall in London, which was discovered and suppressed by the sheriff's officers in June 1567. Although it lasted for only a short period, it would later be recognized as one of the roots of separatism. The Vestiarian Controversy really resolved nothing. Puritans continued to ignore those aspects of the settlement that they found objectionable, and bishops who were sympathetic to their plight of conscience continued to turn a blind eye to the idiosyncrasies of some of their best clergy.

Prophesyings and Presbyterianism

The next stage in the development of Puritanism involved a radical challenge to episcopal church government. The new controversy was initiated by Thomas Cartwright, the Lady Margaret Professor of Divinity at Cambridge, who in the course of his university lectures on Acts in spring 1570 argued that the English church did not conform to the New Testament model in its church government. Although Cartwright had not worked out a fully presbyterian system of church government, his ideas were radical enough for him to be suspended from his position at the university in December 1570, through the influence of the vice-chancellor of Cambridge, John Whitgift. Cartwright then left Cambridge and went to Geneva, but the controversy continued. In June 1572 two London ministers, John Field and Thomas Wilcox, published what was called an *Admonition to Parliament*, in which they condemned the existing system of church government. They maintained that "the names of archbishops, archdeacons, lord bishops, chancellors, etc. are drawn out of the Pope's shop together with their offices, so the government which they use . . . is antichristian and devilish, and contrary to the scriptures."[42] In its stead, they argued for the introduction of a presbyterian system.

Although Field and Wilcox were imprisoned for a year in Newgate Prison, this did not quell their ardor, and others took up the cause. A *Second Admonition* soon appeared, describing the presbyterian system in greater detail. In a controversy marked by a lack of creative titles for the publications involved, Whitgift answered the *Second Admonition* with an *Answer to the Admonition*, and Cartwright responded in 1573 with a pamphlet not surprisingly entitled *The Second Reply*. In the following year Walter Travers, a supporter of Cartwright, published a work entitled *A Full and Plain Declaration of Ecclesiastical Discipline*, which provided a systematic exposition of presbyterianism. Although much effort was devoted to advocating or attacking presbyterianism, the first stage of the controversy involved relatively few people. By 1575 the controversy abated, as both Cartwright and Travers were in Geneva while Field and Wilcox were in prison. Furthermore, a new archbishop of Canterbury, whom Puritans rightly considered a friend, made them hopeful that the reforms they were advocating could be achieved within the existing episcopal system.

The new archbishop was Edmund Grindal, who was moved from York to Canterbury when Matthew Parker died in 1575. Grindal was as close as one could get to a Puritan archbishop. He understood Puritan problems of conscience with the prayer book and was equally committed to achieving an educated preaching ministry for the church. With such a man at the helm and since the first generation of Elizabethan bishops was largely sympathetic to Puritan concerns, the future seemed bright. As noted earlier, one of the biggest problems facing the Elizabethan church was the lack of an adequate educated preaching ministry.[43] Preaching was particularly important because most people could not read the

Bible, and the training of an adequate preaching ministry was one of the major priorities for both the Puritans and Archbishop Grindal. One of the methods Puritans used to bring preaching ministers into parishes was through the establishment of what were called "lectureships." If a minister could not, or would not, preach the number and kind of sermons the Puritan laity wanted, they would hire another minister, called a lecturer, to preach at times when the church was not being used for regular services. Private individuals or corporate bodies such as municipalities, trade guilds, or hospitals might provide the funds to set up a lectureship. Most were temporary foundations set up to meet an immediate problem, but some, such as the Dedham lectureships, were eventually permanently endowed.

Another method designed to aid in the development of a preaching ministry was a type of in-service training called prophesyings, which normally took place in a market town on market day. Sometimes they sprang from the initiative of the local clergy, and sometimes they were even encouraged by bishops. A panel of local ministers, presided over by a moderator, gathered to hear a number of ministers preach on the text for the day. A large public audience might be present, including leading officials of the town. After the speakers had finished, the moderator would ask learned men to react to the doctrine presented, and the audience would sit with their Bibles open searching for the texts cited by the preachers. When the meeting was over, the people would discuss what they had heard, and the ministers would withdraw to comment in private on the sermon in order to aid the preacher. The day ended with dinner, where more informal discussion of matters of common concern could take place. The prophesyings, which have been described as "partly clerical conferences, partly in-service training courses for ministers, partly team missions to the market towns of England,"[44] also served an evangelistic purpose. While the lectureships provided posts for preaching ministers, the prophesyings offered in-service training for less well-trained ministers. Meanwhile the universities were producing the next generation of Puritan ministers, as Puritans gained control of a number of Cambridge and Oxford colleges.

All was going well from the Puritan perspective until Queen Elizabeth I heard of the prophesyings. Elizabeth did not have the same commitment to a preaching ministry as the Puritans and many of her bishops, having once said that she would be happy with ministers "such as can read the scriptures and homilies well unto her people."[45] Elizabeth was above all concerned about keeping peace in her church and did not want clergy who might threaten the fragile religious settlement. In 1576 the

queen ordered her archbishop to suppress the prophesyings. She had
not reckoned with the courage and conviction of Grindal. After trying
very hard to convince the queen to change her policy, he wrote her the
following letter:

> I am forced with all humility, and yet plainly, to profess, that I cannot
> with safe conscience, and without the offence of the Majesty of God, give
> my assent to the suppressing of said exercises; much less can I send out
> any injunction for the utter and universal subversion of the same. If it be
> your Majesty's pleasure, for this or any other cause, to remove me out of
> this place, I will with all humility yield there unto, and render again to
> your Majesty that I receive of the same . . . bear with me, I beseech you
> madam, if I choose rather to offend your earthly majesty than to offend
> against the heavenly Majesty of God.[46]

It was a very courageous statement, but it led to his suspension as
archbishop in May 1577. He remained suspended until he died in July
1583.

Suddenly all the things that had seemed so promising to the Puritans
were being undermined. They had not only lost a sympathetic archbishop,
but between 1575 and 1581 many of the first generation of Elizabethan
bishops who had supported the prophesyings died. They were replaced
by a new generation of hard-line anti-Puritan bishops; Puritans now
faced a dilemma and responded in a number of ways. Some Puritans,
such as Field, Travers, and Cartwright, became even more committed to
introducing a presbyterian system of church government. By the beginning of the 1580s, Cartwright and Travers were back in England, while
Field led the way in organizing an underground presbyterian system
based on local meetings of clergy called *classes*. These local meetings
sprang up spontaneously, partly as a reaction to the suppression of
the prophesyings. The best known of these meetings was the Dedham
Classes, because its record book has survived. Most of the clergy who
attended the meetings were probably not committed to a presbyterian
system but simply wanted to meet with like-minded brethren to discuss
matters of concern, to uphold each other in common problems, and to
continue the in-service training program, which had been suppressed.
The Presbyterian leaders such as Field, however, had another agenda
for the classes. They viewed them as an embryonic presbyterian system
and sought to use them as a means of changing the Church of England
from within. By holding local provincial and national synods, committed Puritan ministers could stay in contact and use the organization to

mount a parliamentary campaign and influence elections, as they tried to do in 1584.

Although the Puritan effort to influence Parliament was unsuccessful, the underground Puritan organization proved quite effective in combating an offensive against Puritanism launched by the new archbishop, John Whitgift. He had been involved earlier in Cartwright's dismissal from his Cambridge professorship, and he considered Puritans "rebels" who needed to be forced to conform to the settlement. In October 1583 he promulgated a series of articles and insisted that all ministers must subscribe to them. One of those articles was especially objectionable to Puritans, stating that "the Book of Common Prayer . . . containeth nothing in it contrary to the word of God . . . and he himself will use the form of the said book prescribed in public prayer and administration of the sacraments and none other."[47]

The wording of the article was so precise that Puritans were confronted with a serious conscience problem. They were in the habit of adjusting the prayer book service to fit their belief that preaching should be central to worship, and one of their most serious objections to the prayer book rubric was "that they make the chiefest part, which is preaching, but an accessory."[48] Besides discarding the surplice and ceremonies to which they objected, they often truncated the service, leaving out portions of the liturgy so they could have longer sermons. They also adjusted the administration of the sacraments to their theological beliefs, refusing to use the sign of the cross at baptism or to kneel at communion and using common bread rather than wafers. In addition, they administered communion in a black gown from a table that in no way resembled an altar. By making these adjustments in the worship service, Puritans were able to remain ministers within the Church of England without violating their consciences, but when they were ordered to sign an article that seemingly made these kinds of compromises impossible, they were faced with a difficult choice. Either they must violate what they believed to be biblical by signing the article, or they were in danger of losing their positions and undermining all the hard work they had done to bring a preaching ministry to the Church of England.

Although hard-liners in London such as Field were unyielding, maintaining that there could be no compromise on this issue, more moderate Puritan ministers struggled with a deep dilemma. They knew they were called to preach the gospel in the Church of England, but if they hoped to continue to do this they would need to sign an article that they felt was in violation of the Scriptures. It is estimated that between three hundred and four hundred ministers refused to make a subscription and were suspended from their ministries. Archbishop Whitgift might have swept Puritans out of the Church of England pulpits if it had not been for the intervention of the Puritan laity and compromises on both sides. Appeals were sent to the Privy Council, which was bombarded with petitions from ministers and their lay supporters. The outpouring of lay support, including important members of the council, eventually forced Whitgift to back down and allow a form of subscription that made it possible for Puritans to give a conditional assent to the articles. Whitgift recognized that he had lost the first round, because he knew that when a Puritan subscribed "as far as the law required," the minister did so under the assumption that the law required no such subscription. He also knew that when a Puritan "promised to use the Book of Common Prayer and no other," he meant that his services would consist of material selected from the prayer book.[49]

Archbishop Whitgift had lost a battle but not the war. Supported by the queen, he would continue his attacks on Puritans, who fought back in Parliament. In 1586 they again sought to influence parliamentary elections. They presented petitions for reform to Parliament, supported by a survey they had made of the parochial clergy to document the need for reform. Although moderate Puritans had considerable support in Parliament, their more radical Presbyterian brethren often undermined their efforts to achieve moderate reform by radical proposals that were unacceptable to the majority in Parliament. For example, in 1586 a Presbyterian member of Parliament named Anthony Cope proposed a bill that would have done away with the Book of Common Prayer and set up a presbyterian system of church government. The bill was so radical that when the queen intervened and ordered Cope and four other Puritan members of Parliament arrested, the House of Commons did not even protest. Most Puritans were not Presbyterians and were committed to work within the Church of England despite their objections to some aspects of the settlement.

Among the exceptions was a group of Puritans who have been labeled "Separatists," who became so frustrated by their failure to reform the Church of England that they decided the only way forward was to separate from that church. Although Separatism was an insignificant movement in the reign of Elizabeth, it grew in numbers and significance in the half century following her death, eventually providing the background for the emergence of Congregationalists and Baptists. The first expression of Separatism is often identified with the meeting in the Plumbers' Hall mentioned earlier; however, the Plumbers' Hall Puritans were not really Separatists because they intended their separation as a temporary expedient until the Church of England was reformed.

True Separatism did not appear until the 1580s, when some Puritans broke entirely with the established church. The best-known Separatists are Robert Browne and Robert Harrison, both at Cambridge when Cartwright was dismissed. Browne came to the conclusion that the Church of England was not a true Christian church and that it could not be reformed. In place of the national church, he proposed that the church should be a "gathered" community of people who joined the body freely and who were bound together by a covenant. Rather than having a hierarchy of clergy, with local congregations served by ministers who were selected by bishops, each congregation would elect its own minister. In 1579 Browne began preaching in Cambridge, attacking the bishops as "ravenous and wicked persons"[50] and even identifying them as Antichrists. In 1581 he and Harrison formed a Separatist church in Norwich, but after Browne spent time in prison, they emigrated to the Netherlands, where they established a new Separatist church. They found themselves at odds with each other over a number of issues, and by 1583 their disagreements were so strong that Browne was expelled from his own church. In the following year he came back to England, returned to the Church of England, and was ordained to a parish in Northamptonshire in 1591.

While Browne was a little inconsistent,[51] others were more committed to the Separatist beliefs. John Greenwood and Henry Barrow, who left the Church of England because they considered it apostate, were arrested in 1586 for setting up a Separatist church in London, and they remained imprisoned for seven years. During that time they continued to produce Separatist literature, until the authorities took extreme action in April 1593 and executed them. A few weeks later another Separatist named John Penry was also hanged. Continued persecution and the threat of death caused other Separatists to leave England. In 1583 Greenwood's old congregation in London, now led by Francis Johnson, emigrated to the Netherlands. By the end of Queen Elizabeth I's reign, Separatism, which involved only a small minority of English Puritans, seemed to have been stillborn. However, it was to return to play a major role in the civil war period.

The Catholic Challenge

While Puritans sought unsuccessfully to alter the Elizabethan
Settlement in order to eliminate those aspects of it that they considered too "Catholic," others sought to achieve the opposite and return
England to the Catholic faith. In this effort they received help from
abroad, which was capped when in 1588 Philip II of Spain, husband of
the late Mary Tudor, sent an Armada to conquer England. For the first
part of her reign Elizabeth had pursued a cautious policy toward English
Catholics in order to avoid alienating them. Although the penalty for
a second refusal to take the oath of supremacy was death, Elizabeth
instructed her archbishop never to offer it a second time. In addition,
although people could be fined for not attending the Church of England
services or for attending mass, in most cases the authorities turned a
blind eye to offenders. Elizabeth was satisfied with what one writer has
called "a token conformity,"[52] and the vast majority of English Catholics
conformed outwardly and remained loyal to the crown. The popes had
also dealt with Elizabeth in a cautious manner, hoping that England
could be won back to Catholicism by diplomacy. After almost a decade
of using diplomacy, Pope Pius V turned to more severe measures when
in 1569 a rebellion in the northern counties gave him hope that Queen
Elizabeth I might be overthrown by her own people.

In February 1570 Pius V issued the papal bull *Regnans in Excelsis*,
which excommunicated Elizabeth as "a heretic and abetter of heretics,"
and deposed her "of her pretended claim" to be queen of England.[53] The
northern rebellion had already failed by the time *Regnans in Excelsis*
was issued, and the bull placed English Catholics in a difficult position.
If they accepted the dictates of the papal bull, they became traitors to
the queen, but if they accepted Elizabeth as their queen, they would be
disobeying their spiritual leader. Parliament added to their problems
when, in response to the bull, legislation was enacted that extended the
treason laws to include all who brought in papal bulls or "reconciled
others to Rome or who were reconciled themselves."[54]

In 1568 an English exile, William Allen, established a seminary at
Douai in the Spanish Netherlands to train priests who would be sent
back into England to minister to English Catholics. Such men were
particularly affected by the new legislation, as many were hunted down
by the authorities and executed as traitors. The first Catholic priest was
executed in 1577, and before Queen Elizabeth I's reign ended more than
two hundred had been martyred. Catholics considered this religious
persecution, but the Elizabethan authorities argued that the priests were

executed for treason rather than heresy. Even the method of execution differed from that suffered by Protestants in Queen Mary's reign. The Elizabethan Catholic martyrs were hung, drawn, and quartered—the method reserved for traitors—while the Marian martyrs were burned at the stake, which was the way heretics were dispatched. Elizabeth's problems were complicated when Mary Stuart (queen of Scotland) fled to England in 1568. Mary wanted Elizabeth's help against the rebels in Scotland, but Elizabeth certainly did not want to help Mary regain the Scottish throne in place of her allies in Scotland. The Puritans wanted Mary executed, but Elizabeth did not want to execute her cousin, so she kept her confined in England in one castle or great house after another for eighteen years. During this time Mary became involved in a number of plots against Elizabeth. Elizabeth always protected her, but when her secret service produced undeniable evidence of Mary's involvement in a plot to assassinate Elizabeth and put Mary on the throne, Elizabeth bowed to the inevitable and allowed Mary's execution in 1587.[55]

The execution of Mary Stuart played a role in bringing about the greatest foreign threat to the Elizabethan Settlement. Philip II of Spain, who had been vacillating about a planned attack on England, was now free of the danger of a pro-French ruler inheriting the English throne, and in July 1588 he sent a mighty Armada to conquer England and restore it to Roman Catholicism. The military force assembled for the operation was one of the most massive ever gathered for a sea attack, consisting of 130 ships, 18,000 soldiers, and 7,000 sailors. In addition the Armada planned to pick up 17,000 battle-hardened troops under the command of the Duke of Parma in Calais, who would be added to what seemed like an invincible force for the invasion of England. Philip also expected the Roman Catholics in England to rise up against their heretic queen once the foreign troops had landed. In July 1588 England was clearly facing a threat that might have brought an end to Protestant England, and as the Spanish fleet approached, England launched a prayer offensive. The council ordered clergy to move their parishioners to pray for God's assistance, and special prayers were written to be used in all parish churches as a kingdom on its knees pleaded for God's assistance against the enemy.[56]

As the Armada approached, England waited in fear. But then everything went wrong for the Spanish. Bad planning, poor communication, some excellent English seamanship, and a "Protestant wind" that blew the Spanish ships up the channel away from England brought disaster to the Armada. Although Philip accepted the defeat stoically, the English viewed it as confirmation that God was on their side and had answered their prayers. Thanksgiving celebrations were held throughout the land in which God was given credit for the victory.[57] The victory continued to be celebrated after Elizabeth's death, and for the next century it provided material for preachers to use to illustrate how the English were a special people in God's sight. Although Roman Catholics had remained solidly loyal throughout the crisis, they were identified with the threat from Spain, which helped to "inflame anti-Catholicism."[58]

The Settlement Secured

The victory over Catholic Spain also increased the popularity of the Church of England. In view of the popular belief that God had given England the victory, it was logical that "if God felt that strongly about England, there could not be too much wrong with its established church."[59] Consequently, there could hardly have been a time when criticism of the church was more ill-advised. Nevertheless, in October 1588 the first of a series of tracts appeared that contained such vicious attacks on the bishops that even Presbyterian leaders such as Cartwright and Travers were shocked. The anonymous tracts were published by a well-known Puritan printer and were clearly associated with radical Puritans. They were called the Martin Marprelate Tracts, after the man who was satirically identified as their author.[60] Although many found the humor of the tracts entertaining, they contained scurrilous attacks on the bishops that helped vitiate the wider Puritan cause. They were especially upsetting to the authorities, who launched an assault on Puritanism.

Archbishop Whitgift, who was called "John of Kankerbury, the pope of Lambeth" and branded "the forerunner of Antichrist,"[61] was understandably upset, and he ordered an investigation under the leadership of the future archbishop, Richard Bancroft. The investigation uncovered the Puritan underground presbyterian organization of classes and synods, which were then suppressed. Cartwright and eight other prominent leaders were arrested and brought to trial. Although they were released, they gave up any further efforts to change the government of the Church of England. With the destruction of the Puritan organization, its political potential was undermined, and the reign of Elizabeth ended with the Puritan challenge to the settlement considerably weakened. In addition, the theological basis for Puritanism was severely challenged in a massive work written by Richard Hooker (1554–1600) entitled *Of the Laws of Ecclesiastical Polity*.

Despite differences over clerical vestments, liturgy, and church government, Puritans and Conformists were united by what has been described as a Calvinist consensus. Even Whitgift, the perennial opponent of Puritans, was a committed Calvinist, but Hooker was clearly not a Calvinist.[62] In a sermon he gave at Paul's Cross in 1581, he argued that God wanted all men to be saved, and those who were not saved were damned because they had not responded to the grace offered to them. In 1585 he engaged in a controversy with Walter Travers. Many of the ideas and arguments that he expressed in those debates were later published in his *Laws of Ecclesiastical Polity*. The work consisted of eight volumes, three of which were published after Hooker's death. He first responded to the Presbyterian challenge and then proceeded to offer a logical and consistent defense of the Church of England, which he saw as a middle road between extremes. Although his arguments were based on Scripture, he did not believe that the Bible provided answers to all questions. Hooker pointed out that some important doctrines, such as the Trinity, which are not explicitly defined in Scripture, need to be deduced by reason. He also did not believe Scripture specified a particular form of church government; he accepted the possibility of different forms dictated by different situations. In addition, he tended to place less emphasis on the Reformation and accepted that the medieval church was part of the true church, and in contrast to the Puritan emphasis on the sermon, Hooker stressed the sacraments and liturgy. Although Hooker's work did not become well-known until long after his death, his volumes provided the classic statement of what was later to become Anglicanism.

When Queen Elizabeth I died in 1603, the Elizabethan Settlement had been secured and significant progress had been made in church reform. In contrast to the sorry state of the ministry at the beginning of Elizabeth's reign, at her death over half the pulpits of England's parish churches were filled with educated preaching ministers, the vast majority of them university graduates. By the time Elizabeth died, England was "undoubtedly a Protestant nation despite the continuance of superstitions and the rudimentary understanding of doctrines."[63] Although the Puritans had not succeeded in their efforts to reform the Church of England in the way they understood reform, they had achieved a great deal, and many of their objectives had been realized. In 1603 the English people could also look back at half a century of relative religious peace, while the Continent was being torn apart by religious war. The Roman Catholic threat had been neutralized, the Presbyterian challenge had been defeated, and although Puritans had failed in their efforts to change the settlement, most remained committed members of the Church of England. England seemed to have succeeded in maintaining a Protestant settlement without religious war—a major achievement. Yet in the next half century the bright hope of continuing religious peace was undermined, and the last religious war of the Reformation era was to be fought in England.

10

THE CATHOLIC
REFORMATION

▼

Concerning ordination: no care is taken. Whoever they are (uneducated, of
appalling morals, under age), they are routinely admitted to the holy order
from which came so many scandals and a contempt for the church. . . .
Concerning Rome: honest manners should flourish in this city and church,
mother and teacher of other churches . . . [yet] whores perambulate like
matrons or ride on mule-back, with whom noblemen, cardinals and priests
consort in broad daylight.

Advice Concerning Reform of the Church[1]

The above statement reads as though it were written by a Protestant
critic of the Catholic Church, but in fact, it was written as part of a report
from a committee set up by Pope Paul III (1534–1549) to investigate
the condition of the church and make recommendations for reform.
The pope was courageous enough to do what many modern politicians
seldom do when they appoint committees to investigate a scandal in
which they might be implicated: he appointed to the committee zealous
reformers who were unlikely to cover up the problems that needed to
be addressed. The report was published in 1537, and its findings were
so embarrassing to Catholics that Protestants eagerly cited them as

evidence that they were right in what they had said about the church. The pope who commissioned the report, as well as the leading cardinals who were represented on the committee, were committed to reform.[2] The publication of their findings provided a major impetus for what was to become a wide-ranging reform movement in the Catholic Church.

Historians have given the Catholic reform movement a variety of names. Protestant historians have tended to label it the "Counter-Reformation," suggesting that its major emphasis was to "counter" the impact of Protestantism.[3] Catholic historians preferred the label "Catholic Reformation," because it emphasized the positive reforming aspects of the movement and suggested that Catholic reform was not necessarily a reaction to the Protestant Reformation. There was a time when one could recognize the bias of the historian by the title used, but this is no longer the case. As religious bias abated, historians began to recognize that both terms had an element of truth. For example, John O'Malley believes that "we need to accept the multiplicity of names as a good thing, for each of them captures an important aspect of the reality."[4] Dickens begins his study of what he has called *The Counter Reformation* by commenting on the usefulness of both terms:

> Counter Reformation or Catholic Reformation? Was it not quite obviously both? Some of the tributaries to the stream of revival are discernible before Luther. And even after Luther's revolt, the highest Catholic achievements were those of men and women who believed themselves to be seeking Christ rather than fighting Luther. Yet on the other hand, it seems equally clear that the Catholic Reformation was a slow starter and the Lutheran Reformation an exceedingly rapid one. . . . Undoubtedly this crisis stimulated self-reforming Catholicism to greater effort, while the tasks of self-defence and counter-attack demanded no small share of its growing resources. In view of these facts either title remains acceptable.[5]

Origins of the Catholic Reformation

Catholic reform began in the late Middle Ages. The conciliar movement, which had reunited the church at Constance in 1414 by ending the papal schism, was also committed to reforming the abuses in the church. However, throughout much of the fifteenth century the struggle between the papacy and the councils blunted efforts at reform. After the conciliar movement had been defeated, Pope Julius II convened the Fifth Lateran Council at Rome in 1512, and it continued meeting into the pontificate of Leo X. This was the last official effort to achieve church reform before the beginning of the Reformation. The council met for almost five years and was attended by church leaders representing much of Latin Catholic Christendom, although it was dominated by Italian and Spanish bishops. It was presented with proposals for significant reforms and it issued reforming decrees; however, it fell short of instituting major reforms or implementing the decrees that were issued. In the final analysis it may even have delayed reform, as the difficulty Pope Leo X had in controlling the council made the popes who followed him more reluctant to call a council during the Reformation. Within six months of the adjournment of the Fifth Lateran Council, Luther wrote his *Ninety-five Theses*.

Although the Renaissance popes were not particularly active in initiating reforms, reform movements originating from sources other than the papacy were widespread well before the beginning of the Lutheran Reformation. One such movement was led by the Spanish Cardinal Francisco Ximenes de Cisneros (1436–1517), who spent the years 1459–1466 in Italy, where he came into contact with humanism. He returned to Spain and became archbishop of Toledo and primate of the Spanish church in 1485. Although he was nearly sixty years old, he began a major reform movement that started with the monastic orders and extended to the secular clergy. In 1507 he received the cardinal's hat and the following year established a university at Alcala with his own funds in order to provide for the education of the clergy. He also financed the printing of the six-volume Complutensian Polyglot Bible, which was produced by the humanist scholars he attracted to the new university. The Old Testament section contained the Hebrew text, the Latin Vulgate, and the Greek Septuagint printed in parallel columns. Volume six included exegetical aids, and in a prologue addressed to Pope Leo X, Cisneros expressed his humanist commitment to studying Scripture in the original languages. The Greek New Testament section of the Polyglot Bible was printed in 1514, two years before Erasmus produced his version. In contrast to his scholarly interests, Cisneros also served as Inquisitor General of Spain; intolerance and persecution of dissenters was also associated with the Spanish reform movement. The Spanish Inquisition had been established in the latter part of the fifteenth century as a special tribunal to bring suspected heretics to trial. It was initially directed against baptized Jews who were suspected of having returned to their Jewish beliefs and practices. It was later also used against Muslims who had been forced to accept baptism and, after the Reformation began, against those suspected of Protestant leanings.[6]

Cisneros died two years after the birth of another reformer who was to become one of the great spiritual mystics of the age, Teresa of Avila (1515–1582). She grew up as the pampered child of a wealthy family that had purchased noble status. She could have led a life of luxury and ease, but as a young woman she committed herself to a religious life. When she was twenty years old she entered a Carmelite convent, where she remained for the next twenty-seven years. Initially she did not adhere to a strict monastic rule and often found it difficult even to pray. She confessed in her autobiography that "very often, over a period of several years, I was more occupied in wishing my hour of prayer were over . . . whenever I entered the oratory . . . I had to summon up all my courage to make myself pray."[7]

At the age of forty, Teresa had a vision of Christ that radically changed the direction of her life, and she committed herself totally to the service of God. She no longer found the lax observances of the Carmelite order acceptable, and with the support of relatives and friends, she founded a reformed convent in Avila in 1562. It was the first of sixteen new houses she founded in Spain as she traveled throughout the country preaching reform. Committed to seeking oneness with God through contemplation and prayer, Teresa wrote some of the great classics of mystical spirituality in the remaining years of her life, including *The Way of Perfection* and *The Interior Castle*. Teresa lived into her late sixties, and she never slackened in her energetic pursuit of reform. She also continued to write: in addition to four major works, she composed poems, meditations, and some five hundred letters. She and her co-worker, John of the Cross (1542–1591), helped popularize a mystical spirituality that was to become one of the major characteristics of the Catholic Reformation and would be reflected in much of the literature and art inspired by the movement. Teresa also had a deep commitment to rescuing non-Christians and Protestants from what she considered false beliefs, and she urged her nuns to pray continually for their conversion.

In Italy groups called Oratories of Divine Love played a major role in church reform. These were small, urban religious societies that sought the inward renewal of their members through religious exercises and prayer as well as frequent communion. They were also committed to putting their faith into practice through service to the poor. The original inspiration for establishment of the oratories came from the life and work of St. Catherine of Genoa (1447–1510), whose life of selfless service in the care of the sick and profound spirituality inspired a wealthy layman to found an oratory in Genoa in 1497. Oratories were also established in a number of other important Italian cities, including Florence, Milan,

Verona, Naples, and Padua. The Genoa oratory eventually moved to Rome, where it included among its members many of the future leaders of the Catholic Reformation, including Jacopo Sadoleto, Gaetano Thiene, Reginald Pole, Giovanni Pietro Carafa, and Gasparo Contarini. The group met regularly for prayer, meditation, mutual encouragement, and discussions about reforming the institutional church, and although it disbanded after the sack of Rome in 1527, its influence continued through the reforming activities of its members.

The sack of Rome had a significant impact on the Catholic Reformation. It occurred when troops in the service of Emperor Charles V, who were in Italy fighting the French and a coalition of Italian powers that included the papacy, marched on Rome. Their leader was killed in the assault on the city, and after they captured Rome the unpaid, leaderless troops, who included some German Protestants, subjected the city to a week-long orgy of pillaging, murder, and rape. Charles, who had not authorized the attack, was deeply distressed when he learned of the sacrilege committed in the holy city, maintaining that he would have "preferred not to win than to be left with such a victory," and that he "felt great pain and shame for the offence given to the Holy See."[8] Church leaders were even more distressed and shocked by the horror of what had happened, and some, such as Giles of Viterbo, used it to document the urgent need for reform. Giles had given the opening address at the Fifth Lateran Council, in which he urged the council to lead the way in church reform. Since the council failed to do so, Giles argued that the sack of Rome was punishment for the church's failure to reform the abuses that were so offensive to God: "You must understand just how wicked are these days and how angry is heaven at the rabble now admitted everywhere to the exalted office of the priesthood (lazy, untrained, disorganized and immoral, mere youths, bankers, merchants and soldiers not to mention usurpers and pimps). . . . The ungodly say 'If God cares for sacred things, why does he allow this?' I reply that it is because God cares that he not only allows this thing, but even carries it out himself."[9]

Gian Matteo Giberti (1485–1543), the bishop of Verona, was one of those who reacted to the sack of Rome as Giles had hoped people might. He had spent the early part of his career as a member of the Roman Curia, serving under both Leo X and Clement VII, but after the sack of Rome he felt compelled to devote himself solely to the reform of his diocese. He returned to reside in Verona and began to work diligently to correct abuses and to institute reforms. One of his first acts was to visit all the parishes in the diocese and examine the clergy personally. He expelled unqualified clergy, forced nonresidents to return to their parish, and punished those living with concubines. He also reformed the religious orders and founded orphanages and almshouses. In contrast to the ostentatious lifestyle of many Italian church leaders, who neglected their spiritual responsibility, Giberti set an example of frugality and hard work. By making Verona a model of what could be achieved by a conscientious bishop, he trusted that other bishops would copy his efforts.

The Theatine Order, which was one of the new monastic orders founded by members of the Roman oratory, produced a number of the reforming bishops who followed Giberti's example. Established by Gaetano Thiene and Gian Carafa in 1524, it was committed to the reform of the church through the reform of the clergy. Although it was never a large order, it attracted idealistic people who were leaders in society and who became leaders in the church, and it had an important impact on the Catholic Reformation by training future bishops who would lead the way to reform in their dioceses.

Contarini, Paul III, and the Regensburg Colloquy

Some of the most committed Reformers were known in Italy as the *spirituali* and included members of the Roman Oratory of Divine Love such as Gasparo Contarini (1483–1542). The latter was a member of a distinguished Venetian family, and in the course of his career in the secular world he held a number of important posts in the government of the city, while between 1528 and 1530 he also served as the ambassador to Emperor Charles V. Earlier he experienced a spiritual crisis similar to that which Luther had experienced. In the course of that crisis he began to doubt his own salvation, as he realized that he could not atone for his sin by his own efforts. Like Luther, he eventually found his answer in the grace of God in Jesus Christ. In 1523 he wrote, "I have truly come to the firm conclusion . . . that no one can at any time justify himself through his works or purge his mind of its inclinations. One must turn to the divine grace obtained through faith in Jesus Christ, as St. Paul says. . . . We must justify ourselves through the righteousness of another, that is, of Christ, and when we join ourselves to him, his righteousness is made ours."[10]

Other *spirituali* held similar views, and although they were not fully in accord with the Protestant understanding of justification, the closeness of their views to the Protestant position on the central doctrine of the Reformation held out hope of reconciliation. Contarini gained the opportunity to work for reconciliation with Protestants and also to confront the problem of church reform after Pope Paul III made him a cardinal in May 1535. He then took up residence in Rome and became one of the pope's closest advisers. In that capacity, he proposed the establishment of a reform commission, which subsequently wrote the report cited at the beginning of this chapter.

Pope Paul III, who brought Contarini to Rome, was in many ways the typical Renaissance pope, patronizing the arts, living ostentatiously, and working for the advancement of his family. Paul III was even guilty of blatant nepotism when he made his fourteen- and sixteen-year-old grandsons cardinals shortly after he was elected pope. Although he was guilty of the very abuses the report criticized so severely, Paul III played a central role in placing the papacy at the head of the reform movement. In his younger years he had kept a mistress who bore him three sons and a daughter; however, he changed his ways after Pope Julius II made him bishop of Parma in 1509. He took his responsibilities as bishop seriously, and after the Reformation began, he became identified with the reform party in the Curia. When Pope Clement VII died, Paul was unanimously elected pope. Although he was sixty-seven years old, he lived fifteen more years and led the way to serious reform. He not only appointed the Reform Commission and staffed it with committed reformers, but he was also responsible for making a number of *spirituali* cardinals in addition to Contarini. He also recognized the new monastic orders that would play a major role in the Catholic Reformation, including the Ursulines, the Barnabites, and the Jesuits. Finally, he convened the long-delayed church council in 1545.

The Papal Reform Commission presented its formal report to the pope in March 1537. The report was brutally honest and very perceptive in identifying some of the areas that needed reform. It began by stating that many of the evils in the church were due to the actions of the papacy. While making a clear declaration of papal authority and praising Paul III for his commitment to reform, the report did not mince words in condemning the actions of previous popes: "Your Holiness knows that these evils arose from the wilfulness of several previous popes . . . [and their belief] that the pope being lord of all benefices, can sell its own, and cannot therefore be guilty of simony. . . . From this, as the Trojan horse burst forth into God's church so many grave ills . . . [which] obeying your command we have examined and here make known to you."[11]

The cardinals were also severely criticized for their worldliness and their failure to give adequate attention to spiritual matters. The report

cited examples of the abuse that needed to be addressed including bribery, abuses of papal power, evasion of canon law, laxity in the monastic
orders, and the abuse of indulgences. As indicated in the quotation at
the beginning of this chapter, the members of the commission were
especially scathing in their criticism of conditions in Rome.

Not surprisingly, the report received a mixed reception. Although
Protestants were delighted, and Luther even published a German translation with a woodcut on the title page showing three cardinals trying
to sweep the church clean with foxtails, the cardinals were not at all
pleased. The conservative majority in the College of Cardinals saw their
vested interest threatened by the proposed reforms and did their best to
frustrate the work of the commission. Pope Paul III also failed to pursue reform vigorously, although at Contarini's urging he did appoint a
commission, which included Contarini and Carafa, to reform the papal
bureaucracy. It is also to his credit that in December 1540 he ordered
eighty absentee bishops living in Rome to return to their dioceses.

By the late 1530s the Catholic reform movement was well under way,
but Protestantism was also gaining in strength and spreading. Catholic
reformers were divided on how to deal with Protestants. Contarini and
other *spirituali* were committed to finding a way to reconcile them to
Rome, while more conservative reformers such as Carafa believed that
suppression was the only way to deal with heretics. Contarini gained
an opportunity to achieve reconciliation when Emperor Charles V, who
desperately needed internal peace within the empire so he could deal
with the other threats outside, promoted conversations between Catholics
and Protestants at Hagenau and Worms in 1540–1541. In April 1541 the
effort to achieve reconciliation moved to Regensburg, where an imperial
diet was in session. As noted earlier, both Bucer and Calvin attended
the Colloquy of Regensburg, where the two sides used as their basis for
discussion the *Regensburg Book*, which had been composed by John
Gropper, a Catholic humanist, and modified by Martin Bucer.

The most surprising achievement of the colloquy was that the participants reached an agreement on the doctrine of justification. The
article dealing with that doctrine was worded in such a way that it took
into consideration the major concerns of both sides. The Protestant
position was that justification is based solely on the merits of Christ,
which are imputed to the believer. Sanctification, or the Christian life,
is a response to justification already completed rather than part of the
process of justification, as Catholics believed. Although the Catholic
delegates were willing to concede that justification was by faith, they
wanted to make sure it was made clear that justifying faith was one

that produced works of righteousness. The final formula seemed to satisfy both concerns, as justification was attributed to the imputation of Christ's righteousness; however, it also stated that justifying faith must result in righteous acts. In this sense there is really a "double righteousness." The first righteousness is imputed, while the second is an inherent righteousness—an inner righteousness brought about by the Holy Spirit, which in turn gives birth to good works.[12] Contarini, who served as papal legate to the colloquy, considered the agreement a major breakthrough, but others were not so sure. Luther called it "a patched up thing," while Carafa and other hard-line Catholics saw it as a threat to Catholic teaching on merit and purgatory.

Although the colloquy had agreed on justification, major stumbling blocks lay ahead, and none was more difficult to overcome than differences over the Eucharist. The *Regensburg Book* taught a real presence of Christ's body and blood "under the form of bread and wine,"[13] but Contarini found that definition unacceptable because it did not include the word *transubstantiation*. Although they debated for nine days, no agreement was reached, and in the end the colloquy failed to reconcile differences in a number of other areas as well. It must have been difficult for Contarini to accept that failure, but he hoped the long-delayed general council might continue the work of reconciliation begun at Regensburg. In a communication addressed to the emperor he wrote, "In several articles the Protestants have departed from the common understanding of the universal church. It is our hope that, with the help of God, they will yet reject these and that in time they will come to agree with us. Everything then should be forwarded and submitted to the pope and the apostolic see, who should take up the matter according to universal truth in a general council to be convened in comparatively short time."[14]

Contarini did not live to see the council that was convened four years later because he died in 1542. Even before his death, the hard-liners in the Curia, who believed that suppression rather than dialogue was the only way to deal with Protestants, were introducing their methods. Carafa, who became acquainted with the Spanish Inquisition while serving as papal nuncio in Spain, proposed establishing a similar institution in Italy, and in July 1542 Pope Paul III bestowed on him the power to do so. One of the supporters of Carafa's proposal to establish the Inquisition in Italy was a Spaniard living in Rome who was to play a major role in the next stage of the Catholic Reformation. His name was Ignatius Loyola (1495–1556).

Ignatius Loyola and the Jesuits

On the basis of his background, it seemed highly unlikely that Ignatius Loyola would become a leader in the reform of the church. His father was a Basque nobleman, and Ignatius was the youngest son in a large family. He was initially destined for the priesthood but showed so little interest that his father sent him to serve as a page at the court of King Ferdinand, where he lived the dissipated life of a young courtier. Three years later, Loyola was briefly involved in military action when the French attacked the fortress in which he was serving. He was wounded when a cannonball broke his right leg and wounded the left. His leg was initially set incorrectly, and it had to be rebroken and reset twice; the injury left him with a limp for the remainder of his life. During the nine months in which he was convalescing, he asked for his usual reading—chivalric romances—but the castle had only a medieval *Life of Christ* and a collection of saints' lives. In his autobiography, written in the third person, Loyola described the impact of this reading: "By the frequent reading of these books he conceived some affection for what he found there narrated. Pausing in his reading, he gave himself up to thinking over what he had read. At other times he dwelled on the things of the world which formerly had occupied his thoughts. . . . In reading of the life of our Lord and the lives of the saints, he paused to think and reason with himself, 'Suppose I should do what St. Francis did, what St. Dominic did.'"[15]

Loyola became convinced that God was working within him and guiding him to a new life. In March 1522 he made a pilgrimage to the shrine of the Virgin Mary at Montserrat, where he dedicated himself to the service of Christ. He gave away his fine clothes, put on a beggar's robe, and left his sword and dagger at the altar. Loyola spent much of the following year in seclusion at Manresa, where he went through spiritual struggles similar to those Luther had experienced in the monastery. He sometimes spent as much as seven hours on his knees in prayer, fasting and scourging himself. Like Luther, he was so tormented by his sins that he tried to rid himself of his guilt by self-mortification. Although the two men's struggles were in some respects similar, the solutions they arrived at were radically different. As we know, Luther came to the conclusion that he could never achieve reconciliation with God or peace of mind by his efforts to live a righteous life, and so he threw himself totally on the mercies of God in Jesus Christ. In contrast, Loyola devised a method by which he could achieve a life that was lived to a great extent in conformity to what he considered God's will.

While at Manresa, Loyola began writing what was to be his most famous work, the *Spiritual Exercises*. This book outlines specially designed exercises that take place over a period of thirty days. The first week is devoted to meditations on sin and its consequences, which is followed by three weeks of meditations on Christ's life, concluding with his passion, resurrection, and ascension. Throughout the book there are instructions on prayer, suggestions for the ascetic life, and ways to evaluate motives and impulses. An appendix entitled "Rules for Thinking with the Church" was added to the *Exercises*; the rules teach total dedication to the church. They begin by stating that "we must put aside all judgment of our own, and keep the mind ever ready and prompt to obey in all things the true spouse of Christ our Lord, our holy mother, the hierarchical church." The thirteenth rule emphasizes submission to the church even more strongly. It reads:

> If we wish to proceed securely in all things, we must hold fast to the following principle: What seems to me white, I will believe black if the hierarchical church so defines. For I must be convinced that in Christ our Lord, the bridegroom, and in his spouse the church, only one Spirit holds sway, which governs and rules for the salvation of souls. For it is by the same Spirit and Lord who gave the Ten Commandments that our holy mother church is ruled and governed.[16]

The *Exercises* proved to be extremely effective, and through the centuries many Christians have found them a useful aid in their spiritual journeys. They also provided a spiritual training manual for the Society of Jesus, the new religious order founded by Loyola. The *Spiritual Exercises* helped to engender in novices a spirit of discipline and unselfish service to the church that made the Jesuits some of the most effective agents of the Catholic Reformation.

In September 1523 Loyola went on a pilgrimage to Jerusalem, where he spent three weeks visiting the places associated with the life of Christ. He then returned to Spain to pursue his neglected education. He needed first to learn Latin, which he did by studying with schoolboys in Barcelona. In February 1528, after studying in two Spanish universities, he enrolled at the University of Paris. He was thirty-seven years old, had a poor academic background, suffered from ill health, and had inadequate financial resources, but through hard work and discipline Loyola was successful in completing his studies and being awarded a master's degree in 1534.

While at the university Loyola gathered around him a group of six equally committed men, including Francis Xavier (whose remarkable

career as a missionary to Asia will be discussed in chapter 12) and Diego
Lainez and Alfonso Salmeron, who were to play important roles at the
Council of Trent. After Loyola left the university, the group took vows
of poverty and chastity and pledged themselves to go to Jerusalem to
convert the Turks. If that were not possible, they agreed they would go
to Rome to serve the pope. They planned to meet in Venice the following year to depart for the Holy Land, but when they got there Venice
was at war with the Turks, so they were prevented from crossing the
Mediterranean to carry out their mission. They remained near Venice
for three years, preaching and engaging in charitable works, and when
they were still unable to go to Jerusalem, they decided to pursue their
alternative plan of service to the pope in Rome.

While in Rome Loyola recommended that, rather than continuing
in an unstructured way, they found a religious order and seek papal
approval. In the summer of 1539 Loyola's group submitted the proposal
for a new order to Pope Paul III, with the support of Contarini, who recognized their potential for becoming a major force for church reform. In
September 1540 the pope issued a bull officially recognizing the Society
of Jesus, or the Jesuits, as they are popularly known. According to the
original charter the society was to be limited to sixty members, each
of whom vowed: "To abandon his will, to consider ourselves bound by
special vow to the present pope and his successors to go without com-
plaint, to any country whither they may send us, whether to the Turk
or other infidels, in India or elsewhere, to any heretics or schismatics,
as well as to the faithful, being subject only to the will of the pope and
the general of the order."[17]

The Jesuits were not only a tightly disciplined order, they were also an
elitist order that attracted only the brightest and most committed men.
Before becoming a full member of the order, the aspirant underwent
twelve years of rigorous training, which included a year of general studies,
three years of philosophical studies, and four years of theological studies.
Training also included preaching, practical theology, and the *Spiritual
Exercises*, and a dominant trait of the order was complete submission
to hierarchical authority. In a frequently quoted letter written in March
1553, Loyola described the Jesuit belief on authority:

> We may allow ourselves to be surpassed by other religious orders in fasts,
> watchings and other austerities. . . . But in the purity and perfection of
> obedience together with the true resignation of our wills and abnegation
> of our judgment, I am very desirous, my dear brothers, that they who serve
> God in this society should be conspicuous. . . . For the superior is to be

obeyed not because he is prudent, good, or qualified by any other gift of God, but because he holds the place and authority of God.[18]

Not surprisingly Loyola became the first superior general of the order, but only after two ballots. On the first ballot all except Loyola voted for him, but he refused to accept unless the vote was unanimous. The second election had the same result, and again he initially refused to accept, but in the end he bowed to the inevitable on the insistence of his confessor. Loyola spent the remaining fifteen years of his life directing the rapidly growing order. Although the papal bull had limited the Jesuits to sixty members, the papacy subsequently lifted that restriction, and by the time of its founder's death in 1556, numbers had increased to one thousand Jesuits living in one hundred different houses. By that time the Jesuits had also established almost a hundred colleges and seminaries. Initially Loyola had planned to establish seminaries purely for training members of the order, but he was eventually persuaded to establish mixed colleges where non-Jesuit students could study as a means of reaching the ruling classes and the educated elite of society. Pope Paul III found the order especially useful in helping him carry out his reforming program and used it in many different ways, including diplomatic missions. In addition, the order was involved in many charitable activities, and the Jesuits led the way in missionary work outside Europe.

Although the Jesuits are well known for their role in serving as papal shock troops to win back areas of Europe to Catholicism, this was not their initial or primary activity. In fact, the order grew fastest in Portugal and Sicily, two areas where Protestantism had made little or no impact. Nevertheless, Loyola was also committed to confronting the challenge posed by the spread of Protestantism. This commitment was clearly expressed in his letter to Peter Canisius, who was to be one of the most effective Jesuit missionaries in Germany. The letter, written in August 1554, pointed out the threat posed by Protestantism and the role of the Jesuits in restoring true religion:

Seeing the progress which the heretics have made in a short time, spreading the poison of their evil teaching throughout so many countries and peoples . . . it would seem that our society, having been accepted by Divine Providence among the efficacious means to repair such great damage, should be solicitous to prepare proper steps, such as are quickly applied and can be widely adopted thus exerting itself to the utmost of its powers to preserve what is still sound and to restore what has fallen sick of the plague of heresy, especially in the northern nations.[19]

The letter suggested that Protestantism should be confronted with "sound theology" and that "dogmas" should be proven "with good arguments from Scripture, tradition, the councils and the doctors." It should be taught to the people in a way that they could understand, using many of the methods Protestants used, including catechisms, booklets, and pamphlets. The letter concluded: "We should use the same diligence in healing that the heretics are using in infecting the people."[20]

Loyola died within two years of writing this letter. He spent his last two decades mainly in Rome, from where he directed the myriad activities of the order. In this effort he wrote many letters, which help provide historians with insights into the mind and character of this remarkable man who played such a vital role in the Catholic Reformation. Like Luther, he was plagued with poor health during his later years but never slackened in his relentless activity to carry out what he considered God's calling. Loyola dictated his final letters on his deathbed, while suffering a painful gall bladder attack. After spending the night in prayer, he died in the early hours of 31 July 1556, before he could even be given the last rites. He was succeeded as superior general of the order by Diego Lainez, one of the original Jesuits, who had played a major role in assuring that the Council of Trent did not make any compromises with the Protestant doctrine of justification.[21]

The Council of Trent (1545–1565)

The long-delayed general council of the church began to meet at Trent in 1545, almost three decades after Luther wrote his *Ninety-five Theses*. Although Luther first appealed to a church council in November 1518 and many others had consistently looked to a council to resolve the problems that caused the schism in the church throughout the early years of the Reformation, its meeting was consistently delayed. Political rivalries, especially the wars between France and the Holy Roman Empire, played a major role in preventing the meeting of a council. The emperor and the papacy also had different goals for the council, which made it difficult to agree on an agenda. Emperor Charles V wanted a council that included Protestants and that would concentrate on moral and disciplinary reforms and would serve to heal the schism in the church. The pope wanted a council controlled by the papacy that would concentrate on moral reforms. Memories of the medieval conciliar movement made popes very cautious about calling a council that might threaten papal power. Members of the Curia were equally concerned about preserving their privileges and feared that a council committed to a thorough reform of the church might adversely affect them. In the end, the differing agendas of the emperor and the pope were reconciled by agreeing to discuss theological and reform issues alternately. A further problem was where the council should meet. If it met in Germany it was more likely to be controlled by the emperor, while the papacy would be in a stronger position if the council met in Italy. Trent provided a good solution, as it was in northern Italy but still within the boundaries of the Holy Roman Empire.

Paul III issued the papal bull convening the council in May 1542, but war between France and the Holy Roman Empire delayed the first meeting for three more years. When the delegates finally assembled at Trent in December 1545, it was not a particularly auspicious gathering. Only thirty-one bishops and forty-two theologians attended the first session, the vast majority of them Italians,[22] so the meeting could hardly be considered representative of the whole church. On that December day there was little to suggest that this council would become one of the most important councils in the history of the church. It met in three separate phases over a period of eighteen years, and it would "produce a body of legislation greater in bulk than the total left by all previous eighteen General Councils of the Church."[23] Cardinal Pole, one of the three presiding papal legates, who had been a member of the Papal Reform Commission of 1537, spoke to the assembly in its second session on 7 January 1546. In a courageous address, he identified "heresy . . . the decline in ecclesiastical morals, and . . . internal and external war" as the three areas that the council needed particularly to address, and he urged the council to begin to deal with the evils in the church by confessing their own sins: "Therefore what in his great love of God the Father and his mercifulness towards our race Christ did, justice itself now enacts of us that we make ourselves responsible for all the evils now burdening the flock of Christ. The sins of all we should take upon ourselves, not in generosity but in justice; because the truth is that of these evils we are in great part the cause and therefore we should implore the divine mercy through Jesus Christ."[24]

The initial doctrinal decrees set the tone for the future direction of the council. In April the decree on authority rejected the Reformation teaching that the Scriptures were the sole source of authority in the church, stating that "unwritten traditions" and the Bible were of equal authority; however, the decree did not define the relationship between Scripture and tradition. The council also pronounced the primacy of the Vulgate translation over all others and condemned those who would "presume to interpret" Scripture "contrary to the sense which holy mother Church, to whom it belongs to judge their true sense and interpretation, has held and holds."[25] The vitally important decree of justification was promulgated in January 1547. By far the longest of the council's decrees, the final version consisted of sixteen chapters and thirty-three canons, which condemned opposing positions. Among the positions condemned were the beliefs that justification was either by works or by faith alone, as well as the teaching that justification was based solely on the imputation of Christ's righteousness.[26] The decree presented justification as a process in which the sinner was made righteous. Justification was described as "not only a remission of sins, but also the sanctification and renewal of the inward man through the voluntary reception of the grace and gifts whereby an unjust man becomes just." Although faith was the beginning of the process of justification, and it began without human merit playing a part, in order to complete the process, human beings must cooperate with God's grace. The eternal punishment for sin was remitted in baptism, but the temporal punishment for sin must be atoned for by "fasts, alms, prayers and other devout exercises of the spiritual life, not indeed for the eternal punishment, which is, together with the guilt remitted . . . but for the temporal punishment, which, as the sacred writings teach is not always wholly remitted." Among the teachings that were condemned was "that no debt of temporal punishment remains to be discharged either in this world or in purgatory before the gates of heaven can be opened."[27]

The decree on justification was particularly significant. In the words of one historian, it "completed the separation of Protestants and Catholics from the shared theological inheritance of the Middle Ages and created a new Catholic doctrinal orthodoxy."[28] Shortly after the decree was promulgated, the first phase of the council came to an end. Once again the rivalry between the emperor and the papacy affected the council, as Charles's victory over the Lutheran princes in April 1547 caused the pope to fear that an overly powerful emperor might impose his will. The outbreak of a serious epidemic in Trent provided the excuse for moving the council to Bologna, in the Papal States, where it would be further from the center of the emperor's power base. Charles was furious and insisted that the delegates return to Trent. Fourteen Spanish bishops refused to leave Trent, and Charles sought his own solution to achieving reconciliation with the Lutherans in Germany through the Augsburg Interim. Pope Paul III eventually bowed to the inevitable and ordered the suspension of the council in February 1548.

Paul III died in the following year, and his successor, Pope Julius III (1550–1555), was elected only after a bitterly contested election: Reginald Pole missed being elected by just one vote. Julius was hardly the ideal candidate to lead a reform movement: he was a typical, pleasure-loving Renaissance churchman, devoted to providing for his relatives. He even created scandal by his infatuation with a fifteen-year-old youth, whom he found in the streets of Parma and had his brother adopt as a son. Julius made his new nephew a cardinal, which hardly seemed an appropriate action for a pope committed to reforming the abuses in the church. Pope Julius III was also not the favorite candidate of the emperor, especially since he had proposed the motion for moving the council to Bologna. Nevertheless, the work of reform continued as the new pope reconvened the council at Trent in May 1551. Although it met for less than a year, the sessions produced important decrees on the Eucharist and penance. The doctrine of transubstantiation was reasserted, and in a series of canons, the Lutheran, Zwinglian, and Calvinist positions on the Eucharist were specifically condemned. On the question of penance, the necessity of oral confession before a priest and of performing satisfaction for sins was affirmed.

A number of German Lutheran representatives were allowed to join the council in January 1555 on the emperor's insistence. This was the only time that Protestants participated in the council, and they were not happy that essential questions had been decided before they arrived. The only matters they were allowed to discuss were communion in both kinds and marriage of the clergy. The Lutherans insisted that the council void all previous doctrinal decisions and begin anew to discuss the doctrines that had already been promulgated. Not surprisingly, they did not succeed in their demands. Shortly afterwards the council was again suspended as the political situation in Germany changed. This time it was not fear of the emperor's power that resulted in the suspension but the defeat of the emperor by the turncoat Lutheran, Maurice of Saxony. When Maurice changed sides in the war and attacked the emperor, the delegates at Trent feared he might also attack them. With the Protestant army just a few hours' march from Trent, Pope Julius III decided it might be wise to move, so in April 1552 he adjourned the council. It did not meet again for almost a decade.

One of the reasons the council was not reconvened sooner was the election of Giovanni Pietro Carafa as Pope Paul IV (1555–1559) in May 1555. Paul IV, who was a deeply committed reformer, was, nevertheless, totally opposed to councils, which he considered "as at best a source of vain theological chatter."[29] In contrast to the pleasure-loving Julius,

Carafa lived a life of strict personal asceticism. He had been involved in the reform movement for much of his life, was a member of the Roman Oratory of Divine Love, served on the Papal Reform Commission, and was the cofounder and the first superior of the Theatine order, which was dedicated to strict poverty and to reforming abuses in the church. He was, as noted earlier, opposed to Contarini's attempt to achieve reconciliation with Protestants and was responsible for the establishment of the Inquisition in Rome.

Paul IV was seventy-nine years old when he became pope, but age had not mellowed him. He was totally intolerant of any form of deviance and zealously sought to impose conformity and reform on all who were guilty of immorality or abusing their office in the church. He sought to prevent simony and to reform corruption in the Curia; he also dealt harshly with monks who were living outside the monastery without permission, scourging them and sentencing them to serve in the galleys. He even attacked other reformers, such as Pole, whom he accused of an unorthodox view on justification. Even though Pole was at the time working with Queen Mary for the restoration of Catholicism in England, Pope Paul IV summoned him back to Rome to face charges of heresy. It was only Mary's support of her archbishop that helped to preserve one of the leading Catholic reformers from being tried for heresy. At the same time as he was expanding the work of the Roman Inquisition, Paul IV also issued the first Roman Index of Prohibited Books in the final year of his pontificate. It was so sweeping in its prohibitions that all vernacular translations of the Bible as well as all the works of Erasmus were banned. Not surprisingly, even those who had once supported Paul IV greeted his death in August 1559 with a sense of relief.[30]

Paul IV's successor was Pope Pius IV (1559–1565), who differed radically from his predecessor. In contrast to the ascetic and despotic Paul IV, Pope Pius IV was open and much worldlier. He was also guilty of nepotism, in that he made his twenty-one-year-old nephew, Charles Borromeo, a cardinal and archbishop of Milan. This proved an excellent choice, however, as Borromeo became one of the important leaders of the Catholic Reformation. Pius IV reversed some of his predecessor's more despotic acts and placed restrictions on the Inquisition. He also began a revision of the Index to make it less unreasonably restrictive. He did not share Paul IV's attitude toward councils and reconvened the Council of Trent in January 1562.

Two hundred bishops attended the new session of the council, and they were much more representative of the church outside of Italy. As a result, this was also the most turbulent phase of the council. Spanish and French bishops—who were present in larger numbers—were determined to protect the independence of their national churches from papal dominance. One of the central questions involved in the debate was whether the papacy could grant dispensations from the requirement that a bishop be resident in his diocese. If bishops derived their power directly from Christ, popes could not grant dispensations, but if their powers were derived from the pope, they could. The wider question was whether Christ granted the power to rule the church to Peter alone or to all the apostles. Both sides appealed to the church fathers, and some of the sessions became so stormy that the delegates denounced each other as heretics and punches were thrown. Meanwhile their lay supporters fought each other in the streets of Trent. In the end the council took refuge in ambiguity, stating that the bishops were the successors of the apostles and the Holy Spirit instituted them to rule the church, yet it did not specifically define the extent of papal authority.

Although the council did not resolve the questions dealing with papal authority, it continued the process of doctrinal definition and issued a series of important reforming decrees. The doctrinal decrees further divided Protestants and Catholics, as the dogma of the sacrificial mass was defined. It was also agreed that purgatory existed, that souls in purgatory were aided by masses and prayers, and that it was good and useful to call upon the saints in heaven for aid. The disciplinary decrees were to play a vital role in correcting abuses. Probably the most far-reaching was the order that a seminary should be erected in every diocese for the training of clergy. Although it would take some time before that order could be implemented, it was the beginning of the process that resulted in the Catholic Church acquiring a well-educated priesthood. In addition, measures were enacted to ensure the residence of clergy and the reform of the clergy's lifestyle, including the suppression of concubinage. Strict norms were set for the appointment of cardinals and bishops, and annual episcopal visitations of the dioceses were to be held. Uncompleted business, such as the preparation of an official catechism as well as the revision of the Missal, the Breviary, and the Index, was delegated to the pope, who confirmed the acts of the council in January 1564.

With all its divisions, the council ended on a note of unity as the delegates broke out in spontaneous cheering for the pope. One eyewitness wrote, "I myself saw many of the most grave prelates weep . . . and those who had only the day before treated each other as strangers embrace with profound emotion."[31] In the closing address Jerome Ragazonus, the presiding papal legate, spoke of the successes and the failures of the council:

> This most happy day has dawned for the Christian people, the day in which the temple of the Lord, often shattered and destroyed, is restored and completed, and this one ship, laden with every blessing and buffeted by the worst and most restless storms and waves is brought safely into port. Oh, that those for whose sake this voyage was chiefly undertaken had decided to board it with us, that those who caused us to take this work in hand had participated in the erection of the edifice! Then indeed we would have reason for greater rejoicing. But it is certainly not through our fault that it so happened.[32]

From one perspective Ragazonus was perceptive in describing the achievements of the Council of Trent. He was also correct in recognizing that the major failure of the council was that it failed to heal the schism, although his assessment of the blame for that failure is more questionable. Except for the insignificant Lutheran representation in its second phase, the council made no real effort to achieve reconciliation with Protestants.

From the perspective of those who believed that no compromise with Protestantism was possible, the council had done its work well. It had defined the theology of the church in such a way as to differentiate Catholic belief from all forms of Protestantism. It had also enacted impressive reform legislation that held out the promise of creating a truly reformed church that would not only save Catholicism from further Protestant inroads but could also begin the process of winning back areas that had been lost in the initial stages of the Reformation. However, for those such as Contarini, who had hoped for reconciliation with the Protestants, the council had virtually eliminated that possibility. The theological decrees condemned Protestant beliefs in such specific terms that future generations would find the canons and decrees of the Council of Trent a major stumbling block to ecumenical discussions. After Trent, it seemed that the only way in which the schism could be healed would be by Protestants surrendering their beliefs or by suppression.

Trent was also a defeat for those Catholics, such as Pole, who were in the Augustinian tradition or who were committed to humanism. The theological decrees of the council signified the victory of certain Catholic traditions over others that could equally claim to be part of the theological heritage of the medieval church.[33] After almost two decades, the work of the Council of Trent was finished. It remained to be seen how effectively its reforms would be put into practice.

The Impact of Tridentine Catholicism

A reformed papacy played a major role in the implementation of the Tridentine legislation. Pope Pius IV died within a year of its ending, after he had confirmed the acts of the council. He was succeeded by Pope Pius V (1566–1572), an austere reformer who was committed to putting the decisions of the council into effect. In contrast to the Renaissance papacy, there was no trace of worldliness either in his personal life or his appointments. He imposed such strict moral standards on Rome that he was accused of turning the city into a monastery. He not only put the reforming decrees of Trent into practice in Italy but also made sure the decisions of the council were circulated throughout the Catholic world. He completed the work of Trent by publishing a Roman catechism as well as a revised Breviary and Missal. Unfortunately, in his commitment to enforcing the decisions of Trent, Pius V relied heavily on the Inquisition and greatly expanded its activities, at times attending its sessions in person. He also lacked political astuteness and, as was noted in the last chapter, his decision to excommunicate and depose Queen Elizabeth I adversely affected the cause of English Catholics.

Equally committed reformers followed Pius V in the papal office. Gregory XIII (1572–1585), although less austere and rigorous than his predecessor, worked hard to carry out the decisions of Trent and to make sure that the men appointed to the episcopacy, or who were made cardinals, were worthy of the office. He was also responsible for the revision of the calendar. Gregory proclaimed the new calendar—fittingly called the Gregorian calendar—by a papal bull in 1582. Although Catholic countries accepted it almost immediately, the divisions resulting from the Reformation were evident even in the much-needed calendar revisions.[34] Protestant states, suspicious of a papal calendar, did not introduce it for more than a century.

The popes who followed Gregory XIII were also concerned about reform and took steps to implement the decisions of Trent,[35] so the papacy, which had at the outset of the Reformation era been one of the major stumbling blocks in the way of reform, became its most zealous proponents. A massive change also occurred in the Curia, as cardinals were no longer appointed largely on the basis of family connections. Spiritual qualities as well as commitment to reform were now important considerations, and this was evident in the way they conducted themselves. The Venetian ambassador in Rome noted the difference in one of his reports: "Cardinals now stand aloof from every kind of amusement. They are no longer seen riding or driving masked in the company of ladies. . . . Banquets, games, hunting parties, liveries and all forms of external luxury are all the more at an end because there are no longer any lay persons of high rank at the courts, such as were formerly to be found there in great numbers among the relatives and intimates of the pope."[36] Sadly, the pope's determination to suppress Protestantism sometimes resulted in actions that are difficult to defend from a Christian perspective. For example, when Pope Gregory XIII learned of the terrible massacre of French Protestants in the St. Bartholomew's Day Massacre, he had thanksgiving services celebrated in Rome and issued a commemorative medallion to celebrate the massacres as a "holy" event.[37]

The Catholic Reformation also benefited from a substantial increase in the number of reforming bishops. One of the most outstanding was Charles Borromeo (1538–1584), the archbishop of Milan, who made Milan into a model archdiocese, reforming the clergy and the monastic orders while also renovating churches and establishing schools and colleges. There are many other examples of reforming bishops. The Irish church had an especially impressive group of conscientious bishops, who used their powers effectively to correct abuses. Other countries were blessed with equally able and committed bishops. However, this was clearly not the case throughout Europe, as "only a minority of bishops in the sixteenth and seventeenth centuries could be accurately described as zealous reformers."[38] A myriad of abuses continued in the French church, where nepotism was rampant, and a significant number of bishops continued to be nonresident or pluralists. Even those bishops committed to reform could not always bring to their diocese the type of reform Trent envisaged. One major problem was finding the resources to establish the diocesan seminaries ordered by the Tridentine decree. Only the wealthier dioceses could afford a seminary, and their establishment proceeded at a relatively slow pace, so that at the end of the Reformation era many priests were still poorly educated. In addition, bishops did not control all clerical appointments, as in many cases private patrons had the right to nominate parish priests, so bishops could do little to prevent the appointment of unsuitable candidates.

Despite the difficulties faced by the bishops in appointing and training able parish priests, there were major improvements in the parishes, where a new type of reformed clergy was becoming more common by the end of the Reformation era. Absenteeism was significantly reduced, and moral offenses were less prevalent.[39] Although visitations still uncovered abuses, regular visitations were being held, and efforts were being made to correct the abuses uncovered by the visitations—marks of a church that was serious about reform. There was also a significant increase in the number of priests who were qualified to preach, as homiletics became part of the new seminary training. A better-trained, more moral, and more spiritually committed clergy worked hard to change the beliefs and lifestyle of the laity, who clearly needed instruction even in the fundamentals of the faith. St. Vincent De Paul noted in 1651: "In truth the greater part of those called Catholics are Catholics only in name, because their fathers were Catholics before them, and not because they know what it means to be a Catholic."[40]

The French historian Jean Delumeau has argued that the majority of the population was never really Christianized in the Middle Ages and that one of the achievements of both the Catholic and Protestant Reformations was the conversion of the masses from popular religion to Christianity.[41] Sermons, catechisms, art, and other forms of visual presentations were used to teach the faith. There was a new emphasis on the sacrament of penance, and private confession to a priest was aided by the use of "a new piece of church furniture: the confessional box."[42] Jesuits became especially skilled in the confessional and used that skill to bring life changes in the laity. They were also skilled in communicating the faith in creative ways, often using theatrical performances and popular presentations. Long before the Salvation Army came up with the idea, Jesuits put religious words to melodies that were familiar to the ordinary person in other settings. For example, in the early eighteenth century "a new French 'Invocation to the Holy Spirit' was set to the tune of a well-known popular song with the rather interesting title, 'I don't know if I'm drunk.'"[43]

A central concern of the Catholic Reformation was winning back areas from Protestants, which was done in many different ways. Using a method Protestants had once used to win areas from Catholicism, better-educated Catholic priests now challenged Protestants to public debates. Trained in the Scriptures as well as Protestant theology and methods of argumentation, the Catholic debaters were more than able to hold their own in these debates. Jesuits also used their excellent schools to attract Protestants and win them over. They even infiltrated schools in hostile Protestant environments. One Norwegian Jesuit acquired a post at a seminary in Sweden, obviously without disclosing his true identity, and subtly won many of his students to the Catholic faith. He not only converted thirty of them, but some even went to Rome for further training. One of the most successful missionaries to Protestants was the Dutch Jesuit Peter Canisius (1521–1597). It is estimated that he covered some twenty thousand miles on foot and horseback, in an era when travel was difficult, spreading the Catholic faith. In addition

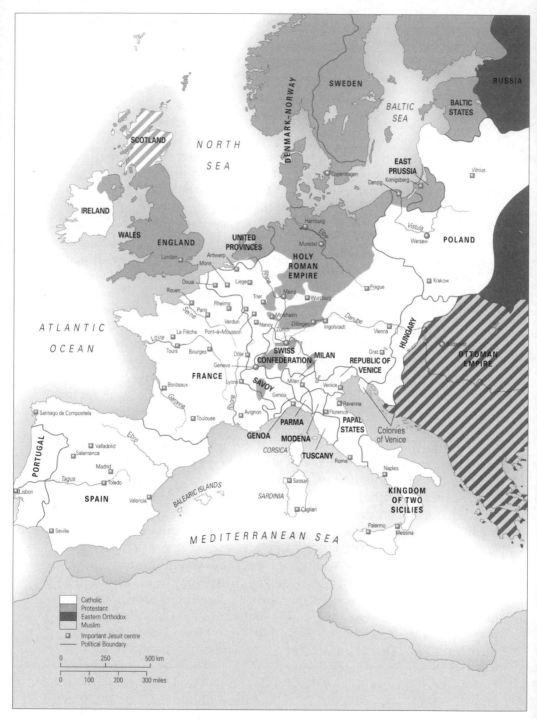

The Catholic Recovery ca. 1650.

to preaching countless sermons and founding five Jesuit university colleges and a series of colleges for boys, he prepared three catechisms for teaching the faith—including a large catechism for priests and educated adults, a mid-size one for adolescents, and a small catechism for children. Canisius was one of many dedicated priests responsible for the success of the Catholic Reformation in winning back areas from Protestantism through education, debate, and preaching. Other successes were achieved in a far less desirable way. In the final century of the Reformation era France, Belgium, Austria, Bavaria, Bohemia, and Poland were all restored to Catholicism, but much of this was accomplished by political manipulation and religious war.[44]

Although the Catholic Reformation was directed against Protestantism and many of its manifestations were anti-Protestant, curiously it also had much in common with the Protestant Reformation. Both Reformations sought to Christianize a European population that was often Christian in only a very superficial way, and for which popular religion was more important than official Christianity. Both the Catholic and the Protestant Reformations launched a frontal attack on popular religion, which the medieval church had tolerated and even in some respects promoted. Both movements produced the kind of educated clergy that had been to a great degree absent in the medieval church. Both movements also stressed the importance of educating the laity, and both Protestants and Roman Catholics produced catechisms and homilies for this purpose. Sadly, the two movements, which had many objectives in common, found it impossible to reconcile the areas where they differed, and the result was religious war and permanent schism in the Christian church. Although Ragazonus was wrong to blame that failure on the Protestants, with the advantage of hindsight one is tempted to echo his lament: "Oh . . . that those who caused us to take this work in hand had participated in the erection of the edifice! Then indeed we would have reason for greater rejoicing."

11

WOMEN AND THE REFORMATION

▼

You remind me that the Apostle Paul told women to be silent in the church. I would remind you of the word of this same apostle that in Christ there is no longer male nor female and of the prophecy of Joel: "I will pour forth my spirit upon all flesh and your sons and your daughters will prophesy." I do not pretend to be John the Baptist rebuking the Pharisees. I do not claim to be Nathan upbraiding David. I aspire only to be Balaam's ass, castigating his master.

Katherine Zell[1]

These words were written by a twenty-six-year-old housewife in Strasbourg named Katherine Zell in response to attacks on her marriage to the Strasbourg reformer, Matthew Zell. They are surprising in that they came from a woman in an age when women were expected to be "silent in the church." Fortunately, many women were not silent, and as a result they made a significant contribution to the Reformation. For four centuries the men who wrote Reformation history paid little attention to the women of the Reformation, unless they were political leaders or unlucky enough to have been married to Henry VIII. Although Luther's wife Katherine received some attention, historians were generally either unaware of the female contribution to the Reformation or did not consider it important enough to devote much space to writing about it. Merry Wiesner has noted that most historians of the Reformation "simply ignored" women, "assuming either that women shared their father's and husband's experience so that gender made no difference, or else that women played no significant part in the Reformation."[2] By the time she wrote that article, historians were no longer ignoring the role of women in the Reformation. In the past three decades a great many studies have centered on this topic. The most recent innovation is gender studies, focusing on "the way societies determine what it means to be male or female and the norms set for appropriate male and female behaviour."[3]

The Impact of the Reformation on Women

One of the first modern historians to give serious attention to the women of the Reformation was the dean of Reformation historians, Roland Bainton. In 1971 he wrote the first of three volumes on the women of the Reformation. Entitled *Women of the Reformation in Germany and Italy*,[4] it introduced the general reading public to women who had been known only to specialist historians, if at all. Among them are three of the women discussed in this chapter: Katherine Zell, Vittoria Colonna, and Wibrandis Rosenblatt. In the preface Bainton discussed the reasons he had undertaken the study:

> I have always had an interest in those who have not had their due, and devoted my earliest studies to the heretics of the Reformation, who were persecuted alike by the Catholics and the Protestants. The second reason is to observe the way in which the reform was disseminated. The women constituted a half of the population, and had they boycotted the movement one may be sure that would have been the end. The third is to assess the impact of the Reformation on the social order. This involves the character of the family, the position of women in society and the role of women in the Church.[5]

Although Bainton was convinced that the Reformation changed the status of women and that their lot improved significantly, many historians today are not convinced that he was correct in that analysis.[6] They argue that although the Reformation may initially have offered new opportunities to women and the new attitude toward the family made marriage and motherhood more honorable than celibacy, as the Reformation progressed women lost the freedom they had initially experienced. In addition, the closing of convents in Protestant Europe eliminated one of the few opportunities women had in the Middle Ages for a vocation that provided them with an education and made it possible—even honorable—to avoid the drudgery of marriage and child-bearing. Feminist historians also point out that Protestants eliminated some of the ways in which the medieval church exalted the position of women in the church by rejecting the veneration of the Virgin Mary and the recognition of female saints. During the Middle Ages women could pray for other sainted women to intercede for them, but the Reformation ended that practice among Protestants.

While feminist historians have tended to stress what women lost as the result of the Reformation, other historians concentrate on what they gained. David Steinmetz maintained that the new role of a pastor's wife was a factor in the liberation of women: "Women who had lived a shadowy existence as a priest's concubine were able to enter into a sexual relationship with their husbands within officially acknowledged bonds of matrimony. . . . It may be difficult for women who are currently seeking ordination to regard the creation of pastor's wife as a great step forward in the liberation of women from unjust repression, but for the women involved the Reformation was a profoundly liberating event."[7]

Although Protestants did not ordain women, Steinmetz was convinced that the Protestant doctrine of the priesthood of all believers provided the foundation for arguing that women should have a significant role in ministry. He also stated that "lay women were given a far greater role in the lives of the Protestant churches than they had ever exercised in the medieval church, even as members of religious orders."[8] Lyndal Roper did not agree with him. In her excellent study of women in Augsburg, she argued that rather than opening up opportunities for women to play a role in the church, Protestant churches limited the role of women: "In the new church hierarchy drafted according to function by the Strasbourg preacher, Martin Bucer, there was no post for women amongst the range of clerical officials. The radical implications of the early Reformation doctrine of the priesthood of all believers, the theological tenet which offered at least the conceptual possibility of a ministering role for women in the Church, were lost."[9]

These are some of the major arguments in the controversy, and at the time of writing, neither side has been able to offer definitive evidence on how the Reformation affected the status of women. Possibly the most convincing conclusion is that offered by Sherrin Marshall in the introduction to a collection of essays on women in the Reformation: "Women were liberated as well as enslaved during the age of Reformation and Counter Reformation. To the extent that they were forced to accept and fit into stereotypes that shaped their behavioural options, women were confined. To the extent that they pursued . . . new activities and created definitions of spirituality not limited by gender, they were liberated."[10]

In this chapter we discuss some of the changes that occurred as the result of the Reformation, and the attitude of the Reformers toward women. We shall also study the lives and ministries of some exceptional women to see how they contributed to the Reformation. In order to see how the Reformation changed the status of women, if at all, we must begin by examining gender attitudes in the Middle Ages.

Women in the Middle Ages

Although the medieval church officially declared that marriage was a sacrament, at the Council of Florence in 1439, the church held that the highest state for the truly spiritual was celibacy. Even though women were intended by nature for childbearing, those women who surrendered that natural function and gave themselves fully to the Lord by retaining their virginity were especially extolled. Celibacy was also considered a more honorable state for men, so the clergy were required to be celibate. However, celibate clergy often found women a source of temptation. Sebastian Brant expressed this allure in his satirical poem *Ship of Fools*, published in 1494:

> Who sees too much of women's charms
> his morals and his conscience harms
> he cannot worship God aright
> who find in women great delight.[11]

Many clergymen were not able to resist "women's charms" and broke their vow of celibacy by taking a concubine, often with the approval of their bishop, who used clerical concubinage as a source of income by taxing them or charging them for a license to keep a concubine. In outward appearances such priests seemed to be married; they lived together with their concubine, often for a lifetime, and had children. The clergyman might benefit from the relationship, but for the woman the relationship fell far short of the benefits she might receive through marriage. She had no right to an inheritance, her children were illegitimate and did not carry the father's name, and she had no protection under the law.

Some clergy found women such a serious threat that they reacted with the worst kind of misogyny. For example in 1486 two Dominican monks, Heinrich Kraemer and Jacob Sprenger, wrote an instructional manual for inquisitors dealing with witchcraft entitled *Malleus Maleficarum* (Hammer against Witches). Although, as the title indicates, the work was primarily directed against witches, it contained some scurrilous passages about women in general, as the authors tried to explain why women were more prone than men to witchcraft. In addition to stating that women were more superstitious and more impressionable than men, Kraemer and Sprenger maintained that because women were "feebler both in mind and body, it is not surprising that they should come more under the spell of witchcraft." They also stated that women were imperfect from creation, offering a novel explanation of why a woman was in their estimation "more carnal than a man": "It should be noted that there was a defect in the formation of the first woman, since she was formed from a bent rib, that is, a rib of the breast, which is bent as it were in contrary direction to a man, and since through this defect she is an imperfect animal, she always deceives."[12]

Kraemer and Sprenger would have agreed with the general assumption of their society that the best women were those who gave up marriage and their natural function of childbearing and spent their lives in a convent. Although it is true that convents opened up possibilities for education and a vocation not available elsewhere, they could also become places of imprisonment for women who did not enter of their own volition. Sometimes women were forced by their families to enter the religious life for a variety of reasons, including trying to avoid having to pay a dowry for marriage. Conversely, those who found fulfillment in the religious life at times used their position as nuns to influence their society and the church. Some extraordinary women, such as Catherine of Siena and St. Bridget of Sweden, not only served their society in impressive ways through works of charity but also made an impact on the wider church with their persistent calls for reform. They severely chastised the papacy for corruption and during the Babylonian Captivity demanded that the pope return to Rome. Other nuns, such as Julian of Norwich, Hildegard of Bingen, and Mechthild of Magdeburg, wrote works that retain their status as some of the outstanding devotional and theological works of medieval literature. Although there were extraordinary women in the Middle Ages, including women who made their mark in the political arena such as Eleanor of Aquitaine and Joan of Arc, the vast majority of medieval women received no recognition and often lived very short lives of drudgery under the domination of men.

Attitude of Reformers

Did the Reformation result in a new attitude toward the role of women in church and society? If it did, one would expect to find the roots of that change in the beliefs of the Reformers. Consequently, historians have devoted much effort in recent years toward uncovering the attitude of the Reformers toward women. This is not always easy, because as a rule they did not write treatises specifically dealing with women, and their beliefs must be culled from occasional references made in their extensive publications.

Not surprisingly, historians have arrived at differing conclusions on the Reformers' views. For example, two recent studies of Calvin's beliefs offer different perspectives. Jane Douglass considered Calvin exceptionally pro-women for that time; she pointed out that he was the only major Reformer to include Paul's injunction regarding women's silence in the church under *adiaphora*, or things indifferent, which suggests that it was a matter that could be changed as circumstances directed. Although for the sake of order and decorum Calvin was not prepared to have women take a role of leadership because the attitudes of society prohibited it, he was open to the possibility that churches in a different culture might permit women's leadership. Nevertheless he was "far too deeply shaped by the prejudices of a patriarchal society to imagine giving up those patriarchal structures in the foreseeable future."[13] John Thompson has questioned some of those conclusions. While accepting that Calvin does stand out from other Reformers in considering Paul's restrictions on women in Corinthians as things indifferent, Thompson maintains that Calvin held traditional views on women's subordination and that he "was not as flexible on women's roles as Douglass has claimed." Although he was prepared to accept "the public ministry of women in time of crisis," it was purely "on the basis of sheer necessity."[14]

Luther was equally ambiguous in his attitudes toward women. Jonathan W. Zophy described Luther's seemingly contradictory attitudes in the opening paragraph of an article on Luther and women: "According to Luther, women are faint-hearted, flighty, haughty, weak in spirit, gossipy, vain, incapable of profound thought, and not up to the demands of public responsibility. Yet Luther had a deep love for his wife and his daughter and was kind to many other women. He also defended women publicly from their numerous detractors, advocated something close to partnership in marriage and worked to increase educational opportunities for girls."[15]

Although at times Luther showed great appreciation and sympathy for women, he continued to hold traditional attitudes and clearly believed that the major role God ordained for women was as mothers and wives. In contrast to the average male outlook in his age, Luther did appreciate that women experienced more suffering than men. In his commentary on Genesis, he wrote: "The female sex has been greatly humbled and afflicted and it bears a far severer and harsher punishment than the men. For what is there of such things that a man suffers in his own body" compared to what a woman suffers?[16] He often defended women and denounced those who reviled them, and he is also credited with advocating the right of women to acquire an education. As early as 1520 he stated in his *Address to the Christian Nobility*: "Would to God that every town had also a girls' school, in which girls might be taught the gospel."[17] In 1533 he helped to establish a school in Wittenberg to train young girls in the basic skills of reading, writing, mathematics, and music. That school served as a model for girls' schools that would later be established in other German towns.

Luther's commitment to women's education did not mean he viewed education as a means by which women could expand their vocational opportunities. Rather it simply provided the tools for them to function more effectively as wives and mothers. It is to Luther's credit that he viewed marriage as a partnership, and in his own marriage he put this belief into practice; however, the wife was clearly subordinate to the husband. The woman's role, Luther believed, was in the home, and she should not be involved in politics or play a leading role in the church. If women usurped men's roles, Luther stated, "There would be a disturbance and confusion of all social standing and of everything."[18] A recent study of Luther's letters to women confirms his contradictory view of women. He wrote eighty-three letters to forty different women for a variety of reasons. Although the letters present a more positive image of women than was common in his time, he seldom corresponded with women on intellectual questions or on theological issues.[19]

Martin Bucer seems to have had more enlightened views on women than any of the other Reformers, as revealed in his beliefs about divorce and remarriage.[20] Bucer viewed marriage as a fellowship in which the partners made a covenant with mutual obligations. Although the wife was still expected to be submissive, the husband was to sacrifice himself for his wife and must not act toward her in a tyrannical manner. Bucer permitted divorce as a last resort for a number of reasons, including adultery, desertion, illnesses that inhibit sexual intimacy, and abuse. In addition to permitting divorce for reasons that most of the Reformers would not have accepted, he allowed remarriage for both the innocent party and the guilty party upon repentance. Although Bucer continued to hold that women were to be submissive in marriage, he was clearly aware of the abuse women sometimes suffered in marriage from violent spouses. His willingness to allow divorce for abuse indicates a concern for abused women that was rare in his age. Bucer was also unique in his beliefs about the reasons for the institution of marriage. He did not teach that marriage was primarily for procreation, as the other Reformers believed; instead, he maintained that mutual service was the primary aim of marriage. Although, in common with the other Reformers, he viewed marriage as a remedy for lust, he stressed the importance of companionship and mutual affection in marriage. He also put his beliefs into practice in his own marriages. Yet despite his advanced views on some aspects of marriage, Bucer continued to believe, with the other Reformers, that a woman's role was largely confined to the home.

Changes Brought About by the Reformation

In view of the traditional beliefs the Reformers held about women, it should not be surprising that the Reformation did not result in women being liberated from the limited role they had in the Middle Ages or in their being given a major role in the church. However, there were clearly changes that had a significant effect on the lives of women. The changing attitude toward marriage and the family was an area in which medieval values were altered, but, as already noted, historians are not in agreement as to whether that was a positive step in the liberation of women. Although the Reformers viewed marriage as a partnership, it was not an equal partnership. Patriarchy was the ideal, and the family was organized according to a hierarchical structure of obedience, in which a wife obeyed her husband and the children obeyed their parents. In his study of the German Reformation, Robert Scribner stressed the limiting aspects of Protestant beliefs about women, marriage, and the family: "It is often said that Protestantism raised the status of women by projecting the ideal image of the Christian wife and mother. But it can also be said to have narrowed the range of acceptable female identities. The choice of an independent and celibate religious vocation in which a woman might develop her own talents was removed. In its place was set only the new ideal of the pastor's wife, to be fulfilled within the patriarchal context."[21] In contrast, Steven Ozment emphasized what women gained as the result of the new attitude toward marriage and showed how the marriages of the Reformers and others were based on mutual affection, respect, and companionship.[22]

The role of women in the church continued to be limited by traditional beliefs about women being silent and not exercising authority over men. Even Calvin and Bucer did not believe women could be ordained, and while Calvin viewed the biblical statements about women being silent in the church as *adiaphora*, he was not prepared to put into practice the implications of his belief. Nevertheless, it can be argued that the theology of the Reformation did open opportunities for women that were not available in the Middle Ages. For example, the Reformation emphasis on the authority of Scripture provided opportunities for women to hold their own against men in theological debate. Roland Bainton noted that "even the comparatively uneducated who appear in the martyrologies and the heresy trials, gave their judges a terrific run at any point involving the word of God."[23] Anabaptists, who did not limit preaching to the ordained ministry, gave women many opportunities to speak the Word, encouraging participation in sharing the message of Scripture in their worship services where women could be involved as much as men. Many Anabaptist women became martyrs, and in their trials and courageous deaths they testified to their faith and exhibited a thorough knowledge of Scripture. For example, Elizabeth Dirks, who was drowned in 1549 after being examined under torture, was accused of being a teacher of the heretic faith, which she did not deny. She also was more than the equal of her tormentors in her understanding of Scripture, being able to quote numerous passages from memory.[24]

Women also played a major role in the Catholic Reformation, but there were inevitably limitations as to how much they could do. Even Teresa of Avila who, as we have already noted, made important contributions to the Catholic Reformation, recognized those limitations when she wrote, "I heard of the miseries France was suffering and of the havoc the Lutherans were making there. . . . I would have laid down a thousand lives to save one of the many souls perishing there. Yet, as I am but a woman, feeble and faulty, it was impossible for me to serve God in the way I wished."[25]

Teresa of Avila also experienced the criticism a woman faced when she stepped out of the boundaries of what was considered acceptable for a female. The papal nuncio Felipe Sega wrote in 1579 that she was "a restless gadabout, a disobedient and contumacious woman, who

invented wicked doctrines, called them devotion . . . and taught others against the commands of St. Paul, who had forbidden women to
teach." Even those who admired and supported her still held that she
had stepped out of the role expected of a woman. The comment made
by a Carmelite friar in the sermon at the celebration when Teresa was
made a patron saint of Spain in 1627 reveals one way in which men
explained women excelling in a role that was not a typical woman's position. "This woman," he said, "ceased to be a woman, restoring herself
to the virile state, to greater glory than if she had been a man from the
beginning, for she rectified nature's error, transforming herself through
virtue into the bone from which she sprang."[26]

A woman who sought to follow a calling and attempted to make an
impact in a man's world had to be an exceptional person, like Teresa.
There were many other women whose exceptional gifts and courage
made it possible to make significant contributions to the Reformation.
They did so in many different ways, but until our own age their stories
were known only to a small group of specialist historians. The rest of
this chapter is devoted to telling the stories of three women whose lives
illustrate the ways in which women played a role in the Reformation.
Wibrandis Rosenblatt fits best the expected role of a woman as a wife
and mother, but she was quite exceptional in that she was married to
four different Reformers and outlived them all. Katherine Zell was also
the wife of a Reformer, but her exceptional achievement is that even in
a church that rejected women's ministry, she was able to carry on an
impressive ministry. Finally, Vittoria Colonna is an excellent example of
a woman who was an outstanding intellectual and who held her own in
the councils of men in the opening stages of the Catholic Reformation.
There are many other women's stories that could—and should—be told,
and not everyone will agree that the three selected best illustrate the
roles of women in the Reformation. But it would be hard to argue that
their tales are not worth telling.

The Marriages of Wibrandis Rosenblatt

Wibrandis was born in Basel in 1504 to a relatively well-to-do family,
her father being in the service of the emperor. As was not unusual in the
sixteenth century, she was married before she reached the age of twenty
to Ludwig Keller, a humanist and an early Protestant, who died in 1526
after they had been married for only two years. Wibrandis was left with
a daughter named after her and an uncertain future, but she did not

remain single for long. Within two years she married Oecolampadius, the Reformer of Basel. Oecolampadius married because his mother, who had looked after his house, had died, and his friend Capito encouraged him to get married. Oecolampadius was forty-five years old when he married the twenty-four-year-old Wibrandis; he had not been married before, so it could have been a difficult marriage. However, Oecolampadius was a gentle man and very appreciative of his young bride. When they got married, he said that he wished she was a bit older but saw in her "no signs of youthful petulance."[27] Wibrandis's second marriage lasted less than three years, but they were busy, productive, and happy ones—they were the years of the Basel Reformation in which she was fully involved. She provided hospitality for the many people who came to visit her husband, including Capito, who would become her third husband. She also corresponded with the wives of the other urban Reformers, including Anna Zwingli, Agnes Capito, and Elizabeth Bucer.

Wibrandis bore Oecolampadius three children, so when he died in November 1531 she was left a widow with four children, but again she did not remain unmarried for long. In the same month that her husband died, Capito's wife, Agnes, died, and Bucer, who was a great matchmaker for his colleagues and friends, already had Wibrandis in mind for his friend Capito. They were married in August 1532, and Wibrandis moved to Strasbourg to become involved in another of the urban Reformations. Again her life was busy, entertaining and providing support for her husband, who was a pastor and a professor, while at the same time bearing children. In less than a decade she had five more children—two boys and three girls—and then disaster struck. An outbreak of the plague in 1541 took a terrible toll, including many children. The Reformer Hedio lost all five of his children, while Bucer, whose wife Elizabeth had borne him thirteen children, of whom five had survived to 1541, lost four. Wibrandis lost three children as well as her husband, Capito. Bucer also lost his wife, Elizabeth, but before she died she urged her husband to marry Capito's widow and also appealed to Wibrandis to take her place as Bucer's wife. Her dying wish was fulfilled in April 1542 when Wibrandis, now in her late thirties, was married for the fourth time, to the fifty-year-old Martin Bucer.

Once again Wibrandis faced the challenge of providing for a very busy husband and taking care of a household, which included her five surviving children and Bucer's single surviving son. Bucer and Wibrandis had two more children in the course of their marriage but only one, a daughter, survived. Bucer appreciated his new wife, but missed his beloved Elizabeth. He wrote to a friend in April 1542, "There is nothing that I could desire in my new wife save that she is too attentive and solicitous. She is not as free in criticism as was my first wife, and now I realize that such liberty is not only wholesome but necessary. . . . I only hope I can be as kind to my new wife as she to me. But oh the pang for the one I have lost!"[28]

Bucer traveled a great deal in his work as a Reformer, and Wibrandis was often left alone to manage the household. She also provided hospitality for many people who came to see Bucer and rarely received recognition for it. For example, Peter Martyr Vermigli, who was one of many guests in her household, wrote a long letter in which he described the busyness of Bucer's life and the hospitality of his household, but he never once mentioned the woman who was responsible for that hospitality and who provided the support that Bucer needed to carry out his many responsibilities. Disaster struck again in 1548, but this time it was of human origin. The Augsburg Interim forced Bucer to flee to England, and Wibrandis was left alone to provide for the children and the household. Eventually she and all the family migrated to England, and once again she had to make all the arrangements. She was just settling into her home in a strange country when, in the winter of 1551, her fourth husband died.

Wibrandis then had to take care of all the financial matters and arrange for the family to return to Strasbourg. During this time she wrote a series of letters in both German and Latin, including one to Archbishop Cranmer, to gather the resources for her move and make the necessary arrangements. She managed to get the family back to Strasbourg and then moved to her home city of Basel, where she lived as a single mother raising her remaining children. Even after they left the household she was still trying to look after them. A letter to her son, John Simon Capito, who went to the University of Marburg to study theology, reads like a typical letter from a concerned mother to a son who is living the licentious life of a college student. She wrote:

> If only I might live to the day when I have good news from you then would I die of joy. Be thrifty, study hard, no drinking, gaming or wenching. If you would follow in the steps of your father, then grandma, the sisters, and the in-laws would lay down their very lives for you. But if you won't behave differently, no one will give you a heller. If you will behave yourself properly, come home. If you won't, then do as you will. I advise you to be saving. I wish you a good year. Your faithful mother.[29]

Wibrandis was a "faithful mother" as well as a committed wife to four Reformers. She died in 1564 from the plague at the age of sixty, largely forgotten. As a mother and wife, Wibrandis made important contributions to the Reformation that were largely unheralded and unrecognized. She was intelligent, resourceful, and able to take care of the many details of everyday life that made it possible for her husbands to carry on their work of promoting the Reformation. Today one might consider that work degrading and unrewarding, but it was as demanding as anything her husbands did, and she had to do it while having one baby after another—a challenge that they never had to face. Furthermore, although the husband was clearly the dominant person in her marriages, evidence suggests that to a great extent they recognized her as a partner in achieving their common goals.

The Ministry of Katherine Zell

Katherine Zell[30] had a remarkable ministry in Strasbourg and was recognized by her husband, Matthew, as his co-worker in ministry. She called herself "a splinter from the rib of that blessed man Matthew Zell," and he referred to her as *"mein helfer"* (my helper).[31] Katherine, whose maiden name was Schutz, was the daughter of a well-respected Strasbourg carpenter, had a minimal education in one of the vernacular schools in Strasbourg, and never seems to have learned to read or write more than a few words of Latin. After a period of spiritual struggle similar to that which Luther underwent, she came to believe the doctrine of justification by faith alone after reading Luther's tracts. In 1523 when Katherine was twenty-five or twenty-six years old, she married the man who had introduced the Reformation to Strasbourg, Matthew Zell. The marriage proved to be a great blessing to both partners. Although they were initially blessed with two children, both died, and so Katherine, in contrast to Wibrandis, was able to devote herself entirely to being her husband's *helfer* in his ministry.

Katherine was certainly not a passive *helfer*. She first showed her spirit in reaction to the bishop's excommunication of her husband for his marriage. Priests' marrying was, curiously, a serious abuse in the eyes of many bishops, who were willing to avert their gaze from priests living with a concubine; as a result, the Strasbourg priests who married were all excommunicated. We have already noted Katherine's vigorous defense of clerical marriage, and she was equally unreserved in what she wrote to the bishop. She admitted that her letter "smoked," and she also wrote a tract that was offensive enough for the bishop to complain to the Strasbourg city council, who forbade future writings of this sort, while continuing to support their married priests.

Katherine's work as Matthew's *helfer* involved more than writing indignant letters to bishops and tracts defending clerical marriage. It included a practical ministry to the thousands of refugees who flocked to Strasbourg because the city was willing to welcome people rejected elsewhere. For example, 150 men from the town of Kensingen were banned from their town after they briefly accompanied the Lutheran minister when he was forced to leave town. After one man was caught and executed, the rest fled to Strasbourg, where Katherine helped to provide for them by accommodating eighty of them in the parsonage and feeding sixty for three weeks. She also found provisions for the others and ministered to their wives by writing them words of comfort and consolation:

> Had I been chosen . . . to suffer as you women I would account myself happier than all the magistrates at Strasbourg with their necklaces and golden chains. Remember the word of the Lord in the prophet Isaiah "in overflowing wrath for a moment I hid my face from you but with everlasting love I will have compassion on you" . . . are not these golden words? Faith is not faith which is not tried. "Blessed are those that mourn." Pray then, for those who persecute you that you "may be perfect as your Father in heaven is perfect."[32]

The Peasants' War of 1525 presented a serious challenge to Strasbourg when some three thousand refugees with their wives and children fled there to escape the retribution of the princes after the defeat of the peasants. Although the peasants had not heeded the pleas of Capito and Matthew Zell, who visited their encampments accompanied by Katherine urging them to avoid violence, the refugees were not turned away when they sought help. The arrival of so many refugees posed a serious problem for a city of approximately twenty-five thousand, and in order to provide for the refugees, two gifted people were put in charge of dealing with the problems of food distribution and housing. The first was Lucas Hackfurt, one of the municipal directors of relief, and the second was Katherine Zell. The emergency lasted for six months before the refugees were able to return to their homes. During this time Katherine and Hackfurt successfully carried out the huge job of seeing they were housed and fed.

In addition to the ministries described above, Katherine also made a major contribution to the worship of the Strasbourg church with the publication of a hymnal in the 1530s. This book was published at a time

when Strasbourg was in the process of making liturgical changes to
introduce a truly Protestant worship service. One of the major contributions of the Protestant Reformation to worship was the introduction
of vernacular congregational singing, which necessitated the production of hymn books. Katherine's hymnal was the first one published in
Strasbourg and was based on an earlier Bohemian Brethren hymnal of
1531, but Katherine added many tunes and wrote a preface explaining
why she published it and what she expected of it for those who used it as
well as providing annotations explaining the content of the hymns. The
modern editor of the hymn book has noted that Zell's major purpose in
publishing the hymnal was to teach the faith to ordinary Christians:

> Katherine was deeply concerned about ordinary Christians and the inad-
> equate resources available for their personal religious nourishment and
> expression. As her preface makes clear, Schutz Zell conceived of this book
> as a "teaching, prayer and praise" book for ordinary Christians, to give
> them Biblical knowledge of their faith, words for their personal devotional
> lives, and the means to praise God and edify their families and neighbours
> as they went about their daily business.[33]

In the preface Katherine also confronted some of the questions on
which the Reformers were divided, including whether or not there should
be singing in the service as well as what type of singing should be permitted. Although Luther was very enthusiastic about congregational
singing and composed some of the great Reformation hymns, not all
the Reformers were of the same mind. Zwingli would not allow any
music at all in public worship, and Calvinists limited congregational
singing to psalms. Katherine did not hesitate to take a stand on these
controversial issues, citing numerous Bible passages to show that God's
people should sing in worship, and she also confronted the belief that only
scriptural words such as the psalms should be sung. Katherine agreed
that what Christians sing should be taken from the Bible, but it was not
necessary to use its exact words—rather it was important that the songs
have biblical content. Katherine's introduction and annotations reveal a
surprisingly sophisticated understanding of Scripture and of Christian
theology for a person who was not theologically trained. Unfortunately,
Katherine's hymnal had a short life as it was not republished; however,
its influence is evident in the official Strasbourg liturgy-songbook published in 1541 and 1545.

Katherine's activities were not limited to Strasbourg. She traveled
extensively with her husband, visiting various centers of reform, including spending time with Luther in Wittenberg. Luther welcomed them,

even though Katherine had questioned his actions after the Marburg Colloquy in 1529. When Luther and Zwingli failed to reach agreement, Katherine wrote to Luther remonstrating with him for not agreeing to intercommunion, pointing out that first and foremost Christian action must be motivated by love. Luther responded that he agreed "except where God's Word is at stake."[34] When Calvin was at Strasbourg, he visited the Zells, who played a role in helping him get over his anger about being expelled from Geneva. Katherine also carried out the expected wife's role in providing hospitality. She housed and fed Zwingli and Oecolampadius for two weeks when they were on their way to Marburg in 1529, and she regularly entertained delegations visiting Strasbourg in her home. One can assume that she did not keep quiet when distinguished visitors were in her house and that she freely expressed her opinions on questions involving the Reformation.

One of the most remarkable things about Katherine was her tolerance in an age of intolerance. It is always difficult to rise above the spirit of the times, but Katherine did so in an impressive way. Although she was an orthodox Christian, she did not merely mouth Christian teaching about love for enemies but also fought for justice and denounced hypocrisy and false teaching of all sorts. Between 1529 and 1533 Strasbourg was flooded with Anabaptist refugees, fleeing both Lutheran and Catholic persecution. Strasbourg was remarkably tolerant, but there were limits even to its tolerance. When the radical Anabaptist Melchior Hoffman was imprisoned in Strasbourg for the last ten years of his life, most people ignored him. Alone and largely forgotten, he must have been depressed that the second coming of Christ, which he had expected to happen while he was in prison, had not come. However, he had at least one visitor, as Katherine put into practice Christ's command to visit those in prison. She also expressed sympathy for others who were rejected and persecuted, even when she did not agree with their theology. When Michael Servetus was executed in Geneva, she was one of the few people who expressed concern for him. In addition, she corresponded regularly with the Spiritualist Caspar Schwenckfeld and even defended him when a Strasbourg minister attacked him in the pulpit. In a statement that reveals Katherine's anger when someone was unjustly attacked, she wrote to the minister:

> Why do you rail at Schwenckfeld? You talk as if you would have him burned like the poor Servetus at Geneva. You say that you have left Strasbourg and gone to Ulm because the ministers here are too lenient. . . . You behave as if you have been brought up by savages in a jungle. The Anabaptists are pursued as by a hunter with dogs chasing wild boars. Yet the Anabaptists

accept Christ in all essentials as we do. They have borne witness to their
faith in misery, prison, fire, and water. You young fellows tread on the
graves of the first fathers of this church in Strasbourg and punish all who
disagree with you, but faith cannot be forced. . . . You say that Strasbourg
by her laxity is a shame and a scorn to all Germany. Not yet my dear fellow. She is rather an example of mercy and compassion. . . . The Good
Samaritan, when he came upon the man who had fallen among thieves,
did not ask him to what denomination he belonged, but he put him on
his ass and took him to an inn.[35]

Katherine wrote these words in 1555, after she had been a widow for
seven years. Matthew had died in January 1548, and Katherine continued to minister in Strasbourg for fourteen years more. At first she was
overwhelmed by Matthew's death, but she still delivered an address at
his funeral in which she said, "I am not usurping the office of preacher
or apostle, I am like the dear Mary Magdalene, who with no thought of
being an apostle came to tell the disciples that she had encountered the
risen Lord."[36] Initially, she left Strasbourg for a year and stayed in Basel
with one of Matthew's friends, but she returned to find Strasbourg in the
midst of the Augsburg Interim. Bucer was forced to leave Strasbourg,
and when he was not able to leave in the time allotted, Katherine hid
him from the authorities. He left behind two gold coins in gratitude.
Katherine responded by sending one of the coins to him in England
with a note explaining why she had not also sent the other:

You put me to shame to think that you would leave money for me, as if I
would take a heller from you poor pilgrims and my revered ministers. I
wish I could have done better for you but my Matthew has taken all my
gaiety with him. I intended to return the two gold pieces with this letter
. . . but a refugee minister has just come in with five children, and the wife
of another who saw her husband beheaded before her eyes. I divided the
one gold piece between them as a present from you. The other I enclose.
You will need it.[37]

By the time Katherine wrote this note, her health had begun to fail,
but her zeal for serving those in need had not. When one of the magistrates of Strasbourg was diagnosed with leprosy and confined to an
institution, she visited him regularly despite the danger of contracting
the disease herself. When she was too ill to continue visiting him, she
sent him a note of consolation and a meditation on Psalm 51 that she
wrote for him. She also ministered to a nephew who was stricken with
syphilis by going to stay with him in the hospital for syphilitics. She was
appalled by conditions in the institution and wrote to the Strasbourg

town council complaining and offering suggestions for correcting the problems. Her last act of ministry occurred when, in 1562, the wife of a Strasbourg physician who was a disciple of Schwenckfeld died. When the pastor who was asked to conduct the funeral insisted that he should say at the funeral that she had fallen from the true faith, the husband understandably decided his wife's memory would be better honored if she were buried without such a minister. He decided to hold the service in the early morning, when no one would be present. But Katherine heard about it. Bainton described the final act of Katherine's ministry as follows: "Katherine Zell, now too weak to walk, was taken at that hour in a carriage to the cemetery and herself conducted the service. The town council decreed that if Katherine got well she should receive a reprimand. It was never delivered, for in that same year Katherine, like Moses, 'died of the kiss of God' and no man knows the place of her burial."[38]

Vittoria Colonna and the Catholic Reformation

Vittoria Colonna differed markedly from Katherine Zell and Wibrandis Rosenblatt in her background and her contributions to the Reformation. She was a noblewoman from the highest ranks of the Italian nobility and a literary figure who was recognized and appreciated by some of the leading intellectual and cultural giants of the age, including Castiglione and Michelangelo. She was a Catholic who never seriously considered adopting Protestantism but was committed to church reform, being a partner in this cause with some of the leading figures in the early stages of the Catholic Reformation, including Pole and Contarini. Like them, she sought to achieve reform without schism and was willing to challenge the vested interests in the church that stood in the way of reform. Vittoria was also on friendly terms with two popes, Clement VII and Paul III, although she eventually had a falling out with the latter. She corresponded regularly with the great woman leader of humanist reform in France, Marguerite of Angoulême, the sister of King Francis I and wife of the king of Navarre. Marguerite provided a haven for humanists and evangelicals in Navarre although, like Vittoria, she never became a Protestant. Marguerite was also an author, and the correspondence between these two gifted women holding similar theological views reveals a great deal about their common concerns.[39]

Vittoria was born in 1490, and at the age of nineteen she married Ferdinand d'Avalos, the Marquis of Pescara, who was separated from her for many years because he was fighting in the wars of Emperor Charles V or confined as a prisoner. In her husband's absence, she took up his responsibilities, governing the papal city of Benevento. She also began to write poetry praising her husband and lamenting his absence. When Ferdinand died in 1525 as a result of wounds suffered in battle, Vittoria planned to enter a convent, but her brother, supported by Pope Clement VII, persuaded her not to do so. By this time, she was not only active in Italian cultural circles but also becoming involved in the campaign for church reform.

Vittoria then began to write poetry with spiritual themes. In 1538 the first edition of her poems was published, to be followed by several other editions, and she became a well-known literary figure in Italy. In the mid-1530s she defended the Capuchins,[40] one of the new reforming orders, founded in 1528 as a branch of the Franciscans committed to the strict observance of the rule of St. Francis. The order was committed to preaching the gospel to the poor—a noble endeavor that should not have met with opposition. However, those church leaders whose lifestyle was challenged by the ideals of the order and who were against reform opposed the order. Vittoria came to its defense, especially after she met Bernardino Ochino (1487–1564), who was to become the vicar-general of the order. In 1536 she wrote to Cardinal Contarini defending the order against the accusation that they were heretics:

> The Capuchins are accused of being Lutherans. If St. Francis was a heretic, then call them Lutherans. If to preach the liberty of the Spirit is a vice, when subject to the rule of the church, what will you make of the texts, "the Spirit gives life?" If those who trouble these friars had seen their humility, poverty, obedience, and charity they would be ashamed. . . . The pope should support them. . . . A cardinal inspired by God well said, "If your holiness does not approve of this rule, you will have to deny the gospel of Christ on which it is founded."[41]

Vittoria interceded with the pope for the Capuchins, and in 1536 Pope Paul III confirmed the early bull of Clement establishing the order. Six years later Ochino, the vicar-general of the order, defected to Protestantism—a devastating blow to Vittoria, who had been deeply influenced by Ochino's preaching. Ochino preached powerful sermons to huge crowds, urging people to repent of their worldly ways. Initially he was very popular and was even supported by Pope Paul III, but as he read Protestant tracts with the intention of refuting them, he became increasingly influenced by them. Vittoria first met Ochino in Rome in 1534, and in May 1537 she went to Ferrara, where she attended sermons in which Ochino preached on the themes of sin, grace, and redemption. She was deeply affected by those sermons as she struggled with her own understanding of justification. Contarini sent her a copy of his letter defending the article on justification that both sides accepted at Regensburg, but it is unclear whether she ever fully accepted this position.

Vittoria and Ochino were both associated with the *spirituali*, committed to Catholic reform and loyal to the church but prepared to make concessions to Protestants and take what they found valuable from Protestant teaching. As noted in the last chapter, the *spirituali* had their greatest influence on the reform movement at the time of the Colloquy of Regensburg in 1541. However, with the failure of the colloquy, things began to go wrong for the *spirituali*. By the time the colloquy met, Ochino's preaching was already becoming suspect, as he seemed to be questioning papal authority and leaning more and more in the direction of the Protestant teaching on justification. When he was summoned to Rome in July 1542, he first met Cardinal Contarini, who was on his deathbed, and then fled to Geneva, where he renounced his Catholicism.[42] Before he left he sent Vittoria a letter trying to explain his actions, but she refused to open it.

Even before Ochino left the Catholic Church, Vittoria was struggling with how to hold a middle line between total rejection and full acceptance of Protestantism. The editor of her letters described her dilemma and that of the other *spirituali* as follows:

> She and the other *spirituali* were being pushed closer to the day when they would have to choose between heresy and obedience, but the external pressure was not the heart of Vittoria's difficulty. She had not made up her mind what she believed: She and other *spirituali* understood and appreciated both the insights of Luther and the necessity of the Roman Catholic Church. They reacted to both, but despite having several firm religious principles and practices, they had no coherent religious position that could stand on its own in making the choice between Reformation and Rome.[43]

In the aftermath of Ochino's defection, Vittoria turned increasingly to another spiritual counselor, Cardinal Reginald Pole. Pole found the spiritual companionship of Vittoria indispensable after he learned of the execution of his mother by Henry VIII in retaliation for Pole's rejection and condemnation of Henry's actions in England. Vittoria became a second mother to Pole and benefited greatly from his wise spiritual counsel.

Pope Paul III moved Cardinal Pole to Viterbo in September 1541 to serve as papal governor, and Vittoria joined him there, becoming the only female member of what was called the Viterbo Circle, a group of reformers who gathered around Pole at his residence in Viterbo to discuss joint concerns. She was able to hold her own in the midst of such distinguished intellectuals and church leaders. Pole also persuaded her to give up the extreme asceticism she had adopted, after the model of the Capuchins. Throughout these years, Vittoria continued to work for reform, as did her friend Marguerite. In 1540 Marguerite wrote to Vittoria urging her to continue the work and stating that they needed to encourage each other in the struggle: "I may lose hope in my struggle, yet I don't want to lose that faith which gives victory to hope against hope, of which victory, through your good offices, God alone will have the glory and God will give you the merit for it. . . . For this reason it is necessary that you continue to pray and write your useful letters without becoming tired of sending them."[44]

The growing power of the more extreme group in the Catholic Reformation saddened the final years of Vittoria's life. The establishment of the Roman Inquisition and the meeting of the Council of Trent, which in 1546 adopted the statement on justification that ruled out any compromise with the Protestant position, were major defeats for the *spirituali*. Along with Pole, Vittoria was herself in danger of being accused of heresy, but she continued to hope that things could be changed by the power of the Holy Spirit working in individual Christians. She found great peace and reassurance in her faith. In her final letter to Marguerite, written in May 1545, she commented on the peace she had found: "Because truly belonging to divine realities purifies desire in this life, and calms the soul that lives in the world, we must therefore never cease to desire the things of God . . . in which is found the true peace and true goal of every desire."[45] Vittoria spent the last years of her life in a convent in Rome, suffering from ill health and under suspicion of heresy. She died in February 1547, leaving Cardinal Pole as her heir. One of her other treasured friends in the last years of her life was Michelangelo. That friendship began in the late 1530s and continued to her death. The artist, who was seventeen years older than Vittoria, addressed sonnets to her, made three paintings for her, and made at least one drawing of Vittoria. It was a beautiful friendship of mutual encouragement, and fittingly he was with her at the time of her death.

Wibrandis, Katherine, and Vittoria provide three examples of the many women who contributed to the Reformation in one way or another. Our knowledge of Reformation history has been considerably enriched because their stories are no longer being ignored. It is likely that scholars will remain divided over whether the Reformation had a positive impact on women, depending on which aspect of the female experience they choose to emphasize: the Reformation opened up some opportunities for women and closed others. Women played a major role in both the Protestant and the Catholic Reformations, and their more perceptive male contemporaries recognized and appreciated that role. Pier Paolo Vergerio, the bishop of Capodistria, who became a zealous reformer and member of the *spirituali* after having served as a papal diplomat, wrote Vittoria Colonna a letter in 1540 expressing his appreciation of the women who had been leaders in reform and commending them for the examples they set in their spiritual lives. After mentioning a number of them by name, including Vittoria, he stated: "If God will raise up spirits of this kind and of both sexes . . . who will wake us up from the sleep that burdened our eyes, then our minds would be kindled toward the knowledge of the way and service of God, more than all the ink of the whole world used to write about reformations and more than all the ideas that one would conceive."[46]

12

NON-WESTERN CHURCHES AND MISSIONARY ENTERPRISES

▼

[The devil's] satellites have published abroad that the Indians of the west and the south, and other people of whom we have recent knowledge should be treated as dumb brutes created for our service, pretending that they are incapable of receiving the Catholic faith . . . [but] the Indians are truly men and they are not only capable of understanding the Catholic faith but, according to our information, they desire exceedingly to receive it.

Pope Paul III[1]

The above quotation is taken from a papal bull entitled *Sublimis Deus* issued by Pope Paul III in 1537. In addition to beginning a serious reform of the church by setting up the Papal Reform Commission, Paul III was also concerned about ending the inhumane treatment of aboriginal peoples in the lands that were being colonized by the Spanish and Portuguese. The original inhabitants of those lands were brutalized by the conquerors, who even questioned their essential humanity. *Sublimis Deus* maintained that the conquered people were not only "truly men" and "capable of understanding the Catholic faith" but they were eager to receive it. The papal bull also stated emphatically that they were not to be deprived of their property or their freedom, even if they did not become Christians. Although *Sublimis Deus* seems to have been largely ineffective in curbing the practices it condemned, it documents the pope's concern for the aboriginal peoples and his effort to encourage missionary endeavors. While the church was suffering schism and conflict in Europe, it was expanding outside Europe at a rate not seen since the early Middle Ages. Europeans brought their religion to lands that medieval Christians did not even know existed as they established colonies throughout the world and came into contact with ancient Christian churches in Asia and Africa.

European Voyages of Exploration and Missionary Enterprises

The Reformation era was an age of exploration and colonization, as new types of ships and navigational technology made possible ambitious voyages of exploration, which eventually led to European colonization and the building of great world empires. The voyages of Christopher Columbus in 1492 and Vasco da Gama in 1497 through 1499 initiated the new age as European sailors ventured well beyond the boundaries of the world known to medieval people. Columbus, who thought he had discovered a sea route to the East by sailing west, planted the Spanish flag on a new continent. This was the initial step in the building of a Spanish empire that brought vast amounts of new wealth to Spain and untold suffering to the inhabitants of the lands settled by the Spanish. Vasco da Gama realized the dream of Prince Henry the Navigator (1394–1460) as he found a sea route to India by sailing around the continent of Africa. In the process, Portugal established bases along the coast of Africa and began building a Portuguese empire in Africa and Asia. In 1493 Pope Alexander VI drew a line on the map from pole to pole west of the Azores; Spain was granted the lands that might be discovered to the west of that line whereas lands to the east of that line were to belong to Portugal.[2] Although it may seem a bit out of character for this most nefarious of the Renaissance popes, he also ordered Spain "to bring to the Christian faith the peoples who inhabit these islands and the mainland . . . and to send to the said islands and to the mainland wise, upright, God-fearing and virtuous men who will be capable of instructing the indigenous peoples in good morals and in the catholic faith."[3] Thus missionary enterprises were concomitant with the age of exploration at its outset and would remain so throughout the period.

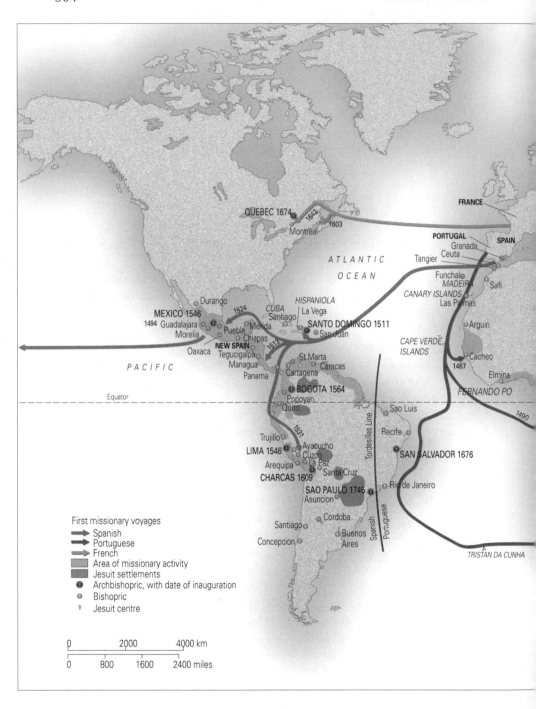

QUEBEC 1674
1642
Montreal
1603

FRANCE

PORTUGAL
Granada
SPAIN
Tangier   Ceuta
Ceuta

ATLANTIC
OCEAN

Funchal
MADEIRA   Safi
CANARY ISLANDS
Las Palmas

Durango
MEXICO 1546
1524   CUBA   HISPANIOLA
1494 Guadalajara   Santiago   La Vega
Puebla   Merida   SANTO DOMINGO 1511
Morelia   Chiapas   San Juan
NEW SPAIN   1513
Oaxaca   Tegucigalpa
PACIFIC   Managua   St Marta
Panama   Cartagena   Caracas

CAPE VERDE
ISLANDS
Cacheo
1467
Elmina

Arguin

FERNANDO PO

Equator

BOGOTA 1564
Popoyan
Quito
Sao Luis
Tordesillas Line
1490
Trujillo
Recife
1531
Ayacucho
LIMA 1546   Cuzco
Arequipa   La Paz
Santa Cruz
CHARCAS 1609
SAO PAULO 1745
Asuncion
Rio de Janeiro

SAN SALVADOR 1676

First missionary voyages
Spanish
Portuguese
French
Area of missionary activity
Jesuit settlements
Archbishopric, with date of inauguration
Bishopric
Jesuit centre

Santiago   Cordoba
Spanish
Portuguese
Concepcion   Buenos
Aires

TRISTAN DA CUNHA

0   2000   4000 km
0   800   1600   2400 miles

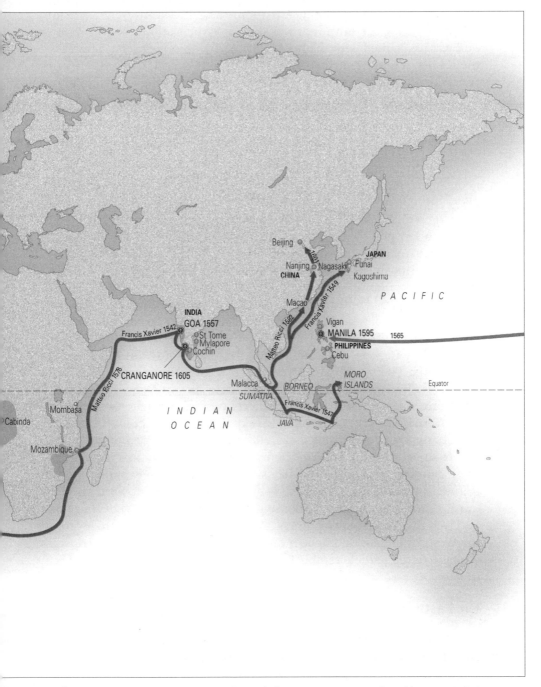

The Catholic Missions, Sixteenth and Seventeenth Centuries.

Another factor in promoting missionary activity was the renewed zeal for propagating the faith that was a part of the Catholic Reformation and was associated with the newly founded religious orders, especially the Jesuits. A reformed and revitalized Roman Catholic Church sent out scores of zealous and courageous missionaries to bring Christianity to parts of Asia that had never before seen a Christian missionary, as well as to areas where the Christian church had been established since ancient times. The record of Western missionary enterprises in the Reformation era is both inspiring and distressing. Although it is a story of great faith, successes in the face of seemingly insurmountable obstacles, and courageous martyrs, the original inhabitants of the newly discovered areas also suffered terribly at the hands of their European conquerors. At the same time missionaries were preaching a gospel of peace and love, the people to whom they were preaching were suffering brutal exploitation and enslavement at the hands of other Europeans. In some areas forced labor and European diseases resulted in the virtual extermination of the native population.

Paul III's papal bull revealed the church at its best when dealing with non-European peoples. There were, as we shall see, other bright spots in the record of colonization and the accompanying effort at conversion, but they do not compensate for the disgraceful behavior of Europeans. The missionaries who followed the explorers came into contact with long-established Christian churches in Asia and Africa in addition to the millions who were adherents of other religions. Although these Christians were originally pleased to make contact with Western Christians, they found that their fellow Christians were neither sensitive to their traditions nor to their needs. The arrogant treatment of these churches was one of the black marks in Western expansion, and it undermined what might have been a positive move toward church unity. Europeans sought to impose their ways upon churches that had survived in a hostile environment for centuries without any help from the West. Understandably the indigenous churches resented European efforts to change their established customs.

The Eastern Orthodox Church

The Eastern Orthodox Church, which had survived the fall of the Holy Roman Empire, the Islamic conquest, and the domination of an often corrupt state throughout the Middle Ages, fell under the rule of the Muslim Ottoman Turks at the beginning of the sixteenth century. In

1453, after resisting foreign conquerors for a millennium, Constantinople, the capital city of the eastern Roman Empire, fell to the Ottoman Turks. By 1526 the Turks had conquered most of the Balkan Peninsula so that within a decade of the beginning of the Lutheran Reformation, most of the lands inhabited by the Eastern Orthodox Church, with the exception of Russia, were under hostile rule. Following the fall of Constantinople, the Turkish ruler, Mohammed II, initially allowed more freedom to the church than the Christian emperors had, and the bishops were invited to elect a new patriarch after the previous one fled to Rome. Although half the churches in Constantinople, including St. Sophia, were turned into mosques, the other half continued as Christian churches and were allowed freedom of worship. In 1516, after the Turks had conquered Syria and Palestine, the churches in these lands were placed under the patriarch of Constantinople. In 1517 Egypt fell, and the patriarch of Alexandria was given special authority over the Christians in that area. The Turks then controlled the Holy Land and the sites associated with Jesus's earthly ministry, which they used to exploit for financial gain the differences among Christians. One of the most revered sites in Jerusalem was the Church of the Holy Sepulchre, which supposedly contained the tomb of Jesus. It was the object of a struggle between various Christian groups who sought to gain control over all or part of the edifice by obtaining *firmans* (royal decrees) from the Turkish authorities validating their claims. The Turks shrewdly sold these *firmans* to competing Christian groups; for example, in the seventeenth century they granted the right to be custodians of the Church of the Holy Sepulchre first to the Franciscans, then to the Orthodox, and finally to the Franciscans again. In 1633 the Eastern Orthodox patriarch, Theophanius, made a bid to win control of the church with a *firman* backdated to the seventh century that supposedly gave the patriarch jurisdiction over a number of holy sites. After this document was exposed as a forgery and withdrawn, various parts of the holy site changed hands half a dozen times, sold each time to the highest bidder by the shrewd sultan, Murad IV.

During the Middle Ages the Coptic church in Egypt, which had been under Muslim rule for centuries, was able to maintain itself despite a number of restrictions on its activities. While the Muslim rulers of Egypt welcomed and utilized the administrative, literary, and commercial skills of the Christian population, the policy of tolerance had its limitations. Christians were not allowed to evangelize and were eventually required to live in ghettos and to wear distinctive clothing. Christian men were not allowed to marry outside the Christian community, and when Christian women married Muslim men, the children were to be raised as Muslims. Relief from the heavy taxes imposed on non-Muslims also encouraged conversions to Islam, so that Christianity eventually became a minority faith in Egypt. The Crusades only increased the difficulties of the Christian community in Egypt, as the Roman church showed little sensitivity to the problems faced by their coreligionists in Egypt. Although the Coptic church survived, by the sixteenth century the once healthy and strong Christian church in Nubia had been decimated, and by 1500 Christianity had all but disappeared in that region.

As the Turks advanced into the Balkan Peninsula, they conquered other Christian kingdoms. The peace treaty of 1533 sealed the status quo, leaving much of the Balkans under Turkish rule. The heartland of the Eastern Orthodox Church was now governed by Muslim rulers and would remain so for centuries. However, once again the Turks were reasonably tolerant in dealing with their Christian subjects. Because Christians and Jews were considered "people of the Book," they were theoretically not to be forcibly converted or persecuted for their faith. They were placed under the supervision of their own leaders, who were made responsible for collecting taxes, maintaining order, and providing civil justice and education. Each of the various Christian churches in the huge area controlled by the Ottoman Empire was under the direct authority of its own bishop, and all were under the overriding authority of the patriarch of Constantinople. The latter's election, however, was in the hands of the Turkish sultan, and the office was normally bought, as were many of the other bishoprics. The sultan also removed the patriarch at his inclination, so the church leadership was thoroughly under the control of the leader of the state. However, this had also been the case under the Byzantine Empire. In practice the patriarch of Constantinople had greater ecclesiastical authority over the church under the sultans than he had had under the Christian emperors because almost all of the Orthodox were under the patriarch's authority.[4]

Christians sometimes rose to high positions in the Ottoman Empire as the result of a much-resented system by which Christian boys were drafted into the military and administrative service of the state. They were taken from their families, required to become Muslims, and forbidden to marry. Known as Janissaries, they became some of the elite troops of the sultan's army, and some acquired important positions of leadership, including that of grand vizier. Although the ruling minority in the Ottoman Empire was Muslim, Christianity remained the religion of the masses, and the Christian church helped to preserve their cultural heritage and national identity. Even though the Eastern Orthodox Church survived under Ottoman rule and served an important role in providing a point of identity for the conquered peoples, it also suffered a serious decline. One historian points out that "theology lost originality and vigor, charitable and educational work was reduced to a minimum, many parish clergy were illiterate and missionary activities ceased altogether."[5]

Throughout their time of troubles, Eastern Christians received very little help from their fellow Christians in the West, even though the two churches had temporarily reconciled their differences at the Council of Ferrara/Florence in 1439. That agreement, which was proclaimed in July 1439 by Pope Eugenius IV in the papal bull *Laetentur coeli*, was arrived at after protracted discussions. The Byzantine emperor John VIII Palaeologus (1425–1448) hoped that agreement between the churches would result in the West providing military aid against the Ottoman Turks, but he was to be disappointed. Although the agreement included some concessions to the Orthodox Church in liturgical practice and clerical marriage and was accepted by the emperor, it was very unpopular in the East. When the West failed to provide the military help necessary to save Constantinople from the Turks, a synod repudiated the agreement in 1472. Although Western leaders such as Emperor Charles V and King Francis I of France spoke of a Crusade to recover Constantinople from the Turks, nothing was ever done. The only major Western victory over the Turks occurred at sea. In 1571 after the Turks had taken Cyprus and attacked Malta, a Holy League, consisting of Spain, Venice, and the papacy, reacted in an effective way. They gathered a fleet of more than two hundred ships, manned by fifty thousand seamen and twenty-eight thousand soldiers, under the command of Don Juan, an illegitimate son of Charles V. On 7 October 1571 Don Juan's fleet defeated a larger Turkish fleet, virtually annihilating it at the Battle of Lepanto. The victory ended Turkish naval domination of the Mediterranean, but it was not followed up with an attack on Constantinople or even the recovery of Cyprus, so it did not really benefit the Christian subjects of the sultan.

One consistent feature of the relations between the Latin Roman Catholic Church and the Eastern Orthodox Church was an ongoing effort by the Roman Church to convince the Orthodox Church to submit to the papacy and to enter into communion with Rome. Some progress was made in 1596 when, in the Union of Brest-Litovsk, the Metropolitan of Kiev and other prelates in the Ukraine accepted union with Rome. It was, however, viewed with scorn by other Russian and Greek Orthodox, who used the name *Uniate* as a term of opprobrium to describe the union. That term is now used to describe a number of Eastern Christian churches that are in communion with Rome but who have retained their own liturgies, liturgical language, and other customs and rites, including communion in both kinds and clerical marriage. Considering the animosity between the Orthodox Church and Rome, it is not surprising that Protestants felt a common bond with the Orthodox. Lutherans were anxious to establish friendly relationships with them, and some Lutherans believed that it would be possible to unite with the Orthodox Church. In 1559 a friend of Melanchthon translated the Augsburg Confession into Greek, and a copy was given to the patriarch of Constantinople, Jeremias II (1574–1584), with the hope that he would see that the two churches had a common theology. Unfortunately for the hopes of the Lutherans, Jeremias did not see it that way. Rather, he responded by pointing out how the Orthodox differed from the Lutherans on questions such as authority, faith, grace, and the sacraments, and he suggested politely that the Lutherans should unite with the Orthodox by accepting their teaching.

Although Jeremias II was not impressed with Lutheran theology, half a century later another patriarch of Constantinople was attracted to the Protestant position, but with tragic results for himself. Cyril Lucaris (1572–1638), who became patriarch of Constantinople in 1620, was seemingly convinced by Protestant teaching while in Poland. While seeking to defend the Orthodox position against Rome, he found Protestants a useful ally. After he became patriarch he corresponded with Protestant leaders, including the archbishop of Canterbury, and sent young men to Europe to study with Protestants. He even allowed the printing of a confession of faith that taught some of the central doctrines of the Reformation, including justification by faith. Lucaris's flirtation with Reformation theology did not win him any friends in the East. He was deposed from his position several times, and each time he had to pay to be reinstated. He was finally condemned to death by order of the sultan, and in 1638 he was strangled and his body thrown into the Bosporus.[6] All this revealed that a Protestant patriarch was not welcome in the East. Whatever the Lutherans might think about the similarities between Orthodox and Reformation theology, the Orthodox did not agree. After Lucaris's execution, a synod of the Orthodox Church anathematized him and his confession. In 1642 another synod condemned Lucaris's confession and Calvinism, leaving no doubt where the Orthodox Church stood in regard to the doctrines of the Protestant Reformation.

The Reformation also failed to have an impact on the one branch of the Orthodox Church that remained free of foreign domination in the Reformation era, the Russian Orthodox Church. In contrast to the rest of the Orthodox Church, the sixteenth century was a healthy period for the Russian Orthodox Church, which experienced significant growth as the Russian state expanded to the east. The rulers of Russia claimed to be the successors to the Christian emperors of Rome. After the fall of Constantinople, which was considered the "second Rome," Moscow claimed to be the "third Rome." In 1547 Ivan IV took the title *czar*, or emperor, indicating that he considered himself the successor of the old Roman emperors. In 1589 the patriarch of Constantinople raised the head of the Russian Orthodox Church from the position of metropolitan to that of patriarch, and four Russian sees were elevated to the rank of metropolitan. The Russian Orthodox Church thereby achieved equal status with the other patriarchates of Alexandria, Antioch, Jerusalem, and Constantinople. The Russians regarded themselves as the defenders of the purity of Christian truth against the perversions of Rome and the Reformation, and they produced polemical writings against all other branches of the Christian church, including the Greeks, Roman Catholics, and Protestants, and proclaimed the superior status of the Russian Orthodox Church as the true Christian church.

The church also served to provide Russians with an identity and source of unity during a time of civil war and foreign invasion at the beginning of the seventeenth century. Known as the Time of Troubles, it began in 1598 with a disputed succession. One of the claimants to the leadership sought the help of the Roman Catholic Poles, who had captured Moscow and imprisoned the patriarch of the Orthodox Church, who died in captivity. However, the nation, led by the church, expelled the Poles from Moscow, and in 1613 a new dynasty was established with the election of Michael Romanov as czar and his father, Philaret, as patriarch of Moscow. For the next twenty-four years a father/son team held the most important political and spiritual positions in Russia. This alliance between church and state would be characteristic of Russia until the Communist Revolution in 1918. The Russian Orthodox Church did experience a schism at the end of the Reformation era when Nikon, who became patriarch in 1652, attempted to introduce reforms that included changes in service books and ritual based on Greek usage. He met such strong resistance that he was eventually deposed. When some of the revisions in the service books were accepted by the church synod, a group known as the Old Believers held that the church had become apostate by following the errors of the Greeks. Under the leadership of Avvakum (1620–1682), they split from the church. Although Avvakum was eventually burned at the stake and his followers severely persecuted by successive Russian czars, the Old Believers survived into the twentieth century.

Portuguese Missions in Africa and Asia

While the Muslim conquest and the resistance of the Russian Orthodox Church to Western influence blocked any further expansion to the east, the age of exploration and colonization provided extensive new opportunities for the expansion of Latin Catholic Christianity. Portuguese explorers began the process by seeking to find a way around the continent of Africa to get beyond the Islamic world. These efforts were led by Prince Henry the Navigator in the 1420s and were partially motivated by the effort to link up with the legendary kingdom of Presbyter John,[7] which was believed to be a powerful and wealthy Christian kingdom that would prove a valuable ally against the Muslims. Portuguese explorations first brought that nation into contact with the peoples of sub-Saharan Africa as their explorers gradually moved down the coast of Africa. In 1482 Portuguese explorers reached the mouth of the Congo, in 1487 Bartholomew Diaz discovered the Cape of Good Hope, and a decade later Vasco da Gama reached India.

The Portuguese also succeeded in linking up with what they thought was the kingdom of Presbyter John when they made contact with the Christians of Ethiopia. Although there was an ancient Christian church in Ethiopia with a Christian emperor, whom the Portuguese insisted on calling Presbyter John even though he had no knowledge of that title, it was not a particularly rich or powerful kingdom. In fact, at the time the Portuguese arrived it was coming under severe pressure from Islam. The Muslims had devastated Christian areas in the highlands between 1529 and 1543, and in desperation the Christian kingdom of Ethiopia sought help from the Portuguese. Although Portuguese intervention may have been decisive in saving the church in Ethiopia, it also brought the Ethiopian church into contact with the West, which in the end proved destructive. A Spanish Jesuit, Father Paez, came to Ethiopia in 1603 and impressed the emperor sufficiently to cause him to look to Rome for assistance against Islam. As a result a Portuguese Jesuit, Alphonsus Mendez, was appointed bishop (*abuna*). However, his arrogance and insensitivity to the traditions and theology of the Ethiopian church led to disaster. He insisted on the rebaptism of Ethiopian Christians, reordination of clergy, and reconsecration of churches. This led to a civil war and the abdication of the emperor in favor of his son, who in 1632 dissolved the union with Rome and expelled the Jesuits. The result of the ill-fated alliance with Rome was a heritage of bitterness and theological controversy within the Ethiopian church.

The Portuguese had a somewhat better record in other parts of Africa. As their explorers sailed down the west coast of Africa seeking to open a new route to the Indies, they came into contact with native African rulers. Second only to their interest in trade and profit was their interest in spreading the faith and their anti-Islamic campaign. African rulers often accepted baptism for diplomatic and military reasons without really converting to the Christian faith, but in the kingdom of Kongo the penetration of Christianity was considerably deeper. After the Portuguese first landed in 1482, the ruler, Nzinga Nkumwa, was baptized, and under the leadership of his son, Afonso, who reigned from 1506 to 1543, real efforts were made to establish Christianity in the kingdom. Afonso's son, Don Henrique,[8] was sent to Portugal for education, and he returned to become bishop of Utica and vicar apostolic of the Kongo. Unfortunately, as in Ethiopia, the greed and arrogance of the Portuguese dissipated the initial positive impact of Western Christianity. After a promising beginning, the Portuguese did not supply the missionaries necessary to continue the Christianization of the Kongo but were zealous in keeping out the missionaries of other countries. It was only with the decline of Portuguese power in the region in 1645, when Italian Capuchin friars came to the Kongo, that progress was again made and Christianity expanded further into the countryside.

As Portuguese explorers pushed on beyond Africa, they came into contact with one of the oldest Christian churches in Asia, which according to legend had been founded by Thomas, one of Jesus's apostles. Although the legend cannot be substantiated, it is clear that there were Christians in India before the fourth century. Initially the Thomas Christians welcomed the Portuguese as valuable allies, and in 1502 the Indian Christian leaders asked Vasco da Gama, on his second trip to India, for protection against the Muslims as well as other enemies surrounding them. The Portuguese provided valuable aid, but once the Islamic foes had been defeated, the European Christians began to impose their rites and authority on the Indian Christians. The Europeans believed Indian Christians to be heretics because of their Nestorian views,[9] and the Indians were shocked by the immorality and cruelty of the Portuguese, who seemed to ignore all the dictates of Christian morality. The long and sad story of the Portuguese efforts to impose their authority on ancient Indian Christianity is too complex to be told here, but it eventually ended in failure, having done serious damage to the Indian church. The Portuguese were totally insensitive to the traditions of that ancient church and the culture in which its followers sought to maintain their Christian faith. For example, the Portuguese missionaries told the Indian Christians that their rejection of images, which distinguished them from the Hindus surrounding them, was heresy.

The arrival of a young aristocrat, Archbishop Alexis Menezes, at the end of the sixteenth century sealed the fate of the ancient church. Menezes was committed to establishing jurisdiction over all the Christians of India and bringing them into conformity with the decisions of the Council of Trent and under the authority of Rome. In June 1599, at the Synod of Diamper, Menezes accomplished his objectives as he destroyed the independence of the Indian church in a disgraceful and totally unnecessary manner. Latin even replaced Syriac as the liturgical language, while Roman practice and order was imposed in every detail. Although the Reformation era ended with the Indian church in subjugation to Rome, that dominance was not maintained. In 1653 about one-third of the Thomas Christians broke from Rome and elected their own archbishop, who took the title Mar Thomas I. One branch of the Indian church was then independent of Rome, although the other remained under Roman jurisdiction. Thus the Catholic Reformation resulted in two rival churches being established among the tiny minority of Indian Christians, and what had started out as a promising relationship ended with a divided church. As was the case in Ethiopia, the insensitivity of the West to the traditions and customs of ancient non-Western Christian churches brought harm rather than benefits to the cause of Christianity.

Portuguese explorers moved on from India and explored other areas of the Asian continent in the first half of the sixteenth century. They established trading posts at Malacca on the Malay Peninsula in 1511 and moved from there into Indonesia and eventually up the coast of China. They began to trade with Japan in the 1540s and established a port at Macao on the coast of China in 1557. Jesuit missionaries were to follow the Portuguese explorers and merchants, bringing Christianity to those areas in the wake of the Catholic Reformation.

The most successful of the European missionary efforts occurred in the Philippines. The Portuguese explorer Ferdinand Magellan, sailing under commission from Emperor Charles V, was killed by natives when he first landed there in 1521, and it was not until the final quarter of the sixteenth century that the Spanish, sailing from Mexico, opened up trade with the islands. Missionaries followed the traders. In 1565 the first Augustinian missionaries arrived, and by the end of the century a number of other monastic orders, including the Jesuits, were working in the island. The Filipinos, who were largely animists with some penetration of Islam in the southern islands, were quickly converted. By 1586 there may have been as many as 400,000 baptisms, and by 1612 there were supposedly over 300,000 Christians on the island of Luzon alone. In 1612 the Dominicans founded a college in Manila that was later to become a university, and within a century the entire population of the islands, with the exception of the Muslims in the south and some remote tribes, had become Christian. However, much of Filipino Christianity was superficial and contained many elements of pre-Christian beliefs. The same was true in Latin America, which was the other area where the Spanish and Portuguese had great success in converting the native population.

Missions in Latin America

Following Pope Alexander VI's line of demarcation, the Portuguese colonized Brazil while the remainder of Latin America fell into the Spanish sphere. Columbus landed in the West Indies in the same year that the Spanish drove the Moors out of their last stronghold in Spain, and the men who followed Columbus brought that same crusading zeal to the New World. Combining the desire for wealth and military success with a deep devotion to Christian mission, they carved out a great Spanish empire in the Americas. Although the men who led Spain's conquest of Latin America were often dreadfully cruel and used highly questionable means to achieve their objectives, they thought of themselves as carrying out a crusade for God to liberate the natives from their worship of idols and superstitious practices. For example, Cortez, the unscrupulous and immoral man who led the conquest of Mexico, was outwardly deeply religious. He attended mass daily, carried a statue of the Virgin Mary with him wherever he went, and had a cross on the flag he carried. The outnumbered Spanish conquered the Aztec kingdom in Mexico and the Incas in Peru using the most brutal and unprincipled methods, including a series of massacres. Cortez slaughtered more than three thousand of the citizens of Cholula in Mexico, and in November 1532 Pizarro, the conqueror of Peru, massacred thousands of Incas who had come with their leader to meet with him. Their leader was later brought to trial and sentenced to death by burning at the stake, but he agreed to be baptized, so his sentence was commuted to death by strangling.

The conquest of Mexico and Peru provided Spain with a huge store-house of precious metals and vast amounts of land, which in turn were granted to the Spanish settlers in huge estates or *encomienda*. The manual labor needed to work the land and mine precious metals was exacted from the conquered native population. In return for protection and instruction in the Christian faith, the landowners were allowed to demand labor from the natives who, although technically free, were virtually treated as slaves. Even though Queen Isabella of Spain forbade the enslavement of the native population and Emperor Charles V tried to protect their rights, the colonists were able to ignore the rules set down by a distant government. Consequently, the exploitation of the native population continued unabated. Considering the way they were treated by the Spanish, it is surprising that so many were converted to Christianity. According to reports, more than one million were baptized between 1524 and 1531, and a letter written in June 1529 states that there were some fourteen thousand baptisms a day. Baptisms did not necessarily mean that the native population became Christian. Christian instruction was normally very rudimentary, and new converts incorporated many of their previous religious practices into the new faith. The confusion between superstition and the Christian faith is illustrated by the following story:

> At one city Cortez left the strictest instructions that the inhabitants were to worship the Christian God and were also to care for one of his horses, which was lame. The inhabitants faithfully obeyed his behest. They fed the horse on fruit and flowers until it died; but their confused minds supposed that the horse and the Christian God were the same and they were later found by two Franciscan missionaries to have made an image of the horse and to be worshipping it believing it was the god of the thunder and lightning.[10]

The Spanish treated the natives as clearly inferior, and although a progressive bishop founded a college near Mexico City in 1536 to train native priests, the Spanish laity rejected the idea of native clergy. In 1555 a church council in Mexico forbade ordaining anyone of the "Moorish race," which in the Spanish definition included all Native Americans, and it was not until 1794 that any were ordained to the priesthood.

The unjust and brutal treatment of the native population did not take place without protest. There were Spanish priests who truly understood the teachings of Christ and who protested and exposed what was happening. The best known of these priests was Bartolomé de las Casas, whose father had sailed with Columbus on his second voyage. In 1502 at the age of eighteen, Las Casas left his native Seville to settle in the new Spanish colonies and was himself involved in the exploitation of the native population. After aiding in the conquest of Cuba, he obtained an *encomienda* on which he used the forced labor of Native Americans.

Although he took holy orders in 1510, he did not change his ways until four years later when, under the influence of the Dominicans, he became convinced that the system from which he benefited was evil and contrary to the teachings of Jesus Christ. As a result, he rejected the system, freed his workers, and returned to Spain where he won the support of Cardinal Ximenes. Las Casas was thirty-one years old at that time, and he spent the rest of his life campaigning for the rights of Native Americans. He worked tirelessly both in Spain and in the Spanish colonies to improve their lot, and his extensive writings provided publicity for his Crusade. In 1552 he published A *Short Account of the Destruction of the Indies* in which he exposed the cruelty of his fellow countrymen: "I was induced to write this work . . . that God may not destroy my fatherland Castile for such great sins. . . . I have great hope for the emperor and king is getting to understand the wickedness and treachery that contrary to the will of God and himself, is and has been done to these peoples; heretofore the truth has been studiously hidden from him . . . by those tyrants who, under pretext that they are servicing the king, dishonor God and rob and destroy the king."[11]

Las Casas crossed the Atlantic fourteen times, at a period when that journey was long and dangerous. He traveled throughout the Spanish colonies, tirelessly promoting the cause of the Native Americans, often in the face of fierce opposition. He accused his fellow countrymen of persecuting those called "the Indians"[12] with "inhuman savagery," even though they were brothers in Christ, who had died for them. The gospel, he contended, should be preached to them "peacefully, with love, charity, sweetness and affection, with meekness and good example," and they "should be persuaded by gifts and presents, and nothing should be taken away from them."[13] His labors were rewarded in 1542 when, largely as the result of his influence, Emperor Charles V promulgated the New Laws, which severely limited the *encomienda* system. He was also rewarded personally by being offered one of the most important sees in the Spanish New World, but he chose instead the bishopric of Chiapas, one of the poorest. Las Casas was seventy years old when he became bishop of Chiapas. After holding this office for three years, he returned to Spain, where he continued his campaign until he died nearly twenty years later. The story of Bartolomé de las Casas is exciting because, in the face of the greed and cruelty of his fellow countrymen who claimed to be acting in the cause of Christ as well as Spain, he stood resolutely for what he knew Jesus Christ had actually taught.

Fortunately Las Casas was not alone in his defense of the native population. Other priests and laymen also came to their defense. The

Jesuits were responsible for a particularly controversial approach to protecting Native Americans from exploitation in a system that consisted of establishing self-sufficient native reservations separated from the white settlers. The Jesuits introduced the system between 1583 and 1605 among the tribe of Guaranis in what is today Paraguay. Thirty of these reservations, known as "Reductions," were established, and they included hospitals, schools, and provision for entertainment and work. The residents led a regimented life, separated from the corruption of the wider society, and the system testified to the Jesuit concern for protecting the Native Americans from white exploitation. But it has also been heavily criticized for paternalism and the regimented life, which is illustrated by the following description of life on a Reduction:

> All members of every community attended mass and vespers daily, hymns were used at work. There was daily catechism for the children. There was a working day of eight hours; orchestral music and the theater and sport were encouraged. In at least one of the early reductions everyone was taught the multiplication table by having to recite it in church after mass on Sunday. They needed to defend the settlements against the land grabbers and slave traders, who destroyed several of the *reductions*, killed or enslaved thousands of Indians and drove the fathers to lead an exodus of 15,000 through the jungle. The Jesuits applied for, and at last obtained, the right to train the Indians in arms and thenceforth private armies preserved those Indian farming societies from contamination.[14]

The Reductions enjoyed their greatest prosperity in the century following the Reformation, but in 1750 the Spanish king, Ferdinand VI, ceded a large part of the area to Portugal in exchange for territory elsewhere. The Portuguese treatment of the native populations in Brazil followed the pattern in the Spanish colonies. Brazil was not as heavily populated as the areas settled by the Spanish, and there were no advanced civilizations like those of the Aztecs and Incas. The Portuguese exploited the native population terribly, and the moral state of the colony was abominable. Here too, courageous men and women, largely from the monastic orders that emerged from the Catholic Reformation, pleaded the cause of the Native Americans.

Jesuit Missions

The new monastic orders, which played such an important role in the Catholic Reformation, also had an impressive record of missionary

Francis Xavier (1506–1552).
Illustration from Beza *Icones*.

activities, with the Jesuits being particularly active. The earliest Jesuit missionary, Francis Xavier (1506–1552), was the son of a Basque aristocratic family. The stories about Xavier's travels and exploits are so remarkable that one needs to separate fact from myth when writing about him, since he left such a powerful impression on future generations.[15] Xavier studied at the University of Paris, where he was influenced by Ignatius Loyola, a fellow Basque, and became one of the original members of the Jesuit order. In 1541 the king of Portugal asked Loyola to give him four missionaries to minister in the Portuguese possessions in India. However, Loyola could only spare two, and one of them became ill, so Xavier went alone. When he arrived in Goa in 1542, his prodigious energy immediately became evident. He ministered to prisoners, taught children, preached, comforted the sick, and founded a college to train Jesuit priests. Xavier also was called upon to instruct the Paravas, a group of newly converted Indian Christians who lived on the very tip of India. They were fishermen, pearl divers, and traders who had been under constant threat from their more powerful Muslim neighbors.

At one point, when the Paravas feared extermination, they called upon the Portuguese for help, and in 1537 the entire community of some twenty thousand Paravas declared themselves Christians and were baptized. In the following year, the Portuguese helped defeat attacking Hindu and Muslim forces, and the newly established Christian community was preserved. However, they understood little or nothing of their newly adopted faith until Xavier was sent to teach them. Although he was ill-prepared for the job because he never learned Tamil and his methods were educationally naïve, in the face of overwhelming obstacles Xavier succeeded in instructing the new converts in the Lord's

Prayer, the creed, and the Ten Commandments. When he left in 1545 he made sure that others would carry on his work. He returned briefly three years later and found that the Paravas had not only survived as Christians but were thriving. Due partly to Xavier's efforts, the Paravas were sufficiently well grounded in the Christian faith for their church to survive until the present day.

During Xavier's three years away from India he visited and preached in Ceylon (Sri Lanka), in Melaka on the Malay Peninsula, and in the Moluccas, which is present-day Indonesia. He spent two years in the islands of Indonesia and supposedly made thousands of converts. Christianity continued to spread after he left, and by 1555 there were thirty Christian villages on the island of Ambon. Unfortunately, the divisions resulting from the Reformation eventually began to plague the mission field. At the beginning of the seventeenth century Dutch Protestants drove out the Portuguese, destroyed monasteries and churches, and introduced Protestant Christianity. Although the Dutch claimed that by the end of the century there were 100,000 Christians in Java and 40,000 in Ambon (where the church has survived to the present day) and the New Testament had been translated into Malay, the missions historian Stephen Neill maintains that "the work was lamentably superficial."[16] Xavier had died by the time of the Dutch conquest, but before his death he also established the Christian church in Japan.

Portuguese traders had reached Japan in 1543, and six years later Francis Xavier arrived. In 1548 he had met a man from Japan named Yajiro who had killed someone in his homeland and had fled to Goa in India. Yajiro told him about his native country, and Xavier determined to bring the gospel to those distant islands. He arrived there in August of 1549 with two Jesuits and Yajiro, who had been converted to Christianity. Initially, Xavier had very little success in Japan; nevertheless, he learned to admire the Japanese, whom he found to be people of high morals, good manners, and intelligence. He stayed for twenty-seven months and left behind the first Japanese converts. He then turned to an even more ambitious mission field as he sought to gain entry into the vast empire of China. He was denied entry, however, and he died in 1552 on an island off the coast of China. Francis Xavier was a remarkable man who willingly endured hardships, extreme danger, and enormous obstacles to bring the gospel of Jesus Christ to the furthest reaches of our planet. Although the Xavier of legend was reported to have been much more successful than can be documented by the facts, the degree to which the real Francis Xavier succeeded is remarkable in view of the obstacles he faced. After his death other Jesuits carried on the work he had begun, and in areas such as Japan they had a significant degree of success.

In 1549 there were only a few Japanese Christians, but the church eventually grew to over 300,000 members before it was decimated by persecution. Initially, the situation in Japan favored the missionaries. Power rested with some 250 *daimyos* or local feudal chiefs, and Buddhism was in decline. The Jesuits who followed Xavier got the support of some local *daimyos* and established a seminary to train Japanese priests. When a central authority was reestablished, the ruler became very suspicious of Christians, whom he thought were subversive and allied with local chiefs. At the end of the sixteenth century, Spanish Franciscans came to Japan, and the rivalries between the Christian powers led the ruler, Toyotomi Hideyoski, to turn against the Christians. In 1597 he crucified twenty Japanese priests and six Spaniards in Nagasaki and also expelled the Jesuits and Franciscans. Fortunately for the Christian cause, Hideyoski died in the following year, and his successor, Tokugawa Ieyasu, initially allied with several Christian *daimyos* and Christians were again tolerated. The church then began to grow, but when the Dutch took the place of the Portuguese as Japan's trading partner, they and the English warned the Japanese ruler about Spanish imperialism. Finally, the Japanese Shogun had enough of these feuding Christians, and in 1614 he issued the following edict: "The Kirishitan [Christian] band have come to Japan, not only sending their merchant vessels to exchange commodities, but also longing to disseminate an evil law, to overthrow true doctrine, so that they may change the government of the country and obtain possession of the land. This is the germ of great disaster, and must be crushed."[17]

This edict resulted in one of the most brutal persecutions in the history of the church, especially after a peasant uprising in which Christians played a leading role was brutally suppressed in 1637–1638. Christians were treated in the most inhuman manner in order to get them to apostatize. They were tortured to the point of death, then the torture was stopped until they recovered sufficiently, and once they had recovered, they were tortured again. This was done over and over again until they gave up their faith. Many Christians were also executed—Japanese Christians were crucified and Europeans burned at the stake. Although we do not know how many were killed, it is estimated that as many as six thousand Christians may have died as a result of executions or their treatment during the time of persecution. In 1640 the Japanese government set up an Office of Inquisition for Christian Affairs to root out Christians. In order to trap secret Christians they instituted the ceremony of picture-stamping, in which everyone was ordered to trample on pictures of Jesus Christ or the Virgin Mary. The most disgraceful part of the story is that Dutch and British traders sometimes aided the government in persecuting Japanese Roman Catholics. The bitter divisions resulting from the Reformation carried over even to the mission field, and the Japanese church was all but eradicated, as only a tiny underground church survived the terrible persecutions.

Although Xavier never succeeded in entering China, another Jesuit, Matteo Ricci (1552–1610), was not only successful in entering China but was able to gain the respect of the Chinese intellectual classes and make a number of converts. Born in the year Xavier died, Ricci was well-educated in mathematics and astronomy, and he also developed a system of memorization that was to impress the Chinese. He began his work in the Portuguese settlement in Macao, on the coast of China, where he studied the Chinese language and customs. His strategy was to win acceptance by the Chinese elite and then try to convince them that Christianity was not in opposition to Chinese beliefs and culture. In 1583 he and a fellow Jesuit were given permission to enter China, and in 1601 he was given permission to go to the capital city, Beijing. He used his knowledge of astronomy and mathematics and his system for memorization to impress the Chinese elite that Europeans were not barbarians. His knowledge of clocks and his skill in map-making also impressed the Chinese, and he was so successful that he was even granted audiences with the emperor.

Once Ricci gained the respect of the Chinese leadership, he began to preach Christian theology, but in such a way as to avoid unnecessary conflict with Chinese beliefs and customs. His effort to accommodate Christian theology with Chinese beliefs included a readiness to honor Confucius and a selective acceptance of the rites associated with ancestor worship. He justified this by arguing these things had only a civil significance and, therefore, Christians could engage in them as long as they avoided practices that were contrary to Christian belief, such as prayers to the dead. Although Ricci's practice of accommodation was so controversial that missionaries from other orders complained to the pope, it resulted in a number of conversions. By the time of Ricci's death in 1610, approximately two thousand Chinese had been converted, including many Chinese intellectuals. Although Christians suffered some sporadic persecution after Ricci's death, the mission continued to flourish, and within a century it is estimated that there were some 300,000 converts as well as Chinese priests and bishops.

Another Jesuit missionary who used methods similar to those of Ricci was Robert de Nobili (1577–1656), who worked in South India beginning in 1606. He recognized that, if he hoped to communicate the faith to Indians, he needed to identify with the people. He learned Tamil and Sanskrit, dressed as an Indian holy man, and refused to wear leather shoes or cut his hair. In addition, he showed respect for the Brahmins by accepting the caste system and their customs. Like Ricci, he felt that Christianity must first reach the ruling classes, and he also practiced accommodation. For example, after he had gained about six hundred converts from the high castes, he allowed them to retain their former customs, even including segregation from Christians in the lower castes. He met strong opposition from other missionaries, who felt he was compromising the faith in order to win converts; however, he had a remarkable ministry lasting for half a century. By accepting the culture of the people to whom they were ministering rather than identifying Christianity with Western culture and seeking to impose it along with the faith, Jesuit missionaries such as Ricci and De Nobili were in advance of their time. Although they avoided the mistakes of many Western missionaries, their policy of accommodation was dangerous because, in the attempt to identify with the culture, they could lose the essentials of the faith.

One of the most successful Jesuit missions in Asia was initiated by the French Jesuit Alexandre de Rhodes (1591–1660) in Vietnam. He first arrived in 1627 and stayed until 1630, when he was expelled. A decade later he was back in Vietnam, and although he faced a good deal of opposition and was forced to leave in 1645, he managed to establish a church that experienced substantial growth, so that by 1658 it is estimated that there were some 300,000 converts. De Rhodes also worked to establish a native clergy. After his return to Europe, he played a significant role in founding the Foreign Missionary Society of Paris in 1659. The French were equally active in missionary activities in their American colonies. In 1632 the first group of Jesuit missionaries arrived in North America. Seven years later three Ursuline sisters came to Canada in response to a vision about Canada that an Ursuline nun, Mary of the Incarnation, had in December 1633. The story of the French mission is one of courage, faith, and martyrdom on the part of many of the missionaries, a number of whom were brutally tortured and even burned alive by the Iroquois, who allied with the English in the wars between the two European powers. It is, however, a sad story for many Native Americans. Although some were converted, more were corrupted by their contact with the white man and his "fire-water." According to Stephen Neill,

"The inhuman cynicism with which the white man engaged the Indian in his own quarrels, setting Indian against Indian and Indian against European makes one of the most shameful passages of colonial history. To make things worse, 'drink and the devil had done for the rest'; the Indian could not resist the temptation of the white man's fire-water, and here as elsewhere the supply of alcohol to a primitive people was almost tantamount to deliberate murder."[18]

English Colonies in North America

While the Catholic Reformation was inspiring worldwide missionary enterprise and Catholic countries such as Spain and Portugal were establishing colonies throughout the world, Protestant countries such as England and the Netherlands were also active in exploration and colonization. They were, however, not as active in evangelizing the people with whom they came into contact. During the Reformation era, both Lutherans and Calvinists focused their evangelistic efforts on Roman Catholics.

English colonization of North America began with the establishment of the Jamestown Colony in Virginia in 1607, largely for commercial reasons. However, in the 1620s and 1630s English settlements motivated almost entirely by religious concerns were founded in New England. The first English colony in New England was established in 1620 by a group of English Separatists, whom we normally call the Pilgrims.[19] They had originally left England to go to Holland because of religious persecution. They then left Holland in order to find a place where they could practice their faith and set up an ideal Christian commonwealth. Their fellow countrymen established the Massachusetts Bay Colony in the following decade. Between 1630 and 1643 some twenty thousand Puritans left England because of their opposition to the introduction of changes in the English church, which they considered to be a surrender to Roman Catholic practices, and the persecution they suffered for refusing to conform. Although united in their opposition to the situation in England, they did not agree on how to respond.

As Separatists, the Pilgrims were convinced that the Church of England could not be reformed, so they decided they must separate from the Church of England and establish a gathered church. In contrast, the settlers in the Massachusetts Bay Colony were committed to staying in the Church of England and working for reform from within. Both groups believed in the ideal of a Christian commonwealth in which the society would be governed by Christian principles. In America they sought to achieve the earthly prototype of the heavenly city, and their model was in many respects Calvin's Geneva. The first governor of the Massachusetts Bay Colony, John Winthrop (1588–1649), stated, "We must consider that we shall be as a city upon a hill, the eyes of all people are upon us."[20] In order to become a member of the church or a citizen in the colony, one had to testify to having experienced a true conversion. All others were simply considered "attendees" of the church and "inhabitants" of the colony. The leaders of the society considered themselves under a covenant with God, and they carried out their secular duties as a religious calling and thought of their society as "God's new Israel." The degree to which they achieved their "holy commonwealth," the problems they encountered, and the eventual result of their efforts is part of another story, because it took place outside the chronological limits of the Reformation era. However, even before the Reformation era ended, diversity and toleration, which were to be a characteristic of American religion, were beginning to be established in the English colonies.

In 1634 Roman Catholics, including two Jesuit priests, arrived in Maryland to settle the area granted to Lord Calvert by the king of England, and in 1649 the Maryland legislature promulgated an act of religious toleration that was well in advance of the times. However, during the English Civil War, Protestants seized control of the Maryland colony and repealed the Toleration Act. Although the Church of England was later made the established church, the Maryland experiment in toleration was to presage the eventual religious settlement in America. A decade earlier, dissenters from New England orthodoxy led by Roger Williams had founded a new colony in Rhode Island that was to be characterized by religious diversity. The Baptists who settled there were committed to yet another characteristic of future American settlement in that they believed in the separation of church and state. Later in the century, William Penn founded a Quaker colony in Pennsylvania, which also attracted Mennonites and Lutherans.

John Eliot and the Praying Towns

Although the English colonies in America provided a home for many Christian traditions that had emerged from the Reformation, in contrast to what Roman Catholics achieved in South and Central America, Protestant colonists had limited success in sharing their faith with Native

Americans. One of the earliest and most enlightened efforts to bring the message about Jesus Christ to the Native Americans of North America was the work of John Eliot (1604–1690). His ministry in North America began at the end of the Reformation era and continued beyond the chronological period covered by this book.

Eliot was a clergyman in the Church of England who went to New England in 1631. He began his work among the Native Americans in 1646, after having learned the language of the Pequot tribe of the Iroquois. His first baptism of a Native American took place in 1651, and when it became clear that converts could not live the Christian life within the tribe, he established so-called "Praying Towns," which were in many ways similar to the Jesuit Reductions in South America. By 1671 Eliot had established fourteen self-governing communities, which included about 3,600 members. He also began the training of Native American clergy and translated the Bible as well as a number of other works, including a catechism, into the language of his converts. His motto, which was printed on his Native American grammar, summed up his faith: "Prayer and pains, through faith in Christ Jesus, will do anything."[21]

Another missionary to the Native Americans, Thomas Mayhew Jr., began work in Martha's Vineyard in 1647, and in a quarter of a century most of the Native Americans in that area had become Christian. It is estimated that by 1675, when King Philip's War disrupted the work, approximately 20 percent of the Native American population of New England had become at least nominally Christian.

Not all New England Puritans had the same benevolent attitudes toward the Native Americans as Eliot and Mayhew. Many were extremely suspicious of them, while others coveted their lands and would do anything to acquire them. When King Philip's War (1675–1678) pitted the colonists against the Native Americans, the Christian Native Americans fought on the side of the English and helped bring about their narrow victory. However, many were treated as enemies and imprisoned by angry colonists, while others were massacred, so the work of John Eliot was undermined before his death. In the end, Puritan missions proved to be a failure, not only because of the disruption and animosity brought about by the attack on the white settlements in King Philip's War, but also because even the most sensitive Puritan missionaries such as Eliot had little appreciation of Native American culture. They considered that culture to be too tied to paganism to be retained when the Native Americans became Christians, so the Praying Towns were set up partly to separate the converts from their own people and "civilize" them—which meant having them make a complete break with their culture.

The story of the Praying Towns is similar to what was happening in other parts of the world, as Europeans sought to bring their faith to the people who inhabited the areas they were colonizing. Eliot cared about the fate of the Native Americans; he was a man of enormous faith and prodigious energy, who had a surprising degree of success in communicating the faith. However, in the end the greed and shortsightedness of his fellow Westerners undermined what Eliot had sought to achieve.

Conclusion

During the Reformation era courageous, gifted men and women of faith who had experienced renewal in the Reformation were willing to undergo enormous hardship and great danger in the face of what often seemed impossible odds to bring the message about Jesus Christ to other parts of the world. In some cases their success was very limited and temporary, but in other cases it was impressive and lasting. At times they showed great sensitivity to the culture and beliefs of the people to whom they ministered, and their ministry was clearly driven by love both for their Lord and those to whom they felt they had been sent.

Sadly, alongside those impressive stories were far too many distressing ones. The zealous Christians of the Catholic Reformation were often totally insensitive to the beliefs and customs of the ancient Christian churches with which they came into contact, and their arrogant treatment of these fellow Christians created lasting divisions and hatred. The brutal treatment and exploitation of Native Americans was a contradiction of the very Christian values missionaries were seeking to impart. Fortunately, other Europeans were moved by their commitment to the teachings of Jesus Christ to raise their voices in protest, and the efforts of people such as Las Casas and John Eliot on behalf of the Native Americans are exciting and inspiring.

Finally, the themes of reform and conflict are evident in the events discussed in this chapter. The reforming movements within both the Roman Catholic and Protestant churches helped to inspire the missions to non-Christian peoples, while such people as Las Casas and such experiments as the Jesuit Reductions and the Praying Towns sought to deal with some of the worst abuses. However, conflict is also an ongoing theme. Conflicts occurred with the ancient Christian churches, with other faiths, between different Christian denominations, and even between different religious orders among Roman Catholics. The saddest part of the story of Christian missions in the Reformation era is that divisions resulting from the Reformation were carried over to the new churches established by the missionaries and in some instances even helped bring about the destruction of churches that had been planted by other Christian denominations. Nevertheless, the overall impact of European missionary efforts was a lasting one, as Christian churches were established and have continued to the present day in areas throughout the world where Christianity had not previously made an impact.

13

THEOLOGICAL CONFLICT, CONFESSIONS, AND CONFESSIONALIZATION

▼

Leaving aside the prophets and the Anabaptists, just look at the spiteful pamphlets written by Zwingli, Luther and Osiander against each other. I have always condemned the venom of the leaders, but they are egged on by the actions of certain people. In actual fact, if you were what you brag of being, they would have set an example of godly and patient conduct which would have made the gospel widely acceptable.

Desiderius Erasmus[1]

In November 1527 Erasmus wrote to Martin Bucer explaining "why I have not joined your church." The portion of the explanation quoted above is a stinging indictment of the viciousness with which theological controversies were fought during the Reformation era. It is not surprising that a sensitive person like Erasmus found the way in which Protestants defended their theological positions and attacked those who differed from them good reason to question the truth of their theology, although vitriolic language was not the exclusive preserve of Protestants. Catholics were equally vicious in the way they attacked their Protestant opponents.

The deep and lasting divisions that occurred between Christians even hampered missionary work. We have already noted how Dutch and English Protestants attacked Roman Catholic missionary outposts in Indonesia and helped to undermine the mission to Japan. In the final century of the Reformation era the conflicts continued and intensified. The battles were fought not only with words but also included the political and military conflicts, which will be discussed in the next chapter. The theological divisions were reflected in what historians have labeled "confessionalization." Each of the major Christian groups produced written confessions, stating their beliefs in a detailed and inflexible manner. These confessions became the identifying mark of the societies that adopted them, and they had a profound effect on the development of the early modern state.

Conflicts and Confessions

The failure of efforts to heal the schism between Protestants and Roman Catholics is probably more understandable than the continuing breach among Protestants, since the latter were agreed on the essentials of the faith. All of the Magisterial Reformers were committed to a belief in *sola scriptura* as well as the rejection of Roman Catholic doctrines and practices. They were also largely agreed on the doctrines of justification and the priesthood of all believers. In addition, they had a common goal as well as a common enemy: the enemy was the newly militant Roman Catholicism that emerged from the Catholic Reformation, and the common goal was to bring real theological and moral reform to the church. However, the Protestants quickly discovered that commitment to the sole authority of Scripture and belief in the perspicuity of Scripture did not necessarily make it easy to agree on what Scripture actually *teaches*. The Marburg Colloquy was only the first of a number of unsuccessful attempts to heal the breach among Protestants. In addition to the divisions that developed among the Lutherans, Zwinglians, Calvinists, and Anabaptists, other conflicts occurred within the major denominations after the deaths of their founding leaders. Lutherans fought bitter internal theological battles after the death of Luther as did Calvinists after the death of Calvin, and even Mennonites divided into a number of feuding groups after the death of Menno Simons. Roman Catholics also experienced divisions. Extended struggles between groups within the church plagued Roman Catholics at the very time they were seeking to win back areas lost to Protestantism.

Although conflict was far more common than consensus, throughout the period there were those who worked hard to achieve reconciliation and who had at least some successes. The committed efforts of Martin Bucer, John Calvin, Philip Melanchthon, Jakob Andreae, and others to restore a degree of unity was a hopeful sign that the prayer of Jesus for his followers to "be one" (John 17:21) had not been totally forgotten amid the conflicts of the age. The period 1550–1650 was also an age of confessions, since one development associated with the theological conflicts was the writing of confessions. These confessions, beginning with the Augsburg Confession of 1530, were written in an attempt to state clearly the beliefs of a particular party in the theological controversies. Sometimes they were designed to bring peace, as was the Augsburg Confession, and sometimes they achieved a measure of accord, as Lutherans did in the Formula of Concord. However, they also defined doctrines in such a clear and uncompromising manner, unequivocally condemning the beliefs that were being rejected, that there was little room for further dialogue. For example, the canons and decrees of the Council of Trent specifically listed and condemned the beliefs of all the Protestant Reformers. Although the Formula of Concord united many Lutherans, it also specifically condemned the beliefs of others, including Calvinists.

Conflicts over Sacramental Theology

Sacramental theology, especially beliefs about the Eucharist, was a central concern of the various confessions as these issues continued to divide Protestants from Catholics and Protestants from each other. The failure of the Zwinglians and Lutherans to agree at Marburg resulted in three confessions being presented to the emperor at the Diet of Augsburg in 1530, each stating differing views on the Eucharist. Although Bucer was able to negotiate an agreement with the Lutherans in the 1536 Wittenberg Concord, the Swiss refused to accept the largely Lutheran position delineated in the concord. We have already seen how efforts to heal the schism between Catholics and Protestants at the colloquies held between 1539 and 1541 were unable to resolve the differences over the Eucharist. Although the participants were able to agree on the central Reformation doctrine of justification by faith, their different views on the Eucharist constituted a major factor in the failure of the final attempt to reestablish unity at Regensburg in 1541. Sadly, the eucharistic meal, which was intended to bind Christians together, became the biggest source of division in the Reformation.

One of the committed peacemakers among Protestants was John Calvin. He recognized that "God has never seen fit to bestow such favor on his servants that each individual should be endowed with full and perfect knowledge on every point." He believed that God did this "to keep us both humble and eager for brotherly communication"; consequently, "we should not hope for what otherwise would be most desirable, that there should be continued agreement among us in understanding passages of Scripture." He also warned against being "driven by fondness for deriding others" or being "goaded by animosity."[2] Throughout his attempts to achieve reconciliation between his feuding fellow Protestants, Calvin tried to avoid polemics and name-calling, although he was not always successful. He was particularly concerned about the divisions over the Eucharist, and in a letter written in March 1557, he lamented that those who were united in the gospel were being distracted by their disagreements on the Lord's Supper, which should have been a source of unity among them. He worked hard to bring that unity but found that he could not fully agree with either the Zwinglian or Lutheran positions. Although he had sympathy for Luther's position, Calvin was unable to accept the Lutheran belief in the ubiquity of Christ's physical body. He also found the Wittenberg Concord unacceptable. In a letter to Bucer written in January 1538, he expressed his dismay that the concord excluded the beliefs of many committed Protestants. He stated, "We are thrice unfeeling and barbarous if we take no account of the thousands who are being fiercely reviled under the pretext of the Concord."[3]

Although Calvin was not able to unite Lutherans and Zwinglians he was able, after lengthy negotiations, to arrive at an agreement with Zwingli's successor, Heinrich Bullinger. Calvin showed great tact and diplomacy in these negotiations, because Bullinger was always suspicious of Lutheran tendencies due to Calvin's insistence that Christ was truly present in the Eucharist. He continually had to assure Bullinger that he did not hold Luther's views, especially after Luther launched a violent attack on the Swiss theologians in his *Short Confession on the Holy Sacrament* written in 1544, which revealed Luther at his worst. Reacting to rumors that he had changed his sacramental theology, Luther allowed his temper, rather than his reason, to dictate what he wrote. The tract was filled with vicious attacks on Zwingli and those whom he believed held Zwingli's view on the sacrament, calling them heretics, hypocrites, liars, and blasphemers. He even said he had ceased to pray for them. He also accused Zwingli of hypocrisy at the Marburg Colloquy because he agreed to so many Christian articles that Luther obviously felt he did not really believe. Luther concluded that Zwingli was worse than a heathen and ten times worse than he had been when he was a papist.[4] He could hardly have been more vicious in his attack on Bullinger's friend and departed colleague, so it is not surprising that Bullinger was furious.

Calvin showed great courage and tact when he wrote to Bullinger in November 1544 in an effort to get him to recognize Luther's contributions, despite the viciousness of the attack. Although Calvin accepted that those whom Luther attacked were justified in responding, he suggested that it might not "be prudent for them to do so." He also asked Bullinger to "consider how eminent a man Luther is, and his excellent endowments." He reminded Bullinger "with how great skill, with what efficiency and power of doctrinal statement" Luther had "hitherto devoted his whole energy to overthrow the reign of antichrist, and at the same time to diffuse far and near the doctrine of salvation." For good measure, he added that even if Luther "were to call me a devil, I should still none the less esteem and acknowledge him as an illustrious servant of God." He concluded by beseeching Bullinger "to consider first of all, along with your colleagues, that you have to do with a distinguished servant of Christ, to whom we are all of us largely indebted."[5] Calvin also reminded Bullinger that he would gain nothing by answering Luther in anger. Even though he would be justified in so doing, it would only undermine rather than serve the cause of the gospel.

Despite Calvin's advice, Bullinger replied to Luther and in 1546 sent Calvin a copy. The following year, Calvin wrote a critique of Bullinger's reply, who in turn replied with a refutation of what Calvin had written. Calvin again showed tact and diplomacy in his response, writing to Bullinger that he did not want to engage in controversy because he would like to arrive at fuller agreement with him. Furthermore, he felt their positions were much closer than Bullinger thought. In January 1547 Calvin paid a visit to Zurich and began negotiations for what would eventually be published as the *Consensus Tigurinus*. The negotiations were difficult, because Bullinger was very sensitive to criticism and the two men held clearly different views, but they continued their dialogue until May 1549, when Calvin returned to Zurich with Farel. Remarkably, they were able to reach an agreement on the Eucharist after just a few hours of discussion. The result was the *Consensus Tigurinus*, a compromise document in which Calvin probably had to make more concessions to the Zwinglian point of view than he might have wanted. The *Consensus* denied Christ's corporeal presence in the Eucharist, because his physical body was in heaven at the right hand of the Father. Although the sacrament was defined in the Zwinglian language as a sign or seal, the two men agreed that it was efficacious and conveyed spiritual gifts to believers.

Conflicts between Calvinists and Lutherans

The agreement with Bullinger led to a conflict between Calvin and conservative Lutherans. Calvin had maintained a good relationship with Melanchthon, who regularly tried to bring Luther and Calvin together and who once told Calvin that Luther held him in high esteem. As we know, Calvin signed the *Variata* of the Augsburg Confession, which simply stated that Christ's body and blood were "truly exhibited" in the Eucharist (changed from the Lutheran "truly present") but omitted the statement in the original version of the confession, which expressed disapproval of dissenting views. Calvin was also anxious to avoid any public debate on the Lord's Supper that might further alienate Christians from one another. However, he found himself involved in such a debate near the end of his life when the Lutheran minister Joachim Westphal (1510–1574) launched an attack on him in 1552 after the publication of the *Consensus Tigurinus*, which a number of Swiss churches had officially adopted.[6]

Westphal was a Lutheran minister who later became superintendent at Hamburg. One historian comments that he inherited "the intolerance and violent temper, but not the genius and generosity of Luther,"[7] and his attack on Calvin made no distinction between Calvin and Zwingli, calling them both "sacramentarians" and heretics who denied the corporeal presence of Christ. He also spoke of their "godless perversion of Scripture" and their "satanic blasphemies."[8] Calvin ignored the first tract, but Westphal was not prepared to let the matter rest, so he wrote a second tract. He also treated those who held differing views on the Eucharist in the most abominable fashion. John a Lasco and his congregation, fleeing to the Continent from Mary's persecution in England, were denied even temporary shelter in the dead of winter because Westphal turned people against them by denouncing them as heretics. When Calvin heard this, he was furious and felt he must respond to Westphal. The result was a heated pamphlet war between the two men, and although both Bullinger and Farel urged him not to respond in kind, Calvin clearly lost patience and wrote to Farel in August 1557, "With regard to Westphal and the rest it was difficult for me to control my temper and to follow your advice. You call those 'brethren' who, if that name be offered to them by us, do not only reject, but execrate it. And how ridiculous should we appear in bandying the name of brother with those who look upon us as the worst of heretics."[9]

In his reply to Westphal, Calvin stated that the revised Augsburg Confession "does not contain a word contrary to our doctrine," and he complimented "its author to whom, as is his due, all pious and learned men will readily pay the honor."[10] He also appealed to "its author," to make an open statement in support of his position. Of course the author was Melanchthon, who, although having made clear in private correspondence that he did not accept the doctrine of the ubiquity of Christ's body, was unwilling to take an active part in the debate between Calvin and Westphal. Calvin was severely disappointed in the reluctance of his friend to support him openly. In March 1555 he wrote to Melanchthon, "Your too great slowness displeases me, by which the madness of those whom you see rushing on to the destruction of the church, is not only kept up, but from day to day increased."[11] Although Melanchthon was unwilling to take Calvin's side in the debate with Westphal, he continued to work for reconciliation with Calvin and his followers.

In 1557 Beza and Farel went to Worms, hoping to gain German support for the French Protestants; there they met Melanchthon, Brenz, Andreae, and a number of other Lutheran theologians. At that meeting Beza said that, with the exception of the articles on the Lord's Supper, the Swiss church would be able to accept the Augsburg Confession. He was wrong! The Swiss hated the Augsburg Confession, and Calvin found himself in the awkward position of trying to repair the damage. Before Calvin died in 1564, he wrote one final treatise on the Eucharist in reply to the strict Lutheran Tilemann Hesshus, who taught at the University of Heidelberg, where he had been involved in a debate over eucharistic theology. In the debate Hesshus stated that he could not celebrate the Lord's Supper with Calvin and Bullinger. The chancellor of the university asked him if he would want to go to heaven if Calvin and Bullinger were there. His answer is unrecorded, but he later wrote a tract on the Eucharist that Calvin answered in 1561. Ironically, Calvin, who had tried to avoid controversy over the Eucharist, ended his life defending his position against the Lutherans. Although he had spent much of his career trying to bring Protestants together, he could not avoid the controversies that plagued the Protestant world.

Beza was equally unsuccessful in his efforts to arrive at an agreement with the Lutherans. Two decades after Calvin's death, he met with the Lutheran theologian Jakob Andreae (1528–1590) at the Colloquy of

Montbéliard. Although the county of Montbéliard was an area within the boundaries of present-day France, it was under the jurisdiction of the Lutheran Duchy of Württemberg. The people of the area, who were largely Calvinist, resisted efforts to get them to conform to Lutheranism, and when French Calvinist refugees arrived in large numbers, they wanted to receive communion according to the Calvinist liturgy. A complicating factor was that Henry of Navarre wanted Lutheran aid in the French religious wars, but they would not give it unless the Calvinists conformed to Lutheran doctrine. Count Frederick of Montbéliard, hoping to find a solution to the standoff, invited Theodore Beza to debate with Jakob Andreae, the chief theologian at the court of Duke Ludwig of Württemberg. The debate, which took place in 1586, dealt with the questions of Christology, baptism, art, and music in the churches, as well as eucharistic theology and the doctrine of predestination. Although some agreement was reached on music and art in churches, no agreement was reached on the other topics.

One interesting question involved in the debate dealt with predestination. Beza held to the doctrine of double predestination, while Andreae was prepared to accept only a doctrine of election, rejecting the Calvinist teaching that God also predestines people to eternal damnation. In order to defend his doctrine from Scripture, Beza had to interpret all the inclusive verses that speak of God loving all people or wanting all to be saved as meaning only the elect, while Andreae was confronted with Beza's insistence that his position was illogical. Beza argued that if God chose the elect, he must have rejected the others, since the choice of one means the rejection of the other. The colloquy ended with Beza expressing the hope that they might eventually arrive at an agreement, and he stated that he prayed God would show to both sides where they were in error and bring them to truth. Andreae was not quite as magnanimous. He said he was also sorry that they had not reached an agreement, but had the other side allowed the Scriptures to speak for themselves, without making them conform to human reason, they might well have arrived at an agreement. He also said he prayed that God would illumine Beza to show him his errors. When Beza extended to him the hand of brotherhood, Andreae refused it but said he would extend the hand of humanity, which Beza then refused. The result of the colloquy suggested that even a common threat could not bring unity among those who were utterly sure that their interpretation of Scripture was correct and the only acceptable view.

Divisions among German Protestants intensified in the last decades of the Reformation era when Germany experienced what some historians have dubbed "the second Reformation."[12] Calvinists considered the Lutheran Reformation to be a halfway house since Lutherans retained so many Catholic practices, which they considered particularly dangerous especially at a time when the Catholic Reformation was seeking to win back areas from Protestants. They considered the Catholic beliefs and practices retained in Lutheranism, such as the doctrine of the real presence and "traditional ceremonial equipage retained in the Wittenberg liturgy," serious compromises with "old papal superstitions" maintaining that:

> The outward form of the mass with altars, communion wafers, candles, liturgical vestments; the baptismal fonts and exorcism rite; the crucifixes, altar retables and other church art; the prescribed pericopes, and the traditional church calendar with its Marian and other festivals . . . were not simply indifferent matters or adiaphora, as Lutherans claimed, but dangerous "papal relics" that were confusing people by blurring Catholic-Protestant differences.[13]

In the second half of the sixteenth century and the early part of the seventeenth century, Calvinists had much success in converting German areas from Lutheranism to Calvinism. The process began in the Palatinate when Frederick III (1559–1576) became Elector of Palatine in 1559. He inherited a university that his predecessor had staffed with the best minds he could find, without discriminating whether they were Lutherans or Calvinists. As a result, the university became embroiled in the controversy over the Eucharist discussed earlier, which included the indomitable Lutheran controversialist Tilemann Hesshus. In the course of the controversy Frederick III became convinced of the Calvinist view and thereupon dismissed the Lutheran faculty members and replaced them with Calvinists. He also "cleansed" the churches in his domain of artworks, organs, vestments, baptismal fonts, crucifixes, and altars. Two of his new appointees to the university, Kaspar Olevianus and Zacharias Ursinus, prepared a new Calvinist confession of faith called the Heidelberg Catechism, which became one of the standard statements of the Reformed faith, and the university became a major Calvinist teaching center. Other German principalities that became Calvinist included Nassau-Dillenburg in 1578, Bremen and Anhalt in 1580, Baden-Durlach in 1599, Lippe in 1604, and Hesse Kassel in 1605. In 1613 John Sigismund of Brandenburg announced his conversion to Calvinism, but he was unable to persuade his subjects that Calvinism was a continuation and completion of the Lutheran Reformation. They were horrified that their ruler had abandoned his Lutheranism, and

after riots broke out in Berlin and several other cities, in 1615 John
Sigismund had to concede that the country would remain Lutheran
while the court would be Calvinist.

Rather than becoming less Catholic, in response to the Calvinist challenge, Lutherans adopted more Catholic practices, such as the elevation
of the host when celebrating the Eucharist, to emphasize the Lutheran
belief in the real presence.[14] Even when the Protestant cause was in
danger of losing all of Germany in the Thirty Years' War, Lutherans and
Calvinists were not able to arrive at a theological agreement. Calvinists
viewed the Lutheran "ubiquitists" (those who believed Christ's body is
everywhere) as having made common theological ground with the papists
and accused them of compromising the doctrine of justification by faith
alone. In 1619 an anonymous Lutheran tract entitled *Why It Is Better to
Ally with Papists Than with Calvinists* argued that Lutherans were better
off trusting Catholics than Calvinists. This confirmed Calvinist suspicions
that Lutherans had chosen the side of Antichrist. In the midst of these
bitter controversies John Berguis, the court preacher in Brandenburg,
tried to get Lutherans and Calvinists to unite in face of a common threat
to the existence of Protestantism in the Holy Roman Empire during the
Thirty Years' War, which led to the Leipzig Colloquy of 1631. Although the
colloquy failed to achieve agreement on the Eucharist and Christology,
the two sides did arrive at a political agreement known as the Leipzig
Manifesto. Facing a common threat from the victorious Spanish and
imperial forces, they agreed to a defensive alliance to protect the liberties
of the German Protestant states. Although the danger had not brought
about theological agreement, at least the participants were able to see
past their theological differences to recognize that they needed to unite
militarily in face of the common threat.

Conflicts among Lutherans

While Calvinists and Lutherans were debating eucharistic theology,
Lutherans were involved in an equally acrimonious debate with each
other. The differences among Lutherans had already become evident
during Luther's lifetime, but as long as he was on the scene, they were
held in check. The Lutheran theology of justification involved maintaining a delicate balance between rejecting the biblical moral law as having
a role in salvation and the teaching that works were a necessary fruit
of justification. Two of Luther's friends dealt with the law in different
ways in their theology. Melanchthon, who was concerned about the

preservation of public morality, stressed the need to preach the law in his articles composed for the Saxon church visitation in 1527. In contrast, Johann Agricola (1492–1566), who had studied under Luther and later taught at the University of Wittenberg, held to the opposite position as he taught that preaching the law was totally unnecessary. He denied any role for the law in the life of the Christian, asserting that it was not even necessary to convict people of sin, because the gospel alone would do that. In 1527 he publicly criticized Melanchthon, but Luther acted as peacemaker and patched up the rift between his two friends.

Although Agricola's antinomianism was clearly not in accord with his view, Luther was surprisingly patient with his erring colleague until 1539, when he challenged Agricola's view in a number of formal disputations at the university. This led to a break between the two men, and Agricola left Wittenberg to take up the position of court preacher for the Elector of Brandenburg. Another of Luther's friends who disagreed with Melanchthon's view was Nikolaus von Amsdorf (1483–1565), who complained to Luther about Melanchthon's position on the necessity of good works. Although he avoided taking public issue with Melanchthon while Luther was alive, after Luther's death the differences among Lutherans became very public as the result of different approaches to the Augsburg Interim.

In his effort to bring religious peace to Germany, Emperor Charles V granted a few minor concessions to Lutherans in the Augsburg Interim, which included allowing communion in both kinds and clerical marriage. Although most Lutherans rejected the Augsburg Interim, Melanchthon found himself in a particularly difficult situation. He was teaching at the University of Wittenberg, which was then under the control of the emperor's Lutheran ally, Maurice of Saxony. Maurice tried to substitute a compromise plan in place of the Augsburg Interim that would still retain the essential teachings of Lutheranism. In December 1548 the Saxon estates accepted that compromise, known as the Leipzig Interim, which attempted to preserve the Lutheran doctrine of justification by making concessions on secondary matters (*adiaphora*, or "matters of indifference") that could be observed without violating the teaching of Scripture. Melanchthon argued that at a time of crisis it was necessary to make some compromises in secondary matters in order to preserve the essential doctrines and to maintain the teaching of the gospel in the church.

Although one can understand Melanchthon's dilemma and the reasonableness of his compromise solution, it did not seem like a reasonable solution to a group of Lutherans who were besieged in the city of

Magdeburg, one of the few German cities that had remained outside the emperor's control. The leaders of the Magdeburg group included Amsdorf and Matthias Flacius Illyricus (1520–1575), a former student at the University of Wittenberg who later became professor of Hebrew there. He had also been Melanchthon's personal secretary, but the two men became opponents as they fought over the issues raised by the Leipzig Interim. From his refuge in Magdeburg, Flacius denounced the compromises of the Leipzig Interim, maintaining that when ceremonies and practices are imposed, they are no longer *adiaphora*. In these cases a clear confession of faith is demanded so they cannot be called "things indifferent." The central question, he maintained, was whether one would obey God or surrender to human directives.

Although the defeat of Emperor Charles V and the Peace of Augsburg of 1555 ended both the Augsburg and the Leipzig Interims, the controversy surrounding them was not resolved. Lutherans were divided into two warring camps. Their opponents pejoratively called the group who followed Flacius "genuine Lutherans" or "Gnesio-Lutherans," while the other was called "Philippists" because they were followers of Philip Melanchthon. Flacius and his supporters were unremitting in their denunciations of Melanchthon and the compromises he was willing to make, even insisting that the Philippists repent publicly for their role in writing and defending the Leipzig Interim. Although Melanchthon was willing to admit he was mistaken in the position he had taken, he and his followers were not prepared to submit to the humiliation of public penance. The controversies were also extended to a conflict between the Universities of Wittenberg and Jena. Duke John Frederick of Saxony had lost Wittenberg to Maurice in the Schmalkaldic War, and when he was unable to move the university to Jena in his territory, he established a new university at Jena, which became the stronghold of the Gnesio-Lutherans, while Wittenberg was the preserve of the Philippists.

The controversies that followed dealt with such a wide range of subjects that it would be difficult even to summarize the major issues. Lutheran theologians fought over such fine points of theology that it is no wonder that Melanchthon in disgust spoke of the *rabies theologorum* or "madness of the theologians." A good example is the so-called Majoristic Controversy. Georg Major (1502–1574), one of the Philippists who agreed with Melanchthon's concern for moral living, had stated that "good works are necessary for salvation." He insisted he had not rejected Luther's teaching that salvation was by grace through faith; rather, he meant that faith will inevitably produce good works, and if it does not, it is not true, saving faith. Despite Major's continual insistence that he was not abandoning Luther's teaching of justification by faith, Flacius pointed out that no matter how often he tried to explain his position, the phrase "good works are necessary for salvation" would inevitably be misunderstood. In an effort to state the Reformation doctrine in a way that emphasized the doctrine of justification by faith, the Gnesio-Lutheran Amsdorf came up with his own radical statement that "good works are harmful to salvation." He meant that if you trusted in works for salvation, they were "harmful," but he could easily be misunderstood. Although both sides were talking past one another, and they probably did not really differ, they continued to argue the point until 1580, when an agreement was reached between Lutherans in the Formula of Concord.

Another issue was debated in the synergistic controversy that dealt with the degree to which the human will played a part in one's salvation. Melanchthon had taught that the human will, along with the Word and Spirit, is a factor in conversion. The Gnesio-Lutherans totally rejected any role for the human will in conversion, while the Philippists maintained that the human will, touched by the Holy Spirit, does have a role in conversion in that it cooperates with God's grace. Another controversial statement was made by one of Melanchthon's friends, Johann Pfeffinger, a professor at Leipzig, who stated that "the Holy Spirit is received . . . by those who seek him, that is, by those who do not spurn or reject him, but who seek his aid with groaning,"[15] which seemed to imply that human cooperation is necessary in conversion. Another issue was the role of the law in the Christian life. Although Luther taught that the law was necessary to convict people of their sins and to act as a curb, he does not seem to have accepted that the law also had a third use—as a guide for the Christian. Not surprisingly, this topic was also the subject of debate among Lutherans after Luther's death. The Eucharist was another divisive issue. When Melanchthon refused to become involved in the controversy between Westphal and Calvin, he was accused of crypto-Calvinism, or secretly being a Calvinist.

Both the Philippists and Gnesio-Lutherans united in their opposition to the position of Andreas Osiander (1496–1552), a Nuremberg Reformer who had become a professor at the University of Königsberg in Prussia. Osiander rejected the belief that Christ's righteousness was imputed to the sinner through faith; rather, he maintained that saving righteousness is the result of the indwelling of Christ in the believer. The righteousness that the believer possesses is the righteousness that Christ has because he is the divine Son of God rather than the righteousness won by him through his death on the cross. Although Osiander claimed he was not disagreeing with Luther, both Gnesio-Lutherans and Philippists rejected his position as a type of creeping Catholicism.

At a time when the "madness of the theologians" threatened to destroy Lutheranism and undermine the achievements of the Reformation, it is fortunate that men of peace were able to work out a settlement that was accepted by most Lutherans. The two men who played the leading role in putting together a Formula of Concord among Lutherans were Jakob Andreae and Martin Chemnitz (1522–1586). At first glance it seems surprising that Andreae should play the role of a man of peace, since at the Colloquy of Montbéliard he had refused to extend the hand of fellowship to Beza, and he also engaged in bitter polemics against Roman Catholics and other Protestants. In addition, he had serious disagreements with his colleagues at the University of Tübingen, where he served as chancellor and professor of theology. Andreae's abrasive personality resulted in the destruction of many friendships, including that with his coauthor of the Formula of Concord, Martin Chemnitz. Nevertheless, he was solidly committed to establishing peace among his fellow Lutherans, even though he experienced attacks from both sides in the controversies.

Martin Chemnitz had a very different personality from Andreae's; he was by nature a quiet, peaceable man rather than a controversial-ist. He had a brilliant theological mind, and although he would have liked to avoid controversy, he was called on again and again to respond in controversial situations. Between 1565 and 1573 Chemnitz wrote a three-volume response to the Council of Trent, which was praised not only by his fellow Lutherans but also by Calvinists. However, he also felt called to write in opposition to the Calvinist position on the Eucharist. Most significantly, it was Chemnitz who framed the position on the Eucharist that was eventually incorporated into the Formula of Concord. Rather than teaching the ubiquity of Christ's human body as Andreae did, Chemnitz taught that according to the "communication of attributes" between the human and divine natures of Christ, his human body could be present wherever, whenever, and in whatever form God wills. This doctrine, which was given the impossible name *multivolipres-ence*, became standard Lutheran teaching as it was incorporated into the Formula of Concord. Chemnitz was, in fact, responsible for much of the theological language in the formula, including article 11, which dealt with predestination and election.

The story of how the Formula of Concord was negotiated is too com-plex to tell here. It emerged as the result of extensive negotiations and the tireless labors of the people in the middle party, between the Philippists and Gnesio-Lutherans, which included Andreae and Chemnitz. The Formula of Concord includes a brief statement of each doctrine, "the Epitome," followed by a detailed discussion in what was called the "Thorough Declaration." Each section begins by discussing the controversies dealing with the doctrine under consideration. The second section, called "*Affirmativa*," presents what the authors believed was the biblical teaching on that doctrine. The final section, called "Antithesis" or "*Negativa*," lists the positions they rejected. The formula was incorporated in a Book of Concord, which included the three ecumenical creeds, the Augsburg Confession, the Apology of the Augsburg Confession, and the Schmalkald Articles as well as Luther's Small and Large Catechisms. It was publicly presented on 25 June 1580, fifty years after the presentation of the Augsburg Confession. The achievement of those who drew up the Formula and convinced others to accept it was considerable. Two-thirds of all the Lutheran territories in Germany accepted it, and 8,811 theologians, ministers, and teachers subscribed to it. "The issues that had threatened to fragment Lutheranism had at long last been settled. Even those German Lutheran churches that refused to accept the Book of Concord generally avoided public condemnation of its teachings."[16]

The Formula of Concord was a balanced work of theology that dealt with controversial questions in a carefully considered fashion. It does not, however, rely on reason to reconcile seemingly contradictory positions based on Scripture. For example, article 11 deals with the doctrine of election and predestination, which divided Lutherans and Calvinists. The article begins by stating that although "no public dissension has developed among the theologians of the Augsburg Confession concerning this article," it was included in the formula "lest at some future date offensive dissension concerning it might be introduced into the church."[17] It warns against probing too deeply into God's mysteries or making judgments on the basis of our reason and states that the doctrine of predestination should be a source of great comfort to Christians, and it should not be logically inferred that because God has chosen some he has rejected the others. Christ's statement that "many are called, but few are chosen" does not mean that "God is not willing to save everybody." Human beings are responsible for their own damnation because they don't accept the Word of God. Rather they "wilfully despise it, stop their ears and harden their hearts, and in this manner foreclose the ordinary way to the Holy Ghost, so that He cannot perform His work in them."[18]

Among the doctrines that were rejected were any teachings that would detract from the comfort this doctrine was meant to bring. This included beliefs held by many Calvinists, as well as the opposing point of view that predestination was based on human merit. The *"Negativa"* included the following beliefs: "That God is unwilling that all men repent and believe the Gospel. . . . That God is unwilling that every one should be saved, but that some without regard to their sins from the mere counsel, purpose and will of God are ordained to condemnation so that they cannot be saved. . . . That not only the mercy of God and the most holy merit of Christ, but also in us there is a cause of God's election, on account of which God has elected us to everlasting life."[19] The article simply cited the relevant passages of Scripture and made no effort to harmonize seemingly contradictory propositions. The Lutheran position, defined in the formula, was to hold opposites in tension and, in accord with Luther's approach, to accept paradox as a way in which God reveals himself. As we shall see, Calvinists were not comfortable with this approach, but efforts to deal with the doctrine of predestination in a logical way would lead to a major theological dispute among Calvinists.

Although the Formula of Concord united most Lutherans,[20] it did not bring Lutherans closer to Roman Catholics or to other Protestants. In fact, the next century in the history of Lutheranism has been labeled the "Age of Lutheran Scholasticism," when Lutheran theologians wrote massive, dogmatic works that emphasized the differences between Lutherans and other Christians. Despite Luther's condemnation of Aristotle,[21] these theologians built their systems on Aristotelian logic and metaphysics. It is called Scholasticism because, like the medieval system, it was the theology of the schools, far removed from the average person, speaking largely to scholars and other theologians. One of the best known of these theologians was Johann Gerhard (1582–1637), whose nine-volume work, *Loci Theologici*, was published between 1610 and 1622 and was to become the most influential work of Lutheran theology, providing an apologia against both Roman Catholicism and Calvinism. The second edition was expanded to twenty-three volumes.

Although Lutherans generally tended to follow Gerhard and the scholastic approach to theology, some continued to try to bring Christians together. For example, George Calixtus (1586–1656), professor of theology at the University of Helmstedt, devoted his life to reconciling the divisions created by the Reformation. Though a convinced Lutheran, he was not prepared to reject all other Christians as heretics, and like Melanchthon, he made a distinction between essential and secondary doctrines. The essential doctrines were those that were necessary for salvation. Although he felt Calvinists and Catholics were in error on nonessential doctrines, he did not believe they were heretics. Not surprisingly, he had little success arguing this in an age of theological orthodoxy. He was viewed with suspicion by all sides and unfairly accused of syncretism—mixing elements from various faiths and accepting all as equally valid. Calixtus aroused the hostility of Roman Catholics, who felt his publications were directed against them, while his fellow Lutherans accused him of being too Catholic. In 1645 he met with Calvinists and Catholics at the Colloquy of Thorn, in Prussia, which had been called by the Polish king, Vladislav IV, in an effort to bring about religious unity. Although some agreements were reached, Jesuit opposition and Lutheran internal quarrels doomed the colloquy to failure. The conference also led fellow Lutherans to accuse Calixtus of Calvinist leanings. He did not succeed in his ecumenical approach, which would have to wait three centuries before it became a popular option.

Confessionalization

One of the reasons that efforts to unite Christians failed was the phenomenon historians have labeled "confessionalization." Heinz Schilling, one of the leading proponents of that concept, has noted that the unified church of the Middle Ages was replaced with "three confessional churches—Lutheran, Calvinistic or Reformed and post-Tridentine Roman Catholic. Each formed a highly organized system, which tended to have an exclusive world-view with respect to the individual, the state, and society, and which laid down strictly formulated norms in politics and morals."[22]

Church and society were so closely united that a society defined itself in terms of its religious belief. The prince stood at the head of both church and state and was the final authority in all church matters; his income was greatly enhanced by control of church lands and resources. Historians believe that the modern state had its origins in this monopoly of religion as "the public confession created the intellectual framework for the state's evolving sense of destiny," and "it was religion more than any other theme in this age which provided the dynamic for social and political relations."[23] The prince was obliged to preserve the faith unspotted from error and also to see that the moral law was enforced in his domain. Educational institutions were harnessed to indoctrinate the public in the true faith, initially through catechetical instruction after church services, then in schools staffed by church officials, and finally in the universities.

Detailed and explicit confessions (or statements) of the faith spelled out the difference between true and false religion and each member of the church was expected to honour the public confession in its entirety. Right belief was not a matter for the individual to decide. The faithful belonged to a distinct religious confession and that confession was legitimized by the state. Moreover, it was the God-given obligation of the state to ensure that unity and purity of faith were observed.[24]

It is not surprising, in view of the thorough indoctrination of the public, that one result of confessionalization was that it became very difficult for even the prince to change a confession or to impose a new confession by princely fiat. Johann Sigismund learned this lesson in Brandenburg when he tried to change the religion of his realm. Confessionalism also meant that it was extremely difficult to convince a thoroughly indoctrinated public to make even modest changes in their confession in the interests of reconciliation and Christian harmony. Rulers were also convinced that religious uniformity was essential for the well-being of the state and that "law and order can only be sustained when all—or almost all—subjects of a state belong to the same religion or to the same church."[25] The church and state thus combined to regulate all aspects of religious life and expression.

They suppressed traditional forms of popular religion; they discouraged magical practices. . . . They tried to wipe out elements of popular medicine, ritual associated with the cycle of sowing and harvest and popular amusements. Religious practices were standardized in accordance with norms laid down by the dominant church and state. Though in some places special churches for dissenters or foreigners might be tolerated, they had to seek and gain permission for deviations in ritual from the established norms.[26]

Confessionalization thus also helped to stoke the fires of religious conflicts that continued both between different religious traditions and within the same tradition.

Conflicts among Calvinists

The conflicts that divided Calvinism in the first part of the seventeenth century are associated with a name that has become notorious among Calvinists, Jacobus Arminius (1560–1609). Ironically, Arminius, who gave his name to a set of doctrines labeled Arminianism, often considered the opposite of Calvinism, considered himself a true follower of Calvin.

Arminius was a Dutchman who had studied theology under Theodore Beza in Geneva. He returned to Holland in 1563 and was named professor of theology at the University at Leiden even though another member of the faculty, a refugee from the southern Netherlands named Franciscus Gomarus (1563–1641), opposed him. Arminius was a popular professor, both because he was an excellent teacher and because he was the only Dutchman on the faculty. In 1604 he came into conflict with Gomarus over his view on predestination, arguing that it was based on God's foreknowledge of those who would have faith in Christ and persevere. Grace, furthermore, was not irresistible. Although Arminius spoke about reconciling differences among Christians in an address to the university in 1606 in which he called for prayer, goodwill, and humility, his teaching created dissension in the church. To strict Calvinists, such as Gomarus, Arminius's position seemed to make salvation dependent on human response and called into question God's sovereignty. It also called into question the teaching of the Heidelberg and Belgic Confessions,[27] which Calvinists wanted to make binding on all clergy. Since those who held Arminius's position would not be able to sign these confessions with their Calvinist teaching on predestination, Arminius called for a synod to revise the Belgic Confession.

Arminius died in 1609, but the debate did not end with his death because his successor at Leiden held to Arminius's position and continued the debate with Gomarus. In addition, students of both Gomarus and Arminius filled clerical posts throughout the Dutch Republic and continued the controversy. The debate ranged beyond the academic world as city councils and church councils were also divided over the issues and two political leaders became involved. Oldenbarnevelt, the unofficial president of the estates of Holland, took the side of the Arminians, and Maurice of Nassau, who controlled the army, took the side of the Calvinists. By this time the two sides in the debate were identified by labels: the Arminians were called "Remonstrants" and the Calvinists were called "Counter-Remonstrants" because in 1610 forty-four ministers, many of whom had been students of Arminius, presented a remonstrance in which they stated their position. The document was made up of five articles dealing with the issues in the debate. The first article contained an ambiguous statement on predestination, stating simply that God determined before the world began who would be saved, but it did not make clear whether the decision was based on foreknowledge, as Arminius taught. The second article stated that Christ's death on the cross gained reconciliation for all, but only believers receive its benefits. The third article stated that human beings cannot come to God for forgiveness unless they are reborn in Christ through the Holy Spirit. However, the fourth article stated that this gift of grace is not irresistible, because many have resisted the Holy Spirit. The fifth article left open the question of whether those who have come to faith can fall from grace, stating that, although believers are aided to persevere in the faith, the Scripture needs to be examined carefully to determine whether they can fall from grace.[28]

The reaction against the Remonstrants was very strong. The Counter-Remonstrants believed that the Remonstrants were threatening the essential teachings of the Reformation and returning to Catholicism, because they allowed human beings to play a role in their salvation. The Counter-Remonstrants stated their position clearly in 1611, but the Remonstrants, supported by Holland and Oldenbarnevelt, seemed to have had the upper hand until Maurice of Nassau sided with the opposition. In 1618 Oldenbarnevelt was arrested and accused of treason. Although there was no substance to the charge, he was convicted and executed in May 1619. At the same time a national synod, often identified simply as the Synod of Dort, was called to meet at Dordrecht. It sat from November 1618 to May 1619 and was international: invitations were extended to other Reformed churches, and delegates from Great Britain, Switzerland, and Germany attended. Thirteen Remonstrant leaders were summoned. After five weeks of clashes, they were dismissed and the synod defined its position in opposition to the Remonstrants in the so-called Canons of Dordrecht.

The Canons of Dordrecht were presented as an elaboration of certain points in the Belgic Confession and were later added to the Heidelberg Catechism and the Belgic Confession as one of the "formulas of concord" for the Dutch Reformed Church. The English language mnemonic TULIP, based on the first letter in each of five points contained in the canons, has traditionally been used to sum up the teachings of the Synod of Dordrecht. The five points were:

Total depravity—everything man does is tainted with sin, and human righteousness is worthless in the sight of God.

Unconditional election—God chooses who is to be saved regardless of any merit they might possess. Predestination is, therefore, not based on God's foreknowledge.

Limited atonement—Christ died effectively only for the elect. In defense of this belief it was argued that since God's work was necessarily efficacious, God does not work in a way that has no effect. Furthermore, man cannot by his own actions make the sacrifice of Christ useless; therefore, it is necessary to maintain that Christ did not die for those who were not chosen for salvation.

Irresistible grace—the grace of God cannot be opposed by human beings.

Perseverance of the saints—no true Christian will ever lose his or her salvation. Believers can, therefore, have full assurance in their hearts that they are saved. Since salvation is entirely the work of God, there is no danger that it could ever be lost.

Immediately after the synod, severe measures were taken against the Remonstrants. Hundreds of Remonstrant ministers were forced into exile or deprived of their ministries. Those who continued to preach Arminian ideas were sentenced to life imprisonment, and laity who attended Arminian services were heavily fined. However, the intolerance that followed the Synod of Dort did not last. After the death of Maurice, his successor, Frederick Henry, allowed Remonstrant preachers to return without fear of persecution. They were allowed to worship in house-churches, and in Amsterdam the same opportunities were extended to Mennonites and Lutherans. Even Catholics, although not allowed to build house-churches, were able to worship in private homes without much harassment. In 1619 the Remonstrants, led by Simon Episcopius (d. 1643), wrote a confession of faith. A seminary was established at Amsterdam in 1634, and Arminianism was openly taught. Thus, while Calvinist orthodoxy was triumphing in the Dutch Republic, the country was also becoming one of the first states in Europe to move toward a policy of official toleration.

Conflicts among Catholics

Curiously, while Calvinists were divided over predestination, so were Roman Catholics. About the same time that Arminius was developing his position, a Spanish Jesuit, Luis de Molina (1535–1600), stated that predestination was based on foreknowledge. Molina's belief was challenged by the Dominicans as being contrary to the teaching of Augustine, because he made the free decision of the human will to accept God's grace a condition of God electing a person to salvation. The result was a bitter controversy among Catholics in which the Jesuits accused the Dominicans of being Calvinists and the Dominicans accused the Jesuits of being Pelagians. The conflict between the two religious orders was as hard fought as the struggles within the Protestant camp or between

Protestants and Roman Catholics, and many of the same issues that had been debated in the conflict within Calvinism were advanced by the two competing religious orders, which went as far as to accuse each other before the Spanish Inquisition. The Inquisition preferred not to get involved and turned the matter over to the pope, who after much delay ruled against both parties, stating that the accusations on both sides were false and the two Catholic religious orders should stop attacking one another. However, the papal ruling did not have the desired effect, and the two orders continued their bitter attacks on each other. The controversy also continued on another level and in another place.

Even before the Jesuit-Dominican conflict in Spain, Michael Bajus (1513–1589), a Catholic theologian from the Spanish Netherlands, had, on the basis of his study of Augustine, stated that human nature is so essentially corrupt that it cannot avoid sin. Many of his arguments, although taken from Augustine, sounded so similar to the position of the Protestants he was seeking to confront that in 1560 the theology faculty at the University of Paris censured a number of propositions supposedly taught by Bajus, who naturally denied he had taught these propositions. Using an old trick of theologians, he maintained he had been misinterpreted. The controversy was in progress during the final session of the Council of Trent, and Rome ordered both parties in the dispute to remain silent until the council ruled on the issues. However, the council did not act on the questions involved in the debate, and further charges were brought against Bajus, who had published three tracts stating his position. Pope Pius V finally ruled against him in 1567; however, since so many of Bajus's statements were direct quotations from Augustine, one of the great fathers of medieval Catholicism, the papal bull had to be very carefully worded so that it did not seem to be condemning the teaching of Augustine. Although Bajus submitted in 1580, he continued to believe that he had accurately taught Augustine's position.

Bajus's submission did not end the debate because the same issues were again a source of controversy among Roman Catholics during the first half of the seventeenth century. A bishop in the Spanish Netherlands, Cornelius Jansen (1585–1638), again used Augustine to confront the semi-Pelagianism of Molina. Jansen had studied at Louvain and was influenced by the ideas of Michael Bajus. He wrote a work entitled *Augustinus*, which claimed to be an exposition of the ideas of Augustine on the subjects of grace and predestination, but he died of the plague before *Augustinus* was published in 1640. Nevertheless, the book became the source of violent controversy between the Jesuits and those who followed Jansen's teaching.

The man most responsible for what was called "Jansenism" was Jansen's close friend, Jean du Vergier (1581–1643), who became the spiritual adviser of a group of nuns in a Cistercian convent near Paris called Port Royal. The convent was the center of a movement of spiritual renewal that included some deeply spiritual young men of the upper classes. These *solitaires*, as they called themselves, sought spiritual and moral renewal by meditation and studying the lives of the saints, whom they sought to imitate. They read the Bible and the works of Augustine and taught their ideas to schoolboys. The movement was in some ways similar to English Puritanism in that the *solitaires* were devout, well-educated young men, seeking to bring moral change to their society. However, the Jesuits accused them of being heretics, and Vergier, or Saint Cyran, as he came to be called, was imprisoned when he came into conflict with the king's chief minister, Richelieu, for criticizing his foreign policy of allying with the Protestants in the Thirty Years' War. He was released after Richelieu's death in 1643, but he died within the year. The movement then continued under the leadership of Antoine Arnauld.

In 1653 Pope Innocent X issued a papal bull condemning Jansenism. He listed as heretical five propositions that he claimed were in *Augustinus*, including the proposition that grace is irresistible and that Christ died only for the elect. Although Arnauld agreed that the pope had every right to condemn these teachings as heretical, he maintained that Jansen had never taught those propositions. The question was referred to the Sorbonne, and in 1656 both the Sorbonne and Pope Alexander VII declared that Jansen *did* teach the condemned propositions. The cause of Jansenism was then taken up by one of the most brilliant intellectuals of the day, who was also one of the greatest Christian apologists of all times, Blaise Pascal (1623–1662). In his *Letters to a Provincial* (1656–1662), Pascal, a mathematician and physicist, launched a clever and effective attack on the Jesuits and helped to breathe new life into the Jansenist movement. The letters were presented as letters written from an inhabitant of the provinces to Parisian Jesuits. They were written with such brilliant humor that the Jesuits became a laughingstock, and for a time it was fashionable in Paris to be a Jansenist. The further history of Jansenism takes us beyond the period covered by this book, but we should point out that Jansenism eventually fell victim to its many enemies, including those in the government of Louis XIV, the new king of France. In 1713 a new papal bull condemned as heretical 101 propositions supposedly held by the Jansenists, and its leaders were imprisoned or forced into exile. The nuns were expelled from Port Royal, and their buildings were destroyed. However, the Jesuits also suffered from the controversy, and in 1762 they too were expelled from France.

This brings us to the end of this sad story of conflict among Christians, which in the end resolved nothing and did untold damage to the Christian faith. Much of the conflict was caused by the attempts of theologians to answer questions that necessitated developing arguments that went well beyond biblical evidence. It is interesting that the same questions were debated between Protestants and Catholics, among Protestants, and among Catholics. Some of the arguments presented by Arminius are, in fact, similar to what was being taught by Roman Catholics; while Roman Catholics such as the Jansenists had at least some affinity to Calvinism. In the end, the real victors in the theological conflicts were those who would have said "a plague on both your houses." As we shall see in the final chapter, the intensity of the religious debate and the accompanying physical violence would lead some to reject entirely inordinate religious zeal as well as any effort to define theology beyond the most basic principles. The theological and political struggles of the Reformation era prepared the way for the triumph of a new Europe in which Christianity would be challenged by belief systems that questioned some of the most fundamental beliefs held by both parties in the Reformation debates.

14

A CENTURY OF MILITARY CONFLICT

▼

Let us not be careless; let us not bring war into the kingdom through sedition or disturb and confuse everything. We must henceforth . . . assail our enemies with charity, prayer, persuasion and the word of God, which are the proper weapons for such a conflict . . . sweetness will achieve more than severity. And let us banish those devilish names—"Lutheran," "Huguenot," "papist"—which breed only faction and sedition: let us retain only one name: "Christian."

Michel de L'Hopital[1]

The chancellor of France, Michel de L'Hopital, included the above plea in a speech he made to the Estates General of Orleans in December 1560. At the time he made the speech, France stood on the brink of religious war, and L'Hopital was one of few members of the royal council who was wise enough to realize that religious peace in France could only be achieved by making concessions to the Protestants. Although his policy was briefly put into practice in the toleration edicts of 1562 and 1563, suppression and religious war eventually replaced his approach of concessions and toleration. Conflict, rather than compromise, was the most common solution to the problem of religious diversity as

353

theological differences combined with political and social tensions to bring about the military conflicts that plagued Europe in the final century of the Reformation era.

The first of these religious wars resulted in the compromise Peace of Augsburg in 1555, which divided the Holy Roman Empire between Lutherans and Roman Catholics. Shortly after that war ended, France and the Low Countries were thrown into protracted religious wars, which also ended with compromise partition settlements. Although both wars were partially the result of a resurgent Roman Catholicism seeking to suppress a growing Protestant movement, nonreligious factors also played a major role. The last of the Continental religious wars, the Thirty Years' War, was even more complex than the earlier wars because of the number of powers that were involved. It ended as a largely political conflict when in the final stage of the war France, a Catholic country, allied itself with Lutheran Sweden to defeat the Catholic Hapsburgs and thereby help ensure the survival of the Protestant cause in the empire. When the Thirty Years' War finally ended in 1648, another religious war was beginning across the English Channel. The English Civil War, which pitted the king against the Parliament, was also partly a political conflict; however, in contrast to the Continental wars, Protestant fought Protestant. The tragedy of the religious wars was compounded by the fact that the terrible blood-letting and inhuman cruelty perpetrated against their religious rivals in the name of the Prince of Peace helped to discredit the faith that those who engaged in the conflicts for religious reasons were trying to defend. In addition, the settlements that eventually emerged could probably have been arrived at by negotiation. Ironically, the solution that Michel de L'Hopital proposed before the French religious wars began was roughly similar to what was granted in the Edict of Nantes thirty-eight years later.

The French Reformation and Religious Wars

The French church in the late Middle Ages was both full of life and characterized by abuses. The same evidences of religious commitment and zeal that we discussed in the first chapter were particularly evident in the French church. The vitality of French religious life in the late Middle Ages has been described as follows:

> This was the golden age of civil mystery plays and Corpus Christi processions. Confraternities multiplied, both devotional associations dedicated to

such practices as the recital of the rosary or the glorification of the blessed sacrament, and guild and parish brotherhoods that combined common banqueting and attendance at church services with obligations of mutual assistance to fellow members in life and death. The economic recovery that followed the end of the Hundred Years War reinforced widely shared concern with the soul's fate in purgatory to bring the number of anniversary masses commissioned by believers to unprecedented levels.[2]

The spread of printing made a growing number of religious publications readily available, and those seeking a deeper religious experience, or a better understanding of the faith, eagerly purchased them.

The same era that witnessed so many signs of religious vitality was also marked by numerous protests about the many abuses in the French church. The higher clergy were hardly a model of Christian piety: pluralism and absenteeism were widespread because members of the great noble families often held a number of bishoprics and seldom visited any of them. Many joined other members of the noble class in the entourage of the king, living the lifestyle of the privileged classes and paying little attention to their religious obligations. The French church was largely independent of Rome, as the result of two agreements between the monarchy and the papacy. In 1438 the Pragmatic Sanction of Bourges provided for the election of bishops and heads of religious houses without papal interference, and in 1516 the Concordat of Bologna granted the French king the right to appoint all bishops. Although there were many dedicated priests among the lower clergy, others did not live up to the standards expected of clergymen. They were often poorly educated and unable to preach, while moral abuses were not unusual. Many violated the rule of celibacy, and even in the monastic houses enforcement of the rules of the order was very lax. The deeply religious public protested and called for reform, but little was done.

Among the most articulate voices calling for reform were those of the French humanists. The best known of these was Jacques Lefèvre d'Étaples (1438–1534), who, like other northern humanists, was devoted to the study of the Bible. He published an edition of the Psalms as well as a number of Bible commentaries, and in 1521 he joined the circle of the reforming bishop of Meaux (1470–1534), Guillaume Briçonnet, who had previously been one of his students. The circle included other Reformers, some of whom were later to become Protestant leaders, such as Guillaume Farel. Briçonnet was so committed to Scripture that he financed a new French translation of the Greek New Testament and encouraged everyone in his diocese to read the Bible. As the Reformation began to spread in France, humanist Reformers such as Briçonnet came increasingly under suspicion. Nevertheless King Francis I continued to protect them, and his sister, Marguerite of Angoulême, was herself a humanist reformer.

When the forces of Emperor Charles V captured the French king at the Battle of Pavia in 1525, the parliament of Paris moved against Bishop Meaux's circle, accusing them of heresy, with the result that the circle broke up and its members went in different directions. Lefèvre, whose understanding of justification was similar to the Reformation doctrine, withdrew to the court of Marguerite of Angoulême, where he spent the remainder of his life. However, he never made an open commitment to the Reformation and was the consummate fence-sitter, avoiding an open declaration of his conformity either to Roman Catholicism or to the Reformation. Briçonnet, in contrast, openly condemned Luther's ideas in 1523, "lest so venomous a plant should extend its roots into the field which has been entrusted to us."[3] Some of those associated with the circle, such as Farel, later became leaders in the Protestant Reformation, while others became Roman Catholic bishops. Meanwhile Lutheranism was beginning to spread in France. Luther's books were already being sold in Paris in 1519, but two years later the conservative Sorbonne reacted by condemning Luther's ideas, and possession of his works became a crime. Nevertheless, the spread of Luther's works continued. During Luther's lifetime at least twenty-two different editions of his writings were published in France, and many of them had been translated into French.

Reformed Protestantism emanating from Switzerland, and especially Geneva, eventually supplanted Lutheranism in France. Here too, printing was a vital means for spreading Protestant beliefs, but French Protestants did not always use the most effective ways to disseminate their faith. For example, in October 1534 they posted broadsheets or placards denouncing the mass in Paris, Orleans, and a number of other cities. The placards were written by a French refugee pastor in Neufchatel, Antoine Marcourt, and smuggled into France. Marcourt had no idea how to present his ideas in a diplomatic fashion to a largely Roman Catholic country in which the mass was the central feature of their worship. His statement that the mass was a practice "in which our Lord is outrageously blasphemed and the people seduced and blinded" was hardly likely to impress those for whom it was a deeply religious experience. Marcourt also used especially vituperative language to denounce the church hierarchy, stating that "the Pope, and all his vermin of cardinals, bishops and priests, monks and other sanctimonious mass-sayers and all those who agree with them are false-prophets, damned cheats, apostates, wolves,

false-pastors, idolaters, seducers, liars, and wretched blasphemers, kill-
ers of souls, renouncers of Christ, of his death and passion, perjurers,
traitors, thieves, rapers of God's honor and more detestable than devils."[4]
The placards seem to have been distributed by a well-organized group,
but where the placards were posted was tactless—one was even posted
on the king's bedroom door in Amboise.

As might be expected, the Affair of the Placards had the opposite effect
to what its perpetrators might have hoped. King Francis I (1515–1547),
who had been very tolerant of the humanists' criticism of the church
and their calls for church reform, began to persecute Protestants. Even
though six Protestants were burned within a month and others were
imprisoned, the radicals were not dissuaded from their campaign, and
in January 1535 they spread other tracts by Marcourt in Paris. This
resulted in yet more executions and a ban on new books. A number of
Protestants, including John Calvin, who, as noted in an earlier chapter,
wrote the *Institutes* partly to convince King Francis I that the French
Protestants were not Anabaptist rebels, fled France to escape the persecutions. Nevertheless, Protestantism continued to grow in France, and
after 1550 Geneva became the chief source of Protestant literature and
pastors. By the 1560s there were at least thirty-four printing presses in
Geneva printing Calvin's and Beza's works for distribution in France.

Protestants also began to organize and set up churches throughout France. Over 1,200 churches were established in France between

1550 and 1565, most of them
before 1562. It is estimated that
two million people—approximately 10 percent of the population—were involved in these
churches, and a steady stream
of ministers from Geneva
came to serve them. As many
as 220 pastors came to France
from Geneva between 1555
and 1562, and in 1559 they
adopted a confession of faith
based on a document drafted
in Geneva. Since many of the
converts were from the leading noble houses, the French

Francis I (1515–1547).
Illustration from Beza *Icones*.

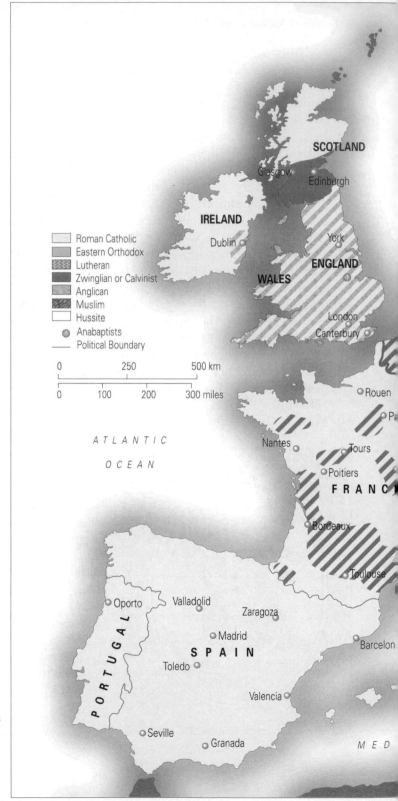

Popular Religious Affiliation in 1560.

Roman Catholic
Eastern Orthodox
Lutheran
Zwinglian or Calvinist
Anglican
Muslim
Hussite
Anabaptists
Political Boundary

0   250   500 km
0   100   200   300 miles

ATLANTIC

OCEAN

SCOTLAND
Glasgow
Edinburgh

IRELAND
Dublin

York

ENGLAND
WALES

London
Canterbury

Rouen
Pa
Nantes
Tours
Poitiers
FRANC
Bordeaux
Toulouse

Oporto   Valladolid
Zaragoza
Madrid
PORTUGAL   SPAIN
Toledo   Barcelon

Valencia

Seville   Granada

M E D

Protestants, or Huguenots[5] as they came to be called, had considerable military potential and could pose a significant challenge to a Roman Catholic monarchy. Thus the religious struggle became inextricably tied to political struggles and eventually to the succession to the French throne. When Francis I died in 1547, his son, Henry II (1547–1559), who did not have his father's humanist sympathies, succeeded him. Persecution increased significantly during King Henry II's reign, and he even set up a special court to try heretics, appropriately named *la chambre ardent* ("the burning chamber") because of its zealous pursuit of heretics. In its three years of existence, before being disbanded in 1550, it condemned thirty-seven people to death. King Henry II was determined to rid France of what he called "this Lutheran scum," but the continuing war with Spain diverted his attention until he made peace with Spain in 1559. Fortunately for the Protestant cause, just as he became free to devote his full energies to ridding France of heretics, he suffered fatal wounds in a tournament arranged to celebrate the signing of the peace treaty and died ten days later.

Henry II left as his heir his teenage son, Francis II (1559–1560), who had married Mary Stuart in 1558. Since the new king lacked experience, his mother, Catherine de' Medici, became the regent. A member of the de' Medici family of Florence, she married Henry II when she was fourteen years old, and he treated her abominably. For ten years she failed to bear children, and the court wanted Henry to divorce her. Instead, he openly took a mistress and pushed Catherine into the background, but not out of his bed. In 1544 she had her first child, and she eventually bore seven more children. When the king died, she used all her cunning to preserve the throne for her sons; members of the Guise family, who were related to Mary Stuart, assisted Catherine in ruling France—including Mary's uncle, Francis, Duke of Guise, and his brother Charles, the cardinal of Lorraine. The Guise family were zealous Catholics, and with King Francis II under their sway, persecution of Protestants increased. The rival noble families of Montmorency and Bourbon resented the Guise dominance. Antoine, king of Navarre, and Louis, Prince of Condé, who were Huguenots, were the leaders of the Bourbons and next in line to the throne. In March 1560 Condé was implicated in a plot known as the Conspiracy of Amboise to remove King Francis II from the control of the Guise family. Condé was arrested, and other conspirators were ambushed and killed or summarily executed, and their bodies hung over the castle wall.

Before further action could be taken against Condé, King Francis II died in December 1560, and his ten-year-old brother became King

Charles IX (1560–1574). Catherine continued as regent, but she adopted a new policy to try to hold the kingdom together for her son; she allied herself with a group of churchmen and intellectuals, including several bishops and the chancellor Michel de L'Hopital. They sought to restore religious unity by a program of reform that it was hoped might persuade Protestants to return to the Catholic fold. The new approach involved treating Huguenots with moderation, releasing Condé, and allowing Huguenot nobles to have their own services at court. L'Hopital distinguished between those Huguenots who should be punished because they resorted to violence and those who eschewed violence, who he argued should be allowed to practice their religion peacefully. Although he was not, as some have suggested, philosophically committed to religious toleration, he recognized that this might be the only way to preserve the kingdom from a disastrous civil war. His speech to the Estates General of Orleans, cited at the beginning of this chapter, was part of his effort to heal the deep divisions in the country. This was followed by the calling of a national assembly at Poissy in 1561, where it was hoped dialogue could take place between the two parties.

The Colloquy of Poissy was a major victory for the Huguenots, as their legitimacy was now recognized, in opposition to some of the Catholic prelates who protested against the very idea of meeting with heretics. The Huguenot position at the colloquy was eloquently presented by Theodore Beza, whose moderation and reasonableness made a good impression upon the assembly until he commented on the Eucharist. According to one account of the meeting, people listened with close attention and a degree of affirmation as Beza summarized Calvin's doctrine. However, when he foolishly stated that in the Eucharist the body of Christ "is as far removed from the bread as the heavens from the earth,"[6] an enormous uproar ensued. Whatever support he had gained by his moderate, well-expressed, earlier statements was dissipated as the Catholic prelates accused him of blasphemy and some even walked out of the meeting.

Although the colloquy lasted for another month, all hope of achieving religious unity was lost. Ironically, the meal in which Christians remember their Lord's sacrifice for them and express their unity in Christ was the rock on which efforts to restore unity foundered. The failure of the Colloquy of Poissy to achieve Catherine's objectives was, however, not the end of her policy of trying to accommodate Huguenots. In January 1562 the Edict of Saint Germain was issued, which granted Protestants a measure of religious toleration and forbade clergy of each faith to insult the other. However, proclaiming a measure of religious toleration was a good deal easier than actually achieving it. A little more than a year after the edict was issued, a violent attack on Protestant worshipers began a process that plunged the country into a ferocious religious war.

One of the leading opponents of toleration was Francis, Duke of Guise, in whose territory lay the small town of Vassy, which had a large congregation of Huguenots. On 1 March 1662 the duke, accompanied by an armed escort of about two hundred men, passed through the area and found a Huguenot congregation of about five hundred people worshiping in a barn near a Catholic church. When he sent his men to disperse the worshipers, they resisted, and many of them were massacred by the duke's men. According to the Huguenot version, fifty were killed and two hundred wounded. Rather than being punished for his actions, the Duke of Guise entered Paris to receive a hero's welcome from the Catholic population. With other Catholic nobles, the Duke of Guise then went to Fontainebleau, where the king was residing with his mother, and brought them both back to Paris. Protestants declared that the king had been kidnapped and in response seized control of some twenty cities. In March 1563 Francis, Duke of Guise, was assassinated. The fragile religious peace had been shattered, and the religious wars began, which would last intermittently for more than three decades interspersed by numerous peace treaties and failed truces.

One of these efforts at peace was shattered by the worst atrocity of the war, the infamous St. Bartholomew's Day Massacre. The massacre began in Paris, where the great nobles of the realm were gathered for the wedding of the Bourbon heir, Henry of Navarre, and the king's sister, Marguerite of Valois, which was to take place on 18 August 1572. The marriage had been arranged as a way of uniting the warring factions, and the Huguenot nobles came to Paris, including the Admiral of France, Gaspard de Coligny, a member of the powerful Montmorency family. Coligny had been a close companion of King Henry II, but he was converted to Protestantism through reading Calvin's and Luther's works. After the massacre in Vassy he joined the Huguenot army and in March 1569 assumed command. He was also much admired by King Charles IX. Although the king was now twenty-two years old, he was still very much under the influence of his mother, who feared Coligny's influence on her son. The Guise family hated Coligny, blaming him for the assassination of Francis Guise. On 22 August, when Coligny was walking from the Louvre to his residence, a hired killer, who may have been in the pay of Catherine or the Guise family, attempted to assassinate him but only succeeded in wounding him in the right hand and left arm. The Huguenots were furious, and Catherine was panic-stricken.

Fearing that the Huguenots would now strike at her and the king, she decided to strike first. In an emergency session of the royal council on 23 August, it was decided that the Huguenot leaders should be killed. The killing began at four in the morning with the murder of Coligny and the other Huguenot leaders; many of them were murdered in their beds, while others were shot as they tried to flee. The bridegroom, Henry of Navarre, was only saved by reconverting to Catholicism. The mobs then turned on Protestants throughout the city, massacring men, women, and children in an orgy of killing that lasted for three days.

In the days that followed the events in Paris, the violence spread to other cities, including Orleans and Lyons, where it is said the Rhone River was red with the blood of thousands of mutilated corpses. It is estimated that as many as six thousand people may have been killed in Paris alone and as many as twenty thousand throughout France. Although unleashed from above, the massacres were often carried out by ordinary Frenchmen who hated the Huguenots, partly because they often expressed their abhorrence of Catholic worship and popular religious culture by interrupting services, desecrating the host, and smashing religious objects. The Huguenots also separated themselves from much of popular religious culture by refusing to take part in the religious festivals and processions and the confraternities.

Reactions to the St. Bartholomew's Day Massacre were surprisingly weak on the part of the Protestant powers and disgracefully triumphal

on the part of Catholic leaders. It is said that Philip of Spain laughed publicly for the first time in his life, and as noted earlier, Pope Gregory XIII decreed that a special thanksgiving service should be celebrated annually. The latter also issued a medallion to commemorate the massacres as a "holy event." Huguenots reacted by abjuring their faith in large numbers; Beza commented that "the number of apostates almost defies counting," and in many areas of France the massacres

Marguerite of Valois (1553–1615).
Illustration from Beza *Icones*.

decimated the Huguenot communities. Many left the faith because they could not understand why God had allowed such terrible suffering to descend on those he had predestined. The Huguenots lost both in numbers and in confidence, and in the years that followed the massacres their strength was largely centered in the southwest, while in the north the once numerous Huguenot congregations shrank to insignificance.

The St. Bartholomew's Day Massacre led to the development of a Calvinist resistance theory. Although Calvin himself did not endorse rebellion against constituted authority, after the massacres, Calvinist writers including Theodore Beza began to argue that resistance and rebellion against the monarch could be justified. In *The Right of Magistrates over Their Subjects*, published in 1574, Beza argued that the king had been granted his powers by the people, and if he proved a tyrant, the representatives of the people sitting in the Estates General could depose him. Other writers, such as the anonymous author of *Vindiciae Contra Tyrannos*, published in 1579, went even further and justified rebellion as well as tyrannicide. Although the mass defections from the Huguenot ranks after the St. Bartholomew's Day Massacre destroyed their hope for winning France, it did not destroy the movement. Huguenots regrouped in their strongholds such as La Rochelle, in southwest France, and fought back.

Henry of Navarre, who had been in captivity for three years after the massacre, escaped, renounced his Catholicism, and took up leadership of the Protestant forces. Meanwhile, King Charles IX died of tuberculosis in May 1574, and his brother became King Henry III (1574–1589). He was a committed Catholic, but he was prepared to make concessions to the Huguenots in order to restore peace to the kingdom. Although previous generations of historians judged him severely as an inadequate king who was more interested in his personal pleasures than governing, more recent interpretations have been kinder in their evaluation. Even though Henry III alienated many of his more zealous subjects by his extravagant living and foppish ways and by surrounding himself with male favorites who lived scandalous lives, he was intelligent and sponsored some reforming legislation. He granted the Huguenots significant concessions in the Edict of Beaulieu in May 1576, which allowed them "the free public and general exercise of the Protestant faith" except in Paris and its suburbs and at court. It stated that "our wise and chief purpose is to reunite our subjects within a single religion, and we hope that God will gradually bring this about by means of a free and holy general council."[7]

The edict infuriated the zealously Catholic Guise faction, which was against any concessions to the Huguenots. They founded the Catholic

League in 1576 under the leadership of Henry of Guise, who had been the king's childhood companion but now became his enemy. A third Henry, the newly reconverted Huguenot leader, Henry of Navarre, became heir to the throne when Henry III's brother, the Duke of Anjou, died in June 1584. The struggle between these three Henries, appropriately called the War of the Three Henries, ended with the victory of the Huguenot Henry. In May 1588, Henry of Guise drove the king from Paris in a popular uprising known as the Day of Barricades. King Henry III responded by having Henry of Guise assassinated in December of 1588. As a result Pope Sixtus V excommunicated him, and in August of 1589 Henry III was assassinated by a Dominican monk. This left one surviving Henry, the Huguenot leader, Henry of Navarre, but despite a series of military victories over his Catholic opponents, he was unable to conquer all of France. The major obstacle standing in the way of a complete victory for Henry of Navarre was the city of Paris, which was by far the most important and the most Catholic city in France. The citizens of Paris were so opposed to having as their king a man whom they considered a heretic that they sought the support of the Spanish, France's traditional enemy, to prevent him from entering the city. Faced with the dilemma of how to win the allegiance of Paris, Henry of Navarre came up with a solution while he was besieging the city in July 1593. The staunchly Protestant Duke of Sully is said to have provided Henry with the counsel that "Paris is worth a mass," and Henry agreed; so he converted back to Roman Catholicism.

In March 1594 Henry of Navarre's forces entered Paris, meeting little resistance, and Henry went to the cathedral of Notre Dame to attend mass. His conversion was clearly politically motivated, but in contrast to his earlier practice, he seems to have taken his new religion seriously. His conversion cost him the support of many of his former Protestant subjects, but over the next four years King Henry IV (1589–1610) won control of the rest of France and defeated the Spanish. He also showed he had not forgotten his former coreligionists, since in 1598 he issued the Edict of Nantes granting a measure of toleration to the Huguenots. The edict stated that its purpose was to give the king's subjects "a general law, clear, precise and absolute to be applied in all the disputes that have arisen amongst them . . . and establish a good and lasting peace."[8] In order to achieve this aim, the Huguenots were granted a reasonable measure of religious toleration and were allowed freedom of worship on the estates of Huguenot noblemen and other places throughout France, but not within the city of Paris. Although Roman Catholicism was declared the state religion, Protestant ministers were to be paid out of public funds, and the Huguenots were granted some two hundred places throughout France where they could maintain garrisons or forts.

Although the war had brought the Huguenots reasonable gains, Calvinist leaders were not necessarily happy with how it ended. Theodore Beza, who had worked so hard to bring about the triumph of Calvinism in France, was disappointed that the Henry whom he had hoped would be the great leader of the Protestant cause had become a Roman Catholic. On 25 November 1600 Henry IV and Beza had a final meeting while the king was encamped near Geneva, and the eighty-one-year-old patriarch of Calvinism rode out to meet Henry, whom he had not seen for some thirty years. It was a poignant meeting as "Henry embraced Beza, calling him his father and friend." The king then had Beza sit while he remained standing and they talked. Henry invited Beza to stay the night, but he declined the invitation and returned to Geneva.[9]

Neither King Henry IV nor the religious peace was to survive for long. In 1610 a Catholic fanatic assassinated the last of the three Henries. The peace that Henry IV had brought to France did not survive either. A decade after Henry's death, civil war broke out again under his successor, King Louis XIII (1610–1643). After an eight-year war, the Huguenots lost their last fortified place in 1629 when the city of La Rochelle fell to the king's forces. The war ended with the Peace of Alais, which took away the political and military rights granted by the Edict of Nantes but reaffirmed their civil and religious rights. A half century later the Huguenots were also deprived of the religious toleration granted by the Edict of Nantes when King Louis XIV (1643–1715) revoked the edict in 1685. In the years that followed the Huguenots were persecuted so severely that many emigrated from France to other countries. However, others stayed, and the French Protestant church survived until the French Revolution, when in 1797 it was finally granted lasting toleration.

The Dutch Religious Wars

The Dutch religious wars began at about the same time as those in France. Although there were many similarities between the two conflicts, there were also major differences. The people of the Low Countries had a style of life and culture that was very different from that of the Spanish and the French. They had the most prosperous economy in Europe with the highest per capita income, due in part to the economic benefits they reaped from the wool trade and cloth manufacturing. They were also helped by their location, which enabled them to become a

center of trade and to develop a very successful herring-fishing industry. Politically they were divided into seventeen autonomous provinces
that had many differences, including linguistic ones. The people of
the northern provinces spoke Flemish or Dutch, which was related to
Low German, while the Walloons, who lived in the southern provinces,
spoke a dialect of French. Although the provinces were united under the
rule of the Duke of Burgundy, they had a fierce sense of independence
and were jealous of their local liberties. In 1509 Charles V became the
Duke of Burgundy after the death of his father, Philip, whose mother
was Mary of Burgundy. Charles was born in the Low Countries, spoke
their language, and respected their culture as well as their local liberties.
Although he taxed them heavily to finance his wars, he left government
in the hands of the local nobility.

During the reign of Charles V, Protestantism began to make inroads
in the Low Countries. The first Protestants were Lutherans, followed by
the Anabaptists, who had a great deal of success. Melchior Hoffman was
active in East Frisia in 1530, and the city of Münster, which the radical
Anabaptists took over in 1534, was on the border of the Netherlands. After
the fall of Münster, the robber-gangs of the so-called Batenburgers (followers of Jan van Batenburg) pillaged farms and monasteries and created
havoc in areas where they were active. They were eventually defeated,
and the peaceable Mennonites became the dominant Anabaptist group
in the Low Countries until Calvinism began to make major inroads in the
1550s. In 1561 Guy de Bray, a French-speaking minister who had been
trained in Geneva, drafted the Belgic Confession, which was accepted by
a Synod in Antwerp in 1566. This confession, which followed the earlier
French confessions of 1559, was written in French but later translated
into Dutch. Although Calvin only listed preaching of the gospel and the
administration of the sacraments as the two marks of the true church,
the Belgic Confession added discipline as a third mark.

In 1562 the Belgic Confession was presented to the new ruler of the
Netherlands, King Philip II, with an affirmation of loyalty to the government. But he was uncompromising in his commitment to Roman
Catholicism and unwilling to make any concessions to subjects he considered to be rebels and heretics. He had become ruler of the Low Countries
when his father, Emperor Charles V, resigned in 1556, and he brought
a very different approach to ruling. He could not speak Dutch, and he
disliked the Dutch. The feeling was mutual. Charles had been a fellow
countryman, but Philip was a foreigner; Charles was able to learn from
his mistakes, while Philip persisted in a policy of persecution even when
it became clear that it was alienating his subjects. Charles had initially

reacted to the growing religious diversity with a policy of suppression: between 1518 and 1528 approximately four hundred people were sentenced for religious deviance. After 1529 even heretics who recanted were sentenced to death. The first to be burned were two Lutherans in 1523; Anabaptists and Calvinists followed, but the persecutions were never popular even among Catholics. Local authorities were reluctant to enforce the law against heresy, and people sometimes rose locally in protest against the executions. By the end of Charles's reign, he had become much more lenient in dealing with heresy, but his son had no sympathy with a cautious approach to either heresy or local autonomy. Philip was determined to stamp out heresy, curb the independent spirit of the Low Countries, and force them to submit to centralized Spanish rule. This policy resulted in a war that, although rooted in religious differences, was inextricably intertwined with the political question of the ancient freedoms of the Low Countries.

The religious war in the Low Countries was to a great extent a revolt against Spain. The Counts of Egmont and Horn and, most significantly, William of Orange were the leaders of the opposition to King Philip II. William—who was nicknamed William the Silent because he often kept his true intentions secret—was hardly the type of man one would expect to lead a religious revolt. He was known for extravagant living and so was constantly in debt, and like Henry of Navarre, William seemed willing to change his religion as circumstances demanded, moving from Lutheranism to Catholicism to Calvinism. Although he was not a particularly good general, he proved to be a courageous, intelligent, and effective leader of his people in standing up to Spanish tyranny. In 1564 William stated unequivocally in the Council of State that the heresy laws could not be enforced and that princes did not have the right to control the consciences of their subjects. In 1566 three hundred nobles petitioned Margaret of Parma, the king's sister, who was his regent in the Low Countries, to abolish the Inquisition. When a courtier contemptuously said, "Why be afraid of these beggars?" it gave the cause a title. "Long live the beggars!" became the Protestant rallying cry. Some of the most effective military campaigns against Spain were carried out by zealous Calvinists who were skilled seamen; they not only managed to defeat the Spanish fleet but also seized the ports in Zeeland and Holland in 1572 and held on to them throughout the war. They called themselves the "sea beggars."

A turning point occurred in 1566 when iconoclastic riots broke out throughout the Low Countries as zealous Protestants attacked churches and monasteries, destroying images. The Protestant leadership was not

prepared to suppress the riots until Margaret granted religious concessions, and when she gave in because the riots were spreading, William,
Egmont, and Horn helped to restore order. The period from April 1566
to April 1567 was called the "wonder year" because there was a brief
respite in the persecution and the Protestant churches experienced
significant growth. Calvinists preaching outside the walls of Antwerp
drew crowds estimated at up to twenty-five thousand, and many were
converted. However, the respite was brief because King Philip II then
took his vengeance on his rebellious subjects. He responded with massive force, often directed against people who were not even directly
involved in the iconoclastic riots. The riots cost the Protestant cause
the support of many neutral or even sympathetic citizens who were
appalled at the violence and disruption of society, but Philip II's actions
horrified people even more. In 1567 he sent his able but brutal general,
the Duke of Alba, with ten thousand troops to the Low Countries, and
he engaged in a reign of terror. Rather than concentrating only on the
leaders of the revolt, Alba struck out against all who were at all tainted
with Protestantism. Egmont and Horn, who had helped to suppress the
riots and who had declared their loyalty to Philip, were publicly executed,
with the result that they became martyrs in the eyes of their countrymen. A special tribunal was set up to try cases. Officially called the
"Council of Troubles," Philip's rebellious subjects labeled it the "Council
of Blood" with some justification because from six to eight thousand
people suspected of heresy were brought before it, and thousands were
executed. Heavy taxation was imposed on the Low Countries, and local
autonomy was suppressed.

The result of King Philip II's policies was that many able and wealthy
people, including merchants and artisans, fled to neighboring countries.
William the Silent, who had his own property confiscated, emerged as
the hero of the struggle against Spain, as only he and a small group of
exiles continued the unequal struggle against Philip II. Unable to get any
significant help from other Protestant powers, William found his best
support came from the northern provinces of Holland, Zeeland, and
Utrecht, where Calvinism had made significant gains. In 1572, the year
of the St. Bartholomew's Day Massacre, William's "sea beggars" captured
a number of ports, and the Spanish fleet was defeated in the Zuider Zee.
The representatives of the northern cities that had revolted then elected
William commander in chief of the army. The rebels, who controlled
the low-lying provinces, were able to use the topography to their advantage—even to the point of opening the dikes to stop the invading Spanish
army. Philip II was never able to regain these northern provinces, and

by 1577 he had lost almost the whole of the Low Countries. The Spanish lost further support when the Spanish garrison in the southern provinces, which had not been paid, sacked the city of Antwerp and murdered as many as eight thousand of its inhabitants. The so-called "Spanish Fury" enraged the people of the southern provinces, and in November 1576 they joined with the northern provinces in a treaty known as the Pacification of Ghent, which granted virtually sovereign authority to William the Silent to conduct the war. In the following year all the provinces joined in the Union of Brussels, and all faiths combined in their resistance to the Spanish tyranny, pledging to fight Spain until Philip II withdrew his troops and restored the privileges of the Low Countries.

The Spanish cause was saved by a new Spanish commander, the Duke of Parma, who arrived with twenty thousand troops in 1578. In addition to winning on the battlefield, he won the loyalty of the southern provinces by appealing to the linguistic, ethnic, and religious differences between the north and the south. In January 1579 he organized the southern provinces in the Union of Arras. They expressed their loyalty to King Philip II in return for a promise that their ancient liberties would be respected and Catholic worship kept. A few weeks later the northern provinces of Holland, Zeeland, Utrecht, Gelderland, Friesland, Overijssel, and Groningen joined in the Union of Utrecht, in which they committed themselves to freedom of conscience for all citizens but banned the public practice of all but "the evangelical reformed religion." In the summer of 1580 Philip II, believing that if he eliminated William the resistance would collapse, declared William the Silent an outlaw and offered a reward of twenty-five thousand crowns for his capture, dead or alive. William responded with his *Apology*, in which he publicly renounced Philip's right to rule because, he declared, Philip had failed in his duty to the people of the Low Countries. In 1581 the arguments in the *Apology* were put into practice when the States-General of the northern provinces declared Philip II deposed and proclaimed the independence of the United Provinces of the Dutch Republic. The act stated: "We have declared and declare hereby by a common accord, decision and consent the king of Spain, *ipso jure* forfeit of his lordship, principality, jurisdiction and inheritance of these countries and that we have determined not to recognize him hereafter in any matter concerning the principality, supremacy, jurisdiction or domain of these low countries."[10]

William the Silent did not live to see independence actually achieved. In July 1584 a man named Balthasar Gerard betrayed William's generosity and murdered him. Claiming that his father had been martyred for

Protestantism and that he wanted to serve that cause, Gerard gained an audience with William, who even gave him money to buy shoes so that he could join the Protestant army. Gerard used the money to buy two pistols. On 10 July he joined a group of petitioners, and when William appeared, he shot him with the pistols he had bought with William's money. William died shortly afterwards, and Gerard, who was apprehended as he tried to make his escape, was executed. After the death of William the Silent, the Protestant cause was in serious danger as Parma was successful in capturing city after city, capped in August 1585 by the capture of Antwerp, which had a large Calvinist population. In desperation, the beleaguered Protestants appealed for foreign help, and in 1585 the United Provinces concluded a treaty with Elizabeth of England by which the Dutch agreed to accept a governor-general sent by England. Elizabeth sent her favorite, Robert Dudley, Earl of Leicester, with a small army to aid them, but Leicester was neither a competent military leader nor a good diplomat. His high-handed methods alienated the ruling elite of the Dutch towns, and he had little military success. Elizabeth's involvement resulted in King Philip II sending the Armada to invade England; however, as we already know, his plan was thwarted by English "sea dogs" and the so-called "Protestant wind."

Meanwhile the Dutch Protestants acquired two able, new leaders: Johan van Oldenbarnevelt provided political leadership, and Maurice of Nassau, William the Silent's seventeen-year-old son, became the military leader. Oldenbarnevelt differed from the ardent Calvinists in that his objectives were more political than religious. He recognized the independent spirit of the various provinces and did not attempt to impose a strong central government. The decentralized system worked remarkably well in providing the funding to support the war, which Maurice of Nassau conducted brilliantly, especially after the death of Parma in 1592. Maurice recovered many of the towns that Parma had captured, and by the turn of the century he had established a line of fortifications that effectively blocked any further advance from the southern provinces.

In 1609 the new ruler of Spain, King Philip III, recognized the status quo and signed a Twelve Years' Truce that divided the Low Countries between the Catholic southern provinces and the Protestant north. During the peace, the United Provinces of the north prospered economically. They maintained a blockade of the Scheldt River, cutting off Antwerp from the sea, and so trade shifted to the northern port of Rotterdam, while the southern provinces suffered an economic decline. Meanwhile the religious divisions within the Calvinist community, which we discussed in the last chapter, cost the United Provinces one of its most able leaders when Oldenbarnevelt was executed for treason in May 1619. Two years later the war began again, but this time the Dutch had all the advantages. When Maurice died in 1625, Frederick Henry, William the Silent's youngest son, took command of the armies and pushed the Spanish forces even further south. The Dutch fleet had great success against the Spanish at sea, even capturing their fleet bringing in silver from their American colonies in 1628. Finally, the Spanish gave up the effort, and in the Peace of Westphalia of 1648 they officially recognized the independence of the United Provinces.

Although Calvinists played the central role in winning independence from Spain, their ministers were not successful in achieving their goal of turning the Netherlands into a new Geneva. As we learned in the last chapter, Frederick Henry was tolerant of the Remonstrants, who had been exiled after their defeat at the Synod of Dordrecht, and they were encouraged to return. Even though Calvinism became the state religion, Remonstrants, Mennonites, and Lutherans were allowed to hold worship services in their homes, and even Roman Catholic house-churches were not harassed by the local authorities. In contrast, Catholicism was restored in the southern provinces and the remnants of Protestantism suppressed. A revived Catholicism flourished in what was called the Spanish Netherlands, which became the state of Belgium in the nineteenth century.

The Thirty Years' War

At about the same time that the French and Dutch religious wars were drawing to a close, the Holy Roman Empire was about to be thrown into an even bloodier and more destructive war. Although the Peace of Augsburg resulted in fifty years of religious peace for the empire, it was always an uneasy peace. The hopes expressed in the peace treaty were a good deal more idealistic than the reality of trying to get Christians to live together in peace during the age of confessionalism. The treaty included the statement that the competing faiths should treat "the disputed religion in no other way than by Christian, friendly and peaceful means and paths to a unanimous, Christian understanding and conciliation."[11] The major provisions of the treaty gave the rulers of the German principalities the right to determine the religion of the area they ruled, with two exceptions.[12] The first was that in the free cities, where both Lutheranism and Catholicism existed, the two faiths should share the churches. The second was the controversial "Ecclesiastical Reservation," which the emperor added without the consent of the Protestant estates. It read:

> Where an archbishop, bishop, or prelate or any other priest of our old religion shall abandon the same, his archbishopric, bishopric, prelacy and other benefices, together with all their income and revenues which he has so far possessed shall be abandoned by him without any further objection or delay. The chapters and such as are entitled to it by common law or the custom of the place shall elect a person espousing the old religion, who may enter on the possession and enjoyment of all the rights and incomes of the place without any further hindrance and without prejudging any ultimate amicable settlement of religion.[13]

In simple terms, this meant that if an ecclesiastical ruler became a Lutheran, he could not take his property and income with him, but a Catholic successor should be elected in his place. In the years that followed the Peace of Augsburg, this clause was violated again and again as ecclesiastical rulers converted to Protestantism and secularized their lands. The so-called "second Reformation" that developed in the half century following the peace presented another problem as Lutheran rulers were converted to Calvinism, which had not been included in the provisions for mutual toleration in the Treaty of Augsburg.

A major threat to the Protestant cause came from the militant Reformed Catholicism of the Catholic Reformation, led by the Jesuits, which began to make serious inroads into the empire in Bavaria and the Austrian lands. Bavaria became a major center of revived Catholicism when Duke Albert V (1550–1579) invited the Jesuits to work in the region. The University of Ingolstadt became a center for their activity. The Austrian lands also experienced the full impact of the Catholic Reformation as Protestant nobles were suppressed and the church was reformed.[14] Another group that suffered from the new reforming zeal of both Catholicism and Protestantism was those suspected of witchcraft. Between 1580 and 1660, forty to fifty thousand people were executed for witchcraft in Europe, and half those executions took place in the Holy Roman Empire. The uneasy peace in the empire between Protestants and Roman Catholics was maintained, to some degree, by the existence of the Ottoman threat. However, in 1606 pressure from the Persians in the east resulted in the sultan agreeing to a truce in the west, and once the common enemy was removed, Protestants and Catholics turned on each other.

German Protestantism in 1618.

War broke out in Bohemia after the Hapsburg heir Ferdinand of Styria
(1578–1637) was elected king of Bohemia in 1617. Bohemia was Protestant,
and Ferdinand was a Jesuit-educated Catholic who had been known for
his persecution of Lutherans in Austria. When Ferdinand sent two ardent
Catholics as his deputies, the Protestants reacted with fury. They marched
to the royal palace on 23 May 1618 and threw the emperor's representatives out of the window. Although the two men survived the fifty-foot fall
(according to the Catholic version, angels rescued them in full flight),[15]
the so-called defenestration of Prague led to war as the Protestants raised

an army, expelled the Jesuits, and confiscated Catholic lands. Although Ferdinand was unanimously elected Holy Roman Emperor in 1619, which meant the three Protestant princes of Saxony, Brandenburg, and the Palatinate voted for him, the Protestant nobles of Bohemia deposed him as their king and elected Frederick V of the Palatinate as king of Bohemia.

They could hardly have made a worse choice. Frederick V was twenty-three years old and without military experience.[16] He lacked the resources to fight a war and the diplomatic skills to acquire allies. Even his own father-in-law, King James I of England, did not come to his aid despite Puritan pressure, and the Lutheran ruler of Saxony fought with the Catholics against him. Emperor Ferdinand II did not have an army or much support in Bohemia, but he acquired the help of Maximilian of Bavaria, his Hapsburg cousin Philip III of Spain, and the Lutheran Elector of Saxony, who joined the coalition for territorial gain. The first stage of the war did not last very long. In 1620 the Bohemian army, led by Frederick V, was routed at the Battle of White Mountain. Poor Frederick, who had only been king for one winter,[17] was deposed from his throne. His troubles were far from over because in the next two years the Bavarian and Spanish armies conquered the Palatinate.

Frederick's disastrous defeat should have ended the Thirty Years' War, but it did not do so because a number of people and nations had vested interests in continuing the struggle. These people included the mercenary captains who raised private armies and fought for plunder and spoils. One of them, Ernst von Mansfeld, had originally fought for the Spanish but then became a Calvinist and sold his services to Frederick. During the course of the Thirty Years' War he was to change sides several times, always selling his services to the highest bidder. The most notorious of the mercenary captains was Albrecht von Wallenstein (1583–1634) who, although he was a Bohemian Protestant by birth, became the most effective of the Catholic commanders. The mercenary armies helped to make the war particularly devastating for the inhabitants of the Holy Roman Empire because the armies lived off the land and both sides pillaged the countryside. In addition, a number of foreign armies became involved in the war. Although it was labeled a religious war, political factors and the simple desire for personal gain played a major role throughout the conflict. In 1625 Christian IV (1588–1648), the Lutheran Danish king, entered the war to try to prevent a total Catholic victory, but he was unable to find German allies because the electors of both Saxony and Brandenburg refused to join him.

After Christian IV's defeat by the Bavarians at the Battle of Lutter in 1626, the Protestant cause seemed hopeless. Wallenstein occupied much

of Denmark as well as Brandenburg, and in 1629 he issued the Edict
of Restitution, which outlawed Calvinism and forced the Lutherans
to give back the ecclesiastical properties that they had secularized.[18]
Meanwhile Wallenstein's troops even occupied Magdeburg, the symbol
of resistance to the emperor in the first German religious war, as well as
the major Lutheran city of Augsburg. Both cities were forced to reconvert
to Catholicism. At the very time that the emperor was in a position to
rescind the Peace of Augsburg and reimpose Catholicism on the empire,
the Swedish king, Gustavus Adolphus (1594–1632), came to the rescue
of his fellow Lutherans. Gustavus Adolphus initially had trouble getting
the help of the German Lutheran princes, but he did get a subsidy from
the French king's chief minister, Cardinal Richelieu, who had ambitions
for imperial territory in the Rhineland and wanted to keep his Hapsburg
enemies distracted by the war in the empire. Gustavus Adolphus was
an outstanding military leader, and in 1631 he won the most decisive military victory of the war at the Battle of Breitenfeld, saving the
Protestant cause. However, the following year he met Wallenstein at the
Battle of Lutzen and was killed. Wallenstein himself was assassinated
in 1634, after the emperor dismissed him from command because he
was negotiating with the emperor's enemies. Although the most successful generals were dead, the war dragged on. In the final stage, the
French became involved on the side of the Protestants and, along with
the Swedes, continued the war for thirteen more years.

When the Thirty Years' War finally ended with the Treaty of Westphalia
in 1648, the major gainers were, as might be expected, the two powers that
had dominated in the final stage of the war—France and Sweden. The
French acquired parts of Alsace and Lorraine, and the Swedes annexed
western Pomerania. A number of German states also gained territory.
Saxony was granted Lusatia, Brandenburg acquired eastern Pomerania
as well as Magdeburg, while Bavaria gained territory in the Palatinate
and became one of the imperial electors. The big losers in the war were
the German people. For thirty years armies had lived off the land, looting, raping, and destroying. The empire suffered very severe population
losses. It is estimated that there may have been as many as eight million
fewer inhabitants in Germany at the end of the war than there were at
the beginning. The war reduced the population of Germany by at least
25 percent, and it may be that the population loss was closer to 35 or
40 percent. Although contemporaries may have exaggerated the losses,
there is no question that the impact on Germany was disastrous.[19] The
religious settlement added Calvinism to the two faiths allowed by the
Peace of Augsburg, so that ruling bodies could now establish Catholicism,

Lutheranism, or Calvinism as the state religion within their areas. The Thirty Years' War ended with a partition settlement, because no party was able to win a total victory. Ironically, the religious wars played a major role in bringing about a degree of toleration, since neither party was able to annihilate the other, and the participants emerged from these lengthy wars too exhausted to continue trying to achieve religious unity by the suppression of the opposition.

The English Civil War

Europe experienced one more religious war, just about the time the Thirty Years' War was ending. When Queen Elizabeth I died in 1603, it seemed as though she had achieved her objective of avoiding religious war in England. During the period that religious wars were raging in France and the Low Countries, Elizabeth was able to prevent the Puritans from changing the religious settlement, while keeping them within the Church of England. Although the radical Catholic opposition sought to assassinate the queen and put the Catholic Mary Queen of Scots on the throne, their efforts at rebellion were easily defeated, and the majority of Roman Catholics remained loyal to the throne. King Philip II's effort to impose Roman Catholicism through military means failed with the defeat of the Armada, and by the end of Elizabeth's reign there was probably less opposition to the settlement from either Puritans or Roman Catholics than there had been earlier. The leading Puritan theologian was William Perkins (1558–1602), and although he was theologically a radical Calvinist and held typical Puritan attitudes about clerical dress and other aspects of the prayer book, he was a reasonable man. For example, in contrast to John Knox's insistence in the reign of King Edward VI that kneeling at communion was idolatrous, Perkins explained that although kneeling was not excluded as an option, he preferred sitting because Christ sat at the first communion. When King James I (1603–1625) came to the throne in 1603, he dealt with his Puritan subjects in an effective and clever way and managed to avoid giving in to their demands while not alienating them.

When James first ascended the throne, his Puritan subjects, who expected that a king raised in Scotland by Presbyterian ministers might be sympathetic to their demands, presented him with a petition, called the Millenary Petition because it was supposedly signed by a thousand ministers. It contained the usual Puritan complaints about clerical dress, keeping the Sabbath, and providing for more preaching. James not only received the petition but, in contrast to his predecessor, he agreed to meet with the representatives of those who had signed the petition at the Hampton Court Conference in 1604. While King James I avoided making major concessions that would have threatened the settlement, he was willing to make some minor ones. He also agreed that there should be one uniform translation of the Bible that would be the only version used in all the churches. This resulted in the translation we now call the King James Version, or Authorized Version, which was the standard translation in the English-speaking world for centuries. Although Puritans suffered some harassment in the reign of King James I, they were largely content to work within the parishes, where they gained a significant following that included many of the gentry. Although James had many personal weaknesses, during his reign the Elizabethan Settlement remained intact and the Church of England was kept broad enough to contain all but the most radical Separatists or thoroughly committed Roman Catholics. All this came to an end in the reign of his son, Charles I.

Although historians continue to debate who was most responsible for the English Civil War, King Charles I (1625–1649) cannot escape responsibility for alienating his Puritan subjects in a way that his father had never done.[20] Charles was not at all sensitive to their feelings and completely alienated people who wanted to be loyal subjects but were appalled by his religious policy. The Puritans were particularly distressed when Charles promoted people whom they considered to be Arminians to leadership positions in the church. A great deal of debate has taken place over whether or not these so-called English Arminians can legitimately be called Arminians, since they expressed their views before Arminius's works were published. Nor were they necessarily united in the doctrines they taught—though they were united in what they opposed. They were against Calvinism, and one writer has labeled them "anti-Calvinists."[21] They were also associated with what might be identified as a "high church party" in the Church of England, because they emphasized beauty of worship. They placed greater stress on the sacraments as a means of grace, while opposing what they considered the overemphasis on preaching by the Puritans. The decisions of the Synod of Dordrecht were particularly distressing to the Arminians and resulted in deepening the divisions in the English church.

Meanwhile, Puritans were unhappy about England's stance in the Thirty Years' War. Although Frederick of the Palatinate was King James I's son-in-law and a Calvinist, James seemingly ignored his plight. In the meantime James pursued a marriage alliance for his son Charles with the Catholic Infanta Maria of Spain at the very time that the Catholic powers, which included Spain, were seeking to suppress Protestantism on the Continent. By the end of King James I's reign, many English Arminians were being appointed bishops, although the king, who had been brought up as a Calvinist and condemned the errors of the Arminians in his *A Meditation of the Lord's Prayer* in 1619, continued to be committed to Calvin's theology. In contrast, his son Charles was not at all sympathetic to Calvinism. He not only married a French Catholic princess but was clearly committed to those whom the Puritans considered Arminians. From the onset of his reign, Charles's policy was anti-Calvinist. Calvinists were virtually excluded from various church committees, and the preacher at the opening session of Parliament was an Arminian Anglican named William Laud (1573–1645), who was appointed archbishop of Canterbury in 1633.

Laud is one of those historic figures whom people either love or hate. The Puritans hated him because he seemed to threaten everything they had achieved, and they believed he was reintroducing Catholicism into the church. His supporters considered him a great hero of the faith who stood for godliness, orderliness, and beauty of worship. As is usual in debates of this nature, the truth lies somewhere between the extremes. Laud was a man of principle and a deeply committed Christian, but he was also determined to enforce the proper use of the Book of Common Prayer. Puritans regularly changed or omitted parts of the authorized service because they believed that some of the practices were idolatrous or stood in the way of what they considered "true religion" and a God-pleasing form of worship. They also commonly left out significant parts of the liturgy so they could have longer sermons. In the year that Laud became archbishop, he received a report from the diocese of Chester that "the Book of Common Prayer is so neglected and abused in most places by chopping, changing, altering, omitting and adding at the ministers' own pleasure, as if they were not bound to the form prescribed. In sundry places the Book of Common Prayer was so disregarded that many knew not how to read the service according to the Book."[22]

Archbishop Laud introduced policies that were designed to change this situation. He was also committed to the restoration of the clerical estate to its rightful place, which he believed had been undermined by the Reformation. Therefore he began to enforce the rules stringently and dismiss ministers who refused to conform. The two policies that caused the greatest controversy and opposition were his restraint of preaching and the campaign to remove the communion table from the nave. Laud believed preaching was subordinate to prayer and the sacraments in public worship. He was concerned to redress what he considered an imbalance in favor of preaching and to place a greater emphasis on the Eucharist by placing the communion table in the chancel and separating it from the congregation by a rail. Puritans found this particularly objectionable because in their view Laud was turning the table into an altar and returning to a doctrine that taught that a sacrifice rather than a meal was taking place in the Eucharist. King Charles I also reissued a *Book of Sports* that commended such Sunday recreations as dancing, maypoles, ales, and archery—all of which the Puritans considered a desecration of the Sabbath.

Archbishop Laud not only offended Puritans by his policies, but he enforced the regulations strictly. Those who would not comply or who criticized his policies were subjected to savage punishments. King Charles I, who backed Laud completely, was equally insensitive to the feelings and consciences of his Puritan subjects, and they were gradually alienated from the crown. Many Puritans left to go to North America, but others stayed to fight in Parliament.

The Puritans had strong support among the gentry who sat in Parliament and brought their grievances to be debated in the Parliament chamber. When King Charles I attempted to stop Parliament from dealing with matters that he considered to be the king's business, they protested vigorously that he was violating their ancient rights. For many who were not Puritans, this became a central issue in the debate. For example, when the Puritans launched a vociferous attack on the appointment of Arminians to high places in the church, Charles tried to adjourn the House of Commons to stop them from talking about these matters. But the Speaker of the House was held in his chair while the Commons passed three resolutions against those who introduced religious innovations. In 1629 Charles decided he could do without such an obstreperous body, so he did not call a Parliament for eleven years and raised money to run his government by quasi-legal means. The result was that resentment built up even more, and without an outlet for protest, the anger simmered beneath the surface, ready to explode. When the king was forced to call Parliament in 1640 because he had stumbled into war with Scotland, he was faced with a tidal wave of protest.

The Scottish war had broken out in 1637 when Archbishop Laud tried to impose on Scotland the same uniformity he was enforcing in England. A new liturgy, based on the Book of Common Prayer, was drawn up for Scotland, and when it was used in a service in St. Giles's Cathedral on 23 July 1637, a riot broke out. When the bishop stood with his back to the congregation in obedience to the new prayer book rubric, the congregation began to shout "the mass has come among us." Thirty or forty women started shouting curses, and someone threw a stool at the bishop, who barely escaped with his life. The Scots then broke into open rebellion against King Charles I, who insisted he would continue his religious policy despite the protest. The Scots then met in an assembly and drew up a National Covenant, in which they denounced the prayer book. In November 1638 they also abolished the episcopacy.

When subsequently a Scottish army began to invade England, the king had no choice but to call Parliament in order to raise money for the war. The first Parliament he called demanded redress of grievances before they would grant the king any taxes, so he dismissed them after three weeks. However, he still had no solution to the Scottish problem, and since he was still without adequate funds, he had to call Parliament again. That Parliament is known as the Long Parliament, because it met for a very long time and made revolutionary changes in the English government and church that eventually resulted in a civil war. The story of the events that led to the civil war is too complex to describe in detail; however, much of the responsibility lies with the king's foolish actions. Charles still had considerable support, and had he been willing to make reasonable compromises, he could have won the day, since the extremists on the Puritan side tended to alienate the moderates in Parliament. Again and again the king acted in a way that alienated the moderates. When the king attempted to arrest five of the leading members of the opposition in Parliament, he provoked Parliament to pass the Nineteen Propositions in June 1642, which would have turned the king into little more than a figurehead. Understandably, King Charles I refused to accept them, and he left London to raise his standard at Nottingham in August 1642. The king's action led to a civil war that very few people either expected or wanted.

Historians are not agreed on whether the English Civil War was a struggle between the king and Parliament over constitutional issues or a war fought primarily about religious issues. Although most would agree that both issues played a role, recently historians have tended to stress the religious motivations for the war.[23] Neither side wanted a military conflict, and both sides suffered terribly from the war. Although the Puritans were successful in defeating the king, in the end the victory was more costly to the Puritan cause than the years of persecution had been. Once they had triumphed, the Puritans were faced with many new problems, including the divisions that developed among them and the enormous difficulty of achieving their vision of a godly commonwealth. They also had to decide what to do with the leaders of the defeated opposition. The much-hated Archbishop Laud was impeached by Parliament for high treason in 1641 and confined to the Tower. After a grossly unfair trial in March 1644, he was sentenced to death, and on 10 January 1645 Laud was beheaded on Tower Hill. Four years later King Charles I was also beheaded after losing the civil war to an army led by the man who was a great military leader and became the political leader of the Puritans, Oliver Cromwell (1599–1658).

Cromwell was one of those enigmatic figures in history who continues to puzzle modern writers attempting to understand a character whose motivation and way of viewing the world were radically different from those held by most people in the twenty-first century.[24] Although understandably hated by the Irish and lovers of medieval stained glass,[25] he had many admirable qualities and was a very able leader. He came from the minor gentry, and most of the first forty years of his life were spent in relative obscurity. The most important event of those years was a conversion experience in 1638 that radically changed the direction of his life. Whatever else we may think of Cromwell, there is no doubt that after his conversion experience the major motivation in his life was to serve God and to use his gifts to achieve what he believed were God's purposes for England.

In 1640 Cromwell was elected to Parliament, and he gradually became more important as he distinguished himself militarily. Even though he had no military experience or training before the civil war, he was an outstanding general who never lost a battle. He raised an army of committed Puritans called the New Model Army, which he led to victory over a far more experienced army led by battle-hardened generals. The decisive battle occurred at Naseby in 1645, when Cromwell's disciplined New Model Army defeated the king's forces. At that point, Cromwell was prepared for a settlement that would provide for religious liberty, parliamentary reform, and the return to power of King Charles I, but Charles escaped, made an alliance with the Scots, and restarted the war. After Charles had been defeated and taken prisoner, Cromwell decided that the king was a traitor and had to pay for his treason with his life. When many members of Parliament hesitated to take such a radical step, Cromwell purged Parliament of over 200 members, and the remaining 154 members, the so-called Rump Parliament, convicted the king of high treason and sentenced him to death. His execution was carried out in January 1649 at Whitehall.

The execution of King Charles I brings us to the chronological end of the period covered by this book, but we need at least to summarize the result of the civil war. Cromwell had less than a decade to live after the king's execution, and during this period he subdued a revolt in Ireland, where he also committed brutal massacres at Drogheda and Wexford. He also defeated the Scots, who had recognized Charles I's son as king, and tried a number of experiments to restore constitutional government to England. However, in the end Cromwell ruled without a Parliament because all his efforts to establish a godly Parliament failed. He did not want to be a military dictator, but he found he could not achieve what he considered God's purposes for England without imposing a military dictatorship on the country. He was deeply concerned about social justice and moral reform and sought to achieve them by a variety of means. He also believed in liberty of conscience, and while he was in power, England had greater religious liberty than it had ever had before or would have again until the Toleration Act of 1689. In the end, when all of Cromwell's constitutional experiments had failed, he divided England into military districts ruled by major generals—a political arrangement that continued until his death in September 1658.

Although as Lord Protector, Cromwell was able to hold together his divided country while he lived, the defeat of the monarchy revealed the deep religious divisions among the victorious Puritans. The Westminster Assembly, which was called to implement the religious settlement, met from 1643 to 1652 and was made up of men who were Calvinists, including representatives from Scotland and North America. Yet they found they were deeply divided over questions concerning church government. The majority of the delegates were committed to a presbyterian system, but others argued for a modified episcopacy, and the independents rejected both forms of church government. Out of the deliberations came one of the great Reformed confessions (the Westminster Confession), two catechisms, and a Directory of Public Worship, but a state Presbyterian church modeled after the Scottish system that the Presbyterians desired was never established nationwide.

Cromwell was personally committed to liberty of conscience, but he was confronted with a proliferation of sects, most of which caused him a great deal of trouble. Some of them, such as the Fifth Monarchy Men, were millenarians who were prepared to use violence to achieve their ends. Others, such as the Levellers or Diggers, had political and socio-economic agendas. Still others, such as the Muggletonians and Ranters, were unrestrained in their radical beliefs.[26]

When Cromwell died, his son Richard succeeded him as Lord Protector, but he lasted less than a year. He had inherited an impossible job in a deeply divided country, and when he lost the support of the army, his situation became hopeless. General Monck, who commanded the parliamentary army in Scotland, marched his disciplined army to London in 1660 and ordered elections for a new Parliament, which met in April 1660 and invited the son of Charles I to return from exile in France. Charles II (1660–1685) came back to rule a kingdom whose religious divisions were all too evident. As Parliament turned to the task of enacting a religious settlement, the king would have been happy with one that allowed a degree of religious tolerance, since he leaned toward Roman Catholicism,[27] but in an angry reaction against the Puritans, the Parliament imposed an extremely intolerant settlement. The Restoration Settlement restored the Church of England as the established church and imposed strict regulations on the Puritans in the so-called Clarendon Code (1661–1665), which eventually drove them out of the Church of England. As a result of the Clarendon Code, many Puritans became Separatists, and the Church of England lost some of its most gifted and zealous ministers. The church also lost much of its religious zeal, as many only went through the motions of religion. London society, reacting against the strict morality of the Puritan Commonwealth, entered one of the more licentious periods in English history, while Puritans engaged in endless theological controversy with each other. Their theological differences and the debates over what most would consider insignificant points of theology were so intricate that it was difficult for outsiders to understand the differences. But those involved considered them serious enough to divide them from each other at the same time as they were suffering persecution under the Clarendon Code.[28]

The civil war was a disaster for English Christianity. It was one of the bloodiest wars in English history. One in fourteen adult males was killed—a higher percentage of the population than was lost in World War I. The terrible blood-letting and atrocities committed under the banner of "the Prince of Peace" helped to undermine the Christian faith in England as it had on the Continent. As a result it helped to prepare the way for the modern age in which religion was relegated to the status of a private matter. The war also led to religious toleration, possibly because one of the effects of the war was that the English no longer took their religion as seriously as they once did. Within three decades after the Restoration Settlement, a form of religious toleration that included all but Roman Catholics and antitrinitarians came to England.

15

THE IMPACT OF THE
REFORMATION

▼

Can we doubt that there has ever been any age which has seen so many admirable things in so short a time? So many changes in kingdoms, religions and estates?

Johann Sleidan[1]

Recent research is leading us to such a different understanding of the Reformation, that many . . . common notions about its impact should be drastically revised.

R. W. Scribner[2]

What was the overall impact of the Reformation? How significant were the "changes in kingdoms, religions and estates" on which the first historian of the Reformation commented in 1537? Throughout this study we have been examining how new research is calling into question older interpretations of Reformation history. So it should not be surprising that "many common notions" about the impact of the Reformation are also being "revised" as historians ask new questions and new research casts doubt on previous "understandings of the Reformation." Although it is not possible to consider all the questions that are being debated in a brief, concluding chapter, we can at least introduce some of the issues in the debate and comment on how the Reformation affected aspects of European culture and society.[3]

The impact of the Reformation on artistic expression was very significant, as the competing churches sought to express their faith in art, music, and literature. The Reformation also led to the development of resistance theories in reaction to the efforts of political leaders to suppress religious diversity. Some historians believe that the scientific Revolution, the modern state, and capitalism had their origins in the Reformation, which has led them to call the Reformation the beginning of the modern world. But others question how far the Reformers can really be identified with things we would normally term *modern*. An equally controversial question is often phrased, "Was the Reformation a success or failure?"[4] Answering this question requires examining how far the Reformers succeeded in communicating their message to the people of Europe. Did the Reformation change the religious beliefs and behavior of the European masses, or did it have an impact primarily on the educated elite? We begin with some of the less controversial questions by first examining how the Reformation affected the arts.

Art and Music

The Reformation had a varied impact on the fine arts. Although Lutherans considered art and music beneficial to worship, Zwingli, Calvin, and the Anabaptists were suspicious of what they considered idolatry in art and had a mixed reaction to the use of music in worship. Nevertheless, visual presentations of various kinds were combined with music and preaching to propagate the doctrines of the Reformation. Peter Matheson, who has studied the popular presentation of Reformation teaching, notes that "poet, artist, musician, painter and pamphleteer allied with preacher so that in Luther's words the Gospel was not only preached, but painted, sung, and—we might add—rhymed."[5]

Woodcuts provided a particularly effective way of communicating the teachings of the Reformers as well as to attack opposing positions. Appearing in cheap broadsides, the woodcut illustrations presented the conflicts between religious traditions in simple terms that the average person could not fail to understand. Woodcuts were also used to illustrate considerably more extensive publications, including the vernacular Bibles that were produced in great numbers on the presses of Protestant printers in addition to some of the major works of Reformation literature.

Although many woodcuts were of poor quality and religious cartoons were often crude and even obscene, well-known Reformation artists such as Lucas Cranach the Elder (1472–1553) and Hans Holbein (1498–1543) were also involved in producing woodcuts. Cranach was responsible for many of the Lutheran woodcuts and book illustrations that played such an important role in the early spread of the Reformation, and Holbein contributed a series of illustrative woodcuts to editions of Luther's Bible translation that were published at Basel. Woodcuts were also used to convey the message of some of the best-known Reformation works in visual form. For example, the title page of John Foxe's *Acts and Monuments* shows the *persecuted church* on one side and the *persecuting church* on the other side. Protestant preaching and courageous martyrs are illustrated in two frames, which are contrasted with popish superstition. The woodcut also portrays Protestant martyrs being ushered into paradise while the papists are expelled from heaven on judgment day.

The different attitudes of Lutherans and Reformed groups toward art resulted in contrasting artistic traditions. Lutherans, who saw the value of art in conveying the gospel, attracted some of the outstanding artists of northern Europe. Albrecht Dürer (1471–1528), who had established a reputation as one of the great artists of the age even before the Reformation, seems to have been an early adherent of the Lutheran Reformation. When in 1521 he heard a report that Luther was imprisoned, he lamented, "I do not know whether he is still alive or was murdered. . . . O all ye pious Christians, join with me in heartfelt mourning for this man, inspired by God. Pray God that another may be sent in his place as enlightened as he."[6] Like Luther, Dürer was disturbed by the radicalism of the Anabaptists, and his last great work pictured the four apostles with scriptural texts warning against false prophets.

Lucas Cranach the Elder (1472–1553) and his son Lucas Cranach the Younger (1515–1586) were two of the most prolific Lutheran artists. The father was a close friend of Luther and godfather to one of his children. In collaboration with Luther, he produced numerous woodcuts and book illustrations that taught Reformation theology. For example, *The Law and the Gospel* presented Lutheran teaching in pictorial form by contrasting the judgment of humankind under the law with the salvation that Christ won under the gospel, and it was produced both as a woodcut and a panel painting. In addition he used his artistic gifts to attack the papacy as illustrated by *Passional Christi und Antichristi*, which contrasted Christ's service to the poor with the ostentatious pomp of the papacy. We are also indebted to the Cranachs, father and son, for many portraits of the Reformers, including Luther and Melanchthon.

The German artist Hans Holbein produced much of the art associated with the English Reformation. After establishing his reputation on the European Continent with paintings that were solidly in the tradition of late medieval religion and producing woodcuts for editions of Luther's Bible translation, he painted Erasmus's portrait in Basel. As a result, when Holbein went to England in 1526 he carried with him letters of recommendation from Erasmus, which brought him to the attention of Erasmus's friend Sir Thomas More, who in turn introduced him to the king, with the result that Holbein became one of Henry VIII's court painters. Historians should be grateful to Erasmus and More, because it is due largely to Holbein's skills that we have a good idea of the physical appearance of Henry and his wives.[7] Holbein was also used by Cromwell to illustrate the title page for the Great Bible, the English translation that was placed in all the country's churches by royal order. Unfortunately, Holbein did not live long enough to paint the next stages of the English Reformation, as he died of the plague in the last years of Henry VIII's reign.

The Reformation also had a negative effect on church art. Injunctions issued in Edward VI's reign ordered the destruction of "all . . . pictures, paintings, and all other monuments of feigned miracles, pilgrimages, idolatry and superstition so that there remain no memory of the same in walls, glasses, windows or elsewhere within their churches or houses."[8] Although efforts to enforce this order were met with resistance and the government tried to prevent popular iconoclasm, much medieval art was destroyed.[9] During Mary's reign efforts were made to restore the art that had been removed in her brother's reign, and images that had been hidden reappeared to decorate the churches once more. However, after Elizabeth became queen a new injunction ordered their removal. The Elizabethan injunctions are sometimes considered less extreme than the Edwardian orders, but the commissioners appointed to enforce them were largely Marian exiles, who were zealous in their efforts to cleanse the churches of what they considered idolatry. Much of the surviving medieval religious art was destroyed by Cromwell's armies, who were responsible for breaking much of the stained glass in English cathedrals and beheading statues in chapter houses throughout England.

The destruction of medieval religious art was a reflection of Calvin and Zwingli's belief that pictorial representations were idolatrous. Calvin argued in the *Institutes* that the use of images and pictures was contrary to Scripture and specifically attacked the belief that "images are the books of the unlearned," maintaining that "everything respecting God which is learned from images is futile and false."[10] Calvin's followers took his attack

on images to mean that churches must be stripped bare of all their medieval decoration, and this often occurred wherever Calvinism triumphed.
The iconoclastic outbreaks in France, the Netherlands, England, and
Scotland all reflected the belief that images and pictures were idolatrous.
Although Calvinism had a negative effect on religious art, it did not discourage other forms: one positive effect of the Reformed attitude toward
religious art was the stimulation of secular art, as artists in Calvinist
areas who might once have concentrated on religious subjects turned
to other subjects. "The energies which in Catholic countries were still
directed toward religious art were poured into developing new secular
genres." As a result, "portraiture, the new art of landscapes, the pictures
of everyday life known as genre paintings and still life . . . flourished in
those parts of Europe where Protestantism had left the smallest scope
for traditional religious art."[11]

The Catholic Reformation also had a significant impact on painting.
Although the Council of Trent said little about the visual arts, it made
it clear that paintings and church decorations must not corrupt faith or
morals. For example, depictions of Mary breast-feeding the baby Jesus
were discouraged in order to avoid an overemphasis on the humanity of
Christ at the expense of his divinity. The new papal moral rigor resulted
in a "breeches painter" being hired to paint clothing on the nude figures
in Michelangelo's *Last Judgment* on the walls of the Sistine Chapel. The
concern about nudity even led the sculptor responsible for the nudes
on a fountain in Florence to repent publicly. Paintings also "reasserted
visually" Catholic doctrines that Protestants denied, such as "the holy
souls in purgatory, and associated with them, the holy guardian angels,"
and "the doctrine of the Eucharistic Real Presence was asserted by the
adoption of the scene of the breaking of the bread at the Last Supper
. . . and the Supper at Emmaus entered the canon of painting in the
same cause."[12] The negative results of these new attitudes were more
than balanced by a great outpouring of artistic expression inspired by
the Catholic Reformation, some of it under the direct supervision of the
papal commissions, such as the painting and sculpture used to decorate
the interior of St. Peter's in Rome, but most of the art was the result of
private patronage.

Spain was where much of the art inspired by the Catholic Reformation
was produced. Three painters who spent their careers working in Spain
provide examples of the diversity and depth of painting. Of the many
names associated with the art of the Catholic Reformation, few are better known than El Greco (1545–1614), whose real name was Domenico
Theotocopuli. Maybe the Spanish had trouble pronouncing that name,

because they simply called him "The Greek" (*El Greco*), since he was born in Crete. After a few years spent in Italy, where he was a student of the great Italian painter Titian, El Greco moved to Spain where he was employed by Spanish King Philip II to paint in his great palace of the Escorial. El Greco later settled in Toledo, and among his many paintings are some powerful and dramatic pictures of that city. The rich color and the elongated figures in his paintings, as well as sharp transitions from light to dark, give the impression of high emotion and deep spirituality characteristic of the Catholic Reformation.

The cult of the Virgin Mary, which became especially popular in the Catholic Reformation, helped to inspire another Spanish artist, Bartolomé Murillo (1617–1682), to paint some thirty different versions of the immaculate conception[13] and the Virgin with child. Murillo, who was almost wholly a religious painter, lived much of his life in Seville, where he completed a large number of paintings for convents and the cathedral. Another Spanish artist, Francisco de Zurbarán (1598–1664), is well-known for paintings that depict ecstatic religious experiences. Zurbaran also worked mostly for ecclesiastical patrons, producing paintings for monasteries, convents, and churches. A deep solemnity and fusion of mysticism and realism are characteristic of his work, as he used light and shade in a dramatic fashion to deepen the spiritual and devotional impact of his painting.

Music was another area that was greatly affected by the Reformation. We have already noted the different attitudes toward music among the Reformers and how Luther contributed to the great musical tradition that became characteristic of Lutheranism. This tradition reached its high point in the seventeenth and eighteenth centuries with the hymn-writer Paul Gerhardt (1607–1676) and one of the greatest of all religious composers, Johann Sebastian Bach (1685–1750). Even among Calvinists, who limited singing to the Psalms, the Reformation resulted in greater congregational participation, and throughout the Protestant world singing in vernacular languages was emphasized. This resulted in "a musically cultured population far wider than that of pre-Reformation society, where the great majority of musical performances were provided by professionals."[14] In 1562 a Calvinist Psalter was published containing psalms versified by the French poet Clement Marot (1496–1544) and Theodore Beza. The metrical psalms, sung to the tunes of popular French songs, became an identifying characteristic of Calvinist spirituality. Huguenot armies sang them going into battle, Calvinist martyrs died singing them, and congregations found great comfort and joy in what others might consider a relatively limited musical tradition.

Although Elizabethan England was strongly influenced by Calvinist theology, the Church of England had a musical tradition that was considerably broader than that of Geneva and most Continental Calvinism. Thomas Tallis (1505–1585), often called the "father of English cathedral music," and William Byrd (1543–1623) are some of the best-known names among English church musicians. Church music also crossed denominational boundaries. Byrd, who was a committed Roman Catholic, wrote settings for Matins and Evensong as well as a large number of English anthems for Anglican worship. He also composed three Latin masses.

The Catholic Reformation helped inspire impressive contributions to church music. Giovanni Pierluigi de Palestrina (1525–1594), who served three different popes and composed a vast amount of varied church music, is one of the best-known Catholic church musicians. St. Mark's Cathedral in Venice was served by two great composers who made major contributions to the musical heritage of the Catholic Reformation: Claudio Monteverdi (1567–1643), who in addition to his religious compositions was one of the pioneers of Italian opera, was music director at St. Mark's for thirty years, and Giovanni Gabrieli (1557–1612), another gifted church musician, was organist there for more than two decades. Music was able to cross the theological divide, as a promising German musician, Heinrich Schütz (1585–1672), was sent by his staunchly Calvinist prince to study in Catholic Italy. Schütz, who was to become one of the great Protestant composers, first studied under Gabrieli, who inspired him to become a professional musician, and he then returned to Venice to study with Monteverdi.

Literature

The Reformation had a huge impact on literature as it promoted theological, devotional, and polemical writing and helped to inspire writing in the vernacular, which contributed to the development of national languages. We have already noted how Luther's biblical translations affected the formation of the German language. Calvin's *Institutes* had an important effect on the French language, and Tyndale's Bible translation is considered one of the most influential works in the history of the English language. The Reformation era was also a period in which some of the great classics of Western literature were written. In England it was the era of Edmund Spenser (1552–1599), William Shakespeare (1564–1616), John Milton (1608–1674), and John Bunyan (1628–1688)—the works of the latter two being directly affected by the beliefs of the Reformers.

Both Milton and Bunyan were Puritans who were on the parliamentary side in the English Civil War. Bunyan served in the army, and after the war he spent twelve years in prison for preaching without a license. Although he was a tinker without a formal education, Bunyan used his time in prison to write and in 1678, inspired by his study of Scripture and Puritan preaching, he published *The Pilgrim's Progress*, one of the great allegories of Western literature. In telling the story of his humble hero, who was fittingly named Christian, Bunyan was describing his own spiritual journey and that of every Christian believer as he taught generations of Christian readers about the perils they face in their earthly pilgrimage and how to reach the celestial city. It was to become one of the most widely read works of Christian literature.

Milton's background was very different from Bunyan's. He was born into a prosperous London family and had an excellent education. He supported Parliament in the civil war and wrote polemical pamphlets attacking episcopacy as well as a pamphlet called *Areopagitica*, advocating freedom of the press from government censorship. In 1649 Milton defended the execution of King Charles I, arguing that monarchs can rule only with their subjects' consent. He was an admirer of Oliver Cromwell and served in his government. Although he became completely blind in 1652, he was still able to write his greatest work, *Paradise Lost*, after the Restoration. Published in 1667, it became one of the great epics of Western literature. Milton's work, which portrays the horrors of hell as well as the glory and beauty of heaven, communicated effectively to his own age and has continued to do so throughout the centuries that followed.

We turn to France for examples of the diverse ways in which the Reformation influenced some writers who remained within the Catholic Church. François Rabelais (1494–1553), one of the literary geniuses of his day, used his skills in the early Reformation period to attack the ecclesiastical establishment. A humanist and brilliant satirist, Rabelais used the stories of the mythical giant Gargantua and his son Pantagruel to poke fun at many of the institutions of his day, including the church. Although his works betray some sympathy for Protestant positions and contain vicious antipapal satire, Rabelais also attacked overzealous Protestants, and his writings reveal a belief in the inherent goodness of human beings.

Michel de Montaigne (1533–1592) and René Descartes (1596–1650) were both distressed by the divisions and hatreds resulting from the Reformation. Montaigne responded with skepticism, while Descartes tried to find a new approach to knowledge that all human beings could accept. Montaigne was a French nobleman who witnessed the bitter hatreds and terrible atrocities that took place in the French religious wars. Although he tried to remain aloof, he could not escape totally, and he was present when the Duke of Guise was murdered. In his *Essays*, initially published in 1580, Montaigne reflected on many different subjects. One long essay entitled "Apology for Raymond Sebond" expressed skepticism about the possibility of knowing God and achieving certainty by rational means. He also commented in bitter satire on the behavior of Christians he had witnessed in the religious wars: "There is no hostility that excels Christian hostility. Our zeal does wonders when it is seconding our leaning toward hatred, cruelty, ambition, avarice, detraction, rebellion. Against the grain, toward goodness, benignity, moderation, unless as by a miracle some rare nature bears it. It will neither walk nor fly. Our religion is made to extirpate vices; it covers them, fosters them, incites them."[15]

Descartes was a committed Catholic who found Montaigne's skepticism and the challenge Protestants raised to the church's authority disturbing. After participating in the initial battles of the Thirty Years' War, he moved to Holland where he lived in seclusion for twenty years and devised a system in which he applied mathematical methods to achieve a certainty in human knowledge that he hoped all could accept. He decided that he must first discard all inherited beliefs and accept only what could be proven by reason, so he began with the one truth that he could not deny: his own existence. This resulted in his famous maxim, *cogito ergo sum* (I think, therefore I am). Descartes then constructed a system using the principles of analytical geometry, starting with what was logically self-evident, moving from the simple to the complex and providing rational proofs for each step in the process. Although he remained a believer in Christian doctrine, Descartes prepared the way for a new generation of thinkers who would call into question the truths accepted by both sides in the Reformation, making reason the ultimate judge of truth.[16]

Blaise Pascal (1623–1662), one of Descartes's fellow countrymen, saw the danger in his approach and denounced him for leaving God out of philosophy.[17] One of the most brilliant men of his day, he wrote a book on geometry and invented a calculating machine while he was still a teenager. As an adult, he made major contributions to early modern science and mathematics. However, while Pascal was prepared to use reason to question and test previous scientific theories and conclusions, he believed that in theology one could not rely solely on reason. On the night of 23 November 1654 Pascal had a powerful experience of God that changed the whole direction of his life and deeply affected the way in which he thought about religious knowledge. He became more and more drawn to the Jansenists in Paris, and (as we noted in an earlier chapter) he wrote effectively in defense of the movement and in opposition to the Jesuits. Pascal also planned to write a defense of the Christian faith, but he died at the age of thirty-nine before he could complete it. The thoughts he intended for the book were later published in what was simply entitled *Pensées* (thoughts). Although they often read like random reflections on various subjects, the *Pensées* have become one of the classic works of Christian apologetics. Pascal pointed out the weaknesses of reason while not rejecting its value, and although one of his best-known statements reads, "The heart has its reasons which reason itself does not know," he also wrote, "If we submit everything to reason, our religion will contain nothing mysterious or supernatural. If we shock the principles of reason, our religion will be absurd and ridiculous." Pascal responded to the skeptics with his famous "wager": He argued that God either exists or he doesn't exist, and we must bet one way or the other. If he exists and we reject him, we will lose everything, but if he does not exist and we bet that he does, we lose nothing. Pascal urged his readers to bet on God, pointing out, "If you win, you win everything; if you lose, you lose nothing. Wager that he exists then, without hesitating!"[18]

Science

Three of the writers we have just discussed were also scientists or mathematicians.[19] They were part of a large group of brilliant men who participated in what has been labeled a "scientific revolution" because the advances made in the sciences radically altered previously held beliefs. It is remarkable how many great scientists and mathematicians were at work during the period 1500–1700. It was an international revolution because the scientists came from many different countries. Rabelais, Descartes, and Pascal were Frenchmen; in astronomy a Pole, Nicholas Copernicus (1473–1543), first advanced the heliocentric theory of the universe; a Dane, Tycho Brahe (1546–1601), made the astronomical observations that provided the evidence for a German, Johannes Kepler (1571–1630), to formulate his three laws of planetary motion; and an Italian, Galileo Galilei (1564–1642), provided supporting evidence for Copernicus's theory and also made major advances in the study of physics by his experiments with the pendulum and the laws governing falling bodies. In medicine, an English physician, William Harvey (1578–1657), made important discoveries in the circulation of blood, and a Fleming, Andreas Vesalius (1514–1564), published the first modern book on anatomy. In biology, a Swiss scientist, Conrad Gesner (1515–1565), made important advances in cataloguing plants and animals. Many of the discoveries were made possible by the new instruments of measurement and observation developed during the period such as the microscope, telescope, micrometer, and pendulum clock. The Dutch made especially important contributions in developing these instruments. Hans and Zacharius Janssen are usually credited with inventing the microscope about 1600, while another Dutchman, Anthony Leeuwenhoek (1632–1723), made significant improvements leading him to become the founder of microbiology. A Dutch optician, Hans Lippershay, invented the telescope in 1608, but Galileo constructed the first refracting telescope used for astronomical observations.

It was once believed that the church, whether Protestant or Catholic, stood in the way of the development of science. The condemnation of Galileo by the Italian Inquisition is often cited as evidence to support the view that science is characteristic of the modern world and that the church was opposed to science and stood in the way of new scientific developments. This interpretation has now been called "at best simplistic and at worst a profound misunderstanding of the complexity of the relationship between science, medicine and theology during the century of the Reformation."[20] Many of the early scientists were committed Protestants whose interest in science was motivated by their desire to study God's creation to reveal the glory of God and to benefit mankind. A large majority of the members of the Academy of Sciences in Paris and the Royal Society of London were Protestants. Many of the Royal Society members were clergymen, including John Wilkins (1614–1672), the society's first secretary and later bishop of Chester. Rather than being opposed to science, Protestant leaders often fostered scientific discoveries. A Lutheran prince, Albrecht of Prussia, subsidized the publication of Copernicus's book On the Revolution of Heavenly Bodies, and a Lutheran theologian, Andreas Osiander, wrote the preface. Other Lutherans aided in the printing and later supported Copernicus's position in their teaching. Although Luther's reaction to Copernicus (which is based on remarks found in what might be considered a questionable source) seems to have been negative,[21] he supported and welcomed other scientific advances. Melanchthon was particularly impressed with Vesalius's work on anatomy and introduced the subject into the University of Wittenberg's curriculum in 1535.

The major evidence of a clash between religion and science is the condemnation of Galileo by the Inquisition. Although the treatment of Galileo was disgraceful,[22] it does not necessarily indicate a clash between science and religion. Galileo was able to publish freely and was, in fact, supported by church authorities for most of his career. The initial opposition to him came from academic conservatives who were upset by his rejection of Aristotle's theories and by the results of his experiments in physics. In 1613 Galileo was attacked for contradicting the passages in Joshua that stated that the sun stood still, and in 1616 Cardinal Bellarmine ordered him not to defend Copernicus's view about the movement of the earth. Nevertheless, Galileo continued to write and to hold an honored position for almost two decades before changes in the political situation in Rome, personal rivalries, and the publication of his *Dialogue of Two Chief World Systems* resulted in an outcry against him. Although Galileo maintained that he had not defended Copernicus's position in the supposed dialogue between three characters discussing various views of astronomy, the person opposing Copernicus's position, who was called Simplicio, clearly had the weaker arguments.[23]

Those who opposed Copernicus's views (including Pope Urban VIII, who had been a good friend of Galileo) felt Galileo had tricked and insulted them, so he was called to answer before the Inquisition. Galileo was sixty-nine years old, in poor health, and in no position to resist the pressures placed on him. Under the threat of torture, he eventually recanted his belief that the earth rotates around the sun. He spent the remainder of his life under house arrest in his villa near Florence, but he was well treated and continued to write new scientific treatises. Throughout Europe many rose to his defense, and the Protestant Dutch Estates General even presented him with a gold chain honoring him. Later generations would look back on the treatment of Galileo and see it as evidence of a clash between the new world of science and the old world of religion, while Protestants would cite it as evidence that Protestantism was more favorably inclined to the new science than Catholicism. Although it was a foretaste of clashes that would occur in the centuries following the Reformation, during the Reformation era those clashes were the exception rather than the rule. Overall the impact of the Reformation on science was positive and constructive.

Economics and Politics

The impact of the Reformation on economics has been the subject of extensive controversy. In the early years of the twentieth century the German sociologist Max Weber (1864–1920) presented an intriguing theory that linked the growth of capitalism to Calvinism. In a classic essay entitled "The Protestant Ethic and the Spirit of Capitalism," Weber argued that the new type of capitalism that appeared in the post-Reformation era was partly the result of a Calvinist ethic. The new capitalism was characterized by the relentless pursuit of profit and limitations on consumption, which resulted in the accumulation of surplus capital, which would be reinvested to produce further economic growth. The Calvinist ethic of hard work, thrift, discipline, and a sense of vocation, combined with an understanding of the doctrine of predestination that sought assurance of election in adhering to the ethic and being blessed with economic gain, helped to stimulate this type of capitalism. The fact that early capitalism thrived in areas such as England and the Netherlands, where Calvinism was strong, tended to offer support to the theory.

Those who have questioned Weber's thesis point out that capitalism existed well before the Reformation and also contend that many of the facile connections between the Calvinist ethic and capitalism made by those who support Weber's thesis are based on a misunderstanding of the Protestant ethic. Both Calvin and Luther opposed many of the practices associated with the growth of capitalism and would have been horrified to have their names associated with a system that made the pursuit of profit the major motivation of economic activity.[24] Some Protestant beliefs, such as the concept of vocation, which raised the status of ordinary occupations, had an economic impact, as did the changing views on usury;[25] however, it is difficult to establish any direct connection between the Reformation and modern economic systems.

The political impact of the Reformation is much easier to trace. It is, for example, evident that the Reformation had a direct effect on the development of resistance theory. Although both Luther and Calvin held to the biblical teaching that the powers that be are ordained by God (Rom. 13:1) and therefore are to be obeyed even if these powers act in a tyrannical way, their followers found ways to justify resistance to magistrates who sought to suppress their religion. Lutherans first justified resistance to the emperor when the latter threatened to eliminate Protestantism by force. The establishment of the Schmalkaldic League in 1531 was based on the contention that the constitution of the Holy

Roman Empire gave "inferior magistrates"[26] the right to resist a tyrannical emperor. After Charles V defeated the Lutheran princes in 1547,
conservative Lutherans in the city of Magdeburg defended the right to
resist the religious settlement imposed by the emperor. Calvinists found
these arguments, which they learned by reading Johann Sleidan's history,
very useful when they faced government persecution in France. French
writers responded to the St. Bartholomew's Day Massacre by defending the right to resist tyrants who imposed their will in opposition to
the will of God. Francis Hotman (1524–1590), a humanist scholar and
Huguenot propagandist who narrowly escaped the massacre, fled to
Geneva where he wrote a work entitled *Franco Gallia* in 1573. Having
researched the early history of France, he maintained that the French
monarchy was originally elected and that it was responsible to a council that had the right to depose the king if he became a tyrant. The
Vindiciae Contra Tyrannos, published anonymously in 1579, went even
further, arguing that government is created and regulated by a contract
between the ruler and his subjects. When a ruler violates this contract,
subjects are no longer obliged to obey him. Minor magistrates serve as a
check on rulers, and foreign powers can intervene in support of subjects
contending with a tyrannical ruler. More radical political theorists even
advocated tyrannicide. In England John Ponet (1516–1556), one of the
Marian exiles, wrote *A Short Treatise of Political Power* in 1556 in which
he defended the right to kill a tyrant.

    Radical resistance theories were not limited to Protestant writers.
Catholic writers such as the Jesuit Juan de Marina (1536–1624) also
maintained that royal authority was based on a social contract and justified the right of deposition—and even tyrannicide—if a ruler violated
the fundamental law of the kingdom. Although the resistance theories
resulting from the Reformation conflicts were quite common, more
radical positions such as tyrannicide did not have widespread support
and were repudiated by most responsible leaders of public opinion.
The Reformers and the resistance theorists would have recoiled at the
suggestion that their theology or theories might be used to argue for
democracy, since they associated democracy with anarchy and radicals
such as the leaders of the Peasants' Revolt. However, the Reformers'
attacks on church privilege and their doctrine of universal priesthood
suggested a basic equality that would one day aid the development of a
political system that in their day was considered anathema by responsible
people. Political theorists would later draw on the resistance theories
first articulated during the Reformation to justify eighteenth-century
revolutions. Finally, as noted in an earlier chapter, many historians

would contend that the Reformation played a major role in the creation of the modern state, which is characterized by "independent councils, written constitutions, complex bureaucracies, standardized legal codes and university-educated ministers of government,"[27] maintaining that "the modern state had its beginning not in its monopoly of taxation and the military, but in its monopolizing of religion."[28]

Education

While there may be some debate about the impact of the Reformation on science and economics, there is no question that both the Protestant and the Catholic Reformations encouraged the development of educational institutions. Protestantism was a religion of the Book, and therefore, it was necessary to educate people so that they could read the Bible and the catechism. Luther wanted to establish a school in every town, in addition to public libraries, and advocated compulsory education for both boys and girls. He considered the office of teacher so important that he rated it as being second only to that of a minister. Philip of Hesse stated that he wanted to have a school in every town and village, an aim shared by most of the Lutheran authorities in Germany. Remarkable progress was made in achieving this goal during the first century of the Reformation era. For example, the number of schools in Württemberg increased from eighty-nine in 1520 to more than four hundred by the end of the sixteenth century. The Reformers were equally committed to the establishment of schools, so wherever Protestantism triumphed, schools were established. In addition to schools that taught reading and writing in the vernacular, Latin schools were established in the cities to teach Latin grammar and composition as well as introductory Hebrew and Greek. In England these were called "grammar schools," and their number increased from approximately thirty in 1480 to more than four hundred by the end of the Reformation era. Opportunities for university education, where the gifted could study theology, law, or medicine, also greatly expanded. In Germany, twenty new universities were added to the approximately fifty that existed at the beginning of the Reformation era. The Catholic Reformation also placed great emphasis on education, and as we have already noted, the Jesuit schools were some of the most respected educational institutions in Europe.

The expansion of educational opportunities had a significant impact on society in general. This ranged from the most elementary level, where many more people learned to read and write, to the universities, which produced a more highly trained clergy than had ever existed in the church's history. The volume of books being printed and the spread of book ownership to a much wider segment of the population is used to document the increase in literacy, but it is more difficult to determine what percentage of the population was literate. In Germany estimates range from 5 to 10 percent of the total population to as high as 30 percent of urban dwellers at the end of the Reformation era were literate. Although other factors, such as the introduction of printing and new ideas, certainly played a role, the Reformation was a major catalyst in producing a more literate population in Europe. However, the Reformers did not advocate establishing schools simply to teach people to read. Their major concern was to produce good Christians who knew the Bible, believed the doctrines of the Reformation, and reflected their faith in their lives. It was hoped that the newly established educational system, which placed great stress on teaching the catechism, would achieve these goals. The degree to which they were successful has been the subject of another major debate among historians, which has resulted in the asking of the simple question, "Was the Reformation a success or a failure?"

Was the Reformation a Success or Failure?

The measure by which the Reformers would have assessed success or failure was the degree to which their goal was achieved of communicating effectively what they believed was God's message of Good News in Jesus Christ. They were convinced that as people came to understand the faith and believe it, their lives would be changed. Their measure of success was therefore changed minds and changed lives among the mass of society. Did they succeed in achieving this? In an oft-quoted article written in 1975, Gerald Strauss offered substantial evidence to show that they did not, and so he maintained that the Reformation was "a failure."[29] Three years later he published a book in which he argued that after an initial hopeful beginning, even the Reformers came to realize that their idealistic hopes about getting "all people" to understand and practice the faith could not be realized. Using largely the evidence from visitation reports, he maintained that the new schools with their methods of rote learning produced resentment and boredom rather than good Protestants. He concluded:

If it was the objective of the Reformation to complete the breaking up of the medieval church, it succeeded. If its goal was to rationalize ecclesiastical administration and co-ordinate it with the goals of the early modern state, it definitely succeeded. If it sought to channel the religious energies of an intellectual elite, it was in large part successful. But if it was its central purpose to make people—all people—think, feel and act as Christians, to imbue them with a Christian mind-set, motivational drive and way of life, it failed.[30]

Other historians agreed with Strauss that the Reformation failed to bring the kind of change to church and society that a previous generation of historians had attributed to it. Tom Scott called "the 'success' of the Reformation . . . highly problematic" and argued that "its appeal to a broad audience was often at variance with what the Reformers themselves believed and taught."[31] Visitation records reveal that laymen did not understand some of the most basic teachings of Lutheran theology, and even the clergy continued to believe aspects of pre-Reformation religion, while magic and superstition remained part of popular religious beliefs. Pastors complained that parishioners often treated them with contempt, and visitors noted that superstitious practices continued despite efforts to suppress them. In some instances, pictures of the Reformers replaced those of the saints, and people attributed miracles to them. In 1634 people maintained that a picture of Luther was miraculously unharmed in a fire that completely destroyed the house where it was kept, and the so-called "incombustible Luther" appeared again in 1689. Earlier, in 1651 it was reported that drops of blood ran from the image of Luther onto the pulpit and preacher during a sermon.[32]

It is not surprising that Strauss's conclusions were not universally accepted or that they stimulated a lot of new research. Some scholars challenged his sources, maintaining that visitation records were not a particularly reliable source for judging the true state of religion in a community. The visitors were, after all, looking for things that were wrong in the parishes they visited rather than things that were right. However, even these records, if carefully used, reveal that the Reformation did not necessarily fail to reach the average person. James Kittelson used visitation records to study the parishes in the vicinity of Strasbourg in the late 1580s and concluded that there was real success in educating the young as committed Protestants.[33] In addition, visitation records are very sparse for cities, where Protestantism often had its greatest impact.

Studies of individual cities such as Strasbourg reveal a very different picture of success or failure in the Reformation from what Strauss found in his study. Lorna Jane Abray, who studied the Reformation in Strasbourg, maintained that it was too complex to describe in simple terms like success or failure because much depended on which element of the population was being examined. Success was clearly greatest among the middle classes but not limited to them. In addition, one needs to take into consideration the degree to which achievements could be labeled a success, even if they did not reach the standard that the clergy, often with "overly ambitious goals," had hoped might be achieved. There was a significant improvement in the quality of clergy, and they "did succeed in winning the respect, and even the affection of their parishioners." Although "not all Strasburghers accepted the clergy's ideals . . . there were no more complaints about clerical laziness, ignorance, immorality, or greed."[34] Abray concluded that change was slow and the Reformers did not fully achieve their ideals. However, she contended that the Reformation "certainly made deep changes in the way the Strasburghers understood the Christian faith and, however slowly and incompletely, had an undeniable impact on the way they lived their lives."[35]

Several authors have pointed out that evaluating success or failure in the Reformation depended on how high one sets one's sights.[36] Although the degree of change that the Reformation brought to Protestant parishes did not always meet the expectations of the Reformers, their expectations may have been higher than was realistically possible, considering the immensity of the task before them. The Magisterial Reformers held to the concept of a church embracing the whole community, and they initially hoped that the whole community could achieve the zealous religious commitment, knowledge, and morality of a gathered community or sect. They were to be disappointed, because an entire community is usually not capable of achieving or even desirous of achieving what the Reformers felt was necessary to consider the Reformation a success. This could, however, be achieved and was achieved by those who have been labeled the "Godly Community." They were the people who took their religion especially seriously, who understood the doctrines of the faith, and who made real efforts to put them into practice. At times Protestant leaders "discussed the possibility that, within a universal disciplinary church there might nevertheless arise an 'inner ring' of devout believers who exceeded the average Christian in evangelical enthusiasm and activity."[37]

In England the "Godly Community" is partly identified with the Puritans, who tried very hard to change the whole of the Church of England but failed in their attempt. In their case there can be little doubt that the Reformation was a success, but they were a minority of English Christians. In the Middle Ages the church recognized that only a minority could ever reach the high standards that the Reformers expected all to reach, so it provided a priesthood who carried out religious duties on behalf of society. Priests acted as intercessors for the wider society and offered eucharistic sacrifices for the sins of the community, both living and dead. The church also sanctified the superstitions of popular religion and provided ways in which the community could participate in religious events. The devoted minority joined the priesthood, entered a convent or monastery, or joined a lay fraternity such as the Brethren of the Common Life. The Reformers substituted the individual's personal responsibility to God for the intercessory priesthood and tried to end the superstitions of popular religion. We should not be surprised that they were not successful in fully achieving their goals. What should surprise us is the degree to which they were successful in changing the religion of a large number of people in European society.

The global dimensions of the Reformation are also too often overlooked when measuring the success of the Reformation. Whatever its successes or failures in Europe, it played a major role in the process of making Christianity a worldwide religion. "Reservations that historians have about the impact of the Reformation often betray a Eurocentric or a Western narrowness. In fact, the Reformation has an extra-European history; it went around the world with European culture as its host."[38] In some instances, Christianity did not survive after the Europeans left, but most sixteenth-century missions had a lasting impact in those areas of the world where Christianity was first planted during the Reformation era.

Was the Reformation the Beginning of the Modern World?

It is sometimes argued that the Reformation inaugurated what we may identify as the modern world—a world of rational practical values, of individual effort and reward, or popular will against dogmatic authority. This view is largely nonsense. The Reformers themselves would have been aghast at the thought of being harbingers of intellectual pluralism, relativism or rationalism.[39]

Although he may have deliberately overstated his case for effect, the author of the provocative statement cited above was correct in his assessment of what the Reformers would have thought about modern society. Luther, Calvin, and the other Reformers had no intention of modernizing

society, and many of the changes that led to the establishment of modern
Europe were already under way when the Reformation began. However,
the Reformation opened the door to other changes that would eventually
produce modern society. Some of those changes occurred in opposition
to what the Reformers wanted or as an aftereffect of regrettable aspects
of the Reformation. One prime example is the growth of skepticism: the
vicious conflicts that dominated the last century of the Reformation era
helped to disillusion some people to the degree that rather than trying to
decide between the many competing truth-claims, they reacted against
all of them. In 1582 a Calvinist minister in Brussels complained to his
colleagues that "one finds atheists and libertines everywhere, of whom
some openly ridicule all religion, calling it a fable and an ornament . . .
others, in order to disguise their contempt for God, say that so many
warring creeds have grown up in our Fatherland that they do not know
which is the true one, nor which they should believe; some others hang
their coats in the wind and, in their outward behaviour, accommodate
themselves to all religions."[40] It is difficult to determine how widespread
this attitude was, but we have already noted that sensitive intellectuals
such as Montaigne planted the seeds of skepticism in their reaction to
the brutality with which Christians treated each other. The terrible religious wars helped to undermine the faith they were seeking to advance
and in the end prepared the way for the Age of Reason.

Allied to the growth of skepticism was the beginning of toleration.
One major characteristic of the modern world is the acceptance of religious pluralism. This is a radically new attitude that would have been
totally unacceptable in both the Middle Ages and the Reformation era.
"Neither tolerance nor religious freedom was an entry in the vocabu-
lary of 16th-century man. . . . All countries, Catholic and Protestant
alike, clung to the notion that religious uniformity was indispensable
to the tranquillity of a political commonwealth."[41] Catholics persecuted
Protestants where they controlled the state, while Protestants persecuted
Catholics in the areas where they had political power, and both persecuted the Anabaptists. During the second century of the Reformation
era, Protestants and Catholics alike executed tens of thousands of people,
largely women, who were accused of witchcraft. This so-called "witch
craze" was another manifestation of the bigotry and brutality that were
all too characteristic of the era.[42]

In the course of the Reformation, some individuals opposed the values accepted by the culture, as they concluded from their study of the
Gospels that persecuting others for their religious beliefs was not in
accord with Christ's teaching. We have already met Sebastian Castellio

and Katherine Zell, who objected to the persecution of Anabaptists. A Spiritualist Anabaptist, Sebastian Franck (1499–1542), also taught mutual tolerance, writing in 1539 that "to me anyone who wishes my good and can bear with me by his side, is a good brother, whether Papist, Lutheran, Zwinglian, Anabaptist or even Turk. . . . I reject no one who does not reject me."[43] Unfortunately, this left quite a number of people whom Franck might reject, since relatively few would have accepted his radical doctrines, which rejected both the visible church and the sacraments.

One of the most influential works on toleration was written by an Italian antitrinitarian, Jacob Acontius (1500–1567), whose *Satanae Stratagemata*, later translated into English as *Satan's Stratagems*, argued for toleration and even pointed out that heretics brought benefits to true believers: "By them godly men are stirred to search the Scriptures much more carefully and diligently, who otherwise would give themselves up to sloth and would gradually sink into a state of general ignorance."[44] Although the first arguments for religious toleration came largely from those who were on the fringes of orthodoxy rather than the mainline churches, failure to resolve the problem of religious diversity by force eventually led to partition settlements that necessitated accepting the legal validity of other religious beliefs. It would take several centuries before Europe fully accepted the concept of religious toleration, but already during the English Civil War Congregationalists argued for a limited form of religious toleration and English Calvinists such as John Owen (1616–1683) wrote in defense of toleration. In 1689 Protestant dissenters in England were granted toleration. Although true religious liberty did not come to England for another century and a half, the initial steps had been taken.

In the making of modern Europe, one can hardly overemphasize the significance of the destruction of religious unity. The Reformation led "to the rise of an ecclesiastical pluralism never previously known or indeed imaginable. A universal church that had long been able to integrate many different religions broke up into several alternative, distinct and mutually exclusive religious systems."[45] This led to a very different Europe in which the political units, once divisions within a single Christian family, became independent sovereign states that had no ties to one another except those of self-interest. In addition, within the individual states the religious and the secular spheres were separated in a way that contrasted sharply with the intertwining of the secular and spiritual characteristic of the Middle Ages. "To be free of secular intervention, the churches were to withdraw from all secular areas . . .

and conversely if the states were to be independent from ecclesiastical opposition they must keep out of all strictly religious matters. . . . These ideas promote . . . the desacralization and secularization of the state."[46] The modern European state system with its secularized societies was, therefore, in one respect an indirect result of the Reformation.

Was the Reformation the beginning of the modern world? Clearly some of our modern ideas and the things we consider desirable today are in marked contrast to the attitudes of most people in the Reformation era, and the Reformers were certainly not "modern" in many of their attitudes and beliefs. However, what they taught and the impact of the Reformation on society in general played a significant role in the making of modern Europe. One can, therefore, conclude that "the effects of the Reformation were part of the process whereby modern society developed, and it gave a powerful impetus to the 'modernization' of Europe."[47]

Conclusion

In conclusion we return to the theme of this book—reform and conflict. Both were part of the Reformation's impact, and both should be considered in a concluding statement. Beginning with the positive aspects of our Reformation heritage, the whole church was reformed. When the Reformation era ended, all branches of the church had to a great extent achieved the goal of acquiring a qualified and spiritually committed ministry. Although we might debate the degree to which the general population absorbed the teachings of the Reformers, the Bible was more widely available in the vernacular than ever before, and more people could read it. Even the illiterate public was being presented with a view of God that differed radically from the stern judge commonly pictured in the late medieval representations that so terrified Luther. Popular presentations tended to present Christ as a gentle and loving Savior. "Christ . . . had come closer to humanity. He was no longer the remote and terrible judge." Children were to think of Christ as "their best, their most faithful, their friendliest friend."[48] Reformation theology taught that human salvation was dependent on what God had done for humankind in the person of Jesus Christ rather than on what human beings were required to do in order to appease God. At the center of that theology was the picture of God as a loving Father whose unconditional love provided assurance of salvation. This was a vital part of the heritage that the Reformation left for future generations. In summing up the impact of the English Reformation, A. G. Dickens reminded his readers that "imperfectly as the Reformers executed their task," they sought to "bring men nearer in love to the real person" of Jesus Christ. He concluded, "This type of aspiration lies at the heart of their message for our own century."[49]

People were willing to die for a God who cared enough about them to sacrifice his life for their salvation. In a recent study, Brad Gregory has sought to understand the martyrs in a sixteenth-century context rather than applying modern theories and beliefs to explain why people were willing to suffer and die a horrible death. In his words, "The act of martyrdom makes no sense whatsoever unless we take religion seriously, on the terms of people who were willing to die for their convictions." He points out:

> The Christian willingness to die in the sixteenth century was shared, in both form and content, by Protestant, Anabaptists and Roman Catholic martyrs. Faith and scripture grounded Christian life in all three traditions. . . . Above all, the martyrs believed that in scripture, God was speaking to them. . . . God's word accomplished its purpose, and Christ sustained them. In these respects early modern Christian martyrs were much alike. But their respective communities of faith were also deeply divided. The martyrs died for their fidelity to Christ, but they disagreed about what it meant to be Christian. They died for God's truth, but they disputed what his truth was.[50]

Sadly, this reminds us of the negative aspects of the Reformation, because alongside the impressive faith commitments of the martyrs are the fears and hatreds of those who were responsible for their martyrdom. It is sad that "quite contradictory movements can coexist within the one religious landscape. Images of light and liberation can alternate with the blackest nights of the soul."[51] The Reformers would not have been surprised that darkness accompanied the liberation from evil, death, and sin, which Reformation theology taught. Reformation theology also included a doctrine about the nature of human beings, which was veri-fied by their behavior throughout human history and was responsible for the conflicts that arose. Historians have contributed to those con-flicts by presenting the story of the Reformation in a one-sided manner. Hopefully, we have moved beyond the writing of propaganda histories and today our study of the Reformation can help us understand differ-ences rather than accentuate them. We turn again to A. G. Dickens for a final word as he described in his usual balanced fashion what should be the objective of every Reformation historian—something we have sought to achieve in this study.

If he entertains any practical objectives in the study of the Reformation, the Christian historian may legitimately hope to close at least some of the old rifts by explaining them with a due blend of sympathy and hard-headed realism. In so doing, he can also underline the obvious truth than none of the parties to the original dispute had anything like a monopoly of virtue, or good sense, of charity, or understanding in the Faith.[52]

Time Line

Date	Major Developments
1302	Pope Boniface VIII (1294–1303) issues Papal Bull *Unam sanctam* claiming papal supremacy in church and state
1304–1374	Francesco Petrarch, Italian poet
1309–1377	Papacy moves to Avignon during "Babylonian Captivity"
ca. 1330–1384	John Wycliffe, English reformer
1337–1453	Hundred Years' War between England and France
1348–1351	Black Death sweeps through Europe
1373–1415	John Hus, Bohemian Reformer
1378–1417	Great Schism ("Western Schism") between two, then three simultaneous popes
1414–1418	Council of Constance ends papal schism and condemns Hus
1438	Pragmatic Sanction of Bourges reduces power of papacy in France
1452–1519	Leonardo da Vinci, Italian painter and inventor
1453	Constantinople falls to the Turks
1455–1485	Wars of the Roses in England
1467–1536	Erasmus of Rotterdam, Dutch Christian humanist
1471–1528	Albrecht Dürer, German artist
1483–1546	Martin Luther, German reformer
1485–1531	Ulrich Zwingli, Swiss reformer
1489–1556	Thomas Cranmer, Archbishop of Canterbury and English reformer
1491–1556	Ignatius Loyola, Spanish reformer and founder of the Jesuits
1492–1503	Pope Alexander VI (Rodrigo Borgia)
1496–1561	Menno Simons, radical reformer, founder of Mennonites
1497–1543	Hans Holbein, German painter
1498?–1526	Conrad Grebel, Swiss radical reformer

Date	Major Developments
1505	Luther enters Augustinian monastery
1505/15–1572	John Knox, Scots reformer
1506	Rebuilding of St. Peter's, Rome, begins
1508–1512	Michelangelo paints frescoes in Sistine Chapel, Rome
1509	Henry VIII (1509–1557) of England marries Catherine of Aragon
1509–1564	John Calvin, French reformer
1512–1517	Fifth Lateran Council in Rome
1515	Pope Leo X (1513–1521) issues plenary indulgence to finance rebuilding St Peter's
1516	Mary Tudor, eldest child of Henry VIII of England, is born Concordat of Bologna grants French King right to appoint all bishops, independent of pope Erasmus's Greek New Testament published
1517	Luther's *Ninety-five Theses* issued
1519	Luther disputes with Eck at Leipzig Debate Charles V (1500–1558) elected Holy Roman Emperor Zwingli begins preaching in Zurich
1520	Luther publishes three Reformation treatises Pope Leo X excommunicates Luther in bull *Exsurge Domine*
1521	Luther refuses to recant at Diet of Worms Henry VIII publishes *Assertio Septem Sacramentorum* opposing Luther
1522	Luther's German New Testament published Luther returns from Wartburg Castle to deal with troubles in Wittenberg
1524	Martin Bucer (1491–1551) comes to Strasbourg Erasmus publishes *Diatribe or Sermon concerning Free Will* against Luther
1525	Peasants' Revolt in Germany Luther marries Katherine von Bora Luther responds to Erasmus in treatise *The Bondage of the Will*
1527	Sack of Rome Anabaptist Felix Mantz executed in Zurich Henry VIII begins seeking to annul his marriage to Catherine of Aragon
1529	Luther and Zwingli fail to agree on Eucharist at Marburg Colloquy "Protestation" at Second Diet of Speyer—hence term *Protestant* Henry VIII calls Reformation Parliament in England Reformation in Basel completed Mass abolished in Strasbourg
1530	Augsburg Confession, first official Lutheran statement of faith

Date	Major Developments
1531	Thomas Bilney (ca. 1495–1531) executed in England for teaching doctrine of justification by faith alone Zwingli killed at second battle of Kappel Schmalkaldic League of Lutheran princes formed
1533	Cranmer appointed Archbishop of Canterbury Henry VIII's marriage to Catherine annulled; he marries Anne Boleyn (1507–1536); their daughter Elizabeth Tudor born
1534	Henry VIII declared Head of Church of England by Act of Supremacy
1534–1535	Anabaptist kingdom in Münster
1535	John Fisher and Sir Thomas More executed in England
1536	Smaller English monasteries suppressed Anne Boleyn executed Henry VIII marries Jane Seymour Bucer and Lutherans reach agreement on Eucharist in Wittenberg Concord Reformation in Denmark and Norway First edition of Calvin's *Institutes* William Tyndale (b. 1494) executed
1536–1538	Calvin's first period in Geneva
1537	Report of Papal Reform Commission Schmalkald Articles summarize Lutheran faith Paul III (1534–1549) issues papal bull *Sublimis Deus*
1538–1541	Calvin in Strasbourg
1539	Six Articles in England mark return to Catholic doctrine Larger English monasteries suppressed
1540	Pope Paul III sanctions Society of Jesus
1541	Colloquy of Regensburg (Ratisbon) fails to heal breach between Protestants and Catholics Calvin returns to Geneva
1542	Francis Xavier (1506–1552) arrives in Goa India to begin mission
1545–1547	First session of Council of Trent
1546	Scots reformer George Wishart (b. ca.1513) burnt at stake
1547	Schmalkaldic War: Lutherans defeated at Battle of Mühlberg
1547	Edward VI reigns in England (until 1553) Six Articles repealed Italian poet Vittoria Colonna (b. 1490) dies
1548–1552	Augsburg Interim attempts to reimpose Catholicism in Holy Roman Empire
1549	*Consensus Tigurinus* agreement between Calvin and Bullinger (1504–1574) First English Prayer Book published Xavier arrives in Japan
1551–1552	Second session of Council of Trent

Date	Major Developments
1552	Second English Prayer Book published Bartolomé de Las Casas (1474–1566) publishes *A Short Account of the Destruction of the Indies*, describing terrible atrocities committed against Native Americans
1553	Antitrinitarian Michael Servetus (b. 1511) executed in Geneva
1553	Mary Tudor reigns in England (until 1558) Edwardian Reformation repealed in England
1555	Peace of Augsburg in Germany ends first religious war Johann Sleidan publishes *Commentaries of Religion and the State in the Reign of Charles V*, first history of the Reformation
1555–1558	Marian persecution in England; Thomas Cranmer executed 1556
1558	John Knox publishes *The First Blast of the Trumpet against the Monstrous Regiment of Women*
1558	Elizabeth I reigns in England (until 1603) Marian Catholic legislation repealed Act of Supremacy declares Elizabeth "Supreme Governor of Church in England" Act of Uniformity establishes 1558 Prayer Book as required form of worship
1559	Final edition of Calvin's *Institutes* Knox returns to Scotland
1560	First edict of toleration in France
1561	Colloquy of Poissy in France assembles Roman Catholic and Reformed leaders Belgic Confession of Reformed faith
1561–1563	Third Session of Council of Trent
1562	Teresa of Avila (1515–1582) founds reformed convent at Avila Katherine Zell (b. 1497) dies
1562–1598	Wars of Religion in France
1563	Thirty-nine Articles issued by Church of England
1564	Calvin dies *Book of Common Order* adopted as official book of worship for Scotland
1564–1616	William Shakespeare, English dramatist and poet
1566	Archbishop Parker's issues his *Advertisements* regulating English clerical dress
1567	Mary Stuart ("Queen of Scots") flees to England
1568	William Allen (1532–1594) establishes seminary at Douai to train priests to minister to English Catholics
1568–1648	Dutch Wars of Religion
1572	St. Bartholomew's Day massacre in France John Knox dies

Date	Major Developments
1574	Walter Travers (1548–1635), English Puritan, publishes *Full and Plain Declaration of Ecclesiastical Discipline* describing Presbyterianism
1575	Edmund Grindal (1519?–1583) becomes Archbishop of Canterbury
1577	Grindal suspended as Archbishop for refusing to suppress Puritan "prophesyings"
1578	Second Book of Discipline in Scotland
1580	Formula of Concord unites most German Lutherans Michel de Montaigne (1533–1592) publishes *Essays*
1581	States General of northern provinces in Netherlands declares independence from Spain
1583	Matteo Ricci (1552–1610), Italian Jesuit, gains permission to enter China
1583–1605	Jesuit *Reductions* established in present day Paraguay
1584	William of Orange (b. 1533) assassinated in Netherlands
1586	Colloquy of Montbéliard fails to unite Lutherans and Reformed
1587	Mary Stuart executed
1588	Spanish Armada fails to invade England First of "Martin Marprelate" Tracts published in England
1595–1596	Union of Brest-Litovsk establishes Uniate church in Russia
1598	Edict of Nantes grants French Huguenots toleration outside of Paris as well as political and military rights
1599	Synod of Diamper in India ends independence of Indian church
1603–1625	Reign of James I in England
1605	Robert de Nobili (1577–1656), Italian Jesuit, arrives in India to begin mission
1608–1674	John Milton, English Puritan poet
1609	Twelve Years' Truce divides Low Countries between Catholic southern provinces and Protestant north
1610	Henry IV of France assassinated
1618–1619	Synod of Dort (Dordrecht) in Netherlands rejects Arminianism
1618–1648	Thirty Years' War in Germany
1620	Cyril Lucaris (1572–1638), "the Protestant Patriarch," appointed Patriarch of Constantinople English Pilgrims arrive in Massachusetts
1623–1662	Blaise Pascal, French religious thinker
1625–1649	Reign of Charles I in England
1627	Alexandra de Rhodes (1591–1660) arrives in Viet Nam to begin mission
1631	Swedish king Gustavus Adolphus (1594–1632) defeats Catholics at Battle of Breitenfeld, saving Protestant cause in Thirty Years' War

Date	Major Developments
1633	Galileo Galilei (1564–1642) called before Inquisition for advocating Copernican theory
1637	René Descartes (1596–1640), French philosopher, publishes *Discourse on Method*
1640	Cornelius Jansen (1585–1638), French Catholic, publishes *Augustinus*
1642–1649	English Civil War
1643	Westminster Assembly begins meeting
1646	John Eliot (1604–1690) begins work among Native Americans
1648	Peace of Westphalia ends Thirty Years' War
1649	Execution of Charles I of England
1656	Pascal's *Provincial Letters* ridicules Jesuits and defends Jansenists
1658	Death of Oliver Cromwell (b. 1599), Lord Protector of England
1660	Restoration of Charles II (1660–1685) of England

SUGGESTIONS
FOR FURTHER READING

Writing the History of the Reformation

Historiography and Bibliography

Dickens, A. G., and John M. Tonkin, with Kenneth Powell. *The Reformation in Historical Thought*. Cambridge: Harvard University Press, 1985. Survey of historical writing about the Reformation.

Maltby, William S., ed. *Reformation Europe: A Guide to Research*, vol. 2. St. Louis: Center for Reformation Research, 1992.

Ozment, Steven, ed. *Reformation Europe: A Guide to Research*. St. Louis: Center for Reformation Research, 1982.

Maltby and Ozment contain bibliographical essays on various Reformation topics that provide an introduction to changing interpretations within the field of study.

Survey Texts

Brady, T. A., Heiko A. Oberman, and James D. Tracy, eds. *Handbook of European History 1400–1600*. 2 vols. New York: E. J. Brill, 1994–1995. Chapters are written by specialists in their areas who introduce the reader to some of the more recent interpretations.

Cameron, Euan. *The European Reformation*. Oxford: Clarendon Press, 1991.

Grimm, Harold J. *The Reformation Era 1500–1650*. 2nd ed. New York: Macmillan, 1973. Standard Reformation textbook for decades after it was first published in 1954, which continues to be a useful source of factual information.

Lindberg, Carter. *The European Reformations*. Oxford: Blackwell, 1996.

MacCulloch, Diarmaid. *Reformation: Europe's House Divided 1490–1700*. London: Allen Lane, 2003; New York: Viking Books, 2004.

Pettegree, Andrew. *Europe in the Sixteenth Century*. Oxford: Blackwell, 2002.

———, ed. *The Reformation World*. London: Routledge, 2000. Includes articles by specialists on a variety of topics including culture.

Tracy, James D. *Europe's Reformations 1450–1650*. Lanham, MD: Rowman & Littlefield, 1999.

Wallace, Peter. *The Long European Reformation: Religion, Political Conflict and the Search for Conformity 1350–1750*. Basingstoke, U.K.: Palgrave, 2004.

Reformation Theology

George, Timothy. *Theology of the Reformers*. Nashville: Broadman Press, 1988.

McGrath, Alister E. *Reformation Thought: An Introduction*. 3rd ed. Oxford: Blackwell, 1999.

Reardon, Bernard M. G. *Religious Thought in the Reformation*. 2nd ed. London: Longmans, 1995.

Primary Source Collections

Hillerbrand, Hans J., ed. *The Reformation: A Narrative History Related by Contemporary Observers and Participants*. New York: Harper and Row, 1964.

Janz, Denis R., ed. *A Reformation Reader*. Minneapolis: Augsburg Fortress, 1999.

Lindberg, Carter, ed. *The European Reformations Sourcebook*. Oxford: Blackwell, 2000.

Naphy, William G., ed. *Documents on the Continental Reformation*. London: Macmillan, 1996.

Noll, Mark A., ed. *Confessions and Catechisms of the Reformation*. Leicester, U.K.: Apollos, 1991.

Chapter 1

Primary Sources

Moriarty, Catherine, ed. *The Voice of the Middle Ages in Personal Letters 1100–1500*. New York: Peter Bedrick Books, 1989.

Strauss, Gerard, ed. *Manifestations of Discontent in Germany on the Eve of the Reformation*. Bloomington, IN: Indiana University Press, 1972. Collection of documents illustrating the grievances of all classes in Germany in the late Middle Ages.

Secondary Works

Allmand, Christopher, ed. *The New Cambridge Medieval History*. Vol. 3, 1415–ca.1500. Cambridge: Cambridge University Press, 1998. New edition that reflects the revisionist interpretations of the late Middle Ages viewing it as period of "innovation and development" rather than "doubt, decline, and division."

Aston, Margaret. *The Fifteenth Century: The Prospect of Europe*. New York: Harcourt Brace, 1968.

Brown, Peter. *Church and Society in England 1000–1500*. New York: Palgrave Macmillan, 2003.

Cohn, Samuel K., Jr. *The Black Death Transformed: Disease and Culture in Early Renaissance Europe*. London: Arnold 2002. Claims that the Black Death was not the bubonic plague.

Dykema, Peter A., and Heiko A. Oberman, eds. *Anticlericalism in Late Medieval and Early Modern Europe*. Leiden, Netherlands: E. J. Brill, 1993.

Ferguson, Wallace K. *The Renaissance in Historical Thought: Five Centuries of Interpretation*. Cambridge, MA: Houghton Mifflin, 1948. Survey of interpretations of the Renaissance.

Hale, John. *The Civilization of Europe in the Renaissance*. New York: Atheneum, 1994.

Huizinga, Johan. *The Waning of the Middle Ages*. London: Penguin; Garden City: Doubleday Anchor, 1955. Classic work that paints a very bleak picture of late Middle Ages.

Kristeller, Paul O. *Renaissance Thought and Its Sources*. Edited by Michael Mooney. New York: Columbia University Press, 1979.

Le Goff, Jacques. *Medieval Civilisation 400–1500*. Oxford: Blackwell, 1988.

Lynch, Joseph H. *The Medieval Church: A Brief History*. London: Longman, 1992.

Oberman, Heiko A. *The Harvest of Medieval Theology: Gabriel Biel and Late Medieval Nominalism*. Cambridge, MA: Harvard University Press, 1963.

———, ed. *The Reformation in Medieval Perspective*. Chicago: Quadrangle Books, 1971. Collection of essays by different scholars on late medieval religion.

Sumption, Jonathan. *Pilgrimage: An Image of Mediaeval Religion*. London: Faber; Totowa, NJ: Rowman and Littlefield, 1975.

Tuchman, Barbara W. *A Distant Mirror: The Calamitous 14th Century*. New York: Knopf, 1978. Very readable popular work that, as the title suggests, views the late Middle Ages as a period of unmitigated disaster.

Waley, Daniel. *Later Medieval Europe from Saint Louis to Luther*. London and New York: Longmans, 1964.

Chapter 2

Primary Sources

Crowder, C. M. D., ed. *Unity Heresy and Reform 1378–1460: The Conciliar Response to the Great Schism*. New York: Palgrave Macmillan, 1977. English translations of conciliar documents.

Olin, John C., ed. *Christian Humanism and the Reformation: Selected Writings*. New York: Harper, 1965.

Secondary Works

Augustijn, Cornelis. *Erasmus: His Life, Works and Influence*. Translated by C. G. Gayson. Toronto: University of Toronto Press, 1991. One of the best comprehensive recent biographies.

Duffy, Eamon. *Saints and Sinners: A History of the Popes*. New Haven, CT: Yale University Press, 1997.

———. *The Stripping of the Altars: Traditional Religion in England 1400–ca.1580*. New Haven, CT: Yale University Press, 1992. Detailed work that portrays late medieval religion in a very positive way as both healthy and popular.

Fudge, Thomas A. *The Magnificent Ride: The First Reformation in Hussite Bohemia*. Aldershot, U.K.: Ashgate, 1998.

Goodman, Anthony, and Angus MacKay, ed. *The Impact of Humanism on Western Europe*. London: Longman, 1990. Twelve essays that provide a good introduction to the subject.

Jansen, Katherine L. *The Making of the Magdalen: Preaching and Popular Devotion in the Later Middle Ages*. Princeton, NJ: Princeton University Press, 2000. Studies the cult of Mary Magdalen, which provides insight into popular devotion in the late Middle Ages.

Kirk, James, ed. *Humanism and Reform: The Church in Europe, England and Scotland 1400–1643*. Woodbridge, U.K.: Boydell and Brewer, 1997.

Lambert, Malcolm D. *Medieval Heresy: Popular Movements from the Gregorian Reform to the Reformation*. 3rd ed. Oxford: Blackwell, 2003. New edition of what has long been a standard study.

Leff, Gordon A. *Heresy in the Later Middle Ages*. 2 vols. Manchester, U.K.: Manchester University Press, 1967.

McConica, James. *Erasmus*. Oxford: Oxford University Press, 1991.

Mollat, G. *The Popes at Avignon 1305–1378*. London: Nelson, 1963.

Oakley, Francis. *The Western Church in the Later Middle Ages*. Ithaca, NY: Cornell University Press, 1979. One of the early revisionist works presenting a positive view of the late medieval church.

Ozment, Steve. *The Age of Reform 1250–1550*. New Haven, CT: Yale University Press, 1980.

Scribner, R. W. *The German Reformation*. Atlantic Highlands, NJ: Humanities Press, 1986. Brief revisionist study that has a very useful analysis of late medieval religion.

Shaw, Christine. *Julius II: The Warrior Pope*. Oxford: Blackwell, 1993.

Stump, Phillip H. *The Reforms of the Council of Constance*. Leiden, Netherlands: E. J. Brill, 1994. Excellent recent work on the most important of the councils.

Swanson, R. W. *Religion and Devotion in Europe ca.1215–ca.1515*. Cambridge: Cambridge University Press, 1995.

Tentler, Thomas N. *Sin and Confession on the Eve of the Reformation*. Princeton, NJ: Princeton University Press, 1977.

Thomson, John A. F. *Popes and Princes 1415–1517: Politics and Polity in the Late Medieval Church*. London: Allen & Unwin, 1980.

Tierney, Brian. *Foundations of the Conciliar Theory*. Cambridge: Cambridge University Press, 1968.

Chapter 3

Primary Sources

Dillenberger, John, ed. *Martin Luther: Selections from His Writings*. New York: Doubleday, 1961.

Pelikan, Jaroslav, and H. T. Lehmann, eds. *Luther's Works*. 55 vols. St. Louis: Concordia, 1955–1975. The most complete English translation, including excellent introductions.

Rupp, E. G., and B. Drewery, eds. *Martin Luther*. London: Edward Arnold, 1970. Very useful selections from a variety of documents including letters.

Secondary Works

Althaus, P. *The Theology of Martin Luther*. Translated by Robert C. Schultz. Philadelphia: Fortress, 1966.

Atkinson, James. *The Trial of Luther*. London: Batsford, 1971.

Bagchi, D. V. N. *Luther's Earliest Opponents: Catholic Controversialists 1518–1525*. Minneapolis: Fortress, 1991.

Bainton, Roland H. *Here I Stand: A Life of Martin Luther*. New York: Abingdon Press, 1950. Brilliantly written study that was a best seller when first published and remains a classic study.

Brecht, Martin. *Martin Luther*. 3 vols. Translated by James L. Schaaf. Minneapolis: Fortress, 1985–1993. Best recent biography. A remarkable work that incorporates a vast amount of new Luther research.

Edwards, Mark. *Printing, Propaganda and Martin Luther*. Berkeley. University of California Press, 1994.

Erikson, Erik H. *Young Man Luther*. New York: Norton, 1962. Psychohistorical study. Useful primary text for illustrating this questionable method.

Hendrix, Scott H. *Luther and the Papacy: Stages in a Reformation Conflict*. Philadelphia: Fortress, 1981.

Iserloh, Erwin. *The Theses Were Not Posted: Luther between Reform and Reformation*. Translated by Jared Wicks. Boston: Beacon, 1968.

Kittelson, James M. *Luther the Reformer: The Story of the Man and His Career*. Leicester, U.K.: InterVarsity Press; Minneapolis: Augsburg, 1989. Well-written short biography very favorable to Luther.

Loewenich, Walther von. *Martin Luther: The Man and His Work*. Minneapolis: Augsburg, 1982.

Lohse, Bernhard. *Martin Luther's Theology: Its Historical and Systematic Development*. Translated by Roy A. Harrisville. Minneapolis: Fortress, 1999.

MacDonald, Stewart. *Charles V: Ruler, Dynast and Defender of the Faith 1500–1558*. London: Hodder & Stoughton, 1992.

Marius, Richard. *Martin Luther: The Christian between God and Death*. Cambridge, MA: Belknap Press, 1999. One of most recent biographies. Interpretations are at times questionable.

Oberman, Heiko A. *Luther: Man between God and the Devil*. Translated by Eileen Walliser-Schwarzbart. New Haven, CT: Yale University Press, 1989. One of the best publications of the Luther quincentenary.

Rupp, Gordon. *Luther's Progress to the Diet of Worms*. New York: Harper and Row, 1964. Short study by one of the great Reformation scholars of our age.

Schwiebert, E. G. *Luther and His Times*. St. Louis: Concordia, 1950. Older work, but still very valuable, which stresses role of University of Wittenberg in spread of the Reformation.

Steinmetz, David C. *Luther in Context*. Bloomington, IN: Indiana University Press, 1986. Excellent series of essays on aspects of Luther's theology.

Yule, George, ed. *Luther: Theologian for Catholics and Protestants*. Edinburgh: T & T Clark, 1985. Collection of essays by well-known Protestant and Catholic scholars exploring the relationship between the teachings of Luther and Catholicism.

Chapter 4

Primary Sources

Lund, Eric, ed. *Documents from the History of Lutheranism*. Minneapolis: Fortress, 2002. Good selection of documents illustrating transition from Luther to Lutheranism.

Scott, Tom, and Robert W. Scribner, ed. and trans. *The German Peasants' War: A History in Documents*. Atlantic Highlands, NJ: Humanities Press, 1991. Documents collection with excellent, detailed introductions.

Vandiver, Elizabeth, Ralph Keen, and Thomas D. Frazel, eds. *Luther's Lives: Two Contemporary Accounts of Martin Luther*. Manchester, U.K.: Manchester University

Press, 2002. English editions of Luther's earliest biographies by Melanchthon and Cochlaeus.

Secondary Works

Blickle, Peter. *The Revolution of 1525: The German Peasants' War from a New Perspective*. Translated by Thomas A. Brady Jr. and H. C. Erik Midelford. Baltimore: Johns Hopkins University Press, 1981.

Bluhm, Heinz. *Martin Luther, Creative Translator*. St. Louis: Concordia, 1965.

Bornkamm, Heinrich. *Luther in Mid Career 1521–1530*. Translated by Theodore Backmann. Philadelphia: Fortress, 1983.

Brecht, Martin. *Martin Luther*. 3 vols. Minneapolis: Fortress, 1985–1993.

Dixon, C. Scott. *The Reformation in Germany*. Oxford: Blackwell, 2002.

Ebeling, Gerhard. *Luther: An Introduction to His Thought*. Translated by R. A. Wilson. Philadelphia: Fortress, 1970.

Edwards, Mark U. *Luther's Last Battles: Politics and Polemics 1531–46*. Ithaca, NY: Cornell University Press, 1983.

———. *Luther and the False Brethren*. Stanford, CA: Stanford University Press, 1975.

Grell, Ole Peter, ed. *The Scandinavian Reformation: From Evangelical Movement to Institutionalisation of Reform*. Cambridge: Cambridge University Press, 1995.

Gritsch, Eric W. *A History of Lutheranism*. Minneapolis: Fortress, 2002.

Haile, H. G. *Luther: An Experiment in Biography*. New York: Doubleday, 1980.

Höpfl, Harro, ed. *Luther and Calvin on Secular Authority*. Cambridge: Cambridge University Press, 1991.

Janz, Denis R., ed. *A Reformation Reader*. Minneapolis: Augsburg Fortress, 1999.

Kolb, Robert. *Martin Luther as Prophet, Teacher and Hero: Images of the Reformer 1520–1620*. Grand Rapids: Baker Books, 1999. Traces impact of images of Luther on Lutheranism.

Lohse, Bernhard. *Martin Luther: An Introduction to His Life and Work*. Philadelphia: Fortress, 1980. Includes a good discussion of Luther interpretation and sources.

Maurer, Wilhelm. *Historical Commentary on the Augsburg Confession*. Translated by H. George Anderson. Philadelphia: Fortress, 1986.

Ozment, Steven E. *Protestants: The Birth of a Revolution*. New York: Doubleday, 1992.

———. *When Fathers Ruled: Family Life in Reformation Europe*. Cambridge: Harvard University Press, 1983.

Scribner, Robert W. *Popular Culture and Popular Movements in Reformation Germany*. London: Hambledon, 1987. Traces relationship between Luther, lay piety, and German culture.

Tjernagel, Neelak S. *Martin Luther and the Jewish People*. Milwaukee: Northwestern, 1985. Traces and attempts to explain the changes in Luther's attitude toward the Jews.

Tracy, James D., ed. *Luther and the Modern State in Germany*. Kirksville, MO: Sixteenth Century Publishers, 1986. Contains articles that deal with the relationship between Lutheran movement and German territorial state.

Chapter 5

Primary Sources

Bromiley, G. W. *Zwingli and Bullinger*. Philadelphia: Westminster Press, 1979.

Furcha, Edward J., and H. Wayne Pipkin, eds. *Huldrych Zwingli: Writings*. 2 vols. Alison Park, PA: Pickwick, 1984. Best translation of Zwingli's major works into English.

Potter, G. R., ed. *Huldrych Zwingli*. London: Edward Arnold, 1978.

Secondary Works

Baker, J. Wayne. *Heinrich Bullinger and the Covenant: The Other Reformed Tradition*. Athens, OH: Ohio University Press, 1980. Major study of Bullinger's theology in English.

Biel, Pamela. *Doorkeepers at the House of Righteousness: Heinrich Bullinger and the Zurich Clergy 1535–75*. Berne, Switzerland: Lang, 1990.

Brady, Thomas A. *Ruling Class, Regime and Reformation at Strasbourg 1520–1555*. Leiden, Netherlands: E. J. Brill, 1978.

Brecht, Martin. *Martin Luther*. 3 vols. Minneapolis: Fortress, 1985–1993.

Chrisman, Miriam U. *Lay Culture, Learned Culture: Books and Social Change in Strasbourg, 1480–1599*. New Haven, CT: Yale University Press, 1982.

Eells, Hastings. *Martin Bucer*. New York: Russell & Russell, 1971. Comprehensive biography in English. Although somewhat dated as it was first published in 1931, still very useful.

Farner, Oskar. *Zwingli the Reformer: His Life and Work*. Translated by D. G. Sear. Hamden, CT: Shoe String Press, 1967. Brief and very sympathetic biography.

Gäbler, Ulrich. *Huldrych Zwingli: His Life and Work*. Translated by Ruth Gritsch. Philadelphia: Fortress, 1986. More critical biography.

Gordon, Bruce. *The Swiss Reformation*. Manchester, U.K.: Manchester University Press, 2002.

Greschat, Martin. *Martin Bucer: A Reformer and His Times*. Translated by Stephen E. Buckwalter. Philadelphia: Westminster John Knox Press, 2004.

Locher, Gottfried W. *Zwingli's Thought: New Perspectives*. Leiden, Netherlands: E. J. Brill, 1981.

McGrath, Alister E. *Iustitia Dei: A History of the Christian Doctrine of Justification*. 2 vols. Cambridge: Cambridge University Press, 1986. Most comprehensive study of central Reformation doctrine.

Moeller, Bernd. *Imperial Cities and the Reformation: Three Essays*. Philadelphia: Fortress, 1972. Contains his classic essay on imperial cities and the Reformation.

Nicholas, David. *Urban Europe 1100–1700*. New York: Palgrave Macmillan, 2003.

Ozment, Steven E. *The Reformation in the Cities*. New Haven, CT: Yale University Press, 1975. Offers a different perspective from Moeller.

Potter, G. R. *Zwingli*. Cambridge: Cambridge University Press, 1977. Standard biography in English.

Stephens, W. P. *The Theology of Huldrych Zwingli*. Oxford: Oxford University Press, 1986.

———. *Zwingli: An Introduction to His Thought*. Oxford: Oxford University Press, 1992. Best studies of Zwingli's theology. Second work is a shorter version of the first.

Walton, R. C. *Zwingli's Theocracy*. Toronto: University of Toronto Press, 1967. Explores political ramifications of Zwingli's thought.

Wandel, Lee Palmer. *Voracious Idols and Violent Hands: Iconoclasm in Reformation Zurich, Strasbourg and Basel*. Cambridge: Cambridge University Press, 1995.

Wright, David F., ed. *Martin Bucer: Reforming Church and Community*. Cambridge: Cambridge University Press, 1994.

Chapter 6

Primary Sources

Baylor, M. G., ed. *The Radical Reformation*. Cambridge: Cambridge University Press, 1991.

Harder, Leland. *The Sources of Swiss Anabaptism: The Grebel Letters and Related Documents*. Scottdale, PA: Herald Press, 1985.

Klaassen, Walter, ed. *Anabaptism in Outline: Selected Primary Sources*. Waterloo, Ontario: Herald Press, 1981.

Liechty, Daniel. *Early Anabaptist Spirituality: Selected Writings*. New York: Paulist Press, 1994.

Secondary Works

Bender, Harold S. *Conrad Grebel, 1498–1526: Founder of the Swiss Brethren, Sometimes Called Anabaptists*. Scottdale, PA: Herald Press, 1971. Reprint of classic work by one of the best-known Mennonite scholars.

Clasen, Claus Peter. *Anabaptism: A Social History, 1525–1618*. Ithaca, NY: Cornell University Press, 1972.

Deppermann, Klaus. *Melchior Hofmann: Social Unrest and Apocalyptic Visions in the Age of the Reformation*. Translated by Malcolm Wren. Edinburgh: T & T Clark, 1987.

Goertz, Hans-Jürgen, ed. *The Anabaptists*. Translated by Trevor Johnson. London: Routledge, 1996. Provides a summary of new approaches to the study of the Radical Reformation.

———. *Profiles of Radical Reformers*. Kitchener, Ontario: Herald Press, 1982.

Gritsch, E. W. *Thomas Müntzer: A Tragedy of Errors*. Minneapolis: Fortress, 1989.

Hillerbrand, Hans, ed. *Radical Tendencies in the Reformation: Divergent Perspectives*. Kirksville, MO: Sixteenth Century Journal Publishers, 1986.

Littell, Franklin H. *The Anabaptist View of the Church*. 2nd ed. Boston: Star King Press, 1958. Classic work that reflects Free Church historiography.

Packull, Werner O., and Geoffrey L. Dipple, eds. *Radical Reformation Studies*. Aldershot, U.K.: Ashgate, 1999. Collection of essays by some of major scholars in Anabaptist studies, introducing recent research.

Rempel, John D. *The Lord's Supper in Anabaptism: A Study in the Christology of Balthasar Hubmaier, Pilgram Marpeck and Dirk Philips*. Waterloo, Ontario: Herald Press, 1993.

Scott, Tom. *Thomas Müntzer: Theology and Revolution in the German Reformation*. New York: St. Martins, 1989.

Snyder, C. Arnold. *Anabaptist History and Theology: An Introduction*. Kitchener, Ontario: Herald Press, 1995.

Stayer, James M. *Anabaptists and the Sword*. Lawrence, KS: Coronado, 1972.

———. *The German Peasants War and the Anabaptist Community of Goods*. Montreal: McGill-Queen's University Press, 1991. Stayer is one of the most important scholars in the redefinition of Anabaptism.

Weaver, J. Denny. *Becoming Anabaptist: The Origin and Significance of Sixteenth-Century Anabaptism*. Scottdale, PA: Herald Press, 1987.

Williams, George H. *The Radical Reformation*. 3rd ed. Kirksville, MO: Sixteenth Century Journal Publishers, 1992. Massive work that remains indispensable for Anabaptist studies.

Chapter 7

Primary Sources

Calvin, John. *Institutes of the Christian Religion*. Translated by Henry Beveridge. 2 vols. Grand Rapids: Eerdmans, 1957.

Dillenberger, J., ed. *John Calvin: Selections from His Writings*. New York: Doubleday, 1975.

Kingdon, R., T. Lambert, I. M. Watt, and M. W. McDonald, eds. *The Registers of the Consistory of Geneva in the Time of Calvin*. Grand Rapids: Eerdmans, 2000. First volume in a major project to edit and translate Consistory records.

Olin, John C., ed. *A Reformation Debate: Sadoleto's Letter to the Genevans and Calvin's Reply*. New York: Fordham University Press, 2000. Useful introduction to Calvin's thought via debate he had with Cardinal Sadoleto in 1539.

Torrance, David, and Thomas Torrance, eds. *Calvin's New Testament Commentaries*. 12 vols. Grand Rapids: Eerdmans, 1972.

Secondary Works

Benedict, Philip. *Christ's Churches Purely Reformed: A Social History of Calvinism*. New Haven, CT: Yale University Press, 2003.

Bouwsma, William J. *John Calvin: A Sixteenth Century Portrait*. Oxford: Oxford University Press, 1988.

Gerrish, B. A. *Grace and Gratitude: The Eucharistic Theology of John Calvin*. Minneapolis: Fortress, 1993.

Greef, W. de. *The Writings of John Calvin: An Introductory Guide*. Translated by Lyle Bierma. Grand Rapids: Baker, 1989. Clear, concise introduction to Calvin's life and his writings.

Höpfl, Harro. *The Christian Polity of John Calvin*. Cambridge: Cambridge University Press, 1982.

Kingdon, Robert M. *Geneva and the Consolidation of the French Protestant Movement 1564–1572*. Geneva, Switzerland: Droz, 1967.

Klooster, Fred. *Calvin's Doctrine of Predestination*. Grand Rapids: Baker, 1977.

McGrath, Alister E. *A Life of John Calvin*. Oxford: Blackwell, 1990. Very readable recent biography.

McKim, Donald K., ed. *The Cambridge Companion to John Calvin*. Cambridge: Cambridge University Press, 2004.

Monter, E. William. *Calvin's Geneva*. New York: Wiley, 1967.

Muller, Richard A. *The Unaccommodated Calvin: Studies in the Foundation of a Theological Tradition*. New York: Oxford University Press, 2000. Controversial new study that seeks to understand Calvin in a sixteenth-century context and to correct accommodation to modern agendas.

Naphy, William G. *Calvin and the Consolidation of the Genevan Reformation*. Manchester, England: Manchester University Press, 1994.

Niesel, Wilhelm. *The Theology of Calvin*. Philadelphia: Westminster, 1978.

Parker, T. H. L. *John Calvin: A Biography*. Tring, U.K.: Lion Publishing, 1975.

Pettegree, A., A. Duke, and G. Lewis, eds. *Calvinism in Europe 1540–1620*. Cambridge: Cambridge University Press, 1994. Contains essays by scholars on various aspects of Calvinism.

Schnucker, Robert V., ed. *Calviniana: Ideas and Influence of John Calvin*. Kirksville, MO: Sixteenth Century Journal Publishers, 1988. Useful essays on aspects of Calvin's theology and impact of Calvinism.

Walker, W. *John Calvin: The Organiser of Reformed Protestantism 1509–1564*. New York: Schocken Books, 1969. Reprint of classic biography first published in 1906.

Wendel, François. *Calvin: Origins and Development of His Religious Thought*. New York: Harper and Row, 1963.

Chapter 8

Primary Sources

Bray, Gerald, ed. *Documents of the English Reformation*. Minneapolis: Fortress, 1994.

Dickens, A. G., and Dorothy Carr, eds. *The Reformation in England to the Accession of Elizabeth I*. New York: St. Martin's Press, 1968. Collection of documents with useful introductions.

Foxe, J. *The Acts and Monuments of John Foxe*. Edited by George Townsend. 8 vols. New York: AMA Press, 1965.

Hughes, P. L., and James F. Larkin. *Tudor Royal Proclamations*. Vol. 1. New Haven, CT: Yale University Press, 1964.

Secondary Works

Brigden, Susan. *New Worlds, Lost Worlds: The Rule of the Tudors 1485–1603*. New York: Viking Penguin, 2001. Good introduction to period that uses the most recent research.

Brooks, Peter N. *Thomas Cranmer's Doctrine of the Eucharist*. 2nd ed. London: Macmillan, 1992. New edition of what remains the best study of the subject.

Daniell, David. *William Tyndale: A Biography*. New Haven, CT: Yale University Press, 1994. Best biography of the translator of the English Bible.

Dickens, A. G. *The English Reformation*. 2nd ed. London: Batsford, 1989. Second edition of classic work.

Duffy, Eamon. *The Voices of Morebath: Reformation and Rebellion in an English Village*. New Haven, CT: Yale University Press, 2001. Study by a leading revisionist scholar of how the Reformation affected a single English village.

Elton, G. R. *Reform and Reformation: England 1509–1558*. London: Edward Arnold, 1977. Extremely well-written survey by an outstanding Tudor scholar of our age.

Haigh, Christopher. *English Reformations: Religion, Politics and Society under the Tudors*. Oxford: Clarendon Press, 1993. One of the major revisionist studies.

———, ed. *The English Reformation Revised*. Cambridge: Cambridge University Press, 1987. Collection of revisionist articles by various authors, including the editor.

Heinze, Rudolph W. *The Proclamations of the Tudor Kings*. Cambridge: Cambridge University Press, 1976.

Jones, Norman. *The English Reformation: Religion and Cultural Adaptation*. Oxford: Blackwell, 2001.

Loades, David M. *The Reign of Mary Tudor*. London: Longmans, 1991.

MacCulloch, Diarmaid. *The Boy King Edward VI and the Protestant Reformation*. New York: St. Martin's Press, 2001. Balanced, detailed study.

———. *Thomas Cranmer: A Life*. New Haven, CT: Yale University Press, 1996. Best biography of central figure in English Reformation.

Marsh, C. *Popular Religion in Sixteenth-Century England: Holding Their Peace*. New York: St. Martin's Press, 1998.

Marshall, Peter, and Alec Ryrie, eds. *The Beginnings of English Protestantism*. Cambridge: Cambridge University Press, 2002.

Scarisbrick, J. J. *Henry VIII*. Berkeley: University of California Press, 1970. Somewhat dated but remains best biography of Henry VIII.

———. *The Reformation and the English People*. Oxford: Blackwell, 1984. First of the revisionist works.

Shagan, Ethan H. *Popular Politics and the English Reformation*. Cambridge: Cambridge University Press, 2003. One of the recent postrevisionist publications.

Chapter 9

Primary Sources

Emerson, E. H., ed. *English Puritanism from John Hooper to John Milton*. Durham, NC: Duke University Press, 1968. Selections of Puritan texts and documents.

Hughes, P., and Larkin, James F. *Tudor Royal Proclamations*. 3 vols. New Haven, CT: Yale University Press, 1964–1969. Volumes 2 and 3 include Marian and Elizabethan proclamations.

Knox, John. *Works*. Edited by David Laing. 6 vols. Edinburgh: Bannatyne Society, 1846–1864. Contains all the works of John Knox as well as his letters.

Secondary Works

Collinson, Patrick. *The Elizabethan Puritan Movement*. Oxford: Clarendon Press, 1990. An excellent introduction to the subject. Still the best study available.

Cowan, Ian B. *The Enigma of Mary Stuart*. London: Gollancz, 1971. Good introduction to controversy over Mary Queen of Scots.

———. *The Scottish Reformation*. London: Palgrave Macmillan, 1983.

Donaldson, Gordon. *The Scottish Reformation*. Cambridge: Cambridge University Press, 1979. Standard work on Scottish Reformation.

Doran, Susan. *Elizabeth I and Religion 1558–1603*. London: Routledge, 1994.

Dures, Alan. *Elizabethan Catholicism 1558–1642*. London: Longmans, 1983. Brief survey with selection of documents.

Durston, Christopher, and Jacqueline Eales, eds. *The Culture of English Puritanism 1560–1700*. London: Macmillan, 1996. Chapters written by specialists on various aspects of Elizabethan and Stuart Puritanism. Especially valuable introduction by the editors.

Heal, Felicity. *Reformation in Britain and Ireland*. Oxford: Oxford University Press, 2003.

Hylson-Smith, Kenneth. *The Churches in England Elizabeth I to Elizabeth II*. Vol. 1, 1558–1668. London: SCM Press, 1996. Useful survey that includes recent research.

Kirk, James. *Patterns of Reform, Continuity and Change in the Reformation Kirk*. Edinburgh: T & T Clark, 1981. Collection of his works; views Scottish reformation as strongly Calvinist and anti-episcopal.

Lake, Peter. *Moderate Puritans and the Elizabethan Church*. Cambridge: Cambridge University Press, 1982.

MacCulloch, Diarmaid. *The Later Reformation in England 1547–1608*. London: Macmillan, 1990.

MacDonald, Alan R. *The Jacobean Kirk, 1567–1625*. Aldershot, U.K.: Ashgate, 1998.

Marshall, Peter. *The Impact of the English Reformation 1500–1640*. New York: St. Martin's Press, 1997.

Mason, Roger A., ed. *John Knox and the British Reformations*. Aldershot, U.K.: Ashgate, 1999.

Neale, J. E. *Queen Elizabeth I*. Chicago: Academic Chicago Publishers, 1992. Reprint of what was once the standard biography of Elizabeth.

Packer, J. I. *Among God's Giants: Aspects of Puritan Christianity*. Eastbourne, U.K.: Kingsway, 1991.

Ridley, Jasper. *John Knox*. Oxford: Oxford University Press, 1968. Detailed, thorough study.

Todd, Margo. *The Culture of Protestantism in Early Modern Scotland*. New Haven, CT: Yale University Press, 2002.

Wormald, Jenny. *Mary Queen of Scots: A Study in Failure*. London: Palgrave Macmillan, 1988.

Chapter 10

Primary Sources

Ignatius Loyola. *The Spiritual Exercises of St. Ignatius*. Translated by Anthony Mottola. Garden City, NY: Doubleday, 1964.

Schroeder, H. J., ed. *Canons and Decrees of the Council of Trent*. St. Louis: Herder, 1941.

Teresa of Avila. *A Life of Prayer*. Edited by James M. Houston. Basingstoke, U.K.: Pickering and Inglis, 1983. Anthology of Teresa's writings with useful introductions.

Secondary Works

Bangert, William. *A History of the Society of Jesus*. 2nd ed. St. Louis: Institute of Jesuit Sources, 1986. Comprehensive study in a new edition.

Bowd, Stephen D. *Reform before the Reformation: Vincenzo Querini and the Religious Renaissance in Italy*. Leiden, Netherlands: E. J. Brill, 2002. Study of Venetian humanist illustrates that Catholic reform preceded Luther's Reformation.

Brodrick, James. *St. Peter Canisius*. Chicago: Loyola Press, 1962. Reprint of what is still the best study.

Dalmases, Candido de. *Ignatius of Loyola, Founder of the Jesuits: His Life and Work*. Translated by Jerome Aixala. St. Louis: Institute of Jesuit Sources, 1985.

Davidson, N. S. *The Counter-Reformation*. Oxford: Blackwell, 1987. Very brief but useful introduction.

Delumeau, Jean. *Catholicism between Luther and Voltaire: A New View of the Counter-Reformation*. Philadelphia: Westminster John Knox Press, 1977. Important study with a provocative thesis.

Dickens, A. G. *The Counter Reformation*. New York: Harcourt Brace, 1969. Clear, well-written introduction, designed for students, with useful illustrations.

Evennett, H. O. *The Spirit of the Counter-Reformation*. Notre Dame, IN: Notre Dame University Press, 1970.

Fenlon, Dermot B. *Heresy and Obedience in Tridentine Italy: Cardinal Pole and the Counter Reformation*. Cambridge: Cambridge University Press, 1972.

Gleason, Elizabeth G. *Gasparo Contarini: Venice, Rome and Reform*. Berkeley: University of California Press, 1993. Study of Contarini's thought and ideas on reform.

Jedin, Hubert. *A History of the Council of Trent*. 2 vols. St. Louis: Herder, 1957.

Jones, Martin. *The Counter Reformation: Religion and Society in Early Modern Europe*. Cambridge: Cambridge University Press, 1995.

Monter, William. *Frontiers of Heresy: The Spanish Inquisition from Basque Lands to Sicily*. Cambridge: Cambridge University Press, 1990.

O'Connell, Marvin R. *The Counter Reformation 1559–1610*. New York: Harper and Row, 1974.

Olin, John C. *Catholic Reform from Cardinal Ximenes to the Council of Trent, 1495–1563*. New York: Fordham University Press, 1990. Useful introduction with illustrative documents.

O'Malley, John. *Trent and All That: Renaming Catholicism in the Early Modern Era*. Cambridge: Harvard University Press, 2000.

Posset, Franz. *The Front-Runner of the Catholic Reformation: The Life and Works of Johann von Staupitz*. Aldershot, U.K.: Ashgate, 2003.

Wright, A. D. *The Counter-Reformation: Catholic Europe and the Non-Christian World*. New York: St. Martin's, 1982.

Chapter 11

Primary Sources

Collett, Barry. "A Long and Troubled Pilgrimage: The Correspondence of Marguerite d'Angoulême and Vittoria Colonna 1540–1545." *Studies in Reformed Theology and History*, New Series, 6 (2000).

McKee, Elsie Anne. *The Writings: A Critical Edition*. Leiden, Netherlands: E. J. Brill, 1999. Second volume in her study of Katherine Zell.

Wilson, Katharina, ed. *Women Writers of the Renaissance and Reformation*. Athens, GA: University of Georgia Press, 1987. Includes selections from Vittoria Colonna and Marguerite of Navarre.

Secondary Works

Bainton, Roland. *Women of the Reformation from Spain to Scandinavia*. Minneapolis: Augsburg, 1977.

———. *Women of the Reformation in France and England*. Minneapolis: Augsburg, 1973.

———. *Women of the Reformation in Germany and Italy*. Minneapolis: Augsburg, 1971.

Brink, Jean R., Allison P. Coudert, and Maryanne C. Horowitz, eds. *The Politics of Gender in Early Modern Europe*. Kirksville, MO: Sixteenth Century Journal Press, 1989.

Charlton, Kenneth. *Women, Religion and Education in Early Modern England*. New York: Routledge, 1999. Study of how women received and provided religious education.

Crawford, Patricia. *Women and Religion in England 1500–1720*. New York: Routledge, 1993.

Douglas, J. D. *Women, Freedom and Calvin*. Philadelphia: Westminster John Knox Press, 1985.

Giles, Mary, ed. *Women in the Inquisition: Spain and the New World*. Baltimore: Johns Hopkins Press, 1999.

Hutson, L., ed. *Feminism and Renaissance Studies*. Oxford: Oxford University Press, 1999. Collection of seventeen essays by feminist scholars beginning with the question, "Did women have a Renaissance?"

Marshall, S., ed. *Women in Reformation and Counter Reformation in Europe*. Bloomington, IN: Indiana University Press, 1989. Nine articles on various aspects of women's experiences in Reformation Europe.

Matheson, Peter, ed. *Argula von Grumback: A Woman's Voice in the Reformation*. Edinburgh: T & T Clark, 1995.

Mattox, Mikey. *Defender of the Most Holy Matriarch: Martin Luther's Interpretation of the Women of Genesis*. Leiden, Netherlands: E. J. Brill, 2003.

McKee, Elsie A. *Katharina Schutz Zell*. Vol. 1. *The Life and Thought of a Sixteenth-Century Reformer*. Leiden, Netherlands: E. J. Brill, 1999.

———. "Reforming Popular Piety in Sixteenth-Century Strasbourg: Katharina Schutz Zell and Her Hymnbook." *Studies in Reformed Theology and History* 2, no. 4 (Fall 1994).

Meek, Christine, ed. *Women in Renaissance and Early Modern Europe*. Dublin: Four Courts Press, 2000. Ten essays examining the status of women within Renaissance culture.

Ozment, Steven. *When Fathers Ruled: Family Life in Reformation Europe*. Cambridge: Cambridge University Press, 1983.

Peters, Christine. *Patterns of Piety: Women, Gender and Religion in late Medieval and Reformation England*. Cambridge: Cambridge University Press, 2003. Believes that the loss of Virgin Mary and saints was detrimental to women in transition from Catholic to Protestant England.

Roper, L. *The Holy Household: Women and Morals in Reformation Augsburg*. Oxford: Clarendon Press, 1989.

Selderhuis, H. J., J. Vriend, and L. D. Bierma. *Marriage and Divorce in the Thought of Martin Bucer*. Kirksville, MO: Thomas Jefferson University Press, 1999.

Snyder, C. Arnold, and Linda A. Huebert Hecht, eds. *Profiles of Anabaptist Women*. Waterloo, Ontario: Laurien University Press, 1998. Biographies of Anabaptist women as well as excerpts from their writing.

Thompson, J. *John Calvin and the Daughters of Sarah*. Geneva, Switzerland: Droz, 1992.

Zophy, J. W. "We Must Have the Dear Ladies: Martin Luther and Women." *Pietas et Societes*. Edited by Kyle Sessions and Phillip Bebb. Ann Arbor, MI: Edwards, 1985.

Chapter 12

Primary Sources

Casas, Bartolomé de las. *A Short Account of the Destruction of the Indies*. Translated by Nigel Griffin. London: Penguin, 1992.

Nobili, Roberto de. *Preaching Wisdom to the Wise: Three Treatises by Roberto de Nobili S.J.* Edited and translated by Anand Amaladass and Francis X. Clooney. St. Louis: Institute of Jesuit Sources, 2000.

Xavier, Francis. *The Letters and Instructions of Francis Xavier*. St. Louis: Institute of Jesuit Sources, 1992.

Secondary Works

Boxer, C. R. *The Christian Century in Japan*. Berkeley: University of California Press, 1951.

———. *The Church Militant and Iberian Expansion 1440–1770*. Baltimore: Johns Hopkins University Press, 1978. Analytical survey of the role of Portuguese and Spanish missionaries in overseas expansion.

Bremer, Francis J. *The Puritan Experiment: New England Society from Bradford to Edwards*. New York: St. Martin's, 1976.

Chatzeantoniou, Giorgios A. *Protestant Patriarch: The Life of Cyril Lucaris (1572–1638)*. Richmond, VA: John Knox Press, 1961.

Chidester, David. *Christianity: A Global History*. San Francisco: Harper, 2000.

Drummond, Richard H. *A History of Christianity in Japan*. Grand Rapids: Eerdmans, 1971.

Elison, George. *Deus Destroyed: The Image of Christianity in Early Modern Japan*. Cambridge: Harvard University Press, 1988.

Friede, Juan, and Benjamin Keen. *Bartolomé de Las Casas in History*. De Kalb, IL: Northern Illinois University Press, 1971.

Gibson, Charles. *Spain in America*. New York: Harper and Row, 1966.

Hastings, Adrian, ed. *A World History of Christianity*. Grand Rapids: Eerdmans, 1999. Chapters written by specialist scholars dealing with different world regions.

Latourette, K. S. *A History of Christian Missions in China*. New York: Macmillan, 1929.

———. *A History of the Expansion of Christianity*. Vol. 3. *Three Centuries of Advance 1500 A.D. to 1800 A.D.* Grand Rapids: Zondervan, 1967. Reprint of outstanding detailed history of Christian missions.

Michalski, Sergiusz. *The Reformation and the Visual Arts: The Protestant Image Question in Western and Eastern Europe*. New York: Routledge, 1993. Has a useful chapter on Eastern churches and the Reformation.

Neill, Stephen. *A History of Christian Missions*. 2nd ed. New York: Viking Penguin, 1986. Second edition of valuable survey work with detailed bibliography.

———. *A History of Christianity in India: The Beginnings to 1707*. Cambridge: Cambridge University Press, 1984.

Ronan, Charles E., and Bonnie C. Oh, eds. *East Meets West: The Jesuits in China 1582–1773*. Chicago: Loyola Press, 1988. Story of earliest contact between Chinese intellectuals and Catholic missionaries.

Schurhammer, Georg. *Francis Xavier*. 4 vols. Rome: Jesuit Historical Institute, 1973–1982.

Spence, Jonathan D. *The Memory Palace of Matteo Ricci*. New York: Penguin, 1984. Fascinating study of how Ricci's method of memorization impressed Chinese intellectuals.

Thornton, John K. *The Kingdom of Kongo: Civil War and Transition, 1641–1718*. Madison: University of Wisconsin Press, 1983.

Ware, Timothy R. *The Orthodox Church*. 2nd ed. New York: Penguin, 1993.

Chapter 13

Primary Sources

Arminius, James. *Works*. 3 vols. Translated by James and William Nichols. Grand Rapids: Baker, 1991.

The Book of Concord: The Confessions of the Evangelical Lutheran Church. Translated and edited by Theodore G. Tappert. Philadelphia: Mühlenberg, 1959.

Cochrane, Arthur C., ed. *Reformed Confessions of the 16th Century*. Philadelphia: Westminster, 1966.

Secondary Works

Abercrombie, Nigel B. *The Origins of Jansenism*. Oxford: Clarendon Press, 1936.

Bangs, C. *Arminius: A Study in the Dutch Reformation*. Grand Rapids: Asbury Press, 1985.

Dixon, C. Scott, ed. *The German Reformation: The Essential Readings*. Oxford: Blackwell, 1999. Has articles on confessionalism as well as other aspects of German Reformation.

Harrison, Archibald H. W. *The Beginnings of Arminianism to the Synod of Dort*. London: University of London Press, 1926.

Jungkuntz, Theodore R. *Formulators of the Formula of Concord: Four Architects of Lutheran Unity*. St. Louis: Concordia, 1977. Discusses Chemnitz, Selneccer, Andreae, and Chytraeus.

Kolb, Robert. *Luther's Heirs Define His Legacy: Studies on Lutheran Confessionalization*. Aldershot, U.K.: Ashgate, 1996.

Maag, Karin, ed. *Melanchthon in Europe: His Work and Influence beyond Wittenberg*. Grand Rapids: Baker, 1999.

Manschreck, Clyde L. *Melanchthon: The Quiet Reformer*. Westport, CT: Greenwood Press, 1975.

Muller, Richard A. *After Calvin: Studies in the Development of a Theological Tradition*. Oxford: Oxford University Press, 2003. Essays dealing with development of Reformed theology in the second half of sixteenth and seventeenth centuries.

Neuser, Wilhelm H., ed. *Calvinus Sacrae Scripturae Professor: Calvin as Confessor of Holy Scripture*. Grand Rapids: Eerdmans, 1994. Includes article on *Consensus Tigurinus*.

Nischan, Bodo. *Lutherans and Calvinists in the Age of Confessionalism*. Aldershot, U.K.: Ashgate, 1999. Fourteen essays dealing with Lutheran and Calvinist doctrinal controversies.

———. *Prince, People and Confession: The Second Reformation in Brandenburg*. Philadelphia: University of Pennsylvania Press, 1994.

Nobbs, Douglas. *Theocracy and Toleration: A Study of the Disputes in Dutch Calvinism from 1600 to 1650*. Cambridge: Cambridge University Press, 1938.

Raitt, Jill. *Colloquy of Montbéliard*. New York: Oxford University Press, 1993.

———. *The Eucharistic Theology of Theodore Beza*. Chambersburg, PA: American Academy of Religion, 1972.

Rorem, Paul. *Calvin and Bullinger on the Lord's Supper*. Cambridge, U.K.: Grove, 1989.

Rummel, Erika. *The Confessionalization of Humanism in Reformation Germany*. Oxford: Oxford University Press, 2000.

Sedgwick, A. *Jansenism in Seventeenth Century France*. Charlottesville, VA: University of Virginia Press, 1977.

Spitz, Lewis W., and W. Lohiff, eds. *Discord, Dialogue and Concord: Studies in the Lutheran Formula of Concord*. Philadelphia: Fortress, 1977.

Wengert, Timothy. *Law and Gospel: Philip Melanchthon's Debate with John Agricola of Eisleben over Poenitentia*. Grand Rapids: Baker, 1997.

Chapter 14

Primary Sources

Abbott, W. C., ed. *The Writings and Speeches of Oliver Cromwell*. 4 vols. Cambridge: Harvard University Press, 1937–1947.

Clarendon, Edward Hyde, 1st Earl of. *History of the Rebellion*. Edited by W. Dunn Macray. 6 vols. Oxford: Oxford University Press, 1888. History of civil war by man who was a moderate participant in first stage, joined Charles II in exile, and became his chancellor after the Restoration.

Duke, Alastair, Gillian Lewis, and Andrew Pettegree, eds. *Calvinism in Europe 1540–1620: A Collection of Documents*. Manchester, England: Manchester University Press, 1992.

Secondary Works

Benedict, Philip. *The Faith and Fortunes of France's Huguenots, 1600–1665*. Aldershot, U.K.: Ashgate, 2001.

Crew, Phyllis Mack. *Calvinist Preaching and Iconoclasm in the Netherlands, 1544–1569*. Cambridge: Cambridge University Press, 1978.

Cunningham, Andrew, and Ole Peter Grell. *The Four Horsemen of the Apocalypse: Religion, War, Famine and Death in Reformation Europe*. Cambridge: Cambridge University Press, 2000. Deals with the many tragic events of the period viewed as an apocalyptic age.

Diefendorf, Barbara B. *Beneath the Cross: Catholics and Huguenots in Sixteenth Century Paris*. Oxford: Oxford University Press, 1991.

Dunn, Richard S. *The Age of Religious Wars 1559–1689*. New York: Norton, 1970.

Greengrass, Mark. *The French Reformation*. Oxford: Blackwell, 1987. Brief survey in Historical Association Studies series.

Hill, Christopher. *God's Englishman: Oliver Cromwell and the English Revolution*. New York: Harper and Row, 1970. Classic biography by one of the great civil war scholars.

Holt, Mack P. *The French Wars of Religion 1562–1629*. Cambridge: Cambridge University Press, 1995.

Kendall, R. T. *Calvin and English Calvinism to 1649*. Oxford: Oxford University Press, 1979. Controversial study argues that English Calvinism reflected the thought of Beza rather than that of Calvin.

Kingdon, Robert M. *Geneva and the Coming of the Wars of Religion in France, 1555–1563*. Geneva, Switzerland: Droz, 1956.

———. *Geneva and the Consolidation of the French Protestant Movement 1564–1572*. Geneva, Switzerland: Droz, 1967. Important study by one of the leading scholars of French Calvinism.

Knecht, R. J. *The French Wars of Religion 1559–1598*. London: Longman, 1989. Brief survey with illustrative documents.

Morrill, John, ed. *Oliver Cromwell and the English Revolution*. London: Longman, 1990. Essays by specialist scholars on Cromwell and the civil war.

Pages, G. *The Thirty Years War, 1618–1648*. Translated by David Maland and John Hooper. New York: Harper and Row, 1970. A very readable and long standard account and survey.

Parker, Geoffrey, and Simon Adams, eds. *The Thirty Years' War*. 2nd ed. London: Routledge, 1997. Second edition of standard work with contributions by a number of scholars.

Prestwich, Menna. *International Calvinism 1541–1715*. Oxford: Clarendon, 1985.

Racaut, Luc. *Hatred in Print: Catholic Propaganda and Protestant Identity during the French Wars of Religion*. Aldershot, U.K.: Ashgate, 2002.

Raitt, Jill. *The Colloquy of Montbéliard*. Oxford: Oxford University Press, 1993.

Richardson, R. C. *The Debate on the English Revolution*. London: Methuen, 1977.

Swart, K. W. *William of Orange and the Revolt of the Netherlands, 1572–84*. Translated by J. C. Grayson. Aldershot, U.K.: Ashgate, 2003.

Tyacke, Nicholas. *Anti-Calvinists: the Rise of English Arminianism 1590–1640*. Oxford: Oxford University Press, 1987. Argues Arminians rather than Puritans were responsible for civil war.

Wedgewood, C. V. *William the Silent*. London: Jonathan Cape, 1948.

White, Peter. *Predestination, Policy and Polemic: Conflict and Consensus in the English Church from the Reformation to the Civil War*. Cambridge: Cambridge University Press, 1992.

Woolrych, Austin. *Britain in Revolution 1625–1660*. Oxford: Oxford University Press, 2003.

Chapter 15

Primary Sources

Galilei, Galileo. *Dialogue Concerning the Two Chief World Systems—Ptolemaic and Copernican*. 3rd ed. Translated by Stillman Drake. Berkeley: University of California Press, 1981.

Montaigne, Michel de. *Complete Works*. Translated by Donald M. Frame. Stanford, CA: Stanford University Press, 1967.

Pascal, Blaise. *Pensées and Other Writings*. Translated by Honor Levi. Oxford: Oxford University Press, 1995.

Secondary Works

Abray, Lorna Jane. *The People's Reformation: Magistrates, Clergy, and Commons in Strasbourg, 1500–1598*. Ithaca, NY: Cornell University Press, 1985.

Cameron, Euan. "The Godly Community in the Theory and Practice of the European Revolution." *Studies in Church History* 23 (1986): 131–53.

Chrisman, Miriam U. *Lay Culture, Learned Culture: Books and Social Change in Strasbourg 1480–1599*. New Haven, CT: Yale University Press, 1982.

Christensen, Carl C. *Art and the Reformation in Germany*. Athens, OH: Ohio University Press, 1979.

Davies, Richard. *Descartes: Belief, Skepticism and Virtue*. London: Routledge, 2001.

Dillenberger, John. *Images and Relics: Theological Perceptions and Visual Images in Sixteenth-Century Europe*. New York: Oxford University Press, 1999. Deals with what theology meant for artists including Dürer, Cranach, Michelangelo, and Holbein within the context of art.

Gregory, Brad S. *Salvation at Stake: Christian Martyrdom in Early Modern Europe*. Cambridge: Harvard University Press, 1999. The significance of martyrdom in the Reformation.

Guggisberg, Hans. *Sebastian Castellio 1515–1563: Humanist and Defender of Religious Toleration in a Confessional Age*. Translated by Bruce Gordon. Aldershot, U.K.: Ashgate, 2002.

Henry, John. *The Scientific Revolution and the Origins of Modern Science*. 2nd ed. Basingstoke, U.K.: Palgrave, 2002. Brief survey written for the nonscientist.

Hillerbrand, Hans J. "Was There a Reformation in the Sixteenth Century?" *Church History* 72, no. 3 (September 2003): 525ff.

Kamen, Henry. *The Rise of Toleration*. New York: McGraw Hill, 1967.

Kittelson, James. "Success and Failures in the German Reformation: The Reform from Strasbourg." *Archiv für Reformationsgeschichte* 73 (1983): 153–75.

Lehmann, Hartmut, and Gunther Roth, eds. *Weber's "Protestant Ethic": Origins, Evidence, Contexts*. Cambridge: Cambridge University Press, 1993. Series of essays dealing with the thesis and its critics.

Lindberg, David C., and Robert Westman, eds. *Reappraisals of the Scientific Revolution*. Cambridge: Cambridge University Press, 1990. Discusses relationship between scientific revolution and the Reformation.

Matheson, Peter. *The Imaginative World of the Reformation*. Minneapolis: Fortress, 2001.

Oberman, Heiko. *The Impact of the Reformation*. Grand Rapids: Eerdmans, 1994.

Oettinger, Rebecca Wagner. *Music as Propaganda in the German Reformation*. Aldershot, U.K.: Ashgate, 2001. Shows role of music in Reformation polemics.

Panofsky, Erwin. *The Life and Art of Albrecht Dürer*. Princeton, NJ: Princeton University Press, 1983.

Parker, Geoffrey. "Success and Failure during the First Century of the Reformation." *Past and Present* 136 (1992): 43–82.

Shea, William R., and Mariano Artigas. *Galileo in Rome*. Oxford: Oxford University Press, 2003. Balanced and well-written account of Galileo's life and work.

Strauss, Gerald. *Luther's House of Learning: Indoctrination of the Young in the German Reformation*. Baltimore: Johns Hopkins University Press, 1978.

———. "Success and Failure in the German Reformation." *Past and Present* 67 (1975): 30–63.

Zapalac, Kristin E. S. *In His Image and Likeness: Political Iconography and Religious Change in Regensburg*. Ithaca, NY: Cornell University Press, 1990.

NOTES

Preface

1. David Bebbington, *Patterns in History: A Christian Perspective on Historical Thought* (Leicester, U.K.: Apollos, 1979), 4.

Writing the History of the Reformation

1. I. B. Vogelstein, *Johann Sleidan's Commentaries*, vol. 1 (Lanham, MD: University Press of America, 1968), 12.

2. A. G. Dickens and John M. Tonkin, *The Reformation in Historical Thought* (Cambridge: Harvard University Press, 1985), 13.

3. Sleidan did not fully succeed in writing an objective history. Despite his attempt to be fair and accurate, he could not escape Protestant bias. "Although he avoids factual untruths and violent condemnations, his selections and omissions end by creating a uniformly antipapal and antiprelatical atmosphere" (ibid., 15).

4. The process of writing polemical history began even before Sleidan wrote his *Commentaries*. In 1549 a Catholic author, Johannes Cochlaeus (1479–1552), published his *Commentaries on the Acts and Writing of Luther*, which contained a vicious attack on Luther and his theology.

5. According to legend, a scholarly woman disguised as a man was elected pope in the ninth century. After two years in office, she gave birth to a child while taking part in a procession. The story was widely believed in the Middle Ages and was used by opponents of the papacy. It is based on such questionable evidence that today no serious scholar would accept its authenticity. See Peter Stanford, *The Legend of Pope Joan* (Berkeley: Henry Holt, 1999).

6. Ten additional volumes, continuing the work to 1565, were published between 1647 and 1677.

7. Two of the most recent survey textbooks use the plural in their titles: Carter Lindberg, *The European Reformations* (Oxford: Blackwell, 1996), and James D. Tracy, *Europe's Reformations 1450–1650* (New York: Rowman and Littlefield, 1999). Tracy considers the Reformation as "the high point in a series of Reformations" that occurred "from the eleventh to the eighteenth centuries" (Tracy, *Europe's Reformations*, 3).

8. See, for example Andrew Johnston, *The Protestant Reformation in Europe* (London: Longman, 1991), 1.

Chapter 1: Church and Society in the Late Middle Ages

1. "Petrarch to Socrates," in Catherine Moriarty, ed., *The Voice of the Middle Ages in Personal Letters 1100–1500* (New York: Peter Bedrick Books, 1989), 322–23.

2. Matteo Palmieri, "On Civic Life," in Margaret Aston, *The Fifteenth Century: The Prospect of Europe* (New York: Harcourt Brace, 1968), 175.

3. Barbara W. Tuchman, *A Distant Mirror: The Calamitous 14th Century* (New York: Knopf, 1978).

4. "Journal d'un bourgeois de Paris sous Charles VI et Charles VIII," in Daniel Waley, *Later Medieval Europe from Saint Louis to Luther* (London: Longmans, 1964), 101.

5. "Petrarch to Gasparo Squaro dei Broaspini of Verona," in Moriarty, *Voice of the Middle Ages*, 158.

6. The Golden Bull codified the procedure of election that had been established in the previous century. Seven electors (the Duke of Saxony, the Margrave of Brandenburg, the king of Bohemia, the Count Palatinate of the Rhine, and the archbishops of Cologne, Trier, and Mainz) were granted the right to elect the emperor. The papacy, which had often interfered in imperial elections in the past, was now excluded from any role in the process.

7. Waley, *Later Medieval Europe*, 198.

8. In order to prevent a struggle over the succession, Mohammed II had initiated a policy that the son chosen for the succession was to kill all his brothers and half brothers, but two of his sons survived and promptly fought each other.

9. The Black Death has traditionally been identified as the bubonic plague, but a recent study questions that association. Samuel K. Cohn Jr., *The Black Death Transformed: Disease and Culture in Early Renaissance Europe* (London: Arnold, 2002).

10. Jakob Burkhardt, *The Civilization of the Renaissance in Italy* (London: G. G. Harrap, 1892). Original German edition Basel, 1860.

11. Aston, *The Fifteenth Century*, 176.

12. The Florentine Academy was a center for the study of Plato. Seeking to fuse Christian and Platonic thought, Ficino edited the complete works of Plato, translated Plato's *Dialogues*, and wrote a commentary on Plato's *Symposium*.

13. Scholars continue to debate the timing of the recovery. Some contend that the economic slowdown was limited and recovery came quickly, especially in Italy. Others contend that the recovery did not arrive until the late fifteenth century.

14. Alister McGrath, *Reformation Thought: An Introduction*, 3rd ed. (Oxford: Blackwell, 1999), 31.

15. Pelagius was a British monk who engaged in a controversy with Augustine over the role of human beings in their salvation. "Pelagius . . . held that God never commands what people cannot perform. . . . Mankind is created with the ultimate grace of freedom, and to it is added the grace of divine commands in Scripture teaching us what we should do." Stuart G. Hall, *Doctrine and Practice in the Early Church* (London: SPCK, 1991), 205. Pelagius's views were condemned at the Council of Ephesus (431), and the Second Council of Orange (529).

16. Gabriel Biel, "The Circumcision of the Lord" (ca. 1460), in Denis R. Janz, *A Reformation Reader* (Minneapolis: Augsburg Fortress, 1999), 51.

17. Unfortunately, Thomas Bradwardine died of the plague forty days after his consecration as archbishop of Canterbury.

18. Thomas Bradwardine, *The Case of God against the Pelagians*, in Janz, *Reformation Reader*, 41–42.

19. Norman P. Tanner, ed., *Decrees of the Ecumenical Councils*, vol. 1 (Washington, DC: Georgetown University Press, 1990), 250–51.

20. Gerald Strauss, ed., *Manifestations of Discontent in Germany on the Eve of the Reformation* (Bloomington, IN: Indiana University Press, 1971), 219.

21. Ibid., 221.

Chapter 2: Reform and Conflict in the Late Medieval Church

1. Thomas à Kempis, *The Imitation of Christ*, in Janz, *Reformation Reader*, 13.

2. Desiderius Erasmus, *In Praise of Folly*, in Janz, *Reformation Reader*, 61.

3. A good example of such a study is Eamon Duffy, *The Stripping of the Altars: Traditional Religion in England 1400–ca.1580* (New Haven, CT: Yale University Press, 1992). See also R. N. Swanson, *Religion and Devotion in Europe ca.1215–ca.1515* (Cambridge: Cambridge University Press, 1995).

4. See, for example, Euan Cameron, *The European Reformation* (Oxford: Clarendon Press, 1991), 71ff.

5. *Boniface VIII, Unam Sanctam*, in Carter Lindberg, *The European Reformations Sourcebook* (Oxford: Blackwell, 2000), 10.

6. It is estimated that Pope John XXII spent 63 percent of the papal income on war.

7. Quoted in Aston, *The Fifteenth Century*, 120.

8. Lindberg, *Sourcebook*, 12–13.

9. Neither the Avignon line nor the Pisan line of antipopes is recognized by the church. Consequently, when in 1958 Angelo Giuseppe Roncalli was elected pope, he could take the title John XXIII, since the church did not recognize the fifteenth-century John XXIII as a legitimate pope.

10. Three of Benedict's remaining cardinals tried to continue the line by electing still another pope, but he finally resigned in 1429.

11. Lindberg, *Sourcebook*, 14.

12. Eamon Duffy, *Saints and Sinners: A History of the Popes* (New Haven, CT: Yale University Press, 1997), 149.

13. Taken from Edigius of Viterbo's description of Rome during the pontificate of Alexander VI, in S. Harrison Thomson, *Europe in Renaissance and Reformation* (New York: Harcourt Brace, 1963), 451.

14. Although Erasmus denied writing it, the modern editor of the work is convinced that he did and offers impressive evidence in support of his belief. J. Kelley Sowards, *The "Julius Exclusus" of Erasmus*, trans. Paul Pascal (Bloomington, IN: Indiana University Press, 1968).

15. Ibid., 8.

16. Ibid., 86.

17. Ibid., 90.

18. Bengt R. Hoffman, *Luther and the Mystics* (Minneapolis: Augsburg, 1976), 33.

19. Luther often misunderstood the mystics. "He unwittingly transformed them, though they were headed in quite a different direction, into confederates and colleagues because in everything that he read, he was always seeking answers to very personal questions and problems which were raised by his own reflections and experience." Heinrich Boehmer, *Martin Luther: Road to Reformation* (New York: World Publishing, 1965), 146.

20. Although Eckhart died before the trial could take place, twenty-eight propositions taken from his writings were condemned by Pope John XXII in 1329.

21. Scholastics were often accused of debating senseless questions, such as how many angels could dance on the head of a pin. Although this seems to have been a false accusation, they did debate questions that seemed to have little relevance to the religious concerns of the wider society, such as: "Could God have become a cucumber instead of a human being?" "Could he undo the past, by making a prostitute into a virgin?" Alister McGrath, *Reformation Thought*, 66.

22. Janz, *Reformation Reader*, 57.

23. Girolamo Aleander, the papal envoy at the imperial court, once stated that Erasmus had done more damage to the church than Luther. The oft-repeated comment that Erasmus had "laid the egg which Luther hatched" is attributed to him.

24. Cameron states that the principles on which humanist reform was based, "education, learning and moral self control," were "essentially elitist principles neither appealing nor practical for all the clergy, let alone the people as a whole." Euan Cameron, *European Reformation*, 68.

25. Lindberg, *Sourcebook*, 15.

Chapter 3: Martin Luther and the Origin of the Lutheran Reformation

1. Philip Melanchthon, *The Life and Acts of Martin Luther* (London: Unwin, 1845), 4–5. Available online at http://iclnet.org/pub/resources/text/wittenberg/melan/lifea-01.txt.

2. Melanchthon was the first to mention that the *Ninety-five Theses* were posted. Since this account was written almost thirty years after an event that Melanchthon did not witness and the posting was never mentioned before that time, some historians have questioned whether they were actually posted. See Erwin Iserloh, *The Theses Were Not Posted: Luther between Reform and Reformation*, trans. Jared Wicks (Boston: Beacon, 1968).

3. The best-known example of a psychoanalytical interpretation is Erik H. Erikson, *Young Man Luther* (New York: Norton, 1962). Most recent historians question Erikson's method as well as his interpretation. For a more sympathetic assessment of Erikson, see Richard Marius, *Martin Luther: The Christian between God and Death* (Cambridge, MA: Belknap Press, 1999), 20ff.

4. E. G. Rupp and Benjamin Drewery, eds., *Martin Luther* (London: Edward Arnold, 1970), 3.

5. Ibid., 2–3.

6. Jaroslav Pelikan and Helmut T. Lehmann, eds., *Luther's Works*, vol. 24 (St. Louis: Concordia, 1955–1986), 260. Hereafter cited as *LW*.

7. *LW* 4:340–41.

8. At one point he stated that he confessed for six hours. Every time a new sin came to mind, he rushed back to his confessor.

9. *LW* 24:24.

10. Walter von Loewenich, *Martin Luther: The Man and His Work* (Minneapolis: Augsburg, 1982), 81.

11. *LW* 49:48. Although Staupitz supported Luther in the first stages of the Reformation and expressed his love for Luther in his last letter to him, he also made it clear that he was not in sympathy with what had occurred in the Reformation. Even though he died in 1524 in full communion with the Catholic Church, his books were placed on the Index of Prohibited Books in 1559.

12. He said he almost regretted that his father and mother were still living, because he could have freed them from purgatory.

13. E. G. Schwiebert, *Luther and His Times* (St. Louis: Concordia, 1950), 187.

14. Compared with Erfurt, Wittenberg was little more than a village. It had only about two thousand inhabitants, "many of whom earned their living by brewing heavy

beer, much of which they drank." James M. Kittelson, *Luther the Reformer* (Minneapolis: Augsburg, 1989), 53.

15. Heiko A. Oberman, *Luther: Man between God and the Devil*, trans. Eileen Walliser-Schwarzbart (New Haven, CT: Yale University Press, 1989), 146.

16. *LW* 54:50.

17. Roland H. Bainton, *Here I Stand: A Life of Martin Luther* (New York: Abingdon Press, 1950), 62.

18. According to some accounts the experience took place in the "cloaca tower." Since *cloaca* is the Latin word for toilet, some have speculated that it took place on the toilet, but since Luther's study was located in the cloaca tower, it is likely it took place in his study. Brecht comments, "No matter how much the conception of Luther making his reformatory discovery while on the privy may accord with the fantasies of polemicists, psychologists, and even theologians, it is really much more probable that he attained his insight at his desk while about his exegetical work." Martin Brecht, *Martin Luther*, trans. James L. Schaaf (Minneapolis: Fortress, 1985–1993), vol. 1, 227.

19. Bernhard Lohse, *Martin Luther's Theology: Its Historical and Systematic Development*, trans. Roy A. Harrisville (Minneapolis: Fortress, 1999), 86–87.

20. Bernhard Lohse commented in 1999, "At present no conclusion to this rather unsatisfactory debate is in sight" (ibid., 88). The writers in a collection of essays on the topic edited by Lohse arrive at a similar conclusion; Bernhard Lohse, ed., *Der Durchbruch der Reformatorischen Erkenntnis bei Luther; Neuere Untersuchungen* (Stuttgart, Germany: Franz Steiner, 1988). For an excellent, although somewhat dated, discussion of the debate on the dating of the tower experience, see W. D. J. Cargill Thompson, "The Problems of Luther's Tower-Experience and Its Place in His Intellectual Development," in Derek Baker, ed., *Studies in Church History*, vol. 15 (London, 1978), 187–212.

21. *LW* 34:336–37.

22. "Later I read Augustine's *The Spirit and the Letter*, where contrary to hope I found that he, too, interpreted God's righteousness in a similar way, as the righteousness with which God clothes us when he justifies us. Although this was heretofore said imperfectly and he did not explain all things concerning imputation clearly it nevertheless was pleasing that God's righteousness with which we are justified was taught." *LW* 34:336–37.

23. Brecht, *Martin Luther*, vol. 1, 230.

24. Ibid., 229.

25. John Dillenberger, *Martin Luther: Selections from His Writings* (New York: Doubleday, 1961), 87–88.

26. Bernard M. G. Reardon, *Religious Thought in the Reformation*, 2nd ed. (London: Longman, 1995), 54.

27. Dillenberger, *Martin Luther*, 89.

28. Rupp and Drewery, *Martin Luther*, 15–17.

29. Lindberg, *Sourcebook*, 31.

30. Rupp and Drewery, *Martin Luther*, 17–18. The actual title of the document popularly known as the *Ninety-five Theses* was *Disputation on the Power and Efficacy of Indulgences*. It was probably posted in the middle of November. Brecht, *Martin Luther*, vol. 1, 201.

31. Dillenberger, *Martin Luther*, 490.

32. Ibid., 490–500.

33. Brecht, *Martin Luther*, vol. 1, 211. Never one to be outdone in vituperation, Luther replied with a bitter personal response in which he questioned Eck's competence as a theologian.

34. *LW* 31:83; Kittelson, *Luther the Reformer*, 114.

35. Oberman, *Luther*, 193.

36. Leo is credited with two comments. Although they are probably apocryphal, they illustrate what may well have been his initial reaction toward a quarrel in Germany about which he understood very little except that it was interfering with his plans for the rebuilding of St. Peter's. One was, "Luther is a drunken German. He will feel different when he is sober." The second was, "Friar Martin is a brilliant chap. The whole row is due to the envy of the monks." Bainton, *Here I Stand*, 85.

37. Lindberg, *Sourcebook*, 34.

38. He commented, "The stupid dolt wrote such wretched stuff that I had to laugh." *LW* 54:83.

39. Luther never contacted Frederick directly because he relied entirely on Spalatin to communicate with his prince. The letters, four hundred of which have survived, are an important source revealing Luther's feelings and reactions.

40. Frederick had a collection of nineteen thousand relics. One could receive an indulgence of one hundred days for every fragment, so viewing them all would result in an indulgence of 1,900,000 days. He did not give up his treasured collection easily, as the relics continued to be displayed until 1522. However, he accepted communion in both kinds on his deathbed, which suggests that at the end of his life he accepted Luther's teaching.

41. Cajetan wrote, "I exhort and beg your highness to consider your honor and your conscience and either to have the monk Martin sent to Rome or to chase him from your lands. Your highness should not let one little friar bring such ignominy over you and your house." Oberman, *Luther*, 16.

42. Schwiebert, *Luther and His Times*, 371.

43. *LW* 48:94; Kittelson, *Luther the Reformer*, 127.

44. Charles's maternal grandparents were Ferdinand and Isabella of Spain, and through them he became heir to Spain, its possession in Italy, and its rich empire in the New World. His father was Philip of Burgundy, the son of Maximilian of Hapsburg, through whom he inherited the Hapsburg lands in Eastern Europe and the Burgundian territories.

45. Brecht, *Martin Luther*, vol. 1, 271.

46. The University of Leipzig owed its origins to the exodus of German students and faculty from the University of Prague in 1409.

47. Schwiebert, *Luther and His Times*, 408.

48. Bainton, *Here I Stand*, 116–17.

49. Ibid.

50. *LW* 18:153.

51. Janz, *Reformation Reader*, 91.

52. Ibid.

53. Ibid., 93.

54. Schwiebert, *Luther and His Times*, 471.

55. Janz, *Reformation Reader*, 99–100.

56. Ibid., 100.

57. Ibid., 104.

58. Ibid., 327–29.

59. Brecht, *Martin Luther*, vol. 1, 424.

60. Bainton, *Here I Stand*, 179.

61. This statement is taken from Spalatin's account of Luther's trial. The entire account is included in James Atkinson, *The Trial of Luther* (London: Batsford, 1971), 149.

62. Atkinson, *The Trial of Luther*, 155.

63. Ibid., 161–62. He may also have included, "Here I stand, I cannot do otherwise," but this statement is only found in later printed versions of the speech.

64. Melanchthon, *Life and Acts of Martin Luther*, 6.

Chapter 4: The Consolidation and Spread of the Lutheran Reformation

1. *LW* 48:356.

2. When in 1521 Luther's followers began to use his name in defense of their actions, he wrote in horror, "I ask that men make no reference to my name; let them call themselves Christians, not Lutherans. What is Luther? After all, the teaching is not mine. Neither was I crucified for anyone. . . . How then should I—poor stinking maggot-fodder that I am—come to have men call the children of Christ by my wretched name? Not so, my dear friends. Let us abolish all party names and call ourselves Christians, after him whose teachings we hold." *LW* 45:70–71.

3. Bainton, *Here I Stand*, 194.

4. Rupp and Drewery, *Martin Luther*, 72.

5. Emser and Luther had engaged in an exchange over Luther's teaching on the priesthood of all believers. Emser, who was one of Luther's most persistent antagonists, accused Luther of obliterating the distinction between the clergy and the laity. Luther responded in a tract with the type of title only Luther could devise; it was called, *Answer to the Hyperchristian, Hyperspiritual and Hyperlearned Book of Goat Emser*. A vicious controversy ensued in which Emser showed himself the equal of Luther in devising titles for his attacks. One of his tracts was called *Reply to the Answer of the Raging Bull of Wittenberg*. However, in addition to name-calling, the exchange between Emser and Luther resulted in Luther clarifying the distinction between the priesthood of all believers and the Christian ministry. In a tract written in 1521 he wrote: "In all my writings I never wished to say more, indeed only so much, that all Christians are priests, although not all of them are ordained by bishops, and so not all preach, celebrate mass or exercise the priestly office unless they were ordained to it and called." *LW* 39:233.

6. *LW* 36:134.

7. Bainton, *Here I Stand*, 328.

8. Rupp and Drewery, *Martin Luther*, 94.

9. Ibid., 75.

10. Ibid., 101.

11. Kittelson, *Luther the Reformer*, 183.

12. All three met with Luther at different times, but Luther was not impressed. Storch died in Munich in 1525.

13. Janz, *Reformation Reader*, 166.

14. Frederick died on 5 May after receiving the Lord's Supper in both kinds for the first time.

15. Rupp and Drewery, *Martin Luther*, 121–22.

16. Martin Luther, *The Small Catechism* in *Book of Concord* (St. Louis: Concordia, 1952), 158.

17. Schwiebert, *Luther and His Times*, 664.

18. Kittelson, *Luther the Reformer*, 209.

19. Heinrich Bornkamm, *Luther in Mid-career 1521–1530* (Philadelphia: Fortress Press, 1983), 616.

20. *LW* 49:297–98.

21. Augsburg Confession, Article VII, *Book of Concord*, 13.

22. Harold J. Grimm, *The Reformation Era, 1500–1650*, 2nd ed. (New York: Macmillan, 1954), 178.

23. Roland H. Bainton, *Women of the Reformation in Germany and Italy* (Minneapolis: Augsburg, 1971), 26

24. *LW* 49:117.

25. Although Katie reminded him that the publishers were making huge profits from his writings, which she could use to help pay the family's expenses, he stubbornly refused to profit from his many publications.

26. Schwiebert, *Luther and His Times*, 597.

27. Only one of Luther's daughters lived to adulthood. Elizabeth died at eight months, Magdalena died at thirteen years. Margaret, the youngest, married a rich Brandenburg nobleman and died at the age of thirty-six in 1570. Luther's sons had varied careers. Hans, his eldest son, became a lawyer and later a royal councillor. Martin studied theology but never took up a clerical post. Paul achieved the greatest success as he became a famous doctor.

28. Bainton, *Here I Stand*, 302.

29. Kittelson, *Luther the Reformer*, 211.

30. The noted humanist Thomas More was equally scathing in his attacks on Luther, stating that he "surpassed magpies in chatter, pimps in wickedness, prostitutes in obscenity and all buffoons in buffoonery. . . . The most absurd dregs of impiety, of crimes, of filth, should be called Lutherans." Neelak S. Tjernagel, *Martin Luther and the Jewish People* (Milwaukee: Northwestern, 1985), 100.

31. In 1544 Luther published his *Short Confession on the Holy Sacrament*, in which he used the most vicious language to attack those who did not agree with his eucharistic theology. In the year of his death he again attacked them in a parody of the first Psalm: "Blessed is the man who walks not in the counsel of the sacramentarians, nor stands in the way of Zwinglians, nor sits in the seat of the Zurichers." B. A. Gerrish, *The Old Protestantism and The New: Essays on the Reformation Heritage* (Chicago: University of Chicago Press, 1982), 33.

32. *LW* 45:229.

33. Eric Gritsch, "The Unrefined Reformer," in *Christian History*, 39 (1993): 37.

34. Rupp and Drewery, *Martin Luther*, 173.

35. Kittelson, *Luther the Reformer*, 397.

36. Oberman, *Luther*, 322.

37. Schwiebert, *Luther and His Times*, 845, n. 162.

38. Robert Kolb, *Martin Luther as Prophet, Teacher and Hero: Images of the Reformer 1520–1620* (Grand Rapids: Baker Books, 1999). Robert Scribner, "Incombustible Luther: the Image of the Reformer in Early Modern Germany," in *Past and Present* 110 (February 1986): 39–68.

39. One Luther bibliography took seventy-seven pages to examine just the German works on Martin Luther.

40. For a new edition of both the Melanchthon and the Cochlaeus biographies with very useful introductions, see Elizabeth Vandiver, Ralph Keen, and Thomas D. Frazel, eds. and trans., *Luther's Lives* (Manchester, England: Manchester University Press, 2002).

41. G. R. Elton, "Commemorating Luther," *Journal of Ecclesiastical History* 35, no. 4 (October 1984): 619.

Chapter 5: The Urban Reformation: Zurich, Basel, and Strasbourg

1. Bernd Moeller, *Imperial Cities and the Reformation: Three Essays* (Philadelphia: Fortress Press, 1972), 41.

2. A. G. Dickens, *The German Nation and Martin Luther* (New York: Harper and Row, 1974), 182.

3. See, for example, Moeller, *Imperial Cities and the Reformation*, 74ff. This interpretation has been disputed by Steven Ozment, *The Reformation in the Cities: The Appeal*

of Protestantism to Sixteenth-century Germany and Switzerland (New Haven, CT: Yale University Press, 1975).

4. Zwingli and Erasmus parted ways in the summer of 1523 when Zwingli gave protection to Ulrich von Hutton, who had attacked Erasmus in writing. When Hutton again attacked him from the safety of Zurich shortly before his death, Erasmus wrote a reply, which he dedicated to Zwingli. He never wrote to Zwingli again.

5. Swiss soldiers were highly regarded because they were courageous and effective fighters; as a result they were in great demand as mercenaries. Since Switzerland was a poor area, mercenary service provided an important source of income.

6. Zwingli defended himself against the charge without denying it. In a letter he confessed: "When I was still in Glarus and let myself fall into temptation in this regard a little. I did so so quietly that my friends hardly knew about it." Janz, *Reformation Reader*, 152.

7. Whether what he called "the gospel of Christ" was actually the Reformation doctrine of justification by faith alone has been called into question. The writer of a popular Reformation textbook comments: "His conception of the gospel in those early years . . . was a kind of Erasmian Christocentric ethic of love, the 'philosophy of Christ.'" Lewis Spitz, *The Renaissance and Reformation Movements* (Chicago: Rand McNally, 1971), 389.

8. Lindberg, *Sourcebook*, 112. Zwingli may not have been as independent of Luther in his theological development as he maintained. It is clear that Zwingli knew about Luther and had read his writings by late 1518.

9. Ulrich Zwingli, "Of the Clarity and Certainty of the Word of God," in *The Library of Christian Classics*, vol. 24, *Zwingli and Bullinger*, ed. G. W. Bromiley (Philadelphia: Westminster Press, 1953), 90–91.

10. William G. Naphy, ed., *Documents on the Continental Reformation* (London: Macmillan, 1996), 38–39.

11. In a single year priests in the diocese of Constance fathered 1,500 illegitimate children, and the bishop received a fine of four or five gulden for each. George R. Potter, *Ulrich Zwingli* (London: Chameleon Press, 1983), 18.

12. Janz, *Reformation Reader*, 157.

13. Moeller maintains that "Zwingli and Bucer . . . both differed with Luther at precisely those points of contact between urban thought and the Reformation where the gulf between Luther and the cities was most clear, i.e., in the concept of the church and in the basis of ethics." Moeller, *Imperial Cities and the Reformation*, 75.

14. Alister McGrath, who is the leading exponent of this position, states: "For Luther, Scripture declares the promises of God, which reassure and console the believer: it is primarily concerned with narrating and proclaiming what God has done for sinful humanity in Christ. For Zwingli, Scripture sets out the moral demands which God makes of believers; it is primarily concerned with indicating what humanity must do in response to the example provided by Christ." McGrath, *Reformation Thought*, 123.

15. Martin Luther, *The Large Catechism*, in *The Book of Concord, The Confessions of the Evangelical Lutheran Church* (Philadelphia: Mühlenberg, 1959), 210.

16. Lindberg, *Sourcebook*, 121.

17. Janz, *Reformation Reader*, 159.

18. Brecht, *Martin Luther*, vol. 2, 309.

19. Ibid., 314.

20. Ibid., 318.

21. Ibid., 322.

22. Schwiebert, *Luther and His Times*, 708–9.

23. Naphy, *Documents on the Continental Reformation*, 100.

24. Schwiebert, *Luther and His Times*, 711.

25. Janz, *Reformation Reader*, 162.

26. Rupp and Drewery, *Martin Luther*, 137.

27. Janz, *Reformation Reader*, 164.

28. Ernest Winter, ed., *Erasmus-Luther Discourse on Free Will* (New York: Ungar, 1961), 113.

29. Ibid., 132–33.

30. Ibid., 137.

31. Philip Schaff, *History of the Christian Church*, vol. 8, 3rd ed. (Grand Rapids: Eerdmans, 1953), 112–13.

32. Erika Rummel, "Voices of Reform from Hus to Erasmus," in T. A. Brady, H. Oberman, and J. Tracy, *Handbook of European History 1400–1600*, vol. 2 (New York: E. J. Brill, 1994), 78.

33. Ibid.

34. The other marks were that "heed is paid to the voice of the Shepherd . . . the ministry of teaching . . . the possession of suitable ministers" and "lawful dispensation of the sacraments." Johnston, *Protestant Reformation in Europe*, 94.

35. Ibid., 95.

36. Brecht, *Martin Luther*, vol. 2, 410.

37. Kittelson, *Luther the Reformer*, 266.

Chapter 6: The Radical Reformation

1. Janz, *Reformation Reader*, 183.

2. Sattler cited that command in article 6 of the Schleitheim Confession. Ibid., 178.

3. Bullinger, who wrote the most comprehensive early history, thought Satan was responsible for the movement. His attitude is betrayed by the title of a work he wrote in 1548: *A Wholesome Antidote or Counter-poison against the Pestilent Heresy and Sect of the Anabaptists*.

4. James M. Stayer, "The Anabaptists," in *Reformation Europe: A Guide to Research*, ed. Steven Ozment (St. Louis: Center for Reformation Research, 1982), 135.

5. Ibid., 136.

6. The classic work presenting this interpretation is Franklin H. Littell, *The Anabaptist View of the Church*, 2nd ed. (Boston: Star King Press, 1958).

7. The provision in Roman law making rebaptism a capital offense was directed against the Donatists, one of the schismatic groups in the early church.

8. The third edition has 1,311 pages of text and 68 pages of bibliography. George H. Williams, *The Radical Reformation*, 3rd ed. (Kirksville, MO: Sixteenth Century Journal Publishers, 1991).

9. Ibid., 1289.

10. Critics have pointed out that "not a single one" of the beliefs that Williams maintained were characteristic of the Radical Reformation "was held by all radicals." James M. Stayer, "The Radical Reformation," in Brady, *Handbook of European History*, 249.

11. Adolf Laube, "Radicalism as a Research Problem in the History of the Early Reformations," *Radical Tendencies in the Reformation: Divergent Perspectives*, ed. Hans J. Hillerbrand (Kirksville, MO: Sixteenth Century Journal Publishers, 1988), 10. See also Hans-Jürgen Goertz, "History and Theology: A Major Problem of Anabaptist Research Today," in *Mennonite Quarterly Review* 53 (1979): 177–88.

12. Stayer, "The Anabaptists," 146; Hans-Jürgen Goertz, ed., *The Anabaptists*, trans. Trevor Johnston (London: Routledge, 1996).

13. Lindberg, *Sourcebook*, 128–29.

14. Eric W. Gritsch, "Thomas Müntzer and Luther: A Tragedy of Error," in Hillerbrand, *Radical Tendencies in the Reformation*, 55ff., contains a good summary of the different interpretations.

15. Lindberg, *Sourcebook*, 84.

16. Ibid., 90.

17. Gritsch, "Thomas Müntzer and Luther," 64.

18. Lindberg, *Sourcebook*, 85.

19. Ibid., 85–86.

20. Gritsch, "Thomas Müntzer and Luther," 69.

21. Janz, *Reformation Reader*, 165.

22. Lindberg, *Sourcebook*, 88.

23. Williams, *Radical Reformation*, 187.

24. He received the name Blaurock, which means blue coat, because at a meeting where he was wearing a blue coat somebody who didn't know his name called him the man in the blue coat.

25. Daniel Liechty, ed., *Early Anabaptist Spirituality* (New York: Paulist Press, 1994), 2.

26. Lindberg, *Sourcebook*, 131.

27. "The Schleitheim Confession," *Christian History* 4, no. 1: 29.

28. Matthew 18:15–17 describes the procedure to be used with a "brother" who "sins against you." You are first to talk to him privately. If that does not resolve the problem, you are to see him again, taking several other people with you. If he still persists in his sin, "tell it to the church; and if he refuses to listen even to the church, treat him as you would a pagan or a tax collector."

29. "The Schleitheim Confession," 10.

30. Catholics used the traditional method of burning at the stake, but as an act of mercy a bag of gunpowder was tied around the necks of the victims to hasten their death. Protestants tended to use drowning or beheading as the preferred methods of execution.

31. Sebastian Franck, quoted in Liechty, *Early Anabaptist Spirituality*, 11–12.

32. Williams, *Radical Reformation*, 263–64.

33. Ibid., 342.

34. Liechty, *Early Anabaptist Spirituality*, 37–38.

35. Claus Peter Clasen, *Anabaptism: A Social History 1525–1618* (Ithaca, NY: Cornell University Press, 1972), 131ff.

36. Klaus Deppermann, *Melchior Hoffman*, trans. Malcolm Wren (Edinburgh: T & T Clark, 1987), 293.

37. Philips was appalled when in Amsterdam in February 1535 a group of extremists ran naked through the streets crying out that they were proclaiming the "naked truth of God."

38. Münster was the chief city of a prince-bishopric in northwest Germany on the border of Holland; it had a population of approximately fifteen thousand.

39. Matthijs had originally announced that he intended to kill all the "godless," but fortunately a colleague convinced him that this would make them hated by all nations.

40. It is argued that John Beukels, who was already married, introduced the law because of his lust for the widow of Matthijs.

41. Those who resisted would be "considered reprobates (and therefore in danger of execution)." Williams, *Radical Reformation*, 568.

42. Günter Vogler, "The Anabaptist Kingdom of Münster in the Tension between Anabaptism and Imperial Policy," in Hillerbrand, *Radical Tendencies in the Reformation*, 115.

43. Menno Simons even wrote a tract against John Beukels, which was probably written before the fall of Münster. But after Münster fell, he decided not to release it, and it was not published until 1627.

44. Among those who have not been discussed are Spiritualists such as Sebastian Franck (1499–1542) and Caspar Schwenckfeld (1490–1561), antitrinitarians such as Michael Servetus (1511–1553), and eclectic Anabaptists such as Pilgram Marpeck (1490–1556), some of whom will be covered in later chapters.

Chapter 7: Calvin and Calvinism

1. John Calvin, *Preface to the Commentary on Psalms*, in *John Calvin: Writings on Pastoral Piety*, ed. Elise Anne McKee (New York: Paulist Press, 2001), 60.

2. Spitz, *Renaissance and Reformation Movements*, 412.

3. Jerome Bolsec, one of Calvin's enemies, published a hostile biography in 1551. His *Life of Calvin* portrayed the reformer in extremely negative terms, maintaining that "he treated his own words as if they were the word of God and allowed himself to be worshipped as God." Alister E. McGrath, *A Life of John Calvin* (Oxford: Blackwell, 1990), 16–17.

4. John Calvin, *Commentary on the Epistle of Paul the Apostle to the Romans and the Thessalonians*, ed. David W. Torrance and Thomas F. Torrance (Grand Rapids: Eerdmans, 1961), 4.

5. Wulfert de Greef, *The Writings of John Calvin: An Introductory Guide* (Grand Rapids: Baker Books, 1993), 135.

6. William J. Bouwsma, "The Quest for the Historical Calvin," in *Archiv für Reformationsgeschichte* 77 (1986): 48.

7. Ibid.

8. When Luther read Calvin's *Short Treatise on the Lord's Supper*, he supposedly told a Wittenberg bookseller that Calvin might have been able to resolve the eucharistic controversy between him and the Zwinglians. The account, which may not be entirely accurate (see Gerrish, *The Old Protestantism and the New*, 286–87, n. 53), cites Luther as stating, "I might have entrusted the whole affair of this controversy to him from the beginning. If my opponents had done the like we should soon have been reconciled." Robert D. Linder, "The Early Calvinists and Martin Luther: A Study in Evangelical Solidarity," in *Regnum, Religio et Ratio*, ed. Jerome Friedman (Kirksville, MO: Sixteenth Century Journal Publishers, 1987), 116.

9. Gerrish, *The Old Protestantism and the New*, 38.

10. Calvin, *Preface to the Commentary on Psalms*, 59.

11. Gerrish, *The Old Protestantism and the New*, 37.

12. Although Theodore Beza maintained Calvin wrote the address, there is no convincing evidence to substantiate his claim.

13. See chapter 14 for a fuller account of the so-called Affair of the Placards.

14. John Calvin, *Institutes of the Christian Religion*, vol. 1, trans. Henry Beveridge (Grand Rapids: Eerdmans, 1957), 3.

15. Ibid., vol. 2, 19.

16. For the 1536 edition, see John Calvin, *Institutes of the Christian Religion* (1536 edition), ed. Ford Lewis Battles (Grand Rapids: Eerdmans, 1986).

17. Calvin, *Institutes*, trans. Beveridge, vol. 2, 206 (book 3, chapter 21, 5).

18. Ibid., vol. 2, 204 (book 3, chapter 21, 1).

19. Ibid., vol. 2, 402 (book 2, chapter 12, 3).

20. Ibid., vol. 1, 475 (book 3, chapter 2, 7).

21. Ibid., vol. 2, 38 (book 3, chapter 11, 2).

22. McGrath, *Reformation Thought*, 125.

23. Calvin, *Institutes*, ed. Battles, vol. 2, 560 (book 4, chapter 17, 5).

24. De Greef, *Writings of John Calvin*, 135. Like Luther, Calvin believed the Eucharist should be celebrated every Sunday, but the Geneva City Council did not agree and, as a result, the Zwinglian practice of celebrating communion four times a year was adopted.

25. Calvin, *Institutes*, ed. Battles, vol. 2, 563 (book 4, chapter 17, 10).

26. McGrath, *A Life of John Calvin*, 94–95.

27. Calvin, *Preface to the Commentary on Psalms*, 61.

28. Johnston, *Protestant Reformation in Europe*, 102.

29. Ibid.

30. Calvin, *Preface to the Commentary on Psalms*, 62.

31. See chapter 10 for a discussion of the Colloquy of Regensburg.

32. Hans J. Hillerbrand, *The Reformation: A Narrative History Related by Contemporary Observers and Participants* (New York: Harper and Row, 1964), 184.

33. "Of the Lord's Supper," article 10 in *The Book of Concord*, 13.

34. Schaff, *History of the Christian Church*, vol. 8, 666. The *Variata* was also stronger and more explicit in denouncing Catholic practices. "The sections on church ministry and penance denounced those who taught a wrong (that is, Catholic) doctrine of justification. The clause on church rites condemned the 'burdening [of consciences] with superstitious opinions' about the need for particular rituals. The discussion on the mass included a new, bitter attack on private masses and the idea that a mass was a 'good work' earning remission of sins." Euan Cameron, "Philip Melanchthon: Image and Substance," in *Journal of Ecclesiastical History* 48 (Oct. 1997): 719.

35. Steven Ozment, *The Age of Reform 1250–1550* (New Haven, CT: Yale University Press, 1980), 365.

36. Calvin first considered a wealthy German woman, but she didn't speak French and didn't seem ready to learn it. In addition Calvin wrote to Farel that he was concerned whether a wealthy woman would be comfortable being married to a poor minister. Farel's candidate was both a French speaker and a devout Protestant, but she was fifteen years older than Calvin. Another candidate, who spoke French and didn't have any money, interested Calvin enough for him to invite her to Strasbourg to be interviewed, but this failed to happen.

37. William J. Petersen, "Idelette: Calvin's Search for the Right Wife," in *Christian History*, 5, no. 4 (1986): 13.

38. Ibid., 15.

39. T. H. L. Parker, *John Calvin* (Tring, U.K.: Lion Publishing, 1975), 96. When Farel tried to persuade Calvin to return by reminding him that the climate in Geneva might be better for his health, Calvin responded that if Farel was really concerned about his health, he should never again mention Geneva to him.

40. Calvin, *Preface to the Commentary on Psalms*, 51.

41. H. Oberman, "Calvin and Farel: The Dynamics of Legitimization in Early Calvinism," in *Reformation and Renaissance Review* 1 (June 1999): 29.

42. Ozment, *Age of Reform*, 366.

43. The doctors were teachers whose role was to teach "sound doctrine." The deacons assisted the pastors in relief for the poor, caring for widows and orphans, visiting the sick and needy, as well as administering the city hospital.

44. Hillerbrand, *The Reformation*, 192.

45. Ibid., 193.

46. At the time of this writing only the first volume has been translated: Robert M. Kingdon, Thomas A. Lambert, Isabella M. Watt, and M. W. McDonald, eds. and trans., *The Registers of the Consistory of Geneva in the Time of Calvin* (Grand Rapids: Eerdmans, 2000).

47. R. Kingdon, "The Geneva Consistory," in *Calvinism in Europe, 1540–1620*, ed. Andrew Pettegree, Alastair Duke, and Gillian Lewis (Cambridge: Cambridge University Press, 1994), 26.

48. Residents of Geneva were either *citoyens*, *bourgeois*, or *habitants*. *Citoyens* were the citizens of Geneva who were born there to parents who were *citoyens*, and they alone had the right to vote and hold office. *Bourgeois* were long-term residents who had purchased civil rights, but they could not be elected to the Little Council. *Habitants* were registered aliens who had no civil rights. Calvin belonged to the third category until he was offered civil rights in 1559.

49. Generations of students who used Harold Grimm's excellent Reformation textbook would have read the following description of the Consistory's activities: "It even invaded the privacy of the family, occasionally questioning children of suspected parents. People were brought before it to answer for the slightest deviations from the extremely straight and narrow path. Absence from sermons, family quarrels, criticism of the ministers, attendance at theaters—especially because women with 'brazen effrontery' were beginning to take women's roles—singing obscene songs, dancing, playing cards, and many smaller infractions fill the pages of the Consistory's records." Harold Grimm, *Reformation Era*, 2nd ed. (1954; repr., New York: Macmillan, 1973), 280–81.

50. Johnston, *Protestant Reformation in Europe*, 103. Calvin probably deserved some of the negative reaction because of the way he treated those who opposed him. For example, when Pierre Ameaux made a remark at a dinner party accusing Calvin of being a false teacher and having too much influence, he was sentenced to apologize to Calvin before the council. Calvin felt the punishment was insufficient and insisted that Ameaux do public penance by repenting on bended knee at every square and crossroads in the city.

51. Although they are often referred to as "libertines" in biographies of Calvin, the term was not actually used until well after Calvin's death. E. William Monter, *Calvin's Geneva* (New York: Wiley, 1967), 91, n. 31.

52. Parker, *John Calvin*, 137.

53. Andrew Pettegree, "Michael Servetus and the Limits of Tolerance," in *History Today* (February 1990): 41.

54. Ibid., 45.

55. Lindberg, *Sourcebook*, 182.

56. Pettegree, "Michael Servetus," 45.

57. McGrath, *A Life of Calvin*, 116.

58. Parker, *John Calvin*, 180.

59. John Dillenberger, ed., *John Calvin: Selections from His Writings* (New York: Doubleday, 1971), 38.

60. Ibid., 43.

61. Ibid., 42.

62. Lindberg, *Sourcebook*, 249.

63. There seems to have been a significant decrease in some activities that Calvin would have considered immoral. For example, the number of illegitimate births dropped dramatically, and a Jesuit traveling through Geneva in 1580 expressed surprise that he "never heard any blasphemy, swearing or indecent language." A contemporary chronicler remarked that after the events of 1555, "Everybody devoted themselves to the service of God . . . even the hypocrites." Philip Benedict, *Christ's Churches Purely Reformed: A Social History of Calvinism* (New Haven, CT: Yale University Press, 2003), 103.

64. Williston Walker, *John Calvin: The Organiser of Reformed Protestantism 1509–1564* (New York: Schocken Books, 1969), 444.

Chapter 8: Origins of the English Reformation

1. Gerald Bray, ed., *Documents of the English Reformation* (Minneapolis: Fortress Press, 1994), 114.

2. Maurice Powicke, *The Reformation in England* (Oxford: Oxford University Press, 1941), 1.

3. A. G. Dickens, *The English Reformation* (London: Batsford, 1964). A second, revised, edition was published in 1989.

4. The word *Lollardy* was first used in the fourteenth century as a term of contempt to designate the followers of John Wycliffe. It may have come from the Middle Dutch, *lollen*, the word for mumble (indicating a mumbler of prayers), or from *lolia*, the Latin word for "tares."

5. J. J. Scarisbrick, *The Reformation and the English People* (Oxford: Basil Blackwell, 1984); Christopher Haigh, ed., *The English Reformation Revised* (Cambridge: Cambridge University Press, 1987); Duffy, *The Stripping of the Altars*; Christopher Haigh, *English Reformations: Religion, Politics and Society under the Tudors* (Oxford: Clarendon Press, 1993); Eamon Duffy, *The Voices of Morebath: Reformation and Rebellion in an English Village* (New Haven, CT: Yale University Press, 2001).

6. Haigh, *English Reformation Revised*, 215. Haigh's conclusion is not accepted by all revisionists.

7. Examples are Peter Marshall, *Beliefs and the Dead in Reformation England* (Oxford: Oxford University Press, 2002); Norman Jones, *The English Reformation: Religion and Cultural Adaptation* (Oxford: Blackwell, 2001); Ethan H. Shagan, *Popular Politics and the English Reformation* (Cambridge: Cambridge University Press, 2003); Susan Wabuda, *Preaching during the English Reformation* (Cambridge: Cambridge University Press, 2002); Christopher Marsh, *Popular Religion in Sixteenth-Century England: Holding Their Peace* (New York: St. Martin's, 1998); Diarmaid MacCulloch, *The Boy King Edward VI and the Protestant Reformation* (New York: St. Martin's, 2002); Susan Brigden, *London and the Reformation* (Oxford: Clarendon Press, 1991).

8. The arguments presented in this paragraph are based on Marsh, *Popular Religion*; Peter Marshall and Alec Ryrie, eds., *The Beginnings of English Protestantism* (Cambridge: Cambridge University Press, 2002); and Shagan, *Popular Politics*.

9. Dickens, whose first publication dealt with Lollardy in the diocese of York (A. G. Dickens, *Lollards and Protestants in the Diocese of York, 1509–1558* [Oxford: Oxford University Press, 1959]), maintained: "Perhaps the only major doctrine of the sixteenth-century Reformers which Wycliffe cannot be said to have anticipated was that of Justification by Faith Alone." A. G. Dickens, *The English Reformation*, 2nd ed. (London: Batsford, 1989), 46.

10. Among other things, the Lollards attacked clerical celibacy, transubstantiation, clerics holding secular office, prayers for the dead, pilgrimages, and confession to a priest. The full text is found in "Twelve Conclusions of the Lollards," in *English Historical Review* 22 (1907): 292–304.

11. Anne Hudson, ed., *English Wycliffite Sermons*, vol. 1 (Oxford: Oxford University Press, 1983). Copies of these sermons were probably produced in almost assembly-line fashion in secret Lollard scriptoria. Thirty-one copies of the cycle have survived.

12. Among the recently published studies dealing with Lollardy are Curtis V. Bostick, *The Antichrist and the Lollards: Apocalypticism in Late Medieval and Reformation England* (Leiden, Netherlands: E. J. Brill, 1998); Richard Rex, *The Lollards* (London: Palgrave Macmillan, 2002); Fiona Somerset, Jill C. Havens, and Derrick G. Pitard, eds., *The Lollards and Their Influence in Late Medieval England* (Woodbridge, U.K.: Boydell, 2003); Norman Tanner and Sharon McSheffrey, eds. and trans., *Lollards of Coventry 1486–1522* (Cambridge: Cambridge University Press, 2003).

13. Christopher Haigh rejects the "tip of the iceberg" argument, maintaining that "the general hostility towards heresy suggests reporting rates were probably high and the submerged section of the iceberg therefore not very large." He contends that "heretics were, like critics of Church courts, refusers of tithes, and complainers against the clergy, far from numerous, even by 1530." Haigh, *English Reformations*, 55. Richard Rex also argues that there were relatively few Lollards and that the movement was insignificant in its impact on the Reformation (Rex, *The Lollards*).

14. In Amersham, ten of the twenty richest citizens were accused of Lollardy in 1522, and in both Coventry and Colchester there were Lollards among "the civic and mercantile elite." Andrew Hope, "Lollardy: The Stone the Builders Rejected?" in *Protestantism and the National Church in Sixteenth Century England*, ed. Peter Lake and Maria Dowling (London: Croom Helm, 1987), 5.

15. In 1497 an Italian visitor to England observed that outwardly the English were very pious and liberally supported their churches. Christopher Harper-Bill, *The Pre-Reformation Church in England 1400–1530* (London: Longman, 1989), 97. Revisionist studies tend to confirm the accuracy of his observations.

16. The first salvo in the debate about anticlericalism was Christopher Haigh's 1983 article entitled "Anticlericalism and the English Reformation," which was republished in Haigh, *English Reformation Revised*, 56–74. He was answered by A. G. Dickens in "The Shape of Anticlericalism and the English Reformation," which was included in Dickens, *English Reformation*, 2nd ed. (1989), 316ff.

17. Chaucer's work went through five editions in the period between 1478 and 1526. Dickens maintains that *Piers Plowman* "attained its highest influence" in the Tudor period. Dickens, *English Reformation* (1964), 318; see 318–19 for a discussion of Gascoigne, Colet, and Melton. See Haigh, *English Reformations*, 8–10 for the revisionist position. Some postrevisionists believe anticlericalism played a significant role in the English Reformation. See Shagan, *Popular Politics*, 160.

18. Johan Huizinga, *Erasmus and the Age of Reformation* (New York: Harper and Row, 1957), 200.

19. W. J. Sheils, *The English Reformation 1530–1570* (London: Longman, 1989), 79. Christopher Harper-Bill has argued that Colet's charges against the clergy were largely unfounded. See Christopher Harper-Bill, "John Colet's Convocation Sermon and the Pre-Reformation Church in England," in *History* 73 (1988): 191–210.

20. Richard Rex, "The Early Impact of Reformation Theology at Cambridge University, 1522–1547," in *Reformation and Renaissance Review* 2 (December 1999): 71. Since the word *Protestant* did not become common until the 1540s, some scholars prefer to use the term *evangelical*.

21. The actual title is *Actes and Monuments*. Foxe was a humanist who became a Protestant in the reign of Henry VIII. He began his history while in exile during the reign of Mary, and it was first published in 1563.

22. Cited in David Daniell, *William Tyndale: A Biography* (New Haven, CT: Yale University Press, 1994), 176. A recent study by Greg Walker considers him more of a schemer than a saint. Greg Walker, *Persuasive Fictions: Faction, Faith and Political Culture in the Reign of Henry VIII* (Aldershot, U.K.: Scolar, 1996), 146–64. Latimer died a martyr to his new faith in the reign of Henry VIII's daughter Mary.

23. Foxe is the source for this story. Barnes acted on the advice of a friend who told him "he should write a letter to the cardinal and leave it on his table where he lay, and a paper by, to declare whither he was gone to drown himself and to leave his clothes in the same place; and another letter to the mayor of the town to search for him in the water." John Foxe, *The Acts and Monuments of John Foxe*, ed. George Townsend, vol. 5 (New York: AMS Press, 1965), 419.

24. David Daniell, who has written the best recent biography of Tyndale, comments that "there is not a scrap of witness that he even knew where the White Horse was." Daniell, *William Tyndale*, 50.

25. William Tyndale, *Select Works* (Lewes, U.K.: Focus Christian Ministries Trust, 1986), 3. At one point Tyndale supposedly told "a learned man . . . that if God spared him life, ere many years he would cause a boy that driveth the plough to know more of Scripture than he did." Foxe, *Acts and Monuments*, vol. 5, 117.

26. The Constitutions of Oxford of 1408 forbade the translation of the Bible into English by any person on his own authority under pain of being punished as a heretic.

27. Lindberg, *Sourcebook*, 222.

28. Tyndale also translated the book of Jonah. The Old Testament translation was completed by Miles Coverdale (1488–1568), who, because he did not know Hebrew, made use of a Latin translation made in 1528 and Luther's German translation. The first complete English Bible was printed by Coverdale in 1535, probably in Zurich.

29. Foxe, *Acts and Monuments*, vol. 5, 127.

30. Ninety percent of Tyndale's words were included in the King James (Authorized) translation, which was the standard translation in the English-speaking world for centuries. Seventy-five percent of his words were included in the Revised Standard Version.

31. Daniell, *William Tyndale*, 141.

32. Dickens, *English Reformation* (1989), 95.

33. Although Henry VIII told Luther, "It is well known for mine, and I for mine avow it," it is likely that he received help from a "committee of theologians" in writing the *Assertio Septem Sacramentorum*. Susan Brigden, *New Worlds, Lost Worlds: The Rule of the Tudors 1485–1603* (New York: Viking Penguin, 2001), 96.

34. J. J. Scarisbrick, *Henry VIII* (Berkeley: University of California Press, 1968), 13.

35. When Henry I died without male heirs in 1135, he designated his daughter Matilda as his successor and had his barons swear loyalty to her before he died. However, the effort to achieve a peaceful female succession failed miserably and led to nineteen years of civil war and lawlessness.

36. Retha M. Warnicke, *The Rise and Fall of Anne Boleyn* (Cambridge: Cambridge University Press, 1989), 48.

37. Clement VII might have been hoping for the death of one of the parties involved or a change in the fickle king's feelings.

38. The Venetian ambassador described Anne as "not one of the handsomest women in the world; she is of middling stature, swarthy complexion, long neck, wide mouth, bosom not raised, and in fact has nothing but the English king's great appetite and her eyes which are black and beautiful." Warnicke, *Rise and Fall of Anne Boleyn*, 58.

39. It is difficult to tell exactly when the relationship with Anne became serious. Scarisbrick believed it was as early as 1525–1526 (Scarisbrick, *Henry VIII*, 149), but there is no evidence in the surviving records to confirm his supposition. The seventeen love letters are the best evidence of how the relationship grew. Curiously, they are in the papal archives, probably because they were stolen and smuggled out of the country by someone opposed to the divorce. See E. W. Ives, *Anne Boleyn* (Oxford: Blackwell, 1986), 102ff., and Warnicke, *Rise and Fall of Anne Boleyn*, 76ff. for a discussion of the letters and their content.

40. In one of his letters Henry VIII wrote, "Ensuring you that henceforth my heart shall be dedicate to you alone, greatly desirous that so my body could be as well, as God can bring to pass if it pleaseth Him, whom I entreat once each day for the accomplishment thereof, trusting that at length my prayer will be heard, wishing the time brief." Ives, *Anne Boleyn*, 107.

41. Bray, *Documents of the English Reformation*, 78.

42. Some historians have argued that Henry VIII did not even attend the christening because he was so disappointed that Elizabeth was not a boy. Warnicke questions this interpretation; see Warnicke, *Rise and Fall of Anne Boleyn*, 169.

43. Both the Ten Articles and the Bishops' Book were Catholic in their overall theology, but they left out certain aspects of Catholic teaching. For example, only three of the seven Catholic sacraments were mentioned in the Ten Articles, and although prayers for the dead were commended, the articles left some doubt about the existence of purgatory, stating that "the place where they be, the name thereof, and the kind of pains there, also be to us uncertain in Scripture; therefore this with all other things we remit to Almighty God." They also did not use the word *transubstantiation*, although they clearly taught the real presence of Christ's body and blood in the Eucharist. Bray, *Documents of the English Reformation*, 173.

44. Warnicke, *Rise and Fall of Anne Boleyn*, 198.

45. Ives believed Anne was undermined by factions at court (Ives, *Anne Boleyn*, 346ff.). Recently Warnicke has advanced the theory that in her miscarriage Anne gave birth to a deformed fetus, which made Henry think she was a witch. Warnicke, *Rise and Fall of Anne Boleyn*, 3–4.

46. There is no convincing evidence that any of the men were guilty of the offenses for which they were executed. Anne went to her death uttering words of loyalty to the king, who had treated her in such a despicable fashion. "I come hither to accuse no man nor to speak of that whereof I am accused and condemned to die, but I pray God save the king and send him long to reign over you, for a gentler nor a more merciful prince was there never, and to me he was ever a good, a gentle and sovereign lord." Ives, *Anne Boleyn*, 410.

47. In 1540 Cromwell arranged a marriage for diplomatic reasons with Anne of Cleves, the daughter of a German prince, but Henry VIII did not find her to his liking, and he had the marriage annulled. The forty-nine-year-old monarch married a nineteen-year-old girl named Catherine Howard in the same month that his fourth marriage was annulled, but she seems to have been guilty of sexual indiscretions both before and after her marriage. She was executed for adultery less than two years later. Henry's last wife was a thirty-one-year-old widow named Katherine Parr, who outlived him.

48. R. W. Heinze, *The Proclamations of the Tudor Kings* (Cambridge: Cambridge University Press, 1976), 139–49.

49. "Outside the court and the Council chamber, their chief support came from people who did not matter in politics: Cambridge dons, a minority of clergy and a swathe of people below the social level of the gentry, all concentrated in south-east England." MacCulloch, *Boy King Edward VI*, 59.

50. In the year following the injunctions, a number of royal proclamations placed limits on preaching. The first restricted preaching to licensed preachers, and in September 1548 all sermons except the homilies were prohibited. Heinze, *Proclamations of the Tudor Kings*, 209.

51. Paul L. Hughes and James F. Larkin, eds., *Tudor Royal Proclamations*, vol. 1, *The Early Tudors (1485–1553)* (New Haven, CT: Yale University Press, 1964), 411.

52. The timing of the first English prayer book may also have been affected by events on the Continent. The negotiations between Calvin and Bullinger, which eventually resulted in the *Consensus Tigurinus*, were taking place at the same time as Cranmer was working on the prayer book. MacCulloch points out that "in 1548–49 it would have been fatal for England, the most important surviving evangelical power in Europe, to make any official pronouncement on the eucharist while delicate efforts were being made abroad to heal the twenty-year-old wounds of the eucharistic quarrel between Luther and Zwingli." MacCulloch, *Boy King Edward VI*, 87.

53. The best study of Cranmer's eucharistic theology is Peter N. Brooks, *Thomas Cranmer's Doctrine of the Eucharist: An Essay in Historical Development*, 2nd ed. (London: Macmillan, 1992).

54. MacCulloch maintains that although much of the ceremony in the prayer book suggested a real presence, the eucharistic theology did not teach a real presence. Diarmaid MacCulloch, *Thomas Cranmer: A Life* (New Haven, CT: Yale University Press, 1996), 414ff.

55. *The First and Second Prayer Books of Edward VI* (London: Dent, n.d.), 212 (spelling has been modernized).

56. These included the *Missa*, which contained the Canon of the Mass, the *Breviary*, which included other services, the *Sacerdotal*, which was the priest's manual, the *Pontifical*, which set forth other sacraments, and the *Processional*, which provided musical settings. In addition, five different rites were in use in England, although the *Sarum Use* was the most common.

57. Peter N. Brooks, *Cranmer in Context* (Cambridge: Lutterworth Press, 1989), 54.

58. For a convincing defense of this position, see Colin Buchanan, *What Did Cranmer Think He Was Doing?* Grove Liturgical Study 7 (Bramcote, Notts, U.K.: Grove Books, 1976).

59. Bucer was one of a number of distinguished refugees from the Continent who came to England fleeing Continental persecution. They also included Peter Martyr Vermigli, who was to become Cranmer's close friend, Bernardino Ochino, and the Polish Reformer John a Lasco.

60. N. Scott Amon, "Martin Bucer and the Revision of the 1549 Book of Common Prayer: Reform of Ceremonies and the Didactic Use of Ritual," in *Reformation and Renaissance Review* 2 (December 1999): 112.

61. *Prayer Books of Edward VI*, 377, 225, 289.

62. Paul Ayris, "The Correspondence of Thomas Cranmer," in *Reformation and Renaissance Review* 3 (June 2000): 30.

63. Hooper had also objected strenuously to the 1549 prayer book, writing to Bullinger in March 1550: "I am so offended with that book . . . that if it be not corrected, I neither can nor will communicate with the church in the administration of the supper." Brooks, *Cranmer in Context*, 72.

64. G. R. Elton, *Reform and Reformation: England 1509–1558* (London: Edward Arnold, 1977), 370.

65. Jones, *The English Reformation*, 149.

66. Foxe, *Acts and Monuments*, vol. 8, 625.

67. Elton, *Reform and Reformation*, 376.

68. For the revisionist position, see J. Loach and R. Tittler, eds., *The Mid-Tudor Polity ca. 1540–1560* (Basingstoke, U.K.: Macmillan, 1980); Jennifer Loach, *Parliament and the Crown in the Reign of Mary Tudor* (Oxford: Clarendon Press, 1986); Haigh, *English Reformations*, 203ff. For an account that considers both points of view, see David M. Loades, *The Reign of Mary Tudor* (London: Longman, 1991).

69. David H. Pill, *The English Reformation 1529–58* (London: University of London Press, 1973), 107.

70. David M. Loades, *Revolution in Religion: The English Reformation 1530–1570* (Cardiff, Wales, U.K.: University of Wales Press, 1992), 83.

71. "Nearly a quarter of the Lower House voted against the change: a comfortingly small minority for pessimists expecting worse, but still alarming." Brigden, *New Worlds, Lost Worlds*, 204.

72. Mary got around her problem by use of the word *etcetera* in her title. She called herself: "queen of England and France, Defender of the Faith, Lord of Ireland *etcetera*."

73. During Edward's reign Parliament had passed an act that allowed priests to marry. Mary's injunction stated that priests who had been monks or friars must give up their wives, but secular clergy could either stay married and live the life of a layman or put away their wife, do public penance, and take up a new living. It seems that most of the married clergy preferred to give up their wives rather than their benefices.

74. Bray, *Documents of the English Reformation*, 316.

75. Revolts had also been planned in Devon, Leicestershire, and Wales, but only the one in Kent actually occurred. Historians are not agreed on the extent to which religion played a role in the rebellion. For opposing points of view, see David Loades, *Two Tudor Conspiracies* (Cambridge: Cambridge University Press, 1965), and M. R. Thorp, "Religion and the Wyatt Rebellions of 1554," in *Church History* 47 (1978): 363–80.

76. Pole had been in exile for twenty years and played a major role in the Catholic Reformation. Although he had been a favorite of Henry VIII, he had broken with him and remained loyal to Rome. Pole was appointed papal legate by Pope Julius III, and he used those powers to absolve England from the sin of schism. See chapter 10 for a discussion of Pole's role in the Catholic Reformation.

77. Brigden, *New Worlds, Lost Worlds*, 203.

78. Loades comments that "Mary had been the victim of sickness and her own desires" (Loades, *Reign of Mary Tudor*, 219). She may have been afflicted with ovarian dropsy, which would explain the abdominal swelling she mistook for pregnancy. Carolly Erickson, *Bloody Mary* (Garden City, NY: Doubleday, 1978), 402.

79. "Her prayer book survives, its pages worn and stained. The queen's tears appear to have fallen most often on a page bearing a prayer for the safe delivery of a woman with child." Erickson, *Bloody Mary*, 421.

80. Haigh, *English Reformations*, 231.

81. See Foxe, *Acts and Monuments*, vol. 6, 647–48, 658–59 for a description of Hooper's execution.

82. Rudolph W. Heinze, "'I pray God to grant that I may endure to the end': A New Look at the Martyrdom of Thomas Cranmer," in *Thomas Cranmer: Churchman and Scholar*, ed. Paul Ayris and David Selwyn (Woodbridge, U.K.: Boydell Press, 1993), 277.

83. Ibid., 279.

84. "Protestants were outraged by the sufferings, but for the curious mass it was drama: the country people flocked to Dartford for the burning of Christopher Wade in July 1555, and fruiterers brought loads of cherries to sell to the spectators." Haigh, *English Reformations*, 233.

Chapter 9: The Scottish Reformation and the Elizabethan Settlement

1. John Knox, "The First Blast of the Trumpet against the Monstrous Regiment of Women," in *Christian History* 46 (1995): 20.

2. The title isn't quite as bad as it sounds. "Monstrous Regiment" means "unnatural government."

3. R. Tudur Jones, "Preacher of Revolution," *Christian History* 46 (1995): 14.

4. The revisionism began in 1960 with the publication of Gordon Donaldson, *The Scottish Reformation* (Cambridge: Cambridge University Press, 1960).

5. Gordon Donaldson on the one hand and James Kirk on the other hold opposing points of view in this debate; see James Kirk, *Patterns of Reform, Continuity and Change in the Reformation Kirk* (Edinburgh: T & T Clark, 1989). For a historiographical article on the Scottish Reformation, see W. Fred Graham, "The Reformation in Scotland," in *Reformation Europe: A Guide to Research*, vol. 2, ed. William S. Maltby (St. Louis: Center for Reformation Research, 1992), 235ff.

6. J. Stephen Lang, "Martyrs and Architects," in *Christian History* 46 (1995): 33.

7. R. L. Mackie, *A Short History of Scotland*, ed. Gordon Donaldson (New York: Praeger, 1963), 127.

8. Dickens, *English Reformation*, 2nd ed. (1989), 346.

9. John Knox, *Works*, vol. 4, ed. David Laing (Edinburgh: Bannatyne Society, 1846–1864), 240.

10. Knox met his future wife, Marjory Bowes, and her mother, Elizabeth, while he was a pastor in England. Marjory gave him two sons before she died in 1560, but Elizabeth continued to live in Knox's household after her daughter's death, taking care of her grandsons. At the age of fifty Knox married a seventeen-year-old distant relative of Mary Queen of Scots, Margaret Stewart, who bore him three daughters.

11. John Knox, *First Blast of the Trumpet*, as cited in Jasper Ridley, *John Knox* (Oxford: Clarendon Press, 1968), 271–72.

12. Ridley, *John Knox*, 190.

13. Ian B. Cowan, ed., *The Enigma of Mary Stuart* (London: Gollancz, 1971), provides a very useful introduction to the controversy. Two recent biographies that present contrasting views of Mary are Jenny Wormald, *Mary Queen of Scots: A Study in Failure* (London: Palgrave Macmillan, 1988), and Gordon Donaldson, *Mary Queen of Scots* (London: English Universities Press, 1974).

14. Ridley is convinced that Knox was part of the conspiracy. Ridley, *John Knox*, 448.

15. Ibid., 458.

16. Margo Todd maintains that the Scots "experienced as remarkably successful a Reformation as anywhere in Western Europe." Margo Todd, *The Culture of Protestantism in Early Modern Scotland* (New Haven, CT: Yale University Press, 2002), 15.

17. *Christian History* 46 (1995): 17.

18. Ridley, *John Knox*, 396.

19. Gordon Donaldson, "The Scottish Church 1567–1625," in *The Reign of James VI and I*, ed. Alan G. R. Smith (London: Macmillan, 1973), 46.

20. Ibid., 51.

21. David H. Willson, *King James VI and I* (Oxford: University Press, 1967), 207. See chapter 14 for a fuller discussion of the Hampton Court Conference.

22. John A. Guy, *Tudor England* (Oxford: University Press, 1988), 251–52.

23. Kenneth Hylson-Smith, *The Churches in England from Elizabeth I to Elizabeth II*, vol. 1, *1558–1688* (London: SCM Press, 1996), 33.

24. J. E. Neale, who pioneered work on Elizabeth's Parliaments, believed that Elizabeth was forced into a more radical settlement than she actually wanted by the radical Protestants in the House of Commons. More recently, Norman Jones has argued that the settlement was the one that Elizabeth desired and that her major opposition came from conservative Catholics in the House of Lords rather than radical Protestants in the House of Commons. J. E. Neale, *Elizabeth and her Parliaments 1559–1581*, vol. 1 (London: Cape, 1953); Norman L. Jones, *Faith by Statute: Parliament and the Settlement of Religion 1559* (London: Royal Historical Society, 1982).

25. Gerald Bray, *Documents of the English Reformation*, 330, 334.

26. Geoffrey R. Regan, *Elizabeth I* (Cambridge: Cambridge University Press, 1988), 28.

27. Brigden, *New Worlds, Lost Worlds*, 227.

28. Hylson-Smith, *Churches in England*, 39.

29. They preferred to call themselves "the godly," "true gospellers," or "the elect."

30. Some historians prefer not to use the term *Puritan* at all because its meaning is so ambiguous. For a discussion of the problems involved in defining Puritanism, see Christopher Durston and Jacqueline Eales, eds., *The Culture of English Puritanism 1560–1700* (London: Macmillan, 1996), 1–9.

31. Patrick Collinson, *The Elizabethan Puritan Movement* (Oxford: Clarendon Press, 1990), 27.

32. Patrick Collinson, *English Puritanism* (London: Historical Association, 1983), 9. A less slanderous depiction of Puritan belief noted that they were people who "would have nothing but preaching," and added, "It was never merry world since that sect came first amongst us." R. Heinze, *Dedham and the Puritans* (Dedham, U.K.: Dedham Ecclesiastical Trust, 1993), 1.

33. Collinson, *English Puritanism*, 10.

34. This was the position of William Bradshaw, who also stated that it was sinful "to perform any other worship to God, whether eternal or internal, moral or ceremonial, in whole or in part, than that which God himself requires in his word." Durston and Eales, *Culture of English Puritanism*, 17.

35. Hastings Robinson, ed., *Zurich Letters 1558–1579*, vol. 1 (Cambridge: Cambridge University Press, 1842), 169.

36. Patrick V. MacGrath, *Papists and Puritans under Elizabeth I* (London: Blandford Press, 1967), 74–75.

37. Collinson, *Elizabethan Puritan Movement*, 69.

38. Sheils, *English Reformation*, 104.

39. Robinson, *Zurich Letters*, 355.

40. Ibid.

41. So there could be no misunderstanding of what was intended, Parker summoned 110 London clergy to Lambeth Palace in March 1566, where he confronted them with a clerical mannequin showing how a minister should properly be dressed. He then commanded subscription to an agreement that they would dress in the same way. Thirty-seven of them declined and were at once suspended from their ministerial functions.

42. Hylson-Smith, *Churches in England*, 58.

43. "A survey of the diocese of Peterborough in 1560 found only nine preachers among 166 clergy; even by 1576 there were just forty preachers among 230 clergy—to spread the gospel through 296 parishes. In Wiltshire in 1561 there were twenty preachers out of 220 clergy, to serve over 300 churches—not much chance of widespread evangelism there. There were more preachers in some areas, and fewer in others: in London itself in 1561 almost half the ministers could preach, in Devon and Cornwall only one in fourteen. But virtually everywhere preaching resources were inadequate and over-stretched." Haigh, *English Reformations*, 268.

44. Ibid., 274.

45. Collinson, *Elizabethan Puritan Movement*, 191.

46. Ibid., 196.

47. Regan, *Elizabeth I*, 71–72.

48. Ibid., 358.

49. Collinson, *Elizabethan Puritan Movement*, 266.

50. Hylson-Smith, *Churches in England*, 65.

51. Browne was never a model Church of England minister. He died in jail in 1633 for assaulting a constable. Hylson-Smith says: "He was no doubt an awkward and cantankerous man, but he had courage and vision and can be considered one of the true progenitors of modern Dissent." Ibid., 67.

52. Alan Dures, *English Catholicism 1558–1642* (London: Longman, 1983), 9.

53. Lindberg, *Sourcebook*, 237.

54. Brigden, *New Worlds, Lost Worlds*, 264.

55. During this time a number of plots against Elizabeth were exposed, but Mary was never directly implicated until 1586. In that year a young Catholic gentleman, Anthony Babington, was involved in a plot to assassinate Elizabeth and make Mary the queen

of England with the aid of foreign troops. When Babington wrote to Mary informing her of the plans, she responded with a letter in which she acquiesced in the plot. What she and Babington did not know was that all her clandestine correspondence was being intercepted by Elizabeth's agents, headed by her Puritan Secretary of State, Francis Walsingham, who allowed the letters to go through so he could acquire indisputable evidence of Mary's treason. He even added a postscript on Mary's response to Babington asking for the names of the people who intended to kill Elizabeth. When the letters were presented to Elizabeth, she bowed to the inevitable and signed the warrant for Mary's execution in 1587.

56. David Cressy, *Bonfires and Bells* (Los Angeles: University of California Press, 1989), 113–14. He notes that "given the shambles of England's military preparations, prayer was, perhaps, the most promising line of defense" (p. 113).

57. "The celebrations were not for the triumph of English arms but for the signal mercy shown to England by an anglophile divinity" (ibid., 117).

58. Ibid., 122.

59. Diarmaid MacCulloch, *The Later Reformation in England 1547–1603* (London: Macmillan, 1990), 57.

60. The actual author was never discovered, but historians have many theories. The most likely candidate is Job Throckmorton, a Puritan gentleman from Warwickshire. Ibid., 56.

61. Powel Mills Dawley, *John Whitgift and the English Reformation* (New York: Scribner, 1954), 184.

62. In contrast to the heavy reliance on Calvin's works found in both Puritan and Conformist writings, Hooker mentions Calvin only nine times in his eight volumes, and three of those times Calvin is mentioned only in order to disagree with him.

63. Susan Doran, *Elizabeth I and Religion, 1558–1603* (London: Routledge, 1993), 66.

Chapter 10: The Catholic Reformation

1. Janz, *Reformation Reader*, 346–47.

2. The committee included some of the leading Reformers in the College of Cardinals including Contarini, Carafa, Pole, Sadoleto, and Giberti.

3. The eighteenth-century Lutheran historian Johann Stephan Pütter first used the term in the introduction of his edition of the Augsburg Confession. He understood it to mean the forced return of Lutheran areas to Catholicism. Throughout the nineteenth century the term was used largely by German Lutherans, inevitably with negative connotations.

4. John W. O'Malley, *Trent and All That: Renaming Catholicism in Early Modern Europe* (Cambridge: Harvard University Press, 2000), 5. O'Malley suggests the neutral title "Early Modern Catholicism" as still another name for the movement.

5. A. G. Dickens, *The Counter Reformation* (New York: Harcourt Brace, 1969), 7.

6. The most infamous Inquisitor General was Tomas de Torquemada, who has been accused of having executed thousands. Although the Inquisition used torture and conducted its proceedings in secret, recent studies argue that its nefarious reputation is not entirely deserved. William Monter, *Frontiers of Heresy: The Spanish Inquisition from the Basque Lands to Sicily* (Cambridge: Cambridge University Press, 1990).

7. Teresa of Avila, *A Life of Prayer*, ed. James M. Houston (Basingstoke, U.K.: Pickering & Inglis, 1983), xxi.

8. Stewart MacDonald, *Charles V: Ruler Dynast and Defender of the Faith 1500–1558* (London: Hodder and Stoughton, 1992), 70.

9. Martin D. W. Jones, *The Counter Reformation: Religion and Society in Early Modern Europe* (Cambridge: Cambridge University Press, 1995), 45.

10. N. S. Davidson, *The Counter-Reformation* (Oxford: Blackwell, 1987), 7.

11. Janz, *Reformation Reader*, 346.

12. The initial draft even used the phrase "double righteousness."

13. Vinzenz Pfnür, "Colloquies," in *The Oxford Encyclopedia of The Reformation*, vol. 1 (Oxford: University Press, 1996), 378.

14. Donald Ziegler, ed., *Great Debates of the Reformation* (New York: Random House, 1969), 168.

15. Janz, *Reformation Reader*, 369.

16. Ibid., 371–72.

17. Ozment, *Age of Reform*, 413.

18. Hillerbrand, *The Reformation*, 442.

19. Ibid., 446. One of Loyola's methods for carrying out this mission to the "northern nations" was the establishment of the Collegium Germanicum in 1552, which became a training school for missions to Germany.

20. Ibid., 446–47.

21. Diego Lainez and Alfonso Salmeron were theological advisers to all three phases of the Council of Trent.

22. Italians dominated throughout the three phases of the council. Almost 70 percent of the 270 bishops attending at one time or another were Italian.

23. Dickens, *Counter Reformation*, 108.

24. Hillerbrand, *The Reformation*, 463.

25. H. J. Schroeder, *Canons and Decrees of the Council of Trent* (St. Louis: Herder, 1941), 18–19.

26. "Canon 1. If anyone says that man can be justified before God by his own works, whether done by his own natural powers or through the teaching of the law without divine grace through Jesus Christ, let him be anathema. . . . Canon 9. If anyone says that the sinner is justified by faith alone meaning that nothing else is required to cooperate in order to obtain the grace of justification . . . let him be anathema. . . . Canon 11. If anyone says that men are justified either by the sole imputation of the justice of Christ or by the sole remission of sins . . . let him be anathema." Ibid., 42–43.

27. Ibid., 33, 39, 46.

28. Davidson, *Counter-Reformation*, 11–12.

29. Dickens, *Counter Reformation*, 118.

30. There was also a violent reaction by the mobs in Rome, who destroyed the buildings housing the Inquisition, freed its prisoners, and burned its records. They also toppled the statue of Paul IV and mutilated it.

31. Dickens, *Counter Reformation*, 118.

32. Schroeder, *Canons and Decrees*, 259.

33. Dickens states that Trent was "a victory for the rising tide of Thomism and a defeat for those Augustinian and biblical humanist emphases which had helped to stimulate the Protestant Reformation and had become so important for Catholics like Contarini and Seripando." Dickens, *Counter Reformation*, 132.

34. The Julian calendar, introduced by the Roman Emperor Julius Caesar before the birth of Christ, exceeded the astronomical year by some ten days in the sixteenth century. A calendar revision was necessary so that the church could follow accurately the decrees of church councils in celebrating various festivals of the church year.

35. Sixtus V (1585–90) pursued the work of reform even more vigorously than Gregory VIII. He reorganized the central administration of the church and introduced a rule that bishops must submit reports on the state of their dioceses to the pope. Clement VIII (1592–1605), who set an example of reform by his personal piety, continued the papal policy of zealously applying the decisions of Trent. Paul V (1605–21) was an equally

committed reformer who tightened the requirement of episcopal residence and enforced discipline in the religious orders.

36. Jones, *Counter Reformation*, 85.

37. The St. Bartholomew's Day Massacre is discussed in chapter 14.

38. Davidson, *Counter-Reformation*, 29.

39. For example, in parts of Brittany more than 35 percent of parish priests had been living with a concubine in 1554, but this had been reduced to fewer than 3 percent in 1665. Davidson, *Counter-Reformation*, 31.

40. Ibid., 37.

41. Jean Delumeau, *Catholicism between Luther and Voltaire: A New View of the Counter-Reformation* (Philadelphia: Westminster John Knox Press, 1977).

42. Michael Mullet, *The Counter-Reformation* (London: Methuen, 1984), 21.

43. Davidson, *Counter-Reformation*, 43.

44. See chapter 14 for a discussion of the religious wars.

Chapter 11: Women and the Reformation

1. Bainton, *Women of the Reformation in Germany and Italy*, 55.

2. Merry E. Wiesner, "Beyond Women and the Family: Towards a Gender Analysis of the Reformation," in *Sixteenth Century Journal* 18, no. 3 (1987): 311.

3. Merry Wiesner, "Studies of Women, Family and Gender," in Maltby, *Reformation Europe*, vol. 2, 159. For an example of gender studies, see Jean R. Brink, Allison P. Coudert, and Maryanne C. Horowitz, eds., *The Politics of Gender in Early Modern Europe* (Kirksville, MO: Sixteenth Century Journal Press, 1989).

4. The other two volumes were *Women of the Reformation in France and England* (Minneapolis: Augsburg, 1973) and *Women of the Reformation from Spain to Scandinavia* (Minneapolis: Augsburg, 1977). Much of this chapter is based on Bainton's work.

5. Bainton, *Women of the Reformation in Germany and Italy*, 9.

6. Bainton maintained that the Reformation had a significant impact on women because it extolled the family in place of celibacy. A large number of female political leaders and women played roles in both the Catholic and Protestant Reformations.

7. David C. Steinmetz, "Theological Reflections on the Reformation and the Status of Women," in *Duke Divinity Review* 41 (Fall 1976): 204.

8. Ibid.

9. Lyndal Roper, *The Holy Household: Women and Morals in Reformation Augsburg* (Oxford: Clarendon Press, 1991), 264.

10. Sherrin Marshall, ed., *Women in Reformation and Counter-Reformation Europe* (Bloomington: Indiana University Press, 1989), 7.

11. Steinmetz, "Theological Reflections," 200.

12. Janz, *Reformation Reader*, 18. Although the work is filled with comments on the weaknesses of women, the authors did recognize that there were also good women in the Bible who "brought beatitude to men and have saved nations, lands and cities" (p. 17).

13. Jane D. Douglass, *Women, Freedom and Calvin* (Philadelphia: Westminster John Knox Press, 1985), 10.

14. John Lee Thompson, *John Calvin and the Daughters of Sarah* (Geneva, Switzerland: Droz, 1992), 280.

15. Jonathan Zophy, "We Must Have the Dear Ladies: Martin Luther and Women," in *Pietas et Societas: New Trends in Reformation Social History*, ed. Kyle C. Session and Phillip N. Bebb (Ann Arbor, MI: Edwards, 1985), 141.

16. Ibid., 145.

17. Ibid., 147.

18. Ibid., 150.

19. Matthieu Arnold, *Les femmes dans la correspondance de Luther* (Paris: Presses Universitaries de France, 1998).

20. For a recent study, see H. J. Selderhuis, John Vriend, and Lyle D. Bierm, *Marriage and Divorce in the Thought of Martin Bucer* (Kirksville, MO: Thomas Jefferson University Press, 1999).

21. R. W. Scribner, *The German Reformation* (Atlantic Highlands, NJ: Humanities Press International, 1986), 60.

22. Stephen Ozment, *When Fathers Ruled: Family Life in Reformation Europe* (Cambridge: Cambridge University Press, 1983).

23. Bainton, *Women of the Reformation in Germany and Italy*, 14.

24. Historians continue to debate the degree to which Anabaptists gave women an expanded role in church and society. Joyce Irwin represents one school of thought that doubts "women's status in sixteenth-century sects was more free and equal than in established churches" (Joyce Irwin, "Society and the Sexes," in Ozment, *Reformation Europe*, 351). George Huntson Williams, on the other hand, believes that women were given almost equal status to men among Anabaptists. He maintains that "nowhere else in the Reformation Era were women conceived as so nearly companions in the faith, mates in missionary enterprise and mutual exhorters in readiness for martyrdom as among those for whom believers' baptism was theologically a gender-equalizing covenant" (Williams, *Radical Reformation*, 763). For a balanced consideration of the question, see Sigrun Haude, "Anabaptist Women—Radical Women?" in *Infinite Boundaries—Order, Disorder and Reorder in Early Modern German Culture*, ed. Max Reinhart (Kirksville, MO: Sixteenth Century Journal Publishers, 1998), 313–27.

25. Jones, *Counter Reformation*, 93.

26. Ibid.

27. Bainton, *Women of the Reformation in Germany and Italy*, 82. Not everybody approved of Oecolampadius's marriage, and at least one contemporary observer expressed concern for his bride, commenting: "A decrepit old man with trembling head and body, so emaciated and wasted that you might well call him a living corpse, has married an elegant and blooming girl of twenty."

28. Ibid., 87–88.

29. Ibid., 94.

30. Katherine Zell has received additional attention since Bainton wrote about her. Elsie Anne McKee has published both a biography and an edition of her works: *The Life and Thought of A Sixteenth-Century Reformer*, vol. 1; *The Writings: A Critical Edition*, vol. 2 (Leiden, Netherlands: E. J. Brill, 1999).

31. Elsie Anne McKee, "Reforming Popular Piety in Sixteenth-Century Strasbourg: Katharina Schultz Zell and Her Hymnbook," in *Studies in Reformed Theology and History* 2, no. 4 (Fall, 1994): 55.

32. Ibid., 61–62.

33. Ibid., ix.

34. Bainton, *Women of the Reformation in Germany and Italy*, 64.

35. Ibid., 73.

36. Ibid., 66–67.

37. Ibid., 68.

38. Ibid., 73.

39. Barry Collett, "A Long and Troubled Pilgrimage: The Correspondence of Marguerite d'Angoulême and Vittoria Colonna 1540–1545," in *Studies in Reformed Theology and History*, New Series, 6 (2000).

40. The name was derived from the four-cornered hood that they wore in imitation of the one St. Francis wore called *cappuccio*. Its wearer was called *cappuccino*, which means "little hooded man."

41. Bainton, *Women of the Reformation in Germany and Italy*, 204–5.

42. Ochino was fifty-six at the time and spent the rest of his life moving from place to place, including a brief time in England during Edward VI's reign. He eventually died in Moravia at the age of seventy-eight.

43. Collett, "Correspondence of Marguerite d'Angoulême and Vittoria Colonna," 74–75.

44. Ibid., 79.

45. Ibid., 117.

46. Ibid., 140. Vergerio was himself faced with heresy proceedings in 1545, and after four years of seeking to establish his innocence, he left the Catholic Church and became a Protestant.

Chapter 12: Non-Western Churches and Missionary Enterprises

1. Pope Paul III, *Sublimis Deus*, in Janz, *Reformation Reader*, 377.

2. The line was modified by the Treaty of Tordesillas in 1494 and moved further east, thereby including Brazil in Portugal's sphere.

3. Stephen Neill, *A History of Christian Missions*, 2nd ed. (New York: Viking Penguin, 1986), 121.

4. There were some exceptions to this in the Balkans, especially in Serbia, where the patriarchate of Pec was restored to govern the Serbian church in 1557.

5. Philip Walters, "Eastern Europe Since the Fifteenth Century," in *A World History of Christianity*, ed. Adrian Hastings (Grand Rapids: Eerdmans, 1999), 286.

6. Lucaris's story is told in Giorgios A. Chatzeantoniou, *Protestant Patriarch: The Life of Cyril Lucaris (1572–1638)* (Richmond, VA: John Knox, 1961).

7. The legend of Presbyter ("Prester") John has its origins in the period of the Crusades, when it was believed that there was a great Christian kingdom located in Asia. In the late Middle Ages, its location was associated with Ethiopia.

8. In addition to proselytizing, the Portuguese also gave their African converts Portuguese names.

9. Nestorius, who was accused of separating the divine and human natures of Christ, was condemned by the Council of Ephesus in 431.

10. Owen Chadwick, *The Reformation* (New York: Penguin Books, 1990), 329–30.

11. Janz, *Reformation Reader*, 379.

12. Columbus believed he had reached the East Indies when he landed at the Caribbean Island of Hispaniola in 1492, so he called the inhabitants of the island Indians. That term was in regular usage until recently, when the misnomer was corrected and the indigenous inhabitants of the Americas were properly called Native Americans.

13. Lindberg, *Sourcebook*, 281.

14. Chadwick, *The Reformation*, 333.

15. Xavier was canonized in 1622, and in 1927 Pope Pius XI named him Patron of Foreign Missions.

16. Neill, *History of Christian Missions*, 191.

17. R. G. Tiedermann, "China and Its Neighbours," in Hastings, *World History of Christianity*, 376.

18. Neill, *History of Christian Missions*, 171.

19. The term *Pilgrim* originated when William Bradford described the Separatists who were leaving Holland as "pilgrims." The settlers were not called the "Pilgrim fathers" until 1799.

20. R. B. Mullin, "North America," in Hastings, *World History of Christianity*, 420.

21. Neill, *History of Christian Missions*, 192.

Chapter 13: Theological Conflict, Confessions, and Confessionalization

1. Naphy, *Documents on the Continental Reformation*, 90.

2. Gerrish, *The Old Protestantism and the New*, 47–48.

3. Ibid., 30.

4. As mentioned earlier (chapter 4, note 30), in January 1546 Luther even wrote a parody on Psalm 1 attacking the Zwinglians: "Blessed is the man who walks not in the counsel of the sacramentarians, nor stands in the way of Zwinglians, nor sits in the seat of the Zurichers" Ibid., 33.

5. Schaff, *History of the Christian Church*, vol. 7, 661.

6. "The Consensus was adopted by the Churches of Zurich, Geneva, St. Gall, Schaffhausen, the Grisons, Neuchatel and, after some hesitation by Basle, and was favorable received in France, England and parts of Germany." Philip Schaff, *The Creeds of Christendom with a History and Critical Notes*, vol. 1, 4th ed. (New York: Harper, 1884), 472. For an English translation of the *Consensus Tigurinus* with commentary, see Ian Bunting, "The *Consensus Tigurinus*," in *Journal of Presbyterian History* 44 (1966): 45–61.

7. Schaff, *History of the Christian Church*, vol. 8, 660–61.

8. Ibid., 661.

9. Ibid., 664.

10. Ibid., 666.

11. Ibid., 667.

12. Bodo Nischan, *Prince, People and Confession: The Second Reformation in Brandenburg* (Philadelphia: University of Pennsylvania Press, 1994).

13. Bodo Nischan, *Lutherans and Calvinists in the Age of Confessionalism* (Aldershot, U.K.: Ashgate, 1999), x.

14. While Lutherans and Calvinists fought over eucharistic theology, they still had to contend with popular religion, which was unconcerned about the finer points of theology and approached the sacrament as a means of dealing with everyday problems. For example, a widow in Brandenburg was prosecuted for removing a host from her mouth and taking it home to kill bedbugs.

15. R. A. Kolb, "Historical Background of the Formula of Concord," in *A Contemporary Look at the Formula of Concord*, ed. Wilbert Rosin and Robert Preus (St. Louis: Concordia, 1978), 30.

16. Bodo Nischan, "Germany after 1550," in *The Reformation World*, ed. Andrew Pettegree (London: Routledge, 2000), 395.

17. *Book of Concord*, 230.

18. Ibid.

19. Ibid., 231.

20. Although the Formula of Concord met with opposition outside Germany and was rejected in Denmark, it was accepted by two-thirds of German Lutherans, and those who did not accept it "avoided public condemnation of its teachings. . . . In the Book of Concord the majority of German Lutheran churches found their substitute for medieval popes and councils and the authoritative source and guide . . . for the interpretation of the scriptures." Robert Kolb, "Formula of Concord," in *The Oxford Encyclopedia of the Reformation*, vol. 2 (1996): 120.

21. Luther once said that in order to be a theologian one must abandon Aristotle.

22. Heinz Schilling, "The Reformation and the Rise of the Early Modern State," in *Luther and the Modern State in Germany*, ed. James D. Tracy (Kirksville, MO: Sixteenth Century Publishers, 1986), 22.

23. C. Scott Dixon, "The Princely Reformation in Germany," in Pettegree, *Reformation World*, 160.

24. C. Scott Dixon, ed., *The German Reformation: The Essential Readings* (Oxford: Blackwell, 1999), 18.

25. Schilling, "Reformation and the Rise of the Early Modern State," 24.

26. Ibid., 29.

27. The Belgic Confession first appeared in 1561 and was the earliest confessional statement of the Reformed church in the Low Countries. See chapter 14 for a fuller discussion of the Belgic Confession.

28. A tract by Peter Bertius published in 1610 stated unequivocally that believers could fall from grace.

Chapter 14: A Century of Military Conflict

1. Lindberg, *Sourcebook*, 194–95.

2. Philip Benedict, "Settlements: France," in Brady, Oberman, and Tracy, *Handbook of European History 1400–1600*, 419.

3. Lindberg, *Sourcebook*, 277.

4. Ibid., 187–88.

5. The word *Huguenots* was first used as a pejorative term. Its derivation is uncertain.

6. Lindberg, *Sourcebook*, 195–96.

7. R. J. Knecht, *The French Wars of Religion 1559–1598* (New York: Longman, 1989), 112–13.

8. Ibid., 80.

9. J. Raitt, *The Colloquy of Montbéliard* (Oxford: Oxford University Press, 1993), 192.

10. Janz, *Reformation Reader*, 215–16.

11. T. A. Brady, "Settlements: The Holy Roman Empire," in Brady, Oberman, and Tracy, *Handbook of European History 1400–1600*, 352.

12. The treaty did not actually include the phrase *"cuius regio, cuius religio"* (whose the rule to him the religion), which is often used to describe its major provision. That phrase was coined later by a German law professor.

13. Lindberg, *Sourcebook*, 161.

14. It was clearly in need of moral reform. A survey of 122 monastic houses in the Austrian lands revealed that they did not take seriously the vow of chastity. It reported that there were 463 monks, 160 nuns, 199 concubines, 55 wives, and 443 children in the houses surveyed.

15. The more believable Protestant version said it was because they landed on a dung heap.

16. One writer says, "He knew more about gardening than fighting" (quoted in Brady, Oberman, and Tracy, *Handbook of European History 1400–1600*, 352).

17. This is why he was known as the *"Winterkoenig."*

18. They included 16 bishoprics, 28 cities and towns, as well as over 150 monasteries and convents.

19. Revisionist efforts to argue that the war was not really as destructive as a previous generation believed have not been very convincing.

20. For another point of view, see Kevin Sharpe, *The Personal Rule of Charles I* (New Haven, CT: Yale University Press, 1992).

21. Nicholas Tyacke, *Anti-Calvinists: The Rise of English Arminianism ca. 1590–1640* (Oxford: Clarendon Press, 1991).

22. Hylson-Smith, *Churches in England*, 150.

23. R. C. Richardson, *The Debate on the English Revolution* (London: Methuen, 1977), is a useful introduction to the debate over the civil war. For a recent interpretation, see Austin Woolrych, *Britain in Revolution 1625–1660* (Oxford: Oxford University Press, 2003).

24. Useful brief studies are found in Barry Coward, *Oliver Cromwell* (Harlow, U.K.: Longmans, 1991); John Morrill, ed., *Oliver Cromwell and the English Revolution* (London: Longmans, 1990); and Christopher Hill, *God's Englishman* (London: Harper and Row, 1970). A popular study that became a best seller is Antonia Fraser, *Cromwell: The Lord Protector* (New York: Dell, 1973).

25. Cromwell's armies were responsible for destroying much of the medieval stained glass in England.

26. Ludowicke Muggleton was a London tailor who had been a dedicated Puritan but was influenced by a man who claimed to be God almighty and to raise prophets from the dead. He came to believe he was one of the witnesses of Revelation 11 sent to seal the elect and reprobate with eternal seals of life and death, after which Jesus would appear in glory and power. The Ranters believed there was no law that applied to Christians, so they openly flouted the Puritan moral code by committing adultery, engaging in communal sex, and dancing naked. The stories told about them were so extreme that some historians have questioned whether they existed, arguing that the stories were simply a projection of society's fears and anxieties. J. C. Davis, *Fear, Myth and History: The Ranters and Historians* (Cambridge: Cambridge University Press, 1986).

27. Charles II eventually converted to Catholicism on his deathbed.

28. In 1695 John Locke wrote: "I have talked with some of their teachers who confess themselves not to understand the difference in debate between them; and yet the points they stand on are reckoned of so great weight, so material, so fundamental in religion that they divide communion and separate upon them." John Locke, *The Reasonableness of Christianity*, cited in Peter Toon, *Puritans and Calvinism* (Swengel, PA: Reiner, 1973), 93.

Chapter 15: The Impact of the Reformation

1. Vogelstein, *Johann Sleidan's Commentaries*, 12.

2. Scribner, *German Reformation*, 55.

3. For an excellent summary of the ongoing debate, see Hans Hillerbrand, "Was There a Reformation in the Sixteenth Century?" in *Church History* 72, no. 3 (September 2003): 525ff.

4. A number of articles have used this very phrase. The debate began with an article by Gerald Strauss in 1975 entitled "Success or Failure in the German Reformation," in *Past and Present* 67 (May 1975): 30–63. A recent article that summarizes the issues and evidence in the debate is Geoffrey Parker, "Success and Failure during the First Century of the Reformation," in *Past and Present* 136 (1991): 41–82.

5. Peter Matheson, *The Imaginative World of the Reformation* (Minneapolis: Fortress Press, 2001), 25.

6. A. G. Dickens, *Reformation and Society in Sixteenth-Century Europe* (London: Thames and Hudson, 1966), 67.

7. This may not be the case with Anne of Cleves, as Holbein has been accused of painting an overly flattering picture, which led Henry to believe that Anne was more attractive than she was in reality.

8. Hughes and Larkin, *Tudor Royal Proclamations*, 401.

9. "In response to central *diktat* the altars were drawn down and the walls whited, windows broken or blotted out to conceal 'feigned miracles.' In 1553 veils and vestments, chalices and chests and hangings the accumulation of generations of pious donations

were surrendered to the King's commissioners, to be unstitched, broken up, or melted down." Duffy, *Stripping of the Altars*, 478.

10. Calvin, *Institutes*, trans. Beveridge, vol. 1, chapter 11, 5.

11. Andrew Pettegree, "Art," in *Reformation World*, 489.

12. A. D. Wright, *The Counter-Reformation: Catholic Europe and the Non-Christian World* (New York: St. Martin's, 1982), 235.

13. Although the doctrine that Mary was free from original sin was not promulgated by the Church of Rome until 1854, the Council of Trent had not included the Virgin Mary in its decree on original sin, and the belief in the immaculate conception was particularly popular in sixteenth-century Spain.

14. Francis Higman, "Music," in Pettegree, *Reformation World*, 502–3.

15. Michel de Montaigne, *Complete Works*, trans. Donald M. Frame (Stanford, CA: Stanford University Press, 1957), 324.

16. "What is clear is that the questions that Descartes touched on were questions which set the agenda not only for Continental rationalism and British empiricism but for Western philosophy in general down to the present day." Colin Brown, *Christianity and Western Thought: A History of Philosophers, Ideas and Movements*, vol. 1 (Downers Grove: IVP, 1990), 184.

17. Pascal is cited as having said, "I cannot forgive Descartes; in his whole philosophy he would like to do without God; but he could not help allowing him a flick of the fingers to set the world in motion; after that he had no more use for God." Ibid., 194.

18. Blaise Pascal, *Pensées and Other Writings*, trans. Honor Levi (Oxford: Oxford University Press, 1995), 158, 60, 154.

19. Rabelais was a physician who is credited with performing one of the first dissections. He also published several scientific treatises. Descartes made important contributions to the development of coordinate geometry. He once said that he preferred mathematics to humanities because the humanities never came up with any definite answers.

20. Charlotte Methuen, "Science and Medicine," in Pettegree, *Reformation World*, 521.

21. The remarks are found in Luther's table talk and were made before Copernicus's book was printed. He supposedly said that Copernicus wished "to turn the whole of astronomy upside down . . . I believe the Holy Scriptures, for Joshua commanded the sun to stand still and not the earth." Owen Gingerich, "Did the Reformers Reject Copernicus?" in *Christian History* 76 (2002): 22.

22. The Catholic Church has since apologized. In 1992 a papal commission formally stated that the church had been wrong in its treatment of Galileo. For a balanced account of Galileo's condemnation, see William Shea and Mariano Artigas, *Galileo in Rome* (Oxford: Oxford University Press, 2003).

23. Simplicio is a fictional character, but his name sounds like "simpleton" in Italian. "Simplicio is neither very bright nor very well informed and sometimes plays the buffoon who gets kicked in the pants." Ibid., 124.

24. For a discussion of the Weber thesis and the ensuing controversies, see Gordon Marshall, *In Search of the Spirit of Capitalism* (New York: Columbia University Press, 1982). Hartmut Lehmann and Gunther Roth, eds., *Weber's "Protestant Ethic": Origins, Evidence, Contexts* (Cambridge: Cambridge University Press, 1993), contains a series of essays dealing with the thesis and its critics.

25. Both Luther and Calvin placed limitations on the taking of interest based on Christian principles, but later writers such as Hugo Grotius (1583–1645) and Claudius Salmasius (1588–1653) justified usury on an economic basis alone without reference to religious principles.

26. Those German ruling authorities who were under the emperor, such as the seven electors who elected him.

27. Dixon, "Princely Reformation in Germany," in Pettegree, *Reformation World*, 158–59.

28. Hillerbrand, "Was There a Reformation?" 538. Richard Van Dulmen maintains that "the early modern state, either in its absolutist and authoritarian or in its estatist and libertarian form, was not a product of the Reformation." Nevertheless, he believes that "the Reformation did leave a particular mark on the shape it took." Richard van Dulmen, "The Reformation and the Modern Age," in Dixon, *German Reformation*, 206.

29. Strauss, "Success or Failure in the German Reformation," 30–63.

30. Gerald Strauss, *Luther's House of Learning: Indoctrination of the Young in the German Reformation* (Baltimore: Johns Hopkins University Press, 1978), 307.

31. Tom Scott, "The Success of the Reformation in Germany," in *Early Modern History* 1, no. 2 (January 1992): 31.

32. Scribner, "Incombustible Luther," 38ff.

33. J. M. Kittelson, "Success and Failures in the German Reformation: the Reform from Strasbourg," in *Archiv für Reformationsgeschichte* (1983): 153–75.

34. Lorna Jane Abray, *The People's Reformation: Magistrates, Clergy, and Commons in Strasbourg, 1500–1598* (Oxford: Blackwell, 1985), 214.

35. Ibid., 222.

36. Euan Cameron, "The Godly Community in Theory and Practice of the European Revolution," in *Voluntary Religion Studies in Church History* 23 (Oxford: Blackwell, 1986): 153.

37. Ibid., 132.

38. Scott Hendrix, "Rerooting the Faith: the Reformation as Re-Christianization," in *Church History* 69, no. 3 (September 2000): 577.

39. Scott, "Success of the Reformation in Germany," 30.

40. Geoffrey Parker, "Success and Failure during the First Century of the Reformation," 80. Parker also cites the example of a Saxon jurist who commented in 1555 that theological disputes were causing "lay people and common folk to doubt the very articles of the faith and to hold the preachers, indeed the whole of religion in contempt."

41. Hans Hillerbrand, "The Legacy of the Reformation," in *The Reformation*, ed. Stephen Thompson (San Diego: Greenhaven, 1999), 229.

42. For a balanced discussion of the witch craze, see Brian P. Levack, "The Great Witch-Hunt," in Pettegree, *Reformation World*, 607–33. Brink, Coudert, and Horowitz, *Politics of Gender*, contains a number of gender studies dealing with attitudes toward witches. See also Lyndal Roper, *Witch Craze Terror and Fantasy in Baroque Germany* (New Haven: Yale University Press, 2004).

43. Henry Kamen, *The Rise of Toleration* (New York: McGraw Hill, 1967), 65.

44. Ibid., 84.

45. Dulmen, "Reformation and the Modern Age," 199.

46. Ibid., 206.

47. Ibid., 219.

48. Matheson, *Imaginative World of the Reformation*, 136.

49. Dickens, *English Reformation*, 2nd ed., 196.

50. Brad S. Gregory, *Salvation at Stake: Christian Martyrdom in Early Modern Europe* (Cambridge: Harvard University Press, 1999), 351, 137.

51. Ibid., 78.

52. Dickens, *English Reformation*, 2nd ed., 394.

INDEX

Page numbers in italics refer to maps and illustrations.